Professional
T·r·a·v·e·l
Counselling

D0770356

DAVID WRIGHT CTC

Canadian Institute of Travel Counsellors of Ontario

Fourth Edition - Revised, Copyright © 2000
Canadian Institute of Travel Counsellors of Ontario

ALL RIGHTS RESERVED

No part of this publication may be reproduced, stored in a retrieval
system, or transmitted in any form or by any means, electronic,
mechanical, photocopying, recording or otherwise, without the prior
written permission of the Canadian Institute of Travel Counsellors of
Ontario.

The Canadian Institute of Travel Counsellors of Ontario (CITC-ONTARIO)
is not responsible for any special, consequential or exemplary damages
resulting, in whole or in part, from the readers' use of, or reliance upon, the
opinions, recommendations, or advice offered in this book. All rates and
descriptions are published for illustrative purposes only. CITC-ONTARIO
is not responsible for the accuracy of the rates or descriptions of the
properties and services of suppliers reproduced in this publication.
Inclusion of suppliers' material in this publication does not constitute its
endorsement by CITC-ONTARIO.

Preface

This text is designed for use by students in community colleges and private training schools in Canada. It will also serve as a useful reference for those in the first year of a career in the travel industry. *Professional Travel Counselling* attempts to describe and explain the roles and skills required by a Canadian travel counsellor. A travel counsellor must be familiar with all aspects of the travel industry and must be able to deal with both its suppliers and clients. As such, the skills acquired in training to be a travel counsellor can be transferred to many other positions within the industry. Trained travel counsellors can, and do, take up positions with airlines, hotels, car rental companies, government tourist offices, and a host of related suppliers and businesses. For this reason, the book begins with a description of tourism ... in effect, the "big picture". This introductory chapter provides a context for the remainder of the book. It describes the importance of tourism, both worldwide and in Canada, discusses the governmental and legislative frameworks of the industry, and introduces the distribution system through which travel products are sold.

Most, though not all, travel counsellors work in a travel agency. Chapter 2 begins with a discussion of this business. Various types of agency organizational arrangements are reviewed and the different types of travel agency clients are discussed. Perhaps most importantly, the chapter describes how travel agencies earn income and identifies their expenses. Thus far, the text has described the environment in which a travel counsellor usually works. The focus of the book now turns to travel counselling itself. The study of this topic, careers available and a typical job description are reviewed. Finally, the role of a travel counsellor is examined. This is the core of the text; all further material is based on this role.

A travel counsellor is the individual who matches a client's needs with an appropriate travel product. To be successful, travel counsellors must therefore develop knowledge of their clients and knowledge of the travel products available in the marketplace. Chapter 3 concentrates on the client. Types of travellers, traveller motivations and needs, and travel trends are studied. Suggestions are provided to assist potential counsellors to develop the people skills necessary to determine the travel needs of their clients.

Client knowledge is one part of the equation. The largest part in terms of volume of knowledge is travel product knowledge. Chapter 4 examines the changing nature of travel products and how they differ from tangible goods. The chapter continues with a discussion of how to acquire and maintain product knowledge. Sources of information on travel products are summarized. Chapters 5 through 12 direct their attention to the travel industry's products. Each segment of the travel industry is in turn studied in depth. Individual chapters follow a similar format. Each discusses a particular travel product, for example the airline industry, identifies and reviews the information sources for that product, describes the application of product sources, and identifies booking and payment procedures. The chapters follow a progression which begins with destinations, moves through the various forms of transportation and accommodation, and ends with chapters on tours and cruises which integrate many of the products discussed in earlier chapters. Chapter 12 discusses travel insurance, a product which is designed to protect clients' investments in other travel products.

By Chapter 13, readers have reviewed the two sides of the travel equation; clients and products. Chapter 13 describes how to integrate the two by matching client needs and travel products to produce a sale. A travel counsellor cannot be considered successful unless a sale is made and this chapter discusses methods for achieving this goal.

The final chapter, Chapter 14, examines the administrative aspects associated with a career in travel counselling. Accounting procedures, BSP reporting methods and filing are reviewed. Client relationships, professionalism and its development, and trade associations are also discussed. The acquisition of travel counsellor skills is the first step in a career in the travel industry. For many counsellors, the ultimate goal is to own their own agency. The book therefore concludes with a brief review of how to open a travel agency and obtain conference appointments.

Although the text attempts to follow a logical sequence from the client through various products and ending with sales and administration, instructors and readers will no doubt progress in an arrangement which most suits their particular needs or course structure. To assist both students and instructors, each chapter begins with a summary and learning objectives, and includes review questions and principal references. Most chapters are illustrated with sample pages reproduced from current travel industry brochures and references. These pages are intended to illustrate particular points in the text and to show formats and layouts of typical industry printed materials. They are meant to reflect industry practices but not industry prices. They can be used as the basis for classroom and homework assignments but should not be quoted as valid rates. Several diagrams and forms have been created to assist readers in acquiring the relevant skills. An extensive bibliography is provided for those who wish to pursue their studies in greater depth.

Acknowledgements

Writing a textbook is a somewhat solitary task, but it is certainly not one that can by accomplished by a single individual. Many people have helped in the development and production of this text and to all of them I extend my sincere gratitude. Several, however, merit special recognition. Karyn Moore CTC, Vice President Education - Publications, CITC-Ontario, supported the project from its inception, reviewed the entire manuscript, provided invaluable feedback and supplied energy when the writer flagged. Dorothy Chase CTC and Carla Roosen CTC diligently scrutinized several chapters. Their timely and relevant comments unquestionably improved the text and their teaching experience ensured its suitability for use by instructors and students. Responsibility for the opinions expressed in this publication and for the accuracy of its content, however, remain the author's alone. I wish to thank my colleague Judith Carson for her capable editing of the text and for resolving the issue of "to comma or not to comma". In spite of the old saying, many people do judge a book by its cover. I congratulate Alan M. Jones and Steven J. Spracklin for a fine job on the jacket design and for creating a highly readable interior layout. Their graphics and design capabilities have considerably enhanced this publication. My thanks also go to John Szauer for his production assistance. I wish to thank Gilbert Bullock CTC of Saunders Travel Service, Toronto for permitting me to deplete his shelves of brochures and for access to tickets, forms and other documents. Rick Rigelhof and Kal Bedder promptly delivered the photostats necessary to complete the production process. No project of this type can succeed without the services of a competent administrator to keep everyone on schedule, arrange collection and delivery of draft manuscripts, provide encouragement, and look after all of the minor as well as major details. Coralie Belman admirably fulfilled this function and more.

This project began with a realization that CITC's basic text, *Principles and Procedures of Travel Counselling*, no longer met the needs of the instructors and students who comprise its principal market. This view was subsequently reinforced by the many travel instructors who completed a survey on how to improve the manual. CITC responded to the challenge by engaging the author to produce a new text that would answer these concerns. I wish to thank CITC for their confidence in me; I hope that both they and the readers of this book will not be disappointed with the results.

Professional Travel Couselling is now in its fourth edition. This is most gratifying, and I thank all the travel students who have purchased the text and the many instructors who continue to comment on and recommend it. Most of the changes in this edition are minor. Statistics have been updated, some remarks have been added on the Internet and fees for service, and the section on consolidators has been expanded. For the first time in many years, the format of the Thomas Cook Timetable altered. This necessitated a rewrite of that section and this task could not have been accomplished without the assistance of Derick McQuarrie of Rail Europe. The most significant change by far, however, has been in the area of travel insurance. New products and services have been introduced, sales procedures and regulations have altered, and there has been a consolidation of insurance companies. These factors made Chapter 12 quite outdated. Rene Rockbrune of Voyageur Insurance Company volunteered to overhaul the material and worked tirelessly to expand and restructure the information. It is a great improvement and I am indebted to him for his expertise and assistance. Thanks also to Ken Khan at Printing Depot who continues to maintain the quality of the publication. Finally, my thanks go to Steve Gillick and Heather Craig-Peddie at CITC Ontario who take care of all the administrative and production details.

David Wright
Toronto
August 1998.

Table of Contents

Preface i

1.   The Tourism Industry 1

What is Tourism? • What is a Tourist? • Tourism in Canada • History of Tourism
National Governments and Tourism • Government and Legislation
Canadian Government and Tourism Legislation • Travel Distribution Systems
Suppliers • The Travel Agency

2.   The Travel Counsellor's Role 27

What is a Travel Agency? • Travel Agency Income • Travel Agency Expenses
Types of Travel Agencies • The Travel Agency's Business • What is a Travel Counsellor?
The Role of a Travel Counsellor

3.   The Client 47

Classifying Groups • General Reasons for Travel
Nondiscretionary and Discretionary Travel • Barriers to Travel
Pleasure Travel as a Need Satisfier • The Needs of Business Travellers
Factors Determining Individual Travel Behaviour • Questioning Skills
Effective Listening

4.   The Travel Product 63

The Travel Product • Sources of Product Knowledge • Product Knowledge and Sales

5.   Destinations and Documentation 91

Tourist Destinations • Tourism Development • Impacts of Tourism
Phases in Destination Development • Types of Destination
Acquiring Destination Knowledge • Destination Analysis
The 24-Hour Clock System • Apparent Flying Time and Elapsed Flying Time
Travel Documentation • Vehicles and Licenses

6.   Air Travel 143

Development of Air Travel • Airline Regulation • Deregulation in the USA and Canada
Route Structures • Classification of Airlines • International Air Regulations
Selling Air Travel • Using the Official Airline Guides • Airline Fares and Tariffs
IATA Traffic Conferences • Fare Construction Principles • Air Fares Used for Tours
Airline Ticketing

7.   Rail Travel 199

Development of Rail Travel • Advantages of Rail Travel • Disadvantages of Rail Travel
Rail Travel in Canada • Rail Travel in the United States • Rail Travel in Europe
Railroad Organizations • European Rail Schedules • Eurailtariff • Rail Passes
Rail Travel in Britain • Rail Travel Worldwide • Specialized Train Services

8. **Ground Transportation** 241
Bus Transportation • Types of Buses • Bus Transport in North America
Bus Transport in Europe • Ground Transportation • Car Rental

9. **Accommodation** 261
History and Background • Importance of the Hospitality Industry • Types of Hotels
Hotel Representatives • Hotel Terminology • Hotel Personnel
Grading of Hotels and Resorts • Checklist for Quality • Rates and Charges
Food Service and Meal Plans • Checking In and Checking Out
Commission Arrangements • Business Relations • Timesharing

10. **Tours** 293
Tours • Types of Tours • Tour Wholesalers and Tour Operators
Independent Tours: The Original Tour • Constructing Independent Tours
Role of Tour Wholesalers • Costing System for Independent Tours
Advantages and Disadvantages of Independent Tours • Group Tours • Escorted Tours
Role of Tour Operators • Preparation and Organization of an ITC Program
Negotiations with Suppliers • Costing an ITC Package • Tour Brochures
Recommending a Tour • Product Analysis • Tour Operator Documentation
Advantages and Disadvantages of Package Tours

11. **Cruises** 347
The Cruise Industry • History of Cruising • The Growth of Cruising • Types of Cruises
Other Types of Marine Transportation • Cruise Ship Features • Cruise Ship Personnel
Cruise Industry References • Cruise Brochures • Cruise Fares
Comparing the Cost of a Cruise and a Package Tour • Selling Cruises
Advantages of Cruises

12. **Travel Insurance** 383
The Need for Travel Insurance • What is Insurance? • Travel Insurance Terminology
Travel Insurance Products and Services • Selling Travel Insurance • Waiver Forms
Claims Procedure • Dealing with Travel Insurance Suppliers

13. **Sales** 409
Marketing • Travel Agency Promotion • Advertising • Publicity • Sales • Types of
Prospects Sales Strategies • The Sales Process • Telephone Sales • Sales Success

14. **Administration** 433
Profitability • Accounting Procedures • Converting Currency • Bank Settlement Plan
Filing Systems • Customer Relations • Professionalism • Trade Associations
Familiarization Trips • Continuing Education • How to Start a Travel Agency

Bibliography 473

Index 481

## Chapter 1

The Tourism Industry

Chapter Summary

This chapter introduces the terms and definitions associated with the study of tourism. There follows a brief history of the tourism industry, and a discussion of its growth and development in both Canada and the world. Government involvement in tourism and the legal framework within which the industry operates are reviewed. The Canadian governmental and legislative climate are discussed. The nature and mechanism of travel distribution systems are then studied. The chapter concludes with an overview of the Canadian travel industry's structure. Its various segments and how they interact are described. The central role of the travel agency is emphasized, and this discussion serves as an introduction to the following chapter.

Chapter Objectives
After completing this chapter you should be able to:

- Define some common terms used in the study of tourism.

- List various methods used to gather information on tourism.

- Discuss the requirements for growth in the travel industry.

- Write a short history of tourism.

- Describe the size and economic importance of tourism worldwide and in Canada.

- Describe government goals in tourism.

- Discuss the functions of local and national tourism offices.

- Provide an overview of international, national, provincial and municipal laws and regulations under which tourism operates.

- Give reasons for the introduction of travel legislation in Canada.

- Describe the goals of Canada's provincial travel legislation and how each province achieves these goals.

- Describe the distribution systems used for travel products.

- Identify the advantages and disadvantages of various distribution systems.

- List the major segments of the travel industry.

- Describe the function of each segment and how it interacts with the other segments.

What is Tourism?

Tourism is a vast worldwide industry which includes the transportation, lodging, feeding and entertainment of tourists. The World Tourism Organization (WTO) estimated that in 1997 international travellers spent US$444 billion dollars (excluding air transportation) and that over 600 million people crossed international borders. This figure represents over eight percent of all world trade and about 15 percent of the global service sector. Tourism and its companion, travel, is the largest single item in world trade and has been since 1965, far surpassing the monetary value of wheat, automobiles and machine tools. WTO projections for 2010 are that tourism arrivals will exceed one billion peole and revenues will reach US$1.5 trillion. Pleasure travel accounts for 60 percent of all worldwide arrivals while 30 percent are for business purposes.

The figures provided above are for travellers crossing international borders but, in fact, most tourism is domestic in nature. That is, the majority of tourists travel within their own country. Estimates are that 91 percent of all tourist receipts worldwide are for domestic expenditures. Similarly, most travel outside of one's home area is to a neighbouring region, whether this be domestic or international. For example, most Ontario residents travel within their home province. Those who venture further afield most often travel to neighbouring provinces or to U.S.

states bordering the province. The same pattern is exhibited in other provinces as well as by international travellers. Thus, Americans comprise the largest percentage of all foreign visitors to Canada. The reverse is also true; Canadians account for over half of all foreign tourists to the USA.

The United Nations regards international travel and tourism as "an economic and social force of major proportions in the world". Most countries today attempt to enrich their balance of payments in international trade through increased tourist receipts. For such countries as Mexico, Spain, Ireland, Britain, Italy and Austria, tourism is a major source of foreign exchange. Many developing countries have found this to be especially true. New nations as well as old have discovered tourism's economic benefits. Some countries, whose economies in the past relied on a single resource, have found that tourism can help offset the cycles of boom and recession associated with such commodities.

What is a Tourist?

As early as 1937, the League of Nations (the forerunner of the UN) realized the importance of collecting accurate tourism information. The League developed a series of definitions for the term "tourist" so that valid comparisons could be made. In 1963 at a conference held in Rome, the United Nations revised the earlier definitions and differentiated between "tourists" and "excursionists".

Several definitions for these and other tourism terms have been proposed. For travel counsellors, the United Nations definition is most appropriate:

A **tourist** is a temporary visitor staying at least 24 hours but less than one year in a country other than his own place of residence when the purpose of his journey is one or more of the following reasons: leisure, recreation, holiday, health, study, religion, sport, business, family, convention, mission or congress.

By this definition, military personnel, diplomats, resident students, and those who accept employment in a foreign country, are not considered tourists.

Excursionists are defined as temporary visitors staying less than 24 hours in the country. Thus, cruise passengers on a shore excursion are classified as excursionists.

The distinction between tourist and excursionist is important, particularly in relation to planning for tourism. Excursionists, for example, require no accommodation but are very concerned with transportation and shopping. Tourists, on the other hand, consider accommodation to be at least as important (if not more so) as the arrangements to reach the destination.

Several other criteria are used to describe tourists or travellers. They can be defined by the **distance** they travel or by their place of **residence** as well as by their **purpose** of travel or **length of stay**. Statistics on tourist visits to developing countries are frequently not as complete. Some of these visitor figures therefore include both tourists and excursionists.

Just as the terms tourist and excursionist can be defined, so travellers can be distinguished from tourists. Generally, tourist refers to those taking a pleasure trip while traveller has a broader meaning which encompasses travel for business or pleasure.

The terms travel, tourism and travel industry are also heard. These are usually treated as having the same meaning.

It is not the purpose of this text to obscure the meanings of these terms by listing a seemingly endless number of definitions. Nor is it the intention to bore or confuse the reader with long explanations of their significance and nuances. Rather, the goal is to provide a hint of the vast territory covered by the study of tourism; a subject which has only recently gained a degree of academic credibility. In fact, there is still debate as to whether tourism is an industry, a phenomenon, or as some have described it, a system. These arguments have been well researched and documented in a number of publications. Readers interested in pursuing this discussion may consult the bibliography for the appropriate references.

Tourism in Canada

The tourism industry in Canada generates about $44 billion annually, two-thirds of which is direct income. It is Canada's fourth largest earner of foreign exchange (about $13 billion annually) and is the largest single employer. The industry comprises some 60,000 businesses employing over 500,000 people directly and almost as many indirectly. (Over 270,000 people are employed in accommodation and catering establishments alone.) The Canadian economy is moving away from one based on resource production, manufacturing and agriculture, to one based on service. Service industries, such as tourism, are highly labour intensive and require a large work force. As tourism continues to grow in Canada and worldwide, even more people will be employed in this field.

Of the revenue generated by tourism in Canada, two-thirds is money spent by Canadians travelling within Canada. This is domestic tourism. Over 85 percent of all person-trips in Canada are taken by domestic tourists. Foreign visitors to Canada (including Americans who by far comprise the largest percentage of incoming tourists) account for the remaining one-third of tourism revenues. In spite of the large number of visitors to Canada (about 40 million annually), this country runs a trade deficit of about $3 billion each year. That is, Canadians

travelling abroad spend about $3 billion more each year than foreign visitors spend within Canada.

Although airline sales in Canada have declined in the 90's, in 1997 they still reached $10.5 billion. Almost half of all air travel sold is for business reasons and the remaining 55 percent is for vacation purposes. Domestic and international airline sales exhibit opposite tendencies. On a dollar basis, over 60 percent of domestic flights within Canada and to the USA are for business, whereas about 70 percent of international flights are pleasure trips.

History of Tourism

Humans are restless animals. Constantly seeking that which is new and different, the human species is motivated in its wanderlust primarily by curiosity. It is ever curious to discover what lies on the other side of the forest, what sights may be seen over the mountains, what experiences may be encountered beyond the seas. History and literature have recorded the observations of many famous travellers and explorers, among them Herodotus, Marco Polo, Christopher Columbus, Captain James Cook, Sir Francis Drake and Jacques Cartier. Historically, travel was a class related phenomenon. Only those with the time and the money (i.e., the elite) could travel. Prior to modern times, travel was limited to this elite, and to nomads, warriors, pilgrims, traders and explorers.

The Romans had a well-developed tourist industry. Their empire was safe and politically stable, there was sufficient technology (an excellent road system), prosperity, and a common means of exchange (a currency system). Such conditions are required for tourism to flourish. Roman tourists visited the Parthenon, the Acropolis, the Sphinx and the Pyramids much as do today's tourists. Similarly, they had guides, guidebooks on parchment, and they left their mark by inscribing various graffiti on the monuments. After the breakup of the

Roman Empire and during medieval times, sometimes called the "Dark Ages", the conditions for tourism deteriorated. Travel in any form was dangerous and was limited almost exclusively to those who had to travel, to pilgrims and to crusaders.

During the Renaissance and the Elizabethan era of the sixteenth century, travel once again began to blossom. During this period travel for educational purposes became fashionable. This means of educating the aristocracy, which took the form of a three year tour of Europe accompanied by a tutor and servant, became known as the **Grand Tour**. The fashion of the Grand Tour continued for some 300 years and became the model for some modern tours. Travel for health also became popular. This led to the rise of spas, many of which are still frequented today. For example, Bath in England and Baden Baden in Germany continue to attract tourists from around the world.

Tourists, however, were first given that name in the nineteenth century. Modern tourism in a form recognizable to us can be said to have commenced with the appearance of the railway in Britain in the late 1830s. Cheap fares and a growing middle class brought with them a heavy growth in this novel type of transport-ation. Coupled with the growth in travel was the equally heavy demand for accommodation at the end of the rail journey.

The first person who could be correctly termed a travel agent was Thomas Cook. In 1841 he arranged what is believed to be the first organized excursion or tour for 540 persons on a 12 mile rail journey to a temperance convention. Realizing the potential demand for travel, Mr. Cook gave up his trade of wood turner and entered the travel business as a full time organizer of excursions throughout England. Soon his scope of operations extended to continental Europe as an operator of escorted tours. The business prospered to the extent that today Thomas Cook and Son is known as one of the world's largest travel organizations, operating retail travel agencies, wholesale tours, banking and transport services. Cook's expansion followed the Industrial Revolution which had fostered the development of a middle class with a disposable income. The railroad network, which had been created to transport goods efficiently from factory to port or marketplace, provided the basis for a cheap and rapid passenger transportation system. The Industrial Revolution brought increased prosperity, although initially the working environment was wretched. Gradually, however, labour laws were introduced to reduce the length of the working week and provide paid vacations. The improved working conditions allowed people the time to travel. Thus, the transformation from a rural agricultural society to an industrial urban one created the conditions for the growth of tourism. As a result, a number of seaside resorts were developed near large urban centres. These resorts had originally (in the late eighteenth century) provided a fashionable retreat for the elite. Later they emerged as a means of escape from the "dark satanic mills". Two well known resorts in Britain were Brighton serving London and Blackpool serving the industrial North. Similar resorts arose in continental Europe and the United States as industrialization and rail transportation spread. Examples were Ostend serving Brussels, Deauville serving Paris, and Atlantic City which served the New York-Philadelphia region. Generally, these resorts offered a beach and sea, attractions such as piers, promenades, casinos, dance halls, amusement galleries and theatres, and a range of accommodation from inexpensive bed-and-breakfast guest houses to luxury hotels.

The development of the Mediterranean and other warmer regions, together with the introduction of cheap air transport-ation organized mainly on a charter basis, led to the demise of many seaside resorts in northern Europe. Many resorts now owe their development to government activity and investment and, to a large extent, the tourist industry is nationalized. Government investment is particularly essential in the developing countries.

Today travel is a reflection of income, education, lifestyle, age, occupation, and place of residence. That is, travel as we know it is a phenomenon shaped by technology, economics and social conditions.

Growth of Tourism

Tourism's growth coincided with the development of technology. As improvements occurred in transportation, tourism grew correspondingly. The train was the first transportation mode to clearly show this trend. By the mid-nineteenth century there was a flourishing rail network throughout many parts of Europe and in other parts of the world. In America the first transcontinental route was completed in 1869. A little later, in 1885, Canada was linked by rail from coast to coast. The growth of railways spurred the development of seaside resorts in Europe and North America. The next one hundred years, until about 1930, was the heyday of train travel. During this period, coast to coast travel time in North America fell from seven days to less than three.

Transatlantic transportation also became popular in the latter half of the nineteenth century. Of course, sailing ships had regularly plied the sea lanes between the old and new worlds but this was an arduous three week voyage. The invention of the steam engine and the development of the steamship changed that. Canada's Samuel Cunard inaugurated the first steamship service between England and America in 1840. As the steam engine was refined technically, and screw-propelled luxury liners came into service, crossing time was reduced from 12 days to five. New sea lanes were opened between Europe and the Middle East, the Far East, and Southeast Asia. Ships grew in size, tonnage and comfort. Passenger traffic between the two hemispheres grew steadily until the mid-1950s.

Meanwhile on land, the railroad companies were faced with a new competitor. The gasoline powered internal combustion engine led to the invention of the motor car in the 1880s and to the development of buses. By the 1920s, Henry Ford's techniques for mass production had revolutionized the automobile industry. Car prices dropped dramatically and private car ownership became widespread. The growth in car ownership and the convenience of automobile travel created a demand for more and better roads. The car became "king of the road", particularly in North America. The development of a national highway system brought with it the growth of motels, motor hotels, and similar services for drivers.

The airline industry developed shortly after the First World War. In the beginning, air travel was restricted to the wealthy and adventurous. For the most part, passenger air travel was confined to shorter connections. The Second World War, however, contributed to the technological development of aircraft. After the war there was a surplus of transport planes and of trained pilots. These factors fostered the formation of many airlines during the late 1940s. At the same time, many servicemen had experienced a plane flight for the first time during the hostilities and this had reduced the mystique of flying. The postwar era saw the growth of a network of air routes within Europe and North America. At this time, domestic coast to coast flights took 12 hours, including a four hour refuelling stop. Introduction of scheduled jet service in 1956, however, reduced the travel time to four hours. Similarly, transatlantic flight was technically possible in the 1940s but the trip took 16 hours or more in a propeller-driven plane. Transatlantic scheduled jet service, initiated in 1958, reduced this time to about eight hours. The jet age had begun.

Over the next decade, as the less efficient piston engine planes were phased out, the jet became the dominant form of international transport in every area of the globe. The total number of passengers crossing the Atlantic Ocean by plane in 1958 exceeded for the first time the number making the journey by ship. In every succeeding year since, the volume of air traffic on this route has increased while the number of sea passengers and of passenger liners has declined to almost zero. Today, air travel is the principal form of transportation with which most Canadian travel counsellors deal. Air transport throughout the world has grown at an average rate of about 15 percent annually. The introduction of the jet aircraft, with its economies of operation, its widespread popularity and acceptance as a means of fast, smooth and dependable transport, has made virtually the entire world accessible to millions.

Reasons for Growth in Tourism

The phenomenal growth and development of tourism within the past 20 years can be attributed to the following factors.

1. **Rising disposable income,** that is, the discretionary dollar left over after the income earner has made provision for the necessities of life: food, clothing, shelter, education, taxes, insurance, and similar demands. Wider income distribution, caused by the increased number of working women and two-income families, is also a contributing factor.

2. **Increasing leisure time** through shorter working hours. The 40 hour week seems to be the norm in Canada and the trend appears to favour an even shorter work week. Thus, long weekend vacations, using either public transport or the family car, have increased. Two to four week annual vacations provide the opportunity for travel within Canada, the United States and overseas. As the trend towards longer vacations continues, it is expected that individuals will choose to break their vacation time into two or more periods, thus permitting a seasonal variation in destinations (for example, Europe in summer, Mexico in winter). The trend, too, is toward earlier retirement. Senior members of the population will desire Caribbean and Mediterranean cruises and resort holidays. In Canada, the demographic profile of the population is changing and this too is contributing to the industry's growth. The number of senior citizens and the proportion of the population in the 40+ age group is rising as the baby boom generation approaches the "golden age". As the population ages, there are more

people whose family responsibilities have diminished. Their children have grown and left home, their mortgages are paid, and they now have the time and resources to enjoy one of life's pleasures, travel.

3. The **technology of transportation.** The impact of the jet airplane is the obvious example. Travel time to distant destinations has been dramatically reduced and the operational range of aircraft has increased, thus bringing far corners of the globe within reach of the two week vacationer. The impact of high speed trains and a growing network of intercity highways have also assisted this trend.

4. The **declining cost** of jet travel. Plane capacities have increased as designs and materials improved. Cheaper fares and low cost promotional and excursion fares, made possible by the relatively cheaper operating characteristics of jets, have been significant contributors to the growth of tourism. The growing trend towards deregulation contributed to an explosion of air traffic in the 1980s.

5. **Higher levels of education.** The desire to travel and broaden one's perspective increases with education. Travel experiences appear to increase the desire to travel. As the sophistication of today's travellers grows, so too does their curiosity, and they seek other destinations to satisfy that curiosity. Research has shown that the more education one has, the greater is the tendency to travel. As the population in general has become more educated, so too has the amount of travel.

Generally, growth in travel occurs when the following conditions are met:

There is **political stability** and **peace.** The rise of mass tourism has coincided with a long period of general peace and prosperity. (This is not to deny that there have been wars in the last thirty years, but these have been regional conflicts rather than worldwide.)

Economic prosperity. The recent boom in travel (outpacing even the growth of the 1960s) has coincided with the longest period of economic expansion in this century. Prosperous times create the conditions for a rise in disposable income. Travel is not necessary for survival (although some would argue that they "must" have an annual vacation), and therefore it is a discretionary expenditure. People spend discretionary income on travel only when their personal financial situation permits. This is most likely during prosperous economic conditions.

An **accepted medium of exchange**. For travel to flourish, travellers require a common currency or a means by which their own currencies can be exchanged. Today the financial system is a world-wide network that includes even the eastern bloc countries. Travellers cheques are commonplace and credit cards are accepted almost everywhere.

An **efficient transportation system**. The world is now linked by a fully integrated air transport system. One airline ticket can take a traveller almost anywhere. On land, one can drive from Canada to South America or from Europe to India. There are railroads connecting the Atlantic and Pacific Oceans not only in North America, but also from Europe to Asia.

Leisure time. Never in the history of humanity have so many had so much free time for recreational and leisure pursuits. Together with the conditions described above, this has contributed to the growth of the travel industry. Beginning with an annual week by the sea, modern tourism has grown to encompass trips ranging from long weekends at the cottage to year long safaris.

National Governments and Tourism

Tourism has exceptional potential to create jobs, to earn foreign exchange and to promote regional development. In some countries, such as those in Eastern Europe, the government has been intimately involved in the planning and ownership of tourism enterprises. This is less frequent in Western Europe and North America. Nevertheless, governments of every

political stripe and system are closely involved with tourism and its development. In recent years many countries have created ministries or departments responsible for tourism, thereby giving the industry a seat at the cabinet table and elevating it in importance.

Through a document known as the Manila Declaration, the WTO has produced a set of basic guidelines to help governments define their tourism role. The WTO has identified three areas, namely planning, employment and coordination. Government's planning role is to attract foreign investment and fund infrastructure development. In the area of employment, its responsibility is to determine manpower needs and ensure that suitable training programs are available. A third task for government is the coordination of public and private sector activities.

Every country that actively encourages tourism has a national tourism organization (NTO). A national tourism organization, usually in the form of a tourist board, represents the country. Its main role is the marketing and promotion of the country, that is, to encourage visitors to the country. NTOs accomplish this function by advertising overseas, by obtaining publicity in the trade press, and by participating in travel industry trade shows, presentations and seminars. In addition, such offices usually conduct research and provide statistical information. Many are involved in the regulation or licensing of various facets of the industry. Some actively participate in tourism planning. Others provide training for the industry or otherwise facilitate its growth and development. A few operate hotels or resorts.

The role of such offices is a broad one. Tourist offices are concerned with the development of the industry as a whole, rather than vested interests within it. An integral part of this development is promoting a country's attractions and facilities. Intimately associated with such promotions is the country's image abroad. Creating a positive overseas image is a major task at any time, however, it can become enormous depending on the circumstances. For instance, in Mexico the tourist board was handed the responsibility for restoring the country's image following an earthquake. Jamaica's tourist board had a similar task after Hurricane Gilbert hit in 1988. Several other countries have employed their tourist boards to overcome the negative impact of similar natural disasters, or political instability, or civil strife.

Most NTOs have both international and domestic goals. In the international arena, NTOs may seek to increase export earnings, promote economic development, develop closer ties with expatriates, create favourable foreign opinion, preserve the national heritage, and promote an increased appreciation of the national culture. Domestically, on the other hand, NTOs attempt to foster national cohesion and identity, promote public health and citizen understanding, assist economic growth and redistribution, improve respect for the environment, preserve local and national traditions, and protect the right to leisure.

Tourist offices also operate at the regional and local levels. All fifty U.S. states and the ten Canadian provinces and two territories run such departments. Their functions are similar to those of the national office but, of course, their concerns and markets are more locally focused. Regions and districts within states and provinces also have tourist associations which promote their specific attractions and events. The principal goal of these regional organizations is to promote tourism as a tool for economic development.

At the local level, many cities operate tourist offices. Such offices are usually titled conventions and visitors bureaus (CVB). CVBs are not-for-profit umbrella organizations which service all types of travellers, whether tourists, business travellers or convention delegates. Convention bureaus like government tourist organizations see tourism as a means of local economic development. As such, they work with the city government (who derive employment and tax benefits from tourism), trade and civic unions, and with travel suppliers such as hotels, restaurants, attractions and transportation companies. CVBs market a specific city or metropolitan region and its attractions. As the name implies, the fact that there are conventions and visitors bureaus indicates one of the most important and growing segments of the travel industry, the convention market.

The meetings and convention business in North America has almost doubled in the last ten years. Attracting a convention to a city can bring in thousands of visitors and millions of dollars. (For example, the 1989 Shriners Convention drew some 20,000 convention delegates to Toronto.) Although the main focus of conventions is business, and they comprise trade shows, meetings and seminars, there is a considerable spillover into the tourism area since the necessary accommodation, meals and ancillary services must be supplied. In addition, convention delegates are often accompanied by their "significant other" and frequently participate in pre- and post-convention tours within the area. Research has shown that convention delegates on average spend a higher daily amount in a city and its environs than do pleasure tourists. Thus, conventions generate considerably more revenue than would at first be assumed.

Canadian Government and Tourism

In Canada, as in other countries, the national government monitors and promotes the tourism industry and its development. This has been achieved through the government's Ministry of Industry, Science and Technology and the creation of a government agency, the Canadian Tourism Commission (CTC), to implement the federal government's tourism policies. The CTC has undergone several name changes and structural reorganizations in its history as governments and the tourism industry changed. The CTC was established in January 1995 as a federal agency with the authority to plan, direct, manage and implement programs to generate and promote tourism in Canada. The two main objectives of the Canadian Tourism Commission are to market Canada as a desirable tourist destination and to provide timely and accurate information to the tourism industry to assist their decision-making.

In the past, federal government tourism agencies implemented various programs which had been developed with advice from the tourism industry. The CTC's mandate, however, is to carry out programs developed by the private sector, that is, the agency was created as a partnership with the tourism industry. This is a significant change from past practice. The agency is administered by a Board comprised of the deputy ministers of the provincial ministries of tourism, representatives of the private sector, and chaired by the federal minister responsible for tourism. The majority of the Board members are from the private sector. Currently, the CTC administers three program areas: Marketing, Corporate Services, and Industry Competitiveness.

Marketing uses research to determine its markets and drive its promotional programs. High-yield customers and focused efforts are keys to the success of this program. Marketing programs include the development and maintenance of data, public and media relations, advertising, promotional projects, and travel trade development. The program also establishes partnering relationships with the private sector and provincial/territorial governments. Management of the marketing program is divided into working committees which cover specific markets: US Leisure, Canada, Europe, Asia/Pacific, US Business Travel and Aboriginal Tourism.

Corporate Services is responsible for the financial management of the agency through the Finance/Administration branch. This program also manages Human Resources, Commission Liaison which provides secretariat services, Communications (including CTC public relations), and the Tourism Reference and Documentation Centre (TRDC).

The **Industry Competitiveness** program works with the tourism industry to develop or improve products that satisfy customers needs. It includes industry assessments on the structure and performance of the tourism industry, program development services such as seminars and training manuals, analysis of domestic and international developments, and development and maintenance of industry data. Management of this program is divided into three sections: Research, Infrastructure, and Animation. Research offers

expert advice for the other programs, manages core surveys, and develops the information base necessary for economic forecasts. Infrastructure concentrates on programs and services to improve Canada's tourism industry and facilities. Animation focuses on programs and activities to improve tourism industry products and services.

The creation of the CTC has established a new working relationship among the private sector, destination marketing organizations, provincial/territorial/national private sector associations, the provincial/territorial governments and the federal government. This attempt to integrate the cooperative efforts of partners to expand tourism to/within Canada is a central focus of the CTC. In addition, the agency's programs and services are customer-driven and research-based. The Canadian Tourism Commission is funded jointly by the federal government, the private sector and other government partners in tourism.

In recent years the federal and provincial governments have divided their responsibilities and streamlined their operations. The creation of the CTC, however, has helped the various governments coordinate their advertising and promotional campaigns. It is the CTC's responsibility to generate tourism traffic to Canada. This is achieved by promoting all of Canada through a "brand name" rather than by a generic approach. That is, specific attractions such as Niagara Falls and events such as the Calgary Stampede are used to tempt travellers to visit Canada. The federal government considers such attractions and events to be travel generators which are competitive in the international marketplace. Once visitors have been drawn to Canada by this strategy, there is a joint responsibility to market specific regions and encourage visitors to travel within the country. Provincial governments also promote their particular region to their own target groups (which can be domestic or international). The majority of overseas promotions are handled by the federal agency. This cooperation has improved Canada's promotional capabilities and has made the marketing of tourism more efficient.

Government and Legislation

As well as its involvement in the promotion and development of tourism, government is also involved in regulating the industry. In some jurisdictions such as transportation, the government's role in North America is declining during the present climate of deregulation. Similar changes are occurring in Europe.

The travel industry is governed by laws and regulations in much the same way as any other industry. Even though most travellers and many travel industry employees are not aware of the nature and content of these laws, they can enjoy their trips or work in the industry with few adverse effects.

International Tourism Legislation

All transportation companies are regulated to some extent internationally, however, there are few such regulations directly affecting other members of the travel industry. Those which are most clearly defined are in the area of air regulations. All travel agencies wishing to sell international airline tickets for commission must be appointed by the International Air Transport Association (IATA). IATA sets the criteria for such appointments. The travel agency signs a contract with IATA and by so doing agrees to abide by the conditions set forth by the association. The criteria are fairly universal although they do vary somewhat according to local conditions and laws. If a travel agency loses its IATA appointment it can no longer earn commission from the sale of international air transportation.

IATA's membership of over 180 airlines is restricted to those offering scheduled air service. Thus Canada 3000 and Air Transat, both of which are Canadian airlines that offer charter service only, are unable to join IATA. The association's main purpose is to resolve problems that airline companies acting alone could not. Its objectives are to encourage safe, regular and economical international air services. IATA also fosters international air commerce and researches problems and issues affecting the airline industry.

Airline tickets are legal contracts that specify the conditions under which a passenger will be transported (see Figure 1.1). Most countries have signed one or more of the many agreements relating to this subject. The agreement which makes up the main body of international rules governing air transportation is the Warsaw Convention which was negotiated in 1929. This agreement describes an airline's liabilities with respect to passenger injuries, and damage to or loss of baggage (see Figure 1.2). The Hague Protocol and the Montreal Agreement were subsequently negotiated and these agreements raised the dollar limit on an airline's liability to an individual passenger. As the airline industry continued to grow, governments realized there was a necessity for technical agreements relating to the safety and operations of air transport. In 1944 a meeting was held in Chicago and the outcome, known as the Chicago Convention, became the first worldwide system proposed for airline regulation. Under this proposal, certain freedoms of the air were suggested. The freedoms proposed, however, were not ratified and it therefore became necessary for governments to establish arrangements through mutual negotiations. The Bermuda Agreement, signed in 1946, provided the example for arrangements between governments regarding the exercise of these different freedoms between countries. Eight freedoms are now recognized which define the conditions under which airlines can use the air space of other countries. The eight freedoms are discussed in greater detail in Chapter 6.

There are, of course, international laws relating to piracy, terrorism and other such criminal acts. The majority of the regulations, however, concern the control of international airline routes and

NOTICE

Sold Subject to Tariff Regulations

If the passenger's journey involves an ultimate destination or stop in a country other than the country of departure the Warsaw Convention may be applicable and the Convention governs and in most cases limits the liability of carriers for death or personal injury and in respect of loss of or damage to baggage. See also notice headed "Advice to International Passengers on Limitation of Liability".

CONDITIONS OF CONTRACT

As used in this contract "ticket" means this passenger ticket and baggage check of which these conditions and the notices form part "carriage" is equivalent to "transportation" "carrier" means all air carriers that carry or undertake to carry the passenger or his baggage hereunder or perform any other service incidental to such air carriage "WARSAW CONVENTION" means the Convention for the Unification of Certain Rules Relating to International Carriage by Air signed at Warsaw 12th October 1929 or that Convention as amended at The Hague 28th September 1955 whichever may be applicable

2 Carriage hereunder is subject to the rules and limitations relating to liability established by the Warsaw Convention unless such carriage is not "international carriage" as defined by that Convention

3 To the extent not in conflict with the foregoing carriage and other services performed by each carrier are subject to in provisions contained in this ticket in applicable tariffs in carrier's conditions of carriage and related regulations which are made part hereof (and are available on application at the offices of carrier except in transportation between a place in the United States or Canada and any place outside thereof to which tariffs in force in those countries apply

4 Carrier's name may be abbreviated in the ticket the full name and its abbreviation being set forth in carrier's tariffs conditions of carriage regulations or timetables, carrier's address shall be the airport of departure shown opposite the first abbreviation of carrier's name in the ticket the agreed stopping places are those places set forth in this ticket or as shown in carrier's timetables as scheduled stopping places on the passenger's route, carriage to be performed hereunder by several successive carriers is regarded as a single operation

5 An air carrier issuing a ticket for carriage over the lines of another air carrier does so only as its agent

6 Any exclusion or limitation of liability of carrier shall apply to and be for the benefit of agents servants and representatives of carrier and any person whose aircraft is used by carrier for carriage and its agents servants and representatives

7 Checked baggage will be delivered to bearer of the baggage check In case of damage to baggage moving in international transportation complaint must be made in writing to carrier forthwith after discovery of damage and at the latest within 7 days from receipt, in case of delay complaint must be made within 21 days from date the baggage was delivered See tariffs or conditions of carriage regarding non-international transportation

8 This ticket is good for carriage for one year from date of issue except as otherwise provided in this ticket in carrier's tariffs conditions of carriage or related regulations The fare for carriage hereunder is subject to change prior to commencement of carriage Carrier may refuse transportation if the applicable fare has not been paid

9 Carrier undertakes to use its best efforts to carry the passenger and baggage with reasonable dispatch Times shown in timetable or elsewhere are not guaranteed and form no part of this contract Carrier may without notice substitute alternate carriers or aircraft and may alter or omit stopping places shown on the ticket in case of necessity Schedules are subject to change without notice Carrier assumes no responsibility for making connections

10 Passenger shall comply with Government travel requirements present exit entry and other required documents and arrive at airport by time fixed by carrier or if no time is fixed early enough to complete departure procedures

11 No agent servant or representative of carrier has authority to alter modify or waive any provision of this contract

CARRIER RESERVES THE RIGHT TO REFUSE CARRIAGE TO ANY PERSON WHO HAS ACQUIRED A TICKET IN VIOLATION OF APPLICABLE LAW OR CARRIER'S TARIFFS, RULES OR REGULATIONS

FIGURE 1.1
The contract between a passenger and an airline.
Source: IATA.

services. These are negotiated between governments and are known as bilateral agreements (when two countries are involved) or multilateral agreements when more than two governments enter into negotiations.

The Chicago Conference of 1944 led directly to the formation of the International Civil Aviation Organization (ICAO) in that year and of IATA in 1945. These organizations paved the way for a number of bilateral agreements. Whereas IATA represents airlines, ICAO is an organization of national governments. Among its objectives are the setting of standards, the promotion of safe and orderly growth, and the development of all aspects of international civil aeronautics.

Other suppliers, such as hotels and tour operators, are not controlled to the same extent as airlines. For example, the International Hotel Association has issued a code of conduct for its members and the World Tourism Organization (WTO) has developed a classification system to standardize various categories of accommodation. Both organizations, however, have met with limited success as their systems and codes are voluntary. Generally, hotels and other such suppliers have few international regulations or conventions controlling them. As with other businesses, however, they operate under the laws of the country in which they carry on business.

Canadian Government & Tourism Legislation

Federal, provincial, and many municipal governments are involved in tourism primarily because of its positive economic benefits. There is also, however, a need to regulate an industry as large as tourism so that its growth can be controlled.

Many countries are organized in such a fashion that one set of national laws is sufficient to regulate the business environment. In Canada, however, the constitutional framework has created two levels of legislation; federal and provincial. Under our constitution, powers are divided between the federal and provincial governments. Any individual, business or organization must abide by the law of the land. Some laws are general and relate to all individuals or businesses. Others refer specifically to the travel industry or some portion of it. Many of the laws related to the regulation of the travel industry are provincial laws and apply only in those provinces.

In Canada, whether at the federal or

provincial level, the topic of law is generally subdivided into two main categories; common law and statutory law. **Common law** is the law of the land, the rules we all must follow. In general, these are judge-made laws. Common law includes civil law and refers to an individual's private rights. It is with this type of law that travel industry personnel are most likely to be involved. **Statutory laws,** on the other hand, are passed by parliament and describe rules by which society or a particular industry must live. For example, the Criminal Code, which covers such federal crimes as fraud, theft, tax evasion or assault, are governed by statutory law. It is rare for members of the travel industry to come in contact with such federal legal proceedings in the course of their business. The following federal statutes, however, do impact on those who work in the travel industry.

Federal Framework

The **Competition Act** applies to all businesses and has some provisions of particular interest to the travel industry. This act prohibits companies from conspiring to reduce competition in the marketplace. For example, under this act two suppliers cannot decide together to divide the market, whether it be a resort destination or the travel agency market, such that one supplier services only one half while the other services the remainder. Such actions would ensure that each supplier had unduly reduced the competition in its market and that is illegal. When company actions are challenged under this act, the allegations are referred to the Competition Bureau, a government body created to mediate disputes and determine if the provisions of the act have been broken. The Competition Act also controls "bait and switch" advertising. For example, suppose an airline advertises a return flight to Fort Lauderdale, Florida for $169.00 return but, in fact, only two seats are available on the plane at that price. Potential customers would naturally be attracted (or baited) by such an advert. When they tried to buy the product, however, they would be told that it had sold out but that the trip could be made at a price of $229.00. This type of selling is prohibited under the act.

Regulations specifically related to the travel industry are the Aeronautics Act, which sets the performance standards for aircraft, and the National Transportation Act. The **National Transportation Act** was passed in 1988 to implement the federal government's revised transportation policy. The National Transportation Agency was created by

FIGURE 1.2
An airline's liability is limited by the Warsaw Convention. The details are shown on an airline ticket.
Source: IATA.

Page 2

ADVICE TO INTERNATIONAL PASSENGERS ON LIMITATION OF LIABILITY

Passengers on a journey involving an ultimate destination or a stop in a country other than the country of origin are advised that the provisions of a treaty known as the Warsaw Convention may be applicable to the entire journey, including any portion entirely within the country of origin or destination. For such passengers on a journey to, from, or with an agreed stopping place in the United States of America, the Convention and special contracts of carriage embodied in applicable tariffs provide that the liability of certain carriers, parties to such special contracts, for death of or personal injury to passengers is limited in most cases to proven damages not to exceed U.S. $75,000 per passenger, and that this liability up to such limit shall not depend on negligence on the part of the carrier.

For such passengers travelling by a carrier not a party to such special contracts or on a journey not to, from, or having an agreed stopping place in the United States of America, liability of the carrier for death or personal injury to passengers is limited in most cases to approximately U.S. $10,000 or U.S. $20,000.

The names of carriers, parties to such special contracts, are available at all ticket offices of such carriers and may be examined on request.

Additional protection can usually be obtained by purchasing insurance from a private company. Such insurance is not affected by any limitation of the carrier's liability under the Warsaw Convention or such special contracts of carriage.

For further information please consult your airline or insurance company representative.

NOTE: The limit of liability of U.S. $75,000 above is inclusive of legal fees and costs except that in case of a claim brought in a state where provision is made for separate award of legal fees and costs, the limit shall be the sum of U.S. $58,000 exclusive of legal fees and costs.

this act to monitor airlines and railway operations within Canada. The Canadian National Transportation Agency (NTA) is a federal body which functions under the National Transportation Act. The NTA controls transportation in Canada and has introduced a measure of deregulation in all forms of transportation. The NTA is also the specific body that regulates and licenses all airlines in Canada, whether they are large or small, scheduled or charter. Carriers must obtain approval from the NTA for a wide variety of operations, including the right to operate on a particular route and the conditions covering the sale of excursion fares. Since airlines are closely linked with tour operators and travel agencies in the promotion and sale of airline seats, these federal laws also, by extension, control some of the operations of those sectors of the travel industry. Technically, however, tour operators and travel agencies are governed by provincial laws rather than federal regulations.

Other federal laws created the National Parks system and established the regulations governing their care. The goal of these laws was to protect and preserve the parks for the enjoyment of everyone, including future generations. Some of Canada's national parks such as Banff and Jasper, however, are now among the country's major tourist attractions. Their popularity has put pressure on the environment and has sparked heated debate on their use by such large numbers. Similar, though less contentious federal legislation, established the criteria for designating national and historic monuments.

The federal government also regulates entry into Canada by tourists and other visitors through its visa requirements. Canada Customs and Immigrations personnel administer these entry regulations at border crossings, and at the various seaports and airports. Their task involves monitoring both the people and products that enter the country.

Provincial Framework

The provincial laws which directly relate to the travel industry are the travel acts that have been passed in British Columbia, Ontario and Quebec. At the present time, only those three provinces have legislation dealing specifically with the travel industry. In all other provinces, the travel industry is governed by the general legislation which pertains to any business operation.

Whether the acts apply generally to all individuals and businesses under common law, or are statutory laws specific to the travel industry, they tend to have similar provisions in each province. Their names, however, are different. For convenience, the titles used in Ontario will be used. The discussion, however, applies generally to any of the provinces.

Considering the general legislation first, in Ontario one statute is the **Consumer Protection Act**. Variations of this act apply in each province. The Consumer Protection Act applies to any transaction valued at more than $50.00 (which is virtually all travel transactions). The act requires that a receipt, which describes the details of the product or service being purchased, be issued for all such transactions. Companies which fail to issue such receipts run the risk that the contract they have made with the client may not be enforceable. (Readers should note that the Ontario Travel Industry Act, which is discussed below, specifically requires a travel agency to issue a receipt for any service sold no matter what it costs.) Now consider a consumer who purchases a package tour close to the departure date such that a penalty of 100 percent of the tour cost applies if the client cancels. Suppose that the client leaves a deposit and promises to pay the balance within 48 hours. In return, the travel agency makes a reservation and issues the tour vouchers but does not issue a receipt. If the client has a change of heart and decides to cancel, the travel agency may be liable to the tour operator for the balance of the payment. Because the agency did not comply with the Consumer Protection Act and issue a receipt, it may have no legal recourse against the client for refusing to pay the balance of the cost of the tour program.

Another piece of legislation common to all provinces is called, in Ontario, the **Business Practices Act**. This act describes the various selling and advertising techniques which are permitted. Under this act, false or misleading advertising is prohibited and sellers are prevented from in various ways taking advantage of buyers. For example, if the buyer does not understand English or cannot read the language, the seller would probably be unable to enforce the terms of a contract that the individual had signed. (Again, the Ontario Travel Industry Act provides specific guidelines for the advertising of travel products.)

Specific Travel Legislation

The introduction of regularly scheduled jet airline service in the late 1950s signalled the start of today's tourism industry. Technological developments in the 1960s brought larger and faster planes and, with them, modern mass tourism. Larger planes with a greater seating capacity had to be filled with paying passengers. Europeans were the first to realise the potential of "bulk buying" for the travel industry and before long low-cost charter flights and tour packages were introduced to the marketplace. These ideas quickly spread across the Atlantic and by the early 1970s, charters and packaged holidays were well established in Canada. Such rapid growth and innovation, however, often bring "growing pains". When new business ideas are developed, there are frequently no rules to govern how the game should be played. This was precisely the case with mass travel. Each day brought more people and more new companies wishing to be involved in this glamorous and lucrative new business. The bubble burst in 1973-74. Instead of glamour, newspapers carried stories of travellers who had purchased a carefree vacation only to find on arrival at the resort that the hotel had no room reserved for them and no record of their booking. In some cases

there was no hotel; only a hole in the ground where it was to be built. In other cases, the holiday went well until the final day when the suntanned travellers arrived at the airport to find that there was no plane to take them home. Still others paid for trips to "travel agents" who disappeared with their hard-earned cash. A rash of such problems, together with the collapse of several tour companies and the resulting media furore, prompted the Quebec and Ontario Governments to take action.

Quebec's Travel Agents Act was passed on December 17, 1974, followed three days later by Ontario's Travel Industry Act. In 1977, British Columbia followed the example of these two provinces by introducing the Travel Agents Registration Act. Each of these acts is designed to protect consumers in various ways but, in particular, they help compensate travellers who pay for services that they do not receive. Such protection was necessary because of the aforementioned bankruptcies and other problems, and because of the special nature of travel purchases. Travel is one of the few products that a person buys before having the opportunity to inspect or try the merchandise. This removes one of the consumer's most effective means of leverage, that of refusal to pay until satisfaction has been attained. Without such recourse, consumers are left with little protection if they are dissatisfied with the product. It is for this reason that specific travel-related legislation was thought to be necessary.

The similar titles of each of the travel acts reveals that they have similar goals and methods for achieving them. Each province uses up to four mechanisms to protect consumers. These are a registration system, a compensation fund, bonding and trust accounting.

Registration

Each province has made it illegal to carry on business as a travel agent or travel wholesaler unless registered with the province as such. The definitions of travel agent and travel wholesaler may differ from one province to another but the intent is the same. Companies must meet certain criteria in order to obtain a license from the province concerned. To qualify for registration a company must generally prove its financial stability, good character, and travel experience.

Compensation Fund

Every licensed travel company (wholesale or retail) must contribute to the compensation fund in the province where it is registered. Generally, an initial levy is assessed and then annual payments are made. With the exception of Quebec, there is a limit to the level of the compensation fund. When that limit is reached contributions cease. (All new companies, however, must still pay the initial levy.) The compensation fund is used to repay consumers who purchase travel arrangements from a licensed company but fail to obtain services. For example, if a tour operator declares bankruptcy before a consumer takes a trip, the compensation fund will cover the consumer's costs for an alternative vacation. Similarly, if a travel agency closes before paying for a charter flight which a client has reserved and paid for, the compensation fund will reimburse the consumer for any costs incurred. Although the basic premise of the compensation fund, consumer protection, is the same for all three provinces, its administration varies from one province to another.

The B.C., Ontario and Quebec statutes operate only within those provinces and so protect only residents of those particular locations who purchase their travel services through companies registered with the province. Consumers in other provinces are, for the most part, not protected (other than by general business statutes) when purchasing travel products. For example, if an Ontario tour operator declares bankruptcy leaving consumers stranded on a Caribbean island, those Ontario consumers who had purchased their vacations from licensed Ontario retailers would be able to claim the compensation fund for their return airfare. Those who had purchased the same package from an unregistered retailer in Ontario would not have this protection. Further, consider consumers in Winnipeg who purchased the same Ontario tour operator's package from a local travel agency. A travel agency in Manitoba cannot be registered in Ontario. Thus, consumers in Manitoba would not be protected by the Ontario compensation fund, even if the tour operator had been legally registered in Ontario and had contributed to that province's compensation fund. This applies even if the consumer purchases the tour from a chain or franchised agency which has branches in both provinces. Similarly, if an Ontario or B.C. consumer bought a package tour directly from an American tour operator in Hawaii, or air tickets from the New York office of a foreign airline, provincial travel legislation would not protect them if the supplier subsequently defaulted. Canadian clients are, however, protected when they book a tour with an active member of the USTOA (United States Tour Operators Association). In 1990, the USTOA created a mandatory consumer protection plan for its members to refund travellers affected by tour operator bankruptcies, insolvencies, or non-performance. Some travel agencies in Alberta and Saskatchewan have attempted to overcome the lack of protective legislation by making it company policy that clients purchase cancellation insurance which includes default protection.

Bonding

Bonding is required only in Quebec. In that province, a company must pay a set amount to a bonding company in case the travel company defaults on its obligations. Should this happen, the bond becomes available to compensate consumers. In effect, bonding is rather like buying insurance protection.

Trust Accounting

Only the Ontario and Quebec acts impose trust accounting on their travel companies. British Columbia takes a middle position which "deems that" certain money is held in trust. Where trust accounting is required, a travel agency must operate two separate business accounts. In the first account are held the agency's general revenues which are used to pay salaries, rent, utilities, and similar operating expenses. The second account, the trust account, is where payments received from consumers are deposited. These funds must remain in the trust account until the consumer actually uses the travel service. Only at that time does the agency become eligible to collect the commission earned on the sale of the travel service. This commission is then transferred to the agency's general revenue account and used, as described above, to pay expenses. With the trust accounting system, the consumer's money is held in a separate account which the agent is not legally permitted to use. Should a tour operator or travel agency declare bankruptcy, the client's funds are protected and can be recovered. Canadian courts have yet to decide the issue of whether a travel agency is holding funds in trust for its clients, or whether it merely owes money to, for example, an airline in much the same way that it has debts to accountants, utilities companies, or suppliers of office equipment.

In the years since the specific travel acts were introduced, tour operators and travel agencies have continued to go out of business and situations have arisen where consumers were not protected. Since consumer protection is the overriding aim of the travel legislation, several modifications and enhancements have been implemented. The result is that the travel industry today operates under conditions which are much more stringently controlled than when the legislation was first introduced in 1974.

Since 1978, when the U.S. Government deregulated the airline industry, there has been a growing movement to curtail the size of government bureaucracy and reduce the number of government regulations. Part of this development has been the move to self-regulation of various industries. In 1997, the Ontario Government delegated the responsibility for administering the Ontario Travel Industry Act and its compensation fund to the Travel Industry Council of Ontario

www. TICO.ON.CA

(TICO). TICO is a not-for-profit corporation, made up of travel industry representatives and Ministerial appointments, that has assumed the registration and consumer protection duties previously carried out by the Ministry of Consumer and Commerial Relations. At this writing there have been no changes to the legislation or regulations described above.

Municipal By-Laws

Municipal by-laws are unlikely to be infringed by travel personnel in the course of their business. Such regulations govern various local matters, such as health, fire and safety conditions in the workplace, hours of business, and the zoning of property for commercial, industrial or residential use.

Travel Distribution Systems

Earlier in this chapter, we examined tourism from several vantage points. Tourism is certainly a phenomenon which can be analyzed, discussed and dissected in a number of ways but this text is principally concerned with tourism as a business. Like other businesses, the travel industry has products which the various companies attempt to sell to consumers. Unlike other industries, however, travel is an intangible product; one cannot taste, touch or otherwise inspect the merchandise in a showroom. Thus, the retailer (the travel agency) has no inventory on its shelves other than the brochures produced by tour operators, airlines, and other suppliers. Travel industry suppliers, such as airlines or hotels, are equivalent to the manufacturers found in other industries. Another significant difference between travel and other businesses is that the product is extremely perishable. Many products, for example food, have what is called a shelf life, a period of time within which they are fit to be sold. Even after

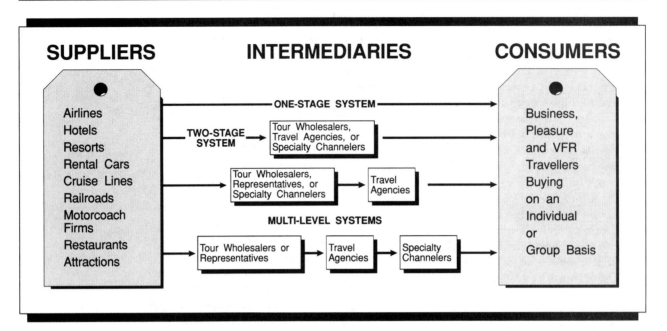

SUPPLIERS

Airlines
Hotels
Resorts
Rental Cars
Cruise Lines
Railroads
Motorcoach Firms
Restaurants
Attractions

INTERMEDIARIES

ONE-STAGE SYSTEM

TWO-STAGE SYSTEM

Tour Wholesalers, Travel Agencies, or Specialty Channelers

Tour Wholesalers, Representatives, or Specialty Channelers

Travel Agencies

MULTI-LEVEL SYSTEMS

Tour Wholesalers or Representatives

Travel Agencies

Specialty Channelers

CONSUMERS

Business, Pleasure and VFR Travellers Buying on an Individual or Group Basis

FIGURE 1.3
Travel distribution systems.
Adapted from Gee et al. "The Travel Industry". 2nd Edition. New York: Van Nostrand Reinhold, 1989.

the expiry date some products can still be marked down and sold at a lower price. Other products, such as furniture, do not deteriorate with age. Their shelf life is limited only by changing trends and tastes. For travel products however, the shelf life is much more critical. If the product is not sold on a given day it is lost to the supplier as a source of income. Once a plane leaves, that empty seat is gone forever. Last night's unoccupied hotel room is lost revenue which cannot be recovered. It is therefore essential that travel products be marketed efficiently.

All industries require a distribution system to create the link between a product's supplier (or manufacturer) and its consumer. The travel industry is no different in this respect. However, for the reasons stated above, there are additional pressures placed on the travel distribution system. Because of its perishable and intangible nature, the travel product requires a large and highly efficient distribution system. This need to distribute the travel product widely and quickly has led to a large number of distributors or intermediaries in the travel industry. The distribution sector for tourism is therefore much stronger than for other products such as automobiles where the producer controls the quality, the price, and who distributes the product. Intermediaries in the travel industry have more power to

influence and direct consumer demand. This influence with consumers gives intermediaries sufficient bargaining power with suppliers to affect their pricing, product policies and promotional activities.

We have briefly mentioned some of the organizations involved in the travel distribution system. Now let us examine it and them in more detail. The distribution system can be extremely simple or rather complex (see Figure 1.3). Much depends on the goals of the supplier. The general goal of all suppliers is to efficiently make their products available to consumers in a cost effective manner. The simplest way to do so is to sell directly to the public. Many travel suppliers do just this. Airlines have sales offices where the public can purchase tickets; hotels accept direct reservations, and hotel chains have central reservations offices which accept bookings on behalf of all properties in the organization; and car rental companies take direct bookings. This is a simple distribution system, sometimes called a one-stage or unilateral system, since there is only one step in the buying process. From the supplier's viewpoint, such a one-stage system is simple and it offers additional sales opportunities (for example, in selling additional services to the client or in upgrading the sale). It also permits greater profitability since there is no intermediary or middleman, and it allows the supplier to better manage key client accounts such as full fare frequent flyers. It may also be necessary for some suppliers to establish a direct sales network. Airlines, for example, compete with each other over the same routes, using similar equipment and timetables, and charging much the same fares. Direct promotion and sales service for clients may therefore be a necessity in such a competitive environment. Its major disadvantage is that it is expensive. Each supplier must maintain sales offices and a sales staff in every location where they wish to sell directly to the client. An alternative is a large (and possibly more expensive or less efficient) central reservation system. Since 1996 many suppliers have developed sites on the Internet which permit them to sell directly to the public. Although it is expensive and time-consuming to establish such a mechanism, the Internet increases a supplier's access to the consumer. Whereas a physical location, such as an office, reaches a local area and a central telephone reservation system has a national range, the Internet market is global. From the consumer's standpoint, the one-stage system provides flexibility and a greater degree of control over the sale. They can buy wherever and whenever it suits them and from suppliers who have earned their confidence. However, this too comes at a price. In the unilateral system, consumers must contact each supplier individually. This can be time consuming and, if it involves overseas communications, expensive and inefficient.

A somewhat more complex system is termed the two-stage or bilevel system. This system places an intermediary between the supplier and the consumer. Most often, this intermediary is a travel agency. The function can, however, be fulfilled by a tour operator with a retail license or by a specialty channeler, such as an incentive travel company or a corporate meeting planner. The two-stage system is employed for a number of reasons. Clients often live far away, perhaps in another town or country, from the tourist services they require. Suppliers must therefore rely on intermediaries to distribute their products or services. Consumers too must rely on intermediaries for information on the services. The principal advantages to suppliers are that they gain a sales force without carrying the overhead, they acquire assistance in dispensing credit and billing clients, and the intermediaries (particularly tour operators) develop off-season promotions to help them sell their product. Clients gain by obtaining unbiased professional assistance (thereby saving time and money), multiple options (in that they can acquire information on a range of suppliers' products), a single charge billing system (in that the intermediary collects once only to cover all supplier payments), and they may have access to out of town assistance through the intermediary's branches or chain offices. In addition, the intermediary, through the cumulative effect of its buying power, can often gain price and/or service advantages with suppliers which can be passed on to the consumer. Thus, the buyer may also obtain a lower price for the product in a two-stage system. Finally, all of these advantages are provided to the consumer at little or no cost since the intermediary earns income from commissions earned on the sale of the suppliers' products.

There are other, more complex distribution systems but they are simply variations on the two-stage system. Generally, the more complex systems separate the intermediaries mentioned above, i.e., the travel agency, the tour operator and the specialty channeler. In such multilevel systems there may be three, four, or more stages in the distribution mechanism. For example, a three-stage system may operate such that suppliers sell their products to tour operators who combine them to create tour packages which are sold through retail travel agencies to consumers. The advantages and disadvantages of this and more complex systems are similar to those of the two-stage system.

The particular channels of distribution selected are determined by suppliers to meet their company goals. The choice is based on factors such as the particular product, the nature and extent of the market, the sales, costs and profit records of various channels, the degree of cooperation expected, the assistance required, and the number of outlets to be used. For example, an operator of budget holidays with a low profit margin that requires a large turnover would, most likely, attempt to obtain the maximum exposure for the product by marketing through all travel agencies. A luxury cruise line with a limited number of sailings, however, might opt for exclusive distribution through one particular travel agency chain with an established high income clientele.

Some companies have attempted to gain more control over the distribution channels by purchasing or forming companies at different levels of the system. For example, Thomas Cook and American Express operate at both the wholesale and retail levels. When a supplier or wholesaler distributes its products through its own retail channel, it is known as vertical marketing. Thomas Cook and American Express are not alone in adopting this marketing strategy. All such companies, however, also distribute their products through other retailers.

Travel Industry Segments

We have discussed the travel industry in terms of its distribution system and learned that the system comprises suppliers, intermediaries and consumers. The following material reviews more closely the components which make up this business side of tourism, that is, the travel industry. In general, the travel industry can be divided into suppliers, related industries, and intermediaries such as retail travel agencies. The suppliers may be primary suppliers or secondary suppliers. Primary suppliers, such as airlines, hotels, or car rental companies, offer direct service to clients. Secondary suppliers, on the other hand, provide service to clients through a primary supplier. For example, an

entertainer on a cruise ship or a musician in a hotel lounge is considered to be a secondary supplier. Our concern here, however, is with primary suppliers, and with related industries and travel agencies. A brief summary of each of these segments follows.

Transportation Suppliers

Transportation is crucial to any tourist activity and the importance of this segment cannot be overestimated. This sector consists of airlines, railroads, ground transportation (bus companies and car rental firms), and marine transportation. Each of these important segments will be discussed in greater detail later in the text. The following material, however, presents a brief overview of their functions and how they interact with each other.

Airlines

Airlines have become the form of transport most closely associated with the tourist business. Although tourist use of airlines is highly visible, commercial (or business) travel actually accounts for about half of all airline business.

Flying's major advantages over other modes of transport are its speed and the time saved by using aircraft. Except in a few countries where high speed trains operate, no other mode of transport can compete with these benefits. Airlines therefore compete almost exclusively with each other rather than with other means of transportation. There is, however, a high degree of cooperation between airlines just as there is between airlines and the other segments of the industry. For example, airlines share routes, accept each other's tickets, and cooperate in scheduling. Airlines also cooperate through the information they share in their computer reservations systems. Each system carries the schedules of its competitors. In addition, these computer systems carry information on the airlines' other "competitors", such as car rental and railroad companies. There is further cooperation with companies offering other forms of transportation. Fly/drive holidays in which airlines cooperate with car rental companies have become extremely popular, as have fly/cruise programs. In fact, it is difficult to imagine any type of vacation which does not include at least a short hop on an aircraft. Airlines also cooperate closely with tour operators in the design and delivery of package tours. Of course, airlines work closely with travel agencies, the chief means of selling airline seats.

Railroads

Although railroads have suffered a decline in North America, they continue to play a significant transport role in Great Britain, continental Europe, Russia, South Africa and Japan. Generally, railroads offer comfortable, convenient service from city centre to city centre. Studies have shown that the central intercity nature of railroad travel offers serious competition to airlines over short to medium distances (up to about 500 km). For such journeys there is no significant time difference between the plane and train. Some countries, such as France and Japan, have developed high speed rail networks to increase this competition and many more plan to do so. Again, cooperation with other industry segments is observed. Rail tours are very popular and in Canada there was a traditional connection between the railroads and the hotel industry.

Bus Operators

Buses offer the most flexible and economical mode of public transportation. Like railroads, however, bus companies have been affected by the dominance of the airlines. Bus companies generally perform one of two types of activity, transportation or sightseeing. Generally, bus lines sell transportation service directly to the public. Few travel agencies, except perhaps in rural areas, are involved in this sales process.

Bus lines offer point-to-point and express service for short haul trips, such as Toronto-London, New York-Washington, Quebec City-Montreal, or Los Angeles-San Diego, as well as for long

haul journeys like Toronto-Vancouver or New York-Los Angeles. Buses are a cheap and efficient means of transportation and compete effectively with railroads and the private car. The main problem with buses as a means of transportation is one of image. Even this is changing, however, with the introduction of new equipment, on-board video entertainment, and attendant service similar to the airlines.

Buses as a transportation mode cooperate with other industry segments by supplying passenger transfer services for airlines, tour operators, and hotels and resorts. Bus companies also work closely with tour operators, who coordinate sightseeing tours by motorcoach with accommodations to create tour packages. Local bus companies, however, may set up their own city sightseeing tours which can be included as part of a stay-put vacation package. Here, cooperation with tour operators and hoteliers is essential. Equally important is the assistance of travel agencies to sell the product. Motorcoach tours can be short local runs or longer regional trips. Tours of the Maritimes and the Calgary-Vancouver region are popular in Canada. Europe is noted for its motorcoach tours.

Car Rental

Cars give travellers more freedom of choice in route, destination and timing of the journey, than any other mode of transportation. This flexibility and freedom of movement appeals to both business and pleasure travellers. Car rental has therefore become an important sector of the transportation field which can provide travel agencies with a lucrative source of income.

Fly/drive packages, available through airlines, tour operators, wholesalers and representatives, are very popular throughout California, Florida, Europe and Britain. A typical fly/drive package arranged by a tour operator will link a charter flight from an airline with accommodation from a hotel chain and a car from a rental company.

Marine Transportation

At one time, more people crossed the

Atlantic Ocean by ship than by airplane. Since the advent of jet aircraft, however, such point-to-point transportation has all but died out. Two types of water travel may still be distinguished.

Long distance point-to-point ship transportation is extremely rare. It is restricted to some summer transatlantic crossings and to repositioning cruises offered by some cruise lines. For example, at the end of a summer season a cruise ship may be repositioned from Mediterranean summer cruises to Caribbean winter cruises. The cruise line may then offer one point-to-point sailing from the Mediterranean to the "new" home port in the Caribbean. Cunard and Polish Ocean Line still offer occasional transatlantic crossings. The Baltic Steamship Line offers transportation service in the North Sea and the Baltic Sea, and the Italian Line operates in the Mediterranean. Travel agencies will sell such transportation services when requested, but this is a very small part of their business.

Limited distance water travel is handled by ferries. Ferry service is important in many parts of the world, such as between Britain and Europe, in the Baltic and the Mediterranean, and in Asia. In Canada, ferries serve the Maritime and West Coast regions. As with long distance marine transportation, travel agencies do sell this product, however, ferry service is usually sold as part of another service such as a train ticket.

Other Suppliers

Accommodation

Accommodation is a major component of the tourism industry and is a part of every trip except a cruise or visits to friends or relatives (known as VFR arrangements). Even a one day business trip may involve meetings arranged at a hotel. The function of the accommodations sector has become much more than just providing shelter and a bed for the evening. The accommodations sector, or hospitality industry, is possibly the largest component in tourism, encompassing lodgings, food, beverage, entertainment, corporate meetings, and transfers. An indication of its importance is that the cost of the accommodation often determines the total price of a packaged tour. Its quality will also have a major impact on how well the client enjoys the vacation or business trip.

Many types of accommodation are available. These range from the well-known hotels, motels and resorts, through bed-and-breakfast establishments, guest houses, *paradores* in Spain, *ryokans* in Japan, villas, apartments, condominiums and castles. The accommodations sector works closely with many other sectors of the industry but particularly with airlines and tour operators in the creation of tours. Travel agencies sell hotel rooms directly but such sales account for only 10-20 percent of hotel bookings.

The most commonly used accommodations are hotels and motels. Hotel chains dominate the industry. Holiday Inn is the largest hotel chain in the world but many others are also important. Some well-known chains are Best Western, Hilton, Ramada, Four Seasons, CP, CN, Sheraton, Hyatt and Intercontinental. Many of the American chains are multinational corporations found around the world. Several European hotels systems, such as PLM, Trusthouse Forte Hotels, Grand Metropolitan, and Novotel, also operate on an international basis.

Wholesale Travel

Wholesalers in the travel industry are involved in the marketing and selling of travel packages and tours. For the present, the following brief survey indicates the range of wholesaler activities.

Tour wholesalers use their knowledge of the industry to help travel agencies who do not have the resources to meet their clients' needs. They provide made-to-measure packages and tours which are sold through travel agencies to the consumer. Wholesalers sell only to travel agencies, not directly to the public. Many wholesalers specialize in certain destination areas, such as Eastern Europe, while others concentrate on particular interests, such as golf holidays. In effect, tour wholesalers are brokers or representatives for suppliers, such as hotels, and act as intermediaries between these suppliers and travel agencies.

Tour operators are an important category of travel wholesaler. Depending on local legislation, tour operators sell holiday packages directly to consumers or indirectly through travel agencies. They often specialize in certain destinations or types of vacation, such as adventure travel. Tour operator packages can be distinguished from wholesaler packages in that they are "mass produced" and all arrangements are made prior to the commencement of a "season". The consumer merely selects a completely preplanned package from the tour operator's brochure. Such mass produced holidays are lower in cost because tour operators buy the tour components in bulk.

We have already discussed tour operator cooperation with bus companies. There are also motorcoach tour operators who have their own equipment and offer sightseeing and land tours. These tours are most popular in North America, Britain and Europe.

Tour operators offer the most obvious example of cooperation within the travel industry. The tour operator must combine the services of airlines, hotels, ground operators such as bus companies and car rental firms, restaurants, and a number of related sectors, if they wish to create successful package tours.

Cruise lines differ from the marine transportation companies discussed earlier in that they sell more than just transportation. Cruises are self-contained vacations which include transportation, accommodation, meals and entertainment. In effect, cruises are floating resorts and cruise lines a type of tour operator. Cruise lines rely almost exclusively on travel agencies to sell their cruises.

Related Industries

There are many related organizations in the travel industry which may or may not create products to sell to consumers. In either case, they play an essential role in the smooth functioning of the tourist business.

We have learned that **tourist boards** are established by national governments to promote travel and tourism to and within their country. They attract tourists and provide them and the travel industry with information. Tourist boards work closely with many sectors of the industry to achieve their goals. For example, a tourist board will generally work closely with the national airline and with the accommodations sector to ensure that there is adequate airline service and lodging facilities to meet demand. The tourist board may also join with tour operators and other companies in advertising overseas. The NTO will often subsidise participation in overseas trade shows. Some NTOs are also involved in the training or regulating of the travel industry or some of its components.

Representative companies are private firms representing clients in major locations where, for various reasons, the client does not wish to or is unable to open an office. Representatives may promote hotels, cruise lines, tourist boards, or car rental companies, and in addition may act as a local reservations centre handling client bookings. Tour operators sometimes act as representatives for cruise lines and promote cruise vacations through their tour brochures. Many tour wholesalers began their company operations as representatives for various hotels. Some wholesalers continue to fulfill this function.

The **recreation and entertainment** segment handles attractions that were built especially for tourists as well as those constructed for local enjoyment. Their range of activity is enormous and includes theatre agencies, stage shows, theme parks, wax museums, animal/marine parks, towers and monuments. Most organizations in this sector deal directly with the consumer but many cooperate with tour operators and airlines to add extra elements to tours.

Travel insurance is one of the unseen sectors of the industry. Insurance is a large business and an essential component of every tour package and trip. Travel insurance companies work with airlines and tour operators to provide protection for the travelling public. The insurance companies have developed a range of insurance coverage to meet most needs of tourists and business travellers. Travel agencies offer travel insurance to all their customers, as much for their own protection as for that of their clients.

Publications are important sources of information for industry members and consumers. Trade magazines assist all travel industry personnel to maintain their knowledge of the industry and its products by supplying accurate and up-to-date information. The consumer's major sources of print information are travel guide books, magazines, and the travel section of daily newspapers.

Individuals and corporations in many fields tend to form associations to achieve common goals with those who have parallel interests. The travel industry is no exception and a number of **trade associations** have been formed for such purposes. Trade Associations are valuable for the educational and support services they provide. ACTA (Association of Canadian Travel Agents), CITC (Canadian Institutes of Travel Counsellors), and TIAC (Tourism Industry Association of

Canada) are significant professional organizations in the Canadian travel industry. In addition to working with its own membership and other segments of the travel industry, each organization lobbies government and informs the public. Trade associations are discussed in greater detail in Chapter 14.

The Travel Agency

The travel agency is the pivotal intermediary in the travel distribution system. Almost every segment of the travel industry, either directly or indirectly, deals with the travel agency. Travel suppliers rely on travel agencies to distribute their products. Consumers rely on travel agencies for impartial advice and professional service. The travel agency is the central link in the chain. The travel agency and particularly its employees, travel counsellors, are the focus of this textbook. For this reason, the role of the travel agency and its employees has been reserved for a more in-depth study. The following chapter examines this topic more closely. At the same time, readers will begin to acquire the skills and knowledge required by a professional travel counsellor.

Review Questions

1. Why is it important for a government tourist office to be able to define the terms "tourist" and "trip"?

2. Discuss the growth of modern tourism and suggest some reasons for its expansion.

3. When, where and why was travel legislation introduced in Canada?

4. Describe the types of companies which make up the travel industry.

5. Discuss the advantages and disadvantages of various travel distribution systems.

Research Assignment

Compare how the national tourist offices of Canada, Australia, and Great Britain promote tourism to their country.

References

Government tourist offices provide travellers and travel agencies with brochures, booklets and maps of their countries free and in ample quantity. Statistics and other information are also available for office use and for consumer distribution. For Canadian information contact Statistics Canada, Tourism Canada, and the provincial and territorial tourist offices.

The Personnel Guide to the Canadian Travel Industry published by The Canadian Travel Press, 310 Dupont Street, Toronto, Ontario M5S 1V9. This publication, which is updated twice yearly, gives the addresses of all national tourist offices and foreign embassies in Canada, as well as a listing of airlines, tour wholesalers, travel agencies and related companies. It is an invaluable reference for anyone working in the Canadian travel industry.

The World Travel Directory published by the Reed Travel Group, 500 Plaza Drive, Secaucus, NJ 07094-3602, USA. For those who have global aspirations, this annual reference provides a worldwide listing of travel agencies, wholesalers and tour operators.

## Chapter 2

Travel Counselling

Chapter Summary

This chapter focuses on the primary distributor of the travel product, the travel agency, and on the work of its employees, travel counsellors. The chapter begins with a discussion of the nature of a travel agency. Following this introduction is a review of how travel agencies earn income. Agency expenses, such as wages, overhead, and payments to airlines and other suppliers, are then described. The chapter continues with a study of the forms of organization found among travel agencies. The types of agency business and the business mix are then discussed.

The latter part of the chapter presents some reasons for studying travel counselling. Careers available are mentioned and a job description for travel counsellors is outlined. Next, the role of a travel counsellor is discussed. This role is the basic focus of the text. The chapter concludes with a discussion of this role and in setting the parameters for the remainder of the book.

Chapter Objectives
After completing this chapter you should be able to:

- Describe the nature and function of a travel agency.

- Determine the importance of travel agencies to the travel industry.

- Report the sources and nature of travel agency compensation.

- Discuss travel agency expenses, e.g., wages, overhead.

- Distinguish between fixed and variable expenses.

- Describe how travel agencies are organized - by size, by affiliation (independent, chain, franchise, consortium), and by type of business.

- Distinguish between each type of affiliation.

- Define the types of travel business which travel agencies sell.

- Distinguish between each type of business.

- Discuss agency business mix.

- Describe the advantages and disadvantages of specialization.

- Identify careers in the travel industry.

- Discuss reasons for studying travel counselling.

- Describe the role and responsibilities of a travel counsellor.

- Recognize a job description for travel counsellors.

What is a Travel Agency?

Chapter 1 introduced the idea that the travel agency is the principal sales force of the travel industry. The discussion on the travel distribution system noted that travel agencies provide the link between the suppliers of travel products and consumers. Agencies sell the industry's components, either individually or in combination, to travellers. This chapter focuses on the travel agency and its employees, travel counsellors. An agency's function is to sell travel products by servicing its clients' travel needs. The travel counsellor's role is to satisfy these needs by matching them with an appropriate travel product.

An illustration of various travel distribution systems is reproduced in Chapter 1. With the exception of the one-stage distribution system, all other methods of selling travel products involve the use of travel agencies. As the industry increases in complexity, more travellers are turning to travel agencies for information and advice on the latest travel opportunities. The diagram on the opposite page (Figure 2.1) represents this central position which the travel agency holds in the selling and distribution of travel products in the marketplace.

Even though some travellers do deal directly with suppliers, the accompanying

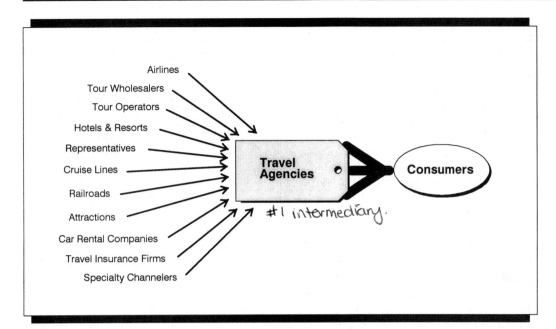

FIGURE 2.1
The travel agency's central place in the travel distribution system.

table (Figure 2.2) emphasizes the importance of the travel agency, particularly in connection with international travel.

Travel Agency Income

Travel agencies act as distributors of travel products for the companies which supply the services. Suppliers, such as airlines and tour operators, make up the bulk of most travel agency sales. In return for promoting and marketing their products, travel suppliers pay travel agencies a commission for each sale. The vast majority of income for daily operations is earned from sales made by the agency's counsellors to its clientele. Income is, however, generated from other suppliers and additional sources. Some travel agencies sell travel accessories, travel guidebooks, and passport photographs. Almost all agencies earn a small amount from the application of cancellation penalties and service charges. A few agencies design independent tours for clients using net rates from suppliers and add a mark-up for their professional services. These additional sources of revenue are, however, quite small by comparison with the income generated from commissions.

The travel agency acts on behalf of and receives a commission from industry **principals**, such as airlines and other transportation companies, tour operators and hotels, for each sale made by the travel agency. For most travel products, the rates of commission are fixed by the suppliers and, to a large extent, are non-negotiable. The average commission rate in the travel industry is 8-12 percent of the retail price of the product. Scheduled airline tickets generally pay less than this rate whereas travel insurance sales usually earn a considerably higher commission. Many industry principals will not pay commission to travel agencies unless the agency possesses certain key appointments or produces a minimum sales quota. For example, a travel agency must be

FIGURE 2.2
Supplier depend-ence on travel agencies.
Source: Bitner, M.J., and B.H. Booms. "Journal of Travel Research", Volume XX, Number 4, Spring 1982.

SUPPLIER		Approximate Sales Volume Booked by Travel Agencies
Air	- Domestic	50 - 65%
	- International	75 - 90%
Hotel	- Domestic	20 - 30%
	- International	70%
Cruises		95%
Rail		Less than 10%
Bus		Less than 10%
Car rentals		20 - 30%
Tour packages		
	- Domestic	66%
	- International	95%

appointed by IATA to receive commission on the sale of international air tickets, and by the Air Transport Association of America (ATA) to receive commission on transborder or domestic U.S. air tickets. There is also a Canadian appointment from the Air Transport Association of Canada (ATAC) which permits agencies to earn commission on tickets sold for travel within Canada. Currently, there is a dollar limit (or "cap") on commissions paid by scheduled carriers for travel within Canada and on transborder fares to the USA. Commissions on the sale of airline tickets for international routings follow IATA procedures (i.e., a percentage of the ticket price) with a cap.

As well as paying commission, suppliers also provide travel agencies with such sales tools as brochures, posters, window displays, and visits from sales representatives. The cost of servicing a travel agency with these sales tools can be quite high. Many tour operators stipulate that agencies reach a minimum production quota over a certain period of time in order to receive commission and/or sales tools. This practice varies among tour operators and no set policy applies. Most hotels, hotel chains, and ground transportation companies require no appointments and set no minimum sales figure for agencies to receive commission. It is always prudent, however, to contact the sales department of any travel principal to check conditions for receiving commission.

Just as there is a minimum sales quota to earn commission from some tour operators, most travel suppliers have a commission structure designed to pay a higher rate of commission as the number of bookings increases. Once a particular sales level is reached a higher percentage, or **override commission**, is paid on all subsequent sales. As an incentive, this higher commission percentage is usually awarded retroactively for all bookings made by the agency within that season or year. For example, a tour operator may pay a standard rate of 10 percent commission on the first twenty sales made by an agency. The commission rate may increase to 12 percent for the next thirty bookings, and 15 percent on fifty or more. If an agency

achieves fifty sales within a given sales period, then the 15 percent commission is paid on all sales made by the agency in that time frame. This system acts as a further incentive to travel agencies to sell the products of particular tour operators. Most travel suppliers allow agencies with multiple offices, such as chains, franchises and consortiums, to combine the sales figures of all branches or organizational members. This strategy establishes higher overall sales volumes for multiple outlet agencies than can generally be achieved by single agencies. The larger organizations therefore reach override commission levels earlier than their smaller competitors. In some cases, the multiple outlet initially receives a higher commission rate than the independent.

One effect of this commission structure and sales quota system is its influence on the products sold by a travel agency. Many travel agencies find it more profitable to promote a limited range of airlines, tour operators and other suppliers' products. By concentrating its efforts on just a few suppliers, the travel agency hopes to more quickly reach the override commission level of sales. Some agencies support such a limited range of product lines that they become associated with particular products and companies. This can have both positive and negative effects. It permits the agency to earn a higher income, to become linked in the consumer's mind with a particular type of product, and to perhaps gain preferential treatment from its suppliers. That is, the agency's reputation becomes more closely related to that of the suppliers it sells. On the other hand, if an agency refuses to sell particular products it can lose some of its business to its competitors. Further, an agency which specializes in a limited product range loses some control over its image and its ability to change product with changing market conditions.

Although the majority of travel agency income still derives from commission on the sale of travel products, several factors are changing the nature of how travel agencies earn revenue.

- Airlines have introduced commission caps which limit the amount they pay for selling an airline ticket.

- In an effort to find the lowest fare for a price-sensitive public, travel consultants increasingly have turned to consolidators who supply airline tickets at a net rate (i.e., without commission).
- Many other suppliers now offer their products to travel agencies at a net rate.
- The Internet has become a competitor for travel agencies since it provides easy direct booking facilities for consumers. In fact, the growth of the Internet threatens the travel agency's central place in the distribution system.

In response to these challenges, travel agencies have begun to impose fees for the services they provide. This is a risky proposition, since consumers may feel that they are being charged for services which once were given freely. The situation compels travel consultants to become more professional. To earn a fee, consultants must give their clients added value. That value is the expert knowledge they possess and the professional advice they offer. In the future, it is expected that travel agencies will earn the majority of their income by selling their services rather than by selling travel products.

Agencies charge fees for a number of services. Generally, fees are charged on an hourly basis and vary depending on the consultant's experience and the complexity of the service. Fees can also be set at a specific amount, again depending on the task. Some of the charges currently in use are fees for:

- Expenses previously absorbed, e.g., long distance calls and faxes, delivery charges.
- Services that provide no income, e.g., booking a B&B in Britain, assisting with visa or passport applications, making airline reservations paid with frequent flyer points.
- Plan to go deposit. The amount is considered a deposit if a booking is made but is treated as a cancellation fee if the client decides not to proceed. Such deposits recognize the time spent in consulting and planning before a reservation is made. Some agencies call

this a commitment deposit. Others label it as a research or consulting fee.
- Last minute requests, which can be time consuming and may be unsuccessful in securing the desired booking, e.g., a flight to Calgary during the Calgary Stampede.
- Cancellation and changes (in addition to those set by suppliers).
- Processing airline reservations.

Travel Agency Expenses

Business expenses are generally divided into three categories; fixed, variable and semi-variable.

Fixed expenses are defined as those expenses which are unrelated to sales volume or the level of income generated. Such expenses can be predicted and are relatively stable on an annual basis. Basic salaries, rent, utilities, business insurance, leases for automation equipment, systems and furniture, subscriptions for reference manuals, and professional fees, such as those for accounting, bookkeeping and trade association memberships, are considered fixed expenses. These items may increase from year to year but they are generally unchanged within any one year period. Telephone line charges are also a fixed expense whereas long distance calls and fax charges are semi-variable expenses.

A **variable expense** is one which is directly related to the company's sales level. Variable expenses rise when sales increase and fall when sales decrease. An obvious example of a variable expense is bonus commissions made to travel counsellors. Another example is the salaries and commissions paid to outside sales staff. Items such as familiarization trips for staff and advertising for the agency are also considered variable expenses. Although advertising may be employed to generate business during a slow period, most agencies usually advertise only during the good times.

Similarly, staff are generally sent on familiarization trips only when the agency can afford the expense. This is most likely when sales volume is high.

Semi-variable expenses have some characteristics in common with both fixed and variable expenses. They exhibit the features of a fixed expense in that they must be paid each year. However, they also tend to rise or fall with the sales level of the agency. Typical of semi-variable expenses are supplies, such as ticket stock, stationery and the like, postage, long distance calls and fax charges, and payments to the compensation fund (if the agency operates in a province with specific travel legislation).

The Travel Agency as a Service Industry

As we have discussed, travel agencies earn their income from the sale of travel products. The travel agency business, however, is generally considered to be a service industry rather than a sales business. With travel products, consumers pay for an intangible item; something that cannot be returned, unlike clothing or an appliance. There is little opportunity to "examine the merchandise" before purchase. Often, there is no more than a picture of a hotel or a beautiful landscape, and a description of the destination's nightlife and attractions on which to base a purchase decision. This attribute affects the debate on travel as a sales or service industry.

A travel agency's income is defined by the range of products it sells and by the commission available on these products. Most travel agencies sell basically the same products at much the same prices. (A few agencies do discount the selling price. Such agencies attempt to boost their earnings by generating a higher sales volume.) The intangible nature of travel products makes it difficult for consumers to compare, for example, one tour with another or one destination with another. The travel counsellor is critical in this

selection process. It is the travel counsellor's knowledge, expertise and service which become the major factors in making a sale, rather than the product itself. Furthermore, as travel becomes more expensive, and the consumer more cost-conscious, the selection of a travel agency by the consumer tends to be based on the service provided by the agency. Agencies that sell travel at discounted prices usually offer a minimum of service. Full service travel agencies pride themselves on the knowledge, professionalism and counselling abilities of their staff. Consumers are free to select the approach they prefer but the majority choose service over sales.

Choosing an Agency

Consumers may purchase most travel products directly from the supplier or through a travel agency. The majority prefer to use the services of a travel agency rather than spend the time and expense needed to make one's own travel arrangements. Several factors influence a consumer's selection of a particular travel agency.

Travel Agency Reputation. The reputation of a travel agency is foremost in the mind of the consumer. "Every client a satisfied client" is the way to keep and build an agency's reputation. Satisfied clients often tell friends and neighbours about the excellent travel arrangements made for them by a particular agency. This "word of mouth" advertising is the most valuable type. It cannot be purchased, it increases an agency's clientele, and it provides a solid base for the agency.

The consumer action column of any large newspaper often contains complaints of "bad pricing" by a particular travel agency, or travel services not supplied as contracted. Even if the travel agency is not at fault, this type of negative advertising will harm the reputation of the travel agency.

Advertising. Many large travel agencies have the financial resources to create extensive multi-media advertising campaigns. This is effective as consumers will constantly see or hear the name and slogan of the particular travel agency. Name familiarity is frequently the prime reason for a consumer selecting a particular agency. Travel agencies located in or near large metropolitan areas can make use of community newspapers or neighbourhood bulletins where advertising rates are lower.

Small or medium size travel agencies do not possess the available capital to launch large advertising programs. Consequently, direct mail and cooperative advertising become more important to them. Cooperative advertising can be used with any medium but is particularly popular in newspapers. In cooperative advertising a number of agencies jointly advertise and thus reduce their individual costs. Such advertisements are most commonly created by suppliers who share the costs with various retailers. For example, a tour operator may produce an advertisement for a particular destination which includes a list of agencies where the product can be purchased.

Repeat Clientele. Nothing is more satisfying to a travel agency or an individual counsellor than having a satisfied client return to make arrangements for future travel. Accurate and competent servicing of clients in conjunction with courtesy, appropriate telephone manners, a warm welcome and a clean office, create the atmosphere for clientele to become repeat clientele.

Convenience. In many cases a client deals with a travel agency because it is convenient. The agency may be located near the client's home or place of business, have adequate parking, or be situated in a shopping mall and have suitable business hours.

Types of Travel Agencies

There are currently over 4500 retail travel agencies in Canada. Retail travel

agencies may be classified in several ways. For example, about half of the 4500 agencies are located in Ontario. Agencies can therefore be classified by location. Of the 4500 or so agencies in Canada, about 4000 are appointed by IATA to sell scheduled airline tickets. Another way to classify agencies, then, is by the appointments they hold. A third system groups agencies by the types of travel business (or clientele) that they have. A fourth classification describes agencies according to their organizational structure. Types of travel business and organizational structure will each be discussed later in this chapter. The simplest and most common method, however, is by agency size, either in terms of the number of staff or in terms of the annual sales volume.

Travel Agency Size

Agencies classified as **small** are often managed by the owner who employs between one and three counsellors. Small agencies usually have annual sales of about one million dollars or less. Often, such agencies specialize in a particular clientele or type of business. These agencies rely on "word of mouth" reputation and the personal contacts of the owner, manager and staff to generate clients. The emphasis is personal service as a basis for customer loyalty. The owner/manager usually takes an active role in the counselling aspects of the business.

Medium size travel agencies commonly have a staff of 8-10 employees. They depend on some personal contact to attract clientele but also have the resources to be involved in advertising and promotion on a small scale. Business is neither heavily commercial nor biased towards vacation travel but is a blend of both. At one time, the medium size travel agency generally possessed an automated reservation and/or ticketing system which the small agency could not afford. Today, however, the majority of travel agencies are automated, no matter what their size.

Larger agencies may operate more sophisticated systems with accounting software, automated ticket printing, and other features beyond the reach of their smaller cousins. Their physical appointments may also be of a higher quality. In recent years competition has been so severe that many companies decided that the only alternatives were growth or death. The result was a consolidation of the travel agency market. A series of takeovers, mergers and reorganizations has occurred which created larger groupings within the travel agency community. Thus there are now more large organizations and multiple outlet agencies than at any stage in the industry's development. The large travel agency may be either a single office outlet employing dozens, or a multi-office organization with branch offices throughout the province or country. Large agencies are often highly diversified and have specialists who concentrate on particular areas of the travel industry to service specific client needs. A large agency is sometimes structured so that there are a number of small, specialized agencies or departments under one company umbrella. Larger agencies can participate in more intense promotional programs and use their advertising budgets in a number of different media. Large agencies generally have the most sophisticated technology available to the travel industry, including completely automated reservation and ticketing systems. The agency may also possess its own in-house computer accounting system.

Travel Agency Organization

The travel agency business has traditionally attracted small businessmen and individuals with an entrepreneurial flare. Most travel agencies are owned as a sole proprietorship, a partnership, or a corporation (that is, a limited company). Regardless of the form of ownership, an agency will be organized in one of four structures: independent, chain, franchise, and cooperative or consortium. Originally, all travel agencies were individually owned and many were family businesses. As the

travel industry grew, so did the size of the agencies which distributed the product. Some agencies began to open branch offices and this led to the formation of chain agencies. By the latter part of the 1970s, the multiple office or chain concept had become the dominant structure in the retail sector. During the 1980s, the franchise concept which had proved successful in marketing fast foods and other products, was successfully introduced into the retail travel business. More recently, cooperatives have sprung up to protect independent agencies and to compete with the other larger agency groupings. Both franchises and cooperatives have experienced rapid growth.

Independent Travel Agencies

All travel agencies were originally independent. Independent agencies have traditionally been single outlet operations. As such, they tend to fall into the category described above as small agencies. Some independent agencies, however, have a large number of employees and a healthy sales income. Nevertheless, the majority show the attributes typical of all small businesses. They tend to be managed by the owner (who may have no management training or expertise), have a small staff, and operate primarily in a local area with local clientele. The advantages of such independent agencies are that they have low overheads and the flexibility to modify their operations according to the circumstances.

Although many newly opened agencies are independents, industry pundits predict that the demise of this form of operation is imminent. There may be some truth to this opinion. Current figures suggest that about seven agencies close their doors for every ten that open and the majority of new agencies are members of chains or franchises. The travel industry, like most others, is becoming increasingly competitive. This type of competitive business climate fosters the growth of some companies at the expense of others, that is, the large companies tend to become larger while the small ones go out of business. Larger companies have the ability to buy travel products and services in bulk and this allows them to offer their clients a lower price. With their larger staff, they also have more expertise and experience at their disposal. These advantages permit them to generate a higher sales volume and thereby qualify for override commissions.

In addition to the disadvantages of smaller size and lower sales volume, independents may suffer from a lack of experience and poor management. They may not be sufficiently well financed and may also find it difficult to acquire the financial backing necessary to develop an efficient operation. Financing is critical, particularly now that the travel industry has become increasingly automated. The independent agency, however, still has a place in the industry. Many clients prefer the personal service associated with a small operation. Clients of independent agencies are often among the most loyal. The growth of the travel industry and the predominance of larger organizations has also given independents an opportunity to identify and fill specific market niches. By specializing in one type of business or clientele, such as the luxury market, senior citizens, the cruise industry or a particular special interest group, independents can build a reputation and business in areas where larger agencies do not have the flexibility to compete.

Chain Agencies (or Multiple Outlets)

A chain agency is one which has several branches operating under the same ownership and management policies. Chains are characterized by standard administrative and operating procedures, and selling and promotional strategies which are directed by a head office.

We have discussed the fact that multiple outlets permit chains to generate higher sales which allows them to make volume purchase agreements with suppliers. Higher sales are also promoted by cooperative advertising with suppliers. The increased sales

volume then provides a higher rate of commission from their suppliers. The higher sales volume means that multiple outlets have more buying power as well as higher commissions. Such agencies can and do sometimes receive preferential service. For example, they may be able to obtain a seat on a "fully booked" plane or reserve a room in a "fully booked" hotel for a client who needs or deserves special treatment. This does not mean that multiple outlets control suppliers or always get their own way in negotiations, but they often gain more attention.

Chain agencies function on centralized administrative and operating procedures. Such an organization can save time and money for all agencies in the chain and it permits certain economies of scale. For example, stationery and supplies, or even office furniture and equipment, may be purchased in bulk to reduce costs. Chains can also pool resources to achieve further economies or a larger impact. For example, chains can afford to sponsor larger advertising and promotional campaigns thereby reaching a wider market and benefiting all members. Some chains, such as American Express, have developed large credit card membership or mailing lists which enable them to negotiate more advantageous cooperative advertising and promotional arrangements with suppliers. Chain agencies, with their network of branch offices, have the resources to service larger accounts than do independents. For example, a chain with a nationwide presence could better meet the needs of a national corporation with offices in several cities. Large companies may prefer the security of knowing that they can contact an agency representative in any of the country's major cities. Often, the chain can provide better service and/or lower costs because such accounts permit economies of scale in its servicing.

In a travel agency chain, all employees work for the same company. The larger organization means that chains can employ staff more effectively. Employees with particular experience or abilities can be accommodated in career paths to match their skills. Employees can be transferred between offices to assist during periods of staff shortage or to cover particular situations. Large staff numbers give the chain agency a great deal of flexibility in how personnel are assigned. At the same time, employees have some advantages. Their job prospects tend to be more secure and they can follow a career path through more positions within the company. They enjoy better fringe benefits, more training opportunities, and often obtain higher salaries or participate in bonus or incentive plans not available to the employees of smaller agencies. Chain agencies also present a greater number of opportunities for counsellors to specialize according to their skills or interests, for example in commercial accounts, marketing, or in particular destinations or activities.

Offsetting these advantages are the drawbacks associated with many larger organizations. Chain agencies can be more impersonal for both clients and counsellors. Their operations are likely to be more rigid than in a small, independent agency. An example of this rigidity is that decisions regarding the products and suppliers to be sold are usually made at the head office rather than by branch or regional managers. Although these products may not meet the needs of local clientele in all regions, individual branches may not have the ability to alter or deviate from head office policies.

Their size and visibility have made familiar names of many travel chains. Thomas Cook Travel and American Express are two of the world's largest companies whose business encompasses financial services and wholesaling, as well as retail operations. Although every company has its own character, structure and style, all chains basically operate on the same principles. All have a head office and regional divisions. If the operation is sufficiently large there will also be a district division which supervises individual branches.

Travel Agency Franchises

A fairly recent type of agency is the franchise operation. Individual offices may be small or large. From the outside, at least, franchises can be easily confused with chains. The difference between a chain and a franchise is that each franchise (or office) is independently owned, whereas the various branches of a chain are under the same ownership. The franchise agency is usually managed by a franchisee (the individual or company that has signed a franchise agreement with the franchiser, the owner of the franchise concept). The franchiser generally remains at "arm's length" from the day-to-day operations of the agency.

When a franchise agreement is signed, the franchiser usually provides a complete turnkey operation. This means that the franchiser agrees to supply a complete business operation, including concept, management system, advertising, sales strategies and techniques, training, store layout and location, and company image. In return, the franchisee (or franchise holder) pays a fee for the rights to the franchise name and system within a specific territory, and a continuing royalty based on a percentage of annual sales.

Franchises tend to have similar business advantages and limitations as chain agencies. These were described above and principally relate to bulk purchasing power and higher commission receipts. Since franchises are independently owned, each office to some extent works for itself. This individual incentive leads franchise holders to claim that they are more motivated than their chain agency counterparts. They also claim that the individual ownership of franchises personalizes the services they offer. Employees of franchises, like those in chain agencies, have considerable job opportunities. Some movement between franchises is also found since all agencies sell the same products (usually selected by the franchise holder) and follow the same administrative procedures and sales methods. In some cases, particularly in the selection of travel products to be sold, franchise policies may be more rigid than those of the chains. As with the chains, extensive promotional programs are undertaken by the franchise central office. Print media advertising generally mentions all agencies under the umbrella of the franchise.

The franchise operation can be highly diversified, with different offices specializing in different aspects of the travel industry. The major Canadian travel agency franchises are Uniglobe and Goliger's Travel. Intra Travel is also a well known travel franchise. This company also operates a retail agency chain and first began as a consortium.

Travel Agency Cooperatives or Consortiums

Another arrangement, usually employed by small to medium size agencies, is the cooperative or consortium. In this system, each agency retains its independence, personal identity and individual ownership, but combines with other agencies under an association title to gain the marketing advantages of a large chain or franchise organization. This structure permits each agency to obtain the benefits of, for example, large scale advertising and promotion campaigns, or increased commission rates based on the total sale volumes of all agencies in the cooperative.

A consortium functions as a sales and marketing organization which promotes the interests of its members. To maintain and operate a cooperative, each member pays an initial membership fee and then a continuing levy for services. In return for a degree of territorial exclusivity, the central office arranges advertising and promotional activities, negotiates supplier agreements, and administers the affairs of the organization.

Critics of the concept maintain that cooperatives cannot compete with chains or franchises in the service they provide. They suggest that the independent nature of consortium membership prevents the application of consistent policies and procedures. Defenders of cooperatives, however, claim that their members can provide the advantages of a chain or franchise (that is, lower costs for consumers) while giving the personal service associated with a small independent operator. As with most such arguments, clients will ultimately decide which type of operation best meets their needs.

Independent Travel Professionals (ITP), GIANTS, the Rider Group, GEM and T-Comm are the best known of the travel cooperatives presently operating in Canada.

The Travel Agency's Business

There are four main classifications for types of travel business. These groupings can be divided into endless sub-categories according to the tastes and interests of the client. The four primary categories are commercial travel, pleasure travel, ethnic travel and group travel.

Commercial Travel

Commercial or business travel refers to travel undertaken by the personnel of an organization to conduct business related to the enterprise. Depending on the size of the business, a commercial traveller may contact the travel agency directly or the travel agency may be contacted by an employee of the traveller's organization to request the necessary travel arrangements. The volume of business generated from a single commercial account can vary from one representative travelling regionally a few times a year to several dozen representatives travelling worldwide. Some large organizations employ one or more staff members whose sole function is to make the necessary arrangements with the travel agency for the company's representatives. If the account is sufficiently large, a travel agency will sometimes establish an office within the company's premises specifically to handle its commercial travel arrangements.

There are two opposing views regarding the value of commercial accounts to a travel agency. On the positive side, commercial accounts generally offer steady, year-round income for an agency. Even in times of economic recession, business people still need to travel although the frequency may be reduced. In addition, business travel tends to have fewer seasonal fluctuations than vacation travel. Since business people usually know where and when they must travel, they tend to require less research and counselling time than do pleasure travellers. The counsellor's task is to efficiently service the client's needs. Revenue received from commercial sales will generally cover overhead costs. Competent servicing of a commercial account may lead to an increase in vacation sales. Employees of the organization often direct their vacation travel requests to the servicing agency. The commercial account frequently uses a credit card and payment is therefore guaranteed immediately to the travel agency. This allows the travel agency to be in a positive cash flow situation.

On the negative side, the majority of commercial or business travel consists of transportation only and therefore offers a small return to the agency. Business commitments may force the commercial traveller to alter arrangements several times, both before and after the trip has commenced. This results in the need to reissue tickets, rewrite files and invoices, or provide refunds. All of these functions increase the labour time to service the account thereby reducing the efficiency of the agency staff. Some agency owners suggest that for this reason commercial accounts are uneconomic. The strongest factor against handling business travel is the payment terms expected by the commercial account. Normal business practices usually extend liberal credit terms between businesses. For example, Company A purchases material from Company B and is allowed 30 days to remit payment without finance charges, or is given a discount for prompt payment. Billing and Settlement Plan Reporting, the system used to remit payment to the airlines for airline tickets sold by a travel agency, dictates that payment must be received by the airline on specific dates

(seven day cycles from the date of issuance of the tickets to the date of drawing the funds from the agency's bank account). This does not allow an agency to extend the credit terms that a commercial account may be accustomed to in its regular operation. Alternatively, if an agency decides to extend credit terms to its commercial accounts, it may find a shortfall in its cash flow. A commercial account may also expect, at no cost, additional services not provided to the vacation client. One example is free delivery of tickets.

Pleasure Travel

As the name implies, pleasure travel involves the arrangements for holiday travellers. Pleasure travel can be and is the mainstay of many travel agencies. Arranging pleasure travel generally earns an agency a higher rate of commission than making business travel reservations. Selling pleasure travel, however, usually demands more time of the counsellor who must research the product, counsel the client, and make the sale. In contrast to commercial travel, however, once a client has booked a vacation changes to the reservation are rare.

In today's travel industry, where competition is fierce and costs are soaring, many agencies are discouraging the "carriage trade" (or up-market) traveller as these arrangements can be very time consuming. Nevertheless, this type of traveller can allow counsellors to use a maximum amount of knowledge and imagination. For example, a counsellor may be required to construct a complex independent tour. At the other end of the scale, the pleasure traveller may be looking for an inexpensive prepackaged vacation. This traveller also demands excellence from a travel counsellor as product knowledge and imagination are extremely important in arranging a suitable vacation for the cost-conscious client. The types of pleasure travel are as varied as the interests of people and include cruises, conducted or escorted tours, special interest tours (e.g., Olympics, Cannes Film Festival), rail and bus tours, theatre tours, pilgrimages and carnivals. For all types of pleasure travel, commissions are higher as usually more than transportation is involved. A higher rate of return to the agency justifies the additional counsellor time necessary to service the client effectively.

Ethnic Travel

Ethnic travel is the movement of specific ethnic groups (or their children) between their adopted country and their country of origin. As Canada has a large ethnic population, ethnic travel has become big business. In fact, many agencies specialize in dealing with a particular ethnic community and often employ staff who are members of or conversant with the particular ethnic population.

Ethnic travel frequently involves transportation only, sometimes on scheduled air carriers. Although the commission return to the agency is less than that for a pleasure traveller, minimum work is involved in making the travel arrangements. In many cases, ethnic travel is by charter carrier and therefore offers a higher return to the agency. For instance, charter air carriers may offer an override commission structure to travel agencies, such as 10 percent on the first 49 passengers booked and 11 percent on 50 plus passengers retroactive to the first booking. An agency involved with a particular ethnic community often has the opportunity to increase revenue due to the frequency of travel. Ethnic clientele are usually recruited on a personal basis through the owner or manager, or are drawn by the counsellors' reputations within the ethnic community. An agency may also increase its ethnic clientele by advertising in specific ethnic newspapers.

Group Travel

Group travel is used to designate a collection of people travelling together by the same mode of transportation, staying together at the same hotels, and partaking of the same facilities for the duration of the travel period. In most cases, persons travelling with a group enjoy maximum economy as services have been purchased in bulk. Group travel can be very lucrative for any travel agency. Many travel agencies specialize in group travel and most handle one or more groups annually.

Group travel is usually generated in two ways. The agency owner or an employee may have personal contact with a group. Alternatively, group business may be produced by the development and promotion of a group sales proposal based on a "cold" or unknown sales call.

Groups tours may be escorted (conducted) or not. The majority of group tours have a tour leader, sometimes called a tour escort or tour conductor. Five common types of group travel are special interest, religious pilgrimages, sales conferences, conventions and sales incentives.

Special Interest. This type of group involves the arrangements for individuals travelling together to pursue common interests such as a hobby, sport or cultural activity. This is the type of group an agency is most likely to handle. The sale is usually generated on a personal basis.

In many cases, transportation is the only travel product required by a special interest group. For groups where all arrangements are serviced through the travel agency, the group organizer or leader (tour conductor) will expect a free ticket, and possibly certain other expenses, in return for booking a given number of travellers. Free or reduced rate tour conductor transportation can be arranged with the carrier or carriers used in transporting the group, subject to specific regulations. Another type of special interest group is one in which the group has characteristics in common (other than a shared interest in the destination or event) which merit the counsellor's special attention. Two examples of this type of group are senior citizens and handicapped travellers.

Religious Pilgrimages. The religious pilgrimage is one of the most specialized forms of group travel. Religious tours are usually sponsored by and limited to travellers of a particular denomination. Such tours are often created for members to attend an outstanding religious event, for example Christmas in Bethlehem. Sometimes the tour combines features of a standard tour with emphasis placed on visiting religious landmarks, such as the Vatican. In general, religious tours are not advertised to the general public. This type of clientele is usually built on a personal basis, with the responsible party in the travel agency being a member of the particular religious community.

Sales Conferences. A sales conference is an event planned by a company to achieve specific results. Conferences are set in surroundings conducive to receiving the complete attention of the sales staff. They are used to foster new sales techniques and strategies, to introduce newly appointed personnel, or to launch new product lines. Most companies hold sales conferences at a hotel or resort, often quite secluded, so that sales personnel will not be interrupted by office and home routines. The sponsoring company frequently secures deluxe accommodations to further enhance the setting of the conference.

Convention Travel. Convention travel comprises a group of people travelling to the same destination for a common purpose, such as the annual meeting of a professional, service or fraternal organization. Convention travel may be local, national or international in scope.

Arranging travel to a convention does not offer a high return for an agency. Accommodation and other services are generally handled by a housing committee in the convention city and thus no commissions are available to the travel agency. The lucrative aspect of convention travel is the pre- and post-convention tour. If, for example, an agency is organizing a convention group to Vancouver, the agency may arrange a one week tour to Hawaii after the convention has concluded. By using certain airfares that allow stopovers on the west coast at a nominal charge, the cost of the entire program may not greatly exceed the

regular airfare to Vancouver. Alternatively, the delegates could be offered a pre-convention tour consisting of air travel to Calgary and rail transportation through the Rockies en route to Vancouver. The possibility of generating additional revenue through such tours, even if sold to only a small percentage of the convention participants, greatly increases the desire of an agency to handle this type of business. A travel agency may also become involved with the convention organizing committee and offer complete travel services for incoming groups. This can include arranging air transportation, transfers of delegates and baggage, the development and implementation of special programs for delegates' spouses, and planning pre- and post-convention tours.

Sales Incentives. This type of group travel is one of the fastest growing and most lucrative in the travel industry. Sales incentive travel programs are introduced by companies to achieve particular company goals. Some of the more common objectives are:

- To introduce or "launch" a new product.
- To increase sales of a particular product which is a "slow" seller.
- To increase overall sales volume.
- To attract new customers.

The incentive (in this case a vacation) may be offered to sales staff (and spouses), to customers, or to both. In the case of sales staff, it is a reward for achieving a particular sales goal in accordance with the criteria set down by the company. For the customer, it is a prize for successfully completing a contest or finding a lucky coupon in the company's product. The prime characteristic of incentive groups is that the clientele is composed of winners. As such, they must receive special treatment. Such treatment usually has a higher price tag and therefore this type of business can generate substantial income. Agencies involved in incentive travel arrange a full service program, including transportation, meals, accommodation, ground transfers and, in some cases, sightseeing tours and entertainment.

Sales conference, convention and sales incentive travel can be generated in either of two ways. These groups can be solicited on a "warm" or personal contact call. Often, particularly for sales conference or sales incentive groups, the agency will already handle the commercial travel for the company. Convention travel may also come from a commercial or business account. The delegates seek assistance from the travel agency and perhaps provide the names of other delegates for the agency to contact. Alternatively, conference, convention and sales incentive groups can be solicited in a similar manner to other types of groups by making cold calls and submitting proposals.

The promotion and successful servicing of sales and convention travel demands that the agency's personnel use maximum imagination and promotional skills. Usually direct mail advertising and personal contact is mandatory to generate and keep the interest of the program's participants. This may include a brochure with a completely detailed program, periodic mailings of general information and, in the case of contests or incentives, the progress of potential participants.

What is a Travel Counsellor?

The foregoing material has described the nature of travel agencies and their various structures and types of business. There would, however, be no travel business without travel counsellors. The terms travel agent and travel counsellor are used interchangeably in the travel industry. The term travel counsellor is preferred in this textbook because it more clearly describes the responsibility of a travel agency employee. The term travel agent, on the other hand, describes the function of the agency or its owner, that is, as the agent for the supplier. This distinction also implies that travel counsellors do more than sell travel. It has already been noted that travel is an

intangible and that this type of product must be sold and handled in a different fashion. Many clients are inarticulate, that is, they are unwilling or unable to express their needs in terms of a travel product. The travel counsellor's role is to guide clients and assist them in making a purchase decision. Counsellors do this by investigating and evaluating the products of travel suppliers and tour operators, and then matching them to the needs of the client. To competently service the requirements of different types of travellers is an extremely complex task.

A capable travel counsellor must have current knowledge of air fares offered to a given destination, schedules of carriers to that destination, available hotel accommodation (including the hotel's amenities and facilities, quality, and prices at various seasons of the year), climatic conditions, customs, health and documentary requirements, currency exchange rates, scenic and cultural attractions, entertainment and recommended dining places and, often of prime importance, the current political situation. A counsellor's personal travel experience can be of great value. A travel counsellor, however, cannot have visited every airport hotel and tourist attraction in the world, nor be familiar with all the technical information, no matter how much time is spent on attending seminars or taking familiarization trips. It is therefore essential that travel counsellors be familiar with the available reference sources and how to use them. Technical travel information such as airfares, routings, and the rules and regulations governing them, can be found in standard computer reservation systems (CRS). The Travel Information Manual (TIM) states the rules and regulations for each country concerning necessary documentation for travellers, health requirements and customs information. The Official Hotel Guide (OHG) gives rates and descriptions of hotels worldwide. Information concerning particular destinations can be obtained from government tourist boards and the brochures they supply at no cost to agencies. These brochures cover almost

Job Description for Travel Counsellors

A skill and comprehension profile adapted from the DACUM Report of the College Affairs Branch of the Ministry of Colleges and Universities, Ontario, updated in 1982 and revised in 1989.

General Office Practice

Organize one's schedule and set priorities for one's own work.

Handle cash accurately, process cheques as per company procedures and prepare bank deposits.

Compose and type business letters and customer itineraries accurately and with a minimum speed of 35 WPM.

Complete client files in a neat and legible manner, and file accurately according to individual office procedures.

With instruction, operate the following office equipment:
postage meter; photocopier; adding machine/calculator/bookkeeping machine; typewriter; word processor; facsimile machine; telephone; CRT set; automated printer for tickets, itineraries, correspondence, and other forms.

Travel Agency Operations

Accurately prepare and complete sales reports according to BSP Canada procedures and/or computerized reporting systems approved by BSP Canada as practised by individual offices.

Demonstrate understanding of the legal liabilities of self and the agency as set out under various provincial and federal acts, such as the Competition Act, the Business Practices Act, and relevant provincial travel acts.

Place orders with suppliers accurately and efficiently, observing suppliers' policies and following ATC and IATA reservations procedures.

Prepare and issue invoices, receipts and other accounting forms.

Accurately calculate commissions due on services sold.

Geography

Use a recognized current world atlas to:
locate capitals and principal cities; locate major rivers, lakes, mountains and mountain ranges;
identify continents and political boundaries;
determine probable climatic conditions based on geographic location in relationship to the equator;
identify the various time zones of the world;

Product Knowledge - *Reference Manuals*

Revise and update manuals and tariffs as required.

Research and analyze (i.e., classify and evaluate) various tours, cruises, hotels, destinations, and other travel products.

Plan itineraries, quote times and fares using the Eurailtariff and Cook's European Timetable, or relevant domestic references.

Plan itineraries using shipline schedules and/or Official Steamship Guides.

Identify the relative merits of cabin locations and ship facilities using comparative deck plans.

Calculate cruise costs using applicable rate sheets.

Identify location, cost and merits of various hotels/resorts and their facilities using the Official Hotel Guide (OHG), Hotel and Travel Index, OAG Travel Planner (North American, European and Pacific editions), ABC Star Reports, or other standard travel publications and guidebooks.

Plan itineraries and quote times, meals available and aircraft used using the Official Airline Guide (OAG - domestic and worldwide editions), the ABC Guide and individual airline timetables.

Accurately quote fares, rules and routing principles using the Airline Tariff Publishing Company's domestic tariff book (ATPCO) and the International Air Tariff.

Plan individual tours using the Consolidated Tour Manual (CTM), confidential tariffs, rack and net rates from hotels, and ground transportation services.

Identify passport, visa and health documents required for entry and/or transiting foreign countries using a current Travel Information Manual (TIM) and/or checking with the tourist board and airlines serving the country.

Advise clients of customs regulations and currency restrictions for destination countries and returning residents to Canada using a current Travel Information Manual (TIM).

Use an airline computer reservation system (CRS) to source any of the above information available electronically.

Ticketing and Fares

For both manual and automated formats, correctly complete airline tickets, MCOs and ATOs (BSP standard forms) according to the fare applicable, and using the rules and regulations laid down by IATA and ATC handbooks.

Correctly complete MCO and compute fares, using applicable bank buying rates where required, to transmit a prepaid ticket.

Correctly complete Credit Card Charge Forms (BSP format) according to IATA and ATC handbooks.

Apply correct commission percentages based on destination and applicable fare level.

Comply with ticket security procedures as laid down by BSP Canada.

Apply principles of domestic and/or international fare construction.

Apply mileage principle and Neutral Units of Construction (NUCs) where required.

Using the appropriate tariff, apply rules and regulations surrounding the use of regular and promotional airfares.

Counselling and Salesmanship

Explain and sell travel accident, baggage, cancellation, flight and medical insurance.

Identify customer needs and recommend appropriate airfare, tour package, cruise, rail or hotels using the relevant reference materials.

Be prepared to offer alternatives to clients.

Using a standard costing format, develop, prepare and cost independent tours and services for clients.

Recommend principal tourist attractions in Canada and abroad to meet client interests.

Calculate elapsed flying times using world time zones.

Accurately convert Canadian dollars to foreign currencies and vice versa at applicable bank buying rates.

Advise clients of expected climatic conditions and recommend appropriate dress.

Describe foreign customs, historical and cultural events, current political climate and economic conditions in destination countries.

Recognize and maximize sources of company income.

Display salesmanship by controlling the sale situation, recommending the optimum (for client and agency) and making the booking.

Follow up on the clients' return.

Make sales calls and phone solicitations.

Prepare and conduct public presentations.

Cope with office workload and stress, and adjust to changing situations.

Diplomatically handle dissatisfied clients.

Display good manners by listening carefully, enunciating clearly and speaking grammatically correctly.

Exercise discretion and confidentiality in dealing with clients.

Maintain product knowledge by regularly reading trade publications and suppliers' bulletins/brochures, and by attending product launches and seminars.

Develop telephone politeness techniques and use telephone system effectively.

FIGURE 2.3

every imaginable facet of the destination from its climate to its hotel facilities. Thus it is unnecessary for a counsellor to be totally familiar with a particular destination, provided that the individual is fully conversant with the references available and how to research the necessary information. It can, in fact, be detrimental for a counsellor to memorize certain technical details, such as air fares and flight times, which constantly change. It is easy for a counsellor to err by quoting such details "offhand" when a quick check would provide accurate and up-to-date information. Today, counsellors access much of this information through an airline computer reservations system (CRS).

A job description for travel counsellors is reproduced in this chapter (Figure 2.3). It provides, in objective terms, a useful set of performance standards. The original list was published in 1973 by the Ontario Ministry of Colleges and Universities in conjunction with CITC members, travel industry executives and educators. It has been updated to reflect current trends and needs within the travel industry, and corresponds with the requirements of the core curriculum developed by ACCESS (ACTA/CITC Canadian Educational Standards System).

Why Study Travel Counselling?

Anyone briefly reviewing the previous material, and giving even a cursory glance at the job description for a travel counsellor, may well ask, "Why study travel counselling?" There is certainly much to learn and considerable responsibility to be shouldered in performing these duties. The financial rewards may not be as high as one would expect or hope for. Yet many people do study travel counselling and a large proportion of them take up employment in that position. There are many reasons proposed for studying this topic. By the time you begin to read this text, you will most likely be enrolled in a course of study for travel counselling. Given the

amount to learn, you may be having second thoughts on whether you did, in fact, make the correct career choice. This text is not the place to convince you that your choice is sound. Rather, the intention here is to suggest additional incentives for staying the course. You have obviously been attracted by the travel industry. Maybe the glamour of the advertisements have drawn you; perhaps it is a desire to travel; or it's just that you like working with people. A career as a travel counsellor can certainly provide these benefits. There is, however, one overriding reason for anyone interested in a career in the travel industry to study travel counselling. Travel counsellors, as you will have noticed from the foregoing material, must know all aspects of the travel business. They must be experts in how the transportation industry works; they must be able to select the best tour for their client from a vast array of available products; they need to be able to interpret a wide range of reference and research materials. Perhaps most importantly, they must know how each sector of the travel industry works; they must be able to sell that component to clients; and they must be able to make reservations with, and disburse payments to, all these suppliers. In short, a travel counsellor must interact with all parts of the travel industry and therefore has to be familiar with each segment's procedures. This makes the travel counsellor a highly skilled and valuable person. For example, someone trained as a car rental reservationist or as a tour operator's destination representative would not have the training to fill the other's position. Neither one would have the skills to work at an airline ticket counter. Travel counsellors, however, receive basic training in all aspects of the travel industry and therefore the world of travel is open to them. Students of travel counselling can and do successfully find employment in airlines, tour operators, cruise lines, tourist boards and hotels, as well as in almost every other segment of the travel industry. So even if you decide not to work in a travel agency as a travel counsellor, there are still a multitude of

FIGURE 2.4
The Travel
Counsellor's role.

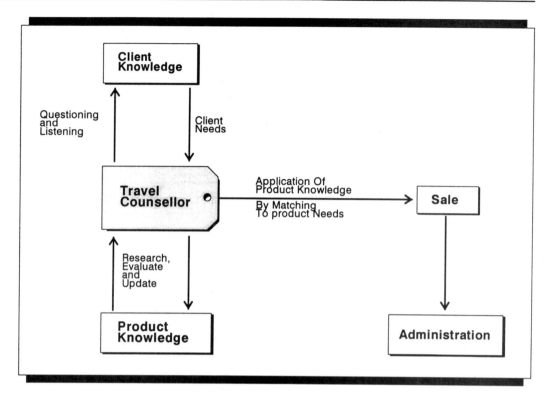

career options available. There are also a variety of travel agency positions. Some demand strong interpersonal and counselling abilities whereas others emphasize technical skills, for example, in agencies specializing in commercial accounts.

The majority of this text is devoted to the specific skills associated with particular segments of the travel industry. As you study each chapter you will acquire the abilities necessary to sell that product as a professional travel counsellor. In addition, however, you will also gain the knowledge and ability to take up a position in that industry. In some chapters, specific positions will be highlighted. Other chapters will generally review the area and the positions available. Where appropriate, there will be a discussion of some of the job opportunities in that industry.

The Role of a Travel Counsellor

To begin the discussion of careers in the travel industry, the role of the travel

counsellor, the individual who is central in the travel industry, will be studied. A successful travel counsellor has a loyal and satisfied clientele. But how does one become successful? There are some who say that the way to keep your clients satisfied is to give them what they want; in the travel industry, however, the key is to give your clients what they need. In essence, *the responsibility of a travel counsellor is to efficiently, economically (to the client) and profitably (to the agency) match the client's travel needs with an appropriate travel product*. The aim of this text is to teach the basic skills which assist potential travel counsellors to become successful.

The essence of travel counselling is the successful matching of client needs with appropriate travel products. The ability to achieve this goal requires skill in four main areas; client knowledge, product knowledge, sales ability and administration (see Figure 2.4).

Client Knowledge

It stands to reason that in order to match a client's needs one must first determine what are these needs. To identify client needs one must develop strong questioning and listening skills. Sometimes clients will not know what they want, other than "a break". Or they may know exactly what they want (such as a romantic adventure) but be embarrassed to state it openly. Each situation requires skill and tact in drawing out the client. On the other hand, clients may think that they know what they want but, in fact, their choices may be totally unsuitable. For example, they may be attracted by advertisements for a coach tour of Europe. After some questioning, however, the counsellor might learn that the potential clients like to be flexible when on holiday; they do not wish to be regimented. Obviously, a bus tour with its rigid schedule would not provide the type of vacation that these clients desire. It then becomes the counsellor's duty to advise (or counsel) the clients accordingly. Again, this requires tact and skill. These issues will be investigated more closely in Chapter 3 which is devoted to a study of the client.

Product Knowledge

If a counsellor is to recommend travel products to meet a client's needs, then product knowledge is essential. There are a number of aspects to product knowledge. First, one must know the product, its content, its availability, and where to find the information. This requires the ability to read, interpret and access a wide variety of reference manuals, printed materials and automated systems. Having discovered this information, a counsellor must then assess the product's quality and characteristics to determine whether it is suited to the needs of the client. Chapter 4 discusses product knowledge, how to acquire it and, more importantly, how to maintain it. The bulk of the remainder of this publication continues with an investigation of the various segments of the travel industry. The focus of these chapters is the study of the particular segment as a travel product. Each chapter reviews the essentials of the product and methods whereby one can acquire the type of product knowledge outlined above.

Sales Ability

Two of the most important functions of a travel counsellor have now been summarized; client knowledge and product knowledge. Knowledge of one or both, however, is not sufficient for career success. While both areas are essential, they are useful to a travel counsellor only when combined as part of another process. This combination is achieved when a client's travel needs are successfully matched with an appropriate travel product, that is, when a sale is made. Without sales, there will be no commissions. Without commissions, there will be no agency income. Without agency income, there will be no travel counsellor positions. For this reason, a complete chapter is devoted to the sales process and to a review of successful sales techniques.

Administration

Congratulations are always in order whenever a sale has been made. But the travel counsellor's job does not end there. Travel agencies earn their income from commissions on the sale of travel products. All businesses require that income and expenses be tracked and recorded. Suppliers wish to ensure that they receive the correct payment, and on time. Agencies want to collect their earned commissions. Furthermore, although the client has been sent on a trip, reports must still be written, new products evaluated, problems dealt with, and files maintained. Even in the era of the paperless office, there is administration and filing to be done. This is the final part of the counsellor's responsibility. The administrative and organizational function is an important one which reflects the professionalism of the counsellor and the agency. These topics are covered in the final chapter of the text.

Review Questions

1. Discuss sources of travel agency income and expenses.

2. Describe the factors which influence a consumer's selection of a travel agency.

3. What are the advantages and disadvantages of independent agencies, chains, franchises and cooperatives?

4. Describe the main types of travel agency business.

5. Discuss the role of a travel counsellor.

References

Noble, Cinnie. *The Disabled Traveller: A Guide for Travel Counsellors*. Toronto: CITC, 1991. This is a valuable reference for counsellors who deal with handicapped clients.

The Client

Chapter Summary

This chapter focuses on clients. Ways of classifying travellers are discussed. Different types of travellers, such as business or pleasure, and different reasons for travelling are reviewed. There follows a study of the client. Theories of individual needs and motivation are summarized. The effects of individual behaviour on travel decisions and on destinations is also covered. It is important for counsellors to develop questioning and listening skills. These skills and their application in determining a client's needs, motivations and expectations are emphasized.

Chapter Objectives
After completing this chapter you should be able to:

- Describe the major reasons why people travel.

- List and describe the different types of traveller such as business, pleasure, ethnic and VFR, group and individual.

- Divide the travel market into motivational groups.

- Identify the main reasons why some people do not travel.

- Identify and describe client needs.

- Discuss travel trends and destinations.

- Describe how to plan a trip and select a destination for maximum benefit.

- Discuss the importance of questioning and listening skills in the counselling process.

- Exhibit these skills.

Classifying Groups

Human behaviour can be analyzed in a number of ways. One technique separates behaviour according to individual or group characteristics. Each method can be applied to travel behaviour and both are helpful in understanding different aspects of it. Group characteristics and population trends are most useful to the suppliers of travel products and services. Individual behaviour, on the other hand, is of greater interest to travel counsellors who must deal with individuals rather than groups. Travel counsellors must understand the needs that drive individuals to travel and the factors that motivate someone to become a tourist. Without a knowledge of these it is impossible to offer appropriate travel choices to a potential client. At the same time, travel counsellors must understand the forces and trends that shape human behaviour in general so that they are aware of prevailing values and opinions. Such knowledge helps travel counsellors to predict which travel products are likely to be or become popular. Clients are individuals but they are also members of various groups. Knowledge of both individual and group behaviour is therefore necessary if travel counsellors are to professionally service client needs.

One method used to categorize people is according to their age, income, sex, occupation, marital status, and similar factors. Other classifications which serve useful objectives are ethnic background, religious affiliation, location of residence, hobbies, travel experience, family size, club and association memberships, and education. This type of information is the main feature of studies known as **demographic** research. Demographic analysis provides objective information in that the data obtained are simply records of particular measurable characteristics, not of opinions. Demographic information is based on statistics and is collected through a census or similar survey. A knowledge of demographics is useful to suppliers as they can base their products on such factors. For example, demographic studies have shown that the population of Canada is aging and that many senior citizens have both the time and money to travel. Travel suppliers are interested in such trends. One result is that tour operators can be expected to develop and market travel programs to appeal to this growing segment of the population. Most of the above classifications can be similarly related to travel behaviour. Some relationships have already been clearly established. For example, many studies indicate that the tendency to travel increases with the level of income and of education. The higher one's income or education, the more likely one is to travel.

Another type of group data is **psychographic** information. Psychographic characteristics tend to be more subjective. They include data on personality traits, activities, interests and opinions, motivations and expectations, and lifestyles. It is more difficult to gather accurate psychographic data because it is more subjective and it changes according to circumstances and other factors. People change their opinions. Motivations and lifestyle can shift depending on an individual's situation. There is therefore no easy or accurate way to measure the information as there is with demographic characteristics such as age or level of education. As the variety of travel products offered to the public increases, more sophisticated research methods are required to determine the particular people to which each product will appeal. Psychographic information has become more important as a predictor of consumer choice. Tours and destination activities can also be geared to trends identified from psychographic data in a similar manner to the way in which trends are influenced by demographic data. For example, the movement to a more active and healthier lifestyle indicated a need for a change from tour packages that simply emphasized sun, sea and relaxation to vacations based on watersports and other activities.

As well as by demographics or psychographics, travel companies attempt to separate the general public into various travel markets according to other criteria. Some firms are interested in travel habits and preferences (whether clients choose to travel first class or economy, for example), some in whether they travel as part of a group or as individual travellers, while others wish to know the purpose of travel (such as business or pleasure) or the frequency. All of this information is obtained through research, either primary research or secondary research. In primary research a company directly investigates the marketplace by, for example, distributing a questionnaire and analyzing the results. Hotels typically conduct primary research when they leave evaluation cards in the rooms for their guests to complete. Such questionnaires provide direct evidence of the views of the hotel's actual market, that is, its guests. Secondary research involves consulting information which has been gathered by someone else, usually for another purpose. An example of secondary research is when an airline consults census data to determine if there is sufficient population in a particular location to merit introducing a new service to the city.

This type of information gathering on the characteristics and preferences of consumers is called market research. In simple terms, market researchers attempt to find out who comprises the market for particular products. Market research is used to help design products to match the characteristics and views of particular groups within the population. Alternatively, market research can be used to solicit the opinions of various sectors of the population to determine whether they will accept and purchase proposed products. The technique of dividing a market into various parts each with similar characteristics is called market segmentation. The characteristics that describe a segment of the travel market are referred to as a traveller profile. A profile of a specific group allows managers to plan and direct strategies at the market segment. The particular segments selected are called target markets. The travel industry is divided into many market segments as each sector of the industry, such as airlines or hotels, appeals to a different market. Furthermore, there are different target markets within each sector. For example, one hotel chain may appeal to budget travellers while another concentrates on the luxury market.

General Reasons for Travel

Chapter 2 discussed various types of travel business sold by travel agencies. These different types of business illustrate some of the many reasons why people travel. In the same way that market research information describes categories of potential travellers, the types of travel business also reflect reasons why people travel. Some of the more popular reasons provided to explain vacation travel choices are:

To visit friends and relatives (VFR). VFR traffic is an important segment of the travelling public. Ethnic travel can be classified as a component of VFR traffic. Many Canadians in particular visit "the old country" to renew acquaintances with family and friends in their native land.

To see new places and learn new things. Education and research are common reasons for travel. Some people have a strong interest in learning how people in other countries live, work and play. The education sought may be structured formally as part of a study tour or it may be expressed simply as a desire for personal enrichment.

To do things one cannot do at home. For example, there may be sights of historical or cultural interest, such as the Tower of London or La Scala in Milan, or special events like the Olympic Games or Broadway shows.

To make religious pilgrimages. Catholics travelling to Lourdes and Fatima, pilgrims visiting the Holy Land, or Moslems making the hajj to Mecca, are some of the reasons stated by travellers.

Other reasons are cited. To escape the weather by visiting Florida or the Caribbean to avoid a Canadian winter. Health and recuperation, or sporting activities such as game fishing in the Bahamas and camera safaris in East Africa, are additional explanations given. Some people travel because their neighbours do so or because they seek status.

To relax. Relaxation, pleasure and escape from the daily routine are high on the list of priorities mentioned by pleasure travellers. Others travel simply to "have a good time", to meet "new" people or possibly to have a romantic or sexual experience.

To purchase special items. Shopping seems to be a major reason for some people to travel. Collecting and bargain hunting are part of the fun. For others, inexpensive living such as spending the winter on a Greek island or the Spanish Mediterranean coast is the motive.

These are broad classifications and it is easy to visualize a travel situation in which a holiday destination offers a combination of some aspects of the cultural/historical with the recreational. One example is Mexico where a vacationer can see and learn about pre-Columbian Mayan culture and history at Uxmal and Chichen Itza and also relax on the beach or snorkel at Cancun. Many potential travellers therefore do not fall neatly into any one of the above categories. In fact, most people who travel do so for a variety of reasons.

Nondiscretionary and Discretionary Travel

There are few industries that cover such a broad range as travel and tourism. Chapter 1, simply by virtue of the different definitions for tourist and tourism, suggested some of this scope. For example, one definition of a tourist is an individual who travels more than 100 miles for a purpose other than to commute to work. By this definition, the term tourist includes those who drive from Edmonton to Calgary to take in a hockey game, those who take a bus from Toronto to North Bay to visit grandparents, as well as those who have booked passage on a Mediterranean cruise or a trek in the mountains of Nepal. Our study of tourism in Chapter 1 provided a number of reasons why people travel and from them spring a vast array of tourism experiences. No matter which definition is used or what the motivation for travel is, there are two categories within the travel industry that are marketed and sold differently because the motivating factors of travellers in each division are quite distinct. Those classifications are nondiscretionary travel and discretionary travel. Each type of traveller has different needs and reasons for travelling and therefore the travel industry applies different marketing techniques to the two groups.

Nondiscretionary travellers do not have a choice as to whether or not they should travel. Such travellers must journey out of necessity; they do not necessarily want to go. Examples of nondiscretionary travellers are business people making a sales call or attending a company meeting, family members returning home for a wedding or funeral, and students returning to college. Business and professional travellers generally select products and services that save time. Their inflexible schedules do not allow for preplanning or purchases at discount prices. Promotions based on performance and efficiency or on brand loyalty, such as frequent flyer programs, are directed to this type of traveller. Business travel accounts for over 50 percent of air travel; many hotels directly target this group of travellers. Conventions, congresses and conferences for business, professional and trade personnel is a growing market within the travel industry. This type of traveller therefore cannot be neglected by travel counsellors.

The main focus of this chapter, however, is the pleasure traveller who engages in the second type of travel. Unlike nondiscretionary travel, discretionary travel is voluntary. Such people have a variety of options, one of which is not to travel. They can choose between staying home, driving somewhere, buying a new car, or flying to the Caribbean on a vacation. They select products and services according to their personal needs. Those who choose to purchase travel often choose packages. Flexible schedules permit vacation and leisure travellers to preplan their travel and to purchase at discount prices. Discretionary travellers are influenced by differences in fares and the advertisements showing travel as romantic or adventurous. Promotional air fares and low season price reductions are targeted at these travellers.

Travellers who are visiting friends or relatives do not always fall into one category or the other. Depending on the situation the travel can be discretionary or nondiscretionary. As a result, these travellers may be susceptible to advertising or special promotions. VFR travellers do not usually require accommodation.

The discussion to this point has provided a basis for classifying groups and individuals and has offered some general reasons why people travel. The remainder of this chapter focuses on vacation and leisure travellers, those who can choose between whether or not they will travel. Nondiscretionary travellers, particularly business people, do have some special needs but our concern here is to determine the main reasons why people choose to take a vacation. It is this group of individuals who present the greatest challenge to the travel agent's counselling abilities.

Individual Travellers

Counsellors must have background knowledge on group behaviour as it is the basis for the inventory offered to travel agencies. It can also indicate trends in both the population and in the products designed to appeal to them. However, the counsellor's prime concern is with the individual who enters the agency. This potential client has individual needs, wants, desires, values, motives, feelings and expectations. How can these be classified? The short answer is that no theory applies to all people in every situation. Counsellors must be aware that each client is an individual. The following material offers some reasons why individuals travel and provides some suggestions for discovering their particular needs and interests.

Although the travel industry's target market is the discretionary traveller, not everyone with the disposable income to travel does so. People must meet certain conditions if they are to become tourists. Prime among them is disposable income, that is, sufficient money over and above that required to meet living expenses and obligations. Travellers also require the time to travel. This means that travellers require the flexibility or ability to drop or change commitments such as school, work or home. People also need sufficient health and ability to travel. For example, old age or young children can pose difficulties. In addition, there are documentary conditions to be met such as a passport and perhaps a visa before the individual can travel.

Barriers to Travel

Apart from these conditions, however, there may be additional constraints or barriers which prevent people from travelling. The principal barrier, apart from time and money, is a lack of desire to travel. An individual may prefer to stay home or to do something else. The person may wish to spend any disposable income on a new stereo or a house renovation project. There may be health barriers as stated earlier. Some people are physically unable to travel because of age, a handicap, or another existing condition. For example, the individual may require continuing treatment which is difficult to obtain away from home, or the person may have a condition, such as AIDS, which limits their freedom of movement. Security fears also prevent individuals

from travelling. The fears may be based on rational thoughts, such as a reluctance to travel because of an increase in terrorism, or they may be psychological in nature, such as a general fear of flying. Family or other commitments can prevent travel. Lack of knowledge may be a barrier if the individual is unaware of or unfamiliar with travel opportunities. Some people see travel as a hassle. Travel is just too much trouble and inconvenience for them. Sometimes the reasons offered are just excuses. The individual may give one reason, such as lack of money, when in reality there is another, perhaps fear of the unknown. Counsellors must discover the reasons for objections so that they can properly counsel prospective clients.

Pleasure Travel as a Need Satisfier

A number of theories have been proposed to explain why people travel. Most are based on theories of need satisfaction or motivation. Some theories have been categorized according to push and pull factors. Push theories suggest that there are factors that generate a drive or motivation for people to travel. These factors are internal to the traveller and are different for each individual. An example of a push theory is the notion that people travel out of curiosity or wanderlust, that they have a need to know what lies on the other side of the mountain. Pull theories focus on the factors that attract individuals to destinations. Pull factors are external, associated with the destination or event, and are generally the same for all travellers. These pull factors generally cannot be experienced in the home environment as, for example, the sun and sand that cannot be found in Saskatoon during a Canadian winter. Push-pull tendencies work together to create the travel patterns we see in the world on a local, national, and international scale. Push factors help explain why people choose to take a vacation. Pull factors help to explain why they choose a particular destination.

According to theories of need satisfaction a person does not buy a motorcycle just to own a motorcycle unless the individual is a collector of motorcycles. The purchase is made because it satisfies a need in the buyer. The need may be that the purchaser requires transport but cannot afford a car. Or the need may be for power, for status, or to fulfill a macho or sexy self image. Although the product is the same, the need can be different for different people. Similarly, people do not travel merely to collect stamps in their passports. They travel to satisfy a need. The needs may differ but in each case travel is the satisfier of the need.

Perhaps the best known theory of need satisfaction and human behaviour is that proposed by Abraham Maslow. Maslow suggested that human beings proceed through five stages of motivation. He further declared that an individual cannot move to a higher stage until the needs at the lower stages have been met. These stages were set out in the form of a hierarchy. It will be clear from the discussion that an individual functions on different levels at different times depending on the activity. The need must be satisfied at a lower level, however, before moving on to a higher one. The five stages in Maslow's hierarchy of human needs are, from lowest to highest, physical and biological needs, safety and security needs, social and love needs, status and esteem needs, and self actualization (see Figure 3.1).

Physical and biological needs are basic. At this the lowest level, needs revolve around survival. People require food, shelter and clothing sufficient to protect against the elements. Individuals operating at this level are not usually involved in tourism. Tourists, however, may operate at this level while on vacation. After all, who can deny the need to eat?

Safety and security needs occupy the second level. People who have satisfied their physical and biological needs will tend to behave in ways that will increase their security. Tourists at this level prefer the safety of escorted tours and familiar destinations. Political and safety conditions operate at this level. People will not travel for pleasure to a location they perceive to be unsafe.

Social needs refer to the need to belong, to feel wanted and loved. This is one reason for the popularity of group travel. People are more comfortable when they are with others with whom they feel compatible. The success of tours aimed at specific groups such as singles or senior citizens is a reflection of this need.

Status or esteem needs are important in marketing tourism. Travel has been linked with status since the days of the Grand Tour.

Self-actualization describes the behaviour of people who express their true nature. They can be characterized by the phrase "be all that you can be". Individuals operating at this level are generally interested in independent travel involving the type of action and activities

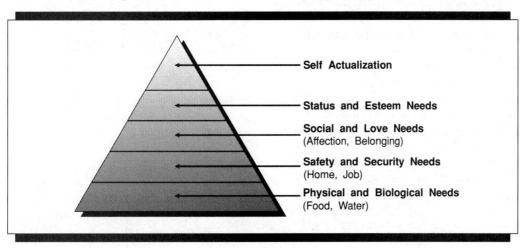

FIGURE 3.1
Maslow's Hierarchy of Needs.

- Self Actualization
- Status and Esteem Needs
- Social and Love Needs (Affection, Belonging)
- Safety and Security Needs (Home, Job)
- Physical and Biological Needs (Food, Water)

found in adventure travel.

According to Maslow's theory, travellers are motivated to buy travel products that satisfy their needs for social interaction, esteem, respect, and self-actualization. A hypothetical example can be used to illustrate that individuals operate at different levels at different times. Consider a lone traveller who is making a first trip to Nepal to trek in the Himalayas. On arrival in Katmandu, the traveller will initially operate at the lower levels. The individual's first priorities will be for accommodation for the evening, that is, for shelter expressing a physical need. Once settled, the traveller will probably explore the city, no doubt in search of food (the biological need) and will determine the lie of the land (the security need). The following day may be devoted to shopping for appropriate clothing (security) and to finding a guide and/or group with which to trek (security and social needs). The choice of a trek may be an expression of the need for status when the individual returns home or a search for self-esteem. The challenge of meeting the arduous demands of a high altitude trek may be an expression of self actualizing behaviour.

The Needs of Business Travellers

The needs of the business traveller are very different from those of the pleasure traveller. The sales and counselling skills required are therefore different. Junior counsellors who service business travellers will soon learn that satisfying their needs involves making efficient connections, changing itineraries and reissuing tickets. There may be little counselling as the airline, hotels and other services may have been preselected by the client, perhaps as part of a frequent flyer program. Business clients (or commercial accounts) are interested in speed, efficiency and costs. An agency's services and price structure will have been negotiated in advance by the manager or a senior corporate account specialist. The counsellor's tasks may therefore require little more than simple order taking.

Corporate travellers are either frequent travellers, those who must travel at short notice, or both. These clients are interested in reducing costs while receiving high service levels. They are also concerned with time and generally desire speedy and efficient service. Where travel arrangements are concerned, they are interested in the time required to travel to and from a destination, in the connections arranged and waiting time. Again, efficiency and convenience are their main preoccupations.

Another common need of corporate travellers is cost control. Business clients expect to receive detailed reports on air, hotel and car rental purchases, they wish to be guaranteed the lowest fare, and they expect their travel agent to negotiate corporate rates with suppliers. Business travellers expect their corporate travel account to be coordinated and administered by the agency. They seek consolidated billing privileges to avoid the paperwork associated with several offices or several individuals. This includes the provision of detailed travel and entertainment expense reports and the use of credit cards. Finally, they expect travel counsellors to have a sound knowledge of the product, especially cities, destinations and airports, and they seek additional services such as ticket delivery.

Factors Determining Individual Travel Behaviour

Travel, whether for business or pleasure, has been identified as satisfying particular needs. Maslow's theory differentiates these needs into levels of action for the individual. There remains the question, however, as to what factors transform an individual into a traveller. The sociological and psychological reasons are complex and varied. These motivations are discussed below. This section does not pretend to provide an in depth study of human behaviour. It will, however, attempt to focus the reader's attention on the differences and similarities between and among individuals, and to suggest some of the forces that determine human behaviour. The determinants of human behaviour may be divided into four main categories: motives, attitudes, knowledge and reference groups.

Motives

A motive is defined as an inner urge that moves or prompts a person to action. This definition indicates just how broad is the meaning of the term motive. Something that motivates one person may have no impact on another. It is therefore difficult to develop a complete list of motives. There is no general agreement among social scientists as to what the list should include or how it should be constructed. One such list, however, is presented below. It attempts to bring together universal motives, classifying them as primary (fundamental drives with which people are born), and secondary (those mainly learned). The terms emotional and rational are often used as rough equivalents.

Primary (Emotional) Motives of Behaviour

- Food and drink
- Comfort
- To attract the opposite sex
- Welfare of loved ones
- Freedom from fear and danger
- To be superior
- Social approval
- To live longer

Secondary (Rational) Motives of Behaviour

- Bargains
- Information
- Cleanliness
- Efficiency
- Convenience

- Dependability
- Style, beauty
- Economy, profit
- Curiosity

Such a listing of motives does not imply that everyone will react the same way to a primary or secondary drive. For example, one person's response to the hunger drive (food and drink motive) may be to buy and consume a candy bar. Another who is diabetic may be motivated by the self-preservation drives (comfort, freedom from fear and danger, to live longer). In this case, the self-preservation drives are collectively stronger and the person may choose a hunger satisfying substance that is dietetically acceptable. Thus, reason and other forces discussed below are always present. These forces temper an otherwise primitive response to basic drives.

Motives are closely related to the expectations one has for the results of the actions one takes. For example, if a client's motive for taking a vacation is comfort then this expectation will determine how the client views the accommodation offered. Once a counsellor understands a person's expectations, their behaviour in a given situation can be predicted.

Motivation can be classified according to primary and secondary drives as discussed above. Another classification suggests four types of motivators. Physical motivators reduce tensions through physical activities, cultural motivators help meet desires to know about other countries, interpersonal motivators fulfill a need to meet new people, and status and prestige motivators assist ego and personal development.

Motives are important to travel counsellors because they suggest reasons why people travel. Some of them are deep and basic while others are at times superficial. Motives provide the clues that allow travel counsellors to suggest alternative ways for potential clients to spend discretionary income. Each person has necessities on which a large portion of income must be spent. Food, shelter, medical fees, clothing and similar expenses fall into this category. The remaining income is discretionary, that is, a person is free to choose which items to purchase. For example, in the course of a year an individual may have a discretionary income of $5,000. There are numerous ways to spend this money each of which may satisfy a number of drives. The person may acquire a sense of superiority by choosing to invest in beautiful possessions, *objets d'art*, a colour television, a new car. Alternatively, the choice may be to spend much of the $5,000 on clothing (beyond the basic clothing needs). Or the individual may delay satisfaction by setting the $5,000 aside in an investment or bank savings account to intensify the realization of the primary motives. The decision, however, could be the purchase of an exotic, unusual or adventuresome form of travel.

This example is, of course, highly simplified. There is an interplay of motives at work. Most likely, the individual would try to satisfy a number of motives with the $5,000 discretionary income. For example, insurance to protect the welfare of loved ones, a subscription to a health club to live longer and to develop a better physique, or an economy vacation in Miami to escape the inconvenience of winter. The latter choice may include a desire to acquire an attractive tan, because the trip is socially acceptable, or because of the possibility of a love affair in the romantic sub-tropics!

The travel industry's target is this discretionary income. To this end travel suppliers design promotional programs that attempt to tap basic and secondary motives. Travel counsellors have the same goal in their interactions with clients. In the face-to-face contact with the potential traveller, counsellors search for clues to the strongest motive for that particular individual.

Attitudes

An attitude can be defined as a predisposition to feel or act in a given manner towards a specific person, group,

object, idea or institution. Opinion and belief are sometimes used as synonyms for attitude or to suggest degrees of intensity. Opinions are less enduring than attitudes while beliefs are more enduring.

Attitudes may be negative, neutral or positive. At the negative and positive levels, attitudes have varying degrees of strength. Whether an attitude is negative or positive depends, of course, on the observer. For example, a person may be strongly opposed to cigarettes. Viewed by a cigarette manufacturer this represents a negative attitude. A health professional concerned by the incidence of lung cancer, however, would consider the attitude positive. The factors that influence the formation of attitudes are strongest during the first five years of life. During this period parents teach their children attitudes on ethics, morals, religion, materialism and behaviour. In the period following the formative years, these basic attitudes are reinforced by exposure to individuals who embrace the same views. Attitudes formed after this period are frequently superficial and are more easily manipulated.

Some marketing people believe that a person's attitude toward a product or service is often largely determined by what it symbolizes to the individual. The symbolism of a product or service refers to its meaning rather than to its function. Thus, the purchaser of an expensive piece of Lalique glass may be accomplishing more than simply purchasing a piece of glassware. To the individual the object may be a symbol of luxury and affluence. Since the President of France sometimes presents a piece of Lalique to visiting dignitaries, the purchase establishes a vicarious link with famous individuals. How does this relate to travel behaviour? First, attitudes and motives are closely related. Motives provide the stimulus for action, attitudes provide the action pathways. Consequently, a desire for adventure might prompt someone to consider an African safari vacation but the person's attitude towards a country's politics or social customs could prevent it from being chosen as the destination.

Knowledge

Knowledge is an individual's state of awareness and/or understanding of a person, group, object, institutions, or ideas.

It is important to know the extent of a customer's awareness or knowledge, the degree to which it should be encouraged, and the areas that are not desirable. For example, consider a couple contemplating a first ever Caribbean cruise, in September, but who are apprehensive of the storms that sometimes strike the area at that time of year. A travel counsellor may convince them that their fears are unfounded by making them aware of the effectiveness of stabilizing equipment used on modern ships. This example illustrates that a lack of awareness can be overcome by knowledge. Sometimes, however, this lack of knowledge is encouraged. For example, airlines avoid stressing safety in their advertising because it focuses awareness on a subject that suggests air disasters.

Reference Groups

Social relationships have a significant influence on human behaviour. All individuals have relationships with various groups such as friends, business associates, or members of a church or civic association. The term reference group is used to designate these and other types of groups that affect individual behaviour. There are four basic types of reference groups: friends, neighbours and relatives; professional (or occupational) associates; social class; race, nationality, religious groups and fraternal associates.

Reference groups influence a person's behaviour in a variety of ways. In general, an individual's reference groups provide a basis for comparison, a source of sanction or approval, or a means of reducing risk. For example, consider a couple that has saved for a long-delayed vacation for themselves and their two teenage children. They are considering three weeks in Hawaii and have limited travel experience, all of it by car in North America. They are apprehensive about their contemplated vacation. They wonder if they are choosing a destination beyond their means. They are concerned as to whether Hawaii is safe for their health. They worry that they will be criticized for "wasting money" which could be spent on something more substantial or necessary. Then they learn that many of their friends have visited Hawaii. By discussing these trips, the couple forms a basis for comparing anticipated behaviour with the actions of others. This reduces the risk in their choice. The enthusiasm of their children and the approval of friends provide sources of sanction for their planned vacation.

No discussion of human behaviour would be complete without mentioning one other theory which has had a major impact on the explanation of travel behaviour. Plog's theory stipulates that an individual's personality determines the travel motivation and choice of destination. Plog's theory describes personality on a continuum from psychocentric to allocentric. A bell curve diagram is usually drawn to represent this continuum (see Figure 3.2). Such a bell curve is called a normal distribution. Psychocentrics and allocentrics are at opposite extremes in this diagram. The travel characteristics of the two groups differ so that different types of

FIGURE 3.2
Plog's Theory

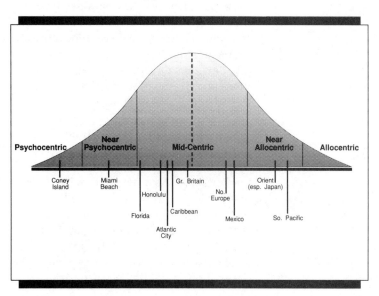

destinations appeal to each. The majority of people are mid-centrics and they exhibit some tendencies and characteristics of each of the other two groups.

Psychocentric personalities tend to be anxious, inhibited and conservative. They prefer familiar destinations and enjoy participating in commonplace activities. Their preference is for sun spots with considerable relaxation and a low activity level. For accommodation they are most comfortable in hotels and family type resorts that closely mirror North American styles and standards. They enjoy tour packages with preplanned activities requiring no decision making on their part. Their meal preferences are hamburgers and other North American fare.

At the other extreme are **allocentrics**. Allocentrics tend to be self-confident, curious, outgoing and adventurous. They prefer to visit non-tourist areas and novel or different destinations. They find pleasure in a sense of discovery and new experiences. They prefer to visit an area before it is discovered by mass tourism and are interested in a high activity level. They are comfortable in adequate hotels and enjoy meeting and dealing with local people. They are FIT type travellers who wish flexibility and freedom in their travel arrangements.

Destination development can be viewed as following a pattern that reflects these personalities. At first a destination may be undiscovered except by a few adventurous travellers, the allocentrics. As the destination becomes better known and develops its facilities, it appeals to more people, the mid-centrics who prefer their destinations to be exotic but "civilized" at the same time. Since Plog's theory suggests that personalities follow a normal curve, destinations that appeal to mid-centrics will attract the largest market share. As a destination becomes overexposed and overdeveloped, it becomes too touristy even for the mid-centrics. The destination now appeals more to psychocentrics who are a much smaller proportion of the population. The destination therefore begins to decline.

Just as personality and destination development are related, so too there exists a link between tourist destinations and an individual's motivations to travel there. Tourist areas must therefore be planned around these motivations or visitor expectations. Since no destination can appeal to everyone, each must develop its own characteristics to satisfy the customers it hopes to attract. There is a risk, however, in linking tourist destinations with a specific tourist type. Travellers have more than one motivation for making a trip and these can and do change from one trip to another. In addition, a destination can offer a range of travel experiences depending on how trips are packaged. For these reasons, it is risky to market a tourist destination to only one type of tourist.

When researching destinations for clients, it is important to be aware of their expressed wishes and needs as well as their personality. Client expectations regarding the suggested arrangements and area must also be considered. Client satisfaction is directly related to how well their expectations of a situation mesh with their perception of the actual conditions. If the level of expectation is higher than the actual experience, the individual will be dissatisfied. Counsellors must therefore be realistic in their counselling advice. If counsellors unrealistically raise their client's expectations by using superlatives such as the best accommodation, wonderful entertainment and the like, they are setting their clients up for a disappointment and themselves for a dissatisfied customer.

No two people have identical personalities or motivations. Similarly, travellers differ in their psychological makeup and needs. They can, however, be grouped according to particular behaviour patterns and attributes. Counsellors who develop the ability to accurately assess and classify potential customers will find that sales can be made more easily and that their clients will ultimately be more satisfied. It is also clear that counsellors must understand the real needs of their clients and not just those they express. Furthermore, counsellors must consider client expectations if they are to satisfy client needs. The conclusion to be drawn is that travel counsellors should study their clients for clues to their motivations, needs and expectations. By understanding how these forces work on client behaviour, they can then be turned to the counsellor's advantage. Some techniques for achieving this are discussed below.

Determining Client Motivations, Needs and Expectations

Vacation travel has been described as a satisfier of needs and wants. This statement implies that the main reason people take vacations is to satisfy, either wholly or partially, various desires. Counsellors must understand these motivations if they are to be successful. Those who do not understand will consider a destination to be no more than a collection of hotel rooms, some sand and palm trees. They will view a cruise as merely a hotel room that floats. On the other hand, those who see a vacation as a means of satisfying tourist needs understand that travel counsellors do, in fact, sell dreams.

The counselling process starts with the needs of the individual. On entering a travel agency a potential customer may be only partially aware of a need. Some may not even have this awareness. Awareness transforms a need into a want. The travel counsellor's role then is to make individuals aware of their need deficiencies. This, however, is only the first step. A person may be stimulated so that their needs become apparent. This may even lead to a desire for satisfaction of these needs. No action will be taken, however, unless that person is motivated. Motives are the key since they cause action, that is, they influence behaviour. Behaviour is of course also affected by

other factors. For our purposes, however, motives are critical to travel behaviour.

The discussion in this chapter has outlined some reasons why people travel. This material and the descriptions of group and individual behaviour have provided a basis for assumptions on client needs, motivations and expectations. A professional counsellor, however, should not base recommendations on assumptions. It is the counsellor's job to uncover these needs, motives and expectations by effective questioning and listening.

Questioning Skills

Two key questions will underlie most of an initial counselling dialogue. What does the client want to do (that is, what are the needs) and where does the client wish to go? Counsellors must also determine the client's previous travel experience. This information can provide an indication of how realistic are the client's expectations. First-time travellers generally have more fears and worries. Counsellors need patience as these travellers usually require more time and reassurance. Counsellors must also ask questions about the client's lifestyle and background. At this point in the discussion, our concern is with questions that elicit information on the client's needs, motivations and expectations. Specific sales questions will be handled in Chapter 13.

Questions are of two types, open ended and closed. **Open ended questions** encourage individuals to offer more than a one word response. There is no right or wrong answer. They are designed to reveal information. Typical open ended questions are: What do you have in mind? What do you like to do? Why were you thinking of a cruise? What other vacations have you taken? What did you like or dislike about them? **Closed questions** expect a specific response. Often the answer is yes or no. Do you enjoy playing tennis? Have you budgeted for luxury or moderate accommodation? Open ended questions are more useful for counselling. Closed questions are useful for closing a sale. When a question has not produced the desired response, follow up questions are necessary to extract more information.

The dialogue between counsellor and client is a communication process. Good communication demands that both parties understand what is being communicated. Counsellors can verify that they understand a client's responses by rephrasing and summarizing the answers. This technique may reveal that further questions are necessary to clarify a point. Questions are also used to obtain more information and to acquire relevant or needed data. It is also important to control the discussion and not to waste questions by asking for irrelevant details. For example, if a client is considering a trip to Banff it is unnecessary to ask whether the client has a passport. Remember that the conversation should be a dialogue. Allow the client to speak freely. The purpose of asking questions is to obtain information on the client's needs so that the counsellor can understand them. It is important to focus on the client. No suggestions or recommendations should be made until a complete picture has been obtained.

Effective Listening

Counsellors must also learn to listen effectively as well as to question clearly. Successful travel counselling requires that the counsellor and client engage in a communication dialogue. Effective listening is essential to clear communication. At least half of all communication is listening; it is the receiving part of communication. Listening is important to everyone. If you do not believe this, just make a list of daily activities that involve listening. Notice how often you require this skill.

Unless one listens effectively it is impossible to clearly understand the sender's communications. If a counsellor does not understand what a client is attempting to communicate then an appropriate response will be impossible.

Effective listening includes not only receiving information through the ears, it also means using one's eyes to observe non-verbal communication. This information must then be interpreted. Only after analyzing the information can an individual respond appropriately to what is heard. Effective listening implies commitment to one's client. Listen closely and clients will appreciate the interest and concern. Successful counsellors find that listening is good business.

Listening effectively has many benefits. It can increase income, improve chances for promotion, increase job satisfaction, improve problem solving abilities, and keep one aware of developments in the organization. Most of us listen to only one quarter of our potential. More than three quarters of what we hear is ignored, forgotten, distorted or misunderstood. This can lead to poor service and loss of clients. For example, a client who ended up on a flight to Birmingham, England rather than Birmingham, Alabama would be unlikely to return to the same agency for future service.

Good listening demands energy and expertise. It is nevertheless a skill which can be developed. Effective listening has four stages. First, one must **listen to the message**. Hearing is involuntary but listening is voluntary, that is, we choose to listen. In order to listen to a message one must pay attention to what is being said, select what is important in the message, and recognize emotional signals. It is obvious that one must concentrate on the client's words. It is also important to separate the statements and issues raised by the client so that the counsellor can begin to determine the reasons why the customer wishes to travel. Recognizing emotional signals will help a counsellor to decide which motives are strongest for the client.

The next stage is **interpreting the message**. It is important that both speaker and listener agree on the meaning of the message. Without this agreement the counsellor and client will be talking at cross purposes and both will be wasting time. Remember that the words spoken convey the thoughts and feelings of the speaker. Listeners filter this message through their own value system of memories, perceptions, attitudes and expectations. Listeners must be alert to the tone of voice and to non-verbal clues such as gestures, facial expression, posture and eye contact. Three factors that assist in interpreting the message are self knowledge, a desire to understand, and asking for clarification. Self knowledge makes a counsellor aware of the filters being applied to a client's words. The counsellor's role is to match client needs with suitable travel products. Counsellors who do not wish to understand their clients' needs are failing in their responsibilities. Clearly, counsellors who do not understand the client's message must ask questions to clarify the misunderstanding.

The third stage of listening is **evaluating the message**. Three techniques that help in evaluation are asking questions, analyzing the evidence, and avoiding the urge to jump to conclusions. The latter skill is the most difficult to acquire. One must ensure that all possible information has been gathered before drawing a conclusion or making a recommendation.

The final stage is **responding to the message**. A response informs the speaker that the message was heard, understood and evaluated appropriately or alternatively that further dialogue is necessary. Following these steps will help develop listening skills and enhance communication.

A person's listening style is a reflection of the individual's attitude and behaviour. How an individual responds when listening can be a barrier or a bridge to communication. Active listeners listen not only to the content of the speaker's words but also to the meaning behind them. They maintain eye contact, ask questions, and give feedback to ensure accuracy.

The following tips will help develop good communication skills. As with many skills, organization is critical to success. Counsellors should always be prepared when a client enters the office. References and materials should be at hand. Taking notes during the conversation will help to focus attention on the key areas of importance. Only the main points need be recorded. It is not necessary to write everything. Remember that counsellors are there to serve the needs of the client. Therefore take an interest in what the client is saying. Listen attentively and do not interrupt. Control the conversation by keeping the client on topic. Do not let the conversation wander.

Be aware of your client's as well as your own body language. Be sure that your posture conveys a positive encouraging attitude, acknowledge the speaker's words, and make good eye contact. Notice the other person's feelings, ask objective questions for clarification and try to see the other person's viewpoint. An effective communication device is to imitate or mirror the speaker. Change your voice rate, tone and volume to match that of the client. Use some of the same words and phrases as the speaker. One should be careful not be too obvious about this. Clients could interpret this as mockery rather than as the empathy that is intended.

Control or eliminate distractions. Do not use distractions as a convenient excuse for not listening. Instead, identify the cause of the distraction and make adjustments. This can be difficult in a busy travel office where telephones are constantly ringing and there is a great deal of surrounding activity. Take a break if you cannot ignore the distraction.

People travel for a variety of reasons and to fulfill a variety of needs. Sometimes they are not aware of which needs they wish to satisfy through a vacation. This lack of awareness makes it difficult for clients to assess a travel experience. Clients may not know whether or not a vacation was of high quality, only that they enjoyed or disliked the experience. Travel counsellors are extremely influential in the selection of a travel experience. They therefore carry a large responsibility for the decision process. To be successful, travel counsellors need to know how to discover what people like and dislike about specific services, why they choose one over another, why they change from one to another, and what they perceive to be the difference. This chapter has laid the foundation for such investigations. Some preliminary suggestions have been made regarding how to classify types of travellers and what their motivations may be. Tips on how to develop effective questioning and listening skills have also been offered. From the material covered in this chapter, counsellors should be able to develop expertise in the first part of their responsibilities, that is, knowledge of their clients. In the following chapter the second area of responsibility, the nature of travel products and product knowledge, will be investigated.

Review Questions

1. Suggest five reasons why people travel and provide examples of possible destinations for each.

2. Discuss the reasons why some people choose not to or are unable to travel.

3. Why is it important that travel counsellors develop effective questioning and listening skills?

4. Compare demographic and psychographic information. Why do travel suppliers require both types of information?

5. Discuss the four main categories that determine travel behaviour.

## Chapter 4

The Travel Product

Chapter Summary

This chapter discusses the special characteristics of the travel product and how it differs from other types of products. Much of the chapter focuses on the sources of product knowledge. The changing nature of the travel product, and its effect on product knowledge, are investigated. Methods by which travel counsellors can keep updated on changes in product are reviewed.

Chapter Objectives
After completing this chapter you should be able to:

- State how travel products differ from other products.

- Identify and discuss sources of product knowledge.

- Acquire and update product knowledge using a variety of methods.

- Distinguish between trade and consumer publications.

- Provide examples of major categories of travel publications.

- Describe the importance of product knowledge in selling travel.

The Travel Product

The previous chapter described the emotional and physical needs of clients and highlighted the fact that the travel industry tends to appeal more to emotional than to physical needs. The travel and tourism industry markets dreams. That is, the industry sells experiences and services rather than physical products. In this respect, the tourism industry is unlike many other industries.

The travel product is unique in that it is primarily **intangible**. Consumers cannot taste, touch or actually inspect a trip prior to purchase as they can a car, clothing, or an appliance. Consumers cannot take a vacation home from a travel agency to see if it fits their tastes and lifestyle. A trip is an experience rather than a physical item of merchandise that can be inspected prior to purchasing.

Chapter 1 noted that there are many definitions for the terms travel and tourist. In Chapter 3 the client was reviewed and the variety of types of travel and motivations were discussed. It became clear that travel is different things to different people. Purpose and motivation vary from one person to another. To a businessman, an airline ticket from Winnipeg to Quebec City may simply be part of getting the job done. This nondiscretionary traveller is likely to be most interested in the airline's efficiency, its ability to follow the schedule, and the

speed of its boarding and baggage handling. For another nondiscretionary traveller, such as someone with a family crisis, the trip may be just one more stress to handle. For tourists, however, the same journey may be the culmination of a dream trip to the Quebec Winter Carnival. For vacationers, travel is the purchase of a dream, an intangible. Most tourists do not focus on the tangible things they can take home, instead they are buying the use of a hotel room, a seat on a train, the culture and friendliness of the local people, the beauty of a sunset, and memories of a pleasant holiday. Other than pictures, souvenirs, and perhaps a credit card bill, nothing tangible remains from a vacation.

This intangible travel product often takes the form of a service. For example, when a client takes a plane trip, the client does not actually buy a seat on an aircraft but instead purchases the right to use that seat on a specific journey. In effect, the client has purchased the services of that airline for that particular trip. Supplier advertisements reveal the service nature of the travel product. Airlines advertise the courtesy of their flight attendants and destinations emphasize their friendly people and atmosphere.

The fact that the travel industry sells services rather than physical products makes it relatively easy for competitors to imitate another supplier's product. The basic components of tourism, such as beaches or transportation, are similar. For example, most airlines fly the same routes using similar equipment, schedules, fares, meals and safety procedures. When a new service is introduced, for example frequent flyer programs, competitors can very quickly mimic the successful service. Manufacturers of tangible goods find it more difficult to copy their competitors' products. The time required to design and manufacture goods is greater and, in addition, products can be protected by patents. Although hotels and resorts do vary in their quality and style, they still follow industry trends, such as all-inclusive resorts. When services are similar, even the smallest change will be publicized in an effort to attract or maintain clientele. For example, an airline will boldly announce a new colour scheme for its aircraft even though this has no bearing on the quality of its service. This similarity and mimicry of services becomes one of the main challenges for travel counsellors. If all products are

basically the same, how can one tell the difference?

Another factor is that there are more variables in services than in products. Manufacturers have a fair degree of control over the quality of their goods. Service industries, however, have a more difficult task in maintaining control of their services. A dissatisfied client cannot return a poor vacation to the manufacturer. Services rely more on people and people are harder to control than products. People are different from each other in ability and personality. Their individual performance also varies from one day to another, or even within the same day. People have good days and bad days; they can be efficient and accurate or the exact opposite; they can be friendly or sullen. A hotel manager can ensure that the rooms are clean and that the furniture is in good condition. It is not so easy to monitor the behaviour of front desk personnel or restaurant staff. An incorrect meal can be returned to the kitchen and

FIGURE 4.1
Airlines sell service and cooperation with travel agencies.

When we make our clients happy we make your clients happy.

We know that when your clients are happy with our service, they're also happy with you. That's why we're continuously striving to offer our customers, your clients, the very best.

This begins with our aircraft. The state-of-the-art Dash 8 offers a level of comfort and convenience that is second to none.

But what really makes an Air Ontario flight special is our service. We're committed to service excellence. When your clients fly

with us, they'll discover a service attitude that says, we care. In fact, we'll do everything we can to make their flight with us the best possible. We'll make it easy for your clients to connect with Air Canada's domestic and international flights at Toronto's Terminal 2. What's more, your clients get all of the advantages of Aeroplan.

So don't just book your clients on any flight, book them with Air Ontario. Your clients will come back to thank you.

WORKING TOGETHER, WE SERVE YOU BETTER.
Member of Alliance of Canadian Travel Association.

AN AIR CANADA CONNECTOR

FIGURE 4.2
Destinations sell
friendly people.
Source: Cayman
Islands Department
of Tourism.

FACTS:

CAYMAN ISLANDS FRIENDLY
The people of The Cayman Islands are known for their warmth, sincere friendliness, and their genuine pleasure in welcoming visitors. They are gracious people who are proud of their Islands, and happy with the lifestyle here. You will find them very glad to answer any questions you may have, and to do whatever they can to make your stay an enjoyable one.

replaced but the same cannot be said of an offensive or inappropriate remark. Similarly, the attitude of the local residents influences travellers to return to a destination or to look for another. Travel counsellors soon learn that when they sell travel products they are really selling people.

Another difference between tourism and other products is the location of the product. Tourism products are located a long way from their customers. In most industries, products are manufactured in factories, packaged and sent to wholesalers who distribute the product to retailers where it is purchased locally by consumers. The consumer then takes the product home for use. With tourism, however, the consumer or tourist has to be brought to the place where the product is produced before it can be enjoyed.

Further, tangible goods are manufactured at one time and used at another. They can be stored and inspected for quality before selling. A service, on the other hand, is produced as it is used. An airplane seat is used on the day of the flight. A meal is eaten on the night it is

produced. Services cannot be produced and put on a shelf for later use. The perishable nature of travel products was discussed earlier and we noted that such products had to be used at specific times or their revenue was totally lost. With tangible products a total loss can be avoided by reducing the price of the goods to sell them at or below cost. Alternatively, they can be stored until a better time such as a new season or a sale. Such sales may not make a profit but some return will be earned; the item will not just be thrown out. After a given date none of the above options are open to the producers of travel products. The perishable nature of the travel product is one reason for overbooking in the airline and hotel industries. Experience has shown that some people do not use the service reserved. Overbooking helps to fill seats and rooms that would otherwise be empty.

Manufacturers have several alternatives for poor quality or unsuitable products. The product can be withdrawn from the marketplace, it can be redesigned, repackaged, repriced, or replaced with an acceptable substitute. Many of these options are not possible with services. Bad experiences leave strong and lingering impressions that are very difficult to change. Thus, it is essential that travel counsellors learn to assess the quality of services.

Just as services cannot be stored, so is it difficult to anticipate demand. For example, who can predict where or when an earthquake will occur or what will be the next fashionable destination? It is therefore difficult to predict the number of airline seats or hotel rooms required on any given day. There is also no easy way to quickly change a supply of tourism products. At any given time and for any destination, the number of hotel rooms or of airline seats is fixed. Although this supply is set, the demand is not. In economic terms, the demand for tourism products is highly **elastic**. This means that an increase in price will decrease the volume of tourists. Conversely, a destination that sharply devalues its currency will most likely experience a sudden increase in tourists. Tourism products are vulnerable to changes in demand which can be caused by fluctuations in currency rates, altered economic conditions, political upheavals, bad weather or other reasons. There are also regular cycles of peak seasons and slumps in demand. We have seen that the industry is extremely competitive. The similarity of services means that tourist demand can be satisfied at a choice of locations. In addition, purchasers of travel products generally have no loyalty to a particular company, destination, or type of vacation, and travellers are subject to fads, fashions, and changes in motivation. All these factors create instability of demand.

Travel products and services therefore exhibit a number of differences from tangible goods, the primary one being their intangible nature. The journey or vacation is an intangible. Once it has been used, it cannot be returned for a refund or an exchange as can be done with a product such as a dress. Although the travel product is an intangible experience, it is nonetheless composed of a number of different and very concrete elements; for example, transportation, accommodation

and attractions. The quality of the facilities provided at a hotel can certainly be inspected, as can the timekeeping record of an airline, or the number of events at a destination. Similarly, the suitability of these products can be assessed against the needs of particular client groups. These components of a pleasure or business travel experience are the products of the travel industry. By extension, the particular quality and combination of elements used by an operator to create tours can be used as a measure of the operator's product. Similarly, features, attractions, weather, culture, infrastructure and other aspects of a destination can be used to assess it in terms of product.

Consumers, however, are unlikely to inspect an aircraft before deciding to fly in it. Similarly, it is not practical to visit a destination and view the hotel room before deciding to purchase the package featuring that particular accommodation. It is equally impractical for a travel counsellor to personally investigate each and every component before deciding to sell a package tour. Neither can clients realistically expect travel counsellors to have previously visited every destination or flown on every airline. Clients can, however, expect to receive professional advice from their counsellors.

Several differences between tourism services and other products have been discussed. Chapter 3 reviewed the nature of the client and emphasized the importance of knowing one's clients, their motivations and preferences. Knowledge of the tourism product is equally important and the foregoing discussion has illustrated that the travel product has several differences from other products. The question remains, then, as to where and how members of the travel industry can acquire the necessary product knowledge.

Manufacturers of tangible goods such as appliances or clothing produce brochures with photographs and technical specifications to support their sales forces. Similarly, travel industry suppliers use brochures, a variety of other materials and techniques, training sessions and promotional campaigns to ensure that their sales force, the travel agency, has sufficient knowledge and information to sell their products. This chapter highlights the main sources of this product knowledge.

Sources of Product Knowledge

Travel products are not only different from other types of products, they are also different from each other. The variety of travel products on the market is so large that it may seem pointless to attempt to categorize them. Added to the variety is the fact that travel industry product is constantly changing; for example, as the seasons change so do the products. An agency's inventory, the brochures on its shelves, will change in step with the seasons. Promotional campaigns, the introduction of new destinations, new types of holidays, and changing tastes, for example, will also affect the composition of an agency's inventory. Consumers, however, rely on the travel industry for knowledge of its products and therefore those in the industry must find an effective way of retrieving this information.

One way to locate information is by trial and error, but this is time consuming and not necessarily effective. A simpler and more accurate method is to develop a system of classifying the sources of product knowledge. There are probably as many classification systems as there are people. This is even more likely when the topic is as diverse as the travel product and the sources range from suppliers to the travel press. Some of the information can be acquired by participation in industry activities. Basic information can be researched from standard sources. This must be sorted, filed, and kept updated. Outdated information is worse than obsolete; it can lead to lost business or in the extreme, to litigation. Here then, is one way of classifying the primary sources of product knowledge:

- Standard References.
- Supplier, Government and Tourist Board Information.

- Computer Systems.
- Travel Trade Publications.
- Industry Presentations, Seminars and Trade Shows.
- Familiarization Trips and Coworkers.
- Clients.
- Other Sources.

You may already be familiar with some of these sources. Others you will encounter as you progress through a travel program or in the course of your travel career. Each is important in developing knowledge of a particular travel industry segment or product. This chapter introduces the most important printed references in addition to other sources and methods of locating product knowledge. The type of information found in the printed references is summarized. Later chapters will review not only their contents but also how to read and interpret them. Their interpretation and use as sales tools is the basis for these later discussions.

Standard References

This category refers to printed materials that are used as standard references throughout the travel industry or within a particular segment. Most are produced by independent publishers or associations of travel suppliers. As such, they do not publicize or promote one specific company but instead record the services of all relevant firms. Many provide basic and indispensable information on tariffs and timetables. Some are issued annually while others are published as often as every two weeks. Although these references are classified as being unbiased, in the sense that they provide information on all services in a particular segment, they are still sales tools. As each is studied in depth, this aspect of their use will be emphasized. Another feature of standard references is that each utilizes a standardized format which does not change from issue to issue. Some other sources of product knowledge, for example tour brochures, vary widely from one issue to the next.

The following review of standard travel industry references has divided them according to their industry segment. The review begins with the transportation sector.

Standard Airline References

The most common and widespread airline reference is the *Official Airline Guide* (OAG). The OAG is basically a timetable of international and domestic flights. It is an essential reference that also contains much additional information useful to travel counsellors. For example, aircraft specifications, airline and city codes, and minimum connecting times are specified. Two editions of the OAG are published. The North American Edition provides information on domestic flights only. Domestic flights are defined as those within and between Canada, the USA including Hawaii and Alaska, Mexico and the Caribbean. All other trips are classified as international and appear in the Worldwide Edition of the OAG. The North American OAG is printed every two weeks whereas the Worldwide Edition is issued monthly.

As well as knowing when a flight will depart and arrive, both of which can be determined by consulting the appropriate OAG, clients also wish to know how much the flight will cost. This information is found in one of two publications known as a **tariff**.

Fares for domestic journeys are published by the Airline Tariff Publishing Company in a series of manuals known as the *ATPCO Passenger Tariff Set*. Here, the term domestic has a narrower definition than that used by the OAG. In the ATPCO, domestic refers to only Canada and the continental USA, plus Hawaii and Alaska. Rules and routings governing the fares for flights within different areas covered by the domestic tariff are printed in a number of books. The separate manuals have different issue dates. Some are distributed every two weeks, others every four weeks, and still others every eight weeks. The contents of these individual books will be reviewed in Chapter 6.

The international equivalent of the ATPCO is the *Air Tariff* which is published jointly by a number of airlines. This reference also comprises a number of separate books with a variety of publishing frequencies. The Air Tariff lists the fares for international flights and contains the rules and regulations which govern the fares printed in it. By definition, international refers to flights to and within any part of the world not covered by the domestic tariff (the ATPCO). Since different sections of the Air Tariff cover different areas of the world, some books are not generally distributed in Canada. For example, the Air Tariff has a section which provides the fares for travel within Europe. This volume is chiefly distributed in Europe and is not generally available in Canada.

The *IATA Ticketing Handbook* is the standard guide for the correct completion of airline tickets and other travel documents. It is published annually by the association and refers to the IATA ticketing format used around the world. This manual is the only correct reference for the completion of IATA documents.

The Billing and Settlement Plan (BSP) is the system developed by the airlines to collect payments for tickets sold through travel agencies and airline ticket offices in Canada. The *BSP Manual* is also published by IATA and is updated periodically. The manual covers the procedures for completing documents and reporting sales through BSP. Occasionally, instructions for ticket completion differ between the IATA Ticketing Handbook and the BSP Manual. In such an event, the IATA Ticketing Handbook should be considered as the decisive reference.

Standard References for Marine Transportation

Standard references in the airline industry concentrate on timetables and tariffs. Information on specific airlines, their services and equipment is left to the individual companies. In part, this is a result of the similarity of the services and equipment of each airline. Airline performance statistics are included in standard reference materials for the simple reason that all DC10s, for example, are designed to the same performance criteria. The seating arrangement, however, is a matter for individual airlines. Such information is better described as supplier information and is discussed below. References for marine transportation, however, follow a different pattern. Its standard references provide details of schedules and fares in much the same way as do airline references but many also include descriptions of the vessels and their services. The notable differences between ships and between ship lines contribute to this decision. Such information naturally falls under the banner of standard requirements.

The most comprehensive guide to cruise lines and cruise ships is the *CLIA Cruise Manual*. Cruise Lines International Association (CLIA) is a trade association of the world's leading cruise lines. As well as providing complete details of all member companies and profiles and deck plans of the ships in their fleets, the manual contains many useful hints and techniques for selling cruises, port maps, sample menus and activity sheets. The association publishes the manual annually.

The *Official Steamship Guide International* is a monthly reference of cruises throughout the world. The guide lists cruises by geographical location and by sailing date. It also contains regular point-to-point voyages for both passenger ships and passenger-carrying freighters.

The *OAG Worldwide Cruise and Shipline Guide* is published every two months. It includes cruise listings, port-to-port sailings, ship profiles and diagrams of pier locations.

The company which publishes the OHG accommodation guide (discussed below) also issues the *Official Cruise Guide* annually. This bound manual describes each ship and cruise line, and provides deck plans, schedules and port maps similar to other cruise references.

Ford's Travel Guides distributes a number of useful references. *Ford's International Cruise Guide* is a quarterly publication which summarizes cruises by departure date and by destination similar to the Official Steamship Guide International. In addition, the guide provides brief histories of the cruise ships and a listing of ships and cruise lines. For those interested in more exotic water transportation, *Ford's Freighter Travel Guide* is published twice yearly. This pocketbook supplies information on passenger-carrying freighters worldwide, as well as details on a variety of waterways of the world. A third publication is *Ford's Deck Plan Guide* which displays large format deck plans of over 130 ships. Its binder presentation permits the information to be easily updated from material made available on an annual basis.

Although the *Thomas Cook European Timetable* is usually considered to be a railroad reference, it also lists shipping services in the English Channel, the North Sea, the Baltic and the Mediterranean. Ferry services and their links to train services are also listed. This timetable is issued monthly.

Standard Railroad References

The *Official Railway Guide* is published five times per year. It is the most comprehensive source of passenger train schedules, fares and principal connecting services for the United States, Canada and Mexico. Listings are shown under a number of categories. Schedules are provided alphabetically by destination within each category.

The *Eurailtariff* is an annual publication based on the calendar year. Fares, regulations, surcharges, reservation procedures, and sleeping car fare charges, are shown for rail journeys between the major cities in western Europe. All cities appear once only in alphabetical order. Thus the fare for the rail journey from Stockholm to Amsterdam would be found under the listing for Amsterdam. To simplify interpretation and to stabilize prices, all costs are quoted in U.S. dollars.

The *Thomas Cook European Timetable*, mentioned above, provides detailed timetables and the principal rail services for Europe and Russia. Shipping services and additional travel information are also listed. The European edition is published on the first of each month. An overseas edition (the *Thomas Cook Overseas Timetable*) is published six times each year to provide information on similar services in the remainder of the world.

Standard Road Transportation References

Most travel agencies do not sell point-to-point bus tickets. For those who require information on such bus schedules, Russell's *Official National Motor Coach Guide* is the standard reference. This monthly publication lists current schedules for all bus lines throughout North America. A Canadian edition, Russell's *Official Canada Bus Guide*, is also published monthly and provides current schedules for all bus services within Canada.

Standard Destination References

The standard destination reference is a world atlas. Every professional travel person or travel agency should be equipped with a good quality atlas that provides clear, detailed and accurate maps, as well as information on climate and vegetation.

The *Travel Information Manual* (TIM) is published monthly by a consortium of international airlines. The TIM contains current entry requirements for nearly 200 countries. Regulations and procedures for passports, visas, health requirements, and customs and currency restrictions, are also described. *also available in GDS*

Standard Accommodation References

Official Airline Guides also publishes an accommodation guide. The *OAG Travel Planner* is the official publication of the American Hotel and Motel Association (AHMA). It is issued quarterly and incorporates the Mobil Travel Guide rating system for accommodation. The publication lists hotels alphabetically by city, and shows their quality, price and location. Other details, such as proximity to airports, transportation services, and a variety of useful destination information, are also provided. The OAG Travel Planner is published in North American, European and Asia Pacific Editions.

The *Official Hotel Guide* (OHG) is a three volume directory. It contains more in-depth descriptions than either the OAG Travel Planner or the Hotel and Travel Index. The reference lists about 30,000 hotels and resorts in about 200 countries and territories. The OHG is available by annual subscription.

The *Hotel and Travel Index*, issued quarterly, lists over 36,000 hotels, motels and resorts, hotel representatives, approximate room rates and commissions payable.

ABC, which publishes airline tariffs and timetables commonly used in Europe, also prints the *ABC Star Service*. This looseleaf manual reports on over 8,000 properties worldwide. Cruise ships are also evaluated. Reviews are often provided by travel counsellors, whose input is solicited by the company, so the comments may be positive or negative. The ABC Star Service therefore presents a unique perspective on hotel quality. The ABC Star Service is updated quarterly.

Standard Tour References

There are no manuals devoted solely to tours such as there are for the transportation segments described above. Tours can, of course, be constructed using standard references from other sources. The nature of tours, however, suggests a combination of services created by a supplier. Most tour product information is therefore found in the following category.

Supplier Information

Supplier materials are possibly the most visible forms of product information. There are two main differences between supplier information and standard references. The first difference is that supplier information does not follow a standard format. Tour brochures, for example, differ from each other and one issue may well differ from that produced by the same operator for the following season. On the other hand, standard references such as airline tariffs tend to have a similar format which do not change. A second difference is that suppliers produce their information specifically to sell their own products. They do not attempt to provide general information on all tours whereas the OAG, for example, lists the schedules of all airlines operating between a pair of cities. Supplier information is produced for promotional and sales purposes rather than for reference as is the first category. In addition, a large proportion of supplier information is targeted directly at consumers, although it is also designed to be used by the industry as a sales tool. Standard references, however, are designed for industry use.

There are at least four categories of supplier information; catalogues (or brochures), flyers, rate sheets and timetables. The following describes their contents and function. Specific details of how to read and interpret them for sales purposes is left until the relevant product chapter.

Catalogues are publications that list various travel industry services for sale. The services may be holiday packages, independent itineraries, cruises, motorcoach tours, hotel packages, or any other type of holiday offerings. Catalogues are based on the same principles as department store mail order catalogues which were once so popular. Most consumers and travel industry personnel know catalogues as brochures. In travel and tourism generally, a brochure is a tour operator publication that provides detailed information on tours, transportation, cruises, accommodation and destinations. Brochures are directed at the consumer and are one of the main sales tools of the travel industry. They are printed in magazine format and include pictures, prices and descriptions. They range from a few pages in length to a hundred or more. In industry jargon a catalogue is often called a "book", especially by tour operators. Folders are less comprehensive than brochures but often provide similar information. For example, a brochure may present a tour operator's complete line of tours for a season whereas a folder may highlight one particular tour package.

Confidential tariffs are a particular type of catalogue published by tour operators and other suppliers. They are intended to be used only by members of the travel trade. Suppliers geared to the independent tours (FIT) market print

confidential tariffs so that travel agencies have access to the information required to construct individual tours. As with other brochures, there is no standard format for confidential tariffs. Although all furnish details of the particular services they provide, some tariffs show prices in dollars while others price the services in local currency. Similarly, some tariffs show gross prices which include the agent's commission in the total price, while others list net prices to which the agent must add an appropriate mark-up. Still others mix both net and gross prices, as well as showing various currencies. As with brochures in general, all confidential tariffs describe the terms and conditions under which the listed services are sold.

The best known confidential tariff is the *Consolidated Tour Manual* (CTM) which is published four times a year. The CTM lists a variety of tours that meet certain specifications required for advertised air tours. This manual shows price and selling instructions for advertised air tour packages within the USA, Canada, Mexico, Central America and the Caribbean. It also contains selected city and area maps, special events tours such as the Rose Bowl Parade, and information on some of the hotels used on the tour packages.

The World Association of Travel Agencies (WATA) also produces a confidential tariff called the *Master-Key*. This confidential tariff contains national tourist information, tariffs for various tour services, hotel listings, and details of WATA membership and procedures.

A **flyer** is usually printed on a single sheet. It is designed and produced specifically to promote a special offering or service, such as a reduced rate fall package or a new branch office. Flyers can be mailed or distributed by hand and can be targeted to either the trade or the consumer.

Rate sheets are used by many suppliers, most often in areas such as car rentals, hotels or resorts, where prices are liable to change due to season, currency or other reasons (see Figure 4.4). In the hotel industry a rate sheet is sometimes called a rack card. A rate sheet is generally a single page listing current prices. It is inserted in folders and is designed to be the same size and format as the enclosing folder. The folders (or sometimes, brochures) are printed in bulk with features and information that do not change significantly over a period of time. For example, a hotel will usually print a glossy, full colour brochure with pictures and descriptions of its accommodations, meeting rooms, restaurants, and decor. A rate sheet describing room rates will then be inserted into this folder. If rates change the rack card can be easily and inexpensively replaced.

Timetables are produced by transportation companies. In many respects, the information repeats that provided in the standard references listed above. The significant difference is that timetables show departure and arrival times only for the particular company producing the timetable. Timetables are printed by all transportation companies and in various styles (see Figure 4.5). The most familiar is the folded pocket timetable issued by airlines.

Computer Systems

Computer systems are the most important source of information in every business and the travel industry is no exception. Although there are several databases that can be accessed by travel agencies, by far the most important and widely used are the airline computer reservation systems (CRS). Airline systems

FIGURE 4.3
Suppliers willingly provide travel agencies with support materials for product knowledge and sales.

PELANGI
BEACH RESORT
LANGKAWI • MALAYSIA

RATE SCHEDULE

EFFECTIVE MAY TO DECEMBER 1989

	SINGLE OCCUPANCY	DOUBLE OCCUPANCY
SUPERIOR	M$130.00	M$160.00
DELUXE	M$150.00	M$180.00
PELANGI SUITE		M$280.00
LANGKAWI SUITE		M$380.00
PRESIDENTIAL SUITE ROYAL SUITE		M$800.00
EXTRA BED	M$ 30.00	

All rates are subject to 10% Service Charge

PELANGI JEEP RENTAL
M. Ringgit 80.00 per day
including Insurance.

Rates are subject to changes without notice.

The Courtleigh

31 Trafalgar Road, Kingston 10, Jamaica, W.I.
Phone: (809) 92-68174-8 (809) 92-95320-4
Fax: (809) 92-67801

SUMMER RATES
EFFECTIVE MAY 1, 1990 – DECEMBER 14, 1990

COURTLEIGH HOTEL

		Rate	Service Charge	Tax	Total
SUPERIOR	SINGLE	US$58.50	5.85	6.00	70.35
	DOUBLE	US$61.00	6.10	6.00	73.10
STANDARD	SINGLE	US$48.50	4.85	6.00	59.35
	DOUBLE	US$55.00	5.50	6.00	66.50
	T. V.				US$3.00

NORBROOK SUITE & TRAFALGAR SUITE

Single & Double		US$65.00	6.50	6.00	77.50

COURTLEIGH HOUSE

ONE BEDROOM					
	SINGLE	US$72.00	7.20	8.00	87.20
	DOUBLE	US$79.00	7.90	8.00	94.90
TWO BEDROOM					
	SINGLE	US$108.00	10.80	8.00	126.80
	DOUBLE	US$115.00	11.50	8.00	134.50
THREE BEDROOM					
	SINGLE	US$145.00	14.50	8.00	167.50
	DOUBLE	US$152.00	15,20	8.00	175.20
	Fridge				5.00
	Stove				6.00

SPECIAL GROUP RATES AVAILABLE ON REQUEST

*All rates are subject to change without notice.
Non-residents are reminded that all hotel bills
are to be settled in Jamaican currency.
Rates are calculated on Daily Bank Exchange
Rates.*

FIGURE 4.4
Hotel and resort rack cards use various formats and can be easily changed.

used in Canada are: Galileo, Sabre, Worldspan and Amadeus.

Deregulation of transportation in the USA, in Canada, and now proposed for Europe, has increased competition between airlines. This competition has affected all aspects of service, not just the fares, routes and schedules offered. One result of this deregulation has been greater rivalry between airline computer reservation systems. Every airline has added more capabilities to its system in an attempt to win travel agents' favour. The result is increasingly sophisticated information and reservations systems.

The Sabre system developed by American Airlines offers a growing array of capabilities and has been rewarded with an increased share of the Canadian travel agency market. At one time, Air Canada and Canadian Airlines International (CAI) operated separate computer reservations systems named Reservec and Pegasus, respectively. As a result of competition from the Sabre system, the two Canadian owned airlines in 1987 formed a joint venture company under the name of Gemini. American Airlines subsequently charged that Gemini operated a biased system and that the merger unfairly restricted competition. Gemini responded by concluding an agreement with United Airlines to share its information and Apollo operating system under the name of Apollo by Gemini (APG). The APG system began operations in Canada in 1990 and completed the system conversion by 1992. APG then concluded an agreement with American Airlines to give its subscribers a direct link with the Sabre system. Further links with other American and European computer systems have occurred. American Airlines subsequently purchased a share of Canadian Airlines with a condition that CAI withdraw from APG and become part of the Sabre network. This transaction was completed in 1995. Air Canada then created Galileo Canada based on the APG system. Galileo is now an independent company.

Joint ventures and consortiums are becoming the rule worldwide in travel industry computerized reservations. In Europe, several airlines have combined to provide a competing computer reservations system named Galileo. In the USA, Delta Airlines (with its DATAS II system), and Trans World Airlines and Northwest Airlines (both of whom use the PARS system) plan to develop a global computer reservations system. In Asia, a system known as Abacus has been developed. The PARS system has already produced a prototype that links the airline's reservations system to a videodisc. This system will allow a travel agency to retrieve pictures of a hotel and its facilities using a videodisc, and then superimpose onto the screen the room rates that are supplied by the reservations system. Such a system will be a powerful sales tool for travel counsellors.

It is obvious that any professional travel counsellor who wishes to keep abreast of current product information must therefore become computer literate in terms of the systems available in the travel industry. This review, although it may have ignited a spark of interest, has not yet established what information can be recovered from such reservations systems. In short, almost everything available in print and described above can now be retrieved from a computer system. For example, OAG schedules, fares and routings from the tariffs, as well as health and entry requirements listed in TIM, are already available through various computer systems. In addition, rail tickets can be purchased, tours can be booked, hotel rooms reserved, and there is the capability to research car rental details. Even tourist boards have entered their destination information in this type of system.

The travel agency's computer terminal (CRT) is linked to the airline's computerized database by means of common carrier lines such as the telephone network. Using the Galileo system as an example, one can readily appreciate the tremendous amount of information stored within the central computer's memory banks and the advantages of having computerized equipment available. For example, a travel agent can access the following types of information directly without having to call the airline:

- point-to-point fares (domestic and international).
- fare rules and regulations.
- baggage information.
- weather information (e.g., ski reports for Banff).
- passport and visa requirements.
- flight arrivals and departures.
- currency exchange rates.
- ticketing endorsements (if the agency issues tickets manually).
- airport facilities and services (e.g., first class lounge).
- elapsed flying times.
- aircraft performance statistics (e.g., how fast a Boeing 767 flies).
- current inflight movies.

Note that the destination information available in the TIM manual can also be accessed through a computer system. The automated manual, known as TIMATIC, permits counsellors to use their reservations terminals to pose specific questions on documentation or health, or alternatively to skim through the complete TIM manual.

The list, however, does not end with the items mentioned above. Almost every conceivable question a client may have can be answered using the information stored in the computer's memory. In addition, an agency equipped with an automated reservations system can also:

- verify whether a specific flight is available for sale.
- determine alternative flights available.
- list the flights scheduled between any two points.
- reserve any flight requested (if available).
- reserve hotels, car rentals, train seats, cruises and tours.
- make special requests for clients (e.g., order special meals or wheelchair assistance).
- preselect particular seats and issue boarding passes.
- control all reservation and client details.

Many agencies have added an automated ticket printer to their computer system. Such agencies can not only make the reservations described previously but can at the same time automatically issue the appropriate ticket.

The above requests and inquiries could be pursued by a travel counsellor without ever having to call the airline in question.

FIGURE 4.5
Timetables vary in format even within the same company.
Source: JAL.

北京・上海 BEIJING・SHANGHAI

G.M.T.との時間差 Difference from G.M.T.	曜日/DAY	Mo.Tu.Th.Fr.Su.	We.Sa.	Sa.	Th.	Mo.	Tu.Fr.Su.	Mo.
	便名/FLIGHT NO.	781	785	795	791	793	793	681
	機種/AIRCRAFT	DC10	B747	DC10	B747	B747	DC10	B747F
	クラス/CLASS	FCY	FCY	FCY	FCY	FCY	FCY	貨物便 CARGO
+9	東京(成田) TOKYO (NARITA) 発dp	1000		0900	0945			0950
+9	大阪 OSAKA 発dp	日曜: B747 Sun.: B747	1040			1050	1120	
+9	長崎 NAGASAKI 着ar / 発dp		土曜: DC10 Sat.: DC10	1055 / 1200				
+9	上海 SHANGHAI 着ar			1330	1245	1305	1335	
+9	北京 BEIJING (PEKING) 着ar	1415	1415					1405

To VANCOUVER from

Day	Dep	Arr	Flight numbers	Stops
SAPPORO				
1-4---	1455	1030	JL562/012	1
-2-----	1455	1130	JL562/018	1
			effective from June 1	
--3----	1455	1305	JL562/016	1
			effective from June 1	
----5--	1455	1130	JL562/018	1
			effective June 1 - August 31 only	
-----67	1455	1305	JL562/016	1
SEOUL				
1------	1455	1030	JL954/012	1
-2-----	1450	1130	JL954/018	1
			effective from June 1	
--3----	1450	1305	JL954/016	1
			effective from June 1	

This alone is advantageous. For example, the counsellor no longer has to call the airline which eliminates waiting time when the lines are in use or passenger agents are busy. Further, it reduces the chance of errors and confusion. For example, a passenger agent might misunderstand the date or the class requested by the travel agent. There may be confusion between Portland, Oregon and Portland, Maine. Using the reservations system can also avoid disappointment. Sometimes counsellors spend time with clients convincing them of the benefits of a discount fare only to discover on calling the airline that all seats are sold out for the day in question. With a computer the availability of the discount fare can be immediately verified.

Automated equipment helps travel counsellors to be more efficient in servicing the needs and wants of clients. The time between an information request from a client and the closing of the sale can be decreased. The agency therefore earns income while saving time and thus reduces costs.

The technology exists to provide more than the above information and tickets through computers. Current airline reservations systems can be used to issue rail tickets, or hotel, car rental and tour vouchers. By combining the reservations system with a common business system, an automated travel agency can print itineraries, reminders, documentation requirements, accounting forms and business letters. Additional systems are being tested and introduced. For example, some tour operators have linked their internal system with that used by the travel agencies to permit counsellors direct access to their tour inventory. Recently, a Canadian tour company introduced an electronic brochure which is being demonstrated in Thomas Cook travel agencies. This system has many similarities to the videodisc project being developed by the PARS system.

Initially, each airline reservations system was biased towards its own product. Legislation has been introduced to change this. There are still some limitations in each system but the similarities now outweigh the differences. Computer systems also present other problems, not least of which is reliance on electricity and the capacity of the system to handle the demands placed on it. Sometimes electricity fails or systems become overloaded. Clients cannot just be told to return for information when it is more convenient. Clients also like the security of having a hard copy of any information they are given by travel counsellors. Materials such as brochures can be taken away by consumers and studied at leisure. For these reasons, the printed materials described earlier will continue to play a major role as sources of travel counsellor product knowledge.

The most significant recent development in computer information has been the emergence of the Internet. The Internet allows both counsellors and consumers to access a huge variety of travel-related material. Today most government tourist offices, travel principals, and associated companies such as travel magazines and guidebooks, have a web site. It has become a simple matter to obtain information on, for example, a destination, airline, hotel, tour operator, cruise line or travel agency. Often, consumers can book directly with the supplier. In other cases, consumers are referred to a local travel agency or a direct booking with the supplier is routed to a local agency.

The rapid and continuing growth of the Internet will pressure travel counsellors to become familiar with this source of information and how to use it to their advantage. This means that counsellors must become more professional and ensure that their knowledge remains current. The public will quickly lose respect for counsellors if they find that they can obtain more information from the Internet than from the counsellor. Although many people believe that the Internet means the demise of the travel agency, professional travel counsellors will remain necessary for two reasons:

• Volume of information.
• Accuracy of the material.

As the Internet grows and the volume of material increases, it becomes more difficult and time-consuming to "surf the web". Although some people will prefer to research their own travels and book directly (as has always happened), many others will not be prepared to spend the time doing so. In addition, much of the public still does not have access to the Internet. However, if travel counsellors are to offer professional advice, they must remain current on new sites and developments in this area of technology.

Perhaps of more importance is the accuracy of the information. The Internet has no government or private body that sets the rules and ensures that the material presented is accurate and current. In the past consumers wanted trained professionals to explain and interpret printed information in brochures and schedules. This desire did not change when the information was transmitted electronically through an airline CRS. There is no reason to believe that consumers will not continue to need this

assistance simply because the information is available through the Internet. Professional travel counsellors have the skills and experience to evaluate the information and determine which products are most likely to meet their client's needs. This service is likely to become even more important given the mass of data that bombards today's consumers.

Travel Trade Publications

Both consumers who wish to travel and travel counsellors wishing to sell vacations seek information from a variety of regular publications in addition to the materials discussed above. Consumers rely on travel magazines, guidebooks and travel supplements in daily newspapers. This is the consumer press. Although the

FIGURE 4.6
Suppliers produce newsletters to keep the travel trade informed.

Sunquest

TRAVEL AGENT UPDATE

PLEASE CIRCULATE TO ALL TRAVEL COUNSELLORS, FILE IN YOUR SUNQUEST BINDER FOR FUTURE REFERENCE **September 7, 1989**

SUNQUEST'S LARGEST PRODUCT LAUNCH

On September 5th we launched our largest Winter Product Launch ever to 4,700 travel industry guests. We've taken a record number of bookings since that launch and as is par for the course at this time of year, we've identified some changes and omissions that we want to make you aware of through this newsletter. Please read it carefully, noting all the details and make sure that you file it for future reference.

DESTINATION 'M'

This is the destination that all the secrecy has been about, a resort so spectacular that we

February 6, 1990, we're offering $150 back per couple. $50 cash (or $25 per person) discount off the brochure price of your holiday, as well as two vouchers worth a total of $100 per couple ($50 per person) towards a future Sunquest vacation. Please note, full payment must be in by November 30. The invoice will reflect the discount only after Sunquest has received full and final payment and then an adjusted invoice will go out.

CHILDREN STAY FREE

At many of our hotels we have arranged for children to stay free when sharing with full paying adults. PLEASE NOTE that the number consumer press can provide interesting and useful background for travel industry personnel, it is not a primary source of product knowledge. By and large, travel counsellors are expected to already possess the general background information found in the consumer press. The counsellor's need is for specialized information on the travel industry, the "inside story" that may not reach the daily newspapers or national media until a later date, if ever. Such details can often be found in the trade press.

Trade papers are directed at individuals and companies within a particular industry. Most travel trade publications are issued on a weekly, biweekly or monthly basis. They contain news of fare and schedule changes, company news, special promotions and events, legal developments, new destinations and properties, sales tips, and similar information. These publications offer a wealth of current product information much of which will be found nowhere else. Regular reading of trade papers is essential to maintain one's product knowledge.

Trade publications appear in a limited number of formats. Most common are the newsletter and newspaper types of presentation. Newsletters, such as *Travel Courier* or *Travelweek Bulletin*, are published once or twice a week. Their presentation is simple and straightforward. They contain current news in capsule form, rarely devoting more than ten lines to an item, and a selection of advertisements and promotional inserts. Photographs are rarely included. The newspaper style, on the other hand, is often printed on glossy paper and usually appears less frequently, although some are published just as often as newsletters. Travel trade newspapers tend to be liberally illustrated with pictures of industry events, personnel and advertisements. These publications have the time and space to cover stories in greater depth than the newsletters. The trade paper with the largest circulation in Canada is the *Canadian Travel Press Weekly*. A number of other trade publications are common throughout Canada, some of

which are American trade papers. For readers with an interest in the academic study of tourism, there are several journals published to meet this need. A list of useful trade publications is printed at the end of this chapter.

Another type of trade publication is a directory. Directories are commonly produced by hotel chains to describe their properties and facilities and by associations to list details of their membership (see Figure 4.7). The directory likely to prove most useful to travel counsellors, however, is the *Personnel Guide to Canada's Travel Industry* which is issued twice yearly by the publishers of the *Canadian Travel Press Weekly*. This is an invaluable guide which lists the major segments of the travel and tourism industry. The guide provides particulars on travel agencies, tour operators and airlines, among others. All are listed alphabetically by province and city.

Industry Presentations, Seminars and Trade Shows

Presentations, seminars and trade shows are used by tourist boards, trade associations, and suppliers such as tour operators, hotels and airlines, to keep the travel industry, particularly retail travel counsellors, informed on their products and services. Each method has its own characteristics and uses.

Presentations

A presentation is an opportunity for travel industry suppliers or associated services to promote products, announce new services, or introduce themselves to their industry distributors. When a new product or service is being announced, or the programs for a new season are being introduced, the presentation is often known as a product launch. Almost all suppliers make presentations. Their frequency varies depending on the company's marketing goals and the nature of the business. As a primary promotional vehicle for suppliers, presentations are targeted directly at retail travel counsellors. The agencies to be

CANADA
British Columbia

Divi at a Glance

VANCOUVER, BRITISH COLUMBIA-AREA MAP

Note: The Number in front of the Name of Each Hotel, Inn or Resort Refers to Its Location on the Vancouver Area Map.

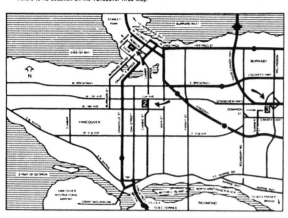

1 VANCOUVER
See number 1 on Vancouver area map

SHERATON LANDMARK HOTEL 762* HOTEL
1400 Robson Street, V6G 1B9
99 Hwy and Trans-Canada #1
☎ 604/687-0511 Telex: 04-55495
FAX: 604/687-2801
360 Rms, Inc Suites, Dntwn, 13 Mi Vancouver Intl Arpt, nr Stanley Pk, Robson Street, English Bay Lobby Cafe, Revolving Dining Rm, Lounges, 20 Mtg Rms Accom 10-600, Sauna & Jacuzzi, 4 Floors Non-Smoking Rms & Disabled Facilities Avail
1 P. $98.00 - $140.00
2 P. 113.00 - 155.00
Suites 190.00 - 390.00

2 VANCOUVER
See number 2 on Vancouver area map

THE SHERATON INN PLAZA 500 763* INN
500 West 12th Avenue, V5Z 1M2
99 Hwy and Trans-Canada #1
☎ 604/873-1811 Telex: 045-5120
FAX: 604/873-5103
153 Rms, 4 Suites, across from City Hall, 8 Mi to Arpt, nr the Financial District, 1 Block to Medical Center Hospital, nr Parks, 1 Mi from New B.C. Stadium, Dining Rm, Ent, Lounge, Pub, 9 Mtg Rms Accom 10-600, 24 Non-Smoking Rms. Disabled Facilities Avail
1 P. $88.00 - $106.00 2 P. $103.00 - $121.00

DIVI RESORTS

	DIVI DIVI	DIVI TAMARIJN	DUTCH VILLAGE	DIVI BAHAMAS	DIVI ST. JAMES	DIVI SOUTHWINDS	DIVI FLAMINGO	DIVI TIARA	DIVI ST. CROIX	DIVI LITTLE BAY	SEA DANCER
(Location)	ARUBA			NASSAU	BARBADOS		BONAIRE	CAYMAN BRAC	ST. CROIX	ST. MAARTEN	
NUMBER OF UNITS	201	236	70	250	131	166	150	70*	86	220	9
STUDIOS OR SUITES	1		70		77	166	40	1	42	3	
AIR CONDITIONED	•	•	•	•	•	•	•	•	•	•	•
TELEVISION			•	•		•	•		•	•	
REFRIGERATORS	•		•			•	•		•	•	
RESTAURANT	•	•	•	•		•	•	•	•	•	
BAR	•	•	•	•		•	•	•	•	•	
FRESHWATER POOL	•	•	•	•	•	•	•	•	•	•	
BEACH	•	•	•	•	•	•	•	•	•	•	
WATERSPORTS	•'	•'	•'	•	•	•	•	•	•	•	
SCUBA DIVING	•'	•'	•'	•	•'	•'	•	•	•'	•'	
TENNIS	•	•	•	•		•	•	•	•	•	
JACUZZI			•				•	•	•		
SQUASH & NAUTILUS					•						

FIGURE 4.7
Directories provide a variety of information.

invited, and the number of staff from each, are determined by such factors as the nature and purpose of the host company and its product. Any or all industry sectors may be invited, however.

The number of people invited determines the location of the presentation. Most are held in hotel suites, meeting rooms, ballrooms and convention areas of major hotels. Centrally located hotels are popular but sometimes suburban or airport area locations are chosen for cost reasons, for convenience, or because the hotel has an affiliation with the company making the presentation. For example, a tour company whose program offers overnight accommodation at an airport hotel for out-of-town clients may also use the location for its presentations.

Presentations are usually held in the evening. They can be small receptions for a few invited guests or large events for all travel counsellors in a particular area. The simpler affairs are often based on a short speech from the host, a brief vote of thanks for the support of the industry, and an introduction to the presentation. Refreshments or snacks are often provided. A film or other audiovisual of the product or service may be shown. Some presentations are planned around breakfasts while others are designed around lunches. The cost of providing such meals naturally restricts the number of participants. Breakfast or lunch meetings tend to be by invitation only and demand a RSVP. Although more costly, hosts generally consider these presentations more productive. A travel counsellor who takes the time to attend an early morning (probably 8:00 a.m.) or midday session is likely to be more interested in the product and, in theory at least, will be more productive. Breakfast meetings are less expensive for the host as the meal is cheaper and alcoholic beverages are rarely offered. Lunches cost the most as they comprise a full course meal, drinks, wine and perhaps a liqueur. Small gifts, usually a promotional item related to the product, are sometimes included. Travel industry hosts recognize that their presentations are a reflection of their image and product and therefore strive for high quality.

Although presentations can be offered at any time according to the needs and goals of the host, they are most often held during seasons that correspond with the peak booking times for various products. Summer/fall programs are introduced from September to late November while winter/spring programs are promoted between February and May. Meetings are rarely called in summer when employees usually take a vacation. At other times, such as early September and during December, travel agencies are too busy and the period following New Year is often a time of recovery.

Transportation companies offer presentations on an occasional basis. Most of these companies have presentations only when they have something special to promote. Airlines, for example, may announce a new type of aircraft, a new route or service, or perhaps a new tour program. A few companies hold regular promotions on a large scale each year.

Wholesalers tend to deal with individual agencies and therefore rarely put on special presentations. Tour operators, on the other hand, attempt to sell their tours through all agency outlets. They regularly conduct presentations for each season's programs, usually twice a year and sometimes more frequently. Tour operator presentations follow the format outlined above and are often very large events. Evening presentations usually begin around six-thirty to ensure that counsellors have time to reach the

venue after work. Tea, coffee and sandwiches may be served to encourage attendance and to allow time for people to arrive. The presentation itself is usually one hour or less in length, and is often an audiovisual with large- or multi-screen format. The message will detail the sales features and benefits of the product and there may also be a speech from a senior company representative. At the conclusion of the business portion of the meeting there may be an open bar and social evening. A cash bar often operates, sometimes after an hour or so of drinks supplied by the host.

Cruise lines, unless they are represented by a tour operator, hold presentations only on occasion. Such occasions are usually reserved for more select groups of travel agents, those that sell or are likely to sell cruises.

Individual hotels and resorts do not usually have the budget to offer more than the occasional small reception for selected potential producers. Hotel representative companies, like the small properties they usually represent, do not have sufficient funds for large, industry-wide events either. Some have smaller affairs in a hotel suite and invite regular producers. The majority, however, limit their participation to attendance at larger presentations in which their clients have an interest. Sometimes the staff of representative firms attend functions on their own. More commonly they accompany clients from the head office or a regional base. In such cases the client normally pays any expenses involved, such as booth rental, room rental or refreshment costs. Major hotel chains, on the other hand, can afford regular presentations. These are often used to publicize the opening of a new office, the expansion of the system, or to announce new policies or package programs.

Associated travel services, such as tourist boards, attractions representatives and insurance companies, vary in their use of presentations. Tourist boards and attractions representatives generally participate with tour operators, airlines, or any other industry component with which they are associated. Unless there is a

You're Invited

TO SUNQUEST'S LARGEST EVER
ENGLAND, SCOTLAND IRELAND & EUROPE
PRODUCT LAUNCH &
TRADE SHOW

- Introducing our first stand alone SCOTLAND brochure in addition to our England brochure & Ireland brochure.
- Introducing exciting INSIGHT COACH TOURS to more great places.
- A fantastic consumer booking incentive that's so hot, we won't announce it until Jan. 8.
- Door prize draw for a trip for 2 to England, Scotland or Ireland.

- Free hot roast beef sandwich buffet.
- Exciting informative audio visual show.
- Reception with free bar refreshments.
- Live band and dancing at the Toronto presentation.
- Pick-up supplies of our new brochures.
- Formal trade show with over 70 hoteliers and suppliers from Britain, Ireland and Europe.

TORONTO SHOW
DATE: Monday, Jan. 8, 1990.
PLACE: Regal Constellation Hotel, 900 Dixon Road.
TRADE SHOW HOURS:
5:00 p.m. to 7:00 p.m. and 7:30 p.m. to 10:00 p.m.
BUFFET: In trade show room at 5:30 p.m.
AUDIO VISUAL PRESENTATION: 7:00 p.m.
RECEPTION/ENTERTAINMENT: 7:30 p.m.

Free Transportation
Depart from York Mills Subway at 6:15 p.m.
(south east corner at Old York Mills Road).
Return from the Regal Constellation Hotel at 10:00 p.m.

Sunquest
The Quality Package Holiday People

SUNQUEST PRODUCT LAUNCH SPONSORS:

 Air Canada

 BTA

 Bord Fáilte Irish Tourist Board

 Scottish Tourist Board

 ISLE of MAN

FIGURE 4.8
Product launches are often sponsored by a group of related suppliers and frequently include additional incentives as well as an opportunity to gain product knowledge.

special reason, such as the opening of a tourist board office in a country, associated suppliers do not usually give individual presentations. Other companies, such as travel insurance firms and trade publications, attend most functions usually at the specific invitation of the host. These events provide an opportunity to increase their exposure in the industry.

The number of presentations and their cost has increased considerably in recent years. The increasing number of presentations has reduced both

participation and their effectiveness. Those who accept an invitation but then neither attend nor cancel their commitment, called "no-shows", have added to the costs. The travel industry has developed three strategies in an attempt to reduce overcrowded travel agent calendars and the financial burden on hosts.

Travel Fairs or **Trade Shows** attended by all suppliers have been produced. Such presentations may be aimed at the travel industry, the consumer, or both. Some are sponsored by industry associations such as CITC and ACTA, others by newspapers (The Globe and Mail or the London Free Press), some are operated by private companies (the Henry Davis Show) and a few are combined efforts of these groups. Trade associations based on specific geographical areas, such as the Pacific Asia Travel Association (PATA) or the Caribbean Tourism Organization (CTO), may also operate mini-trade shows to provide opportunities for their members to promote the area and its products.

Combined Product Launches for suppliers related by destination or product have been introduced. For example, all tour operators servicing a particular Caribbean island may combine their presentations in one show. Alternatively, there may be a Ski Show in which the appropriate suppliers participate.

Clearing Houses operated by industry associations such as ACTA have been formed to reduce duplication of presentation dates.

To a large extent the presentations themselves supply the product knowledge sought by counsellors attending the function. Another reason to attend, however, is the generous supply of product literature made available. These materials, the only "inventory" and physical representation of product knowledge for travel agencies, are essential sales tools and are the main attraction at trade presentations.

After attending a presentation, particularly if it is a trade show, travel counsellors will find that they return to their offices with large quantities of printed material. Often, they will have several carrier bags of brochures, posters and promotional items. Sometimes this material is left "until later". This is a mistake. Product material is useful only if it can be found when required. It is therefore essential that travel counsellors read and file the information as soon as possible after attending a function. It is equally important to discard outdated material at the same time.

Seminars

At first glance seminars are similar to presentations but their aims are different. A seminar's emphasis is education and training rather than promotion and marketing. It is a working session led by a sales or training instructor. Involvement of the participants and the teaching of skills or knowledge are the goals of a seminar.

To increase their effectiveness, seminars are usually held for smaller groups of twenty to thirty. Participation and learning are encouraged. Another difference is that seminars are usually offered during business hours (see Figure 4.9). Morning and afternoon sessions of about two hours are popular. In the evening people are tired and hungry after a day's work and they may not respond well. Alcoholic beverages are not usually served at seminars although refreshments are customary. Unless the seminar is a full day session, meals are generally not offered to participants.

Topics that require study and explanation are most appropriate for seminars. Tour operators often illustrate their programs with slides and commentary. Airlines and rail companies use seminars to teach tariff and ticketing procedures. Such training sessions are almost always held at the company's offices where well equipped training rooms and training staff are available. Cruise lines employ seminars to brief agents on selecting cabins, reading deck plans and generally teaching them to use brochures to sell clients on the merits of cruising. Seminars are often sponsored by trade associations that have an interest in education, or they may be promoted by private training companies.

Familiarization Trips and Coworkers

Much of the allure of working in the travel industry is based on a perception of free holidays that can be taken by employees. The industry does indeed offer opportunities for travel but these are rarely free and they are certainly not

FIGURE 4.9
Seminars stress
education and are
often held during
business hours.

holidays. This false impression is based on a lack of knowledge of the nature and purpose of familiarization trips, popularly known in the industry as **fam trips** or simply, **fams**. Such trips do provide an opportunity for relaxation and they do meet basic desires to travel and see places but they are offered to travel industry personnel for other reasons. It has long been recognized that to acquire product knowledge, as with any type of learning, there is no substitute for first-hand experience. It is this thirst for first-hand

knowledge and facts and perhaps even more, the very real need to face clients with confidence that motivates counsellors to participate in fam trips. All other ways of gaining product knowledge use vicarious methods, such as media or intermediaries.

Fam trips are designed by tourist boards, tour operators, and other suppliers to provide industry personnel, particularly travel counsellors, with the first-hand experience required to successfully sell a travel product. By

Canadian Institute of Travel Counsellors
O n t a r i o

CITC-ONTARIO presents :

COME-ON-I-WANNA-LUAU:
(HOW TO MARKET HAWAII TO YOUR CLIENTS)
Presented during the afternoon of PATAMART 2000, The Old Mill

A Hawaiian vacation may be the magical answer to your clients' dream. They want sun, culture, adventure, palm trees, beaches, resorts or bed and breakfasts, and a relaxing safe atmosphere. Hawaii consists of over 200 islands and atolls but seven islands are inhabited and offer a plethora of activities.

Learn all the details you need to know to suggest Hawaii to your clients. This seminar will include map work, a short language lesson, advice on accommodation, transportation, foods, niche markets, activities, the differences amongst the Islands, package tour costs, independent visit costs and more.

Course Date: March 28th, 2000   1:00-4:00 pm The Old Mill Conference Centre, Toronto
Course Fee:
Save by booking on or before March 14th: CITC & PATA Members $10.70 Non Members: $16.05
Book After March 14th: CITC Members $16.05 Non Members: $21.40

ACCESS Value: 3 PRODUCT/DESTINATION Credits PD Point Value: 1 Point

Nile Kingdom

*10 DAYS: CAIRO, ASWAN, AND LUXOR
BY DELUXE SLEEPER TRAIN*
Guaranteed Departures Every Friday

Rates are per person:	Deluxe	First Class	Tourist
Triple	$810.00	$650.00	$560.00
Double	$825.00	$710.00	$610.00
Single	$975.00	$810.00	$710.00

Tour Features:

- Roundtrip positive space air ticket: JFK/CAIRO/JFK on EgyptAir's 747.
- Six nights hotel accommodations including tax and all meals while in Egypt except on the day of arrival.
- Roundtrip deluxe sleeper train ticket Cairo/Aswan-Luxor/Cairo (overnight each way).
- Positive space air ticket Aswan/Luxor.
- Guided sightseeing in Cairo, Aswan, and Luxor exactly as outlined in Land of the Pharaohs Package.
- Full day excursion to Abu Simbel by motorcoach including lunch.

Egypt for the

**Travel Agents
&
Airline Employees**

SPECIAL RATES

Including positive air space **JFK/CAI/JFK**

visiting the product locations, counsellors can assess the quality of the facilities, and experience the atmosphere and other intangibles associated with a vacation. Fam trips are therefore a promotional device employed by suppliers to increase sales of their product. As such, the participants are often given special treatment not accorded to the tourist. For example, the tour is offered at a reduced cost; it is always escorted by representatives of the various services; only the best features are presented; and all operations run smoothly. Some agents therefore like to travel "incognito" to experience the services from a client's viewpoint. Fam tours provide an excellent opportunity for agents to assess transfers for service and convenience, and to

determine whether local transport is safe and practical. In addition, fams encourage counsellors to meet and discuss the product or service with the people who supply it.

Fams are business ventures, not holidays. As such, they are usually designed to expose participants to the largest number of facilities, events and attractions in the time available. Fam trips are always escorted by one or more hosts. They are working trips and though the hosts may arrange fun and relaxation as part of the program, they are still serious about ensuring that each participant learns as much as possible about their product. Both host and employer invest time and money to achieve particular results. The purpose is to educate and

**FIGURE 4.10
Fam trips have reduced rates to encourage counsellor participation.**
Source: Naggar Tours.

impress travel counsellors so that sales will increase.

The cost of a hotel room influences the price of a tour package and its quality affects a client's enjoyment of a vacation. Since accommodation is the most important component of any tour, hotel inspections are a standard feature of all fam trips. Travel counsellors also investigate transportation, shopping, restaurants, nightclubs and discos, attractions and events. On most hotel inspections travel counsellors are escorted by a manager, public relations supervisor, or senior member of the sales team. Guest rooms, suites, restaurants, ballrooms, pools and patios, are reviewed and mental comparisons are made with other hotels in the area. There may just be time to sample the bartender's special following this whirlwind tour before the group moves on to the next hotel. Many experienced travel agents make time to inspect hotels on their own rather than as part of a management-escorted tour. This permits them to check the natural operations of the hotel, for example the time when rooms are made up, rather than to see the perfect execution which is the norm on a conducted tour. A checklist to assess the quality of a hotel is described later in this text.

Selection Process for Fam Trips

The fam trip has become an institution and for some in the industry today it is almost a condition of employment. Most employers see fam tours as a necessary part of every counsellor's training and education. Other industry employees are also offered fams by tourist boards, airlines or cruise ships. Tour operators and their staff are often encouraged to attend. People in other positions and categories, who represent the host firm or who have legitimate business reasons for being included, will also be invited to take fam trips.

Participants are usually selected by the host organization, often based on either previous or potential sales to the area or with the host firm. Within an agency the owner or manager generally selects the employee who will participate. This internal employee selection process is often based on seniority or sometimes on the destination itself. For example,

destinations such as Florida, the Bahamas and the Caribbean are aimed at new counsellors. European spots such as Copenhagen, Amsterdam, Rome or the Greek Islands may be more suited to those with some experience. The more exotic locations such as East Africa, South America, the South Pacific and Asia are geared to senior personnel.

Most agencies use a rotation system to ensure that all employees are treated fairly. Agencies rarely send someone to an area they have already visited. Every agency, however, has its own policy. Some have been known to never offer a fam to their staff unless it is taken on vacation time at the employee's expense. Others guarantee two or three trips per year paid by the agency. On most fam trips the employer usually pays all costs involved other than those of a personal nature such as laundry, valet, hair appointments, shopping and personal entertainment.

Fam tours are considered to be business travel by hosts, employers and participants. Participants represent both the Canadian travel industry and their employer. For these reasons, correct behaviour is important. ACTA, the trade association, has developed guidelines for appropriate behaviour on fam trips and tour sponsors usually set conditions for participants. Employers commonly demand a report or presentation from staff returning from a fam trip. Reports can be circulated to colleagues while presentations allow opportunities for discussion and questions. Either method encourages current product knowledge to be spread to all coworkers. Fam trip behaviour and reports are discussed in more detail in Chapter 14.

Over the years most counsellors manage to travel quite a bit, whether through vacations, business meetings, fam trips or by attending conventions. The novelty and thrill of just travelling may eventually wear off but the value of the experience often grows in the estimation of participants. The need to acquire or maintain knowledge of destinations and products never seen, to inspect hotels that are recommended but not experienced, or to investigate changes, are the reasons for the continuing popularity of fam trips.

Clients

Clients are often overlooked as a source of product knowledge but, in fact, their views offer invaluable insights into current standards, quality and services. The best alternative to personal experience is a client who has just returned from a business or pleasure trip.

From a professional perspective, every client should receive a follow-up call. This not only encourages the individual to remain a client of the agency, it also provides an opportunity to question the client about the trip. Counsellors who follow this suggestion can avoid surprises and ensure that their knowledge is updated. The client may have visited a destination which the agent has not in which case the agent can learn of the location from the client's viewpoint rather than that of the operator. Perhaps a new airport tax or transportation service has been introduced. There may have been civil unrest or inclement weather and the agent can learn the extent (if any) of the damage or disruption. Such an approach has mutual benefits. The client is gratified by the concern and interest of the agent and the counsellor has an opportunity to expand his or her expertise and knowledge. This in turn helps to make the agent better informed and able to assist other clients. Better client service should increase the agent's business.

Other Sources

Acquiring product knowledge from other sources means that travel counsellors must develop sound research skills. Research involves the systematic investigation and study of a variety of sources. Reliance upon a single source is not research since the information may be false, outdated or distorted. Counsellors should try to develop a complete view of the topic before drawing conclusions. The ability to conduct research and to accurately assess information will assist counsellors in all areas of product knowledge. For example, many of the sources described above are materials and information produced by suppliers and other organizations with a vested interest in selling the product. By reading and researching from other sources, counsellors will develop a healthy scepticism for the claims made in some promotional materials. This will permit travel counsellors to offer professional unbiased advice to their clients. Research skills can also be especially useful when searching for the unusual.

An obvious source of alternative or additional information is the public library system. Histories, geographies, political reports and cultural studies provide a perspective or foundation for trade information. Public libraries stock a varied selection of consumer magazines, newspapers and guidebooks. The travel sections carried in the Sunday New York Times and the Saturday editions of most Canadian newspapers are especially noteworthy.

Counsellors can also acquire product knowledge by consulting guidebooks and contacting trade associations. Both areas are reviewed in detail elsewhere in this text.

Product Knowledge and Sales

The travel counsellor's responsibility is to match the client's needs with the most appropriate travel product. To do this, counsellors must be able to quickly locate the correct information and to accurately interpret it for the client. Only then can a sales dialogue begin.

The location and interpretation of information, however, is not the end point for professional travel counsellors. Some counsellors complain that their time is taken up by "shoppers", consumers who browse through brochures with no intention of buying. Regardless, many of those same counsellors will spend thirty minutes or more displaying their product knowledge, answering questions, and describing features to someone who offers thanks for the information and a promise to return later. Such agents may impress the public but they are unlikely to put a smile on the manager's face. They "tell" rather than "sell". They have given away their most valuable resources, their time and knowledge, and have received nothing in return. This type of "salesperson" is found not only in travel agencies but also in other positions in the industry. No matter one's position, the end use or application of product knowledge in the travel industry is a sales transaction. Unless a sale is made, whether it be a travel counsellor selling a package tour to a consumer, a hotelier arranging a block of rooms for a tour operator, or a supplier sales representative attempting to influence travel agencies to promote the company's services, product knowledge is not being used effectively.

Travel counsellors who sell services need more and better skills than those who market physical products. In general, they cannot just take orders. They must stay with a prospect longer and they must know how to turn a visitor into a client. Clients of travel agencies buy their services sight unseen. Further, travellers must spend both time and money before actually using the product. These differences can lead to unprofessional marketing practices such as exaggerated claims of the product's quality and value. The role of the counsellor in assessing a product and interpreting it for clients is critical in this process. Travel agency managers understand that a client whose travel plans have been spoiled, perhaps through no fault of the agency, will soon look for another agency. Acquiring and maintaining product knowledge is therefore essential for success in the travel industry.

Product knowledge can be defined as the total of all training, experience and materials. It is a combination of destination details ranging from geography to climate and from culture to current affairs. It includes information on suppliers and industry segments, news, services and trends. But product knowledge is more than the simple learning and storage of facts. It encompasses skills and techniques. Any knowledge is useless unless it is applied. Product knowledge is no different in this respect. Product knowledge is effectively applied when a sale is completed.

From a counsellor's viewpoint, there are three important parts to product knowledge in the travel industry. The first is knowing what to look for. This type of information is acquired by studying and questioning clients. Once a counsellor has determined a client's needs, the second part of product knowledge becomes primary, that is, where to find the required information. This chapter has summarized the sources of product knowledge and their contents. The final area of product knowledge is its application, that is, how to use it to complete a sale. The following chapters consider the sources to be consulted for particular products or segments of the industry. The interpretation and application of these sources to a sales situation will be the focus of these chapters. For the moment, it is important to remember only that there is a direct connection between product knowledge and sales. Specific sales techniques will be covered in Chapter 13.

Review Questions

1. Discuss the differences between travel products and manufactured goods.

2. Describe the various sources of product knowledge.

3. Pick up a copy of a travel trade newsletter, a travel trade newspaper and the travel section of a consumer newspaper. Compare how the different publications treat the same stories. Discuss some of the differences in the types of advertisements that each carries.

4. Discuss some of the reasons why product knowledge changes.

5. Which is the most important method of acquiring and maintaining product knowledge? Give three reasons to support your opinion.

References

Standard References

ABC Star Service, ABC International, 131 Clarendon Street, Boston, MA 02116, USA, Telephone (617) 262-5000.

The Air Tariff, 86 Hartford Avenue, Pointe Claire, Quebec H9R 3E1.

ATPCO Passenger Tariff Set, Airline Tariff Publishing Company, Dulles International Airport, P.O. Box 17415, Washington, DC 20041, USA, Telephone (703) 471-7510.

Cruise Lines International Association (CLIA), 500 Fifth Avenue, Suite 1407, New York, NY 10110, USA, Telephone (212) 425-7400.

Consolidated Tour Manual (CTM), 11510 NE Second Street, Miami, FL 33161, USA, Telephone (305) 759-8002.

Eurailtariff, Eurailpass Distribution Centre, Box 300, Succursale R, Montreal Quebec H2S 3K9.

Ford's Travel Guides, 19448 Londelius Street, Northridge, CA 91324, USA, Telephone (818) 701-7414.

Forsyth Travel Library, Inc., P.O. Box 2975, 9154 West 57th Street, Shawnee Mission, KS 68201-1375, USA, Telephone (913) 384-3440, Fax (913) 384-3553.

Hotel and Travel Index, 500 Plaza Drive, Secaucus, NJ 07096, USA.

International Air Transport Association (IATA), 2000 Peel Street, Montreal, Quebec H3A 2R4.

Official Airline Guides (OAG), 2000 Clearwater Drive, Oak Brook, IL 60521, USA, Telephone (708) 574-6000.

Official Cruise Guide, 500 Plaza Drive, Secaucu, NJ 07096, USA.

Official Hotel Guide (OHG), 500 Plaza Drive, Secaucus, NJ 07096, USA, Telephone (201) 902-1861.

Official Railway Guide, International Thomson Transport Press, 424 West 33rd Street, New York, NY 10001-2604, USA, Telephone (212) 714-3100.

Official Steamship Guide International, 111 Cherry Street, Suite 205, New Canaan, CT 06940, USA.

Russell's Guides, Inc., P.O. Box 278, 834 Third Avenue S.E., Cedar Rapids, IA 52406, USA, Telephone (319) 364-6138.

Thomas Cook European Timetable and *Thomas Cook Continental Timetable*. Subscriptions are available from the Timetable Publishing Office, P.O. Box 36, Peterborough PE3 6SB, England. Timetables can also be ordered from the Forsyth Travel Library.

Travel Information Manual, P.O. Box 902, 2130 EA Hoofddorp, The Netherlands.

WATA Master-Key, World Association of Travel Agencies, 37 quai Wilson, P.O.B. 852, 1211 Geneva 1, Switzerland, Telephone 731 47 60.

Trade Papers

Business Travel Weekly, 600 Community Drive, Manhasset, NY 11030, USA, Telephone (516) 562-5000.

Canadian Travel Press, 310 Dupont Street, Toronto, Ontario M5R 1V9.

MLD Canadian Traveller, Suite 210, 1015 Burrard Street, Vancouver, B.C. V6Z 1Y5.

The Travel Agent, 2 West 46th Street, New York NY 10036, USA.

Tour and Travel News, 600 Community Drive, Manhasset, NY 11030, USA, Telephone (516) 562-5000.

Travel Courier, 310 Dupont Street, Toronto, Ontario M5R 1V9.

Travel Weekly, One Park Avenue, New York, NY 10016, USA.

Travelweek Bulletin, 282 Richmond Street East, Suite 100, Toronto, Ontario M5A 1P4.

Academic Journals

Annals of Tourism Research, Pergamon Press, Inc., Fairview Park, Elmsford, NY 10523, USA.

International Tourism Quarterly, The Economist Intelligence Unit, 27 St. James's Place, London SW1A 1NT, England.

Journal of Travel Research, The Travel and Tourism Research Association, Business Research Division, University of Colorado, Boulder, CO 80302, USA.

Tourism Management, Butterworths, 80 Montvale Avenue, Stoneham, MA 02180, USA.

## Chapter 5

Destinations and Documentation

Chapter Summary

This chapter discusses destinations and the documentation required by travellers. The chapter begins with a review of tourism development and its impact on countries and communities. This is followed by a discussion of destination phases and types. A framework is provided to help counsellors analyze destinations thereby acquiring product knowledge. Destination analysis is followed by an examination of world time zones, the 24-hour clock system and calculation of apparent and elapsed flying times. The latter portion of the chapter is devoted to a study of travel documentation. Passport, visa, customs and currency regulations are assessed in detail. The chapter concludes with a few brief tips for travellers.

Chapter Objectives
After completing this chapter you should be able to:

- Discuss the importance of planning tourism and destination development.

- Provide examples of the factors to be considered in tourism development.

- Describe both the positive and negative effects of tourism development.

- Compare the costs and benefits associated with tourism development.

- Identify external factors that may affect tourism and describe their effects.

- Discuss phases of destination development.

- List and describe types of destinations.

- Review the importance of destination knowledge with respect to selling the travel product.

- Analyze and evaluate a destination based on a classification identifying basics, character, documentation and details.

- Exhibit knowledge of the world time zone system.

- Apply the 12-hour clock and 24-hour clock systems and convert one to the other.

- Define and calculate apparent and elapsed flying times.

- Discuss the importance of correct traveller documentation.

- Locate and correctly apply sources of information on travel documentation.

- Complete an application for a Canadian passport.

- Describe passport and visa requirements and customs regulations.

- Identify resources which can assist travellers.

- Describe potential health problems for travellers and appropriate preventive measures.

- Offer advice on suitable dietary precautions, safety procedures and packing.

Tourist Destinations

To this point travel has been discussed in terms of the traveller's motivations. Associated with these needs and wants are certain expectations. The travel counsellor's task is to reveal these influences and attempt to find travel products that match them.

Almost everyone who enters a travel agency with the intention of travelling has a destination or activity in mind. Sometimes clients have extensive destination knowledge but frequently they look to travel counsellors for this information. Travel is a world industry and knowledge of destinations is an essential part of a counsellor's product knowledge. Before attempting to provide a basis for acquiring and maintaining knowledge on destinations, however, a brief review of the factors associated with tourism development is necessary. This discussion will provide a framework for understanding destinations and the features that attract travellers to particular locations.

Tourism Development

Countries or communities did not formerly plan in a deliberate manner to attract tourism, it "just happened". Later it was thought that tourism planning simply meant building new hotels, increasing airline flights to the destination and encouraging tourists to visit. Today, however, tourism has become a large and sophisticated business. Many countries rely on tourism to generate employment and foreign currency. Its development requires large investments in services and facilities. Tourism had effects on so many areas that governments were compelled to take a broader perspective. The use of tourism development principles has increased with the growth in pleasure travel. Tourism development is now considered to encompass all aspects of the planning and marketing of a destination to attract visitors. Destinations can no longer rely on tourism "just happening". To be successful they must now develop tourism. The following discussion presents a brief summary of the issues involved in tourism development.

Tourism development actually encompasses three steps; planning, development and marketing. Each stage requires close cooperation between government, developers, investors and perhaps other professionals. **Destination planning** consists of a number of phases.

The first step is to conduct a **market analysis** to determine the needs in the marketplace and the type of destination and attractions to develop. This analysis attempts to understand the patterns of demand by studying past and present trends, traveller profiles, traveller preferences and habits, market position and destination image.

The market analysis should be followed by a **product assessment**. This requires taking an inventory of available resources at the destination and assessing them in terms of their acceptability as tourist products and how best to develop them. For example, the available attractions will be rated for their variety and appeal. Destinations attempt to not only draw visitors but also to hold them for a time. Visitor attractions must meet this need. The local culture will also be considered. An appropriate development promotes and preserves an area's cultural heritage rather than weakens or destroys it. Since a trained labour force is required for tourism, the available human resources and training capabilities must be examined. A destination also requires an adequate **infrastructure** to support tourism. For example, a destination may have beautiful beaches and spectacular snorkelling but unless these attractions are accessible by land or air they will be worthless. Similarly, there must be sufficient water, electricity and sewage utilities to meet tourist requirements. The roads, transportation terminals, electric lines, sewage and water systems, and related services that comprise infrastructure are normally developed by government. As well as infrastructure, destinations obviously require hotels, restaurants, entertainment facilities, stores and other enterprises. These facilities comprise a **superstructure** which is built after the infrastructure has been put in place. A complete product assessment must consider the need for a superstructure, transportation and support services such as police and fire protection.

Further research is required before a comprehensive **master plan** for the tourism development can be generated. Any tourism development plan must be placed in the context of national, social and economic development. The type of tourism to be developed should be considered. For example, a decision must be made on whether it is better to develop a destination for a package tour market that attracts 500 average consumers or an exclusive market that attracts 50 high price big spenders. Market research must be conducted to select a target market, establish objectives, set strategies and coordinate promotion efforts. All factors must be considered. The 500 tourists will result in additional service costs as there will be more wear on sewers, hydro, roads and the like. However, this group will generate more employment than the 50 big spenders. Further, the plan must comply with existing laws or new laws must be drafted to control the development. An increase in tourism also means an increased demand for employees. A proper training plan is therefore necessary to complement the physical development. Before a plan is implemented, the effects of tourism on the community must be assessed. An economic and financial analysis should therefore be conducted to determine the development's feasibility and costs. This study will include an analysis of economic conditions and financial requirements, the cash flow requirements, available capital, prevailing interest rates and the effects on the balance of trade. In addition to the economic effects of developing tourism, the environmental and cultural impacts on the area must be studied.

Impacts of Tourism

All tourism has an impact and its effects can last for a long time. They may also contribute to or detract from future tourism. For example, the Phoenicians left archaeological traces of their existence that continue to generate interest. Similarly, the Roman city of Bath is still a thriving town and remains a tourist attraction. Conversely, riots in Jamaica during the late 1970s reduced tourism to that country for almost a decade. Tourism's effects therefore can be historical and long term but they are not exclusively so. Destinations and countries must also determine whether tourism is

good or bad. Value judgments cannot be applied. One must look at the consequences for both the destination and for tourism. Tourism can be good or bad or both. The value of tourism to a destination is determined by how well the tourism is planned and how well it is implemented.

Tourism affects all areas of a society with which it comes in contact. These effects can be separated into a number of areas generally considered to be political, economic, environmental, social and cultural.

Political Impacts

The political situation in a country usually sets the tone for its tourism activity. Changes in a country's politics will be reflected in changes in its tourism operations. For example, just a few years ago it would have been inconceivable to consider China as a tourist destination. Then for five years or so it became increasingly popular with western tourists. After the incident in Tienanmen Square in June 1989, however, China suffered a serious decline in tourist arrivals. Similarly, it is hard to believe that Beirut was once considered the rest and relaxation capital of the Middle East. The city attracted tourists and business travellers from all over the region and from Europe to sample its nightlife and entertainment. More recently the "iron curtain" between Eastern and Western Europe has suddenly and dramatically "rusted out" prompting mass crossings in both directions.

Terrorism (e.g., in the Mediterranean) and political instability (e.g., in China and Sri Lanka) have an obvious effect on tourism. Media coverage, however, can be even more influential. Perception becomes more important than reality. As an example, in 1985 more Americans were killed in the USA from the effects of tornadoes (about 100 people) than in terrorist incidents in the Mediterranean (about 25). However, the *Achille Lauro* hijacking and the Rome airport massacre also occurred in 1985. The result was that tourism to Europe from North America fell by almost 50 percent even though it was statistically more dangerous to remain in the USA.

Politics then obviously affects tourism. Government policies affect how a country or region will deal with tourism and tourists. All countries control entry through passport and visa restrictions. Some countries also implement specific tourism policies; for example, at one time the Canadian government discouraged travel to South Africa. Cuba was a favourite tourist destination for Americans (primarily for gambling) prior to the 1958 revolution. After Fidel Castro came to power the casinos were closed and relations with the USA were broken off. Cuba has once again emerged as a tourist destination but its clientele is much different from the gamblers it once attracted. Cuba now appeals to families and senior citizens, however, the U.S. government discourages its nationals from visiting the island.

One aspect of government policy is to generate wealth and employment for the country's people. Tourism is seen as a way to achieve this. For some countries, tourism provides additional income to an economy which is based on resource development, on manufacturing or on trading. For other countries, often in the developing world, tourism is the sole or major source of foreign currency. Some of these countries have initially embraced tourism with enthusiasm only to regret their lack of foresight and planning at a later date.

In centrally planned economies, tourism was an instrument for expressing government policy. Central planning, covering every facet of tourism from its location to its level of activity, was the norm in socialist countries. In Cuba, for example, the government not only determined how many tourists were permitted to visit the country (based on the facilities and infrastructure available to cope with them) but it also actively negotiated with tour operators to decide on the market mix which it desired. Cuba used this strategy in an attempt to avoid swings in the number of visitors should

there be a recession or collapse in the economy of one of its markets. As was mentioned in Chapter 4, however, one problem in tourism planning is the difficulty of anticipating demand. Canada on the other hand encourages tourism development by private entrepreneurs. Planning policies are often local or provincial government affairs, with the exception of national parks and other areas under federal jurisdiction. The Canadian government's role tends to be that of marketing the country overseas and encouraging tourism development within the country. Another consideration is the creation and maintenance of the infrastructure needed for tourism development. Here, the political decisions revolve around who pays for the facilities and services. Should it be the government that will derive economic and employment benefits or the developer who will make a profit? For example, should the ski operator or the local municipality pay for snow removal on the roads leading to the ski resort? Since both wish to benefit from tourism, it is essential that private industry and government cooperate if tourism development is to be successful.

Economic Impacts

For many nations tourism plays a leading part in international trade flows and balance of payments. Its major economic impact is as an export industry. That is, tourism generates foreign exchange in the same way that selling a manufactured product overseas brings foreign currency into the country. Consider the influence the tourist dollar has on the economy of a country. Any money spent by a tourist abroad is "new" money to the economy of the country visited. It has the same consequence as if that country had exported a tangible commodity such as machinery or agricultural products. Furthermore, this newly created capital is spent a number of times thus adding to the wealth of the host country.

When tourists visit an area they

naturally spend money. The amount of money which remains in the area is a source of income for its residents and businesses. This is called a **direct effect**. Naturally these expenditures are in turn used by residents and businesses to pay for goods, services, supplies, wages and similar items. These expenditures are considered to be **secondary effects**. Thus, the dollars spent by tourists in an area will circulate within it and generate further sales and expenditures. This process when "new" money is introduced to an area and circulated within it is called the **multiplier effect**. Multipliers result from all types of expenditures, however, here the concern is only with the tourism multiplier effect, i.e., the effect of tourist expenditures on an area.

The following example of a tourist visiting Jamaica illustrates the multiplier effect at work. The tourist brings money into the country and uses it to pay the hotel bill in Jamaica. The money received by the hotel will be used to pay various debts incurred and the obligations due as a result of that tourist's visit. A considerable percentage of the tourist's dollars will be distributed by the hotel to pay staff, food, wine and spirit suppliers, insurance, commissions to the tourist's travel agency, laundry services and other items. The money paid to the staff for salaries will be spent by each employee to pay bills in the local economy such as food, shelter, education and clothing. Similarly, dollars expended by the hotel to purchase food for its dining room and liquor for its bars will also filter down through the Jamaican economy.

Some of these visitor expenditures will be used to purchase items which are produced outside the area. For example, the hotel in Jamaica might use part of its tourist income to purchase imported Scotch, Rye or steaks for its clients to consume on vacation. Such import purchases mean that the funds are effectively removed from Jamaica and are considered to be **leakages** from the local economy. Similarly, profits that leave a country are also considered to be leakages. The same leakage applies if a commission payment is made to a travel agency outside of Jamaica. The percentage of the tourist's fresh dollar which remains in Jamaica for purchases or savings or investment as a part of a first or second round of spending stimulates different sectors of the Jamaican economy. These may not even be directly related to tourism. These varied transactions of tourist dollars within a given country constitute the multiplier effect. The more hands through which tourist money passes, the greater the benefits of the multiplier effect to the gross national product of that country. Economically speaking, successful tourism development maximizes the tourism multiplier effect on the local economy and minimizes leakage. The more money that remains in the economy, the fewer the leaks and the higher the multiplier effect.

This is but one instance of the multiplier effect at work, namely, in a hotel transaction. There are many other examples that could be cited ranging from the millions of dollars spent by hotels, airlines and other transport organizations within a country to the modest impact made by a one person sightseeing operation. The most immediate and direct side benefit of the multiplier effect is the creation of jobs. In some countries new industries have been created solely to cater to the needs of tourism. In many nations schools have been established to train local citizens as waiters, bartenders, cooks and hotel clerks.

Tourism can and does therefore have a positive economic effect simply by introducing money into a local economy. However, the amount of foreign exchange can be quite limited if the tourism sector is foreign owned and profits leave the local economy. In addition, most package tours are arranged so that tourists pay almost all their expenses in the country of origin. Thus, direct tourist expenditures are limited to drinks, souvenirs and other incidentals. Even these purchases have been reduced with the growth in popularity of all-inclusive packages where personal expenses such as drinks and tips are included in the tour price. It should be noted, however, that all-inclusive resorts are popular with tourists as they provide value for money. They are also popular with travel counsellors as they are easy to sell. All-inclusive holidays also pay a higher commission since the selling price includes more items that are commissionable to the counsellor.

There are also, however, other economic effects which may not be positive. For example, the very fact that tourists come to an area creates an increased demand for certain products and services. This can lead to higher prices and/or shorter supply of some goods. Thus, an inflationary situation can be created where locals must also pay higher prices. Additional costs must also be considered. For example, with increased tourism there inevitably comes an increased need for garbage collection and disposal. Other maintenance costs also rise because of the increased use of facilities and resources. Frequently, these services are supported by local taxes and yet their use is disproportionately in favour of tourists.

A further economic effect is the instability which can be created by tourism. Vacation travel as discussed in an earlier chapter is a discretionary item. Economies tend to be cyclical in nature and during an economic slowdown or recession, pleasure travel is one of the items which people choose not to purchase. Economies that rely on tourism to provide employment and produce foreign exchange will therefore be severely affected by economic downturns. Instability can also be caused by the seasonal nature of tourism as well as by the cyclical nature of economies. Seasonality imposes economic and other stresses because of the cycle of high and low demand. Governments and employers need to consider what happens to those tourism jobs during the off season.

Tourism generates employment. Although this is a positive impact many of the positions created demand low skills and consequently are low paying. If tourism merely creates a nation of busboys, chambermaids and waiters, for example, one must ask whether in the long term this type of job creation is positive. Employment also has a social impact which is discussed later. Where employment is created the government's income tax revenues will increase and where money circulates within the economy, the government will also receive other tax revenues such as sales tax, hotel tax or airport departure tax. These tax revenues are used to benefit the country and sometimes also improve cultural, historical and other tourist attractions. Governments use tourism as a means of economic development. Attractions can be built and tourism encouraged to regions which have poor socioeconomic conditions. Employment can thus be created in areas which have little manufacturing or resource capabilities. For example, some might consider Arizona as being little more than the Grand Canyon and desert. No one would dispute that the Grand Canyon is spectacular and an attraction in itself but many would give no thought to visiting the southern part of the state. This region, however, has capitalized on the romance and history of the Old West to attract tourists to Tombstone and Tucson.

A characteristic of tourism is that it consists of a large number of small businesses. Many are directly involved in tourism but even more support it or are associated marginally with it. The income from tourism is therefore widely distributed so that the economic advantages are shared throughout the population.

Environmental Impacts

Tourism's environmental impact is one of the most basic issues and one which is increasing in importance as environmental awareness grows. To be successful, tourism depends on an unspoiled environment. Since tourism is not associated with smokestacks it has been described as a non-polluting industry but this is debatable. One need only visit the beach after a holiday weekend or a sports stadium after a major event to glimpse the scope of the problem. However, the question is more basic than one of "people pollution". All tourism developments require a certain minimum of infrastructure whose construction undoubtedly has an environmental effect. Whether these effects are positive or negative is to some extent determined by the general level of development of the host community. For example, if tourism in an underdeveloped nation brings with it a sewage treatment plant, then tourism could be considered to have a beneficial environmental effect (assuming that the residents' sewage is also treated). If, however, the influx of tourists strains the already existing facilities such that raw sewage is emptied untreated into a picturesque lagoon, then tourism's effects are certainly negative. If an area is accessible by road the exhaust fumes from large numbers of cars will contribute to air pollution. Alternatively, the facilities may be sufficient to deal with the invasion of tourists but the large number of tourists in some eyes spoils the ambience and beauty of the area. Whether "people pollution" is positive or negative, however, may depend on whether one is a local resident seeking a peaceful retreat or the owner of an ice cream parlour.

There are also many examples where the natural beauty of a region has been conserved through tourism development. Frequently, this conservation is part of local planning policies and has been undertaken at the expense of the developer. Land, of course, is not the only thing which can be conserved through tourism. History and wildlife are but two other examples. Ecuador has used a policy of controlled tourism in the Galapagos Islands to generate funds for scientific research and to protect the environment from the effects of human intrusion. Belize is attempting to promote ecotourism, that is, tourism that is in keeping with the ecology of the country. This includes the preservation of natural environments such as the barrier reef and rainforests as well as its cultural heritage derived from the Mayan civilization. In the 1960s the French government drained swamp land in the Languedoc-Rousillon region to make the area more attractive for tourism. By doing so, it helped eradicate malaria.

When considering the effects of tourism on the environment, we generally speak specifically of vegetation, water quality, air pollution and wildlife. However, its impact on intangibles such as atmosphere and noise cannot be ignored. Tourism can therefore support and promote environmental improvement or it can have a detrimental effect. Underdeveloped areas tend to benefit while developed areas tend to be adversely affected. This effect, however, may only be short term. On a long term basis, the environment can be protected only through proper planning.

Social Impacts

The most obvious social impacts are also economic. For example, tourism can create jobs which brings new income to an area. Increased employment is usually seen as an economic benefit but it also has social implications. For example, whenever jobs are generated immigration normally increases. This can contribute to social dislocation as migrants are attracted, for example, from the rural areas to seaside resorts. One must then consider whether these new migrants are compatible with the local community. Are they perceived as enriching the community or do they appear to be taking jobs which rightfully belong to the local population? Is the long term effect of such migrations positive or negative to the region? Increased immigration also places further demands on housing, social services and other local amenities. Alternatively, tourism development may reduce the availability of the local labour force. For example, construction of hotels will generate jobs but if residents fill these jobs there will be a reduced labour pool for local agriculture or industries.

Further, many jobs created by tourism have fairly low skill requirements and as a result their pay is low. As tourism matures, however, the need for skilled and professional positions increases as does the need for management personnel. This can benefit the local community by developing local human resources. It can backfire, however, if these skilled positions are filled by "foreigners" or "outsiders". This has frequently been the case in the past in, for example, international hotel chains. Importing of skilled personnel can cause resentment and contribute to a negative community attitude towards tourism and tourists. The problem is intensified if local personnel replace foreigners but do not receive the same recognition or pay from the employer. Tourism may disrupt the local social structure in other ways. The low pay and nature of the work available causes many of the positions that arise from tourism to be filled by women. This has a profound effect on societies, particularly those where males dominate and women traditionally do not go to work.

Similarly, the seasonal and fashion-conscious nature of tourism can have detrimental effects. Tourist resorts may boom for a time, drawing immigrants and straining resources, and then fade. They are no longer the "in" place to see and to be seen. Large tour operators may direct tourists to other destinations for profit motives. Mass media also plays a part in redirecting tourist patterns, perhaps by creating the cult of "newness" or by providing a distorted view of the country. For example, the 1985 earthquake in Mexico had little physical effect on tourism areas. Unfavourable media coverage, however, contributed to a large decline in tourism during the following year. It should be noted that travel trade papers accurately reported the extent of the damage but these publications are not seen by the travelling public. This points up once again the need for counsellors to obtain current and factual information and to pass this on to prospective travellers.

Tourism changes the social relations between people. For example, if tourists only come in contact with local people when they are being served or sold something, these interactions will colour their perception of the residents and will affect how they interrelate. Similarly, because tourists wish to buy something and local people wish to earn a living, local exploitation can occur. Tourist demand can, for instance, bring about prostitution.

Cultural Impacts

The cultural effect of tourism is one of the most difficult areas to assess. Tourism can enhance and degrade local art forms at the same time. For example, tourism can encourage local artists and artisans to practise their craft thus realizing employment and remuneration for their skills. Such employment can also spark renewed interest in or awareness of the local cultural heritage. When ceremonies are performed only for pay, however, the cultural value and respect which local residents have for their own art forms, religions and traditions breaks down. They now become merely a means of making money. Another cultural problem associated with mass tourism is its impersonal nature. Many tourists make contact with local people only under the stage managed, standardized interactions described above. Such tourists often pursue only beaches, sunshine and low prices and desire only western-style accommodation and "normal" food. This tends to blur the image of different destinations and to the tourist one culture could become indistinguishable from another. For these reasons, the host often stereotypes the tourist as much as the reverse. It then becomes questionable whether either tourist or host community is learning much that is accurate about the other's culture.

A number of outcomes are possible when tourists interact with a local culture. One consequence is that both tourists and residents coexist in a tolerant fashion. This often happens when destinations are well planned or when there are few tourists. In destinations that are well established, either or both groups borrow or adapt from one another. For example, in Asia residents wear T-shirts and tourists wear wraps. A less positive result is segregation where tourists stay in luxury ghettoes isolated from the residents. This avoids conflict and is the policy pursued by the Maldives, an archipelago in the Indian Ocean. The country is muslim and tourism is permitted on only some islands. The separation is enforced by law and no tourist may spend a night in a native village. All-inclusive resorts employ the same strategy to a lesser extent. A third repercussion is that tourists can be rejected by residents and vice versa. Local behaviour is surly and discourteous while tourists are condescending and scoff at local customs and accents.

Costs and Benefits of Tourism Development

Tourism has a number of impacts in a variety of areas. Some are positive while others have the opposite effect. Governments must decide whether a development is in the overall interest of the country, area or destination or whether its outcome will be largely negative. One technique used to resolve the question is a **cost-benefit analysis**. This technique attempts to assign specific costs to the various planning and development factors discussed above. It also tries to place a figure on their economic benefits. These costs and benefits are then compared with other options, such as a resort development versus the construction of a small manufacturing facility. This is relatively simple when comparing the economic factors associated with various projects. It becomes considerably more complex, however, when social and cultural elements are added to the equation.

Initially most economists saw tourism as a positive force while sociologists viewed it as a negative power. As the study of tourism has advanced these rigid views have been modified. It is now accepted that the effects of tourism and their magnitude will be determined by

the level and quality of planning that precedes the tourism development. In addition, a number of analytical frameworks have been proposed to evaluate tourism activity and development. The impacts of tourism are large and far reaching. It is therefore essential that it be planned according to accepted practice and that a cost-benefit analysis be conducted on all the potential impacts prior to any implementation.

Phases in Destination Development

Several writers have suggested that destinations pass through different phases or cycles. As discussed in Chapter 3, Plog related these phases to different personality types. Other writers apply marketing concepts such as product life cycles to describe destinations. Such life cycles can be short term, medium term or long term. Short term cycles are those that take place within a year or less. Seasonal cycles are a typical example. Sometimes tourist destinations have two cycles within a year. Medium term cycles follow a pattern of a few years. The change is often slow and can be caused by many different factors ranging from changing tastes to currency fluctuations or poor maintenance. Long term cycles are often described as having four stages; inception, growth, maturity and decline. Analogous to the life cycle theory of a destination is a sociological perspective that follows five phases; discovery, development, conflict, confrontation and destruction.

The first stage of the life cycle theory is the inception or discovery phase. This stage has a low tourist volume and hence residents are not really exposed to the effects of tourism development. Only allocentrics or adventurous tourists find the destination. Some stay and become a factor in the development process by opening guest houses, restaurants, souvenir shops and tour services. Initially the destination is comparatively unknown. It is unspoiled, uncrowded and has nice hotels which are relatively empty. The destination is scenically beautiful with good beaches and is potentially fashionable. Tourists are generally welcomed by locals.

During the growth or development phase, local residents begin to respond to the growing demand. Residents welcome tourism enthusiastically for its contribution to the economy, namely improved infrastructure, more jobs and higher incomes. The number of tourists increases largely through word of mouth and these tourists tend to coexist or adapt to local culture. At this stage, facilities and services are not standardized although the tourist industry begins to adapt to tourist needs. The destination becomes fashionable and it acquires an image of where the smart people go. Soon a surge of cheaper hotels is built.

Increased interaction causes residents to measure their values and goals against those of tourists. There is a movement away from traditional vocations and lifestyles and contact between tourists and residents becomes more impersonal and formal. Local services and resources can no longer keep up with the volume of tourists and the development begins to attract crime and juvenile mischief.

Subsequently this leads to the next phase when there is a tourist boom. This is the mature stage of development where services, itineraries and roles are formal. The destination now appeals to mid-centrics. More hotels are built and many are affiliated with international corporations. The residents become dependent on decisions made by foreign owners and procedures and facilities become standardized. The destination becomes more commercialized and begins to look overcrowded and spoiled. At the same time the local population becomes disturbed about tourism. Rising stress is caused by the large number of tourists and increased population growth. Problems occur if the developments hinder traditional leisure activities and are for tourists only. Costs escalate and many residents may be excluded from participation. Conflicts can arise. The end of this stage is identified by hostile attitudes to visitors resulting from competition for local water, energy, facilities and services.

By the time the destination is in the decline phase it is saturated with tourists. The boom is over. There are now too many hotels so that rooms are almost being given away. The area is overcrowded and its services and facilities are stretched beyond their limits. The beach may be dirty and smelling of

FIGURE 5.1
Phases in destination development.

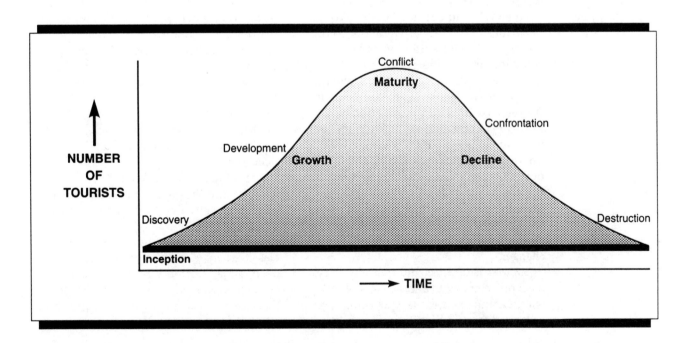

sewage. Residents are disenchanted that tourism has not produced all of the promised benefits. If conditions continue to deteriorate confrontation can occur and there may be organized opposition to new developments. The destination may even decline to the point where there is active antagonism towards tourists and there is sabotage, rampant crime, lack of safety and outflow of capital. Factors such as cleanliness and friendly people that initially attracted tourists to the destination have now disappeared. Many hotels close and workers are unemployed.

This deterioration is not inevitable. Some destinations go through these stages while others move from discovery to maturity with no intervening phase. Proper planning can prevent the decline which was once considered inevitable. To avoid decline a tourist destination may have to adapt to new markets. Suppliers may have to introduce new products and ideas to replace older ones. Destination life cycles can be extended if change is anticipated and if steps are taken to adapt to the change. Destinations can be also be rejuvenated. Atlantic City is an example of such renewal.

During the early stages of tourism, when attitudes to tourism are positive, the values and behaviour of the host population are most likely to change towards those of the tourists. Local residents start to mimic tourists in dress, behaviour and lifestyle. There is also the spread of western culture to consider through, for example, rock music and fast foods and drinks. Depending on whether or not one thinks that western culture is the pinnacle, this may or may not be a positive effect. Later, attitudes to tourism begin to change and become negative. Tourism then provides a focus for opposition to western culture and it can become a barrier to cultural change. Thus, tourism contributes to changing attitudes and values. It has become an agent of, as well as an impediment to, cultural change.

Standards of dress and morality vary from one country to another (and even within countries, for example rural versus urban values and lifestyles). Shorts may

be acceptable in downtown Toronto but not in Mexico City or New Delhi. Similarly, topless sunbathing is commonplace in much of Europe but is considered offensive in many countries. It is the tourist's responsibility to demonstrate social or cultural awareness and to behave appropriately. Travel counsellors, however, must know the prevailing standards and inform clients of them.

Types of Destination

A destination can be defined as a specific area that travellers choose to visit. As far as travellers are concerned destinations are not restricted to a particular size. They can be as large as a continent or as small as a museum or theme park. In Chapter 3 it was indicated that people choose to travel to satisfy certain needs. Their choice of destination is made for the same reasons. The pull factors that draw tourists to various destinations were also discussed. Chief among these are the attractions at the destination. The type and quality of a destination's attractions plays an important part in its success as a magnet for tourists. Here, attractions refers not only to such obvious sites as Niagara Falls or the Taj Mahal but also to the appeal of the destination's sightseeing, recreation, shopping, entertainment and other forms of pleasure travel. Some destinations rely on one specific attraction but the majority have multiple attractions that can appeal to a broad segment of the market. The quality as well as the number and variety of attractions at a destination affect travel decisions. The quality of services, transportation and hospitality complement the attractions at a site and can help ensure that tourists enjoy their visits to the destination.

In terms of tourism, destinations can be classified as primary or secondary destinations. **Primary destinations** have sufficient attraction to draw tourists to the area and to hold them for a significant amount of time. **Secondary** or **stopover**

destinations, on the other hand, are interesting or necessary places to visit on the way to a primary destination. Certain areas can be primary destinations for one segment of the market and stopover destinations for other segments. For example, London may be the final stop or merely a transit point en route to, say, Rome. It is essential that counsellors become familiar with airline routings so that they can sell secondary destinations as well as primary destinations. For example, a Toronto to Singapore flight can be sold using London and Bombay as stopover points. Depending on the client's motives and interests, however, it may be better to offer travel via Hawaii and Hong Kong.

A primary destination must offer sufficient things to do and see to interest the visitor for a few days. The length of stay at a secondary destination, however, is shorter and there is less need for a variety of attractions. People stay longer at primary destinations which can prosper while drawing fewer tourists than secondary destinations. Secondary destinations must rely on a high turnover. When a primary destination becomes too popular, congestion and other problems

**FIGURE 5.2
Destinations use attractions and events as demand generators.**

can occur. The British Tourist Authority (BTA) has encountered this difficulty with London. It is now so difficult to find accommodation during the summer season that the BTA is promoting travel to other parts of Britain.

Destinations can also be categorized according to their peak and low seasons which tend to be related to their climate. For example, ski resorts are obviously winter destinations. The Caribbean is also a winter destination but is considered to be a winter sun destination. Places such as Europe are considered to be summer destinations in seasonal terms while Banff has attempted to market itself as a year-round destination. Ultimately, destinations that are restricted to particular seasons are effectively reducing their market. Most seasonal destinations therefore attempt to develop attractions to counteract low season characteristics. For example, Jamaica offers the Reggae Sunsplash music festival to attract visitors during the slower summer months and for similar reasons Europe markets cultural tours in the low season. Care must be taken with such seasonal generalizations, however, since the seasons change depending on whether one is discussing the northern or the southern hemisphere. Thus, Whistler in B.C. is a winter ski resort for Canadians whereas Chile may be a summer ski destination for the same group of tourists.

Destinations can further be arranged according to the interests that they meet. In this fashion, the attraction of a destination can be based on its history, culture, religion or any number of other interests.

Acquiring Destination Knowledge

Destinations, however, are much more than simply a list of attractions. Since counsellors must know and sell all travel products, including destinations, it is critical that they develop the ability to clearly describe what a client is likely to

encounter at a given destination. This must move beyond such generic terms as "nice", "friendly" or "fantastic". After all, clients turn to counsellors for their professional advice not their personal opinion. A complete description of a destination should therefore include a rating or recommendation. This is an extremely difficult task as there are no criteria available as there are with hotel star ratings. Europe has, however, started to rate its beaches primarily according to cleanliness. A blue flag rating for a beach is equivalent to awarding five stars to a hotel. This system is not very widespread as yet but it can help to develop an overall assessment for a destination. Travel counsellors must recognize that they do business on a global scale. Success in any profession demands that individuals be regarded with credibility by clients and peers. Ignorance of the more popular tourist destinations will undermine this credibility. Product knowledge of destinations and their locations is as important as product knowledge of air fares, routes and hotel tariffs.

The most fundamental aspect of a destination is its location. One of the most important aspects of retail travel counselling that counsellors often overlook is a knowledge of where places are. Travel agency owners and personnel managers regularly decry this deficiency in employees who are otherwise technically competent and suited to their tasks. Some refer to this as geography. Destination geography, however, encompasses much more than simply identifying location. It includes political and physical geography as well as the study of cultural and economic geography. Tourist destinations or tourist geography can be learned by individual study of atlases, maps and other sources of destination information. This technique is by far the most effective way to acquire this crucial product knowledge.

An understanding of basic geography is demanded on an almost daily basis for practically any travel career. Airlines, tour operators and travel agents deal with international destinations, government employees promote national or provincial attractions, and tour guides concentrate on local areas. Employers have continuously emphasized the importance of a solid knowledge of not only political geography but also of social and cultural geography. The following material is not intended as a primer in geography. That topic deserves more than a cursory glance and should be studied throughout one's career. Rather, the goals of this chapter are to indicate why an understanding of destinations is required and to provide a basis for studying them. The ensuing material reviews the information of greatest significance for travel counsellors. For example, consider mountain ranges. Mountains influence the climate in the surrounding area and climate affects the way of life. A general knowledge of the locations of mountain ranges will therefore supply considerable background information on these and other attributes of the particular destination. Individual mountains or ranges become relevant to tourism when they are used for some recreational purpose. For example, the Rockies and Alps have well-developed ski resorts and are significant tourist attractions. The Alaska Range which has similar physical attributes is nonetheless of little recreational importance because of its remote location. Similarly, although the jungle-covered mountains of Borneo and those surrounding Lake Victoria in East Africa share the same latitude, they have very little else in common and each attracts very different types of tourism. Similar comparisons can be made regarding the attraction of the sand found in deserts and that found at beaches. The Gobi Desert, for example, does not draw many visitors whereas the beaches of the Mediterranean at approximately the same latitude are a prime attraction for tourists.

As well as the locations of physical features and tourist attractions, counsellors must also understand why some locations have developed while others with similar natural attributes have not. The reason may be as simple as advertising. One government may promote tourism while its neighbour does not. Alternatively, the destination may be too far from major markets to take advantage of its natural highlights. Some countries have built a tourism infrastructure while others do not have the wealth to invest in tourism development. Other potential destinations may have weighed the costs and benefits of tourism and decided against development.

The many reasons why people travel have already been discussed as has the need for travel counsellors to match these motivations with a suitable vacation experience. The world, however, is a very large place and the choices are virtually unlimited. No travel counsellor can expect to have travelled everywhere or to have examined every aspect of the planet. Yet clients often demand exactly that. From the counsellor's viewpoint, there are two aspects to travel motivation. The first is to learn the general reasons why people visit particular places, such as Britain for culture and history, the Mediterranean for rest and relaxation, France for its wines and cuisine, or Florida for its many tourist attractions. These are the main features among the pull factors of tourism. Counsellors must also learn the particular reasons why individuals select a specific destination. For example, the needs of an ethnic client who is returning to Rome to visit relatives will be very different from those of a business traveller, or a tourist interested in Roman history or Italian cuisine.

Only after these travel motivations have been ascertained can travel counsellors turn to the servicing of client needs. This demands diverse and in-depth destination knowledge to correctly respond to the range of client questions. Travellers are primarily concerned with three features of a destination. They generally want to know where it is and how to get there. They are interested in its physical qualities such as climate, topography, facilities and attractions. They will also seek information on what to expect in terms of culture, language and daily life. Travel counsellors must know these attributes but in addition they must offer advice on some of the more routine aspects of visiting the destination. In particular, counsellors will need to know the documentation required to enter and leave the destination, and they should be able to discuss its nature in terms of the types of visitors it attracts, its peak seasons and its specialties. Not all questions will be as straightforward. The request may be as simple as how to book a round of golf for a visitor at the famous Old Course in St. Andrews, Scotland or as complex as an inquiry from a businessman about appropriate business and social conventions in Malaysia.

Destination Analysis

The dilemma for travel counsellors is how to prepare for such assorted and intricate demands. Travel counsellors must develop techniques to assess all travel products. Destination material is no different in this regard. One way to evaluate destinations and ensure client satisfaction is to develop a method of classifying and rating the information. It is important to learn the essentials first and then add the secondary details to this information. How to find and arrange this destination information in an orderly manner is one of the objectives of this chapter. The following is one suggested way of analyzing a destination. You may wish to develop an alternative method or simply expand or rearrange these categories. The foremost consideration is to develop a format that will assist you to investigate a destination. This structure can then be used to create a destination reference binder for use in your career. Destination analysis falls into four categories:

- Destination Basics
- Destination Character
- Destination Details
- Destination Documentation

Destination Basics

Destination basics are the fundamen-tals of an area that every travel counsellor must know and which all travellers require. It is the overview of the destination. The information in this category does not change quickly or significantly over time, thus it can be studied and recorded.

The foundation for this analysis concerns the destination's location and geography. It is essential that counsellors can use an atlas to locate destinations and interpret facts on climate, vegetation and temperatures. They must understand that climate is affected by location and altitude as well as by physical features such as mountains. These factors also interact and can moderate or exaggerate particular effects. Climates, season changes and cycles are not the same in all parts of the world. Canada, for example, experiences four seasons with radically different temperatures. Thailand on the other hand has a wet season and a dry season while temperatures remain much the same all year. Seasons are reversed in the southern hemisphere and it is quite possible to ski in Chile in July. Certain climatic effects such as hurricanes and monsoons can be expected at particular times of the year. Clients will as a rule ask about the typical high and low temperatures. A simple temperature grid for a complete year can be constructed for reference. Terms such as wet season or monsoon should not be taken for granted. For example, clients should understand that the wet season does not necessarily mean that it rains all day every day.

In selling a destination, its location is important in terms of the climate to be found there. Clients are also particularly interested in how to reach the destination. The destination may be relatively close but inaccessible because of insufficient infrastructure or because the travel arrangements are circuitous. Thus, not only is the location important but also the travel arrangements by which it can be reached. To provide professional service, counsellors must have details of a wide variety of information such as airlines that service the destination, the most convenient routings, whether connections are required, the number of airports and their locations. It is important to create itineraries that provide simple arrangements. Sometimes, however, clients cannot fly directly to their final destination but must make a connection. Clients most often prefer direct flights but where this is not possible convenient connections should be scheduled. Clients do not wish to waste vacation time in an airport waiting for a connection. Other destinations necessitate a change of transportation mode. For example, Monte Carlo cannot be reached directly by air. Travellers to this destination must fly to

Nice and then make a rail or road connection. When the journey involves more than one mode of transport counsellors must also check transfers between terminals as well as schedules. It may be that connections force the traveller to take overnight accommodation.

Counsellors should not consider that their job is simply to sell airline tickets. Remember that clients will be arriving in an unfamiliar country and the more information they have in advance of their arrival the better they will be prepared.

FIGURE 5.3
Basic information on destinations can be found in the OAG Travel Planners.
Reprinted by special permission from the January-March 1990 of the Pacific Asia Edition of the OAG TRAVEL PLANNER Hotel & Motel RedBook. Copyright © 1990, Official Airline Guides, Inc. All rights reserved.

NEW CALEDONIA

THE BASICS

DOCUMENTARY REQUIREMENTS

U.S. CITIZENS: Passport—Required. **Visa**—Not required for stays of 30 days or less. **Other**—Ticket to leave. **Vaccination Certificates**— None required unless arriving after leaving or transiting an infected area. Typhoid and paratyphoid vaccinations recommended.

CANADIAN CITIZENS: Same as for U.S. Citizens.

(FRANCE) CONSULATE OFFICES IN NORTH AMERICA

UNITED STATES

EMBASSY:
Washington, DC 20007-2184, 4101 Reservoir Rd., NW. Tel. 202/944-6000.

CONSULATE GENERAL:
Boston, MA 02116, 3 Commonwealth Ave. Tel. 617/266-1680, Telex: 940985. **Note:** Visas issued **only**, at 20 Park Plaza, Tel. 617/482-3650.
Chicago, IL 60611, 737 N. Michigan Ave., Ste. 2020, (Olympia Center). Tel. 312/787-5359/85, Telex: 190229.
Honolulu, HI 96813, 2 Waterfront Plaza, Ste. 300, 500 Ala Moana Blvd. Tel. 808/599-4458. Tlx: 7238129.
Houston, TX 77019, 2727 Allen Pky., Ste. 976. Tel. 713/528-2181. Telex: 825078.
Los Angeles, CA 90211, 8350 Wilshire Blvd., Ste. 310. (Beverly Hills). Tel. 213/653-3120. Telex: 691183.
Miami, FL 33131, One Biscayne Tower, 2 S. Biscayne Blvd., 17th Fl. Tel. 305/372-9798/99.
New Orleans, LA 70115, 3305 St. Charles Ave. Tel. 504/897-6381/82. Telex: 161850.
New York, NY 10019, 934 Fifth Ave. Tel. 212/606-3600/80. **Note:** Tourism & Business Visas issued in person **only**, at 75 Vanderbilt Ave. Tel. 212/983-5660.
San Francisco, CA 94108, 540 Bush St. Tel. 415/397-4330. Telex: 34225, Visa Information: 415/397-4893.
San Juan, PR 00918, Mercantil Plaza, Ponce de Leon Ave., Ste. 720., Stop 27 1/2, Hato Rey. Tel. 809/753-1700/01, Tlx: 325432.
Washington, DC 20007, 4101 Reservoir Rd., NW. Tel. 202/944-6000.

CANADA

EMBASSY:
Ottawa, ON K1M 2C9, 42 Sussex Dr. Tel. 613/232-1795.

CONSULATE GENERAL:
Edmonton, AB T5J 3L8, Highfield Pl., 10010-106 St., Ste. 300. Tel. 403/428-0232.
Moncton, NB E1C 8P6, 250 Lutz St., Box 1109. Tel. 506/857-4191.
Montreal, PQ H5A 1A7, 2 Elysee, Pl. Bonaventure. Tel. 514/878-4381. Ext. 70/71/72.
Quebec, PQ G1S 3C3, 1110 Ave. Laurentides. Tel. 418/688-0430.
Toronto, ON M5S 1N5, 130 Bloor St. W. Tel. 416/925-8041; Visa Info. 416/925-8233.
Vancouver, BC V6Z 1H9, 736 Granville St., Ste. 1201. Tel. 604/681-4345.

CLIMATE

Average Temp		Jan	Feb	Mar	Apr	May	June	July	Aug	Sept	Oct	Nov	Dec
Countrywide	(F)	78°	79°	78°	75°	72°	70°	68°	68°	69°	72°	75°	77°
	(C)	26°	26°	26°	24°	22°	21°	20°	20°	21°	22°	24°	25°

COMMUNICATIONS

When dialing direct to New Caledonia, dial the proper International Access Code + **687** (Country Code) + Local Number. The International Access Code if calling from the U.S. is **011**.
When transmitting telex messages from the U.S., the code **714** for New Caledonia must precede the telex number.

CURRENCY

French Pacific Franc (CFP). Coins: 1, 2, 5, 10, 20, 50, 100. Notes: 500, 1000, 5000, 10000.
Currency Conversion Rate: At presstime, $1 U.S. = 120.44 Central French Pacific Francs.

ELECTRIC CURRENT

220 volts AC, 50 cycles (Two prong plug).

LANGUAGE

French. English is commonly spoken.

TAXES/TIPPING

Airport Taxes: Departure taxes are not collected of passengers at the airport.
Tipping: Tipping is not customary.

TIME

New Caledonia is 19 hours ahead of U.S. Pacific Standard Time.
Banking Hours: 8:00 AM-3:45 PM (Mon-Fri)
Business Hours: 7:30-11:30 AM; 1:30-5:30 PM
Shopping Hours 8:00 AM-6:00 PM

TOBACCO/LIQUOR

Import Allowances
Tobacco: 200 cigarettes or 50 cigars or 8¾ oz. of tobacco.
Liquor: 1 bottle of liquor (except alcoholic uniseed or absinth).

TOURIST BOARD OFFICES

New Caledonia Government Tourist Office:
Noumea, New Caledonia, 25 Ave. Marechal Foch, Box 688. Tel. 687/27-26-32. Telex: 3063; FAX: 274623.
North America
Los Angeles, CA 90212, 9401 Wilshire Blvd., (Beverly Hills). Tel. 213/272-2661. Tlx: 194674.
Montreal, PQ H3A 2W9, 1941 Ave. Mc Gill College, Ste. 490. Tel. 514/288-4264. Tlx: 5267335. FAX: 514/845-4868.
Pacific Asia
Auckland, New Zealand, Box 430, 57 Fort St., 3rd Flr. Tel. 375257. Tlx: 60321. FAX: 792874.
Brisbane, QLD. 4000, Australia, Windsor Towers, Cnr. Ann St. & Wharf St. Tel. 8322277. Tlx: 141999. FAX: 8320430.
Singapore 0923, 400 Orchard Rd., 14-05 Orchards Towers. Tel. 7377166.
Sydney, NSW 2000, Australia, 39 York St., 11th Fl. Tel. 292 573. Tlx: 176581. FAX: 2902242.
Tokyo, Japan c/o French Government Tourist Office, Akasaka Park Bldg., No. 2, 10-9 Akasaka 2-Chome, Minatoku. Tel. (03) 582-6965/67.
Europe
Paris, France 75001, Maison de La France, 8, Ave. de L'Opera. Tel. 42961023. Tlx: 214260.

DESTINATIONS AND ACCOMMODATIONS

Individual city entries with airport mileages, air carrier, ground and hotel/ motel information immediately follow the Charter/Rental/ Tour Operator category.

The New Caledonia Tourist Office has established ratings for hotels. The rating classification appears after the "Gov't Rating" comment within individual hotel listings. A decode of the classification follows:

★★★★ = Deluxe Hotels
★★★ = First Class Hotels
★★ = Second Class Hotels
★ = Tourist Class Hotels

★★☆ = Comfort Relay (between Three/Two Stars)
★☆ = Tourist Relay (between Two/One Star)
☆ = Halting Place Relay

All room rates presented are for guideline purposes only and should be confirmed, directly with the hotels, their system offices, or their Sales Representatives. In some instances, service charges and/or taxes may be included in the room rate range.

Please note, in line with our listing policy, no more than 8 facilities/ services may be presented per hotel. If the maximum number is shown with a hotel listing, it is possible that additional facilities/services are available.

For Credit Card decoding, see How To Use section.

GETTING INTO THE CITY FROM THE AIRPORT

There are a variety of ways to get from Narita to central Tokyo and Yokohama; or to get to central Osaka, Kyoto and Kobe if you land at the Osaka Int'l Airport. Choose one that fits your schedule and budget.

Airport—Downtown Transfer

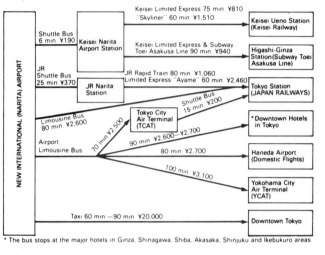

* The bus stops at the major hotels in Ginza, Shinagawa, Shiba, Akasaka, Shinjuku and Ikebukuro areas

FIGURE 5.4
Many references provide airport transfer information.
Source: Japan National Tourist Organization.

For example, do clients understand the procedures when they arrive at a destination? References such as the OAG Travel Planners provide maps of airport terminals to help counsellors advise their clients. Similarly, information on the transfers available, their cost and frequency, and the distance from the airport to downtown can be ascertained in advance. The costs and availability of taxis, limousines, subways and trains must also be researched. Much of this information is available in the standard travel industry reference books or in the airline computer systems described in Chapter 4.

The distance of a destination from the client's home town has a strong effect on whether it will be selected as a vacation spot. Distance here refers not only to kilometres but also the time it takes to reach the destination. For example, clients with a two week vacation period are unlikely to travel from North America to Asia, a journey requiring two travel days in each direction. Here, counsellors must

explain the difference between the actual flying time and the apparent flying time. Actual flying time is the amount of time spent commuting to the destination, including transit stops for connections. The apparent flying time refers to the local time at the destination and therefore demands a knowledge of time zones. These topics are discussed later in this chapter.

It is important to be accurate when creating itineraries or researching information. Place names and correct spellings can be confused. For example, Georgetown can be found in Canada, the Cayman Islands, Guyana and Texas to name but a few. None of these cities, however, should be confused with the George Town found in Australia or the similarly titled settlement in Malaysia. It is also important to know the correct local spellings for place names so that travellers are prepared for road signs and rail schedules. For example, European schedules frequently refer to Koln (for Cologne) and to Praha (for Prague).

Sources of basic destination information are atlases, the OAG, the OAG Travel Planners, airlines and other transportation companies, tourist boards, and tour companies.

Destination Character

Like the basics described above, a destination's character does not change significantly in the short term. Here, the counsellor should attempt to answer the questions, "What is it like?" and "What makes it different?" To answer these inquiries it is essential that counsellors have at least a superficial knowledge of the area's culture, language, religion, politics, history and art.

Every country develops a distinct set of values and way of life influenced by its history and geography. These values are expressed through the country's religion, music, art, politics and language. This combination of standards, values and traditions is described as culture. A destination's culture creates a unique atmosphere that more than any physical feature makes one destination different from another. Counsellors should grasp the significance of cultural characteristics and their effects on conditions at the destination. Tourists must be advised of the implications. For example, the religion practised at a destination can influence the days when stores are closed and the dress codes that are followed. Language and gestures differ, as do opinions of acceptable behaviour. Travellers who are not prepared for these differences can become bewildered and suffer culture shock. Clients do not merely wish to know the language spoken at the destination. They also inquire whether English is commonplace and, if not, which other languages are understood and spoken. In some places English is spoken in particular areas such as markets or major cities but is not understood elsewhere. Clients will seek information on luggage and packing. For example, how much should be packed and what types of clothes should be worn? What attire is suitable in various situations? For instance, can swimsuits be worn while shopping? Such questions require a knowledge not only of the climate but also of the social norms and standards of the country.

A destination's character will also indicate the general rather than the individual reasons why people travel there. Counsellors must therefore be able to answer the general question, "Why do people go there?" In other words, what do people expect when they travel to Acapulco, Aruba, Austria or Australia? The specific answers to this question are discussed in the following section, Destination Details. The most relevant consideration for travel counsellors, however, is whether travellers discover what they expect or are surprised by what they find. For example, a person travelling to the Middle East should not be shocked to learn that many countries strictly forbid the consumption of alcohol, that eating meals with the fingers and taking food from a common platter is usual, and that there are strong restrictions on the interaction of the sexes. Part of a travel counsellor's job is to make sure that there are no surprises.

The type of travellers who visit a destination also help determine its character. Some destinations are purely vacation centres while others are business hubs. Cities such as London and New York attract both business and pleasure travellers. Knowledge of the reasons why people visit a destination will help to describe its character. Some destinations attract an international clientele. Others appeal to particular nationalities. Counsellors should learn whether a spot is popular with Canadians and which other nationalities travel there. Psychocentrics will travel only to places that seem like home with North American style food, accommodation and people, that is, other Canadians. Others are more adventurous and prefer to travel where

Table 27

AUSTRIA EXPRESS

For summer service from May 29, see page **497**.

Train D217 arr.	dep.		Train D216 arr.	dep.
....	0940d	London (Liverpool St.) **66**	1957	....
1049	1115	Harwich (P. Q.) **66**	1745	1840
1900	1954	Hoek van Holland **66**	1055	1145
2014	2017	Rotterdam (C.S.) **229**	1028	1034
2122	2124	Eindhoven **229**	0914	0917
2155	2204	Venlo ⊞ **229**	0825	0835
2228	2244	Mönchen-Gladbach **229**	0742	0800
2323	2336	**Köln** (Hbf.) **229**	0652	0703
2356	2358	Bonn **662**	0627	0629
0036	0040	Koblenz (Hbf.) **662**	0548	0552
0135	0138	Mainz (Hbf.) **662**	0453	0455
0225	0232	Mannheim (Hbf.) **662**	0344	0405
0245	0253	Heidelberg (Hbf.) **662**	0328	0331
0410	0420	Stuttgart (Hbf.) **662**	0154	0211
0531	0542	Ulm (Hbf.) **662**	0042	0048
0637	0643	Augsburg (Hbf.) **662**	2349	2352
0722	0745	**München** (Hbf.) **662**	2241	2310
0930	0954	Salzburg (Hbf.) ⊞**684**	2016	2047
1036	....	Bischofshofen **759**	....	1935
....	1056	Bischofshofen **760**	1854s	....
1239	1250	Selzthal **760**	1651s	1702s
1403	1406	Leoben **760**	1540s	1542s
1500	....	**Graz 760**	....	1445s
....	1043	Bischofshofen	1923	....
1057	1106	Schwarzach St. Veit **759**	1905	1910
1138	1140	Badgastein **759**	1833	1835
1227	1230	Spittal **759**	1732	1737
1255	1306	Villach **759**	1653	1708
1340	....	**Klagenfurt 762a**	....	1620

CONNECTION BY VORARLBERG EXPRESS:

Train **1419**			Train **1418**	
....	0555v	Ulm (Hbf.) **667**	2325x	....
0742v	0755v	Lindau (Hbf.) ⊞ **667**	2115x	2135x
0804v	0806v	Bregenz **667**	2103x	2105x
0900v	0903v	Bludenz **667**	1950x	2001x
0931v	0931v	Langen **667**	1921x	1923x
0943v	0943v	St. Anton **667**	1911x	1912x
1116v	....	Innsbruck (Hbf.) **667**	....	1747x

FIGURE 5.5
Many references use local spelling.
Source: Thomas Cook European Timetable.

LOCALITY NAME OF HOTEL Abbreviation of booking centre Address ☎ telex, telefax	Number of rooms ⚬ single ⚭ double = total	Number of beds	Single rooms Discount prices FIM	Double rooms Discount prices FIM	Weekend discounts (W) Discount period Group prices person/day/double room FIM	Facilities in rooms	Facilities in hotel or vicinity
ALAJÄRVI KANTAKIEVARI .... KR Paavolantie 1 62900 Alajärvi ☎ (9)66-2455	⚬ 6 ⚭ 5 = 11	16	200—330**	240—380**	W 120 for groups of 15—20	♨ (1) ⌐ (1) WC (1) ☐ (1) ☎ (1) Sa ⊡ (1) ⊡ (1) ◆	WC ⌐ ✕ AG D ⚲ C (2) 12—25 s. F Sa (1) ⌐ ⊡ ⚘ ⊟ ✓ ⤸ ⚲ Ø ⤫ ▲ △ ⚌ (68 km) ✈ (50 km) ⎚
ALAVUS ALAVUS .... FINHO Järviluomantie 4 63300 Alavus ☎ (9)65-12 881	⚬ ⚭ 18 = 18	54	450**	530**		♨ (18) ⌐ (18) WC (18) ☐ (18) ☎ (18) ⊡ (18) ⊡ (18) ◎ (18) ◆ ♣ (2) ⊖ (2)	✕ AG D ⚲ C (2) 18—44 s. F Sa (1) ⊡ ⤸ ⊟ ✓ ⤸ ⤫ ⚴ Sq ⤫ (1 km) ⚌ (4 km) ⎚
ANJALANKOSKI KANTAKIEVARI INKEROINEN .... KR Päätie 21 46900 Inkeroinen ☎ (9)51-71 901	⚬ 3 ⚭ 29 = 33	80	340**	460**	W Net price 110—130 for groups of 11 →	♨ (33) ⌐ (33) WC (33) ☎ (33) ⊡ (33) ⊡ (33) ◎ (33) ◆ ♣ (2) ⊖ (2)	WC ⌐ ⊟ ✕ AG N D ⚲ C (3) 8—50 s. F Sa (1) ⌐ ⊡ ✓ ⤸ ⚲ Ø △ ⎈ ✈ (130 km) ⎚

FIGURE 5.6
Tourist boards can provide accommodation details.
Source: Finnish Tourist Board.

there are few tourists or where the tourists generally come from another culture. Part of their enjoyment is escaping from the everyday and meeting new people.

A destination's popularity also indicates its level of development and the facilities that can be expected. If a destination attracts 500,000 tourists annually, one can anticipate a comprehensive infrastructure, a range of accommodation with varying standards and prices, and many attractions. If, however, the destination attracts only 20,000 visitors each year, its characteristics will be very different. Counsellors should also be aware of the destination's seasonal qualities beyond simply a description of the climate. Clients are not only interested in who goes to a destination but also what time of the year they go. Again, some clients want to be part of the crowd whereas others for reasons of privacy or budget prefer to travel in the off-season.

Knowledge of the character of a destination is most easily acquired by visiting it. Sources of this information, however, are Statistics Canada, the World Tourism Organization, tourist boards, embassies and consulates. Guidebooks, a series of pamphlets called *Culturgrams*, libraries and newspaper travel sections also provide reliable information.

Destination Details

Any destination analysis naturally requires particulars of the area's features and attractions. This section should provide answers to such questions as "Where can I stay?" and "What can I do there?" It is perhaps the most comprehensive classification and can be further subdivided into four categories; accommodation, attractions and sightseeing, dining and entertainment, and activities.

Accommodation

No matter how much the sun shines or how tasty the meals, clients will not enjoy a vacation experience unless the accommodations are satisfactory. Given that the price of a hotel room often determines a holiday's cost, accommodation is possibly the most important part of a trip as far as the client is concerned. It is therefore crucial that counsellors have a sound knowledge of the types and quality of accommodation offered. One suggestion is to create a picture file for each destination with examples of budget, moderate and deluxe accommodation. Counsellors must remember that different countries have different categories and definitions for the quality of hotel rooms. "First class" does not mean the same everywhere. For each group of accommodation counsellors must know the number and types of rooms as well as the facilities and amenities available. This can be a time-consuming but worthwhile exercise. Types and standards of accommodation will be studied in Chapter 9. As you become more experienced through familiarization trips and talking with clients, you can develop a more thorough and personal review of the properties in each destination. Just as you need to know the airlines that service a destination, you should also develop a knowledge of which chains operate in the country. It is also important to become familiar with the tour companies that service the destination, the properties that they use, and the types of tours they offer. For example, some tour operators concentrate on a particular market segment, such as budget tours or tours for senior citizens, whereas others offer a variety of products. As you gain travel industry experience you can add notes and comments on the merits of various tour operators.

Attractions and Sightseeing

Destinations have already been discussed in terms of the pull factors that draw tourists to the area. This section considers the specific attributes and attractions of the area. Again, the simplest way to develop this knowledge is to classify attractions in some fashion. For example, the following discussion groups them according to whether they are physical attractions or special events. Physical attractions are further subdivided into natural, cultural and man-made attractions. Almost any way of classifying attractions has a fair degree of overlap. It is less important to agree on the categories, however, than to create a system which is useful for remembering details.

Natural attractions are those where a natural resource is the attraction of the destination. The feature may be a warm climate, excellent beaches, national parks or spectacular mountains. Often, it is a specific site such as Niagara Falls, Ayers Rock or the Grand Canyon.

Cultural attractions possibly form the largest group. Our earlier discussion mentioned the breadth and variety of influences on a destination's culture. Cultural attractions naturally reflect this diversity. The common attribute shared by these attractions is that all reveal an aspect of a destination's culture. The attraction may have a historical significance such as the Sphinx, the Pyramids, the Tower of London, or Quebec City. It may focus on the arts such as the Louvre or the National Art Gallery. Lourdes and Mecca reveal the influence of religion. The ideas of culture are represented in museums such as the Smithsonian Institute. Almost all cultural attractions can also be classified as educational attractions although some, such as the Ontario Science Centre, are specifically designed for this purpose.

Man-made attractions are those that have been designed especially to attract tourists. Ontario Place and Disney World are but two examples in this category. Some attractions are established to take advantage of an existing tourist trade. These range from the fairs and amusement parks which often spring up close to natural attractions such as Niagara Falls to a new ride at Canada's Wonderland or the EPCOT Centre addition to Walt Disney World. Theme parks is just one of the many subcategories that can be developed for man-made attractions. For example, marine attractions such as Sea World, animal and bird attractions such as the San Diego Zoo, towers such as the Eiffel Tower, and miscellaneous attractions such as wax museums and movie studios are a few more types. More important than simply developing lists of attractions, however, is the additional information that should be collected. As well as recommending a destination for specific attractions, counsellors should inform clients whether there is an entrance fee and, if so, its cost. Some museums have times and days when the entrance price is reduced or eliminated.

This information as well as the general opening hours should be communicated. The location of the attraction and whether it is accessible by public transport and by the handicapped should be noted.

Sightseeing and events are also destination attractions. The best advice to offer a client who wishes to learn about a destination is to recommend sightseeing tours. Some of the most popular tours in any city, and an ideal way for clients to quickly become familiar with the location, are the half-day and full-day coach tours offered by local transportation companies in every major city. Many of these tours can be booked from Canada. They will not only provide clients with a pleasing orientation to the destination but they also contribute additional income to the travel agency and counsellor. Events such as the Calgary Stampede and Carnival in Rio are major attractions in themselves. All destination files should contain the dates of significant events.

Dining and Entertainment

Dining is a leading diversion on everyone's vacation. As with accommodations, it is worthwhile to acquire information on a range of eating experiences from fast food to haute cuisine. A knowledge of the expected costs and the location of restaurants specializing in local or other types of cooking will help clients to budget and realistically anticipate their vacation experience. Two frequently asked questions are, "Can I drink the water?" and "What is the food like?" All counsellors should be able to advise their clients regarding what to drink. It is also important to state whether fresh fruits can be eaten, whether the food is highly spiced, and if American-style food is available. Describing the food of another culture is very difficult but not impossible. Descriptions such as "good"

FIGURE 5.7
Sightseeing tours help clients become familiar with a destination.
Source: Australian Tourist Commission.

DAY AND HALF-DAY TOURS

Here is a sample of the many tours available.

In Australia contact: Western Australia Tourism Commission 772 Hay Street, Perth, WA Tel: (09) 322 2999

Tour	Days	Depart	Duration	Price
Australian Pacific Tours - Bookings: (800) 821 9513 USA; (800) 263 5612 CANADA				
The All About Perth Tour ....Tu Th	0910	FD		$A45.50
Perth Fremantle City Sights & Swan River Cruise ....M F	0910	FD		$A42
Perth, River Cruise & Fremantle .M F	0910	FD		$A45
Atlantis Marine Park & YanchepW Sa	0910	FD		$A44
Wildflowers, Aussie Farm & Sheep Sheering.......................Tu Sa	0910	FD		$A48
	(Aug-Oct)			
Cohunu World Park/ Pioneer Village ....Tu Th	1315	HD		$A27
Underwater World, King Park .....Tu Th	0910	HD		$A27
Historic Fremantle........................M F	1315	HD		$A25.50
Swan River Cruise & Fremantle..M F	1315	HD		$A30
Pinnacle Tours - Bookings: (800) 445 0190 CA; (800) 551 2012 USA; (800) 235 8222 CANADA				
The Pinnacle & Wildflowers coach..............................Daily	0800	FD		$A65
Pinnacles Express.......................W F	0800	FD		$A46
Wave Rock York Express ....Sa	0800	FD		$A54
Margaret River. Southwest Vineyards & Caves ....Tu	0800	FD		$A65
Safari-Trek Australia - Bookings: (800) 472 3325 CA; (800) 268 8900 CANADA				
4WD Pinnacles Adventure ....M W F	0800	FD		$A78
FD = Full Day HD = Half Day *Price is AUD and a guide only.				

FISHING EQUIPMENT RENTALS–SHORE FISHING

Establishment	Equipment	Deposit	Rates
Fly Bridge Tackle Across from Hamilton City Hall, Church Street, Hamilton **Tel:** 295-1845	Rod, reel & tackle	$20.00	$10.00 per 24 hours $35.00 per week
Four Winds Fishing Tackle Ltd. 2 Woodlands Road Pembroke HM 07 **Tel:** 292-7466	Rod & reel rentals	$30.00	$10.00 per 24 hours $50.00 per week
Mangrove Marina Ltd. End of Cambridge Road Mangrove Bay, Somerset **Tel:** 234-0914 or 234-0331 ext. 295	Rod, reel & tackle for bone and reef fishing	$20.00	$ 6.00 per 4 hours $10.00 per day
Salt Kettle Boat Rentals Ltd. Salt Kettle Paget **Tel:** 236-4863 or 236-3612	Rod, reel & tackle	$20.00	Available with motor- boat rental only— $8.00 per rod.

or "I don't like it" do not really tell the client very much. If the counsellor has not tried the particular dishes even this scant information is dishonest. Counsellors must learn to be adventurous enough to try different foods at least once. They must also learn to describe food by relating it to particular dishes and spices that the client may be familiar with. Cook books can act as an invaluable resource for such research.

Entertainment means different things to different people. It ranges from daytime pursuits, such as demonstrations and festivals, to the nightlife available in theatres, shows, bars, discos, dancing and cabarets. Additional information on cover charges, minimum orders and other costs will help you project a competent and professional image.

Activities

Not everyone seeks rest and relaxation on a vacation and even those who do will often desire an occasional change of pace. Many travellers currently prefer active holidays. Destination knowledge will therefore include a study of sports and other activities available at the destination. Again, a mere listing of

potential pursuits is insufficient. Counsellors should research tennis, swimming and golf, for example, for both their price and location. For such pastimes, membership fees, advance booking requirements, and whether non-members are admitted will be important. Spectator sports like horse racing and less common pursuits such as hiking cannot be ignored. The professional counsellor's goal is to develop a comprehensive picture of the variety of activities available at the destination. Other recreational facilities such as skiing and marinas may also be popular. Some destinations are known for specific activities such as gambling in Las Vegas or Monaco.

One activity indulged in by almost everyone who travels is shopping. Shopping may in fact be the attraction, as it is at destinations such as Hong Kong. Alternatively, clients may simply wish to purchase souvenirs or perhaps they seek particular items for which the destination is known, such as opals from Australia or batik from Thailand. Many travellers eagerly search out "bargains". Part of a counsellor's task is to advise clients where the best buys, in terms of price,

FIGURE 5.8
Tourist boards supply activity information.
Source: Bermuda Department of Tourism.

DESTINATION ANALYSIS CHECKLIST

DESTINATION: _____

DESTINATION BASICS:

Climate (tropical, temperate, etc.): _____

Seasons (number, type and months): _____

Transfers (type and cost): _____

DESTINATION CHARACTER:

Language(s): _____

Religion(s): _____

Culture (customs/dress): _____

Visitors (type and number): _____

Development type (resort, adventure, etc.): _____

DESTINATION DETAILS:

	Type	Price	Quality	Dates
Accommodations:				
Main Attractions:				
Special Events:				
Dining:				
Activities:				

SPECIALTIES: _____

OVERALL IMPRESSION: _____

FIGURE 5.9
A destination analysis checklist developed from the discussion in this chapter.

quality and variety, are to be unearthed.

The details described here must be sufficient to provide a complete picture of the destination. It also supplies an opportunity for counsellors to display their product knowledge and proficiency by discussing the destination's specialties. Some of these may already have been described in other parts of the destination analysis, however, there should be a place for the special features of the locale. The area may be known for the best scuba diving in the Caribbean, for its dazzling nightlife, or for particular special events. The counsellor's knowledge, however, may be more personal such as a unique dish at a quiet little restaurant or a remote beach away from the tourist crowd.

Counsellors will have advised clients how best to reach a destination when the basics were covered. Clients will also need details of how to travel around within the country. Counsellors therefore need to know the local and national transportation links. Is it customary to travel by plane within the country? Are ferries and trains typically used for travelling around? What are the timetables, services, costs and standards of each mode of transport? Can reservations be made and tickets bought in Canada? Is local transport cheap, reliable and safe? Is it better to rent a car? If so, how do the rules of the road, signs, cars and driving habits differ from those in Canada? Counsellors also require the answers to such questions.

The standards and values of a destination would have been reviewed under destination character but there are also some mundane aspects of this subject that affect travellers on a daily basis. For example, is bargaining the accepted way of buying or are prices fixed? Similarly, is tipping the general custom or are service charges included? What is the common tipping percentage or amount? Who should be tipped and when? In some cultures almost everyone expects a gratuity whereas others consider it rude to tip. In some countries only those in specific occupations expect to be tipped.

Destination details may be found by consulting the Hotel and Travel Index,

hotel directories, OAG Travel Planners, OHG, tourist boards, CTM, sightseeing tariffs, clients, guidebooks, newspapers, television, radio, magazines, clients, libraries and world almanacs.

All travel industry information constantly changes. This may be due to the regular fluctuations caused by the change in seasons or because a new product has been introduced. Airfares and currency values can alter practically every day. The weather is naturally variable. Hotels and resorts open, are

---

FIGURE 5.10
Tourist boards provide promotional materials to help counsellors sell the destination.
Source: The Netherlands Board of Tourism.

Sales Promotion Materials

A variety of promotional items is available from The Netherlands Board of Tourism.

Brochures
A bulk supply of NBT Brochures is, in most case, free of charge or available at cost. Just use the Reader Service Card in the back of this guide.

Display Material
We offer window displays and other items for promotional support and to decorate your office.

Posters
A set of attractive posters shows Holland, both past and present.

Photo Library
Slides for audiovisial presentations, transparencies and black & white photos of scenic Holland are available for travel agents, tour operators and travel writers.

Shell Folders
Personalize your mailings and tour promotions with NBT shells. Material worth up to US$ 100 is provided free of charge, after which items are priced at cost.

renovated or change ownership and style. Restaurants come and go. New tour operators appear. Destinations mature or decline. For these reasons, it is critical that travel counsellors maintain and update accurate product knowledge. Incorrect or outdated information is at best embarrassing and at worst hazardous. As a professional you are responsible for the advice you offer.

Many events cannot be foreseen. Storms and hurricanes can develop in hours. Currency fluctuations and inflation can radically affect the cost of a trip. To counteract negative and embarrassing scenes, and be successful and effective in the travel industry, counsellors must not only take an interest in the physical features of the world, they must also develop a regard for current affairs and international events. A daily reading of the newspaper and/or viewing of world news is integral to product knowledge and is necessary to properly prepare your clients.

Destination Documentation

The specifics of documentation are discussed later in this chapter. When analyzing a destination, however, counsellors must be aware of the preparations that travellers must make prior to travelling. Passport and visa regulations are of prime importance but documentation also includes health and other entry requirements and exit restrictions. The *Travel Information Manual* (TIM) is the most valuable source of this information which can also be obtained from airline computer reservation systems (CRS).

Clients and counsellors require currency information, not only the name and the denominations of the local currency but also the exchange rate. The rate for Canadian dollars should always be given, as well as for any other major currencies that the client is likely to carry. Every Friday, *The Globe and Mail* prints a table of international currency and exchange rates (Figure 5.11) which were set on the previous day. This information is used by much of the travel industry as the standard guide for that week. Banks and currency dealers also supply these rates. Since members of the travel industry frequently use codes, the standard international code for the country's currency should be documented. This information can be found in the OAG Worldwide Edition and in airline computer systems.

Clients must be informed whether Canadian currency is easily exchanged or if another international currency, such as U.S. dollars, Swiss francs, German marks or Pounds sterling, is more suitable. Many cruise ships use U.S. dollars exclusively. Some countries, for example Belize, freely mix their own and U.S. currency. In addition, clients will desire advice on traveller's cheques and credit cards. They need to know which brands of traveller's cheques are commonly recognized, the denominations and currency to carry, and which credit cards are readily accepted. Tourist boards are an additional source for this advice.

Clients also ask how much money they should take on holiday. Counsellors must be aware of local living costs and standards if they are to accurately answer these requests. The price of meals, drinks and other tourist goods varies extensively from one destination to another. Many Caribbean islands, for example, must import much of the food they serve tourists. Meals can therefore be comparable in price to those found in Canada. There may be a shortage of adequate accommodation leading to relatively high hotel charges. Alternatively, destinations with an abundance of local produce and an inexpensive labour force may have living costs that are radically lower than those found in Canada. The economy and culture of a destination can also influence tourist costs. For example, some countries cannot afford to import tourist items that are considered to be luxuries while other nations restrict certain goods that conflict with their beliefs. For instance, Muslim countries generally prohibit or restrict the sale of alcohol. The result is that these items will be seldom available and will be expensive when they can be found. The more isolated a destination is, or the earlier its development phase, the more likely that tourist goods will be rare or highly priced. Currency rates of exchange also affect the cost of living for tourists.

Travel Guidebooks

Guidebooks which are generally targeted at the public can also prove to be valuable references for travel counsellors. Many include an account of the history and culture of a destination as well as its geography and attractions, accommodations and restaurants.

Guidebooks traditionally attempt to inform the reader of what to see and what to buy. Guidebooks often try to be all things to all people but this generally results in a publication that satisfies no one. Today, however, there are so many different guidebooks, some on destinations and others based on particular interests, that counsellors and consumers alike have considerable choice and need not depend on just one handbook. Each manual has a slightly different emphasis and content depending on its client market and the personal biases of the writer. Some guidebooks focus on the destination's history or culture, others stress its attractions, nature, museums or restaurants. Different publishers emphasize different income or interest

FIGURE 5.11
Currency exchange rates.
Source: The Globe and Mail.

Foreign Exchange

Cross Rates

	Canadian dollar	U.S. dollar	British pound	German mark	Japanese yen	Swiss franc	French franc	Dutch guilder	Italian lira
Canada dollar	—	1.3591	2.1678	0.9766	0.015470	1.1681	0.2803	0.8721	0.000844
U.S. dollar	0.7358	—	1.5950	0.7186	0.011383	0.8595	0.2062	0.6417	0.000621
British pound	0.4613	0.6269	—	0.4505	0.007136	0.5388	0.1293	0.4023	0.000389
German mark	1.0240	1.3917	2.2197	—	0.015841	1.1961	0.2870	0.8930	0.000864
Japanese yen	64.64	87.85	140.13	63.13	—	75.51	18.12	56.37	0.054557
Swiss franc	0.8561	1 1635	1.8558	0.8361	0.013244	—	0.2400	0.7466	0 000723
French franc	3.5676	4.8487	7.7339	3.4841	0.055191	4.1673	—	3.1113	0.003011
Dutch guilder	1.1467	1.5584	2.4857	1.1198	0.017739	1.3394	0.3214	—	0.000968
Italian lira	1184.83	1610.31	2568.48	1157.11	18.329384	1384.00	332.11	1033.29	—

Mid-market rates in Toronto at noon, July 14, 1995. Prepared by the Bank of Montreal Treasury Group.

		$1 U.S. in Cdn.$ =	$1 Cdn. in U.S.$ =	Country	Currency	Cdn. $ per unit	U.S. $ per unit
U.S./Canada spot		1.3591	0.7358	Fiji	Dollar	0.9826	0.7230
1 month forward		1.3600	0.7353	Finland	Markka	0.3190	0.2347
2 months forward		1.3607	0.7349	France	Franc	0.2803	0.2062
3 months forward		1.3612	0.7346	Greece	Drachma	0.00602	0.00443
6 months forward		1.3638	0.7332	Hong Kong	Dollar	0.1757	0.1292
12 months forward		1.3702	0.7298	Hungary	Forint	0.01077	0.00793
3 years forward		1.4026	0.7130	Iceland	Krona	0.02158	0.01588
5 years forward		1.4521	0.6887	India	Rupee	0.04330	0.03186
7 years forward		1.5156	0.6598	Indonesia	Rupiah	0.000604	0.000444
10 years forward		1.6221	0.6165	Ireland	Punt	2.2273	1.6388
Canadian dollar	High	1.3465	0.7427	Israel	N Shekel	0.4624	0.3403
in 1995:	Low	1.4267	0.7009	Italy	Lira	0.000844	0.000621
	Average	1.3874	0.7208	Jamaica	Dollar	0.04144	0.03049

groups. It may therefore be necessary for counsellors to consult more than one guidebook before deciding on the most appropriate source for destination knowledge.

Although many guidebooks are updated annually, some allowance should always be made for price increases since the titles are researched up to one year prior to the publication date. Historical and cultural attractions do not change much from one year to another and therefore books that emphasize such information provide much that is useful for counsellors. Counsellors should, however, exercise caution when consulting hotel and restaurant listings as changes can occur rapidly. One way to evaluate guides is to compare how different books describe the same hotel or attraction. If possible, choose a hotel or attraction with which you are familiar and check that each guide has the same publication date. All guidebooks reflect the opinions and experiences of the writers. The writers have stayed in the hotels, eaten at the restaurants, and investigated shopping and prices. In this respect, a good guide can replace a fam trip. They can also balance the promotional information and descriptions published by tourist boards or found in tour brochures. Some guidebook publishers, such as tourist boards or credit card companies, have a vested interest in the information they provide. For example, tire companies emphasize automobile tours. These factors would be considered when assessing a guidebook. The value of a travel guidebook is to some extent determined by the type of information that is sought. Features which are likely to prove useful are:

- An explanation of the culture, history, art and customs of the destination
- The relative importance or value of attractions and suggestions for the order in which sights should be seen
- Accurate and well-drawn maps that are large enough and have sufficient detail to be easily followed
- Practical information on the climate, what to wear and the prices to anticipate
- Honest descriptions which point out both the good and bad features

The 24-Hour Clock System

The travel industry is filled with terms and definitions, some of which are quite complicated. It would be difficult, however, to find anyone unable to explain the term "day" to everyone's satisfaction. This was not always the case. Prior to 1885 a day meant different things in different parts of the world. In Austria the day began at sunset while in the Arab world it started at noon. In Japan, however, the day commenced at sunrise and was divided into four equal parts. Similarly, there was a bewildering variety of time zones. For example, there were seven time zones between Halifax and Chicago. Up to the mid-1800s these variations caused little concern. However, as technology developed, the time between places started to shrink and the differences began to create confusion. To resolve the problem Sandford Fleming, a Scottish immigrant to Canada, proposed that the world be divided into 24 equal time zones and that a Universal Day begin at longitude zero degrees (the Prime Meridian) which runs through the Greenwich Observatory in England. He further proposed that a 24-hour clock be universally adopted to end the confusion of "a.m." and "p.m." Fleming's concepts were implemented by the Greenwich Observatory on New Year's Day, 1885. All countries quickly agreed on these standards and they were soon introduced in all continents.

Since the Universal Day begins at longitude zero degrees, and since the circumference of the earth is described by a circle of 360 degrees, it is clear that each of the world's 24 time zones coincides approximately with each 15 degrees of longitude. Further, each time zone represents a difference in time of one hour. In practice, however, time zones do not exactly match lines of longitude. Time zone boundaries have been altered in certain locations to avoid causing inconvenience in populated areas. Time is measured from Greenwich, England which is located at longitude zero degrees. Time here is referred to as Greenwich Mean Time, or more commonly GMT. All time zones around the world are related to GMT. Local time advances by one hour for each 15 degrees east of the Greenwich meridian. For example, European cities are east of Greenwich and observe GMT+1, i.e., one hour ahead of GMT. Conversely, local time is retarded by one hour for each 15 degrees west of the Greenwich meridian. Montreal is five time zones west of Greenwich and therefore observes GMT-

5, i.e., five hours behind GMT. At longitude 180 degrees east, then, local time is 12 hours ahead of GMT. This line, however, coincides with longitude 180 degrees west which is 12 hours behind GMT. Thus, there is a 24 hour difference from one side of this line to the other. If it is just approaching noon on a Sunday in London (GMT), the local time in the zone 180 degrees east will be just approaching midnight on the Sunday. However, the time in the zone 180 degrees west of London will be just approaching midnight on the Saturday. The day changes at the 180 degree meridian which by convention is the International Date Line. When travellers cross the International Date Line from west to east they "gain" a day. When travelling

FIGURE 5.12
The world is divided into 24 time zones.
Source: Korean Air.

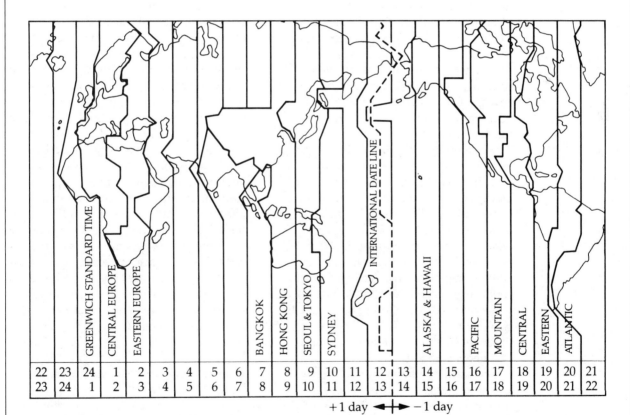

International Standard Time Conversion Table

The map shows how the world is divided into 24 time zones. As a person travels from one zone to another, he moves the clock one hour ahead when going east, one hour back when going west.

The time table along the bottom of the map has 24 columns that correspond to the 24 time zones on the map. If you know the time in any place in the world, you can find the time in any other zones by reading the times to the left or right.

westbound they "lose" a day.

Time zones in North America have been given names. Commencing on the east coast, these time zones are:

- Newfoundland Standard Time NST (GMT-3 1/2)
- Atlantic Standard Time AST (GMT-4)
- Eastern Standard Time EST (GMT-5)
- Central Standard Time CST (GMT-6)
- Mountain Standard Time MST (GMT-7)
- Pacific Standard Time PST (GMT-8)

Note that although each time zone normally varies from its neighbour by only one hour, Newfoundland Time is an exception to this rule. It varies by 30 minutes from its neighbour, Atlantic Time.

Time in North America during the winter months is called Standard Time. GMT is on the Prime Meridian and for the purpose of calculating time is at zero (0) hours. Eastern Standard Time (EST) is minus five (GMT-5). Thus, when it is 12:00 noon in Greenwich it is five hours earlier or 7:00 a.m. in New York. A further complication is that different countries and states adopt Daylight Savings Time at different times of the year. For example, from late April until the end of October most places in North America observe Daylight Time. During this period clocks are advanced by one hour from standard time. Thus, during Daylight Time the times are one hour closer to GMT. For example, Montreal observes EST or GMT-5 during the winter. In the summer months Montreal observes EDT (Eastern Daylight Time) or GMT-4, one hour closer to GMT. Some countries change their clocks in this way while others do not. Still others make the change on different dates. There may therefore be some confusion during the changeover period.

The earth's rotation makes the sun appear to travel from east to west across the globe. At 6:00 p.m. in Toronto it is 3:00 p.m. in Vancouver which is three time zones west. By the time it is 6:00 p.m. in Vancouver, it will be 9:00 p.m. in Toronto. To determine local time, generally, subtract one hour for each time zone entered when travelling west. If travelling east add one hour for each time zone entered.

Counsellors require a working knowledge of time zones, Greenwich Mean Time (GMT), the International Date Line (IDL), and the 24-hour clock system to correctly interpret timetables and schedules, and to make reservations throughout the world. The 24-hour clock is the accepted method of reading time. It is truly a simple and foolproof way of stating hours and minutes. For this reason, it has been adopted by airlines around the world not only for internal use but also for publishing passenger timetables. Counsellors will generally use conventional time (a.m. and p.m.) in conversations with their clients but must be able to convert from one system to the other to assist their clients. Conversions from conventional time to the 24-hour clock are quite straightforward. Clients are more likely to require help in converting the 24-hour time to the conventional form of "a.m." and "p.m.".

In the 24-hour clock time is always shown by a group of four digits. The first two numbers represent the hours (one to twenty-four) and the second two represent the minutes after the hour (one to fifty-nine). Where the hour or minute is a single digit figure it is preceded by a zero. For example, 0101 is one minute after one o'clock in the morning. By convention, time starts at one minute after midnight (0001) and runs through to the following midnight (2400). Noon hour is shown as 1200. As time progresses past noon the hours are added to the 12. Thus, 1:00 p.m. is 1300, 4:00 p.m. is 1600, and so on. Shown below is a step-by-step summary for converting to and from the 24-hour clock system.

Converting from a.m. times to 24-hour clock times

Examples: 11:49 a.m. and 8:05 a.m.

Step 1: Omit the "a.m." and the ":" (colon)
Step 2: Use four digits for all times.

Answers: 11:49 a.m. = 1149
  8:05 a.m. = 0805

Note: The first hour of the day is 0000, thus, 12:01 a.m. = 0001.

Converting from p.m. times to the 24-hour clock times

Examples: 1:08 p.m. and 11:40 p.m.

Step 1: Omit the "p.m." and the ":" (colon)
Step 2: Use four digits in all times.
Step 3: Add "12" to the hours.
Answers: 1:08 p.m. = 1308
  11:40 p.m. = 2340

Note: The 12th hour of the day remains constant in both systems, thus, 12:05 p.m. = 1205.

Converting from the 24-hour clock system to a.m. times

Examples: 0845 and 1120

Step 1: Remove the "0" if it appears as the first digit.
Step 2: Separate the hours and minutes by a ":" (colon)
Step 3: Add "a.m." after the time.
Answers: 0845 = 8:45 a.m.
  1120 = 11:20 a.m.

Note: The first hour of the day changes from 0000 to 12:00 a.m., thus, 0001 = 12:01 a.m.

Converting from the 24-hour clock system to p.m. times

Examples: 1820 and 1301

Step 1: Subtract "12" from the hours.
Step 2: Separate the hours and minutes by a ":" (colon)
Step 3: Add "p.m." after the time.
Answers: 1820 = 6:20 p.m.
  1301 = 1:01 p.m.

Note: The 12th hour of the day remains constant in both systems, thus, 1230 = 12:30 p.m.

Apparent Flying Time and Elapsed Flying Time

Clients commonly wish to know how long it takes to fly to a destination and what time they will arrive. Since both departure and arrival times of an aircraft are always given in local time, and the origin and destination may be in different time zones, determining the actual flying time of a flight can be a very confusing proposition for a client. For example, consider a flight from Toronto (EST) to London (GMT). Flights usually depart from Toronto around 8:00 p.m. in the evening and arrive in London the following morning at about 8:00 a.m. local time. The apparent flying time is 12 hours. From experience, however, actual transatlantic flying time is about seven hours. The five hour difference between apparent flying time and elapsed flying time is caused by travelling between time zones that are five hours apart (EST and GMT). Counsellors must be able to calculate both the apparent flying time and the elapsed (or actual) flying time to deal with client queries. Both can have a significant effect on travellers. For passengers on the Toronto-London flight discussed, arrival will be at 3:00 a.m. according to their "body clock" but it will be 8:00 a.m. London time. The travellers will no doubt feel tired after the trip and will probably be suffering from jet lag. Travel professionals should ensure that their clients understand this disruption of time and body and should offer ways to help them overcome jet lag. One way to do so is to encourage transatlantic travellers to reserve a hotel room at the destination for the night before they arrive. Since check-out time at most hotels is around 1:30 p.m., arriving transatlantic passengers run the risk of finding that their hotel room is not available before that time. A booking for the previous night, however, will not only guarantee that a room is immediately available when clients arrive, but will earn appreciation and commission for the counsellor.

If the origin and destination are in the same time zone, the apparent flying time and the elapsed flying time are equal. It is simply the amount of time that has elapsed between departure and arrival. The elapsed flying time for such a flight can be easily calculated by subtracting the departure time from its arrival time. When the departure city and arrival city are in different time zones, however, an adjustment must be made because subtracting one time zone from another is like subtracting apples from oranges. If several time zones and the International Date Line are involved the calculation becomes more complex and the 24-hour clock must be used. The first step is to convert both the departure time and the arrival time to their GMT equivalents. The converted departure time is then subtracted from the converted arrival time. Some examples showing how to convert local times from one zone to another are provided before taking the next step.

Example 1: When it is 1600 hours in Ottawa (EST), what time is it in Amsterdam (GMT+1)?

EST is GMT-5. Amsterdam is therefore six time zones east of Ottawa. That is, Amsterdam is six hours ahead of Ottawa. When it is 1600 hours in Ottawa it is 2200 hours in Amsterdam.

Example 2: When it is 1400 hours in Frankfurt (GMT+1), what time is it in Calgary (MDT)?

MDT is GMT-6 (since Daylight Time is one hour closer to GMT than Standard Time). Calgary is therefore seven time zones west of Frankfurt. That is, Calgary is seven hours behind Frankfurt. When it is 1400 hours in Frankfurt it is 0700 hours in Calgary.

Example 3: When it is 0130 hours in Halifax (ADT), what time is it in Victoria (PDT)?

ADT is GMT-3 and PDT is GMT-7. Victoria is therefore four time zones west of Halifax. That is, Victoria is four hours behind Halifax. To subtract four hours from 0130 hours (1:30 a.m.), the problem could be written:

0130
-400

(When subtracting, do not confuse minutes and hours. The first two digits represent hours, the last two are minutes.) Since one cannot subtract four from one, the problem is solved by adding 24 (24 hours in a day) to 01. The problem is then written:

2530
-400
=2130

of the previous day. Remember, Victoria is behind Halifax.

Having mastered converting local times from one time zone to another, it is an easy step to calculate the actual flying time of a flight. Before proceeding with some examples, however, it should be noted that clients are usually more interested in total elapsed time rather than with how much of that time is spent in the air (unless they happen to be smokers "trapped" on a non-smoking flight). The total elapsed time is the time from departure at the origin to arrival at the final destination. Consequently it is not necessary to compute the length of each segment and the actual amount of time the aircraft is flying. This is useful when considering flights with en route stops or flights where connections are involved.

Example 1: Air Canada flight leaves Toronto at 8:50 a.m. and arrives in Vancouver at 10:40 a.m. Calculate the elapsed flying time.

Arrive Vancouver
      10:40 a.m. = 1040 GMT-8
Depart Toronto
      8:50 a.m. = 0850 GMT-5

Looking only at the conventional times, it appears that the flying time is 1 hour 50 minutes. However, by converting both times to local Vancouver time using the 24-hour clock:

Arrive Vancouver 1040
Depart Toronto 0550 (Vancouver time)
Elapsed flying time of 4 hours 50 minutes is found by subtraction.

Alternatively, both times could have been converted to local Toronto time:
Arrive Vancouver 1340 (Toronto time)
Depart Toronto 0850
Elapsed flying time of 4 hours 50 minutes is found by subtraction.

The calculation for the reverse journey is equally straightforward.

Example 2: Air Canada flight 790 leaves Vancouver at 8:30 a.m. and arrives Toronto at 4:00 p.m. after a non-stop flight. Calculate the elapsed flying time.

Arrive Toronto
    4:00 p.m. = 1600 GMT-5
Depart Vancouver
    8:30 a.m. = 0830 GMT-8
Looking only at the conventional times it appears that the flying time is 7 hours 30 minutes. However, by converting both times to local Toronto time using the 24-hour clock:

Arrive Toronto 1600
Depart Vancouver 1130
Elapsed flying time of 4 hours 30 minutes is found by subtraction. (The same answer could have been reached by converting both times to local Vancouver time.)

It should be noted that prevailing winds are always from the west in the northern hemisphere. A westbound flight takes longer than an eastbound flight for the same journey because the aircraft is heading into the wind.

To summarize, elapsed flying time can be calculated by first converting the arrival and departure times to the same local time using the 24-hour clock and GMT equivalents. The converted departure time is then subtracted from the converted arrival time. It should, however, be apparent that another method is also available. That is, first determine the apparent flying time and then:

- If travelling westbound, add the number of time zones between origin and destination (since the point of origin is ahead of the point of destination).
- If travelling eastbound, subtract the number of time zones between origin and destination.

A third method, commonly used to calculate the elapsed flying time for international flights, is to convert the local departure and arrival times to their GMT equivalents and then subtract the former from the latter. For example, consider a flight which departs Edmonton at 2:00 p.m. and arrives in Paris at 7:00 a.m. the following morning. The apparent flying time is 17 hours. Edmonton is in Mountain Standard Time (MST) which is GMT-7 while Paris is one hour ahead of GMT (GMT+1). The calculation proceeds as follows:

Arrive Paris at 7:00 a.m. the following day. In the 24-hour clock this is written as 0700+1 (the "+1" denotes the following day). Since Paris is one hour ahead of GMT, one hour must be deducted to give the converted arrival time of 0600+1.

Depart Edmonton at 2:00 p.m. = 1400. Since Edmonton is seven hours behind GMT, seven hours must be added to give the converted departure time of 2100. The elapsed flying time is therefore:

$$0600 \ +1$$
$$-2100$$

As shown in an earlier example, 24 hours (denoted by the "+1") is added to the converted Paris time.

$$3000$$
$$-2100$$

Elapsed flying time of 9 hours is found by subtraction.

Most elapsed time calculations will not prove more difficult than the examples above. To establish the difference in time zones, it is necessary to refer only to the OAG (Worldwide Edition) where an international standard time chart is published showing time zones for all countries in relation to GMT (see Figure 5.13).

Travel Documentation

Travel documentation refers to the passport, visa and health requirements, customs regulations and currency restrictions imposed by a country on travellers entering or leaving its jurisdiction. All travellers who enter or leave Canada must have valid travel documentation. Travel counsellors are obliged, sometimes legally so, to inform their clients of the specific documents needed to enter a destination, regardless of whether that country is the end of the journey or is merely an in-transit stop. Clients must also be made aware of the documents required to exit from the destination and to re-enter Canada at the conclusion of a visit abroad. These documents are essential to the completion of a journey and can even have an impact on the client's physical health. Travel counsellors must therefore be thoroughly familiar with the requirements and must know where to find current information. Travellers who fail to carry proper and valid documentation may be refused entry by the authorities at the destination. Indeed, the passenger may not even be allowed to board the plane at the outset. Such an occurrence would greatly inconvenience the client and may lead to possible legal action against the counsellor or agency. As a matter of sound retail practice, therefore, counsellors should give attention to the necessary travel documents immediately after arranging a client's transportation. This is so important that counsellors should personally check their clients' documents and the validity of each credential.

Passports

A passport is an official document issued by a government to its nationals. As an official credential, a passport verifies an individual's identity and citizenship. It also permits the holder to leave and return to the individual's country of citizenship.

In Canada, the passport office under the jurisdiction of the Department of Foreign Affairs and International Trade, is the authority responsible for issuing Canadian passports. The main passport office is located in Ottawa. Regional offices are located in a number of cities across Canada for the convenience of the public

FIGURE 5.13
OAG publications reproduce an international standard time chart to aid counsellors.
Reprinted by special permission from the January-March 1990 Pacific Asia Edition of the OAG TRAVEL PLANNER Hotel & Motel RedBook. Copyright © 1990, Official Airline Guides, Inc. All rights reserved.

INTERNATIONAL STANDARD TIME CHART

STANDARD TIME: Legal time for each country fixed by law and based on the theoretical division of the world's surface into 24 zones each of 15° longitude with certain deviations due to frontiers or local option.
DAYLIGHT SAVING TIME (DST): Modified (advanced) legal time adopted by certain countries for part of year, especially during local summer.

COUNTRY	STANDARD TIME Hours from GMT	STANDARD TIME Time at 1200 hours GMT	DAYLIGHT SAVING TIME Hours from GMT	DAYLIGHT SAVING TIME Effective Period (first and last day)
AFGHANISTAN	+ 4 1/2	16 30		
ALBANIA	+ 1	13 00	+ 2	Mar. 25E—Sep. 29. 1990E
ALGERIA	+ 1	13 00		
AMERICAN SAMOA	− 11	01 00		
ANDORRA	+ 1	13 00		
ANGOLA	+ 1	13 00		
ARGENTINA	− 3	09 00	2	Oct. 15, 1989—Mar. 3. 1990
ARUBA	− 4	08 00		
AUSTRALIA				
Lord Howe Is.	+ 10 1/2	22 30	+ 22	Oct. 29, 1989—Mar. 03. 1990
New South Wales*	+ 10	22 00	+ 11	Oct. 29, 1989—Mar. 03. 1990
Northern Territory	+ 9 1/2	21 30		
Queensland	+ 10	22 00	+ 11	Oct. 29, 1989—Mar. 03. 1990
South Australia and Broken Hill	+ 9 1/2	21 30	+ 10 1/2	Oct. 29, 1989—Mar. 17. 1990
Tasmania	+ 10	22 00	+ 11	Oct. 29, 1989—Mar. 17. 1990
Victoria, Australian Capitol Territory (A.C.T.)	+ 10	22 00	+ 11	Oct. 29, 1989—Mar. 17. 1990
Western Australia	+ 8	20 00		
AUSTRIA	+ 1	13 00	+ 2	Mar. 25—Sep. 29, 1990
BAHAMAS (excluding Turks and Caicos Islands)	− 5	07 00	− 4	Apr. 1E—Oct 27, 1990E
BAHRAIN ISLAND	+ 3	15 00		
BANGLADESH	+ 6	18 00		
BARBADOS	− 4	08 00		
BELGIUM	+ 1	13 00	+ 2	Mar. 25—Sep. 29, 1990
BELIZE	− 6	06 00		
BENIN PEOPLES REP. (Dahomey)	+ 1	13 00		
BERMUDA	− 4	08 00	− 3	Apr. 1E—Oct 27, 1990E
BHUTAN	+ 6	18 00		
BOLIVIA	− 4	08 00		
BOTSWANA	+ 2	14 00		
BRAZIL ■ — East (Including All Coast and Brasilia)	− 3	09 00	2	Oct. 15, 1989—Feb. 10, 1990
West	− 4	08 00	3	Oct. 15, 1989—Feb. 10, 1990
Territory of Acre	− 5	07 00		
Fernando De Noronha	− 2	10 00	− 1	Oct. 15, 1989—Feb. 10, 1990

COUNTRY	STANDARD TIME Hours from GMT	STANDARD TIME Time at 1200 hours GMT	DAYLIGHT SAVING TIME Hours from GMT	DAYLIGHT SAVING TIME Effective Period (first and last day)
LEBANON	+ 2	14 00	+ 3	May 1—Oct. 15, 1990
LEEWARD ISLANDS				
Antigua, Dominica, Montserrat, St. Christopher, St. Kitts, Nevis, Anguilla	− 4	08 00		
LESOTHO	+ 2	14 00		
LIBERIA	GMT	12 00		
LIBYAN ARAB JAMAHIRIYA	+ 1	13 00	+ 2	Apr. 1—Sep. 30. 1990E
LUXEMBOURG	+ 1	13 00	+ 2	Mar. 25—Sep. 29. 1990
MADAGASCAR	+ 3	15 00		
MALAWI	+ 2	14 00		
MALAYSIA	+ 8	20 00		
MALDIVES	+ 5	17 00		
MALI	GMT	12 00		
MALTA	+ 1	13 00	+ 2	Mar. 25—Sep. 29. 1990
MARTINIQUE	− 4	08 00		
MAURITANIA	GMT	12 00		
MAURITIUS	+ 4	16 00		
MEXICO				
Baja California Sur and N. Pacific Coast (States of Sinaloa and Sonora)	7	05 00		
Baja California Norte (Above 28th Parallel)	8	04 00		
States of Durango, Coahuila, Nuevo Leon, Tamaulipas	− 6	06 00		
General Mexico, States of Campeche, Quintana Roo and Yucatan	6	06 00		
Cities of Ensenada, Mexicali, San Felipe, Tijuana	8	04 00	− 7	Apr. 1—Oct 27, 1990
MIDWAY ISLAND	− 11	01 00		
MONACO	+ 1	13 00	+ 2	Mar. 25E—Sep 29. 1990E
MONGOLIA (Ulan Bator)	+ 8	20 00	+ 9	Mar. 25—Sep. 29. 1990
MOROCCO	GMT	12 00		
MOZAMBIQUE	+ 2	14 00		
MYANMAR (Formerly BURMA)	+ 6 1/2	1830		
NAMIBIA	+ 2	14 00		
NAURU, REPUBLIC OF	+ 12	23 59		

and travel agencies. These offices process about one million passport applications each year. Approximately 5,500,000 Canadians currently possess a valid passport. Canadian passports can be issued only in the legal name of individuals who are Canadian citizens by birth or by naturalization. Evidence of citizenship (such as birth certificate or certificate of citizenship) must be submitted to the passport office when applying for a passport. Care must be taken in determining whether a client is indeed a Canadian citizen or is simply a resident of Canada. A resident is someone living in Canada as an immigrant or as a visitor. Residents cannot obtain a Canadian passport. They can, however, apply to the embassy or consulate of the country of which they are nationals to acquire a passport from that country. A Canadian citizen who mails an application to the passport office in Ottawa can expect to receive a passport within two weeks. Regional offices also issue passports and applications may be dealt with more quickly than by the head office in Ottawa. Local submissions, though, must be presented in person by the individual. A regional office can usually issue a passport in five working days.

Every retail travel agency needs a stock of Canadian passport application forms to distribute to clients. Supplies of these forms can be readily obtained by writing to the Canadian Passport Office, 125 Sussex Drive, Ottawa K1A 0G3. Regional offices do not carry bulk reserves of application forms, however, post offices stock small quantities. Two types of passport application forms are available. Form A (printed in blue) is for Canadian citizens 16 years of age or over. Form B (printed in green) is for Canadian children under the age of 16 years who will be travelling without their parents accompanying them.

Passport application forms are relatively simple and contain clear and explicit instructions for proper completion. Part of a travel counsellor's destination knowledge is to become familiar with all the details needed to accurately complete the most commonly used application, Form A (Figure 5.14). Incorrectly or partially completed forms can lead to unnecessary delay and possibly cancellation of travel arrangements. The following points should therefore be inspected after a client has completed a passport application:

- Evidence of citizenship available
- Application signed by applicant
- 2 passport-type photos, taken within the previous 12 months and duly signed
- Guarantor's declaration, completed and signed
- All questions answered in full
- Fee enclosed (cash, certified cheque or money order payable to "The Receiver General")

A businessman's passport is available at a higher price. This passport contains 48 pages instead of the usual 24 and is useful for the client who plans to be abroad on a regular basis.

A guarantor is one who has personally known the applicant for two years or more. A signed declaration to this effect is needed to identify the document and photograph of the applicant. A guarantor must be a resident Canadian citizen selected from a specific list of persons generally regarded as occupying positions of authority or trust. These include mayor, lawyer, judge, police officer, school principal and postmaster. A complete list of eligible guarantors is provided on each application form (Figure 5.15).

Many couples elect to include their children on the passport of one of the parents. Although less expensive, this practice can lead to problems. For example, a crisis may occur which necessitates that one parent cut short a family vacation. Difficulties can arise if there are children on that parent's passport. Conversely, there are benefits to children having their own passports. The [not true anymore] child may then travel unaccompanied or with either parent.

For clients who already possess a

External Affairs
Canada

Affaires extérieures
Canada

File No

PASSPORT APPLICATION FORM A
(APPLICANTS 16 AND OVER)

FOR OFFICIAL USE ONLY

1. NAME

(a) NAME TO APPEAR IN PASSPORT

Surname

First Name

Middle Name(s)
(optional)

(b) FORMER SURNAME(S)

Surname at Birth

Former Name
(if changed)

2. PERSONAL INFORMATION

Date of departure if known

Date of
Birth
Year   Month   Day

Place of
Birth

City

Province

Country

Do you want the place of birth shown in
the passport?

Write yes or no

See instruction 2 ◄ —

Sex   Occupation
M   F

Hair
Colour

Eye
Colour

Height

Weight

Marital
Status
Single   Married   Widowed   Divorced·   Separated

Permanent Address
No   Street   Apt   City   Province   Postal Code

Telephone
Area Code   Home   Business   Extension

Mailing Address
No   Street   Apt   City   Province   Postal Code

3. IN THE LAST 5 YEARS HAS A CANADIAN PASSPORT BEEN ISSUED TO YOU?

Write yes or no

Passport Number   Date of Issue

IF YES, SUBMIT it and indicate

IF YES, AND THE PASSPORT HAS BEEN LOST, COMPLETE AND SUBMIT FORM PPT 203 "STATUTORY DECLARATION" AVAILABLE FROM ANY
PASSPORT ISSUING OFFICE.

4. YOUR CHILD(REN) UNDER 16 — Children's names may be included in only one passport at a time. Complete only if you want their names
in your passport and submit evidence of Canadian citizenship for each child. If the space below is inadequate, attach a separate sheet giving

FIGURE 5.14
Part of a Canadian passport application (Form A).

passport, a counsellor should determine that the document is valid well beyond the duration of their forthcoming trip. The maximum validity of Canadian passports is five years from the date of issue. Passports cannot be renewed or extended beyond that time. It is important to check a passport expiry date not only to ensure that it will be valid for the entire trip but also to make certain that it meets the destination's entry conditions. Some countries demand that passports be valid for at least six months beyond the proposed return date. All documentation should therefore be checked against the destination requirements as well as the traveller's plans.

A passport is a valuable document and travellers should be cautioned to treat it with the same care and security as their cash, traveller's cheques and personal belongings. Canadian passports have some value in international criminal circles and should be protected against theft or loss. Counsellors should recommend that their clients carry their Canadian birth or citizenship certificate but that it be kept separate from the passport. With this documentary evidence of citizenship a new passport can be obtained from a Canadian consulate or diplomatic post abroad, should the need arise. A passport also serves as an excellent means of identification both at home and overseas since it contains the bearer's photograph and a specimen of the person's signature.

As such, it is commonly required to exchange cash or traveller's cheques at a hotel or bank in a foreign country.

Canadians visit the United States in far greater numbers than they visit any other country. In fact, the total number of individual crossings by Canadians of the Canada-United States border averages almost twice the population of Canada. Most Canadians enter the USA with a minimum of formalities. Frequently, the U.S. Immigration Officer asks only a few simple questions regarding place of residence and length of stay before allowing the traveller to enter the United States. Nonetheless the immigration laws of the United States compel Canadian citizens and residents to present proof of such citizenship or residence when seeking to enter the USA as a visitor. Travellers should therefore be made aware of the importance of carrying such proof. Individuals should not rely upon a verbal declaration alone to gain admittance to the USA.

Canada is a nation of immigrants not all of whom are able to or wish to acquire Canadian citizenship. As a service to such residents who require passports, it is good practice to have readily available a list of the consulates or other diplomatic offices where they can apply as nationals. The list of relevant countries will depend to a large extent on the ethnic mix of the region or of the agency's client mix. The *CTP Personnel Guide* has a complete inventory of embassies and consulates in Canada.

Visas

Passports are official travel documents which permit the holders to travel from and return to their own country. A visa, on the other hand, is a permit or authorization to enter into and depart from another country. Visas are usually issued by the embassy, consulate, or *chargé d'affaires* of the intended destination country. Although visas are sometimes issued at border crossings, it may prevent delays or difficulties if travellers obtain them prior to embarking

on their trip. Each country has the sole right to determine whether or not a traveller will be permitted entry, therefore a visa does not guarantee admission.

A visa usually takes the form of a rubber stamp impression in the traveller's passport. The visa imprint should not be confused with the entry and exit stamps that are put in a passport by the immigration officer encountered at the port of entry. A visa normally shows the issue date and period of validity. The length of stay permitted in the host country and the number of entries authorized before the visa expires are also specified. Visas are usually issued for either single or multiple entries. In some cases, a visa may also list the ports of entry and exit. Visas are generally issued in accordance with the traveller's purpose

**FIGURE 5.15
List of eligible guarantors for a Canadian passport application.**

Your guarantor must be a Canadian citizen residing in Canada and be included in one of the following groups:

— Minister of Religion authorized under provincial law to perform marriages

— Signing Officer of bank or trust company or full-time Manager of credit union

— Judge, Magistrate, Police Officer (RCMP, Provincial or Municipal)

— Person occupying senior university administrative position or teaching appointment in a university

— Person occupying senior administrative position in a community college (includes CEGEP)

— Principal of secondary or primary school

— Professional Accountant (member of C.A., CMA (formerly R.I.A.), C.G.A., A.P.A.)

— Professional Engineer (P. Eng., Eng. in Quebec)

— Mayor

— Lawyer (member of a provincial bar association)

— Notary Public

— Medical Doctor, Dentist

— Postmaster

— Veterinarian

— Chiropractor

for visiting the host country. Many countries record visa applications, in conjunction with actual entries at border points, to create tourism statistics.

Three types of visa are generally available. A **tourist visa** is issued for those visiting as a bona fide tourist. Tourist visas do not permit individuals to conduct business while in the country. Such travellers require a **business visa** which enables the bearer to engage in business at the destination. Some countries require travellers to possess a **transit visa** simply to travel through, without stopover, en route to a destination in another country. This is normally necessary only if the passenger is travelling across country by rail, bus or private car. Most countries waive the need for a transit visa if the traveller is making a direct connection by plane and will not leave the airport holding room. When transit visas are not required, references usually note that transit without visa (TWOV) is permitted.

Canadians are fortunate in that most of the world's nations admit them as tourists without a visa. A valid passport is all that is needed to enter Great Britain, Western Europe, nearly all the member countries of the Commonwealth, and many South American and Oriental countries. Visas are essential for travel to Russia and to most Eastern European nations. The nations of Eastern Europe are changing rapidly and many travel restrictions are being lifted or reduced. Currently, however, some of these countries issue visas only upon receiving prepayment for the traveller's hotel accommodations, meals and sightseeing for the total number of days for which the visa is required. Such prepayment is made to the official state travel bureau or representative of the country concerned. Tourists, such as those visiting friends or relatives, who do not require prepaid accommodations must generally exchange a set amount of money for each day they intend to visit.

Tourist Cards

For travel to many Caribbean, Central and South American nations, a tourist card is needed. A tourist card is the same as a tourist visa except that it takes the form of a separate document instead of a rubber stamp impression in the passport. The most likely instance where Canadian travel counsellors will be involved with tourist cards is for those clients visiting Mexico. An application form for a tourist card to Mexico is reproduced in the text (Figure 5.16). Tourist card applications may usually be obtained from the tourist office, consulate or embassy of the country concerned. For the sake of traveller convenience many Latin American nations, including Mexico, have empowered the airlines and tour operators which serve their countries to issue tourist cards.

The specific requirements for visas or tourist cards vary from country to country and can be influenced by external circumstances. For example, during a recent period of increased terrorist activity France imposed visa requirements on all nations except members of the European Community. Diplomatic spats can also cause countries to temporarily alter visa requirements. Only by checking with the consulate or embassy of the country concerned can the current guidelines be verified. The standard requirements include a valid passport (which must be submitted to the consulate or embassy), two or three passport-type photographs of the applicant, and the payment of a visa fee. In some cases the issuing consular officials may require proof of onward or return transportation from the host country or evidence of support while the traveller is there. Visa issuance can sometimes be delayed for many weeks, either for procedural reasons or because of location. The counsellor should ascertain how long this process might take so that travel arrangements and reservations may be made accordingly. In the usual procedure, visas for the destination countries are first obtained. Any transit visas required for travel through enroute countries are then sought. Most embassies are located in Ottawa although some countries also have consular offices in other Canadian

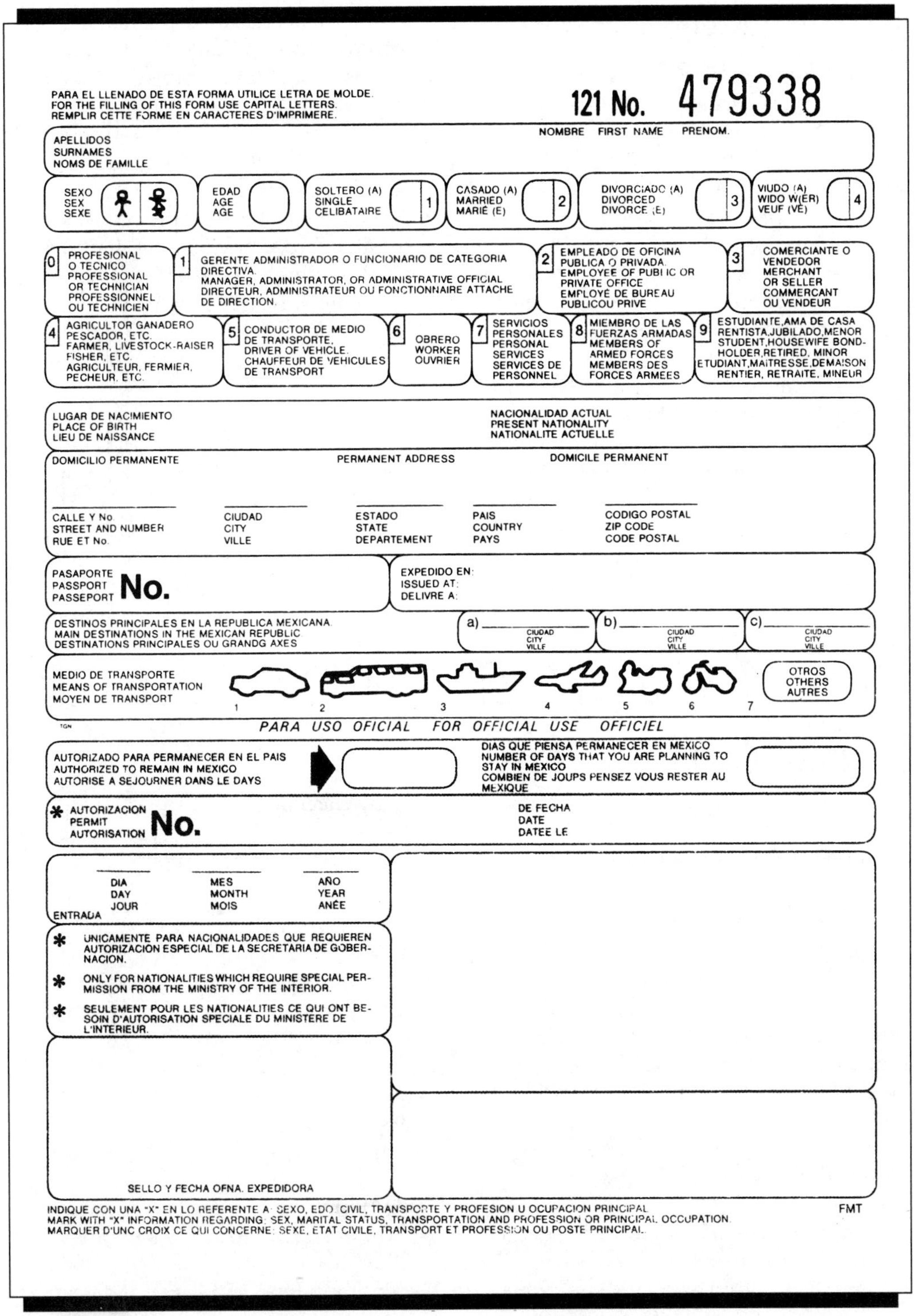

PARA EL LLENADO DE ESTA FORMA UTILICE LETRA DE MOLDE.
FOR THE FILLING OF THIS FORM USE CAPITAL LETTERS.
REMPLIR CETTE FORME EN CARACTERES D'IMPRIMERE.

121 No. 479338

APELLIDOS / SURNAMES / NOMS DE FAMILLE — NOMBRE / FIRST NAME / PRENOM.

SEXO / SEX / SEXE — EDAD / AGE / AGE — SOLTERO (A) / SINGLE / CELIBATAIRE 1 — CASADO (A) / MARRIED / MARIÉ (E) 2 — DIVORCIADO (A) / DIVORCED / DIVORCE (E) 3 — VIUDO (A) / WIDO W(ER) / VEUF (VE) 4

0 PROFESIONAL O TECNICO / PROFESSIONAL OR TECHNICIAN / PROFESSIONNEL OU TECHNICIEN
1 GERENTE ADMINISTRADOR O FUNCIONARIO DE CATEGORIA DIRECTIVA. / MANAGER, ADMINISTRATOR, OR ADMINISTRATIVE OFFICIAL / DIRECTEUR, ADMINISTRATEUR OU FONCTIONNAIRE ATTACHE DE DIRECTION.
2 EMPLEADO DE OFICINA PUBLICA O PRIVADA. / EMPLOYEE OF PUBLIC OR PRIVATE OFFICE / EMPLOYE DE BUREAU PUBLICOU PRIVE
3 COMERCIANTE O VENDEDOR / MERCHANT OR SELLER / COMMERCANT OU VENDEUR
4 AGRICULTOR GANADERO PESCADOR, ETC. / FARMER, LIVESTOCK-RAISER FISHER, ETC. / AGRICULTEUR, FERMIER, PECHEUR, ETC.
5 CONDUCTOR DE MEDIO DE TRANSPORTE, / DRIVER OF VEHICLE / CHAUFFEUR DE VEHICULES DE TRANSPORT
6 OBRERO / WORKER / OUVRIER
7 SERVICIOS PERSONALES / PERSONAL SERVICES / SERVICES DE PERSONNEL
8 MIEMBRO DE LAS FUERZAS ARMADAS / MEMBERS OF ARMED FORCES / MEMBERS DES FORCES ARMEES
9 ESTUDIANTE, AMA DE CASA RENTISTA, JUBILADO, MENOR / STUDENT, HOUSEWIFE BOND-HOLDER, RETIRED, MINOR / ETUDIANT, MAITRESSE, DEMAISON RENTIER, RETRAITE, MINEUR

LUGAR DE NACIMIENTO / PLACE OF BIRTH / LIEU DE NAISSANCE — NACIONALIDAD ACTUAL / PRESENT NATIONALITY / NATIONALITE ACTUELLE

DOMICILIO PERMANENTE — PERMANENT ADDRESS — DOMICILE PERMANENT

CALLE Y No. / STREET AND NUMBER / RUE ET No. — CIUDAD / CITY / VILLE — ESTADO / STATE / DEPARTEMENT — PAIS / COUNTRY / PAYS — CODIGO POSTAL / ZIP CODE / CODE POSTAL

PASAPORTE / PASSPORT / PASSEPORT No. — EXPEDIDO EN: / ISSUED AT: / DELIVRE A:

DESTINOS PRINCIPALES EN LA REPUBLICA MEXICANA / MAIN DESTINATIONS IN THE MEXICAN REPUBLIC / DESTINATIONS PRINCIPALES OU GRANDG AXES — a) CIUDAD CITY VILLE — b) CIUDAD CITY VILLE — c) CIUDAD CITY VILLE

MEDIO DE TRANSPORTE / MEANS OF TRANSPORTATION / MOYEN DE TRANSPORT — 1 2 3 4 5 6 7 — OTROS / OTHERS / AUTRES

PARA USO OFICIAL FOR OFFICIAL USE OFFICIEL

AUTORIZADO PARA PERMANECER EN EL PAIS / AUTHORIZED TO REMAIN IN MEXICO / AUTORISE A SEJOURNER DANS LE DAYS — DIAS QUE PIENSA PERMANECER EN MEXICO / NUMBER OF DAYS THAT YOU ARE PLANNING TO STAY IN MEXICO / COMBIEN DE JOUPS PENSEZ VOUS RESTER AU MEXIQUE

* AUTORIZACION / PERMIT / AUTORISATION No. — DE FECHA / DATE / DATEE LE

DIA / DAY / JOUR — MES / MONTH / MOIS — AÑO / YEAR / ANÉE — ENTRADA

* UNICAMENTE PARA NACIONALIDADES QUE REQUIEREN AUTORIZACION ESPECIAL DE LA SECRETARIA DE GOBERNACION.
* ONLY FOR NATIONALITIES WHICH REQUIRE SPECIAL PERMISSION FROM THE MINISTRY OF THE INTERIOR.
* SEULEMENT POUR LES NATIONALITIES CE QUI ONT BESOIN D'AUTORISATION SPECIALE DU MINISTERE DE L'INTERIEUR.

SELLO Y FECHA OFNA. EXPEDIDORA

INDIQUE CON UNA "X" EN LO REFERENTE A: SEXO, EDO. CIVIL, TRANSPORTE Y PROFESION U OCUPACION PRINCIPAL. FMT
MARK WITH "X" INFORMATION REGARDING: SEX, MARITAL STATUS, TRANSPORTATION AND PROFESSION OR PRINCIPAL OCCUPATION.
MARQUER D'UNC CROIX CE QUI CONCERNE: SEXE, ETAT CIVILE, TRANSPORT ET PROFESSION OU POSTE PRINCIPAL.

FIGURE 5.16 Application form for a Mexican Tourist Card.

cities. Other countries, however, may not have a representative in Canada and the closest authority may be in the USA or even Europe.

The most reliable source of information on passport and visa requirements is the TIM booklet or its automated equivalent. Embassies, tourist boards and airlines serving the destination can also provide these details.

Entry Requirements for Visitors to Canada

All foreign citizens except U.S. nationals require a valid passport to enter Canada and, in addition, some visitors need a visa. Visitors should direct their enquiries regarding visa applications and valid travel documents to the Canadian embassy, consulate or office of tourism in their home country prior to embarking on their trip. Many travel agencies handle travel arrangements on a prepaid basis. Here, a client pays a local travel agent to arrange transportation for another person living in a distant location. One example is the client who arranges from Canada for an overseas relative or friend to visit this country. In this case, the agency is responsible for ensuring that the visitor is advised of the documentation required for entry to Canada. Before being admitted to Canada, visitors must be in good health, law-abiding, and have enough money to support themselves and accompanying dependents during their stay. Visitors who wish to study or work in Canada must obtain special authorization before their arrival.

Health Requirements

The growth of international travel has exposed many travellers to the risk of contracting diseases abroad and infecting others upon their return. To control and minimize the extent of this threat the World Health Organization, a branch of the United Nations, has established a set of international health regulations observed by Canada and most other countries. These regulations are designed to protect travellers by requiring them to be immunized against certain diseases commonly found in a specific country or geographical area. As with requirements for passports and visas, travel counsellors must be aware of the particular health requirements applying to their clients' journeys abroad. Again, each country determines its own restrictions and health regulations are subject to change. Some conditions apply even when the visitor is only in transit and other regulations govern re-entry to Canada at the end of overseas trips. Travel counsellors must always check:

- The most recent health regulations required to enter the destination.
- The latest health regulations of any country through which the client will travel en route to the destination.
- The latest Canadian health requirements for returning from the countries of destination and/or transit.

The most valid source of current health information is the Medical Services Branch of the Federal Department of National Health and Welfare. The *Travel Information Manual* (TIM) described below also has detailed information on present requirements and infected areas. Most health guidelines concern the control of three diseases which are endemic in many parts of the world; yellow fever, cholera and malaria. Yellow fever and cholera are preventable by vaccination but malaria is not.

Yellow fever is a tropical virus disease typified by fever, jaundice and vomiting. Protection requires one injection which is valid for ten years beginning the tenth day after vaccination. The disease is common in Equatorial Africa and Equatorial South America. Yellow fever is transmitted primarily by a bite from an infected mosquito. Travellers arriving from a yellow fever zone without evidence of protection may be vaccinated and quarantined for ten days until the vaccination takes effect.

Cholera is endemic in some parts of the Middle East, Europe, Africa and Southeast Asia. It is spread by a bacterium in food and water and can be prevented by refraining from consuming any water or food that has not been heated to the boiling point prior to serving. A vaccination is available but the medical community debates its effectiveness. The vaccination is administered in a series of two injections separated by a one week interval. The vaccination is valid for six months beginning the sixth day after the first injection. There are few countries which require this vaccination although several recommend the procedure.

At one time the threat of **smallpox** was substantial and vaccination was required by most countries. The disease has now been virtually eradicated and there are currently no infected smallpox areas. No country demands smallpox vaccination unless an outbreak has been reported at either the traveller's origin or destination. Smallpox can be prevented by one vaccination which is valid for three years beginning the eighth day after it is first successfully administered.

Smallpox and cholera vaccinations can often be obtained free of charge from

local public health units in many municipalities and provinces, or from one's personal physician. Yellow fever vaccinations are obtainable only from special centres across Canada (usually the Medical Services branch of the Department of National Health and Welfare in provincial capital cities). Clients should be advised to obtain their vaccinations well in advance of departure as immunity takes time to develop. There is also the possibility of side effects. Travellers would prefer to discover whether they are susceptible to such effects prior to travelling. Failure to observe the health requirements can result in a traveller being refused entry into a country or being required to submit to quarantine detention at the traveller's expense. It is therefore important that

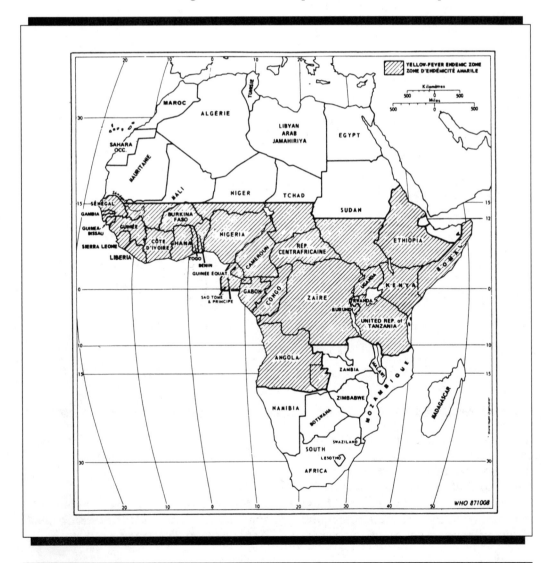

FIGURE 5.17
Map of Yellow Fever endemic area.
Reproduced courtesy of TIM.

Health and Welfare Canada   Santé et Bien-être social Canada

INTERNATIONAL CERTIFICATES OF VACCINATION
INTERNATIONAL HEALTH REGULATIONS

CERTIFICATS INTERNATIONAUX DE VACCINATION
RÈGLEMENTS SANITAIRES INTERNATIONAUX

Issued by :   Health and Welfare Canada Medical Services

Délivré par :   Santé et Bien-être social Canada Services médicaux

QS 2006 (6-82)
7530-21-036-8083

– 6 –
CERTIFICATE OF OTHER VACCINATIONS – CERTIFICAT D'AUTRES VACCINATIONS

DATE	NATURE OF VACCINE GENRE DE VACCIN	DOSE	SIGNATURE AND OFFICIAL POSITION OF PHYSICIAN SIGNATURE ET FONCTION OFFICIELLE DU MÉDÉCIN	STAMP CACHET
1	*Typhoid / Tet Polio*	*5cc / 1cc*	*(signature)*	
2	*Schicktest*			
3 *June 8, 1989*	*(handwritten)*	*o*	/Dr. MARIA DEL JUNCO PALMERSTON HEALTH CENTRE 543 Palmerston Blvd. Toronto, Ont. M6G 2P4 Tel. 535-1958	

FIGURE 5.18
All vaccinations are recorded in an International Certificates of Vaccination booklet.

travellers carry evidence of vaccination and protect it against loss. In Ontario there is a legal requirement that travel counsellors inform their clients of the criteria for entering a destination. Many countries recommend but do not require vaccination against certain diseases such as typhoid and tetanus. Here too it is the travel counsellor's duty to advise travellers of such suggestions.

All vaccinations must be recorded in a special document called the **International Certificates of Vaccination**. An

International Certificates of Vaccination booklet is an official travel document that when properly completed and bearing the individual's signature can facilitate disembarkation formalities. The illustration (Figure 5.18) shows an example of a certificate. Note that the certificate must be fully completed, signed and validated by the physician performing the vaccination and have the stamp or seal of a municipal, provincial or federal health department or office on it. A supply of International Certificates of Vaccination can be obtained free of charge from the Department of National Health and Welfare. These booklets should be stocked for distribution to clients. Travellers should be informed of the importance of proper completion of the certificate, and the necessity for keeping the booklet with the other travel documents such as a passport. It should not be packed in luggage.

A growing danger to travellers is **malaria,** a sometimes fatal disease transmitted by mosquitoes. More than five million Canadians and Americans travel each year to malaria-risk countries. The disease is spread by 65 different types of mosquito and its incidence has increased dramatically in recent years to almost 60 million cases annually. The malaria belt where malaria exists and can be carried by local mosquitoes includes parts of Mexico, Haiti, the Dominican Republic, much of Central and South America, Africa, India and Southeast Asia.

Most forms of malaria can be prevented. Although no vaccination exists for immunization against the disease, the Department of National Health and Welfare currently recommends a weekly tablet of the standard suppressant drug, *chloroquine.* Though the drug is readily available overseas, dosages are not standard everywhere. Travellers should therefore be advised to consult their personal physician and stock up before leaving home. According to the Centre for Disease Control in Atlanta, Georgia, the most dangerous malarial organism, *Plasmodium falciparum,* has developed immunity to chloroquine in some areas of South America and Southeast Asia. Alternative drugs such as Fansidar, Proguanil, and Mefloquine have been developed as daily supplements to a weekly dose of chloroquine in areas

FIGURE 5.19
Maps showing areas where there is a risk of Malaria.
Reproduced courtesy of TIM.

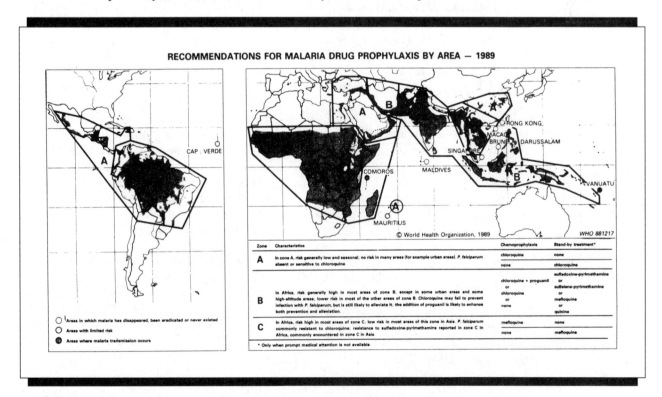

where mosquitoes are resistant to chloroquine. However, some of these drugs have adverse side effects and not all are available in Canada. Counsellors should always urge their clients to consult their doctor for details. Travellers must take anti-malaria medication at least one week before departing for an infected area, continue during the stay and carry on with the treatment for four to six weeks after leaving the region. There is no drug in current use that guarantees protection against malaria. Clients should therefore be advised to take preventive measures such as using mosquito nets, wearing long-sleeved clothing and applying insect repellents. Malaria can take a considerable time to develop. For this reason, any traveller who visits the malaria belt and subsequently becomes unwell should mention the trip to a physician. This is particularly the case if the traveller's symptoms are the chills and fever more commonly associated with influenza. Even if several months have elapsed since the visit to the infected area, the trip should be reported.

One of the most common infections experienced by travellers to tropical areas is **hepatitis** (or yellow jaundice) which can be contracted from an infected person or in food or water. The virus can be prevented by avoiding contact with infected persons and by consuming only thoroughly cooked food and boiled water. An injection of gamma globulin will give some protection against the virus for up to six months. This procedure, however, is not currently required by any country as an entry condition.

The most likely ailment facing tourists is traveller's diarrhea, an uncomfortable condition with a variety of colourful names. Although it can be contracted anywhere, this illness is most often associated with warmer climates and with countries which have poor sanitary conditions. The standard effective remedy is Pepto Bismal which can be purchased without a prescription from any drug store. More serious cases require treatment by a physician. In general,

visitors can reduce the prospect of traveller's diarrhea and several other health problems if they follow the directions below.

- Drink only boiled or bottled water and insist that all bottles are opened in your presence.
- Avoid adding ice to drinks unless you are sure that it has been prepared with boiled or bottled water.
- Ensure that food is thoroughly cooked
- Avoid leafy greens.
- Eat fruits only if they can be peeled and only if the skin is unbroken.

A recent medical development concerns the treatment for motion sickness. Although not a disease, motion sickness may adversely affect some clients' travel plans. *Scopolamine*, the oldest and most effective anti-motion sickness drug, has been available in pill form as Gravol for many years. In low doses, however, its effects are of brief duration and in high doses the side effects (drowsiness and a dry mouth) are often unacceptable. These consequences can be reduced by placing a disc containing the drug behind one ear. This permits controlled release of the drug through the skin rather than by swallowing a pill. Administering the drug in this manner prevents the peaks and valleys associated with taking a drug intermittently. Scopolamine in disc form may be purchased over the counter in most provinces. Alternatively it may be obtained by prescription. Clients should be advised to begin their medication prior to embarking on the journey as the drug takes some time to take effect.

A useful source of health information for both counsellors and travellers is the International Association for Medical Assistance to Travellers (IAMAT). IAMAT is a non-profit organization that can assist travellers who have health problems while abroad. IAMAT has a list of English-speaking physicians who will provide medical assistance to travellers on a 24-hour basis. Participating doctors must:

- Be licensed to practise in their native country and belong to its national medical association.
- Agree to medical standards established by IAMAT.
- Speak English and have at least one year of medical training in the USA, Canada or the United Kingdom.
- Agree to charge the fees established by the association.

IAMAT also has an information program for travel agents, Alliance of Travel Agencies for Traveller Protection Against Malaria. This organization offers members a variety of health information including a leaflet "How to Protect Yourself Against Malaria" and a country-by-country "World Malaria Risk Chart". Membership in IAMAT is available without charge although donations, used to finance the construction of medical clinics in Africa, are encouraged.

Customs Procedures

All nations have the right to protect their security and national interests by controlling the amount and kind of goods imported into the country. The responsibility for monitoring arriving travellers and their accompanying possessions falls on the customs department. Personal belongings, typically defined as used clothing and similar articles, are exempt from duties and taxes. Customs regulations vary from country to country but import restrictions are most commonly placed on tobacco products, alcoholic beverages, perfume and currency. Non-prescription drugs and weapons are forbidden by all countries. There may also be strict limitations on the importation of seeds, plants, meats and fresh fruits. Many of the worst pests and diseases in plants and animals reached Canada in such agricultural items. Dutch elm disease among Canada's native elm trees and an outbreak of foot-and-mouth disease in Saskatchewan cattle during the 1950s are two examples of the devastation that can be caused. The latter epidemic cost

Canadian taxpayers $800 million to eradicate. It is the travel counsellor's responsibility to make clients aware of specific restrictions which apply to the planned destinations. In all cases, the consulate, embassy or tourist office of the country concerned can furnish information on its customs regulations.

Canada Customs for Returning Residents

Travel counsellors are also obliged to inform their clients of the Canadian customs regulations affecting their return to Canada from abroad. Information brochures on Canada customs are available free of charge and should be stocked for distribution to clients. Returning residents can avoid delay and perhaps customs duty by registering valuables such as cameras and jewellery prior to leaving Canada. This can be done by presenting the appropriate goods at any regional customs office. The individual will receive a card, stamped by a customs officer, which lists the goods, their serial numbers and any other information required. The card is also available from customs officials at airports and border crossing points, however, it is preferable to acquire it before leaving on a trip rather than attempting to obtain it at such busy locations. On re-entering Canada, travellers then simply display the card and appropriate goods to the customs officer on duty to eliminate the need for lengthy explanations.

The accompanying illustration (Figure 5.22) shows a declaration form which travellers may be required to complete upon returning to Canada.

Any resident of Canada returning from a trip abroad may qualify for a personal exemption and be able to bring goods into Canada free of duties. There are, however, some limitations based on frequency of travel, length of stay abroad and age of the traveller. As of November 1999, the value of the exemptions accorded to residents returning to Canada are:

FIGURE 5.20
A listing from the
January 1990
edition of the TIM.
All listings follow a
similar format.
Reproduced
courtesy of TIM.

■ **RWANDA**

Geographical information: Capital - Kigali (KGL).

1. **Passport:** Required.
   Admission and transit restrictions: The Government of Rwanda refuses admission and transit to nationals of Burundi without the proper entry documents.
   Visa free transit by nationals of Burundi is only permitted by same flight and without leaving the airport.
   In case of non-compliance the passenger will be deported.

2. **Visa:** Required, except for:
   1. nationals of Rwanda;
   2. those holding a ''permis de retour'', issued after July 1, 1962;
   3. nationals ⧫ of Germany Fed. Rep. (West), Tanzania and Uganda;
   (TWOV)
   4. those continuing their journey to a third country the same day without leaving the airport.
   Issue:
   1. by representations of Rwanda in Belgium (Brussels), Burundi (Bujumbura), Canada (Ottawa), Ethiopia (Addis Ababa), France (Paris), Germany - Fed. Rep. (West) (Bonn), Kenya (Nairobi), Tanzania (Dar-Es-Salaam), Uganda (Kampala), U.S.A. (Washington), Zaire (Kinshasa) and the U.N.O. (New York);
   2. by the Service Immigration, B.P. 40, Kigali, Rwanda to passengers in a country where no representation of Rwanda is established;
   3. on a limited scale only, border air traffic is possible between Kigali (Rwanda) and Kivu Province (Zaire). Passport, arriving and departure details should be available at station manager of transporting airline at Kigali at the latest 72 hours prior to arrival. Do **not** embark those passengers without prior consent of station manager Kigali. (information only obtainable 24 hours prior to arrival). Fee RWF 1000.- per transit visa. Defaulting passengers will be deported.
   Notes:
   ⧫ Visa exemptions are generally for a stay of 3 months.

3. **Health:** Required — except for transit passengers not leaving the airport — vaccination against:
   yellow fever.

Recommended:
Malaria prophylaxis. Malaria risk — mainly in the malignant (P. falciparum) form — exists throughout the year in the whole country. Highly chloroquine-resistant P. falciparum reported (see Terms and Definitions).

4. **Tax: Embarkation Tax** levied on all passengers embarking in Rwanda on domestic flights: RWE 250.-; on international flights: USD 15.- or equivalent in freely convertible currency.
   Place of payment: Airport of Rwanda.
   Exempt are:
   1. Passengers travelling with free or service tickets;
   2. Diplomats travelling on official missions;
   3. Transit passengers not leaving the airport.

5. **Customs:**
   Import: free import by passengers of 16 years and older
   2 cartons of cigarettes and 2 litres of alcoholic beverages.
   Pets: dogs and cats must be accompanied by a veterinarian health certificate issued at point of origin.
   Dogs: vaccination Flury LEP (against rabies) and cats: vaccination Flury HEP.
   Export: Game trophy can only be exported with special permit of the Game Department.

6. **Currency:**
   Import: allowed
   local currency (Rwandesa Franc-RWF): up to RWF 5000.-;
   foreign currencies: unlimited provided declared. Compulsory currency exchange by national residents within 8 days after arrival.
   Export: allowed
   local currency (Rwandesa Franc-RWF): up to RWF 5000.-;
   foreign currencies: up to the amounts imported and declared.

■ **SAMOA (AMERICAN)**

Geographical information: Main city - Pago Pago (PPG).
These islands are situated in the Pacific Ocean along the International Date Line and north of Tonga. American Samoa has entry regulations of its own. Pago Pago is not a port of entry to the United States and passengers intending to proceed to the United States, must comply with the appropriate regulations.

ROMANIA/RWANDA/SAMOA (AMERICAN) 277

1. After 24 hours or more absence from Canada, a traveller may bring in articles up to a value of $50.00, not including tobacco or alcoholic beverages. There is no limit to the number of times per year that this exemption may be claimed. The traveller may be required to make a written declaration.

2. After 48 hours or more absence from Canada, a traveller may bring in articles up to a value of $200.00 duty free. Again, there are no limits to the number of times each year that this exemption may be claimed and a written declaration may be required.

3. After seven days or more absence from Canada, a traveller may bring in articles up to a value of $750.00 duty free. There is no limit to the number of times per year that this exemption may be claimed. A written declaration will be required.

Only one of the above provisions may be claimed on the same trip. Under items 2 or 3 the traveller is entitled to claim up to 1.14 litres of wine or liquor, 200 cigarettes, 50 cigars and one kilo of tobacco. The dollar value of these items forms part of the duty free allowance mentioned above. In addition, travellers must carry all tobacco products and alcoholic beverages in hand or checked luggage, and must meet the provincial age requirements to import such goods. These exemptions are subject to change and to certain modifications in the case of children. Specific and current information

FIGURE 5.21
Most countries obtain their tourism statistics from the arrival and departure information requested by immigration officials.
Source: Immigration Department of Malaysia.

DEPARTURE CARD — AN 771495
Please write clearly

Full name (*Use block letters. Underline surname*)

Passport No.

Number of children travelling on Parent's Passport

FOR OFFICIAL USE

**BE FOREWARNED
DEATH FOR DRUG TRAFFICKERS UNDER
MALAYSIAN LAW**

ARRIVAL CARD — AN 771495
Please write clearly

Full name (*Use block letters. Underline surname*) | Male ☐
| Female ☐

| Passport No. | Place of issue | Date of expiry |

| Visa No. | Place of issue | Date of expiry |

| Country of birth | Date of birth |
| | day   month   year |

| Nationality | Occupation |

Address in country of residence

| Number of children travelling on Parent's Passport? | Travelling on group tour? |
| | Yes ☐   No ☐ |

| Last place of embarkation | Next destination |

Flight No MH

Purpose of visit:
1. Transit ☐   2. Social/Holiday ☐   3. Conference ☐   4. Business ☐
5. Visiting friends/relatives ☐   6. Employment ☐   7. Others ☐

Address in Malaysia

Signature

NOTE: Tick (✓) Appropriate box

FIGURE 5.22
Customs declaration form used by all travellers entering Canada.

can always be obtained from regional customs offices.

All countries do not follow the same procedures as Canada for making customs declarations. In Europe travellers are generally given the choice of entering the country through one of two gates. One opening is designated as a green channel which signifies that the traveller has nothing to declare. Most travellers using this door simply walk through unimpeded although random spot checks are made. The alternative is a red channel which denotes that a customs declaration will be made. In other countries, however, every piece of luggage is checked.

Currency Regulations

Currency regulations are also the responsibility of the customs department. Since foreign exchange controls exist widely in many nations, it is important that one is aware of any restrictions which may affect the import and/or export of currency. Many countries, particularly those in Eastern Europe, place limits on the currency that can be brought in or taken out. Currency restrictions do not usually impose hardship on tourists. Where such controls exist, tourists can generally take unlimited amounts of foreign currency (either cash or traveller's cheques) into the country although several countries ban the importation of local currency. The export of local currency, however, or of foreign currency greater than the amount imported, is usually prohibited. The penalties for breaking these regulations are serious. Travel counsellors must inform their clients of such controls before departure. The TIM manual, foreign exchange dealers, banks and tourist offices are the best sources of up-to-date information on this subject.

Before leaving Canada travellers should consult a bank or foreign exchange dealer for advice on the most appropriate form in which to carry funds. Hotels, stores and banks in some countries do not accept traveller's cheques in Canadian funds. Similarly, some credit cards may not be honoured. A small amount of local currency will be worthwhile for initial tips to porters and taxis. Although banks and dealers do not usually supply small denomination currency, most airports and train stations in major European cities have bank facilities for changing money. These services are open as long as departures and arrivals are busy. Lineups, however, are quite common. Clients should be aware that although these booths may have longer operating hours their rates are often not as good as at a bank in town. They should also be informed that the exchange rate for bank notes is different than the rate for traveller's cheques. In some countries a better rate will be offered for bank notes

while in others the reverse applies. Further, clients should be advised that purchases made with a credit card will be subject to the exchange rate on the date the bill is processed. This may work to the traveller's advantage or disadvantage depending on the stability of the currencies involved.

Before starting a trip, clients should be encouraged to make a list that includes all traveller's cheque serial numbers, the name and account number on all charge cards, and the numbers of any personal bank cheques being carried. One copy of this list should be left with a friend or relative. Another copy should be carried by the traveller but kept separate from cheques and cards so that they may be promptly cancelled and replaced if lost or stolen. Some credit cards now offer insurance schemes to protect their clients against such loss. The average traveller probably carries more funds on a trip than when at home and should therefore be more cautious.

After Ontario introduced tougher travel rules in August 1988, a company named International Travel Information Systems (ITIS) began offering travel advisories for each country. Retail agencies can subscribe to this service and receive printouts directly or through a computer system. The service provides travel information on the relevant laws, customs and documentation necessary to visit specific countries and return to Canada. These printouts can be personalized for individual clients and are a valuable sales tool. The three page printout per country contains such information as entry requirements, health guidelines, customs and duty free allowances, Canadian embassies, local laws, major airports, languages, currency, public holidays, banking, office and shopping hours, and requirements for re-entry to Canada.

Vehicles and Licenses

More clients these days wish to drive in another country. They will, of course, need a valid driver's license and perhaps an **International Driving Permit** (IDP). Although not necessary for all countries, an IDP is a useful document. It is a special license for long term tourists which allows them to drive vehicles in foreign countries without the inconvenience of taking local driving tests. The permit also provides photographic identification and proof that the bearer holds a valid driver's license from the country of residence. An IDP denotes the categories of vehicles which the holder is allowed to drive. This information is translated into ten languages. The permit, in the form of a booklet, is valid for one year from date of issue and is recognized in over 180 countries throughout the world. The Canadian IDP is issued to any person over 18 years of age who presents a valid Canadian provincial driver's license, two passport size photographs and the appropriate fee to a provincial motor club affiliated with the Canadian Automobile Association (CAA) which has over 80 offices to serve the public in Canada.

A second document which some travellers may require is a *Carnet de Passages en Douane*. A carnet is a temporary circulation permit, normally issued in the country where the vehicle is registered, which allows the driver to take a motor vehicle across international borders. This document eliminates the need to pay duty on a motor vehicle when entering a foreign country. It is required to temporarily import a vehicle into many countries, particularly those where vehicles are subject to high import duties. Full details of how to obtain a carnet may be obtained from any of the motor clubs affiliated with the Canadian Automobile Association. In addition, some countries control vehicle imports by entering details of the vehicle in the driver's passport. The driver then cannot leave the country unless accompanied by the vehicle.

Drivers also require proof of insurance. If taking one's own car abroad insurance coverage can be obtained prior to leaving Canada. If driving a friend's car it is the owner's responsibility to ensure that the insurance covers guest drivers. Rental companies provide insurance coverage for their vehicles. Several jurisdictions now have no-fault insurance legislation and travellers should ensure they have sufficient collision insurance. A list of states and provinces where no-fault insurance provisions apply may be obtained from the Canadian Automobile Association.

Travellers who purchase a vehicle abroad can arrange insurance at the time of purchase. They should, however, be aware of the duty and taxes due if the vehicle is brought back to Canada. This information can be obtained from any regional customs office.

Other Traveller Tips

As well as the documentation requirements described above, clients will also seek other recommendations from their travel counsellors. These generally relate to preparations for the upcoming trip and advice for safety and pleasure at the destination.

Before leaving on a trip all travellers should be encouraged to purchase travel insurance. This topic is dealt with more fully in Chapter 12. Some travellers may be interested in joining IAMAT which was described earlier. All clients should be reminded to discontinue mail and newspaper delivery and to lock up before they leave. Other preventive measures include informing the police of the dates they will be away from home, leaving a house key, contact addresses and phone numbers with a relative or friend, and setting lights on a timer. Depending on the season, arrangements should also be made for garden care or snow removal. Many clients will also solicit advice on packing. Details will of course depend on personal preferences and the purpose of the trip. Appropriate clothing in terms of the climate and culture should already have been discussed with clients during the destination review stage. However, novice travellers should be reminded that too much luggage can spoil their enjoyment, particularly if they are embarking on a coach tour where packing and unpacking may be frequent. Generally, clients should be advised to use sturdy, lightweight luggage and to carry a change of clothing and toiletry articles in hand baggage in case luggage is lost or delayed. Clothes should be comfortable. While wash and wear garments are convenient, natural fibres are more suitable than synthetics in warmer climates. Two pairs of shoes will usually suffice. One pair should be comfortable walking shoes and neither pair should be new. Finally, a plastic bag will be convenient for separating a wet bathing suit or laundry items from other articles. Clients should also be reminded to leave space for gifts and souvenirs.

Again, suitable behaviour at the destination should already have been discussed. Some clients, however, may be concerned about hotel safety. Standard advice includes locking doors and luggage at all times and placing valuables in the hotel safe. To reduce concerns about hotel fires, clients should be reminded to become familiar with the hotel layout and alarm system and to contact the front desk if they need any type of assistance. In addition to the precautions on health discussed earlier, clients who wish to remain healthy should be counselled to maintain their regular exercise and diet habits when on vacation. This is not to suggest that clients should avoid new experiences such as windsurfing or an exotic meal. Rather, the counsellor should recommend that such pursuits be followed in moderation. For example, an individual who does not exercise regularly would be unwise to engage in strenuous sporting activities just because it is vacation time. The same advice applies to eating and drinking habits. An added incentive is that moderation can reduce the effects of jet lag.

Review Questions

1. Discuss the benefits and disadvantages of tourism development.

2. Describe the phases of destination development.

3. Outline one method of analyzing a tourist destination.

4. Describe three methods of calculating the elapsed flying time for an international air journey.

5. What advice on travel documentation would you offer to a client wishing to take a camera safari holiday in Kenya?

Research Assignment

Select a tourist destination and prepare a reference binder using the method described in this chapter.

References

Bon Voyage, but... Information for Canadians Travelling Abroad. A publication of the Department of External Affairs. Available free of charge and in quantity, this little booklet provides useful and important information about passports, visas, foreign laws, dual nationality, consular assistance, etc. The booklet can be obtained at passport offices. A film version may also be borrowed. Canada Employment and Immigration Commission can provide free literature on such topics as visiting Canada, students, and temporary workers.

Culturgram is a series of pamphlets summarizing the culture, history, geography and customs of almost one hundred nations. It is published by Brigham Young University, Publication Services, Provo, UT 84602, USA, Telephone (801) 378-1211.

Diplomatic Corps and Consular and Other Representatives in Canada. Available through Government of Canada bookstores. This booklet lists addresses of all diplomatic offices in Canada from whom official regulations and information may be obtained for entry requirements, health and customs. Most such offices are capable of issuing visas and/or tourist cards. The information is also listed in the *CTP Personnel Guide* available from Baxter Publications, 310 Dupont Street, Toronto, Ontario M5S 2V9.

Don't Bring It Back. A pamphlet published by Agriculture Canada which provides a table describing the limitations on animals, foodstuffs and other products.

I Declare. A publication of Revenue Canada, Customs and Excise. Available free of charge and in quantity, this booklet gives a brief outline of duty free exemptions, customs reporting requirements, federal controls on certain goods and more. It is divided into three sections; before you leave, while you are abroad, and when you return to Canada.

Immunization, a Guide for International Travellers. This pamphlet is published periodically by the Medical Service Branch of the Department of National Health and Welfare. It provides up-to-date information concerning health requirements for travel to most countries and re-entry to Canada.

International Association for Medical Assistance to Travellers (IAMAT), 1287 St. Clair Avenue West, Suite 1, Toronto, Ontario M6E 1B8, telephone (416) 652-0137.

International Travel Information Services, 390 Edgeley Boulevard, Unit 18, Concord, Ontario L4K 3Z6, telephone (905) 660-0008, fax (905) 660-0036.

Travel Abroad: Frontier Formalities. A looseleaf format publication of the World Tourism Organization. It provides details about entry and health requirements for many countries as well as entry requirements for private cars. WTO, Capitan Haya 42, 28020 Madrid, Spain.

Travel and Health: A Guide for Canadians published by the Department of National Health and Welfare. This publication lists travel information offices and discusses travel and health hazards in warm climates, immunization and countries with risk of malaria.

Travel Information Manual (TIM). A monthly publication by a consortium of international airlines. It contains up-to-date requirements for entry into nearly 200 countries. It is also available in an automated version (TIMATIC) and can be obtained from TIM, P.O. Box 902, 2130 EA Hoofddorp, The Netherlands.

World Travel Guide. An invaluable destination reference which incorporates the ABTA/ANTOR Factfinder. Recommended by many travel associations including ACTA. Columbus Press Ltd., 5-7 Luke Street, London EC2A 4PX, England.

## Chapter 6

Air Travel

Chapter Summary

This chapter begins with a brief history of air transportation including the circumstances leading to the current deregulated environment. Domestic and international air transport regulations are discussed. There follows an examination of the product knowledge necessary to sell air travel. Airline categories, route structures, equipment, services and procedures, are highlighted. Selling features are reviewed, as are the competition and cooperation between carriers. The chapter concludes with a study of the principal reference sources for airline schedules, fares, and ticketing procedures.

Chapter Objectives
After completing this chapter you should be able to:

- Describe the importance of the airline industry to the travel industry.

- Provide a brief history of deregulation in Canada and the USA.

- List the advantages and disadvantages of deregulation.

- Describe the major regulations controlling the airline industry and how they are changing.

- Define the categories of airlines.

- Discuss airline networks and routings.

- Recognize the more common aircraft types and configurations.

- Describe sales features of air transport.

- Design itineraries using the OAGs.

- Discuss the role of Transport Canada, ATAC, the ATA and IATA regarding fares and routings.

- Research air fares using the ATPCO, the Air Tariff and airline rate sheets.

- Locate the IATA Traffic Conference Areas.

- Book flights.

- Select appropriate airline traffic documents for a given transaction.

Development of Air Travel

The dramatic rise of the air transport industry since the end of World War II can be directly related to circumstances created by those hostilities. The war produced a pool of experienced pilots, increased the number of people who had flown (thereby reducing the mystique of flight), and left a surplus of aircraft that could be put to commercial use. There were also technical advancements, such as the development of radar, and an increase in the number of airfields constructed. The single largest technological breakthrough, however, was the invention of the jet engine which increased travel speeds and permitted a longer travel range. Scheduled jet service was inaugurated in the late 1950s with the introduction of the Boeing 707. During the 1970s wide-bodied aircraft such as the Douglas DC-10, the Boeing 747 and the Lockheed L1011 were developed and began operations. These jumbo jets had about triple the passenger capacity of earlier planes, which led to the construction of new or enlarged hotels at destinations to accommodate the expanded number of visitors. Mass tourism, which had been created with the introduction of jet aircraft and package tours, became even larger. Air travel is now standard throughout the business world and is a powerful influence on the tastes, attitudes and habits of millions. The technological growth and expansion of commercial aviation is an ongoing phenomenon. Supersonic transatlantic flights on a scheduled-service basis commenced in 1976. By the 1980s airlines were flying versions of the jumbo jets which were more fuel-efficient, had larger seating capacities, and could travel further without stopping. At the same time, the growth of commuter airlines has increased interest in STOL (short take-off and landing) aircraft.

For retail travel agencies, air transportation is the single most important element in the tourism industry. Selling aircraft seats to business and pleasure travellers is the foundation on which most travel agencies are built. Few travel agencies can exist without some involvement in the handling, promotion and sale of air transportation. Some agencies did begin operations during the 1970s with the intention of specializing in and dealing exclusively with package tours based on group departures and group fares. These agencies, however, soon realized the need to expand their business to include regular air transportation, if for no other reason than to offer this service to their clients and thus build repeat business. More recently, other agencies have elected to concentrate on cruises. However, these agencies are few in number and even such products usually involve a flight to the port of embarkation.

Airline Regulation

Airlines are regulated domestically and internationally. Each of the world's airlines must abide by the rules and regulations set by its national government. In Canada, Transport Canada controls civil aeronautics and is responsible for all safety matters. It establishes the specific rules governing the licensing of pilots, engineers and mechanics, the number of hours an

aircraft may fly between maintenance checks, the total weightload allowable for different types of aircraft, and many other factors. The agency operates most of the airports in Canada, as well as air traffic control offices and airport towers to manage air traffic between major airports. Smaller airports are often run by the area's local or regional government. The federal government is presently privatizing airport construction and operation. Transport Canada's counterpart in the USA is the Federal Aviation Authority (FAA) which was created to ensure air safety and to promote the growth of aviation. International flying safety regulations are monitored by the International Civil Aviation Organization (ICAO), a specialized agency of the United Nations based in Montreal, which regulates the technical, legal and operational aspects of the industry. In addition to these technical considerations, each national government historically also regulated the airline industry in terms of the fares charged and the routes flown. Internationally, regulation consisted of a system of agreements between governments covering the specific routes to be flown, the capacity to be offered and the airlines to fly them.

Until 1978 in the USA and 1988 in Canada, the respective federal governments strictly controlled the licensing of airlines, the schedules and routes they could offer, and the fares they could charge. Government agencies controlled these elements of airline operations to ensure a safe, reliable and economic transport service for the public. For example, overcharging the public was prevented by regulating the fares assessed by airlines. Fare regulation was also considered an effective way to ensure that an airline would not, for competitive reasons, undercharge its passengers. Undercharging could force an airline to cut operating costs to the point of perhaps jeopardizing safety or service. Government's objective was to exercise control over the routes operated by airlines, the fares they could charge and at the same time closely monitor the competition between them. It was considered to be against the public interest for an airline to fail due to too much competition, or to unfairly restrict competition over routes where competition was possible. As a result of such government policies, practically all airlines had a monopoly over some part of their route pattern. Competition with other airlines was limited mainly to routes where there was a high volume of traffic.

In a regulated environment it was extremely difficult to obtain an airline license. Even after a license was issued, airlines had to apply for rights to operate specific routes. If the application was successful no other carrier would be permitted to fly that route, unless it could prove that the service would be profitable and would not undermine another carrier's profitability. Fares in Canada were regulated by the Air Transport Committee, a subcommittee of the Canadian Transport Commission (CTC). The same function was performed by the Civil Aeronautics Board (CAB) in the USA. In effect, airlines were permitted to compete only on frequency of service, aircraft capacity and in-flight services. Similarly, airlines that wished to discontinue service on a route had to apply for and receive approval from the CTC before that service could be stopped. If another carrier could not be found to fly the route, the CTC could force the carrier to continue its operations.

Deregulation in the USA and Canada

Attitudes in the United States began to change during the 1970s. The rules which government had seen as necessary to protect both carriers and consumers were now considered to be preventing competition and causing unnecessarily high fares. This debate led to the Airline Deregulation Act which was passed by Congress in 1978. Under this act the CAB was gradually dismantled, losing its authority over the entry of new airlines in

1982 and over fares in 1983. The CAB was phased out on January 1, 1985. Its authority was transferred to the Department of Transport (DOT) which was created to consolidate U.S. transportation policy and to abolish separate agencies for each mode of transportation. The DOT replaced the CAB in regulating entry, mergers and acquisitions, consumer protection, and international air routes. The immediate effect of deregulation in the USA was that airlines rushed to drop unprofitable routes and cut services on mediocre routes. They competed fiercely for the most popular itineraries and introduced competitive cut-rate fares to attract customers. Competition was greatest on the most lucrative routes (e.g., New York-Los Angeles), fares were reduced drastically, and service to smaller centres was reduced. Travel agencies were offered higher incentive commissions and business became quite cut-throat.

The introduction of airline deregulation in the United States affected the Canadian environment. Although all airlines in Canada were still regulated, and scheduled carriers still had to obtain government approval to change fares and routes, controls were relaxed. Canadian airlines began to operate in a partially deregulated environment which gave them greater flexibility to set fares, routes and flight times in order to be more competitive with other carriers. Pressure for deregulation continued to mount and a measure of deregulation was introduced to Canada in January 1988 with the passage of the National Transportation Act. Because of the differing conditions between Canada and the USA, total deregulation was not considered appropriate for this country. The National Transportation Act deregulated the airline industry in southern Canada but northern routes continue to be regulated. The act created the National Transportation Agency (NTA) to replace the CTC as the body which issues air carrier licenses for both domestic and international services. In the past, an airline wishing to start a new service had to prove that it was required by "public convenience and necessity". Currently, a carrier needs only to confirm that it is "fit, willing and able" to serve a route for NTA authority to be granted. In practice this means that an airline must have sufficient insurance coverage and a safety certificate from Transport Canada. Regulations for terminating air service have been similarly relaxed. Carriers now need only give 120 days notice that a service will be discontinued. Pricing regulations in Canada have been similarly loosened under deregulation. Tariffs are no longer filed with the government agency and the regulations are limited to ensuring that the travelling public is informed of fares. Thus, carriers need only make a copy of their tariffs available at all business offices. In addition, they are not permitted to charge a fare that is not in the tariff. Bulk contracts (for cargo or for passengers) are exempt, and tariffs can be changed at any time. The NTA and its rules impose only a few requirements on airlines.

During the initial flurry of U.S. deregulation the situation was quite hectic. Travel counsellors were pressed to stay abreast of the many fares that were regularly introduced without warning. As Canada did not deregulate to the same extent or in the same manner, Canadian agents did not face such turmoil. Prior to deregulation, about six airlines controlled approximately 90 percent of the air traffic in the USA. This was considered unhealthy and it was felt that consumers were paying higher fares due to the protection afforded by industry regulation. Deregulation in the USA removed most restrictions and permitted competition on any domestic air route. As a result, large numbers of airlines were formed to take advantage of the new open policy. Over 130 airlines were started in the year following the introduction of deregulation and the situation became chaotic. Fares fell so low that operating costs could not be covered. Safety and operating procedures were questioned. Many airlines went bankrupt trying to compete and others were absorbed by larger carriers. Some measure of calm has now returned to the

marketplace but ironically eight airlines again control about 95 percent of the market. The eight companies, however, are different from those existing in 1978.

Deregulation was intended to increase competition, thereby lowering fares and improving service. Certainly the initial flurry of activity encouraged competition and forced major airlines to become more efficient. Fierce price wars occurred and the number of passengers practically doubled in ten years. Consumers benefitted from more discounts, new airlines, increased service in some areas, and better commuter services. Airlines gained greater flexibility in their pricing, scheduling, marketing, personnel and aircraft. They could also start and end operations more easily. However, there were also drawbacks to the new system. The rush to serve new routes sometimes led to a mismatch of equipment which increased maintenance costs. The fare wars caused serious financial problems and some major carriers (e.g., Braniff) went bankrupt. Others (e.g., People Express, a no-frills airline) emerged briefly before succumbing to the pressures of competition. Many of the smaller companies were acquired by or merged with larger carriers (e.g., TWA or American Airlines), or went out of business. Safety and maintenance procedures have been questioned, and companies have been accused of using deregulation to introduce job layoffs, break contracts and attack unions. Consumers in smaller communities have found that service has diminished. Fares have increased as the number of airlines has shrunk and the industry is again dominated by a few mega-carriers. Of the 215 carriers created in the USA since deregulation only 59 have survived. The larger airlines have again acquired almost a monopoly on their routes. Travellers now complain of overcrowded planes, busy airport terminals, overbooking and flight delays. The situation can only worsen since domestic air traffic is expected to almost double by the end of the century to 800 million passengers. There has also been concern that the distribution system tends to be

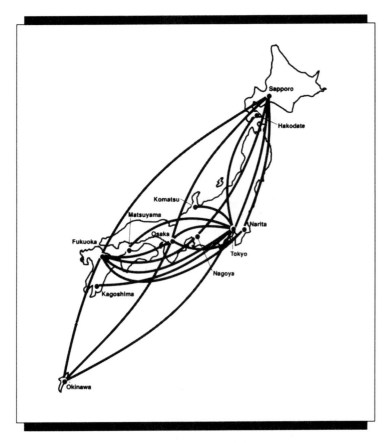

FIGURE 6.1
A linear route structure.
Source: Japan Air Lines.

dominated by a few computer reservation systems. Current legislation proposes that carriers must divest their computer reservations systems and give smaller carriers more room at airports, especially hub airports.

At the heart of deregulation is the debate over whether air transportation is a public service or a strictly commercial enterprise geared primarily to making a profit. Supporters of deregulation believe in market forces. In many countries, however, airlines are viewed as an arm of the state designed to serve broad national interests, including the provision of a public transportation service. These opposing beliefs are illustrated by the different manner in which Canada and the USA introduced deregulation.

Route Structures

The route structure of an airline refers to the network of destinations that it serves. An airline's route structure is one of its strongest selling features. Airline

passengers prefer to travel on direct routes and where possible select itineraries which avoid connections or changes of airline. For their part, airlines choose to develop the routes which have most traffic and greatest potential for profit. The early days of deregulation exemplified this intent when every airline attempted to serve the most lucrative routes. Airlines with more comprehensive route structures therefore have a marketing advantage over their competitors.

Before deregulation, U.S. route structures were assigned by the Civil Aeronautics Board which considered convenience when distributing routes. The CAB, however, placed a greater emphasis on the need to balance competition between the private carriers with a realistic return on their investment. The act introducing deregulation provided for the withdrawal of the CAB's powers in stages until it was formally wound up in 1985. The CAB's remaining powers were then split among other branches of government.

Linear Routes

Prior to deregulation route structures typically followed a linear model. In this pattern, an airline flies to a destination (preferably at the limit of the aircraft's range), deposits passengers, picks up a new load, and returns on the same route (see Figure 6.1). The flights need not be nonstop. Stops in transit permit an airline to pick up additional passengers. This model is the most efficient operating method for jet aircraft and is most effective on long haul routes. In the linear model competition is reduced to whether or not an airline services a particular destination. Connections with other airlines are more common in this format.

Hub and Spoke Routes

One outcome of deregulation was the development of a different type of route structure known as the hub and spoke system. Airlines using this system designate a large centre, such as New York or Chicago, as a traffic hub. Larger aircraft, for example wide-bodied jets, are used to fly between these hubs where traffic is heaviest. Smaller aircraft are used to transfer passengers from surrounding towns to these larger centres. These commuter routes form the spokes of a wheel with the hub at the centre (see Figure 6.2). This hub and spoke system permits airlines to operate more efficiently. In some cases, a major airline owns and operates all of the aircraft in the hub and spoke system. Alternatively, major airlines make marketing agreements with smaller carriers to feed into their national network. Major airlines can then offer their clients more convenient on-line service and a choice of more destinations within their system. Since deregulation and the advent of the hub and spoke system, airlines market their route structures more vigorously. Different airlines designate different cities as hubs. Schedules are arranged so that many commuter routes feed into major hubs at about the same time. This strategy enables airlines to increase their

passenger loads for flights between hub cities. At the same time, passengers are encouraged to remain within the airline's system by being offered convenient schedules. This technique combines both the linear and the hub and spoke models of route structure. That is, the spokes are linear routes which connect the hub with outlying towns, just as connections between hubs themselves form linear patterns. Competition is then based on which hubs and connecting cities offer the most convenient service for travellers. Airlines generally reproduce maps of their route structures in in-flight magazines and timetables. Major hub cities internationally are identified in the route map section of the OAG North American Travel Planner. There are currently about 35 major hub cities in the USA. After deregulation fostered the hub and spoke system, many linear routes linking smaller centres were discontinued. Where such service remains, travellers often have to connect through hub cities.

FIGURE 6.2
An example of a hub and spoke route structure using Phoenix and Las Vegas as hubs.
Source: America West Airlines.

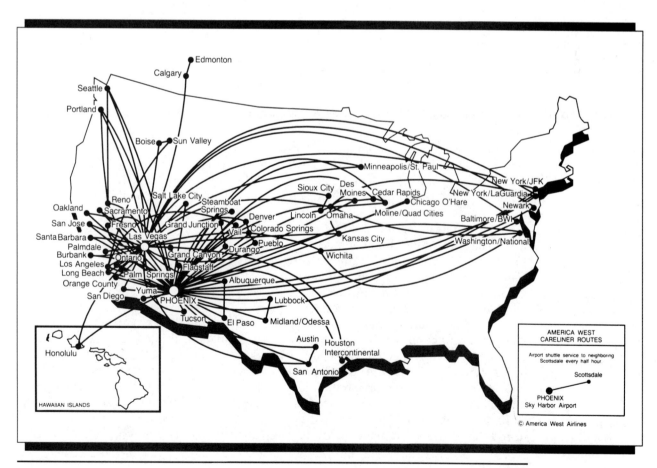

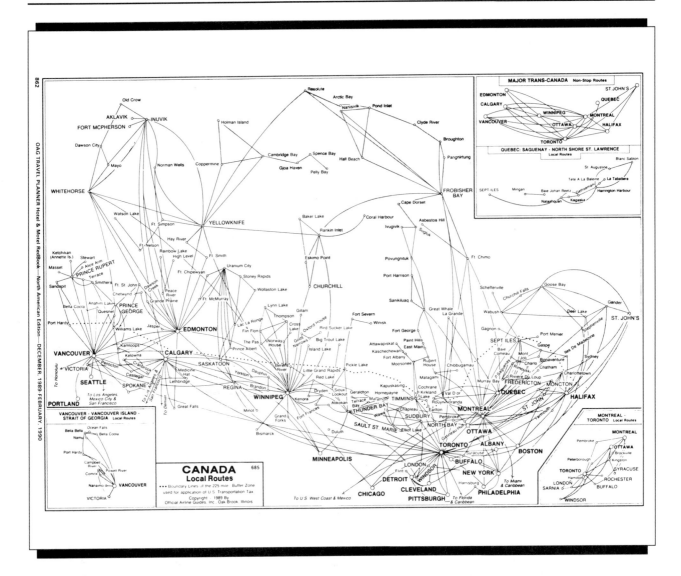

OAG TRAVEL PLANNER Hotel & Motel RedBook – North American Edition – DECEMBER, 1989 – FEBRUARY, 1990

FIGURE 6.3
Canada's airport hubs and linear routes.
Reprinted by special permission from the Winter, 1989 issue of the North American Edition OAG TRAVEL PLANNER Hotel & Motel RedBook. All rights reserved.

A basic transcontinental route structure exists in Canada. The dual bases from which most travel originates are Toronto and Montreal. Canada's two major transcontinental carriers are Air Canada with headquarters in Montreal, and Canadian Airlines International Limited (CAI) whose headquarters are in Vancouver. Both are truly national in the scope of their service. After airline regulations were relaxed in Canada, the charter carrier Wardair briefly offered scheduled service on certain high density routes. However, it was quickly acquired by CAI. Air Canada and CAI developed a hub and spoke system in preparation for deregulation in Canada. Each purchased or started a number of commuter (or third level) carriers and made feeder

arrangements with others. The hub cities in Canada are Vancouver, Calgary, Edmonton, Winnipeg, Toronto, Montreal and Halifax (Figure 6.3).

Classification of Airlines

Even with the introduction of deregulation, airline licensing in the domestic market still follows fairly strict financial and operational criteria. Airline licenses are issued in various categories depending on the type of service offered, the routes desired and the aircraft used. Considering first the types of air service offered, airlines can be licensed as scheduled carriers, charter carriers, or as a combination of both.

Scheduled Carriers

Scheduled carriers fly regularly advertised flights on definite routes according to a published timetable. Flights, routes and fares may not be changed without government permission. Prior to deregulation these rules were rigidly enforced. Today, however, more flexibility is permitted in all of these areas. Air Canada and Canadian Airlines International are examples of this type of carrier.

Charter Airlines

Charter airlines do not offer a systematic service but function on a purely charter basis. Such airlines may arrange occasional, seasonal or once-only flights. Canada 3000 and Air Transat are examples of Canadian charter carriers. Charter airlines are frequently owned by tour operators to ensure a supply of aircraft for their vacation packages. Charter carriers have fewer and less restrictive regulations than scheduled airlines. For example, they may more easily alter routes, change travel plans and cancel flights. For these reasons some airlines such as Air Canada and CAI obtain both scheduled and charter licenses to be able to offer both types of trip. Such combination licenses permit these carriers to compete with flights offered by the exclusively charter carriers as well as with the discount fares offered by competing scheduled airlines.

When charter flights were first introduced to Canada in the 1960s a strictly regulated environment controlled the airline industry. To be eligible for lower cost charter tickets, travellers had to belong to a society, association or group that was travelling together on the same flight. This was known as the affinity rule. Since large numbers of people were travelling together, the

operators of these charter flights were assured of full planes and could therefore drop the charter price to well below the cost of a scheduled airline ticket. Consumers flocked to these charter flights and although IATA (the representative of the scheduled airlines) at first enforced the affinity rule, enterprising business people constantly devised ways of circumventing the regulations. Eventually the scheduled carriers stopped fighting the affinity rule and applied for permission to offer charter flights themselves. One result is that there is sometimes little to differentiate scheduled and charter carrier operations.

Licensing Levels

Airlines are licensed at various levels. The first three levels emphasize the airline's route structure and are important to travel counsellors. Subsidiary licensing levels, such as helicopter services and bush pilots, have little impact on the retail travel industry.

Level 1 carriers are large airlines which fly nationwide and internationally. Such airlines are sometimes known as **trunk carriers**. Air Canada and CAI in Canada, and United Airlines and American Airlines in the USA, are in this category.

Level 2 airlines are known as **regional carriers** and, as their name implies, they fly within a smaller area. In Canada, WestJet serving the western provinces, and Bearskin serving the north region, are important regional airlines. Several regional airlines have been purchased by either Air Canada or CAI.

Level 3 carriers operate within a smaller area than regional airlines. They are often called **commuter airlines**. Air BC, Air Ontario and NWT Air are some of the many airlines offering this local service.

As deregulation progressed in the United States, Canada's regulations became less restrictive. Canadian deregulation has affected the licensing of carriers in each of the above levels but particularly those in level 2. Historically, a series of regional carriers licensed at level 2 served specific geographic areas of the country according to the federal government's Regional Carrier Policy. That policy had long since broken down by the time the regional airlines were consumed by one or other of the two national carriers in the mid-1980s. Third level carriers remain, however, and serve specific areas within the country. Some of these commuter airlines are associated with or owned by Air Canada or CAI. Air Canada presently has affiliates covering all regions except the prairies and Yukon (Figure 6.4) while CAI's partners serve all regions except Quebec, northern British Columbia, Yukon and the Northwest Territories. These airlines then link with either of the two major carriers in a hub and spoke system. In the Canadian

environment, level 2 and 3 (regional and commuter) carriers feed into larger (level 1 or 2) carriers in various major centres or hubs. This has produced a more efficient use of the resources available to each airline.

Before deregulation, airlines in the USA were classified according to trunk, regional, commuter and a fourth level, intra-state carriers, which were somewhat equivalent to commuter airlines in Canada. The distinction between these groups has since blurred and American carriers are now ranked according to their annual earnings. Major carriers earn over $1 billion, national carriers collect $0.75-1 billion, large regional carriers make $10-75 million, and medium size commuter airlines draw less than $10 million.

Airlines, then, may be categorized according to their route structures. Level

FIGURE 6.4
Air Canada's affiliated commuter and regional airlines (May 1990).
Source: Air Canada.

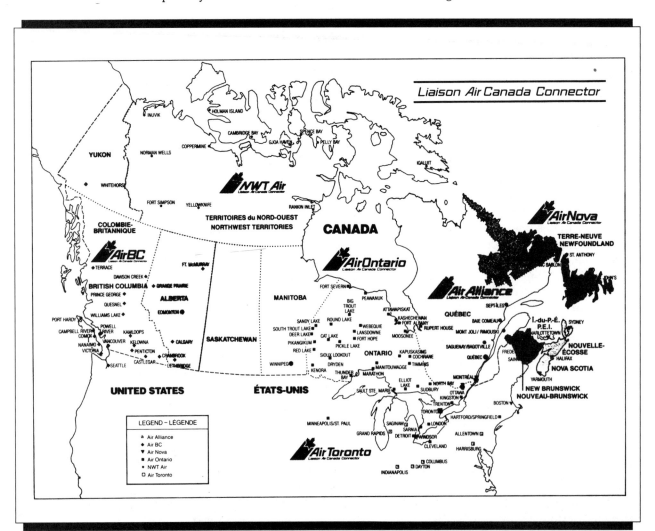

1 carriers can be subdivided into domestic or international airlines. From our viewpoint, domestic airlines operate within North America and Hawaii while international airlines service overseas routes. International carriers can be further classified in the following way.

Domestic Airlines Serving International Destinations

Air Canada, CAI and United are carriers in this category. Such airlines are based in North America and fly domestically but they also service scheduled routes to foreign destinations. Because these airlines operate both domestically and internationally they are subject to two different sets of regulations. Domestically they are controlled by the national government regulations described above. In Canada, Transport Canada, the National Transportation Agency and Air Transport Association of Canada (ATAC) perform these functions. IATA, a body comprised of scheduled airlines from around the world, plays a major part in the administration of international routes and fares. International regulation, however, is a matter for national governments.

Foreign Airlines Serving North America

Airlines such as British Airways, Air France and Japan Airlines comprise this group. They differ little from those in the previous category except that they are based outside of North America and operate international flights to North America. In addition, they may be permitted to fly domestic routes.

Off-Line Carriers

Off-line carriers are airlines which do not fly to any part of North America but only between overseas points. They may be international airlines such as Estonian Air, they may serve a smaller region, such as Cyprus Airways which operates in the Mediterranean, or they may be domestic carriers like Sunflower Airlines which flies only within Fiji. Canadian travellers often use their services on overseas trips. Travel counsellors must therefore be aware of these off-line carriers and which companies maintain sales and booking offices in major North American cities.

International Air Regulations

Deregulation is the term used to describe the reduction of many government controls on the airline industry and its operations. In Europe this is known as liberalization. However, deregulation applies only to a country's domestic airline functions. The right to provide air service into a community is controlled by the government of the country concerned. World tourism requires an international air transport system, however, all governments agree that a completely deregulated arrangement is impractical. International flights are therefore subject to negotiations between two or more countries. The original proposal for a worldwide system of airline regulation was offered at meetings known as the Chicago Convention of 1944 and the Bermuda Agreement of 1946. The Chicago Convention initiated debate on the freedoms of the air, that is, the rights of airlines operating in or over foreign countries. The Bermuda Agreement provided the prototype for all bilateral agreements concerning the application of the different freedoms between countries. Eight freedoms of the air have been identified (see Figure 6.5). The first and second freedoms are widely approved while the seventh and eighth are normally allowed only in special circumstances. The remainder must be negotiated through a bilateral agreement between the countries concerned. Such agreements describe the conditions under which airlines from each country may operate. They specify the permissible routes and rights that are permitted over them, the number of airlines allowed as well as their capacities, frequency of service, and fare regulations. These agreements do not usually cover charter operations.

FIGURE 6.5
The eight freedoms of the air.
Adapted from "Passport: An Introduction to the Travel and Tourism Industry" by David W. Howell CTC, South-Western Publishing 1989.

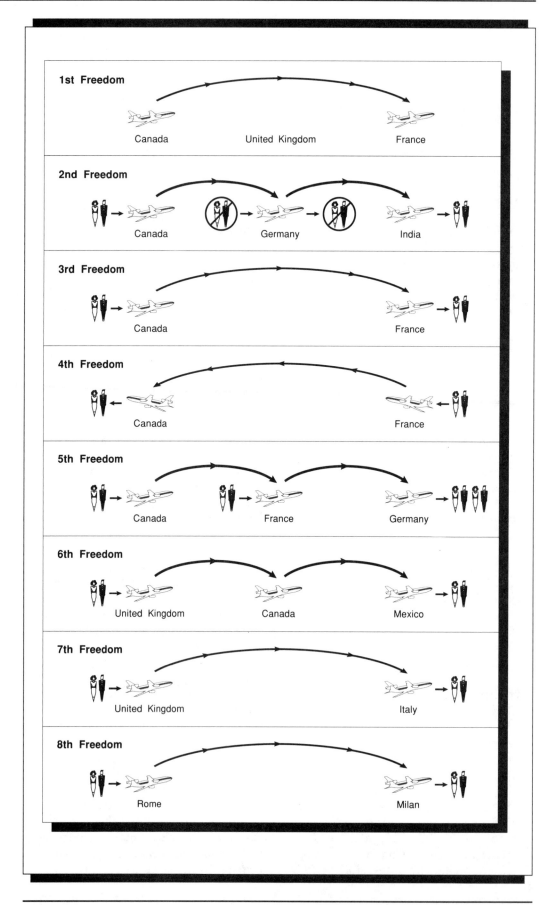

The **first freedom** is the right of transit which allows an airline to fly over one country to reach another. Without this right an airline may have to detour around a country to reach its destination adding to the journey time and cost.

The **second freedom** is the right of technical stop which permits an airline to land in another country to refuel, to change crews, or for maintenance, but not to pick up or drop off traffic.

The **third freedom** is the right to discharge passengers in another country. For example, the third freedom would permit Air Canada to carry passengers from Canada to France.

The **fourth freedom** is the right to pick up foreign passengers in their own country and transport them to the country where the airline is registered. This is effectively an extension of the third freedom. It would permit Air Canada, for example, to pick up passengers in France and carry them to Canada.

The **fifth freedom** is the right to carry passengers into another country and to pick up people there for onward travel to a third country. Continuing with the example of Air Canada, this right would permit Air Canada to collect passengers in France and fly them to Germany provided that the flight originated in Canada. Under this freedom, the reverse journey would also be permitted, that is, passengers may be collected in France as long as the flight terminates in Canada.

The **sixth freedom** is the right of an airline registered in a country to carry passengers to a gateway point in that country and then abroad. The traffic has neither its origin nor ultimate destination in the country. An example of this freedom would be Air Canada carrying British passengers from London to Mexico City with a stopover in Halifax.

The **seventh freedom** is the right of an airline registered in one country to operate entirely outside of that country by carrying traffic between two other countries. An example of this freedom would be Air Canada operating a regular route between London and Rome.

The **eighth freedom** is the right of an airline registered in one country to carry passengers between any two points in another country. This right is also known as cabotage. An example of this freedom would be Air Canada operating a regular route between Rome and Milan.

International Route Structures

International air routes are negotiated between countries through **bilateral agreements**. For example, the governments of Canada and the United Kingdom might negotiate an agreement on a route connecting Toronto and London which specifies the number of airlines each country will allow on that route. Subsequently, each government nominates a carrier or carriers to service the route. Bilateral agreements are renegotiated on a periodic basis to reflect changes in travel patterns, consumer demand or changing political climates. In this example, London and Toronto are referred to as **gateways**. A gateway can be the source of originating traffic, a destination of high consumer demand, or sometimes both. Countries that have more than one important gateway are in a better negotiating position.

The structure of international routes becomes highly complex when the freedoms of the air are introduced into the negotiations. To illustrate the difficulties involved, consider just one of these freedoms, the fifth freedom right, which is the privilege most debated by governments. The air traffic from Rome to Cairo can be the subject of negotiation between the Italian Government and the Egyptian Government, with both an Italian carrier and an Egyptian carrier enjoying traffic rights on that segment. Now, consider air service originating in Rome that travels Rome-Cairo-Bombay. If the Italian carrier wishes to carry traffic originating in Cairo and terminating in Bombay, it must secure permission from the Egyptian Government and from the Indian Government (since each country controls its own air space and landing rights). Both the Egyptian Government and the Indian Government will be reluctant to give rights to the Rome/Cairo route as it will undercut their own airlines on that route. Each will therefore wish to negotiate something in return before granting that permission. The Egyptian Government might settle for permission to carry passengers on a flight from Rome to London (which under the fifth freedom would originate in Cairo). The Italian Government might grant that permission and it would be a straight exchange of the Cairo/Bombay rights for the Italian carrier with the Rome/London rights for the Egyptian carrier. However, now the British Government is involved. It may very well permit the Egyptian carrier to land in London if, in turn, it is granted some other right; for instance, the rights to carry passengers on a flight from Rome to Cairo which originates in London. Not all negotiations are as simple as this, and even this example has not addressed the Indian Government's part in the discussions. However, it is sufficient to illustrate the complexity of the process.

It sometimes happens that a carrier is granted the rights over a certain route but does not exercise them immediately. After several years, however, when the time appears more advantageous for the carrier, it will then exercise these rights and schedule services.

A further complication will soon enter bilateral negotiations with European nations. The fifth freedom right allows an airline under the flag of one nation to transport passengers between two foreign countries. After 1993, when internal barriers were removed between the countries of the European Community (EC), it effectively became one nation and the region became a quasi-domestic market. The fifth freedom right then became cabotage (or eighth freedom) rights for U.S. and Canadian carriers. (Cabotage rights allow carriers to transport passengers between two points within a foreign country.) The United States, however, currently denies cabotage rights to foreign airlines arriving in the USA. It seems likely, therefore, that

this issue will have to be negotiated between the relevant governments.

Until recently, most countries except the United States had at least one airline which was wholly or partially owned by the national government. Air Canada was owned by the federal government until 1989 when it was privatized. Similarly, British Airways was once owned and then sold by the British Government. When a government designates a particular airline (or airlines) to fly a given international route it is called a **flag carrier**. These are often nationalized airlines. Almost all of the major European carriers are owned by their governments. When a country's airline is nationalized the government has an incentive to regulate the routes it controls. For example, countries may restrict the size of planes used by other nations' carriers for flights into and out of its borders. These and other factors have created a European environment characterized by high airfares and few discounts. When national borders were eliminated in 1993 some restrictions were lifted as liberalization occured. Another consequence of European deregulation is the formation of mega-carriers similar to those in America. Many European airlines are currently setting up alliances with a various international airlines in an effort to create a global transportation network. Air Canada and CAI are forming similar partnerships in an attempt to remain competitive in a rapidly changing marketplace. International partnerships allow affiliated airlines to coordinate marketing and synchronize scheduling. Allied carriers feed into each other's network. In effect, this practice extends the hub and spoke system to international routes and gateways.

Mutual Cooperation between Airlines

The airline industry is noteworthy for its policy of mutual cooperation between airlines of the world. A person may contact any airline office and be given information regarding the schedules, services and fares of any of the world's airlines. If so desired, reservations anywhere in the world will be made, the fare computed and collected, and the ticket issued. The airline industry is the only form of transportation that offers this kind of service. This cooperation among international carriers is a result of agreements negotiated through IATA. These agreements enable passengers to journey across the world on a number of airlines using a single ticket. IATA also acts as a clearinghouse for ticket administration and ensures standardization of travel documents and baggage checks. One of IATA's objectives is to organize a system of international fare rates followed by airlines and nations. For many years IATA strictly controlled international fares but it has recently come under attack, particularly in the USA, from those who see this function as obstructing deregulation.

As mentioned earlier, Transport Canada is the government agency responsible for domestic airline safety. The association which looks after such matters internationally is the International Civil Aviation Organization (ICAO), a branch of the United Nations. It was created to encourage cooperation between countries on airline matters. In particular, ICAO helps develop standards for aircraft, training, security and communication. Countries that wish to exchange airline routes negotiate such agreements through the ICAO.

Airline Marketing and Promotion

Airlines pursue business from two markets, the travelling public and the travel industry. Each client group is approached in a different manner. The general public is solicited directly by media advertising, and through window displays in airline offices and travel agencies. Airlines inform consumers of the routes they fly, the quality and reliability of their services, and their comfort, speed and price (see Figure 6.6). It therefore follows that potential purchasers will request more details on these areas. These topics form the basics of airline product knowledge required by

FIGURE 6.6
Airline consumer marketing emphasizes price, reliability and service.
Source: Canada 3000.

Canada 3000: Reliability and Service

FIGURE 6.7
Airline trade marketing emphasizes customer service.
Source: American Airlines.

NOBODY KNOWS AMERICA BETTER THAN AMERICAN.

When your clients' business takes them to the United States, there's no better way to get them there than American Airlines®. Because nobody knows the way better.

Through Terminal 3, we give your clients access to over 200 U.S. destinations - more than any other airline. So it's no surprise we also have the most daily non-stops to New York, Chicago, Dallas/Fort Worth and Nashville.

Meticulous service from the ground up has always been the American way. And your clients will be glad to benefit from our A'Advantage® travel awards program. In total, it's what your clients would expect from America's premier business airline. After all, we've made it our business.

BUSINESS IN AMERICA IS THE BUSINESS OF AMERICAN.

AmericanAirlines®
Something special in the air®

counsellors. Airlines also canvass business travellers through media advertising and by having their representatives make sales calls on companies. The sales message is different than that promoted to pleasure travellers. Emphasis is placed on frequency of service, convenience of routes, quality and comfort, and customer loyalty promotions such as frequent flyer programs. Again, these areas indicate the type of product knowledge that counsellors need.

When promoting their services to the travel industry, airlines employ media advertising and direct sales calls. Such advertising is placed almost exclusively in travel trade publications and has a different message from consumer promotions. Rather than attempting to persuade clients of the benefits of travelling on a particular carrier, as they do with consumers, airlines promote their services to the travel industry by informing them of the advantages of selling their particular airline to clients (see Figure 6.7). Airlines generally emphasize commissions and overrides, satisfied clients, and sales support such as trade presentations, special training seminars and familiarization trips. The main sales support for travel counsellors is the assistance provided by airline sales representatives. These individuals explain new fares and schedules, and ensure counsellors are updated on new

programs and promotions. Sales representatives also contribute by helping counsellors to arrange group travel.

In today's competitive environment, there is frequently little to choose between one airline and another. Airlines often fly the same routes, use the same types of aircraft, follow similar schedules and charge basically the same fares. An airline's marketing expertise thus becomes critical to its success. Even in a deregulated environment where there is considerable flexibility on pricing and route structure, airlines generally compete on reliability and service. Their marketing usually concentrates on the comfort of the seating, the excellence of the meals, or the convenience of the schedules (and sometimes of their hubs). These promotions are designed to attract passengers and, more importantly, to gain their loyalty. Perhaps the most successful marketing program in recent years is the frequent flyer plan. Under these plans, passengers become members of a particular airline's program and are awarded a number of points (usually based on distance travelled) each time they fly on the airline. For the same itinerary, higher points are generally earned by members who travel on a higher fare such as first class. At various point levels the credits can be traded for airline seats on the carrier as well as for other travel benefits. The more one flies with a carrier the more points and benefits one accumulates. These programs therefore encourage loyalty to particular airlines at the expense of their competitors. Almost all airlines have introduced such plans. As these became more popular, competition increased. Bonus points and special awards were introduced. Later, marketing agreements were made with other travel suppliers, such as hotels and car rental companies, to allow clients to gain points by staying at hotels or renting a car from specific companies associated with the airline's frequent flyer plan. The trend towards globalization in the airline industry has also been reflected in the frequent flyer programs. Joint agreements between airlines permit members of a program to gain points by flying on any associated carrier. Frequent flyer plans have proved so popular that there is now concern regarding the airlines' ability to meet their commitments if all outstanding points are redeemed as travel benefits. One consequence has been the introduction of shopping catalogues which permit plan members to use points for discounts on purchases. Several airlines have announced the official end of their program only to extend the deadline for fear of repercussions from the public. Other carriers have considered discontinuing their programs but are concerned that they will lose market share to airlines that decide to retain their plans. Frequent flyer programs have also created a dilemma for some counsellors. For example, a counsellor's responsibility to corporate clients is to arrange the most efficient and economical services. Some employees, however, request a counsellor to book a particular airline or hotel, simply because this will award frequent flyer points to the individual, even though the agency may have negotiated lower corporate rates with a competing airline or hotel chain.

Selling Air Travel

Earnings from the sale of airline tickets represent one of the components of travel agency income. Counsellors must therefore become thoroughly familiar with every feature of this product. The basics of airline product knowledge relate to the equipment used, the services offered, the fares available, and the governing rules and regulations. Deregulation radically changed these factors and many of them continue to vary on an almost daily basis. Two consequences of deregulation for travel agencies are increased retail competition and substantially more information. Travel agencies must be aware of the services and prices offered by their competitors, and counsellors must keep informed and updated on available schedule and fare options, as well as on changes to this information.

Airline Equipment

Travel counsellors should have at least a passing knowledge of equipment, the term used in the airline industry to refer to aircraft, and the fleets operated by different carriers. Since aircraft are extremely expensive machines, carriers must use them efficiently. Airlines attempt to do this by matching aircraft types with their routes, markets and clientele. Most airlines try to operate fleets with a minimum variety of aircraft types and manufacturers. This strategy reduces repairs and maintenance costs, decreases the amount of training required and improves the carrier's efficiency. A major carrier with a large route structure may opt to fly only Boeing aircraft, ranging from the wide-bodied 747 and 767 to the workhorse 737. Another company may choose Airbus products, whereas a small commuter airline may find turboprops such as the Dash-8 or Fokker F27 more appropriate to its needs. Each aircraft has different characteristics and counsellors will discover that clients have personal preferences. Travel counsellors therefore need to know the features of the most common airplanes in which clients will travel.

Aircraft information is found in two

locations. A complete list of aircraft performance statistics is given in both editions of the *Official Airline Guide* (OAG). This list identifies the dimensions, number of engines, flying range and seating capacity of the planes currently in use (Figure 6.8). It is a useful reference for help in answering basic questions posed by clients. Most passengers have at least a passing interest in the plane that will carry them on their journey. First-time travellers will generally ask more fundamental questions while experienced flyers may have very specific queries. The OAG can provide information on the size of aircraft, that is, whether it is a jumbo jet (wide-bodied aircraft), a regular jet (such as a DC-9 or 727), or a "puddle jumper" (Dash-8 or similar small aircraft). It also gives the aircraft's designation, such as a DC-8, DC-9 or DC-10. Note that size does not always increase with number. Another client concern may be which company manufactured the aircraft. The major aircraft manufacturers, such as Boeing, McDonnell Douglas and Lockheed, are American. There are, however, several smaller European aircraft manufacturers such as Fokker that build aircraft widely used around the

world. Other companies compete with the larger American companies by forming a consortium. Most notable is the European Airbus group. Some clients prefer to travel in particular types of aircraft either from experience, superstition or some other reason.

A major interest of clients is the number and type of engines on the plane and where they are located. For example, some clients feel safer in an aircraft with three engines rather than two. Others may not realize that many small commuter airlines use propeller-driven planes rather than jets. The location of the engines can be a critical factor in seat selection. Seats ahead of the engines are less noisy than those located behind them. It is clear then that planes with engines located in the tail section tend to be quieter for all passengers than those with engines under the wings. One of the simplest ways to identify different aircraft is by the number and locations of the engines. The Boeing 737, 757 and 767, and the Airbus 300, 310 and 320, have one engine under each wing. The DC-8 and Boeing 707 and 747 have two engines under each wing. The DC-9 and MD 80, however, are powered by two engines

FIGURE 6.8
Partial listing of aircraft performance statistics.
Reproduced by special permission from the April 1992 issue of the "Official Airline Guide Worldwide Edition." Copyright © 1992, Official Airline Guides, Inc. All rights reserved.

Aircraft Performance Statistics

Aircraft Categories: J-Jet T-Turboprop P-Propeller H-Helicopter A-Amphibian #-Passenger capacities may vary widely between carriers and between First Class or Tourist configuration. Aircraft performance statistics represented here are to be considered only as "typical" of an aircraft type. Due to the various series (models) of individual aircraft types and the engine options available, it is not feasible to show all the various combinations of performance statistics.

Code	Aircraft Type	No. of Engines	Aircraft Categories	Wide Body	Span ft.	Span in.	Length ft.	Length in.	Gross Weight lbs.	Passenger Capacity #	Pay Load lbs.	Cruising Speed m.p.h.	Range miles	Pressurized
NDE	Aerospatiale AS 350 Ecureuil/AS 355 Ecureuil 2	1 or 2	H		35	3/4	42	5 1/2	5,600	5/6		143	437	NO	
CRV	Aerospatiale Caravelle (All Series)	2	J		112	6	118	10 1/2	127,868	140		513	2,153		YES
ND2	Aerospatiale N 262/Frakes Mohawk 298	2	T		71	10 1/4	63	3	23,369	26/29	5,810	233	864		YES
NDC	Aerospatiale SN 601 Corvette	2	J		42	2 1/2	45	4 1/2	14,550	12/14		352	1,588		YES
ATR	Aerospatiale/Aeritalia (All Series)	2	T		88	9	89	1 1/2	44,070	42/74	15,763	286	2,785		YES
AT7	Aerospatiale/Aeritalia ATR72	2	T		88	9	89	1 1/2	44,070	64/74	15,763	286	1,657		YES
SSC	Aerospatiale/British Aerospace (BAC) Concorde	4	J		83	10	203	9	408,000	100	28,000	1,354	3,870		YES
AGH	Agusta A 109A	2	H		36	1	42	9 3/4	5,732	6/7		145	402	NO	
AB3	Airbus Industrie A300 (All Series)	2	J	YES	147	1	177	5	363,765	220/375	95,544	567	4,272		YES
310	Airbus Industrie A310 (All Series)	2	J	YES	144		153	1	330,695	218/280	79,560		5,113		YES
320	Airbus Industrie A320 (All Series)	2	J		111	3	123	3	162,040	164/179	45,686		3,305		YES
AN4	Antonov An24	2	P		72	2	37	6 1/2	7,935	44/55	1,590	112	444	NO	
BEC	Beechcraft (All Series)	2	P or T		54	6	43	9	12,500	4/14	4,786	325	2,170		YES
BE9	Beechcraft C99 Airliner	2	T		45	10 1/2	44	8 3/4	11,300	15	3,250	286	1,048	NO	
BE1	Beechcraft 1900	2	T		54	6	57	9 1/2	15,245	19	4,000	303	860		YES
BH2	Bell (All Series)	1 or 2	H		48	2 1/4	57	9 1/2	11,200	3/14		181	485	NO	
DHP	Boeing Canada DHC-2 Beaver	1	P		48		30	3	5,100	7		143	733	NO	
DHT	Boeing Canada DHC-6 Twin Otter	2	T		65		51	9	12,500	13/20	4,280	210	806	NO	
DH7	Boeing Canada DHC-7 Dash 7 Passenger	4	T		93		80	8	44,000	50/54	11,310	261	795		YES
DH8	Boeing Canada DHC-8 Dash 8 (All Series)	2	T		90		84	3	41,100	36/56	12,500	329	1,249		YES
707	Boeing 707 Passenger (All Series)	4	J		145	9	152	11	333,600	14/181	114,935				YES
727	Boeing 727 Passenger (All Series)	3	J		108		133	2	169,000	145	40,000				YES
72M	Boeing 727-100C/100QC Mixed Configuration	3	J		108		133	2	169,000	28/66	36,000				YES
72S	Boeing 727-200 (All Series)	3	J		108		153	2	209,500	14/189	42,500				YES
737	Boeing 737 Passenger (All Series)	2	J		93		94		110,000	103	30,000		2,500		YES
73S	Boeing 737 Passenger (All 200/200C Series)	2	J		93		100	2	115,500	120/130	34,493	541	2,596		YES
73M	Boeing 737-200C/200QC Mixed Configuration	2	J		93		100	2	115,500	65	31,445	541	2,913		YES
733	Boeing 737-300	2	J		94	9	109	7	124,500	128/149	35,600		1,860		YES
734	Boeing 737-400	2	J		94	9	119	7	138,500	146/170	40,300		2,487		YES
735	Boeing 737-500	2	J		94	9	101	9	60,554	108/132			2,996		YES
74M	Boeing 747 Mixed Configuration (All Series)	4	J	YES	195	8	231	10	775,000	452	166,200				YES
747	Boeing 747 Passenger (All Series)	4	J	YES	195	8	231	10	775,000	452/548	203,500	622	7,542		YES
74D	Boeing 747-300 Mixed Configuration	4	J	YES	195	8	231	10	775,000	496	177,900	630	7,254		YES
743	Boeing 747-300 Passenger	4	J	YES	195	8	231	10	775,000	496/592	151,100	630	7,254		YES
74E	Boeing 747-400 Mixed Configuration	4	J	YES	213		231	10	800,000	496	144,000		8,406		YES
744	Boeing 747-400 Passenger	4	J	YES	213		231	10	800,000	496/592	144,000		8,406		YES
74L	Boeing 747SP	4	J	YES	195	8	184	9	630,000	331/440	78,000	622	7,658		YES
757	Boeing 757-200 (All Series)	2	J		124	10	155	3	220,000	178/239		593	3,247		YES
767	Boeing 767 (All Series)	2	J	YES	156	1	159	2	300,000	216/290	43,200	593	3,639		YES
783	Boeing 767-200/300ER	2	J	YES	156	1	180	3	300,000	216/290	27,238	593	3,639		YES
B11	British Aerospace (BAC) One-Eleven (All Series)	2	J		93	6	107		104,500	89/119		472	1,865		YES
VCV	British Aerospace (BAC-Vickers) Viscount (All Series)	4	T		93	8 1/2	85	8	72,500	71		350	1,725		YES
HPH	British Aerospace (Handley Page) Herald	2	T		94	9	75	6	43,000	56		265	1,110		YES
DHH	British Aerospace (Hawker Siddeley) Heron	4	P		71	6	48	6	13,500	14/17	2,100	195		NO	
HS7	British Aerospace (Hawker Siddeley) 748 Passenger	2	T		98	6	67		46,500	40/58	11,894	281	1,543		YES
ATP	British Aerospace ATP	2	T		100	6	85	4	50,550	64/72	14,830	308	2,140		YES
J31	British Aerospace Jetstream 31	2	T		52		47	1 1/2	15,322	8/19	3,980	264	1,208		YES
146	British Aerospace 146 (All Series)	4	J		86	5	101	8 1/4	93,000	82/112	23,100	440	1,924		YES

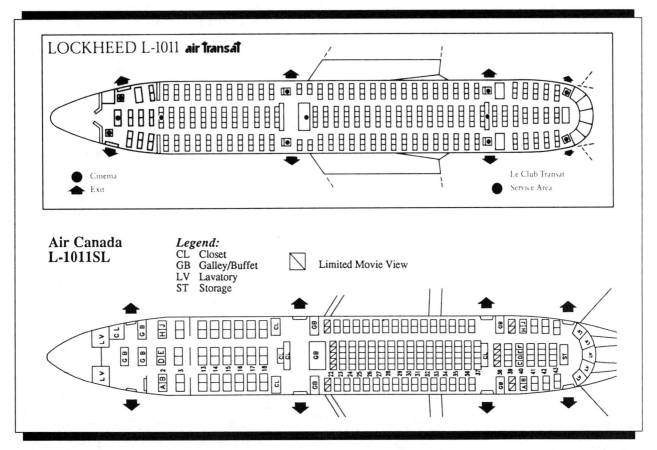

Air Canada
L-1011SL

Legend:
CL Closet
GB Galley/Buffet
LV Lavatory
ST Storage

⬜ Limited Movie View

located on either side of the tail while the Boeing 727 has three engines located on the tail. The L1011, DC-10 and MD 11 have one engine under each wing and one on the tail. As fuel costs continue to escalate, fuel efficiency has become a major consideration when airlines establish their fleets. Newer aircraft have more fuel-efficient engines. Environmental concerns have also led to a reduction in noise pollution created by aircraft.

The aircraft performance statistics in the OAG also display the seating capacity, or how many passengers a particular plane can carry. However, this information is usually shown as a range since each airline designs and modifies the interiors to suit their own needs and specifications. Of greater relevance, therefore, are the details of the particular fleets operated by individual airlines and the seating configurations they use. This information is often reproduced in company in-flight travel magazines and timetables, and is available directly from the airlines. Depending on an airline's route structure and market, its fleet may consist of long haul, short haul or a mix of aircraft types. If it is a commuter carrier it may fly only short take-off and landing (STOL) aircraft. STOL equipment is designed to operate from small airports close to city centres where long runways cannot be built. Commuter carriers have an advantage in that they reduce or eliminate the time required to travel between suburban airports and downtown. For short air trips the driving time can be longer than the actual flying time. Some carriers also operate special purpose aircraft such as those converted to carry freight or for charter operations.

One of the most important details of a carrier's fleet is the seating configuration in its aircraft. Seating configuration refers to the number and arrangement of the seats. For example, an aircraft may have two rows of two seats separated by a centre aisle, two rows of three seats separated by a centre aisle, or on wide-bodied aircraft ten or more seats

**FIGURE 6.9
An aircraft's seating configuration depends on its market and function.**
Source: Air Transat, a charter carrier (top) and Air Canada, a scheduled airline (bottom).

separated by two aisles. The number of seats on an aircraft depends on its size and intended purpose (see Figure 6.9). Planes dedicated to charter service usually have more seats with less legroom than those used for scheduled service. Similarly, seats in first class are wider than those in economy. The seating capacity of identical aircraft models therefore varies widely depending on the number of rows, and the number and type of seats in each row. As with seating, the number of galleys on a plane differs according to the type of equipment and its proposed use. Some clients have seating preferences while others can be guided by a counsellor's knowledge. For example, although seats over the wings usually give a smoother ride the view may be impeded. The location of engines in relation to the seating has already been noted. Since access to emergency exits must not be blocked, seats in those locations often have more legroom. Seats in front of a bulkhead sometimes have more legroom but may make it difficult to view the film. Since there is no seat in front of such seats, passengers must put carry-on luggage elsewhere. Counsellors should know where galleys and bathrooms are situated since these areas can be noisy and crowded. Window seats permit a view but make using the facilities an awkward experience. Aisle seats, on the other hand, allow passengers to conveniently reach facilities or take a brief exercise break. Where smoking sections exist they tend to be in the rear of the compartment.

FIGURE 6.10
First class seating offers passengers the most comfort.
Source: Korean Air.

Classes of Service

Airlines try to provide transportation to meet the needs of all their customers. Thus they compete in the classes of service they offer. At one time there were just two classes of service, first and economy (sometimes called coach or tourist). Today a third type, business class, has been added. Competition is greatest for business travellers since they generally travel on a full price fare. However, these clients often select a carrier for its schedule rather than for the comfort of its seats.

First class in all jet aircraft is located in the forward section of the plane. Seats are wider, have more padding, and there is more legroom to allow for a greater pitch in reclining the seat (Figure 6.10). On some routes first class passengers can pay a surcharge for premium service which offers a seat that almost totally reclines to become a sleeper. Other carriers have introduced a limited number of berths for first class passengers on long flights, such as across the Pacific Ocean. First class offers a choice of meals which are frequently served on china and accompanied by cutlery and linen napkins, wines, champagne and liquor. Bar service is complimentary, as are the high quality earphones supplied for listening to movie soundtracks or music tapes. The first class cabin has a higher ratio of galleys and flight attendants to passengers and therefore service is better and more personalized. First class passengers are generally boarded and disembarked prior to other travellers. Special baggage service and VIP lounge service are provided.

Business class was introduced in the 1980s to recognize the carriers' reliance on business travellers who provide year-round income, and usually pay full fare since their plans are often changed or made at the last minute. The business class section is generally located between the first class cabin and the economy class cabin. Business class is reserved for those passengers paying full economy airfare as opposed to those benefiting from various reduced or discounted excursion fares.

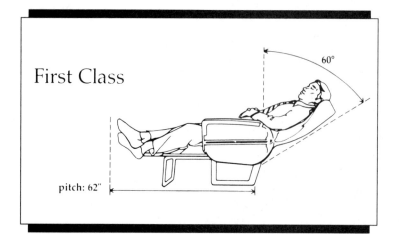

First Class

60°

pitch: 62"

Seats are wider and meal service is somewhat more elaborate than in economy class. Bar service is complimentary. On longer flights many airlines offer an upgraded business class with higher quality wines and other extras.

The economy class section occupies the largest part of the aircraft. Seats are not as wide, legroom is more restricted and the reclining pitch is not as great as in the other sections (Figure 6.11). However, it is still comfortable, adequate accommodation. Bar service is available, sometimes at a charge. Meals, though not as extensive as in first class, are complimentary. The economy class section of the aircraft may be divided between full economy and various promotional fares. The remaining seats are designated as seat sale product.

The fare paid by a passenger determines the class of service and thus the area of the plane where the traveller is seated. Airlines like any other business enterprise seek to make a profit. To this end, carriers have experimented with planes dedicated exclusively to high revenue passengers such as all first class or all business class service. Since this is impractical for most routes airlines offer a mix of classes of service. Many different types of fares may be available within a particular class of service. Depending on the route, season and other factors, carriers adjust the number of seats in each fare type on a plane to achieve the most profitable arrangement. The number of low priced seats, particularly seat sale products, is restricted and sells very quickly. The seating arrangements, however, are somewhat fluid. The number of seats in a given category changes according to how many have been sold, how far in the future is the flight, and how popular it is likely to be. Airlines must try to balance the need for full flights with the fact that there are always passengers who book a seat but do not arrive for the flight (no-shows). The result is that almost every airline overbooks its flights. Counsellors should therefore check to see whether seats are available in the class of service desired by a client before quoting fares.

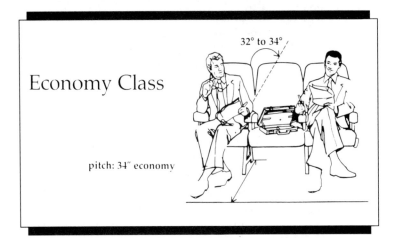

pitch: 34″ economy

32° to 34°

FIGURE 6.11
Economy class is quite comfortable but passengers have less space than in first or business class.
Source: Korean Air.

Catering

Most airlines promote the choice and style of meals served during flight as a selling feature. In fact, a small number of catering companies supply in-flight meals and snacks for all airlines according to the individual wishes of each carrier. Passengers' meals are generally prepared and cooked some hours prior to flight time and then immediately chilled to reduce bacteria growth. Approximately one hour prior to departure the meals are placed on board the aircraft and refrigerated. Meals are then reheated for serving. Complete meals are usually served on the same tray at the same time. Some airlines have, however, experimented with different schedules. For example, passengers can choose when to eat or which dishes to receive. Airlines discovered that many business travellers prefer to sleep rather than have dessert so they serve dessert separately. This procedure not only increases customer satisfaction, but it also cuts serving time by half and reduces wastage.

Over 2000 items are placed on board any aircraft. Cigarettes and reading material are packed, as well as meals, snacks, alcoholic beverages and soft drinks. The inventory of goods loaded demands considerable planning and coordination to ensure satisfied passengers. Individual dietary requirements can be met if requested sufficiently in advance of the travel date. Airlines and computer reservations systems can supply details of the variety of cuisine available. The following special meals are currently offered: low cholesterol; low sodium; diabetic; low calorie; gluten-free; bland; lacto-ovo vegetarian; pure vegetarian; Moslem; Hindu; kosher.

Check-In Procedures

Passengers must arrive at the airport in good time for their flight. Most carriers retain the right to cancel the reservation of any passenger who fails to appear at the aircraft departure area at least ten minutes prior to departure time. However, travellers also need sufficient time to check their baggage, have boarding passes issued by the airline, and pass through the security checks which have become more stringent and time-consuming with the growth of hijacking and terrorism. Passengers may also wish to shop at a duty-free store. Carriers set check-in time limits ranging from one to three hours prior to the flight time to allow for these procedures. Security checks generally take the form of an X-ray examination of both checked and carry-on luggage, and an electronic screening of individual passengers. Anything potentially dangerous is removed and may be claimed at the destination. Refusal to undergo such examination may cause a passenger to be denied permission to board the aircraft. At some airports each item of baggage may be opened for a thorough inspection. Airlines now require all baggage to be accompanied by a passenger.

Each airline has a different procedure for seat selection. Passengers typically choose their seats when checking in, however, the practice of offering seat selection at the time the reservation is made is becoming more common. Seating charts for some airlines can be reproduced on computer terminal screens so that counsellors can advise clients which seats are available at the time of booking. At enroute cities and on certain services no seats are assigned or may be selected. Passengers simply choose from the empty seats available on the plane.

This practice is fairly common in more remote locations, on local services, and in smaller aircraft.

On occasion, too many passengers arrive for a flight and late passengers are bumped, that is, not allowed to board the aircraft. Bumped passengers will usually be accommodated on the next available flight. To avoid being bumped, passengers should confirm or reconfirm onward and return flights. They should also arrive with enough time to check in and to reach the departure lounge. Extra time should be allowed when travelling at the peak periods of 7:00 a.m. to 9:00 a.m. and 4:30 p.m. to 7:00 p.m. on weekdays. Thursday, Friday or Sunday evenings, and Monday or Saturday mornings are also busy at most airports. Passengers who are bumped may be compensated if they possess valid tickets for the flight and a confirmed reservation which has been properly recorded in the carrier's reservation system. In addition, they must check in at the gate within the time limits specified by the carrier and they must comply with the carrier's reconfirmation requirements. Deregulation appears to have increased the incidence of overbooking, particularly in the United States, and bumping has become a feature of air transportation in that country.

As well as ensuring sufficient time to check in, passengers who make a connection (change planes at an airport) must be certain that they meet the minimum connecting time requirement. This is the minimum time which is permitted between the arrival of a flight and the departure of its connecting flight. Connecting passengers may have to walk from one end of a terminal to the other to make their connection. Or it may be necessary to board a bus and transfer to another terminal. Such transfers take time. Airlines have therefore calculated the minimum connecting time required at various airports for various journeys. This information is reproduced in the OAG (see Figure 6.12). The time varies depending on the size of the airport, on whether the connection is on-line (with the same carrier) or interline (changing to another carrier), and on the location of the relevant airline gates. Airlines will not accept a reservation for an itinerary that does not allow sufficient time between connections. A client may, however, ask a counsellor to book a connection which does not meet this requirement. In this situation, counsellors should advise the client that the minimum connection time must be complied with for insurance policies to be valid. If, for example, sufficient time has not been allowed between a flight arrival and a scheduled cruise departure, the client would not be covered for missing the sailing. If the client persists in requesting the shorter connection, make the booking and note the advice on the client file so that the client becomes responsible for the decision.

Baggage Handling

The purchase of an airline ticket permits the traveller to take a certain quantity of luggage on the trip. The amount varies depending on the carrier, the type of fare and the area of the world. In general, passengers may check two suitcases and bring one piece of carry-on luggage. Airlines regard baggage as anything that is considered necessary for the wear, use, comfort and convenience of the passenger for the purpose of the journey. Baggage is classified by piece or by weight according to the region where the flight operates. For example, the piece concept is used in North America and on transatlantic flights whereas within Europe carriers follow the weight concept. Baggage regulations are printed in the OAG. Under the piece concept, two pieces of baggage may be checked free of charge provided that one piece does not exceed a linear measurement (length + width + height) of 62 inches and the other does not exceed 55 inches. In addition, no single piece weighing more than 70 pounds will be accepted. For baggage assessed by weight, any number of pieces including carry-on luggage may be checked to a total weight of 20 kilos (44 pounds) for economy class passengers and 30 kilos (66 pounds) for first class passengers. Carry-on baggage is limited to 9" x 16" x 20" in size. For safety reasons, such luggage must be placed under the seat in front of the passenger or in an enclosed overhead storage bin in the aircraft. Travellers with more than the allowable weight of luggage must pay an extra fee if they wish their additional baggage to be carried. The charges differ for each airline and again the amounts are noted in the OAG. Airlines require that

FIGURE 6.12
Minimum connecting times are listed in the OAG.

Reprinted by special permission from January 1990 issue of the "Official Airline Guide Worldwide Edition." Copyright © 1990, Official Airline Guide, Inc. All rights reserved.

FOR ANY CITY/AIRPORT NOT LISTED ALLOW 20 MINUTES DOMESTIC; 60 MINUTES INTERNATIONAL

CITY	INTERLINE	ON-LINE	CITY	INTERLINE	ON-LINE
DILLINGHAM, ALASKA, USA			**EDMONTON, ALBERTA, CANADA-CONT.**		
STANDARD	:20		TRANSBORDER TO DOMESTIC	1:15	
AS TO BE	:15		NW TO AC	1:00	
DINARD, FRANCE			AC TO AC (FLTS 1950-1976		
DOMESTIC STANDARD	:30		& 1982-1989)		1:00
INTERNATIONAL			INTERNATIONAL		
DOMESTIC TO INT'L	:50		DOMESTIC TO INT'L	:45	
INT'L TO DOMESTIC	:50		TRANSBORDER TO INT'L	1:15	
INT'L TO INT'L	:40		INT'L TO DOMESTIC	1:30	
JY		:30	INT'L TO TRANSBORDER	1:30	
DIPOLOG, PHILIPPINES			INT'L TO INT'L	1:00	
STANDARD	:20		YXD (MUNICIPAL)		
PR		:30	DOMESTIC STANDARD	:30	
DIRE DAWA, ETHIOPIA			INTERNATIONAL		
DOMESTIC STANDARD	:30		DOMESTIC TO INT'L	:30	
INTERNATIONAL			INT'L TO DOMESTIC	:30	
DOMESTIC TO INT'L	1:00		INT'L TO INT'L	:30	
INT'L TO DOMESTIC	1:00		INTER-AIRPORT SURFACE		
INT'L TO INT'L	:45		CONNECTIONS:		
DJIBOUTI, DJIBOUTI			YEG TO YXD & V.V.:		
INTERNATIONAL			DOMESTIC STANDARD	2:00	
ALL SERVICES	1:00		TRANSBORDER TO DOMESTIC	2:00	
DOHA, QATAR			DOMESTIC TO INT'L	2:00	
DOMESTIC STANDARD	1:00		INT'L TO DOMESTIC	2:00	
GF		:50	INT'L TO INT'L	2:00	
INTERNATIONAL			**EINDHOVEN, NETHERLANDS**		
DOMESTIC TO INT'L	1:00		DOMESTIC STANDARD	:30	
GF		:50	INTERNATIONAL		
INT'L TO DOMESTIC	1:00		DOMESTIC TO INT'L	:30	
GF		:50	INT'L TO DOMESTIC	:30	
INT'L TO INT'L	1:00		INT'L TO INT'L	:30	
GF		:50	HN		:10

the passenger's name appear on the outside of all checked baggage. In 1983 IATA airlines made it mandatory for each piece of luggage to have external identification.

When baggage is checked each item is tagged to its destination. The passenger receives baggage claim checks which are attached to the ticket cover. These stubs should be retained until baggage is collected at the end of the flight. On occasion, however, baggage will be lost or damaged in transit. An airline will pay an amount equal to the proven loss up to the limit specified in its tariff for lost or damaged baggage. This sum should not be confused with the travel insurance which can be purchased separately for baggage. Carrier liability on international flights is limited by international treaty to approximately US$20 per kilo for checked baggage. The limit for carry-on baggage is US$400 per passenger. A higher value can be declared on baggage for an additional charge. Since there are variations between carriers, counsellors should consult the airline concerned for details. Passengers should be advised to immediately report misplaced or delayed baggage at the airport. If the baggage is not located within three days the carrier should send claim forms to the passenger. To be valid, claims must be filed within 45 days for domestic flights and within 21 days for international flights. Damaged luggage should also be reported immediately. The claim period for damaged luggage is 45 days for domestic flights and seven days for international flights.

Basic product knowledge of airline equipment, route structures, services and operations have now been discussed. Some factors involved in selling airline tickets have been reviewed. Closing the sale, however, depends to a large extent on the schedules and availability of suitable flights, and on the fares charged. The remainder of this chapter discusses sources of this information. The growth of automation in the airline industry means that these details can be accessed through airline reservations systems. For reasons already covered, however, knowledge of the print resources and their use are essential for professionals in the travel industry.

Using the Official Airline Guides

The Official Airline Guide (OAG) is one of the travel industry's standard references. It may in fact be the most frequently used resource in a travel agency. Two printed editions of the OAG are available. The North American or domestic edition (NAOAG) is published twice monthly. It lists all flights within and between Canada, USA including Alaska and Hawaii, Mexico, Bermuda, the Bahamas, and the Caribbean. Flight schedules for all other destinations are listed in the worldwide edition (WWOAG) which is published monthly. An electronic edition of the OAG can be accessed through any computer terminal connected to a modem and telephone line. Rather than paying a subscription as one does with the printed editions, subscribers to the electronic edition pay a one-time initial fee and a monthly charge based on usage. The same format for schedules is used in both the printed and electronic editions.

The OAG electronic edition provides flight schedules updated weekly and domestic fares updated on a daily basis whereas the printed editions show a fare range. The main application of the OAG, however, is in constructing flight itineraries. Fares should be used only as a guide and should never be quoted to a client. The schedule for any itinerary in the world, no matter how simple or how complex, can be created using a current OAG. The counsellor's principal goal when planning trips is to find the most convenient routing for the client. The most convenient routing is generally the most direct itinerary, involving the shortest travel time and the minimum of connections or stops. Typically, this routing will also lead to the lowest fare.

Since air transportation is the mainstay of most travel agency income, and since flight schedules and routings form the basis of airline systems, it is essential that counsellors know how to read and apply the OAGs. Each edition of the OAG contains a page showing how to read the listings. The publisher also sells programmed instructional booklets to train beginners in its use. It is therefore unnecessary to explain these aspects in detail in this text. However, a few general comments will be made. By and large, the NAOAG and WWOAG follow the same format and contain the same type of information. Both have a table of contents indicating all of the information that can be found in the publication. In addition to flight schedules, OAGs contain flight itineraries, minimum connecting times, baggage allowances, carrier details and aircraft performance statistics, and other points. Codes and abbreviations are used extensively to assist in presenting the volume of information and these too are explained. Airlines are given a carrier code, comprising two letters or a number and a letter, which not only appears in the OAG but is also used on airline tickets and on arrival and departure screens at airports. Airports and cities have a three-letter code. These codes are used to identify cities with more than one airport, to reduce confusion over places with the same name, and to avoid language difficulties.

Both the NAOAG and the WWOAG display all flight schedules alphabetically by destination city. The listing begins with information on the destination city, such as airport code(s) and ground transportation data. The originating cities are presented alphabetically following the destination city. The listings are displayed chronologically, first showing the direct flights and then specifying the connections. Each listing indicates the days the flight operates, the departure and arrival times (in local time), the flight number, classes of service available on the flight, the equipment used, and the number of stops made. There are some differences between the displays shown in the NAOAG and those in the WWOAG. In the NAOAG times are shown in the 12-hour clock, employing "a" for "a.m." and "p" for "p.m." For example, 1:15 p.m. is displayed as 1:15p (see Figure 6.13). In the WWOAG, however, the 24-hour clock is used. Here, 1:15 p.m. is displayed as 1315. The NAOAG listings indicate each city's time zone, whereas the WWOAG contains an International Standard Time Chart but does not show individual time zones in its displays. Similarly, the NAOAG listings identify the meal service available

Freq.	Leave	Arrive	Flight	Class	Eq	Ml	S
To LITTLE ROCK, ARKANSAS					**CST LIT**		
	8:10a	9:34a MEM	NW 870	FYBMH	D9S	S	0
D- 8JAN	10:25a MEM	**11:20a**	NW 1562	FYBMH	D9S		0
	11:35a	12:57P MEM	NW 872	FYBMH	DC9	S	0
	2:05P MEM	**2:43P**	DL 758	FYBMQ	M80		0
	12:30P	1:44P DFW	AA 684	FYBMV	72S		0
D-30JAN	2:33P DFW	**3:41P**	AA 506	FYBMV	M80		0
X6	**1:25P**	2:20P MCI	ZV 1608	YQBMK	SWM		0
	2:50P MCI	**4:50P**	ZV 1537	YQBMK	SWM		1
X6	**5:00P**	6:20P MEM	NW 876	FYBMH	DC9	S	0
D- 8JAN	7:30P MEM	**8:22P**	NW 857	FYBMH	D9S		0
X6	**5:00P**	6:20P MEM	NW 876	FYBMH	DC9	S	0
E- 9JAN	7:35P MEM	**8:24P**	NW 857	FYBMH	D9S		0
X6	**5:57P**	7:12P DFW	AA 502	FYBMV	72S		0
D- 7JAN	7:59P DFW	**9:05P**	AA 1016	FYBMV	M80		0
	5:57P	7:12P DFW	AA 1203	FYBMV	72S		0
E- 8JAN	7:59P DFW	**9:05P**	AA 1016	FYBMV	M80		0
D-30JAN							
6	**5:57P**	7:12P DFW	AA 486	FYBMV	72S		0
D- 6JAN	7:59P DFW	**9:05P**	AA 1016	FYBMV	M80		0
To LLOYDMINSTER, SASK					**MST YLL**		
8.0 MI NW 15 MIN R							
From **CALGARY, ALBERTA**					**MST YYC**		
X67	6:25a	7:35a	CP★ 1164	YBHV	BE9	S	0
X67	9:30a	10:40a	CP★ 1166	YBHV	BE9		0
X67	4:45P	5:55P	CP★ 1168	YBHV	BE9	S	0
7	5:00P	6:10P	CP★ 1164	YBHV	BE9	S	0
COLD LAKE, ALBERTA					**MST YOD**		
7	7:15P	7:50P	CP★ 1165	YBHV	BE9		0
To LONDON, ONTARIO					**EST YXU**		
7.0 MI NE 30 MIN L $3.50 R							
From **ANTIGUA, WEST INDIES**					**AST ANU**		
1	**10:00a**	1:35P YYZ	BW 600	FYB	L15		0
	4:55P YYZ	**5:35P**	AC★ 1217	YMBHV	DH8		0
ASHEVILLE, NORTH CAROLINA					**EST AVL**		
X67	7:00a	11:20a	DL★ 3174	YBMQH	SWM		2
			DL3174 EFFECTIVE		3JAN		
CALGARY, ALBERTA					**MST YYC**		
X7	**12:40a**	6:10a YYZ	AC 146	FJYMB	767	B	0
	9:00a YYZ	**9:40a**	AC★ 1231	YMBHV	DH8		0
7	**12:40a**	6:10a YYZ	AC 160	FJYMB	767	B	0
	9:00a YYZ	**9:40a**	AC★ 1231	YMBHV	DH8		0
X6	**7:20a**	12:50P YYZ	AC 110	FJYMB	767	B	0
	1:40P YYZ	**2:20P**	AC★ 1209	YMBHV	DH8		0
	7:20a	12:50P YYZ	AC 110	FJYMB	767	B	0
	2:30P YYZ	**3:10P**	AC★ 1211	YMBHV	DH8		0
7	**9:25a**	2:55P YYZ	AC 118	JYMBH	72S	L	0
	3:55P YYZ	**4:35P**	AC★ 1215	YMBHV	DH8		0
X67	**9:25a**	2:55P YYZ	AC 118	FJYMB	767	L	0
	4:55P YYZ	**5:35P**	AC★ 1217	YMBHV	DH8		0
	12:00n	5:30P YYZ	AC 120	FJYMB	767	L	0
	7:00P YYZ	**7:40P**	AC★ 1221	YMBHV	DH8		0
X6	**4:00P**	9:30P YYZ	AC 140	FJYMB	767	D	0
	10:15P YYZ	**10:55P**	AC★ 1239	YMBHV	DH8		0
CINCINNATI, OHIO (C-CVG)					**EST CVG**		
X67	9:05a C	11:20a	DL★ 3174	YBMQH	SWM		1
			DL3174 EFFECTIVE		3JAN		
CLEVELAND, OHIO (C-CLE)					**EST CLE**		
X67	10:35a C	11:20a	DL★ 3174	YBMQH	SWM		0
			DL3174 EFFECTIVE		3JAN		
X6	7:50P C	8:35P	DL★ 3150	YBMQH	SWM		0
			DL3150 EFFECTIVE		3JAN		
			EX		5JAN		
DETROIT, MICHIGAN (M-DTW)					**EST DTT**		
X67	9:45a M	10:30a	AC★ 1482	YMBHV	DH8		0
6	11:30a M	12:15P	AC★ 1484	YMBHV	DH8	S	0
X67	12:15P M	1:00P	AC★ 1484	YMBHV	DH8		0
X67	4:30P M	5:15P	AC★ 1494	YMBHV	DH8		0
67	5:00P M	5:45P	AC★ 1494	YMBHV	DH8		0
X6	9:50P M	10:35P	AC★ 1498	YMBHV	DH8	S	0
EDMONTON, ALBERTA (I-YEG)					**MST YEG**		
X7	**12:45a** I	6:10a YYZ	AC 158	FJYMB	767	B	0
	9:00a YYZ	**9:40a**	AC★ 1231	YMBHV	DH8		0
	7:45a I	1:15P YYZ	AC 106	FJYMB	767	B	0
	2:30P YYZ	**3:10P**	AC★ 1211	YMBHV	DH8		0
	12:00n I	5:28P YYZ	AC 126	FJYMB	767	L	0
	7:00P YYZ	**7:40P**	AC★ 1221	YMBHV	DH8		0
X6	**2:10P** I	8:44P YYZ	AC 196	JYMBH	72S	SD	1
	10:15P YYZ	**10:55P**	AC★ 1239	YMBHV	DH8		0
6	**11:15P** I	6:10a YYZ	AC 160	FJYMB	767	B	1
	9:00a YYZ	**9:40a**	AC★ 1231	YMBHV	DH8		0
HALIFAX, NS (H-YHZ)					**AST YHZ**		
X7	**6:33a** H	8:00a YYZ	AC 603	YBHV	D9S	B	0
	9:00a YYZ	**9:40a**	AC★ 1231	YMBHV	DH8		0
7	**6:33a** H	7:56a YYZ	AC 603	JYBHV	72S	B	0
	9:00a YYZ	**9:40a**	AC★ 1231	YMBHV	DH8		0
	8:20a H	9:45a YYZ	AC 605	JYBHV	72S	B	0
	11:00a YYZ	**11:35a**	CP★ 1984	YBHV	J31		0
	11:45a H	1:08P YYZ	AC 127	FJYMB	767	L	0
	2:30P YYZ	**3:10P**	AC★ 1211	YMBHV	DH8		0
6	**2:35P** H	3:58P YYZ	AC 615	JYBHV	72S	S	0
	4:55P YYZ	**5:35P**	AC★ 1217	YMBHV	DH8		0

FIGURE 6.13
The OAG publishes airline schedules in a standard format.
Reprinted by special permission from the January 1, 1990 issue of the "Official Airline Guide North American Edition." Copyright © 1990, Official Airline Guides, Inc. All rights reserved.

on a flight. The WWOAG, however, does not give this information but instead it has a different column which states the starting and ending dates for particular services.

Counsellors will occasionally be unable to locate a listing, either direct or as a connection, for a client's itinerary and will have to construct an itinerary. Several factors must then be considered. Clients prefer a routing that involves the fewest number of changes and the fastest travel time. However, this requires a knowledge of geography and carrier route structures. The widespread use of the hub and spoke system means that the most direct routing is not always the most convenient for the client. Another consideration is the minimum connecting time required to make the connection. A table of minimum connecting times is reproduced in the OAG to assist counsellors to plan itineraries. The minimum connecting times section tends to be more important in the WWOAG as there are direct flights to fewer international destinations than in the domestic market.

Airline Fares and Tariffs

The topic of airline tariff and ticketing merits special attention by working and prospective travel counsellors. Fares, rules, references and procedures change with such speed and regularity that the subject cannot be treated here in sufficient depth, or with the certainty that the information will remain accurate. However, the basic sources of information and the general principles involved are discussed below. Readers are referred to current issues of the sources mentioned for up-to-date information.

Types of Airline Fares

At one time the price of a scheduled airline ticket was determined by the distance travelled. To some extent this is still the case for international fares. Since deregulation, however, this method is no longer used to price domestic flights. Four other factors help determine the price of an airline ticket:

- Class of service.
- Type of journey.
- Type of service.
- Restrictions on the fare.

Type of Journey

The class of service was discussed above. Four types of journey are possible and each influences the pricing of an airline ticket. Journeys may be one way, round trip, circle trip or open jaw. **Circle trips** are similar to round trips except that one leg of the trip has a different carrier, routing or class of service. An **open jaw** trip is one in which the traveller either departs on the return leg of a jour-ney from a destination other than the original, or alternatively returns to a point which differs from the original starting point of the trip. For example, a client may fly from Toronto to London for a vacation in Britain. After travelling around the country, the client returns to Toronto but begins the return journey in Glasgow. Alternatively, a client may fly Vancouver to San Francisco and return from San Francisco to Calgary. Both ex-cursions are examples of open jaw trips.

Type of Service

Carriers offer a variety of services on their routes. Nonstop service does not stop between origin and destination. On a **direct** or **through service**, the plane flies directly from one city to another. The aircraft, however, may make stops en route but the passenger must remain on the plane or in the in-transit lounge. Passengers on a **connecting flight** must change planes at some point between the origin and destination. On-line connec-tions are made when the passenger changes aircraft but continues to fly with the same carrier. An interline connection is made when the passenger not only changes planes but also transfers from one airline to another at the connecting city. Stopover flights permit passengers to disembark the aircraft at intermediate cities and remain there for some time before continuing with the next leg of the journey.

Fare Restrictions

Airfares may be normal or restricted. Normal fares are first class, business class and economy. These fares have no restrictions such as advance reservation requirements or minimum stay stipulations. Such tickets are valid for one year from the date of the first flight and can be extended if not used within that period. Even before deregulation, competition between airlines led to the introduction of excursion and discounted fares. Since these fares are less expensive than normal fares, they are sold with a number of conditions attached. Most require advance reservation and a minimum (and sometimes maximum) stay limit is placed on the trip. Travel dates are predetermined, changes or cancellations are permitted only on the payment of a penalty (and sometimes are not allowed at all), and travel is usually confined to the airline which issues the ticket. As discussed earlier, airlines limit the number of seats available at these fares to encourage travellers to book early. Excursion fares are targeted at vacation travellers committed to their travel plans. On the other hand, promotional fares such as seat sales are aimed at those who had not intended to travel or whose plans were uncertain. Promotional fares are also used to increase traffic during slow periods and to boost new routes. There is a tendency for the conditions governing promotional fares to become more restrictive as the price drops. Further, the nature of promotional fares means that they tend to appear, disappear and change according to circumstances. Counsellors must therefore make a special attempt to stay abreast of this aspect of product knowledge. The more restrictions there are on a fare, the more time it requires to explain and sell it to a client.

As discussed earlier, even in the current deregulated environment each airline must document its fares and routes with the appropriate government agency. When travel counsellors sell an airline ticket they must do so at the fare set by the carrier. Since air fares can and do change with a speed which can be alarming, a counsellor cannot guarantee a fare quoted to a client unless an airline ticket is issued at the time the fare is received from the carrier. The correct fare can be found in several places:

- Filed in the relevant airline tariff books (the ATPCO for domestic air fares and the Air Tariff for international travel).
- Airline reservations departments.
- Airline computer reservations systems (CRS).
- Bulletins or rate sheets issued by carriers.

The tariff books were once the prime sources of accurate information, but automated reservations systems are now so sophisticated, accurate and up-to-date that most agencies consider the tariffs obsolete. Nevertheless, travel counsellors should be familiar with these sources and their use. Computer systems sometimes break down and it may be neither convenient nor appropriate to ask a client to return at another time. Similarly, one cannot always rely on being able to communicate with an airline by telephone (particularly if the computer system is "down"). In addition, clients may request a fare quote for an itinerary which is not in the airline CRS. Finally, travel counsellors may simply wish to maintain their professional expertise and product knowledge. A travel counsellor who can accurately and efficiently construct fares and routings for any itinerary, no matter how complex, is a highly prized employee.

In general, tariffs remain an accurate reference for air fares. However, even a current tariff may be partially incorrect for any of several reasons. Tariffs consist of several parts that are issued on a regular basis varying from two weeks to one year. Since fares constantly change, and do so at different times in different parts of the world, a fare or rule that was correct when the tariff was printed could change just before publication. Alternatively, a fare may simply become outdated during the life of the tariff. Alternatively, a fare that was scheduled to come into effect on a certain date does not receive the necessary government approvals. In an effort to remain as current as possible, the international tariff often publishes fares which are subject to government approval. It is always necessary to ascertain if approvals for such fares were in fact obtained. Since many international fares from Canada and the USA are constructed using special fares which are added to a standard fare from designated gateway cities, occasional changes to these add-on fares may result in a situation where the fare is correct from the gateway city, say Montreal, but incorrect from an interior city such as Edmonton. In addition, most international fares are subject to currency procedures which can increase or decrease the selling fare; a change in this area can also affect the accuracy of a given fare. It is therefore common to have a tariff which is partly correct and partly incorrect. For this reason, both the domestic and international tariffs print a disclaimer which notifies the user that fares and rules contained in the tariff are subject to change.

Domestic Fares and Tariffs

Just as the term "domestic" has a specific meaning when used in connection with the OAG, domestic air fares and rules are similarly defined. Domestic air traffic is that performed:

- Solely within the USA, including Hawaii and Alaska.
- Solely within Canada.
- Between Canada and the USA, including Hawaii and Alaska.

Thus, Toronto to Boston, Chicago to San Francisco, New York to Honolulu,

Anchorage to Seattle, Calgary to Hilo (Hawaii), and Winnipeg to Montreal, are defined as domestic air journeys.

Airline fares and rules in the domestic area are monitored by the Air Transport Association of Canada (ATAC) and the Air Transport Association of America (ATA), organizations which serve somewhat similar needs in Canada and the USA, respectively. Both are airline conferences similar to IATA. ATAC consists of airlines which operate scheduled routes within Canada while the ATA's members are carriers operating within the USA and between Canada and the USA. (CAIL and Air Canada are associate members of the ATA and as such follow ATA procedures within the USA.) Neither body has the power to set fares. However, they help standardize ticketing procedures, baggage handling and interline agreements between their member airlines.

The ATA based in Washington, DC is the trade organization of virtually all scheduled carriers operating in and between Canada and the USA. The ATA follows appointment procedures similar to IATA in the matter of Sales Agency Agreements with appointed travel agents. Some areas the ATA does not control are Canada/USA transpacific flights, whether or not via Hawaii, and flights between Canada/USA and the Bahamas, Bermuda or Caribbean Sea (including Puerto Rico which is a U.S. possession), Mexico and Europe. The ATA exerts jurisdiction only within the USA.

Using the Domestic Tariff

Although the domestic OAG is an extremely useful publication which can be a reasonably accurate guide to air fares, it is not an official tariff and should not be used as such. A fare from the OAG should be verified by checking with the airline concerned or by checking with the official tariff for domestic travel, the ATPCO. The tariff's publisher, Airline

PUBLICATION	CONTENTS	FREQUENCY
PART 1: The Official United States Passenger Tariff.	Local fares and fare rules for transportation wholly within the continental United States, Hawaii and Alaska.	Issued every four weeks.
PART II: The Official Canadian Passenger Tariff.	Local and joint fares, and fare rules for transportation wholly within Canada, and between the United States and Canada.	Issued every two weeks.
PART III: The Official North American Routing Guide.	Local routings for North America.	Issued every eight weeks
PART IV: The Domestic General Rules Tariff.	General rules for transportation within the United States.	One issue, with revisions supplied as required.
PART V: The Canadian General Rules Tariff.	General rules for transportation within Canada, and between the United States and Canada.	One issue, with revisions supplied as required.
PART VI: The Joint Passenger Fares Tariff.	Joint fares to, from and within Canada.	Issued every eight weeks.
PART VII: The Visit Another Country Tariff.	Fares and rules for travel in another country. Used only for residents of countries other than Canada or the United States.	Issued every four weeks.
PART VIII: The Western Hemisphere Passenger Tariff.	Fares and rules within and between the Western Hemisphere, except within and between the United States and Canada.	Issued every two weeks.
PART IX: The International General Rules Tariff.	General rules for international transportation. Since this tariff deals with international destinations subject to IATA regulations, fares and rules are also published in the Air Tariff.	Issued every four weeks.

Tariff Publishing Company Inc. of Washington DC, acts as agent for all airlines which submit their tariffs for publication.

The ATPCO consists of a number of sections published with varying frequency (see Figure 6.14). Some sections are issued in looseleaf form so that revisions may be easily inserted and the accuracy of the information maintained. Others are bound volumes which are replaced with a new issue on a regular basis. It is not possible to subscribe to only part of the tariff; a subscription

FIGURE 6.14
Contents of the ATPCO.
Source: Airline Tariff Publishing Company.

includes all sections and subsequent revisions.

There are basically three types of manuals in the ATPCO tariff set: passenger tariffs contain air fares and fare rules for specific areas; a routing guide describes the permissable routings which can be used with given air fares; and rules tariffs contain the general regulations governing transportation within the region. Only the rules tariffs are looseleaf; the remaining parts of the tariff set are bound volumes.

Domestic Passenger Tariffs

The passenger tariffs of most relevance to Canadian travel counsellors are those listing fares and rules for travel within Canada, within the USA, and between Canada and the USA. These tariffs use a similar format (as shown in Figures 6.15 and 6.16). The Official United States Passenger Tariff (Part I) contains all local fares and fare rules within the continental USA, Hawaii and Alaska. It is consulted

only to find a fare within that area, such as from Miami to Chicago, or Los Angeles to Honolulu. Part I is the largest of the fares volumes and comprises two books (Section A and Section B). Listings are in alphabetical order showing fares between cities. Thus, fare listings are not repeated. For example, a fare from Dallas to Boston will be found under the heading "Boston". All fares are quoted in U.S. dollars.

Part II (The Official Canadian Passenger Tariff) lists all fares for scheduled service within Canada and between the United States and Canada. For example, this tariff would be consulted to determine the fare from Montreal to Edmonton or from Toronto to Los Angeles. The main difference between Part I and Part II is that the Canadian tariff lists fares in both U.S. and Canadian dollars. All Canadian dollar fares are preceded by the letter "C". Any fares without this designation are priced in U.S. dollars. An airline ticket must be calculated in a single currency (either USD or CAD) and counsellors must ensure that the same currency is used for all sector fares on a ticket. Since transborder fares, such as Vancouver-Seattle, are published in both currencies it is a simple matter to select the correct figure. If the ticket is being paid in Canadian dollars, simply ignore the USD fare and use the CAD fare. The tariff uses a set exchange rate and no calculation is required. If, however, a fare is quoted only in USD but will be paid in CAD, it is necessary to convert from one to the other using the bank buying rate (published in *The Globe and Mail* on Fridays or obtainable from the airline). Similarly, U.S. airlines and travel agencies convert CAD to USD using the bank rate published in the *Wall Street Journal* each Tuesday.

FIGURE 6.15
A listing from the Official United States Passenger Tariff.
Source: ATPCO.

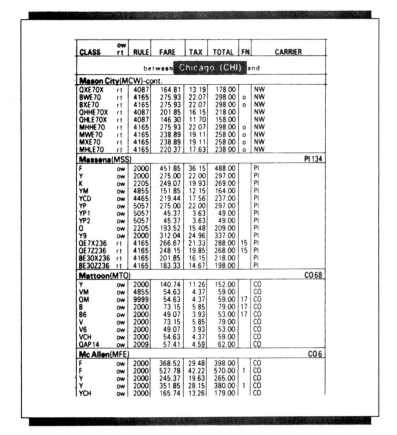

Domestic Routing Guide

All fares in the Canadian and U.S. passenger tariffs specify routings and carriers which apply to the particular fare. There are occasions, however, when it is not possible to book a client on a direct flight. For example, all direct flights may be fully booked or the flight times may be unsuitable so that the client must be booked on an indirect routing. In such cases, the Official North American Routing Guide (Part III) is consulted. If connecting flights on the same airline are required, this tariff must be checked to ensure that the routing proposed on the connecting service is allowed at the direct fare. Occasionally, depending on the route and number of stops made en route, direct flights on the same carrier have different fares between two cities. The routing guide may then compel a counsellor to charge the higher fare.

In addition to fares and fare rules, the passenger tariffs contain two important segments: Definitions and General Provisions. The Definitions section explains the terms used in the tariff. The General Provisions section describes the conditions which apply to the majority of the rules in the tariff. This section provides the standard rules (or provisions) for the tariff and is subdivided into several areas, such as reservations and ticketing procedures, stopover privileges, and cancellation and refund policies. Every air fare has a rule associated with it which states the regulations governing the use of that fare. However, only those parts of a rule which deviate from the general provisions are reproduced (Figure 6.17). For example, if there is no entry under the "children's discounts" section of a particular rule, then the relevant conditions described in the general provisions apply.

Domestic Rules Tariffs

As well as the general provisions and the specific rules for particular fares, there are a number of general rules which apply to all carriers. These general rules for regulating transportation within and between Canada and the USA (the areas covered in the above tariffs and routing guide) are published in separate looseleaf volumes, the Domestic General Rules Tariff (Part IV) and the Canadian General

Rules Tariff (Part V). These rules include those concerning the application of fares, baggage, general rules, fares and routings, currency and fare construction. In addition, this tariff contains exceptions to the common rules which relate to particular carriers. The general rules tariff is consulted whenever the rules summary in the passenger tariff does not provide the information required for the fare being used.

The ATPCO also publishes a Joint Passenger Tariff (Part VI) containing joint fares to, from and within Canada. Joint fares are through fares which two or more airlines agree to offer. A joint fare permits an airline to charge a through fare to a city even though it does not actually fly there. By having an agreement with another airline to provide a through fare to such a point, it is possible to capture at least part of the market to that city. For example, Air BC and Time Air operate scheduled service exclusively in western Canada. By filing joint fares with the transcontinental airlines of Air Canada

CLASS	ow rt	RULE	FARE	TAX	TOTAL	FN	CARRIER	
between Edmonton (YEG) and								
Providence(PVD)-cont.								
BHE14C	rt	4125	632.00				NW	
BHE14C	rt	4125	664.00			n	NW	•29JUN89
BHE14C	rt	4125	C 802.00				NW	
BHE14C	rt	4125	C 843.00			n	NW	•29JUN89
BLE14C	rt	4125	550.00				NW	
BLE14C	rt	4125	578.00			n	NW	•29JUN89
BLE14C	rt	4125	C 698.00				NW	
BLE14C	rt	4125	C 734.00			n	NW	•29JUN89
BG18	rt	4210	672.00				NW	
BG18	rt	4210	706.00			n	NW	•29JUN89
BG18	rt	4210	C 853.00				NW	
BG18	rt	4210	C 897.00			n	NW	•29JUN89
Pueblo(PUB)								HP 102
Y	ow	2000	236.00				HP	
Y	ow	2000	C 300.00				HP	
YCH	ow	2000	177.00				HP	
YCH	ow	2000	C 225.00				HP	
Quebec(YQB)								AC 46,CP 1
J	ow	2000	C 628.00			r	AC	
J	ow	2000	C 640.00			56	AC	
J	ow	2000	C 628.00			o	CP	
J	ow	2000	C 640.00			u	CP	
JS	ow	4070	C 314.00			r	AC	
JS	ow	4070	C 320.00			56	AC	
Y	ow	2000	C 571.00			r	AC	
Y	ow	2000	C 571.00			z	CP	
YCD	ow	4470	C 457.00			z	AC	
YCD	ow	4470	C 457.00			z	CP	
Z	ow	4460	C 286.00			r	AC	
Z	ow	4460	C 286.00			z	CP	
BDG	ow	4598	C 428.00			r	AC	
HHCD	rt	4476	C 628.00			ru	AC	
HHCD	rt	4476	C 628.00			mz	CP	
HLCD	rt	4476	C 514.00			ru	AC	
HLCD	rt	4476	C 514.00			mz	CP	
BR14	rt	4123	C 742.00			p	CP	
BRCH14	rt	4123	C 571.00			p	CP	
HLE14	rt	4593	C 548.00			mz	CP	
HLE14	rt	5000	C 548.00			rv	AC	
HHE14	rt	4593	C 605.00			mz	CP	
HHE14	rt	5000	C 605.00			rv	AC	
VXMAS	rt	5000	C 548.00			55	AC	

FIGURE 6.16
A listing from the Official Canadian Passenger Tariff.
Source: ATPCO.

FIGURE 6.17
Only the parts of a
rule that deviate
from the General
Provisions are
reproduced in the
domestic tariff.
Source: ATPCO.

RULE 4063 EXCURSION FARES

A) **CARRIER(S) AND CLASS(ES) OF SERVICE**
    NW--Coach.
B) **FARE APPLICATION**
    BRAP3C--Booking Code: B.
F) **RESERVATIONS AND TICKETING**
    1) Reservations must be made at least 3 days before departure.
    2) Tickets must be purchased within 3 days after reservations are made and at least 3 days before departure.
    3) PTAs are permitted provided ticketing time limits are met.
        NOTE: Purchase of a PTA does not constitute ticketing.
    4) Tickets may be mailed provided ticketing time limits are met.
    5) Tickets must be issued on carrier's ticket stock or standard ticket stock imprinted with carrier's identification plate.
    6) Seats are limited.
H) **COMBINATIONS**
    These fares may be combined with fares governed by Rules 4125, 4165, 4311, and 4547 to construct **Open-Jaw/Circle Trips.**
L) **REROUTING/FLIGHT CHANGES**
    1) After tickets are issued, voluntary changes in flights/dates must be made at least 3 days before departure of the new flight.
    2) Rule 255 (Reroutings) does not apply.
Q) **SPECIAL CONDITIONS**
    Rules Not Applicable--6000 (Family Fares).

and CAI respectively, they are able to participate in a broader market area than provided by their own scheduled services alone. In a similar fashion, Air Canada can penetrate the Hawaii market by offering joint fares, thus overcoming the disadvantage of not being able to offer direct service. Joint fares usually provide a mutually beneficial arrangement, since the other participating airlines also reach markets beyond their own system.

The ATPCO tariff set contains other passenger tariffs which quote fares for travel to and within other countries, however, these are used rather infrequently by Canadian travel counsellors. When clients travel outside of the domestic area, the accepted reference source for fares and rules information is the Air Tariff which is discussed below.

International Fares and Tariffs

Just as ATAC and the ATA have input into domestic air fares, IATA is involved in the area of international air fares. At one time, IATA had the power to set air fares but this is no longer the case, although the organization still has a major influence on the rates charged. Fare rules and ticketing procedures, however, continue to be set by IATA.

IATA Traffic Conferences

To simplify rules and procedures, and to control rates and services within and between different regions, IATA has divided the world into three areas (or traffic conferences). These are illustrated in Figure 6.18.

IATA Area (Traffic Conference) 1 or TC1 comprises all of the North and South American continents and adjacent islands, Greenland, Bermuda and the Caribbean, Hawaii, and the Pacific as far west as the International Date Line.

IATA Area (Traffic Conference) 2 or TC2 comprises all of Europe (including Russia east of the Ural Mountains) and adjacent islands, Iceland, the Azores, all of Africa and adjacent islands, and Asia as far east as Iran (principally the Middle East).

IATA Area (Traffic Conference) 3 or TC3 comprises the remainder of Asia, the Orient and East Indies, Australia, New Zealand, and the Pacific islands as far east as the International Date Line.

The three conferences are subdivided into four traffic conferences for routes between the different areas:

- TC12 covers North, Mid and South Atlantic routes.
- TC23 covers routes between Area 2 and Area 3.
- TC31 covers routes between the North, Central and South Pacific regions.
- TC123 covers routes between the conferences via the Atlantic.

International air fares and the rules governing them are defined according to these traffic conferences.

Using the International Tariff

The most common tariff source used in North America for fares and rules for international travel is the Air Tariff. This reference consists of several parts, each in the form of a bound book with varying issue dates (see Figure 6.19). Some volumes have separate sections, each printed on a different colour to simplify their use. All are distributed within IATA Area 1, except for Europe Book 3 which is circulated only within Europe. The following discussion is restricted to Books 1 and 2 which are commonly used by Canadian travel counsellors. Just as the ATPCO separates the domestic tariff regionally, the Air Tariff is divided into sections covering the world, the western hemisphere, and Europe as defined by the IATA traffic conferences. Similarly, the Air Tariff consists of basically three types of manuals: fares books primarily contain air fares and add-on fares; rules, routings and mileages books contain the regulations governing the use of the fares; and maximum permitted mileages books list the maximum distance which a passenger may travel at a given fare.

International Fares Books

The Worldwide Fares Book 1 is used most frequently. It lists fares on a worldwide basis with literally thousands

FIGURE 6.18
IATA Traffic Conferences.
Source: IATA.

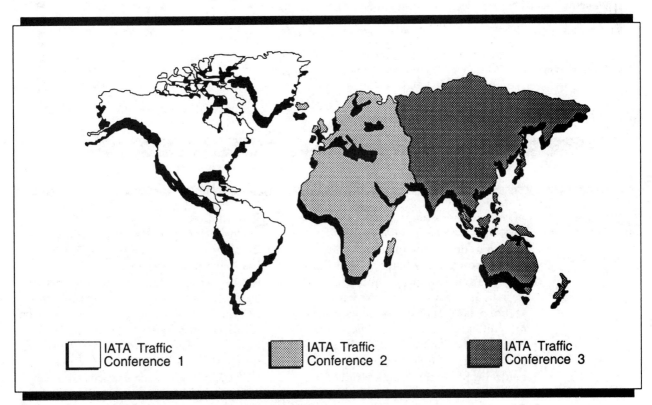

IATA Traffic Conference 1

IATA Traffic Conference 2

IATA Traffic Conference 3

PUBLICATION	CONTENTS	FREQUENCY
Wordwide Fares Book 1.	Fares, add-ons, routings and currency adjustments for travel worldwide, validity indicators for special fares tickets, the excess mileage percentage table and its application.	Monthly.
Worldwide Rules, Routings and Mileages Book 1.	Fare rules, general rules, fare construction rules, routings and ticketed point mileages.	Quarterly, with bulletins issued monthly as required.
Worlwide Maximum Permitted Mileages Book 1.	Global indicators, maximum permitted mileages, the excess mileage percentage table and its application.	Once yearly, with bulletins issued as required.
Western Hemisphere Fares Book 2.	Fares, rules, add-ons and routings for travel in North and South America, and validity indicators for special fares tickets.	Monthly.
Western Hemisphere Rules, Routings and Mileages Book 2.	Fare rules, general rules, fare construction rules, city and airline codes, routings and ticketed point mileages.	Quarterly, with bulletins issued monthly as required.
Western Hemisphere Maximum Permitted Mileages Book 2.	City codes, maximum permitted mileages, the excess mileage percentage table and its application.	Once yearly, with bulletins issued as required.
Europe Book 3.	Fares, add-ons, rules and routings.	Four times yearly, with bulletins issued on the remaining eight months.

FIGURE 6.19
Contents of the Air Tariff.
Courtesy of The Air Tariff.

of combinations of fares available. This reference is consulted if a counsellor wishes to determine the fare from Mogadishu to Zanzibar, Ho Chi Minh City to Tegucigalpa, or Gander to Peshawar. It comprises two main sections, fares and add-on fares printed on white and pink paper respectively. Fares are listed alphabetically by origin city and shown in local currency and neutral units of construction (NUCs). Since the same fare may not be available in both directions, all fares are shown under each city. For example, fares from Bombay to Toronto are listed under Bombay while fares for the reverse journey are listed under Toronto (Figure 6.20). Add-on fares, sometimes called proportional fares or arbitraries, are often confused with local (or sector) fares. A local fare for a given route can be used to purchase transportation between two points. An add-on fare, however, is always used in conjunction with another fare in order to provide a through international fare that is not necessarily published.

There are also several other important sections in this volume. An Editorial section summarizes the fare and rule changes made since the previous issue, advises which fares are subject to government approval (and which governments), reports fares that are subject to further changes in the near future, and mentions fares which have been omitted from the tariff. A Stop Press section immediately follows the editorial section. This contains fare and rule changes received too late to be included in the main section. Many of these changes may not be relevant to tickets issued in Canada. However, both sections should be reviewed before using a new tariff issue. Worldwide Fares Book 1 also includes the rules which deal with currency regulations (General Currency Rules CO5). These are extremely important and are used whenever there are calculations involving neutral units of construction (NUCs) or whenever a fare is quoted in a currency other than that of the country in which the ticket is issued. Although fares and other charges in the Air Tariff are generally quoted in local currency and NUCs, there are some exceptions where fares are quoted in U.S. dollars. The currency regulations section defines and identifies the bank rates and conversion factors to be used in fare calculations. This volume of the tariff also describes how to use the fares printed in it, and deciphers fares, reservations and ticketing codes.

While some fares between the USA/Canada and Mexico, the Caribbean and South America are listed in the worldwide edition, a more complete selection of fares and add-on fares is reproduced in the Western Hemisphere Fares Book 2. Some local domestic fares, such as those available within Brazil or within Mexico, are also included in a separate section. The formats of these two listings differ from each other and from the format of the worldwide fares listed in Book 1 (Figure 6.21). An editorial section and instructions on how to use the fares are again printed in this edition.

International Rules, Routings and Mileages Books

The second type of manual (for rules, routings and mileages) is divided into separate volumes for worldwide and western hemisphere applications in the same manner as the fares books. The Worldwide Rules, Routings and Mileages Book 1 is again the larger of the two volumes. It is colour coded and includes an editorial and a stop press section. The

FARE TYPE	CAR CDE	HEADLINE CITY CURRENCY	NUC	RULES	GI MPM *RTE REF* VIA PT.
BOMBAY (BOM) India			Indian Rupees (INR)		
To TOKYO					
YPX		15352	902.26	E727	EH
To TORONTO					AT 9896
Y		18412	1082.11	G310	AT
J/C		20117	1182.31	G310	AT
F		33933	1994.31	G310	AT
YLAPO		11487	675.11	G600	AT
YHAPO		12679	745.17	G600	AT
YLE4M		17797	1045.96	G482	AT
YHE4M		18928	1112.43	G482	AT
YLGV4		19521	1147.28	G221	AT
YHGV4		20800	1222.45	G221	AT
To TOWNSVILLE					EH 6804
Y		18068	1061.89		EH
J/C		19876	1168.15		EH
F		25769	1514.49		EH
P		25769	1514.49		EH
YLAB		10246	602.17	E808	EH
YHAB		11647	684.51	E808	EH
YLGV		13122	771.20	F821	EH
YHGV		15609	917.37	F821	EH
To TRIPOLI					EH 4539
Y		8811	517.84		EH
J/C		9693	569.67		EH
F		13447	790.30		EH

FARE TYPE	CAR CDE	HEADLINE CITY CURRENCY	NUC	RULES	GI MPM *RTE REF* VIA PT.
TORONTO (YYZ) Ontario, Canada			Canadian $ (CAD)		
To BOMBAY					AT 9896
Y		2017.00	1677.92	G310	AT
Y2		1690.00	1405.89	G310	AT
J/C		2209.00	1837.64	G310	AT
F		3720.00	3094.63	G310	AT
YLXAP		1600.00	1331.02	G582	AT
YLWAP		1650.00	1372.62	G582	AT
YHXAP		1820.00	1514.04	G582	AT
YHWAP		1870.00	1555.63	G582	AT
YLXE		1736.00	1444.16	G483	AT
YLWE		1775.00	1476.60	G483	AT
YHXE		1945.00	1618.02	G483	AT
YHWE		1995.00	1659.62	G483	AT
To BRATISLAVA					AT 5215
Y		1421.00	1182.11	G303	AT
J/C		1483.00	1233.69	G303	AT
F		2615.00	2175.39	G303	AT
YLAP		884.00	735.39	G652	AT
YKAP		1012.00	841.87	G652	AT
YHAP		1109.00	922.56	G652	AT
YKCD		1012.00	841.87	G510	AT
YLE6M		1442.00	1199.58	G427	AT
YHE6M		1589.00	1321.87	G427	AT
YLCD		884.00	735.39	G510	AT
YHCD		1109.00	922.56	G510	AT

FIGURE 6.20
The Air Tariff lists fares in each direction.
Reproduced courtesy of the Air Tariff from Worldwide Fares Book 1.

FIGURE 6.21
Western Hemisphere fares have a different format from the worldwide listings and many are quoted in USD rather than local currency or NUCs.
Reproduced courtesy of the Air Tariff.

FARE TYPE	CUR IND		FARE	RULE NO.	ROUTE
From CARACAS CCS To					**USD&**
Havana			**HAV**		**MPM1857**
F	USD		431	500	VAm
F1	USD	Z	431	2600	YYm
C	USD		347	500	VAm
Y	USD		302	500	VAm
Y1	USD	Z	302	2600	YYm
YPX7	USD	Z	295	2601	YYm
YPX14	USD		295	2601	VAm
YE21	USD		410	502	VAm
YE21	USD	Z	410	2621	YYm
Honolulu			**HNL**		**MPM7407**
F	USD		1291	100	AA4
F	USD		1832	100	PAm
F	USD		1832	1700	VAm
C	USD		1367	100	PAm
C	USD	M	1367	1700	VAm
Y	USD		932	100	AA4
Y	USD		1305	100	PAm
Y	USD		1305	1700	VAm
V2V	USD		887	742	AA4
B2S	USD		990	742	PAm
BE21V	USD		1744	784	AA4
M	USD		990	490	VAm
ME21	USD		1602	763	PA265
ME21	USD		1602	1709	VAm
Houston			**HOU**		**MPM2707**
F	USD		572	100	PAm
F	USD		572	1700	VAm
C	USD		477	100	PAm

remainder of the book is divided into various segments. A General Rules section provides the basic definitions of the terms used and covers virtually all aspects of international air travel including baggage, children's fares, refunds, stopovers, ticketing and validity. Exceptions to the general rules which apply to particular carriers are also described. As with the corresponding section in the ATPCO, the general rules are consulted whenever the rules summary in the relevant book does not provide the information necessary for the fare being used. There follows a section on fare construction rules which is a summary of the existing IATA regulations concerning the worldwide calculation of air fares. Since these regulations tend to change little over the years, both this section and the general rules section are usually reliable, even if the fares are out of date. Fare calculation and fare construction rules are discussed in more detail below.

The major portion of these tariff books comprises worldwide fares rules. Unlike the general rules, these are specific rules which pertain directly to the published fares. Each fare in Book 1 is listed with an associated rule number. The regulations governing the use of the fare are found by looking under the rule number in the

rules section. Three standardized formats, known as Standard Condition A, B and C, are used to simplify the interpretation of the fare rules. Standard Condition A is the most common format and governs rules for all fares except Group Fares and Inclusive Tour Fares. Standard Condition B is used for all Group Fares except Inclusive Tour Fares, and Standard Condition C is used, with a few exceptions, for all Inclusive Tour Fares. The Standard Condition identifies each part of the rule by a paragraph number. For example, permitted stopovers are always discussed under paragraph 10 and cancellations and refunds procedures are always noted under paragraph 20. Whenever a paragraph is omitted from a specific fare rule, the corresponding paragraph in the Standard Condition applies (see Figure 6.22). The Standard Condition in the Air Tariff compares with the General Provisions found in the ATPCO.

The final section of the rules book consists of lists of permissable routings and ticketed point mileages (TPMs). The routings identify which routes are allowed for a given fare with a given carrier. The TPM figures are used to determine whether a given routing lies within the maximum permitted mileage (MPM) for the fare quoted. If the routing exceeds the MPM, the Excess Mileage Percentage Table on the inside back cover of the MPM book must be consulted to calculate the surcharge payable. Although the TPM chart lists each city alphabetically by name, the TPMs to other cities are shown alphabetically by the three letter city code.

The Western Hemisphere Rules, Routings and Mileages Book 2 covers the rules, permitted routings and TPMs applicable to the fares printed in the corresponding fares book. The format is similar to that used in the Book 1 equivalent. Airline and city codes, and an excess mileage percentage table are also reproduced in this edition.

Maximum Permitted Mileages Books

The Maximum Permitted Mileages Book 1 lists the maximum permitted mileages (MPMs) identified beside the fares in the Worldwide Fares Book 1. Each MPM appears only once, in alphabetical order, as the figure is the same in either direction. Again, an editorial section is included to alert users to changes. The excess mileage percentage table and how to use it are also printed in this book. The format and use of the Western Hemisphere Maximum Permitted Mileages Book 2 is the same as its Book 1 counterpart. It is used in conjunction with the fares shown in Book 2.

International Air Fares

The foundation for IATA's rules is that all fares and other fees are set in the currency of the country where the passenger starts the journey. In some countries where the currency is unstable, however, all charges are quoted in U.S. dollars. At

---

G 603   N.ATL. ADVANCE PURCHASE BUSINESS
CLASS FARES: CANADA ◀▶ UK

1. **Application** RT/SOJ via CP.
   A. **BETWEEN** Vancouver/Calgary/Edmonton/Toronto
      AND London/Manchester
   B. **BETWEEN** Montreal/Ottawa
      AND London
4. **Fares** Date of commencement of travel on the first Transatlantic sector shall determine the season fare to be charged.
5. **Children and Infants Fares** Not applicable.
6. **Minimum Stay** 14 days.
8. **Maximum Stay** 6 months.
10. **Permitted Stopovers** Not permitted en route.
11. **Routings** One online transfer permitted in Canada.
12. **Permitted Combinations** These fares are combinable end on with domestic fares only. Combinations with arbitraries are not permitted.
14. **Reservations**
   A. **Deadline:** 45 days (except between Vancouver/Calgary/Edmonton and London/Manchester: 30 days).
   B. **Changes:**
      1. **Outbound Reservations/Routing:** Not permitted after payment of deposit.
      2. **Return Reservations:** Changes to the return segment are allowed any time provided that a charge of CAD 250/GBP 100 is collected at least 30 days prior to the original return segment or new flight reserved, subject to reassessment of fare.
15. **Payment** Reservations made 30/45 days or more prior to departure: A non-refundable deposit of CAD 250/GBP 100 is due within 48 hours. Payment of the remaining balance and all ticketing must be completed 30/45 days prior to departure.
16. **Ticketing**
   A. Tickets must show confirmed reservation for entire journey.
   B. Tickets must be endorsed NONREF/JAP in the form of payment box.
   C. No alterations may be made to the ticket after it has been issued except in the case of involuntary rerouting or as provided in cancellations and refunds below.
20. **Cancellations and Refunds**
   A. **Prior to departure:**
      1. In the event of cancellation the non-refundable deposit of CAD 250/GBP 100 shall be forfeited.
      2. In the event of failure to use reservations there will be no refund, apart from taxes.
   B. **After departure:**
      In the event of cancellation, the amount of refund is the difference between the fare paid and the applicable fare for the transportation used, less CAD 250/GBP 100 (or the equivalent amount converted at the bankers rate).
   C. **Credit towards further transportation:**
      The non-refundable amount as specified in **A** and **B** above may be used as a credit towards payment of a higher applicable fare in which case the original non-refundable amount will not be refunded.

FIGURE 6.22
Rule G603 from Worldwide Rules Book 1. Standard Condition A applies to the sections not covered in this rule. *Reproduced courtesy of the Air Tariff.*

one time, tariffs automatically changed with currency fluctuations. The current practice is that IATA monitors all currencies and sets the conversion factors on a quarterly basis. Only major currency fluctuations interrupt this regular mechanism.

When trying to determine a fare for a client, counsellors should first check the tariff to see if there is a published through fare from the point of origin to the desired destination. This is the simplest and most direct method of determining a fare. If no through fare is published for the itinerary, then a counsellor must construct a fare following the rules set by IATA.

Fare Construction Principles

There are a number of basic fare construction rules and principles that dictate how air fares are calculated worldwide. These are described in the IATA Ticketing Handbook and in the Air Tariff. The particular fare construction principle used and how it is applied to calculate an air fare is determined by the type of transaction made to purchase the ticket. Four possibilities exist:

- SITI - Sold in, ticketed in the country where travel commences.
- SITO - Sold in, ticketed outside the country where travel commences.
- SOTI - Sold outside, ticketed inside the country where travel commences.
- SOTO - Sold outside, ticketed outside the country where travel commences.

Since these four transactions affect how the fare construction rules are applied and what the final air fare will be, the four-letter code must be entered on an airline ticket to show which transaction was used for the fare calculation. In essence, however, all air fare calculations are based on five basic principles:

- Neutral units of construction.
- The routing system.
- The mileage system.
- Add-on fares.
- Higher intermediate points.

Neutral Units of Construction

Most passengers purchase airline tickets in the country where the journey commences (usually their home) using local currency. However, tickets can be bought with another currency provided that the fare is converted at the local banker's buying rate on the date the ticket is issued. Sometimes a client wishes to buy an airline ticket for a journey which starts elsewhere. For example, a client in Thunder Bay may wish to bring a relative from Oslo for a visit. The Air Tariff quotes the fare from Oslo to Thunder Bay in Norwegian Krone. For a simple itinerary involving a single currency, the fare is converted to Canadian dollars at the prevailing bank rate. The fare could, however, be paid in any acceptable currency converted at the rate of exchange.

The Air Tariff lists all fares in the local currency and in its equivalent neutral unit of construction (NUC). (There are exceptions in which fares are quoted in U.S. dollars and NUCs.) The value of the NUC is calculated using an IATA rate of exchange which is set every three months. (However, the rate-setting mechanism allows for monthly updates should any currency fluctuate by more than 10 percent within a 20-day period.) The NUC amount assigned to each fare is then used when converting a fare to another currency. When an itinerary involves fares in a combination of currencies, each fare is converted to a common currency (that of the country where the itinerary commences) using the NUC amounts quoted in the tariff rather than the local currency fare. The NUC amounts are then added together and multiplied by the NUC conversion factor (found in the General Rules section of the Air Tariff) for the country where travel begins.

The Routing System

Some international fares are based on specific routings and/or certain carriers. Such fares are listed in the Air Tariff with an accompanying routing number. The particular routings and carriers which can be used are found by consulting the corresponding section of the routing tariff. Routing diagrams are also reproduced in this tariff, however, these are seldom used. Although the routing system is still applicable on some fares from Canada, it is not as common as fares based on the more flexible mileage system.

The Mileage System

In general, the price of an international airline ticket is based on the distance travelled. The greater the distance, the higher the fare is likely to be. The distance which can be flown at the published direct fare for a given itinerary is determined by the maximum permitted mileage (MPM) associated with it. A client may, however, wish to fly between origin and destination using a route which exceeds the MPM. Whenever a desired itinerary between two points is not published as a specific routing, as described above, the mileage system is used to determine the fare.

The Air Tariff listing for most fares shows a number printed in the last column. This number represents the MPM for the fare. If the sum of the mileage on each sector of the itinerary is less than or equal to the published MPM, the itinerary is permitted at the published direct fare. To determine whether an itinerary exceeds the MPM, the ticketed point mileage (TPM) for each sector of the itinerary is obtained from the tables printed in the Air Tariff. The total TPM for the particular routing is then calculated by addition. If this total is within the MPM, the published direct fare may be used; if it exceeds the MPM, the published fare must be surcharged by a specific percentage (based on the amount that the TPM surpasses the MPM). The additional amount, or mileage surcharge, is determined by consulting the Excess Mileage Percentage Table printed in the tariff.

Unless specifically forbidden by the rules governing the fare, stopovers may be made at any point on a routing. In general, regular first and economy class fares do not restrict stopovers. Clients on such fares are therefore permitted to make an unlimited number of stopovers, provided that they remain within the limits imposed by the mileage system. There are some exceptions to this generalization, however, so counsellors should consult the tariff rules and check with each airline involved to determine the number of stopovers allowed in any given situation.

Add-On Fares

It is first necessary to comprehend the gateway principle to understand add-on fares. IATA members meet on a regular basis to establish or adjust groups of fares. This procedure would be extremely time consuming if everyone concerned had to agree on the fares between all points in Canada and points in Europe, for example. Instead, fares are established for a limited number of routes between points in Europe and certain Canadian cities designated as gateways. Traditionally, Montreal is Canada's eastern gateway city for transatlantic flights and Vancouver its western gateway for transpacific flights. The fares decided are known as **specified fares**. Transatlantic fares from Canadian cities west of Montreal are then established by using predetermined add-on fares (which are sometimes set at a different time from the specified fares). These add-on fares do not necessarily reflect the local fare amounts and are often substantially lower. Fares from U.S. cities are established in the same manner using New York City, Miami and Los Angeles as gateways.

Since the Air Tariff publishes through fares from most major cities, it is generally unnecessary to refer to the add-on pages. To conserve space, however, fares from smaller cities such as Sault Ste. Marie or Whitehorse are not published. This makes it necessary to construct a through fare using the add-on tables. Add-on tables show amounts for different types of fares. The correct add-on amount must be added only to the corresponding type of gateway fare; first class add-ons to first class fares, and excursion fare add-ons to excursion fares, for example. Although gateway cities are used to construct a through fare, it is not necessary to actually travel via such points. For example, the fare from Saskatoon to

Amsterdam is established by applying an add-on to the Montreal-Amsterdam fare. The routing, however, might be Saskatoon-Toronto-Amsterdam.

Lowest Combination of Fares

If a required fare is not published and cannot be produced using an add-on fare, it is constructed by combining two or more fares along the route to be travelled. By selecting the lowest fare for each segment, the lowest combination comprises the fare. However, the rules dictate that a published through fare always takes precedence over any combination of fares (of the same type and class of service) between the same points. In other words, the lowest combination of fares method cannot be used to undercut a through fare. The combination procedure is used only if there is no published through fare.

Combining Special Domestic Fares with International Fares

There are sometimes exceptions to the lowest combination of fares rule. For example, a counsellor may be able to construct a lower fare than the published through fare by combining a special domestic fare with an international fare. This exception is permitted as long as most conditions on the special domestic fare, such as minimum and maximum stay, are obeyed. However, the routing does not necessarily have to follow that of the domestic fare. In such cases the domestic fare is used in the same manner as an add-on. Counsellors should, however, always check with the airline(s) concerned to ensure that the combination is approved.

Higher Intermediate Point (HIP)

Fare construction rules generally prohibit someone from creating a fare for an itinerary which undercuts the fare to some other point en route to the destination. Typically, the fare is calculated to the city on the itinerary which has the highest fare. There are times, however, when the fare is calculated to a city having a lower fare. Most often this is caused by the routing involved. When this occurs, there are several rules designed to ensure that the passenger does not obtain a lower fare than applicable to the highest point.

One-Way Backhaul. If the journey involving the higher intermediate point (HIP) is one way, the one-way backhaul rule is applied. This rule makes it impossible to buy two tickets that would undercut the round trip fare to the HIP. For example, if a client is travelling from Toronto to London and Amsterdam, and the fare to London is higher than the fare to Amsterdam, the one-way backhaul rule stipulates that the client cannot travel at the Toronto-Amsterdam fare. The rule demands that the difference between the Toronto-London and the Toronto-Amsterdam fares be added to the Toronto-London fare. The client then pays this total. This rule only applies if there is a HIP (that is, the fare to the further point is less than the fare to the intermediate point) and there is an interruption in the journey at the HIP.

Circle Trip Minimum. On a circle trip involving a HIP, the circle trip minimum rule ensures that the total fare is not less than the round trip fare from the point of origin to any ticketed point on the routing. For example, consider a client who is travelling on an excursion fare from Toronto to Milan and back to Toronto, with Rome as a connection (no stopover) on the outbound journey. If the Toronto-Rome excursion fare is higher than the Toronto-Milan excursion fare, the circle trip minimum rule must be applied. In this case, half of each excursion fare is charged. However, half of the difference between the two excursion fares is then added to ensure that the total fare does not undercut the round trip fare between Toronto and Rome.

Air Fares Used for Tours

Transportation is an essential element of a tour. The companies which create and market tours have several options regarding which air fare to choose for a particular tour. Naturally, the tour company can select any of the air fares available using the tariffs described earlier. Most tour operators, however, have little interest in regular scheduled air fares, although some may occasionally take advantage of discount fares. Instead, they concentrate on specific promotional air fares that are available only to group passengers. Four types of fares are commonly sold by airlines and tour operators; GITs, IITs, CBITs and ABCs. Each is sold under particular conditions. GITs, IITs and CBITs are tour-basing fares which are found in the tariffs (see Figure 6.23). Such air fares are used by airlines to promote air travel, particularly during slow periods and low seasons. ABCs are charter fares which are not published in the tariffs. Tour companies (commonly called tour operators) use whichever fare most closely matches the requirements of the tour being planned.

Group Inclusive Tour (GIT) Fare

The best known promotional fare is the Group Inclusive Tour (GIT) fare which was first introduced by IATA member airlines for travel across the North Atlantic. GITs are special group fares sold by tour operators for seats on regularly scheduled flights. These airline seats may not be sold independently, however, but are available only to those who purchase a tour consisting of accommodation and other arrangements. The minimum number of passengers required to comprise an eligible group varies according to the destination and routing. Conditions are also placed on the tour. For example, there may be a minimum tour cost, and a minimum and maximum tour length.

Airlines permit tour operators to release back to the carrier for resale any seats

FIGURE 6.23
Tour basing or IT fares and rules are found in the Air Tariff.
Reproduced courtesy of the Air Tariff.

---

146 GIT FARES:
    CANADA ◀ ▶ MEXICO

1. **Application** Y RT/CT/SOJ.
3. **Minimum Group Size** 7 passengers.
5. **Children and Infants Fares** Not applicable.
6. **Minimum Stay** 3 days.
8. **Maximum Stay** 21 days.
9. **Extension of Ticket Validity** Not permitted.
10. **Permitted Stopovers** One in each direction.
12. **Permitted Combinations** End to end with other fares provided travel is via the point of combination.
14. **Reservations**
    A. Deadline: 72 hours.
    B. Booking Code: Y.
17. **Ticket Entries** Fare Basis: YGV7.
24. **Tour Conductors Discounts** One for each group of 15 passengers.
29. **Travel Together** All members must travel together on the outbound portion of the journey.
30. **Minimum Tour Price** The air fare plus USD 50.

FARE TYPE	CUR IND		FARE	RULE NO.	ROUTE
From **TORONTO YYZ** To					CAD
Cancun	CUN				MPM2109
Y	NUC	W	300.31	100	AA1
YE21	CAD		659.00	912	LR5
YE21	NUC		548.21	912	LR5
YGV7	CAD		424.00	146	LR5
YGV7	NUC		352.72	146	LR5
YWIT21	CAD		539.00	935	LR5
YWIT21	NUC		448.38	935	LR5
YXIT21	CAD		506.00	935	LR5
YXIT21	NUC		420.93	935	LR5
BWR	CAD		548.00	790	NW910
BWR	NUC		455.87	790	NW910
BXR	CAD		510.00	790	NW910
BXR	NUC		424.26	790	NW910
BE	CAD		639.00	101	MX201
BE	NUC		531.57	101	MX201
BWER	CAD	W	639.00	106	AA1
BWER	NUC	W	531.57	106	AA1

unsold by a given date. Depending on the contract between the two parties, a tour operator may not have to pay for the unsold seats. Tour operators prefer to use GITs for some tours because there is a lower financial risk if the tour does not sell. GITs are most often selected for low season periods when it may become difficult to fill a chartered aircraft. Similarly, GITs are used when tour operators introduce a new tour program or a new destination.

Group Inclusive Tour fares are offered to many distant destinations where higher air fares may prevent travellers from choosing to holiday in a relatively faraway location. Rules and regulations for GITs are found in the appropriate airline tariff.

Individual Inclusive Tour (IIT) Fare

An IIT fare is similar to a GIT in that it is a special tour-based fare sold for travel on regularly scheduled flights. Again, passengers must purchase an approved package of accommodation and other tour arrangements. The major difference between an IIT and a GIT is that it does not require a minimum number of participants. It can be sold to individuals. Again, IIT fares are published in the relevant tariff.

Contract Bulk Inclusive Tour (CBIT) Fare

CBITs are similar to GITs in that the rules and regulations governing them are reproduced in the relevant airline tariff. Similarly, they must be sold in conjunction with land arrangements and the group must travel together. They are, however, marketed in a different manner. Seats are sold to tour operators at a wholesale price. The tour operator then markets the seats according to the conditions set by the airline. Tour operators who purchase CBIT tickets are responsible for filling all seats that they contract. The number of destinations to which CBIT fares are offered has grown considerably in recent years. CBIT fares have in fact become a major alternate form of airline fare, particularly for travel to the Caribbean region.

Advance Booking Charters (ABCs)

Information on scheduled flights is found in either of the OAGs. Air fares and the rules governing them are found in the ATPCO, the Air Tariff, and in airlines' computer reservation systems. Tickets issued for scheduled flights follow the guidelines discussed below. Many clients, however, do not fly on scheduled carriers or with tickets purchased for scheduled flights. Instead, they take a charter flight, on either a charter carrier or a scheduled airline that offers charter flights. Charter flight information is not found in any of the tariffs discussed above. It is obtained directly from the operators who publish brochures containing their fares and conditions (Figure 6.24). Charters have different regulations and require different selling features and techniques.

A charter is a flight operating between certain points on specific dates only. Unlike scheduled flights, all passengers on a charter flight are subject to the same terms and conditions (Figure 6.25). It is important not to confuse Advance Booking Charters (commonly referred to as ABCs) with discounted or excursion fares offered by scheduled carriers on scheduled flights. In practice, airlines offer a certain number of seats to the public at a reduced fare rate provided the passenger meets the booking conditions of the fare. Many of these booking conditions are similar to the booking conditions for ABCs.

The charter industry began in Canada in the early 1970s. Originally, the advance booking requirement was 45 days, the choice of destination was very limited, and all charters were strictly point-to-point. Charter regulations are now much more flexible and cover a broader range of conditions. Although the National Transportation Agency supervises all air carrier regulations, including charter regulations, the charter situation is extremely volatile. Rules and regulations are constantly changing and vary according to the destination. It is a travel counsellor's responsibility to keep informed of current conditions.

Charter operations do, however, have some common elements and some

FIGURE 6.24
Charter fares are published in brochures.
Source: Regent Holidays.

TORONTO TO GLASGOW GLA
WED/THUR/FRI/SUN VIA B757/L1011

HALF ROUNDTRIP FARE	ADULT	SENIOR	CHILD
APR 2, 9, 16, 23, 30, MAY 1, 7	249	229	209
MAY 8, 14, 15, 21	279	259	239
MAY 22, 28, 29, JUN 4, 5, 11, 12, 17, 18	299	279	259
JUN 19, 21, 24, 25, 26, 28, JUL 1, 2, 3, 5, 8, 9, 10, 12, 15, 16	329	309	289
JUL 17, 19, 22, 23, 24, 26, 29, 30, 31, AUG 2, 5, 6, 7, 9, 12, 13, 14, 16, 19, 20, 21, 23	379	359	339
AUG 26, 27, 28, 30, SEPT 2, 3, 4, 6, 10, 11	349	329	309
SEPT 17, 18, 24, 25	329	309	289
OCT 1, 2, 8, 9, 15, 16	289	269	249
OCT 23, 30	259	239	219

GLASGOW TO TORONTO
THURS/FRI/SAT/MON VIA B757/L1011

HALF ROUNDTRIP FARE	ADULT	SENIOR	CHILD
APR 3, 10, 17, 24, MAY 1, 2, 8, 9, 15, 16	250	230	210
MAY 22, 23, 29, 30, JUN 5	280	260	240
JUN 6, 12, 13, 18, 19, 20, 22, 25, 26, 27, 29, JUL 2, 3	300	280	260
JUL 4, 6, 9, 10, 11, 13, 16, 17	330	310	290
JUL 18, 20, 23, 24, 25, 27, 30, 31, AUG 1, 3, 6, 7, 8, 10, 13, 14, 15, 17, 20, 21, 22, 24, 27, 28, 29, 31, SEPT 3, 4, 5, 7	370	350	330
SEPT 11, 12, 18	330	310	290
SEPT 19, 25, 26, OCT 2, 3, 9, 10	300	280	260
OCT 16, 17, 24	270	250	230
OCT 31	240	220	200

CLUB TRANSAT CLASS: ONE WAY ADD $135 PER PERSON; ROUNDTRIP ADD $270 PER PERSON

NOT INCLUDED: CDN AIR TRANSPORTATION TAX $30/TRANSPORTATION RELATED FEES $25/UK AIR PASSENGER DUTY $48   CHILD= 2-15 YRS SENIORS = 60+

standard terms. All charter passengers must pay a non-refundable deposit, but this can be protected by purchasing air fare cancellation insurance. All charter passengers must also book and pay for their flights in advance of departure. The advance booking requirement ranges from seven to 21 days. Canadian regulations permit charter operators to "top off" (or fill) a charter flight before departure. This condition, however, applies for a certain number of seats only and is dependent on the government of the destination country agreeing to such an arrangement. Seats on some charters can therefore be booked up to the day prior to departure. Charter operators may charge an additional fee to clients booking flights at the last minute. For charters within Canada, the advance booking and "top off" requirements are generally less restrictive than those described here. Another variable in the process is the type of aircraft being used. The number of seats that can be "topped off" varies according to the size of the aircraft. For example, depending on the maximum certified takeoff weight, up to 20 or 30 seats can be "topped off" in narrow-bodied planes whereas for wide-bodied aircraft the limit is 40 seats.

Open jaw trips are permitted. This means a client may book a seat into one city (for example, London) and return from another city (for example, Frankfurt) provided that the charter operator has flights to those cities. The loosening of open jaw regulations has promoted the growth of car rental programs attached to charter flights. Co-mingling is also permitted. That is, passengers originating in Canada may return on flights carrying passengers originating in the country of destination. For example, passengers booked on a Toronto-London-Toronto charter may return on the same flight with passengers booked London-Toronto-London. This was not always the case. At one time, Toronto-originating passengers could return only with other Toronto-originating passengers. Similarly, London-originating passengers could return only with other London-originating passengers. Co-mingling means that these passengers can now take the same flight. Most charters impose a minimum stay restriction ranging from the first Sunday after departure to six days. There are no federal government restrictions regarding maximum stay. A foreign government or charter operator, however, can impose a maximum stay restriction. Tour companies

"The Fine Print"

[1] How to book: A non-refundable deposit of $150 per person is payable at time of booking. Balance is due 42 days prior to departure. Non-Ontario residents (or travellers who book with a Travel Agency outside Ontario): a Cdn$10 per passenger indemnity bond is payable with deposit.

Your ticket will be valid only for the flights/dates you have booked and will be 100% non-refundable. May we strongly recommend that you purchase travel insurance to cover you should you have to change flights or cancel due to illness.

[2] Special inflight meals must be requested at least 2 weeks prior to departure (preferably at time of booking).

[3] Infants under 2 (at date of *completion* of travel) travel free but do not receive seat or baggage allowance. Max. 1 infant per adult. Sorry, Skycots not available. **Child fares** refer to the age of the traveller at date of *completion* of travel. **Children under 5** must be accompanied by a travelling companion at least 16 years. **Unaccompanied minors 5-12 years old pay full adult fare,** and must (a) hold confirmed reservations to the destination (b) be accompanied to the airport by a parent/guardian who must wait until the flight has departed (c) be met by a responsible adult at Canada 3000's destination (d) have in their possession the name, address, and phone number of the responsible party at embarkation and on arrival, and an Unaccompanied Minor form (available at airport check-in). **Senior fares** refer to the age of the traveller at date of *commencement* of travel.

[4] There is no minimum stay; maximum stay is the duration of the program.

[5] Tickets are valid only for flights /dates purchased and once travel has commenced, changes not permitted. Tickets for bookings made (or not paid for) within 8 business days of travel are automatically Airport Pick-Up. In the case of prepaids, it is the Travel Agent's responsibility to forward the tickets to the traveller. **IF YOU ARE FLYING FROM ANOTHER CANADIAN CITY TO CONNECT WITH THESE FLIGHTS** and have purchased a special fare e.g. seat sale to fly to Toronto to connect with these flights, we strongly recommend you purchase Adventure/ Fiesta's Tourist Insurance comprehensive policy which, unlike many other travel insurances, covers you for up to $800 to cover additional airfare required should Adventure/Fiesta announce a schedule change precluding your use of a pre-purchased special fare ticket. Rates and details can be found in our current brochures.

[6] Check-in opens 3 hours prior to and closes 30 minutes prior to departure. We regret that passengers arriving after that time will not be permitted to board nor will they be entitled to any tour refund. Sorry, advance seat selection is not possible. **Documentation** Ask your Travel Agent regarding necessary identification. We regret we can't issue refunds or reimburse costs for anyone denied boarding due to incorrect identification. **Baggage allowance** is 2 checked pieces (max. 20kgs/44 lbs) per person. Limited facilities are available for excess baggage, on a first-come basis, at a rate of Cdn.$5 per kilo. **Hand luggage** is limited to 1 piece per passenger, not to exceed 26 x 38 x 15cm (10" x 15" x 20").

We strongly recommend that you purchase baggage insurance as we cannot be responsible for loss or damage of luggage.

[7] Cancellation charges (GST inclusive) apply from date that we are advised of your cancellation and issue a cancellation number. **22+ days prior to departure:** lose deposit • **21 - 14 days prior to departure:** lose 50% of total cost • **14 days to date of departure:** lose 100% of total cost.

[8] Changes to bookings more than 42 days prior to commencement of journey $40 (incl. GST) administration charge. Within 42 days, a change of name, departure date, or itinerary makes the booking subject to the equivalent cancellation penalties. The passenger will be assessed additional amounts for any taxes, levies, currency or fuel surcharges imposed after publication. We reserve the right to reduce published fares for new bookings only. All flights are charters, and are subject to NTA approval. Fares contained herein are valid for new bookings only and are subject to change without notice.

Printed in Canada January/1995.
Akard Enterprises Ltd d/b/a Adventure Tours
Ont Reg 1539989: Fiesta Ont Reg 1748075 JKA#2703

FIGURE 6.25
Terms and conditions for charter fares differ from those for scheduled fares. *Source: Canada 3000.*

to relatively nearby destinations, such as the Caribbean, have taken advantage of the first Sunday minimum stay requirement to create and market long weekend or four day holidays.

Usually ABCs are round trip flights but they can be sold on a one-way basis. Both the outward and return portions must be booked in advance. The charter operator can, however, stipulate that the passenger may either leave the return open or change its travel date by paying a penalty. This option must be included at the time the application to run charters is made and the amount of penalty to be paid must also be stated.

For charters from Canada to the USA, the rules have been loosened since the "Open Skies" agreement was signed in 1995. ABCs to the USA can now be sold on a one-way basis, and there is no minimum stay requirement.

The above summarizes the regulations governing the operation of charter flights. Some of the regulations are not applicable to some charter operators. For example, if a charter operator wishes to operate charters to London, U.K. only, the open jaw regulations do not apply. Similarly, if a charter operator has charters to Bermuda once a week on Wednesdays only, a minimum stay until the first Sunday is irrelevant since there is no flight before the following Wednesday. Charter operators can impose additional restrictions if they so wish, or if they feel it will be beneficial to them. For example, most charter operators do specify a maximum stay period for their clients. A brief comparison of some of Canada's charter operators will indicate how two very different sets of booking conditions may be attained within the federal government's charter regulations. The travel agent cannot automatically quote one rule and assume it applies to all charters. Each charter operator must be studied separately. Some of the ABC destinations popular from Toronto, Montreal and other Canadian cities are London, Manchester, Birmingham, Dublin, Shannon, Amsterdam, Paris, Lisbon, Frankfurt, Rome and Athens.

Features of ABCs

All passengers on an ABC flight are subject to the same terms and conditions outlined above. If a client is travelling on equipment designed exclusively for charter service, there will generally be more seats and less legroom available. Meals, however, are comparable to those available on scheduled service and bar service is usually complimentary. ABCs appeal primarily to vacationers as the advance booking and minimum stay requirements are inappropriate for most business travellers. By their nature, charter flights usually operate at peak times to popular destinations rather than on a daily basis. Charter tickets are issued by the airline or tour company. ABCs and other discount fares can be combined with various land arrangements to create a tour for vacation clients.

Selling Procedures

Before selling a charter flight, counsellors should compare the benefits of ABCs with the discounted fares and excursion fares offered by scheduled carriers on international routes. The prices of these discounted fares are comparable to ABCs. Since excursion fares are available for scheduled flights they also offer more flexibility in the choice of destinations and travel dates.

Most charter flights are available on a round trip basis only, and usually on specific dates or specific days of the week. Counsellors must remember the restrictions and limitations which apply to charter bookings and always check the minimum advance booking date. Once a client has chosen travel dates, a non-refundable deposit must be paid to hold the airline seat. The travel agent then forwards this deposit to the charter operator. Final payment is due 42 days before departure (or within seven days of booking if reservation is made less than 42 days before departure). It is the counsellor's responsibility to remind the client of this due date. The commission (usually 10 percent) is deducted before the balance is forwarded on time to the charter operator.

Certain penalties apply if a client has to cancel a charter flight. As the departure date approaches the penalty increases. At the minimum, the client will lose the non-refundable deposit. The maximum penalty is the cost of the charter fare. Some charter operators offer clients the option of changing travel dates but a rebooking charge is applied to this transaction. Since travel plans are usually changed only because of unforeseen emergencies, travel counsellors should always recommend trip cancellation insurance to their clients. Either the charter operator's own trip cancellation insurance (also called fare protection insurance) or that offered by one of the insurance companies may be recommended. Be sure the client is aware of the conditions governing insurance coverage. Generally, trip cancellation insurance is valid only if the client cancels for medical-related reasons. Travel insurance is discussed more fully in Chapter 12.

Charters are often the least expensive way for a client to reach a destination. In addition, most charter operators carry infants under two free of charge and offer a discount (usually 25 percent) to children between two and eleven. By comparison, regular fares on scheduled flights charge from 10 to 50 percent for comparable carriage. There may also be other discounts on charter prices for senior citizens or for those booking early. Further, charters pay 10 percent commission plus overrides whereas regular fares are restricted to 5-8 percent commission. (The smaller commission, however, may apply to a higher ticket price.) For these reasons travel by charter has become very popular. However, deregulation has increased the number of discounted fares available. These fares are sometimes less expensive than charters.

Consolidators

A consolidator is any company that purchases tickets from an airline at a rate less than the tariff, with the intention of reselling the tickets to either the public or travel agencies for ultimate resale to the public. Consolidators buy tickets in bulk from airlines and can therefore offer substantial savings to travellers and travel counsellors. Generally, consolidators sell tickets for international routes rather than domestic flights. The main reason is that international flights are subject to IATA rules and regulations that officially

prohibit discounting by member airlines. (The domestic airline industry has been deregulated.) There are no restrictions, however, on how much commission an airline can pay an agent for selling a ticket. Consolidators therefore act as wholesalers or intermediaries between airlines and retail travel agencies.

As well as savings, there is less flexibility and a need for caution when choosing a consolidator (just as there is when choosing any supplier). The risks can be minimized if an agency uses a local consolidator, drops off a cheque and collects the tickets at the same time, limits the volume with any one consolidator, contacts other agents in the area to check the consolidator's reputation, uses consolidators who deal solely with travel agencies, uses scheduled carriers over charter services, and books directly with the carrier but then has the consolidator pick up the ticketing. Clients should be made aware of the risks and limitations on the fare. Consolidators can offer low fares not because airlines sell them discount tickets, but because airlines sell them regular tickets and pay a commission of 30 percent or more compared with the standard 5-8 percent paid to travel agencies. Most consolidators sell only to travel agencies. Tickets usually have restrictions such as advance booking, minimum stay requirements, and no itinerary changes. They are usually nonendorsable meaning that the traveller cannot switch to another airline. Further, flights might not be available every day.

Since airline CRSs show only published (i.e., non-discounted) fares, travel counsellors usually contact consolidators by telephone to determine the price for a particular ticket. The price a consolidator quotes will be based on a number of factors such as its contract with the airline and the volume of business conducted with the travel agency. The travel counsellor then adds a mark-up to this price before selling the ticket to the consumer. This process is used because consolidators rarely provide travel agencies with brochures, rate sheets or other printed records of their prices. That information is confidential and changes frequently, as do airfares and the arrangements between airlines and consolidators.

The role of consolidators can be expected to continue expanding as long as air carriers operating primarily in international markets have excess seat capacity that can be sold to consolidators at discounts reaching 50 percent.

Making Flight Reservations

Before selling an airline ticket to a client, a travel counsellor must learn the client's name, destination, dates of travel and number of seats required. In sales terms, this is known as qualifying the buyer. This qualifying information forms the basis of the reservations details required by the carrier. Most travel agencies have preprinted forms to remind agents of the essential details. The following information is needed from clients in order to reserve their airline seats.

- Client's surname, initial and title (e.g., Mr., Ms or Dr.). The names, initials and titles of other travellers in the party. If children are travelling, their ages should be recorded.
- Client's address.
- Client's phone number, both home and business.
- Destination. Note whether the client is departing from the same city and is returning to the point of origin.
- Departure and return dates. Note whether the client's travel dates correspond with any fare restrictions
- Form of payment, either cash, cheque or credit card.

Counsellors require some additional information to complete the booking. Again, most agencies have preprinted forms to assist counsellors. In automated agencies the prompts appear on the computer terminal screen as part of the reservations process.

- Flight details. Airline and flight number, class of service and itinerary.
- Fare details. The cost of the fare, applicable taxes, class of service, fare basis, ticket deadline, cancellation and change penalties, minimum and maximum stay requirements.
- Special client requests. This includes seat and meal preferences, and whether preboarding assistance is required.
- Administrative details. These include the date the booking is made and the name of the airline reservation agent.
- Agency details. These include the agency's name, address, telephone number, IATA number and the name of the counsellor making the booking.

In return for this information (not all of which may be required on every occasion), the airline reservations department will make the booking (if space is available) and issue a reference or locator number. This locator number and all of the above client and booking information is recorded on a client file. Confirmed reservations are denoted by the code OK.

Sometimes the airline cannot immediately confirm a reservation. This occurs most frequently when more than one airline is involved in the passenger's itinerary and one airline has to contact another to obtain space. In such cases, the airline reservations department will inform the counsellor that the space is on request. This is denoted on the file by the code RQ. It may also happen that a requested flight is sold out. Counsellors should immediately book an alternative flight for their client. This procedure, however, does not prevent the client from being given the chance to register on a waitlist for the preferred flight. Any passengers who cancel are replaced in order by people on the waitlist. If space does become available for a client, counsellors should immediately cancel any other confirmed reservations. The IATA Travel Agent's Handbook and Guide to Automation contains a code of reservations ethics which counsellors should follow when dealing with carriers.

Airline Ticketing

After a counsellor has researched the best fare and made a client's reservation, the necessary airline tickets are then pre-pared. Part of a travel counsellor's re-sponsibility is to ensure that such tickets are accurately completed and issued.

An airline ticket is a legal contract between the airline and the passenger (see Figure 1.1). The carrier agrees to provide air transportation under certain conditions printed on the ticket while the passenger, by purchasing the ticket, accepts those conditions. Further, an airline ticket authorizes a passenger to travel. When properly prepared, an airline ticket is a complete and accurate record of the itinerary, the fare paid, how that fare is constructed, and any special conditions or restrictions that apply to the itinerary. It is therefore essential for counsellors to become thoroughly familiar with all ticket entries required and to learn the correct procedure for properly completing the document. One seemingly small error in writing a ticket can not only invalidate the entire ticket or cause serious delays or difficulties for the passenger, but the travel counsellor might also be held accountable for such problems.

In Canada, IATA regulates airline ticketing procedures through an organization called BSP (Billing and Settlement Plan). At one time each airline had its own ticket stock which was distributed to appointed Canadian travel agencies. Agencies then issued tickets on the relevant airline's stock following the format and procedures set down by the carrier. IATA introduced the BSP system in 1978 to standardize procedures and reduce the administrative problems caused by such a variety of ticket formats and procedures. (BSP administrative procedures are discussed in Chapter 14.) The BSP system introduced four improvements in the handling and processing of airline tickets and other traffic documents:

- Agencies are issued with a single standard ticket stock instead of separate stocks for each airline.
- Airlines supply appointed agencies with a Carrier Identification Plate (CIP) which permits a counsellor to validate a standard airline ticket in the name of the issuing airline.
- Agencies complete a single, combined sales report for all airline sales and pay a single amount to BSP to cover these ticket sales. This procedure eliminates the necessity for agencies to report and pay each airline individually.
- The BSP bank acts as a clearinghouse which analyzes agency sales reports and distributes the appropriate amount due each member airline.

Approved travel agencies receive one free copy annually of the standard ticketing references. The *IATA Ticketing Handbook* describes in detail how to issue and reissue airline tickets, miscellaneous charges orders (MCOs), prepaid ticket advices (PTAs), and other processing operations. Illustrations and examples of each document are provided. The *BSP Canada Manual for Passenger Sales Agents* is primarily an administrative reference which describes the procedures and rules which IATA-approved agents must follow. It also contains illustrations and examples of traffic documents. The two references occasionally differ in their instructions for completing a ticket or other traffic document. In such cases, the guidelines suggested in the IATA Ticketing Handbook should be followed. The *IATA Travel Agent's Handbook and Guide to Automation* is a reference which contains the IATA agency resolutions that outline an agent's rights and obligations. It also describes automated airline reservations and ticketing systems, the traffic documents used with such systems, and the procedures to be followed when using them.

There are two types of airline documents and forms; traffic documents and administrative forms. Traffic documents are numbered sequentially, and each document must be carefully protected and reported by the agent as either a sale or voided. These forms must be stored in a locked safe when not in use. The traffic documents used by a travel agency are airline tickets (Manual & OPTAT) and miscellaneous charges orders (MCOs). Administrative forms are not numbered and therefore do not require the same security procedures (unless they have been issued). These forms include the universal credit card charge form (UCCCF), ticket exchange notices, cash refund notices, and credit card refund notices. They are used to process sales, issue refunds or make adjustments through BSP. Other administrative forms are discussed in Chapter 14. Appointed travel agencies can order the above documents at no charge from authorized suppliers. Some items, such as revalidation stickers, are issued to an agency directly by the airlines.

Since airline tickets are legal contracts, travel counsellors must pay meticulous attention to detail when issuing them. There are some general guidelines which apply when issuing any traffic document. Specific ticketing rules and procedures are identified in the relevant references. All traffic documents are in the form of a booklet with varying numbers of detachable pages (called coupons) which are printed on carbonized paper. Each document typically comprises an audit coupon on which the information is entered, and which is used to process payments and administer the transaction. There is also an agent's and a passenger's coupon which are retained by the relevant parties for record-keeping purposes. Airline tickets contain passenger flight coupons which the other documents do not. Entries are made only on the audit coupon but with sufficient pressure to reproduce the information on all other coupons. Commission information and some other details appear only on the audit and agent coupons; the coupons for any traffic document are the same in almost every other respect. Most entries on an airline ticket are confirmed by another entry. Changes and erasures are not permitted. If an error is made on a traffic document, it must be voided according to the correct procedures; administrative forms may simply be destroyed. Airline tickets can be used only by the person named on the document and are not transferable for use by any other person.

Before any document is legitimate it must be validated using a ticket imprinter.

Each agency purchases a ticket imprinter when it receives its appointment to sell airline tickets. A ticket imprinter is a machine similar to that used to record the details of a credit card transaction for goods purchased in a store. The imprinter contains a date wheel which can be adjusted. An agency validation plate containing the details of the travel agency is obtained from BSP and affixed permanently to the top right corner of the ticket imprinter. Airlines that wish to do business with an agency supply their carrier information plate (CIP) which can be inserted at the bottom right corner of the ticket imprinter in the same way as a credit card is inserted into that machine. A CIP is the property of the issuing airline and may be withdrawn from an agency at any time. To validate a traffic document, the appropriate CIP is selected, placed in the imprinter and the document placed on top. A document is validated in the same manner as a credit card by placing it in the imprinter and pulling the handle across. This action simultaneously reproduces the following:

- The carrier identification plate (CIP) details, i.e., the airline's identification number, name and logo.
- The agency's validation plate details, i.e., name, address and IATA code number.
- The date.

The ticket imprinter, the agency validation plate, airline CIPs, and all traffic documents such as tickets, MCOs and tour orders must be stored in a locked safe at the close of the agency's business day.

Airline Tickets

Airline tickets are available in various forms. Those issued by an airline differ slightly from those prepared by a travel agency. There are generally two versions of each. One type is completed manually by a counsellor and the other is issued through an airline CRS and printer as an automated document (called a transitional automated ticket or TAT).

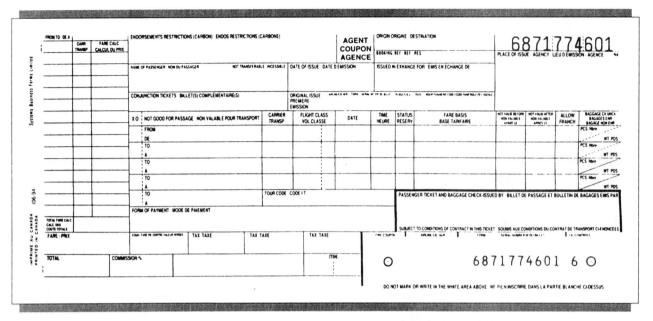

FIGURE 6.26
The audit coupon from a four-coupon manual ticket.
Source: IATA.

Automated tickets issued by travel agencies are known as OPTATs (the OP signifying off-premise). Several carriers in the USA have introduced a document called an automated ticket/boarding pass (ATB) which combines a passenger ticket, boarding pass and baggage identification tag. These combination documents are also proposed for use in Canada. In addition, different forms of tickets are used for individuals and for groups. However, all tickets contain basically the same elements and types of coupons, although their number and format vary.

Manual airline tickets for individuals are available as booklets with four flight coupons. Four-coupon tickets have a blue cover. All automated tickets comprise four flight coupons and have a blue cover. In addition, there is a four-coupon standard group ticket with a brown cover used only for travel wholly within Canada or entirely within the USA.

Every airline ticket booklet comprises a cover, and contains descriptions of the airline's legal and liability obligations (see Figures 1.1 and 1.2). There are also several detachable coupons printed on carbonized paper: an audit coupon, an agent coupon, and either two or four flight coupons. The ticket ends with a passenger coupon

which receives the final reproduction of the information entered on the audit coupon. After a ticket has been completed by a counsellor, each of these coupons is handled and distributed in a different fashion as discussed below and in Chapter 14. There follows a brief review of these segments of an airline ticket.

Front Cover. The presence of the cover is required during travel. The front cover of a standard IATA ticket issued by a travel agency does not bear the logo or colour scheme of any particular airline. (Note that airline offices, however, continue to issue tickets on their own stock.) The IATA symbol is shown in the upper left corner, the ticket number in the upper right, and the ticket title (PASSENGER TICKET and BAGGAGE CHECK) and a stylized impression of an airliner in the centre.

Audit Coupon. Ticket entries are made on this coupon and carbon impressions reproduce the information on the remaining coupons. After the ticket is completed, the audit coupon is detached and sent to the BSP Processing Centre with a weekly sales report. It will eventually be forwarded to the accounting office of the airline whose CIP was used to validate the ticket. The audit coupon is numbered (see Figures 6.26 and 6.27).

Agent Coupon. After completing the ticket, the agent coupon is retained by the issuing agency as a record of the transaction. The agent coupon is also numbered.

Flight Coupon(s). A separate flight coupon is required for each change of carrier and for each portion of the journey where a change of flight, a change in class of service, or a stopover is involved. Either a two-coupon or four-coupon ticket is selected as appropriate. All flight coupons must remain in the ticket booklet until the passenger is about to board a flight. The flight coupon for that leg of the journey is then handed to a ticket agent who exchanges it for a boarding pass for the flight. When a passenger has completed all legs of an itinerary as ticketed, no flight coupons will remain in the ticket booklet. For itineraries involving more than four flights, two or more four-coupon tickets are used in numerical sequence. Tickets issued in this manner are known as conjunction tickets. Each ticket is cross-referenced with the other ticket(s) by entering the numbers in the conjunction ticket box of the coupons.

Passenger Coupon. The passenger coupon must be retained by a passenger during travel. It is the passenger's official receipt and copy of the transaction and is usually kept by passengers for their personal records.

Miscellaneous Charges Order (MCO)

This accountable form is used for many purposes when funds are exchanged between an airline and another supplier (see Figure 6.28). For example, it can be used to record payments for such services as car rentals, tours, hotels, deposits, baggage charges and surcharges. An MCO can also be used to guarantee payments or to send funds in advance. For example, a prepaid ticket advice (PTA) authorizes a carrier to issue an airline ticket or perform a service at a point other than where payment is made. A PTA can be used to prepay tickets, baggage charges or other expenses related to transport. All MCO payments are drawn on the specific carrier whose CIP is used to validate the document.

Universal Credit Card Charge Form (UCCCF)

This form is used to record credit card sales of manually issued airline tickets (Figure 6.30). It is validated on a ticket imprinter by inserting the client's credit card where the airline CIP is normally placed. Automated tickets have a universal charge form inserted between the audit coupon and the flight coupons

FIGURE 6.27
The audit coupon from an OPTAT.
Source: IATA.

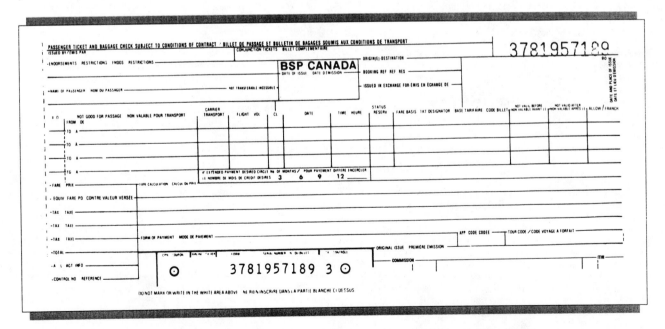

FIGURE 6.28
An MCO can be used to pay for a variety of travel services.
Source: IATA.

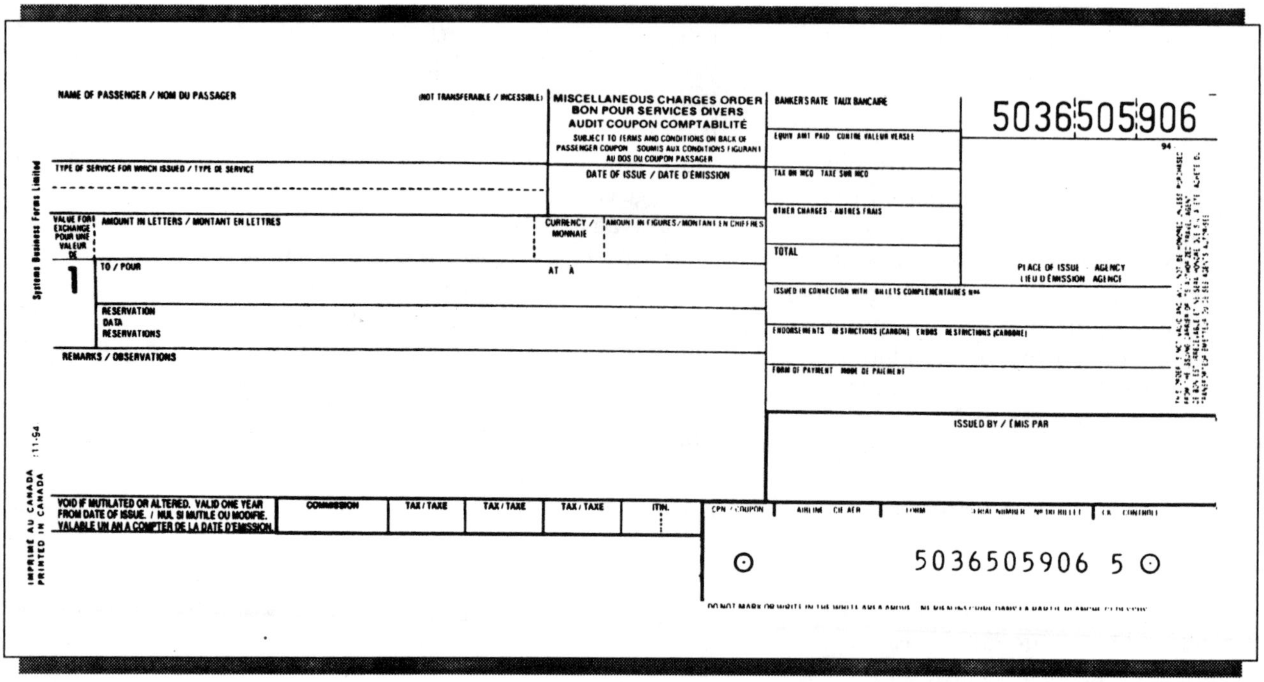

NAME OF PASSENGER / NOM DU PASSAGER

(NOT TRANSFERABLE / INCESSIBLE)

MISCELLANEOUS CHARGES ORDER
BON POUR SERVICES DIVERS
AUDIT COUPON COMPTABILITÉ
SUBJECT TO TERMS AND CONDITIONS ON BACK OF PASSENGER COUPON SOUMIS AUX CONDITIONS FIGURANT AU DOS DU COUPON PASSAGER

BANKERS RATE TAUX BANCAIRE

5036 505 906

EQUIV. AMT. PAID CONTRE VALEUR VERSEE

TYPE OF SERVICE FOR WHICH ISSUED / TYPE DE SERVICE

DATE OF ISSUE / DATE D'EMISSION

TAX ON MCO TAXE SUR MCO

OTHER CHARGES AUTRES FRAIS

VALUE FOR EXCHANGE POUR UNE VALEUR DE

AMOUNT IN LETTERS / MONTANT EN LETTRES

CURRENCY / MONNAIE

AMOUNT IN FIGURES / MONTANT EN CHIFFRES

TOTAL

1

TO / POUR

AT À

PLACE OF ISSUE AGENCY
LIEU D'ÉMISSION AGENCE

ISSUED IN CONNECTION WITH BILLETS COMPLÉMENTAIRES

RESERVATION DATA RÉSERVATIONS

ENDORSEMENTS RESTRICTIONS (CARBON) ENDOS RESTRICTIONS (CARBONE)

REMARKS / OBSERVATIONS

FORM OF PAYMENT MODE DE PAIEMENT

ISSUED BY / ÉMIS PAR

Systems Business Forms Limited

IMPRIMÉ AU CANADA 11-94
PRINTED IN CANADA

VOID IF MUTILATED OR ALTERED. VALID ONE YEAR FROM DATE OF ISSUE. / NUL SI MUTILÉ OU MODIFIÉ. VALABLE UN AN A COMPTER DE LA DATE D'EMISSION.

COMMISSION

TAX / TAXE

TAX / TAXE

TAX / TAXE

ITIN.

CPN / COUPON

5036505906 5

(Figure 6.31). The necessary information is therefore entered automatically for automated tickets paid by credit card; a separate form need not be completed.

Ticket Exchange Notice

For a variety of reasons, passengers may need to have a ticket reissued or exchanged. This form is used on such occasions (Figure 6.32). When one ticket is exchanged for another, there are three possibilities: an even exchange (when the fare on both tickets is the same); an additional collection (if the new ticket is more expensive); or a refund (when the reissued ticket is less expensive). The ticket exchange notice identifies these options and a corresponding box. Counsellors need only enter a check mark in the appropriate box. The amount of collection or refund must also be entered. A refund transaction can only be processed with this document when the original ticket was sold for cash or cheque.

Cash Refund Notice

This form is completed and attached to partially or wholly unused tickets originally paid by cash and returned for voluntary refund.

Credit Card Refund Notice

This notice is used in connection with voluntary refunds on partially or wholly unused credit card sales.

Charter and Tour Tickets

Counsellors who sell ABCs based on tariff information issue airline tickets in the same manner as above using the same documents. Airlines and tour operators generally issue group tickets such as CBITs and GITs. Some tour operators and

charter airlines have their own tickets (Figure 6.33); others issue vouchers rather than tickets for charter flights. All of these options reduce a counsellor's workload to that of selling the product and inspecting the documents supplied by the airline or tour operator.

Ticketing, whether performed manually or through an automated system, is a skill which demands care and concentration. It is also one which must be continually maintained. Each April IATA issues a revised version of its Ticketing Handbook which identifies additions, changes and cancellations from the previous edition. Similarly, periodic revisions are made to the BSP Manual. In addition, air fares and regulations constantly change and these too have an impact on ticket entries. The move to automated reservations systems in recent years has dramatically changed the way travel counsellors sell and issue airline tickets. However, one fact is likely to remain constant; air travel will continue to be the foundation of most travel agency business.

FIGURE 6.30
A manual credit card charge form.
Source: IATA.

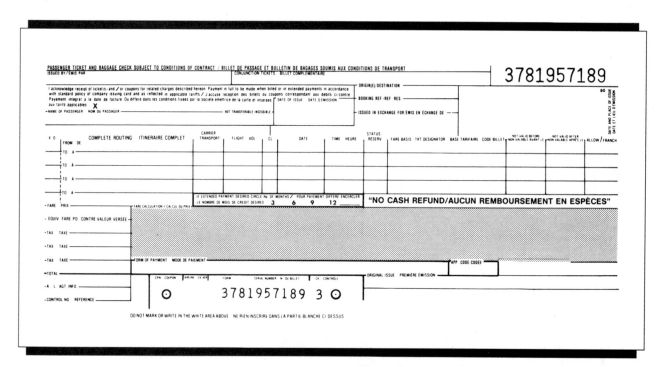

FIGURE 6.31
In an OPTAT the credit card charge form is one of the coupons in the booklet.
Source: IATA.

FIGURE 6.32
A ticket exchange notice.
Source: IATA.

TICKET EXCHANGE NOTICE
AVIS D'ÉCHANGE DE BILLETS

PROCESSING CENTRE COPY
EXEMPLAIRE DU CENTRE DE TRAITEMENT

EXCHANGED TICKET NUMBER(S)
N°(S) DU OU DES BILLETS REMPLACÉS

A/L # # DE AÉR	FORM & SERIAL # # FORMULE & SÉRIE	CPN # # CPN

Date of Issue / Date d'émission

Issuing Agency / Agence émettrice

NEW TICKET NUMBER(S)
N°(S) DU OU DES NOUVÉAUX BILLETS

CHECK APPLICABLE BOX / COCHER LA CASE APPROPRIÉE

1 ☐ EVEN EXCHANGE / PARITÉ
2 ☐ ADDITIONAL COLLECTION / PERCEPTION SUPPLÉMENTAIRE
3 ☐ REFUND / REMBOURSEMENT

ADDITIONAL COLLECTION OF REFUND VALUE DIFFERENCE (PERCEPTION OU REMBOURSEMENT)	Comm.	Tax / Taxe	Tax / Taxe	Tax / Taxe	Change Penalty Pénalité d'échange	Itin.	
TOTAL		Tax / Taxe	Tax / Taxe	PFC AP Code XF _ _ _ _ XF _ _ _ _ XF _ _ _ _		Issued By · Émis par	

O

FIGURE 6.33
A charter flight ticket issued by a tour operator.
Source: Sunquest Vacations.

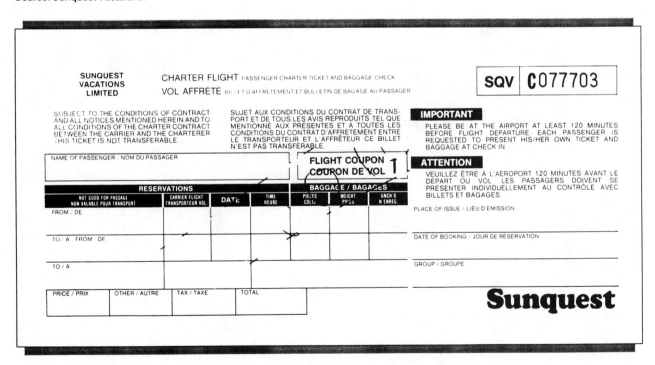

Review Questions

1. How has deregulation affected air transportation in Canada and the USA?

2. Discuss route structures and their relation to an airline's marketing capabilities.

3. Discuss the product knowledge necessary to sell air transportation.

4. What information does a counsellor need to make a flight reservation and where can this be found?

5. Describe the basic principles on which air fares are set and constructed.

References

Air Tariff, 86 Hartford Avenue, Pointe Claire, Quebec H9R 3E1.

Air Transport Association of America (ATA), 1709 New York Avenue NW, Washington, DC 20006-5206, USA.

ATPCO Passenger Tariff Set, Airline Tariff Publishing Company, Dulles International Airport, 400 West Service Road, Chantilly, VA 22021, USA.

Bank Settlement Manual For Passenger Sales Agents - Canada. International Air Transport Association, 2000 Peel Street, Montreal, Quebec H3A 2R4.

IATA Ticketing Handbook, International Air Transport Association, 2000 Peel Street, Montreal, Quebec H3A 2R4.

IATA Travel Agent's Handbook and Guide to Automation, International Air Transport Association, 2000 Peel Street, Montreal, Quebec H3A 2R4.

National Transportation Agency (NTA), Ottawa, Ontario K1A 0N9.

Official Airline Guides, 2000 Clearwater Drive, Oak Brook, IL 60521, USA.

Systems Business Forms Ltd., 1595 Buffalo Place, Winnipeg, Manitoba R3T 1M1. This company supplies manual and automated ticket stock and other traffic documents to travel agencies. Voided tickets are also available for training purposes.

## Chapter 7

Rail Travel

Chapter Summary

This chapter reviews the role of rail transportation in today's travel industry. The key sales features, benefits and disadvantages of train travel are discussed. Rail travel in Canada, the USA, Europe, Great Britain and the rest of the world is then considered. Each section examines the terminology, equipment, facilities and services, fares and reservations procedures. Special attention is given to the use and application of the Thomas Cook European Timetable and the Eurailtariff. The growth of rail passes and their sales features are also mentioned.

Chapter Objectives

After completing this chapter you should be able to:

- Use rail terminology.

- Describe the development and current condition of rail transportation in Canada, the USA, Europe and the rest of the world.

- Recall how rail travel is marketed.

- Report the key sales features of rail service.

- Discuss the importance of rail travel in Europe.

- Interpret the Cook European Timetable and the Eurailtariff.

- State the benefits of various rail passes and outline the conditions under which they are sold.

- Describe the types of trains, facilities and services offered by various railroads.

- Make rail reservations and issue tickets.

Development of Rail Travel

Railways, the first mechanically powered form of transportation, were initially developed to move heavy freight over long distances. As the industrial revolution took hold, rail networks grew in the industrialized countries. Two of the first railways in the world (the Stockton to Darlington line in England and the Baltimore to Ohio line in the United States) were constructed to move raw materials, minerals and finished goods between the mines and factories where they were produced and seaports where they were shipped to overseas markets. Only later did railways become involved with passenger transport. The steam engine was first used as a means of transporting passengers in England over 150 years ago. Railway systems were also started in North America and many European countries before 1840. Steam powered railways spread rapidly throughout the world and for the next one hundred years railways expanded by an average of 200,000 km every 20 years. The earliest and largest increases came in the nineteenth century in the industrialized countries. Later, colonizing activities of the European nations led to the construction of railways in previously remote areas. By 1900, railways had been set up in Tunisia, Mozambique, Angola and Indonesia, and were flourishing in South America. In the century to 1960, the means of power also changed from coal-fired steam engines to diesel locomotives and electric trains. Today, all these types of trains still operate in various parts of the world.

The development of a passenger rail network brought with it the beginnings of the modern tourist industry. Railways were fast, convenient, safe, comfortable (by the standards of the time) and inexpensive. The industrial revolution brought not only a growing rail network but a large workforce with a measure of free time and disposable income. By 1900 a number of seaside resorts, such as Atlantic City on the eastern seaboard, and Blackpool and Brighton in England, had sprung up to service the leisure needs of the new working class. Each of these resorts was linked by rail to nearby industrial cities. As the rail network grew, more distant resorts became accessible to those with the time and money to make the journey. Those in the Northern States could escape the cold winters by travelling to Florida, Arizona and California while their European counterparts journeyed to the warm Mediterranean. As the rail system expanded and became more popular with travellers, the railways began to extend the scope of their operations to include the running of hotels.

Except for crowded commuter routes, railways in many countries were considered obsolete by the early 1960s. Long distance routes in the United States had lost almost all of their passenger business to airlines and shorter routes could not compete with the private car. Many railroad companies experienced serious financial difficulties. Construction began to slow down although major projects were started in Australia and South Africa. For social and political reasons, however, Europe and Japan began to upgrade their rail networks. Trains were converted to electric power, tracks and equipment were upgraded, and services were improved. This modernization led to improved speed, better time performances, smooth running and reliability, and helped change travel habits. This was particularly so in Europe where shorter distances allowed the advantage to pass to railways. In recent years there has been a further burst of upgrading and new construction, primarily in Europe, to build high-speed rail networks. Britain, France, Germany, Italy and Spain are just some of the countries that have invested heavily in refurbishing their rail systems. The result is that worldwide passenger rail traffic more than doubled from 398 million passenger miles in 1948 to 899 million passenger miles in 1976.

Recent technological improvements have helped the railway networks of the world to remain competitive with other modes of transport in attracting passengers. Railways also have some intrinsic advantages over other means of travel. Many railway lines helped pioneer the development of a country. The railway station was often located at the heart of the city and most towns grew around the station. Thus rail travel is always from city centre to city centre and the delay and frustration of travel to and from airports, the inevitable formalities at crowded terminals, and the dependence on weather conditions can all be avoided. Train travel has the greatest advantage over air travel on distances up to 500 km. Given that passengers must now arrive at airports from one to three hours in advance of their flights and that airports are usually located on the outskirts of town, even conventional trains can compete with aircraft over relatively short distances. High-speed services in Europe and Japan make a stronger claim in terms of time savings and have recaptured much of this market. Further, hazards such as fog which can interrupt air traffic do not have that effect on train service. In the Japanese high-speed train system, for example, there are no trackside signals; the correct speed for the conditions is displayed in the driver's cab. Thus the increased speed of passenger trains has not been achieved at the expense of safety. In addition, there are still many travellers who do not wish to fly or who have no desire to drive long distances. Others are "train buffs" or are simply attracted by the romance, comfort and experience of train travel.

Train travel in North America has not undergone the extensive upgrading that has occurred in Europe and travel counsellors may find that few clients seek their advice on domestic rail transport. Rail travel in Europe, however, continues to be popular not only with local residents but also with tourists. Professional travel counsellors must therefore know the essentials of this product. The basics of rail service include knowledge of the equipment, services, routes and schedules in Canada, the United States and elsewhere, as well as the ability to make reservations for clients. In addition, travel counsellors must be able to sell this mode of transport by discussing its advantages, features and benefits.

Advantages of Rail Travel

Every form of transportation possesses its own distinctive travel benefits. Railroads offer certain features which are unique within the transportation network.

Relaxed and Comfortable Travelling Conditions. The seating available on a train is larger and offers more legroom than on a bus or plane. Comfort has been improved with reclining seats. In general, passengers are not confined to their seat as they are on a bus or airplane but can move freely between any of several spacious coaches, designed specifically for relaxed comfort. There are bars and lounges, restaurant facilities and observation cars. On overnight journeys passengers can choose from a wide selection of sleeping facilities. Trains offer a way to see the countryside from ground level without stress and in comfort. Trains also offer facilities which permit business people to work in comfort. Arriving relaxed and rested is also important to this group of travellers.

European trains are among the most modern and most comfortable in the world. The EuroCity network of luxury trains has individual reclining seats, air-conditioning, soundproofing and many other amenities such as a boutique and a hairdresser. Passengers may also enjoy a drink in the bar car or savour a five-course dinner in the dining car or at their seat.

Excellent Sightseeing. Trains travel on the surface and are built with wide windows and often with special observation cars. These afford passengers an excellent opportunity to view sights along the route. Canadian railroads offer superb views of Canada's foremost natural

attraction, the Rocky Mountains. Europe offers the Alps, castles and glimpses of a different lifestyle.

Economical. Passenger trains provide comfortable, efficient transportation at rates which are significantly lower than air fares. In addition, there are the advantages of various rail passes which permit unlimited travel for a specific duration at a single price. Canada, the United States and many European nations each offer national and regional passes. The European railroad system also offers several different Eurail passes which allow unlimited travel in seventeen countries. When comparing rail versus air travel, however, fares are frequently a secondary consideration. The travel experience and service on trains are often more enjoyable than on airplanes.

Convenience (Downtown to Downtown Transportation). Railway terminals are normally located at or near the business and commercial centre of a city. This can become a major factor in deciding how to travel when one considers the time involved in transferring between city centres and airports. A prime example of this situation is illustrated on the Toronto-Montreal route where the elapsed time by air from city centre to city centre, including airport limousine time, waiting time, and the like is comparable to the rail time from Union Station, Toronto to Central Station, Montreal. European high-speed links magnify this advantage. Deregulation has led to congestion and delays at airports, and increased the number and variety of airfares available. These inconveniences and complexities are causing many travellers to reconsider train over air travel.

The European rail network is so extensive that almost any place in Europe can be reached by train. No other carrier, except perhaps the automobile, can claim such convenience. European railroad stations are located in the centre of town and usually constitute focal points around which the city spreads. Furthermore, railroad stations in large metropolitan areas are themselves little towns, in some cases with shopping centres and/or hotels attached. No matter whether it is on a weekend or late at night, the station is the place to find a restaurant open, a bookstore, a currency exchange office and many more conveniences. In addition, European railroads have adopted a system of signs which makes it possible to find one's way through almost any of the facilities available (see Figure 7.1).

Generous Baggage Allowance. Passengers may check 70 kilos of personal baggage free of charge with every adult ticket. Two bags can be taken on board as carry-on luggage. In comparison, aircraft passengers are restricted to 20 or 30 kilos of checked baggage and one carry-on bag. Railways can also easily carry sports equipment such as skis and golf clubs. They will also carry pets when securely confined to cages.

Mystique and Romance. Rail travel recaptures the image of a different time and a different style of travel. This image acts as a stimulus for many travellers.

Safety. Statistically, rail travel is the safest mode of transport. This factor attracts those who have a fear of flying and whose safety need is high.

European rail travel has some additional advantages which cannot be claimed to the same extent by its North American counterpart.

Frequency of Service. European trains are frequent. For instance, from Amsterdam to Cologne there are 12 trains a day; from Paris to the Chateaux Country 14 trains run each day. There is much more track in Europe than in Canada. This permits passengers to make contact with every part of the continent on frequent schedules.

Dependability. European railroads pride themselves on their punctuality. Not only do they leave on time but more important, particularly if your clients are travelling on a tight schedule, they arrive on time. No matter the weather or the density of traffic,

the train will leave on time and make connections at the other end.

Speed. It is claimed that European intercity trains are generally faster than those in North America. This is certainly so in terms of normal operating speeds. Many European trains average speeds of 160-200 km per hour and can reach 270 km per hour. France has the high-speed TGV (*Train à Grande Vitesse*) which can travel at 350 km per hour and easily competes with air and automobile travel. Since the energy shortage of the 1970s all European countries, with the exception of Germany's

FIGURE 7.1
Some of the symbols seen in European stations. *Source: Eurail.*

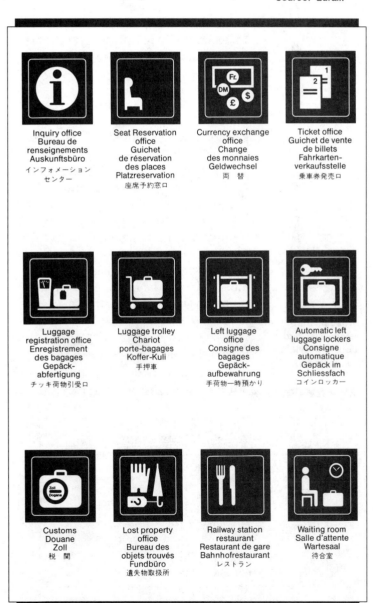

autobahns, have set speed limits on their roads. The limit is about 130 km per hour on highways and 100 km per hour on major arteries. European trains are not only faster, but journey times are also shorter (see Figure 7.2). Europe is densely populated and space is scarce, so airports are built far from city centres. Further, the distances between cities are so short that the time saved in flying from one to another is usually wasted in travelling to and from the airport. If one counts on spending one hour minimum to reach the airport, another hour from the airport to the city, plus the required check-in time for security, and the frequent stacking over congested airports, it is rare when a flight takes less than four hours. In four hours by train, one can travel from Paris to Brussels to Amsterdam and cross three countries.

Scenic Views of Europe. European trains have wide picture windows to provide a breathtaking view of Europe. Since trains follow scenic routes through mountain passes, along lake shores and sandy beaches, passengers gain a sightseeing tour of Europe while travelling from one place to another, with every country offering its own special attraction. Many routes have been retained for their scenic value. A stay-put vacation cannot match this experience. In a car, there are problems with traffic, unfamiliar driving habits and unusual road signs; it is often difficult under such conditions to take time to enjoy the scenery. The driver not only

finds the trip more stressful, but it is impossible to both drive and view the scenery.

A Chance to Meet People. Seating arrangements on European trains make it conducive to start conversations with fellow passengers. Many Europeans understand English and, for those who do not, sign language is a practical and fun solution. The atmosphere on a train can be quite friendly and informal. No other method of touring Europe provides such an opportunity to interact with the local inhabitants. Tourists who travel by car are confined to the security and limitations of their vehicle; on organized bus tours they are generally confined with other North Americans and never really feel the heartbeat of the country they came to see. Train travel is also more convenient than travelling by road. No stops are necessary to share a meal or take a restroom break.

Disadvantages of Rail Travel

Inflexible. Trains can only travel where there are tracks and they have relatively inflexible departure times. These are limitations for some travellers and for some journeys.

Slowness. On longer journeys travel time by train is considerably more than by plane. However, for some travellers the trip is more important than reaching the destination.

Outdated Equipment. This complaint is heard most often about Canadian trains. Generally, equipment in Europe is new and of a high standard.

Poor Quality Food Service. Again, this criticism is most often heard in Canada. The quality of food served on some trains, particularly the snacks available, could be improved in some areas.

FIGURE 7.2
European trains provide fast and frequent service.
Source: Eurail.

From	To	Distance (Miles)	Shortest Travel Time	Frequency (Daily)
Amsterdam	Cologne	162	3 hours	12
Barcelona	Madrid	430	6 3/4 hours	5
Bern	Zurich	81	1 1/4 hour	19
Brussels	Paris	195	2 1/2 hours	11
Frankfurt	Munich	287	3 3/4 hours	17
Geneva	Paris	391	3 1/2 hours	5
Lisbon	Madrid	404	10 hours	2
Paris	Lyon	265	2 hours	22
Rome	Florence	198	2 1/4 hours	18
Stockholm	Göteborg	285	4 hours	14

Passengers can, however, overcome this drawback by packing a lunch.

Rail Travel in Canada

The first rail journey in Canada took place on July 21, 1836. It linked Laprairie on the south shore of the St. Lawrence River with Saint-Jean-sur-Richelieu, Quebec, a distance of 23 km. From that date railroads played a vital role in the development of Canada. They established the first permanent, regularly scheduled transportation routes across the country. Trans-Canada rail service has existed since the "last spike" was driven on November 7, 1885, over one hundred years ago. As the sole national transportation link from about 1890 to 1950, railways enjoyed considerable growth in both passenger and freight traffic. During this time railroads developed complex route systems concentrated not only in heavily populated areas but also connecting major centres across the country. As an enticement for the western part of the country to join Confederation, the federal government made significant concessions to the railroad companies to encourage the development of rail transportation on transcontinental routes. By the 1950s, however, their favoured position in the transportation field became threatened by long distance motorcoach and truck routes, by automobiles and by airlines. The widespread acceptance of automobile travel and the rapid building of multiple highway systems seriously eroded short haul railway markets. Long haul routes were threatened, especially in recent years, by the growing acceptance of air travel as a fast, comfortable means of transport. These developments led one major Canadian railroad to give more attention to freight as a source of revenue and to reduce its passenger service.

Passenger sales, however, were still an important source of revenue for the railroads. To combat the decline in the passenger market, VIA Rail Canada was established as a crown corporation on April 1, 1978. Its objective was to provide Canadians with an attractive, economical and efficient rail passenger service. VIA combined the passenger services of Canadian National and Canadian Pacific Railways to form a single rail network throughout Canada. Passenger service employees from both railways, such as on-board personnel, ticket and reservations agents joined VIA. Today, VIA Rail is responsible for the operation of all intercity and transcontinental passenger services previously operated by CN and CP. The most important route by far is the Quebec City to Windsor corridor. This corridor is the most densely populated region of Canada and offers the most opportunity for profitable service.

VIA does not own the railway beds but instead contracts with both CN and CP to operate passenger trains over their lines and to use their operating employees to run the trains. This arrangement has led to a number of problems over the years. Most notable are the poor condition of the railway beds, which are designed to carry freight rather than passengers, and outdated equipment. VIA has attempted to overcome the latter by undertaking an extensive program to refurbish its passenger equipment. Large sums of money were invested in the development of faster, more comfortable trains capable of competing with airlines and surface vehicles on short and medium range routes. At the same time, an extremely high standard of personal passenger service was provided. For example, between Toronto and Montreal LRC (light, rapid and comfortable) service has decreased travel time and fares are lower than for comparable air travel. On long haul routes, railroads are concentrating on the development of more comfortable accommodation, service is more personalized and the relaxation aspects of rail travel are stressed. Service on many uneconomic routes was cut in an effort to make the railroad profitable. In addition, a variety of marketing programs were implemented. The results were promising. Rail travel in Canada enjoyed an unprecedented increase in the early

1980s as VIA carried more passengers on both scheduled services and on tours. Technical difficulties, however, hampered many of these developments and VIA Rail continued to lose money.

In 1986 the federal government produced a new National Passenger Transportation Act as part of its "Freedom to Move" deregulation policy. The act specified that most of VIA's routes had to earn a specified proportion of their operating costs by 1990 or be cut from the network. The act also allowed for the sale of rail lines. These proposals were intended to increase the efficiency of the rail system by allowing for the conversion of certain lines into specialized, more cost-effective, short-line operations. A recent government review of VIA's operations upheld the views put forward in its deregulation policy. Commencing January 1990, half of VIA's routes were eliminated and service on many others was trimmed. In addition, the rights to operate the southern transcontinental route were purchased by a private tour company to operate a luxury cross-Canada service comparable with that available on the famed Orient Express. Despite these setbacks, VIA continues to offer service in the Quebec City to Windsor corridor and in various other regions of the country. When operating close to capacity, the train has proven to be the most fuel efficient and nonpolluting means of transportation compared with private automobile, bus or air travel. VIA offers its passengers a wide variety of accommodation ranging from economically priced coach seats to first class treatment in the club car. On longer trips, travellers may purchase reasonably priced upper and lower berth space or the more private and luxurious bedroom compartments. VIA also operates various types of dining cars, lounge and scenic dome cars which are available on certain trains.

There are three main sources of VIA Rail information; VIA Rail, airline computer systems, and standard railway references. VIA Rail publishes a number of references for travel agencies appointed as sales agents. Such agencies can issue rail tickets using VIA Rail ticket stock. The publications supply the information necessary for an agent to answer enquiries, quote fares and charges, provide train information and issue tickets. The most important of these references is the *VIA Rail Selling Guide* which describes train services, tours, fares, reservations, ticketing and reporting procedures, and the support services available from VIA. This manual is used in conjunction with a system timetable (see Figure 7.3) which outlines frequency and type of service over all VIA Rail routes in Canada. Other VIA publications describe VIA's tour policies and procedures in greater detail and assist agencies that have access to VIA through airline computer systems. Agents are also provided with brochures outlining the details and features of passenger service on trains.

A second source of VIA Rail information is the *Official Railway Guide*, one of the standard references discussed earlier. The North American edition is the most complete source of passenger train timetables and fares for the United States, Canada and Mexico. The reference contains useful additions to its itinerary planning and ticketing information, such as accommodation and car diagrams, route maps and principal connecting rail, bus and water service. It is published five times per year. A third source of product knowledge is an airline computer reservation system. VIA is linked to travel agencies through a system known as Reservia II which can be accessed through airline computer systems. Ticketing can be done on automated airline ticket stock. This system permits automated agencies to access VIA products and obtain complete information on the various pricing plans and schedules. Counsellors can also reserve and issue coach tickets and create and modify passenger name records.

VIA Rail Equipment

A variety of equipment is used by VIA but its fleet consists of three main types of trains.

Railiners are diesel-powered trains that provide service on shorter regional lines and on intercity commuter routes. These trains, also known as Rail Diesel Cars (RDCs), can be used individually or in combination according to ridership requirements. They are typically employed on routes where the passenger traffic is insufficient to warrant a larger train. These units offer coach accommodation and can reach speeds of 135 km per hour.

Conventional trains offer day and overnight service and are used for transcontinental service. These trains consist of a diesel locomotive hauling standard, air-conditioned, heated passenger cars. Coaches usually have at-seat buffet cart service, takeout and coffee shop facilities, and a lounge. VIA plans to upgrade these trains by installing showers in sleepers, renovating the car interiors, and adding electric heating and ventilation.

The LRC (light, rapid and comfortable) unit is specifically designed for Canadian travel needs with detail paid to climate, track conditions and the latest passenger comfort and services. It is designed for high-speed corridor service and has an improved suspension system that tilts the car bodies when the train enters a curve at speed. LRCs have large panoramic windows with tinted glass, reclining seats with individual foldaway trays, individual reading lights, an intercom system for

FIGURE 7.3
How to read a VIA Rail timetable.
Source: VIA Rail.

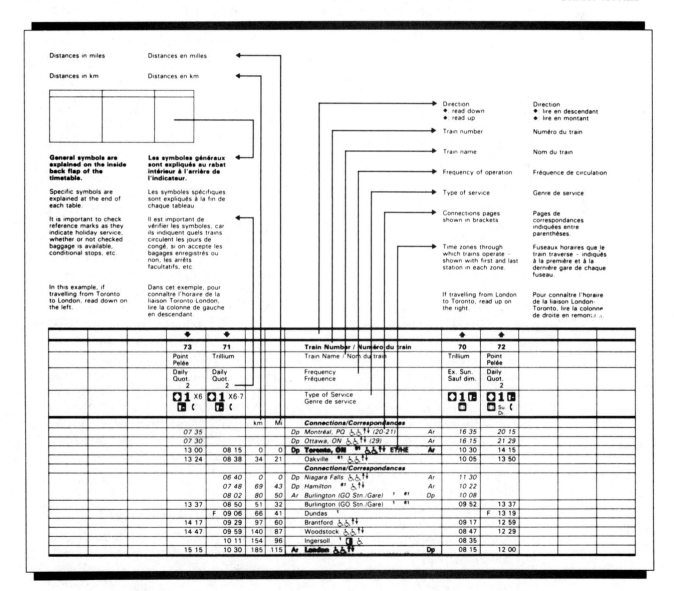

announcements and music, storage lockers for carry-on luggage, and the ability to accommodate handicapped travellers. LRCs provide intercity connections in the Quebec City-Ottawa-Windsor corridor at speeds up to 150 km per hour.

VIA Rail Accommodation and Services

Coaches provide basic rail transportation. They are divided into smoking and non-smoking sections on all VIA trains. Standard coaches are equipped with up to 76 reclining, turnaround seats, adjustable foot rests, end-of-car and overhead luggage racks, portable tables, toilet facilities and a water cooler (see Figure 7.4). LRC trains have one service attendant in each coach. Dayniters are more luxurious coaches which contain 52 deluxe reclining sleeper seats with leg rests, trays and directional lighting. VIA 1 First Class has some additional features. Passengers receive complimentary newspapers and magazines and have priority boarding up to 30 minutes before departure. The surcharge for this service is approximately 30 percent above regular coach fare. The accommodation in these coaches is more luxurious. There are fewer reclining seats (each with leg rests), carpeted floors, individual folding tables at each seat, individual reading lights and superior washroom facilities. This coach offers first class facilities and full course meals served at the passenger's seat. Two service attendants are assigned to each car to provide passenger assistance.

VIA's conventional trains offer four types of sleeper accommodation; sections, roomettes, bedrooms and drawing rooms.

Sections provide open accommodation with either lower or upper berths. A berth typically consists of unfolded facing seats, or a shelf or frame fixed to a wall. Privacy is obtained by closing curtains. Passengers use washrooms located at the end of the car. Roomettes are designed for one passenger only and contain a fixed seat, toilet and folding or sliding bed. Bedrooms, for use by

more than one passenger, exhibit a variety of seating and sleeping accommodation. Enclosed accommodation consists of rooms with a door, private washroom facilities, drinking water, mirrors, luggage space, porter's bell and clothes hangers. Each room has its own set of controls for air-conditioning, fans and lighting. This type of accommodation is available in a variety of designs and can accommodate from one to three persons. Four people can be boarded by removing the daytime wall between ensuite bedrooms which are two connecting rooms in a sleeping car. Bedrooms can be adapted for day or night use. By night they are twin bedrooms featuring an upper and lower berth. During the day they can be converted to a private living room with two armchairs, a fold-down table and picture window. Toiletries are supplied and smoking is permitted at all times.

A drawing room is a sleeping car with three berths and an enclosed toilet. It is approximately 25 percent larger than a standard bedroom. During the day it has a sofa and armchair. At night it can be transformed into one upper and two lower berths with a private toilet closet as in the bedroom. Again, all toiletries are supplied and smoking is permitted at all times.

Meal services on VIA trains are provided in either dining cars or lounge cars. Dining cars offer formal dining service and a complete menu. Snack and meal service is available in a variety of lounge cars.

Not all of the above coaches and services are available on every route. In addition, VIA offers a number of other facilities including the popular bilevel Dome Car. On the upper level there is a wide-vision observation dome lounge while the lower level has a bar and dining area with takeout service. Dome Cars also offer sleeping accommodation in bedrooms.

VIA Rail Fares

Until recently VIA's rail fares were established on a taper principle which reduced the cost per mile as the distance travelled increased. Fares were set for each route and these were published in the tariff as basic transportation charges for coach travel. In January 1990 a new, market-based pricing structure was introduced. Fares were no longer based on the distance travelled but instead were assessed according to the nature of the market, that is, prices were determined to some extent by supply and demand. Under this structure passengers on the most popular routes, such as through the Rockies, pay a premium. VIA's goals for market-based pricing attempt to address specific, local

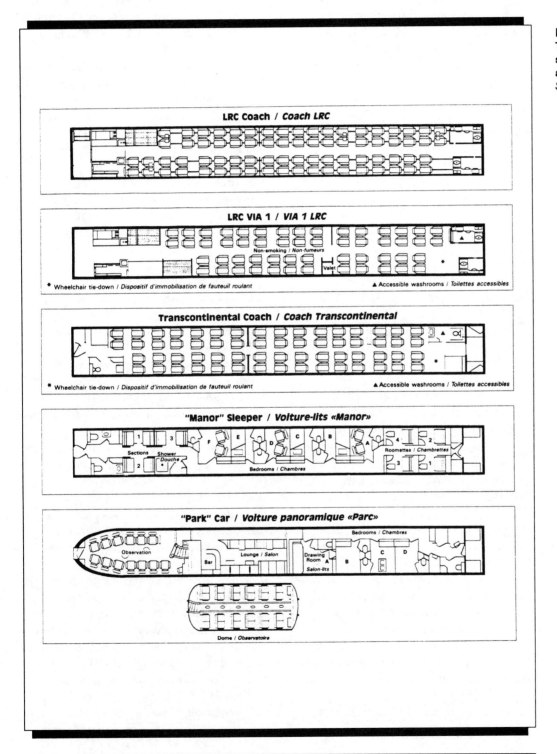

FIGURE 7.4
Typical VIA seating arrangements.
Source: VIA Rail.

market conditions, to simplify the pricing scheme, and to stimulate travel during off-peak periods by offering attractive fares. At the same time as the new pricing scheme was introduced, about half of VIA's routes were cut. The southern transcontinental (The Canadian) route was eliminated in January 1990 and the Supercontinental service (which takes the northern route through Ontario and the prairies) was reduced to three times per week.

In January 1994, VIA moved to segment pricing. VIA defines a segment as a single- or multi-leg trip confirmed in the same class of service where there are no stopovers or where stopovers are permitted. Trips then have one or more segments.

Five distinct regions have been identified in the current pricing scheme. These are the Corridor (Quebec City to Windsor), Intercity East (Nova Scotia and New Brunswick), Transcontinental East (the Corridor to the Maritimes and Gaspe Coast), Transcontinental West (the Corridor to Vancouver), and Essential Services (e.g., Winnipeg - Churchill or Sudbury - White River). Basic fares are set for each route. Three fare levels (peak, off-peak and super saver) apply in these five regions. For the Corridor market, discounted fares are available daily, subject to availability. Discounted fares are available daily for Intercity East trains, except on specific holiday periods. In both regions a 40 percent discount is available in coach and dayniter transport if off-peak tickets are purchased five days in advance. This discount does not apply to VIA 1 First Class tickets or to the supplemental dayniter charge. For long distance travel in the Eastern Transcontinental market the super saver period is seasonally based and operates from January 6 to June 18 and from September 10 to December 14, inclusive. A 40 percent discount from the basic one-way fare is available for off-peak tickets purchased seven days in advance. The discount does not apply to supplemental charges for dayniters or sleeping cars. Discounts are also seasonally based in the Western Transcontinental region. Peak season is June 1 to September 30. A 25 percent

reduction from the basic one-way fare is available during the remainder of the year without an advance purchase requirement. Tickets purchased seven days in advance are eligible for a 40 percent discount during the super saver periods of January 6 to April 30 and November 1 to December 4. For Essential Services, a 40 percent discount is available year-round except from December 15 to January 5. Tickets must be purchased seven days in advance.

Seniors (those 60 years or over), youths (12-24) and students can receive a 10 percent discount from the basic transportation charge without having to make an advance purchase. These reductions can be combined with off-peak discounts for a total reduction of 50 percent provided that tickets are purchased according to advance purchase requirements. These groups do not receive a discount on accommodation supplements. Aboriginal people receive a 33 percent discount in economy class in certain territories.

All regular rail fares are quoted on a one-way basis. They are valid for one year from the date of issue, can be used for accommodation on all trains and allow unlimited stopovers. Children aged two to eleven travel at half the basic fare although children aged seven or less must be accompanied by an adult to qualify for this reduction. Supplemental charges are levied on basic coach fares for each type of accommodation available. These charges are designed to reflect the various degrees of comfort, privacy, space and convenience. Reserved accommodation is charged on a through fare basis whereas supplemental fees are charged on a point-to-point basis. Travel agencies earn 11 percent commission on the sale of VIA Rail tickets.

VIA also offers a rail pass under the name Canrailpass. This travel card provides unlimited transportation on VIA trains at a fixed cost. The pass is available for the entire system (Coast-to-Coast). The pass is valid for travel on any 12 days within a 30 day period. Up to three additional days may be purchased. Canrailpasses are not valid for travel between December 15 and January 5 inclusive, on Holy Thursday or on Easter

Monday. Youth (under 25) and Senior (60+) Canrailpasses are also available at a lower price.

VIA Rail Reservations and Ticketing

Train reservations may be made by contacting VIA by telephone or through the airline CRS in automated agencies. Counsellors must first identify the agency appointment as either IATA or VIA. IATA appointed agencies provide their IATA agency code number and use the CIP (Carrier Information Plate) supplied by VIA to ticket on IATA airline stock. VIA appointed agencies give their VIA agency number and issue tickets on VIA stock. Once agency identification has been supplied, the VIA sales agent will require the following client information.

- Itinerary. List the itinerary beginning with the origin and destination. Identify any stopovers being made. Give the dates and departure times.
- Client Information. Give the names and number of passengers. Provide the ages of any children, specify whether any passengers are senior citizens or students, and identify the discounts that apply.
- Service. Request the appropriate class of service (Coach or VIA 1), smoking or non-smoking if applicable, and the sleeping accommodation desired (section, roomette, bedroom, drawing room).
- Form of Payment. State whether the client will pay by cash, cheque, credit card or Canrailpass.
- Special Service Requests. Identify any special services requested by your client, e.g. wheelchair, oxygen, special meals.

If the counsellor is ticketing at the same time as the reservation is being made, the travel counsellor must also provide the VIA sales agent with:

- Reservation Number (PNR locator).
- Control Number (to validate the ticket sale).

- Total Fare (rail and accommodation combined).
- Fare Restrictions.

If ticketing will not be done until later, the VIA sales agent requires a reservation number (or locator) for reserved space only and an option date. The space and fare will automatically be cancelled if VIA does not receive a ticket number by the option date and issue a VIA Control number authorization.

VIA Rail introduced the Reservia system in March 1980. This system permitted automated travel agencies to book and confirm reservations through an airline CRS and issue tickets on IATA airline ticket stock through an automated ticket printer. This system has since been upgraded and linked with airline reservations systems such as Galileo and Sabre. It now operates as Reservia II. Tickets for Amtrak, ONR (Ontario Northland Railway), Terratransport (CN Newfoundland) and connecting buses may also be written on VIA stock. Reservia II also allows counsellors to locate available space on a given train for a period up to seven days.

Tickets can also be issued on VIA ticket stock and on IATA manual ticket stock. VIA Canrailpasses and VIA Tour products should be ticketed on MCOs which are used as exchange documents. These are forwarded to VIA ticketing locations or presented by clients at VIA locations for ticketing at the point of departure, if applicable.

Rail Travel in the United States

Rail travel in the United States and in Canada shares many characteristics and has a similar history. This common tradition, however, appears to be diverging as rail transport in Canada is being reduced while in the USA it is expanding. Privately owned American railroads reached their peak in the nineteenth century just as they did in Canada. The railways gradually deteriorated through neglect and competition from the plane and private car. By the late 1960s the situation was critical and most railways cut their passenger services to a minimum. Had the legislation permitted it many of them would, in fact, have abandoned passenger services completely. At that time, however, all transportation in the United States was regulated by the government. In 1970 Congress passed an act which established the National Railroad Passenger Corporation (Amtrak) to support the operation of intercity passenger trains with federal government funds. Amtrak began operating the following year with the intention of being a profit-making corporation. Amtrak provided a network of main line passenger services which included all but two of the remaining passenger routes in the United States. The reorganization of Amtrak, together with major company mergers, allowed the railroads to win back much of the freight traffic it had lost to trucking companies. The largest merger occurred in 1976 when Conrail, supported by federal government loans, was formed from six bankrupt eastern railways (including the well known Pennsylvania and New York Central). These privately owned railway lines cooperated with the Amtrak network by providing information and by promoting the sale of passenger transportation. The actual operation of the railways, however, was left to the individual railroads. The remaining private passenger railroads joined Amtrak in 1983.

Amtrak's function in the USA is similar to that of VIA Rail in Canada. It is a marketing organization set up by the federal government to promote and encourage passenger rail service. Amtrak combines the sales and reservations operations of all major American railroads into one organization. Unlike VIA Rail which is a government owned crown corporation, Amtrak is neither nationalized nor a private enterprise but instead is arranged as a partially public organization. Amtrak receives a subsidy from the federal

government but American rail passengers pay a higher proportion of the actual cost than do Canadian riders on VIA.

Amtrak's most important route is the northeast corridor from New York to Washington which accounts for half of all passengers. Other important routes in terms of customer demand are Virginia to Florida (the Autotrain) and San Francisco to Los Angeles which offers parlour car sightseeing tours. The longest distance covered by Amtrak on its 38,400 km network is Chicago to Seattle via Salt Lake City. The closing of the southern transcontinental route by VIA Rail may increase Amtrak's business on this route. Amtrak has been successful in raising both passenger ridership and gross revenue across the system. Several factors helped Amtrak to attain this position. Equipment was modernized, facilities and services were improved, and high-speed service was offered in the northeast corridor to compete with airline shuttle service. Pricing and marketing plans were developed to make rail travel more attractive. Reservation and ticketing procedures were enhanced by linking Amtrak with travel agencies through airline computer systems. This resulted in a higher proportion of rail tickets being sold through travel agencies. Amtrak also cooperates with local bus services through three different agreements. Some buses are operated by or for Amtrak. Secondly, bus tickets for routes not serviced by rail are sold by Amtrak. In a third arrangement, certain bus lines accept rail passenger tickets on routes they have in common with Amtrak. This feature applies throughout the Amtrak system although the rail company does not honour bus tickets in return. The routes of VIA and Amtrak connect at various points, providing north-south rail service between the United States and Canada.

Amtrak Equipment

American and Canadian railroads exhibit only minor differences in their equipment, baggage arrangements, types of service and

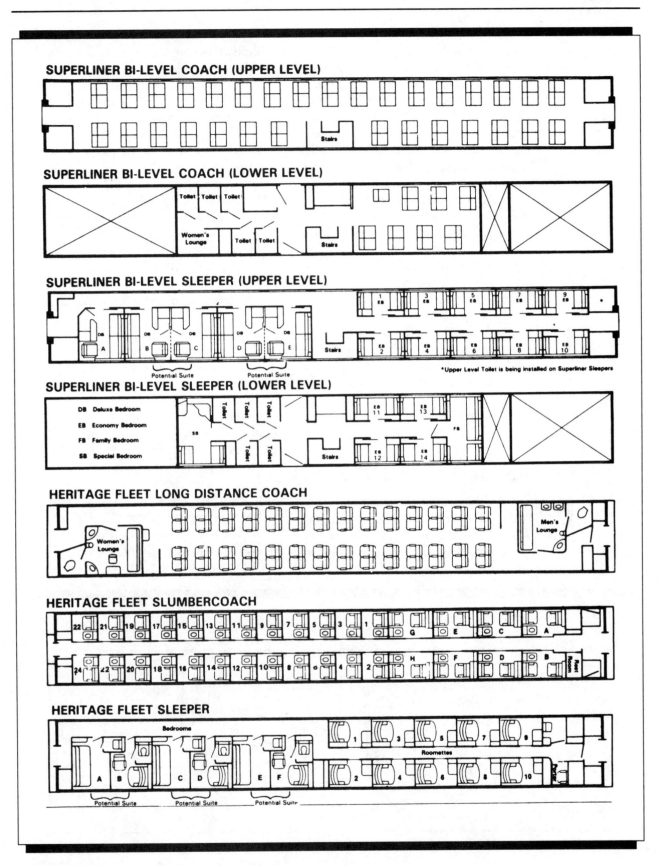

FIGURE 7.5
Some Amtrak seating arrangements. *Courtesy of the Official Railway Guide.*

standards of accommodation. Key sales features are also similar.

Amtrak uses standard coaches, called Amfleet, for day travel. Reservations may be made on this service but they are not a requirement. Standard coaches have two reclining seats on either side of a centre aisle. Washrooms are located at one end of the car and luggage racks are located above the seats. Night coach seats have a leg rest that folds out from under the seat. More luxurious equipment is used on several routes and is available at a surcharge. Seats are wider and have more padding, are arranged two-and-one on either side of a centre aisle, and must be reserved. Metroliners offer high-speed, first class service in the northeast corridor. Heritage coach cars and bilevel Superliners are used for long distance routes (see Figure 7.5). Club Service and Custom Class offer upgraded coach service. Vista Dome Cars are used on eastern and midwestern long distance trains.

FIGURE 7.6
Day and night arrangements of a single slumber-coach.
Source: Amtrak Sales Guide.

Amtrak Accommodation and Services

Amtrak has three categories of sleeping accommodation; slumbercoaches, roomettes and bedrooms. Each category is equipped with private washroom facilities, reading lights, attendant call systems and individual climate controls.

Slumbercoaches are single rooms that offer the most economical sleeping accommodation. A single consists of a seat that becomes a foldaway bed at night (Figure 7.6). Double slumbercoaches have an upper and a lower bed that converts into a sitting area during the day. Slumbercoaches have limited baggage space.

Roomettes accommodate one person but are larger than slumbercoaches. They have a fold-down bed and toilet facilities that are covered when the bed is folded down.

Bedrooms accommodate two people and are less cramped than roomettes. Bedrooms have sufficient luggage space for three average suitcases and a closet for hanging clothes. Four types of bedroom are available. Economy bedrooms can comfortably accommodate two people. Family bedrooms are designed for two adults and two children. Neither economy nor family bedrooms have private toilet facilities. On Superliner sleeper cars, the toilet facilities for these bedrooms are located on the lower level. A deluxe bedroom has a sofa and a reclining swivel chair for day use. At night there are two beds (Figure 7.7). Deluxe bedrooms are equipped with private toilet facilities and a coat closet. A special bedroom designed to meet the needs of a

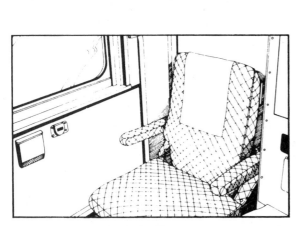
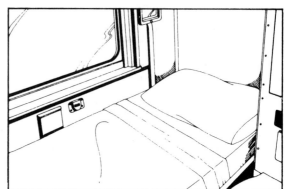

handicapped person and travelling companion is also available. Special bedrooms are located on the lower level. Since passengers on Superliners can pass between cars only on the upper level, attendants provide meal and beverage service to handicapped passengers. Some adjoining bedrooms have a wall that can be withdrawn to make a bedroom suite for family travel.

Amtrak Fares

Few Canadian travel agents possess reference manuals and tariffs for American rail travel. After Canadian agents received permission to write Amtrak tickets on VIA Rail stock, Amtrak withdrew its appointments from Canadian travel agencies. Amtrak does, however, provide mailings such as national timetables, brochures and other materials to Canadian travel agencies. Access to this information is available from VIA Rail passenger sales offices or by contacting Amtrak. Fares, rules and schedules for Amtrak are also found in the Official Railway Guide (see Figure 7.8).

Amtrak Reservations and Ticketing

Counsellors who make a reservation with Amtrak will find that the procedure is similar to that used with VIA Rail. The same information should be supplied in the same order as given to VIA. An Amtrak sales agent will give a reference or locator number when the space is confirmed. Passengers who do not appear for their reserved seats or who cancel within 30 minutes prior to scheduled departures will be assessed a service charge by Amtrak.

**FIGURE 7.7
Day and night arrangement of a deluxe bedroom.**
Source: Amtrak Sales Guide.

Rail Travel in Europe

Most European railroads are owned, subsidized and operated by national governments. Railroads in Europe are more important to the passenger transportation system than they are in North America. A number of factors contribute to this prominence. European governments regard passenger railroads as a source of national pride and as an essential service. Governments therefore continue to invest heavily in rail transportation with the result that track mileage in Europe is increasing while in Canada it is decreasing. Europe occupies a relatively small land mass in comparison with North America. Central and Western Europe and the British Isles possess about one third the area of Canada. Over 300 million people, about twelve times Canada's population, live in this region. Distances between population centres are therefore relatively short. The large

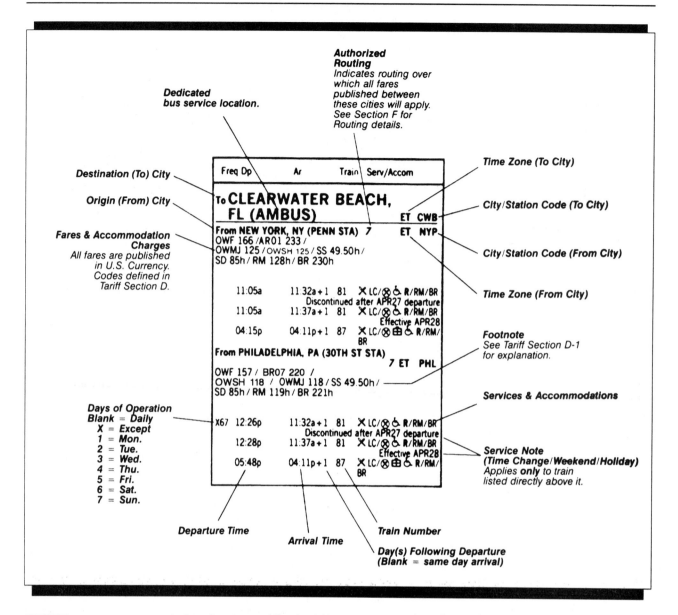

Dedicated bus service location.

Authorized Routing
Indicates routing over which all fares published between these cities will apply. See Section F for Routing details.

Time Zone (To City)

Destination (To) City

Origin (From) City

City/Station Code (To City)

Fares & Accommodation Charges
All fares are published in U.S. Currency. Codes defined in Tariff Section D.

City/Station Code (From City)

Time Zone (From City)

Footnote
See Tariff Section D-1 for explanation.

Services & Accommodations

Days of Operation
Blank = Daily
X = Except
1 = Mon.
2 = Tue.
3 = Wed.
4 = Thu.
5 = Fri.
6 = Sat.
7 = Sun.

Service Note
(Time Change/Weekend/Holiday)
Applies only to train listed directly above it.

Departure Time

Arrival Time

Train Number

Day(s) Following Departure
(Blank = same day arrival)

FIGURE 7.8
How to use the listings in the Official Railway Guide.
Courtesy of the Official Railway Guide.

population density and the facilities to provide transportation almost anywhere in Europe have created the conditions for track mileage that far exceeds that in Canada. Added to these factors are the high cost of car ownership, high gas prices and limited parking. In addition, European railways generally offer a wide selection of routes, frequent and reliable service, and modern equipment.

Railroad Organizations

Each country has its own national railway system offering clean, fast, safe,

efficient and economical transportation. These national railroads use their own equipment and operate on internal routes according to their own tariffs and route schedules. Many lines are electrified and others have been converted to high-speed service where speeds of over 200 km per hour are common. Rail travel is a popular means of transportation for both residents and tourists. Fares are less expensive than for air travel and distances between major centres are relatively short. A tourist can travel from Paris to the Riviera on a luxury class overnight train leaving in the evening and arriving the next morning at a lower price than for flying. If time is a consideration, travellers can take a high-speed train which easily competes with air travel. Standards of service, accommodation and operation are excellent but vary among countries. The German Railroad and Swiss Railways enjoy a fine reputation. In Switzerland, pleasure travellers are offered extras such as the ability to rent bicycles at most stations. French National Railroads (SNCF) also provide outstanding service. In 1978 France pioneered the development of high-speed rail connections in Europe. Its TGV (*Train à Grande Vitesse*) service originally linked Paris and Lyon and has now been extended to other areas. The TGV can carry passengers at speeds up to 350 km per hour. Similarly, Germany introduced an Intercity Express (ICE) network in 1991 which operates in much the same manner as the TGV with high-speed trains running on special tracks. This network will ultimately link all of Germany's major cities. Another proposal will see several countries united in a high-speed European rail network. Plans call for a 30,000 km network of high-speed trains running from Italy to Scandinavia and from Germany to Spain. The first stage was completed in 1995. Spanish National Railways (RENFE) converted its network to standard-gauge width from the traditional wide gauge to link with the French high-speed rail network. The first step joined Madrid and Seville in 1992 in time for the World Exposition held there. This cut travel time by 50 percent to about three hours. The European high speed train network continues to expand and now extends through much of Western Europe. Another development has been the growth of trains operated by independent companies rather than by government owned rail organizations. Luxury, high speed trains such as the *Eurostar* from London to Paris or Brussels and the *Artesia* from Paris or Lyon to Milan or Turin now compete with airlines for business travellers. The trend to privately operated train services is expected to grow. Railroad travel will therefore remain an extremely important means of transportation within Europe, not only to meet the needs of residents but also those of tourists.

In addition to operating national rail networks, the European railways cooperate through an international railroad system established to coordinate transportation between them. These international trains run on routes connecting major European centres and may cross several boundaries between origin and destination. They function according to internationally agreed upon tariffs and timetables. The standard of service and accommodation on international trains is uniformly high. During the past twenty years Canadians and Americans have discovered that the European rail network is one of the finest in the world and that every year it improves.

The major sources of European rail product knowledge are the *Thomas Cook European Timetable* and the *Eurailtariff*. The Thomas Cook European Timetable provides information on major lines only. It displays detailed timetables of the principal rail services in Europe, North Africa and Russia as well as local shipping and ferry services. It is by far the most useful publication when dealing with travel in these areas. Travel counsellors require only the October and the June issues which provide the winter and summer schedules, respectively. The Eurailtariff is published annually by participating European railroad members of the International Union of Railways. It is available free of charge to travel agencies from the Eurailpass Distribution Centre. The Eurailtariff lists fares, regulations, surcharges, reservation procedures and sleeping car fares for all rail journeys between principal points in Western Europe. Although both the Thomas Cook Timetable and the Eurailtariff continue to be published in Canada, they can be difficult to obtain and most travel agencies now retrieve European rail information from computer software or the Internet. For example, Rail Europe supplies travel agencies with a software program called T.R.A.I.N. which can be downloaded to the agency's computer system. This program, which is updated three times annually, provides schedules and fares for over 4,000 city pairs in Europe and Britain. In addition, each country publishes a timetable at least as thick as the Cook and often much thicker. This

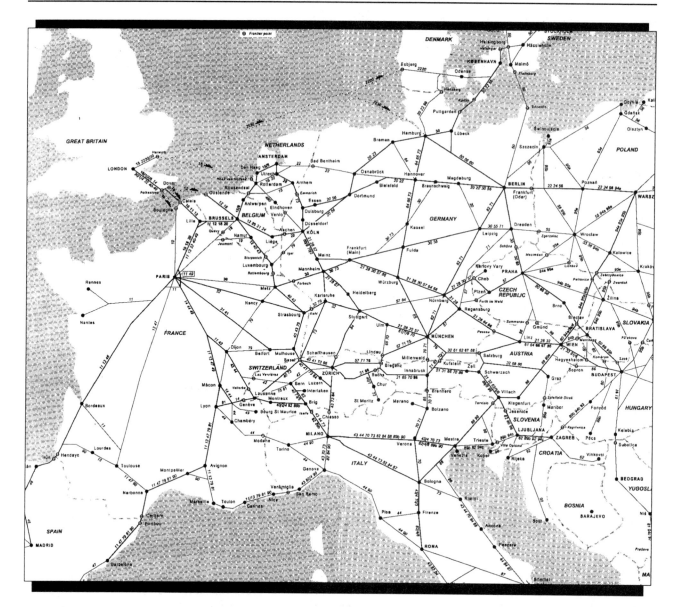

FIGURE 7.9
International Rail Services in Europe.
Source: Thomas Cook European Timetable.

indicates the large number of trains that run through Europe every day. The national tourist board or national rail company (if it is represented in Canada) also provide consumer-oriented material to travel agencies and the public.

European Rail Equipment

Railway cars in Europe are referred to as carriages. European day trains have two basic seating arrangements, compartments and coaches. The compartment type consists of spacious cabins connected to a side corridor which runs the entire length of the car. Each compartment has a picture window for maximum visibility. First class compartments seat six people (three on each of the bench-type seats). Eight passengers are usually accommodated in second class compartments although many have been renovated to seat six persons. The coach type is similar to a North American coach. Seats are arranged two-and-one on either side of a centre aisle in first class. Second class coaches have two seats on either side of the aisle. Today most high speed trains have coaches with a centre isle rather than the corridor style which was once favoured.

Classes of Service

There are two classes of service on European trains. In first class, there are fewer seats which are wider, are upholstered with plush fabric and have individual arm rests, head rests, more leg room, ashtrays, reading lamps and spacious luggage racks. Second class transportation is comfortable but less luxurious. There are more seats per coach which allows less leg and elbow room. Seats are usually covered in leatherette and there is less luggage space.

Fast, limited-stop express trains connect major European centres. In 1957 the European railroads introduced Trans-Europ Express (TEE) service to provide a network of fast intercity trains with comfortable accommodation. The network was targeted at business and other regular travellers. The TEE system attempted to combat the loss of rail travel to air service by providing out-and-home journeys on the same day with sufficient time for business at the destination. The TEE system proved so popular and was expanded to such an extent that the original out-and-home concept could not be maintained for all routes. During the 1980s, the TEE train was virtually phased out in favour of the IC (Intercity) service which provided both first and second class transportation at the same speed, comfort and reliability as the TEE but at a greater frequency.

Beginning in 1987 the TEE and international IC services were replaced by a new network of high quality, first and second class trains called the EuroCity (EC) network (Figure 7.9). The EC system comprises 50,000 seats daily on trains connecting 200 cities in 13 countries. The service is faster and more efficient than offered by the TEE. EuroCity Trains provide premium international travel between European city centres using high-speed, air-conditioned equipment. The trains must meet strict criteria concerning cleanliness, on-board services and punctuality. There are also specially trained English-speaking staff on board to assist passengers. Most EuroCity trains require a reserved seat and charge a supplementary fare. EuroCity trains offer meal service, operate at a minimum average speed of 90 km

per hour including stops, and can attain speeds of 270 km per hour. The French TGV service forms part of the EC network.

All EC and international express trains are given a name, for example, the *Hamlet* (Copenhagen-Hamburg) and the *Ile de France* (Brussels-Paris). Some of the more famous international express trains are the *Orient Express* (Paris-Vienna-Bucharest) and the *Rembrandt* (Amsterdam-Basle). Not all name trains, however, operate on international services. For example, the *Trinacria* (Rome-Milan) and the *Konsul* (Munich-Hamburg) operate wholly within one country. These trains have comforts not found on other services and offer excellent sightseeing. Spain's Talgo train interiors feature videos and overnight Talgo trains (deluxe *Gran Clase*) carry elegant restaurant cars. Some Talgo first class compartments are equipped with showers. Many express trains and particularly the EC services offer tourists special facilities such as shops, boutiques, information bureaux, secretarial service, hairdressing salons and newsstands. There are now fewer EC trains on international routes than in the past. These trains have been replaced, especially on daytime services, by the TGV from France to Switzerland and Italy, and by independently operated trains such as the *Thalys* from Paris to Brussels, Koln and Amsterdam and the *Cisalpino* from Switzerland to Italy. The EC trains remaining now operate primarily in Central Europe and on overnight international routes.

Some Intercity (IC) trains still operate.

FIGURE 7.10
Couchette compartments can have four or six berths.
Source: Eurailtariff.

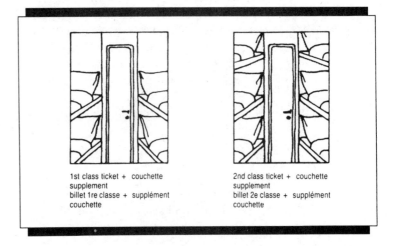

1st class ticket + couchette supplement
billet 1re classe + supplément couchette

2nd class ticket + couchette supplement
billet 2e classe + supplément couchette

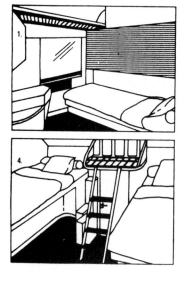

1–First class Single compartment.

2–Standard double compartment (second class in Britain and Norway, first class elsewhere).

3–Second class tourist compartment (upper, middle and lower berths).

4 and 5–Type T2 car with two-berth upper and lower compartments (first class in Spain, second class elsewhere). The lower compartments can also be used as first class (Special) singles.

FIGURE 7.11
Sleeping cars on European trains.
Source: Thomas Cook European Timetable.

These trains are luxurious but perhaps a little less plush than the EC service. IC trains offer both first and second class transportation. In addition, every European country has a comprehensive network of local trains.

Accommodation

European trains are quite comfortable and passengers travelling overnight can sleep in the regular seats. Many clients, however, prefer to reserve a couchette or a sleeper. Travelling at night allows visitors to spend the daylight hours touring a city and sleeping accommodation often costs less than a hotel. (The price varies with the degree of comfort and privacy.) Large railway stations have bath and shower facilities if the sleeping accommodation does not. Clients can therefore save both time and money by travelling overnight in Europe.

Couchettes

The least expensive accommodation is a couchette. Couchettes are acceptable for young travellers or others on a budget, and are appropriate for a family travelling together. A couchette is a bunk bed with a mattress, sheet, blanket and a pillow (Figure 7.10). Couchettes, however, provide no real privacy and sexes are mixed without discrimination. First class sleeping compartments contain four couchettes, two upper and two lower. There are also second class couchettes in which seats are converted into six bunks (two upper, two middle and two lower) on either side of a compartment. Couchettes are often self-service and passengers make up their own beds. The lowest berth is the easiest to reach but travellers can be jostled or feel crowded as others prepare for bed. The middle berth has little head room and no access to one's suitcase. The top berth is out of the way and has a spacious shelf for clothes. A hidden feature is the table under the seats that can be set up for breakfast once the berths are folded up. Couchette reservations are subject to a flat rate surcharge per person (plus any communication fees) regardless of the distance travelled or the class of service reserved. Since couchettes offer the most economical form of sleeping accommodation, they may be in great demand. Clients should therefore be advised to book ahead. Note that clients who miss their train are not eligible for a refund on the couchette charge. Timetables contain information on which trains carry couchette cars.

Sleepers

Sleeper cars in Europe are known as wagon-lits. Four types of accommodation are available; tourist, double, single and special (Figure 7.11). The most economical accommodation is the tourist sleeper. Some tourist sleepers have two berths (one lower and one upper) while others have three (lower, middle and upper). Passengers require a second class ticket to reserve a tourist sleeper whereas a first class ticket is necessary to reserve any other type of sleeper. A double sleeping compartment contains a lower and an upper berth while a single compartment contains one berth only. A special sleeper is a small single, less expensive than a regular single. Some specials have an upper berth, others a lower berth. If a choice is available, take the upper section as it has more head room. All berths are regular beds with sheets, blankets and pillows. Each compartment is equipped with an electric outlet for shavers and a washbasin with hot and cold water. Air-conditioning or fresh air ventilation is standard. Surcharges depend on the distance travelled and the accommodation reserved. A single sleeper is approximately

**FIGURE 7.12
How to use the
Cook European
Timetable.**
*Source: Thomas
Cook European
Timetable.*

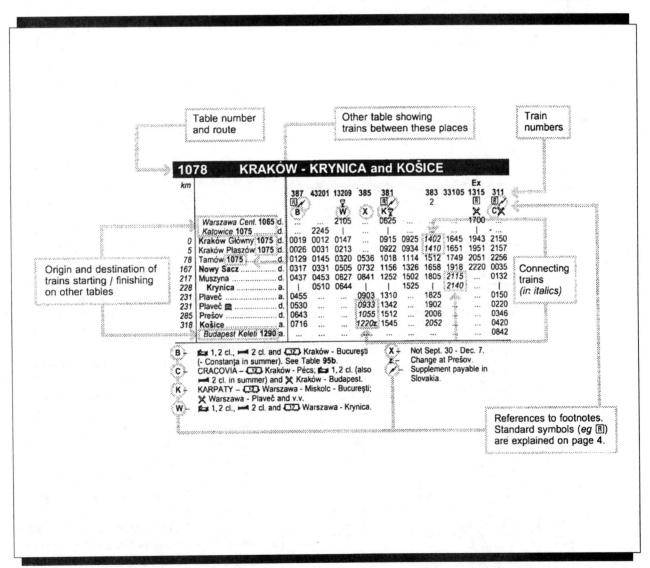

twice the price of a double and about four times that of a tourist sleeper. Special sleepers are priced between single and double accommodation. Requests must be processed via telex, cable or fax and a communication fee is charged for each reservation. The offices of the European railways in North America do not hold allotments for sleepers.

The growth of the high speed rail network has prompted the development of more luxurious accommodation as rail companies compete with airlines by offering increased comfort as well as faster travel times. A new generation of trains, known as Hotel Trains, run on selected routes. They offer higher standards of accommodation than regular overnight sleepers. Many are sold as singles or doubles only, they offer a choice of private or shared shower and toilet facilities, and meals may be included in the price. Hotel Trains now operate throughout most of Western Europe.

Accessibility for physically challenged passengers has also improved. Most high speed Intercity trains have at least one wheelchair space, as do all TGV trains and most EC or IC trains.

Meal Services

Meals are not included in rail fares, unlike travel undertaken by air or ocean. Every national and international main line train in Europe, however, offers its passengers some type of meal service. Long distance trains have conventional dining cars (also called restaurant cars) with table service and menus for breakfast, lunch and dinner. Dining car reservations are usually made while on board and meals are served in two sittings. On short runs, many trains are equipped with snack bars, or buffet or cafeteria cars. On some routes, sandwiches and beverages are served at the bar or purchased from vendors patrolling the aisle of the train.

European Rail Schedules

European train travel offers tremendous potential for designing appealing and innovative tours for clients. To be successful, however, travel counsellors must develop skill in reading timetables and tariffs. The most important timetable is the Thomas Cook European Timetable. This book contains train schedules for all of Europe as well as Russia and the former Soviet Republics. It includes a list of all shipping companies, ferry and/or steamship services in the English Channel, the North Sea, the Baltic Sea and the Mediterranean Sea. In addition, the Cook European Timetable contains maps of railroad terminals in about 60 cities, subway plans for London and Paris, passport and visa requirements, foreign currency restrictions, and a wealth of other information.

The composition of the book follows a standard format and numbering system that rarely changes (Figure 7.12). For example, the schedule for Paris to Vienna via Munich has the same table number no matter which issue of the timetable is consulted. Similarly, schedules within any one country (for example, Rome-Florence-Milan) are given the same table number within a range set aside for that country. Table 1 shows international car sleeper trains and Table 2 lists internal car sleeper trains. Cruise trains are found in Table 3 and airport city centre

FIGURE 7.13
The index identifies table numbers for train schedules.
Source: Thomas Cook European Timetable.

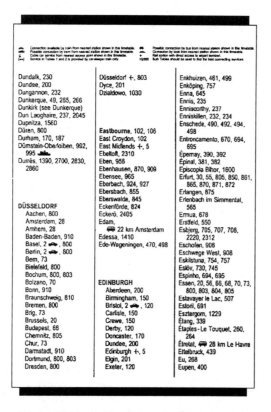

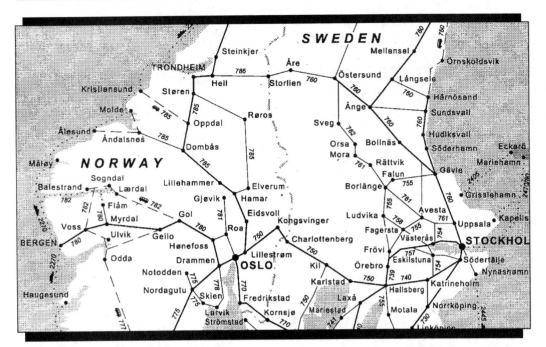

FIGURE 7.14
Maps show rail connections and the table numbers for their schedules.
Source: Thomas Cook European Timetable.

links in Table 5. Tables 8 through 99 are reserved for international services. Rail services within individual countries are displayed in Tables 100 to 1999. These start with Great Britain (Tables 100-229) and generally progress from west to east (Denmark is shown in Tables 700-729 and Greece in Tables 1400-1499) ending with Russia and Belarus. Ferry and shipping services are exhibited in Tables 2000 through 2899 and follow a regional pattern similar to the train schedules. That is, the listings begin with services in the Irish Sea (Tables 2000-2075) and are printed in order from west to east ending with the Adriatic, Eastern Mediterranean and the Black Sea (Tables 2700-2899). All times are based on the 24-hour clock and schedules always name the actual stations since many towns have more than one station. When planning an itinerary try to provide clients with connections at the same station. If this is not possible, remember to leave them sufficient time to travel (with luggage) from one station to another in a strange city.

System maps of the international rail and ship networks are reproduced as well as maps of national and regional railway services. These maps show the key cities and indicate how many railroad lines link every city. There may not always be a through train just when your clients wish to depart but

they can travel to the nearest junction or key city and from there to the final destination. Remember that the timetable shows only the main line trains; there may also be several local trains to your client's destination.

Reading the schedules reproduced in the Cook European Timetable is a fairly straightforward exercise. The first step is to find the appropriate schedule by looking in the alphabetical index of place names (Figure 7.13). Several cities are printed in boldface capital letters, for example **DUSSELDORF**, followed by a list of cities. This format indicates that all connections are given for that particular city. Other key cities, for example **EDINBURGH**, are marked in bold letters. All other towns and cities appear in regular print. Every listed city is followed by one or more numbers. These numbers refer to tables which show train service to or through that city. Connections are also shown on the maps of each country (although you must know the approximate location of the city to find them). The number of the table where the schedule is displayed is written on the line connecting the relevant cities. For example, the map of Norway, Sweden and Denmark shows a rail connection from Oslo to Stockholm. The number 750 appears on the line joining every city pair (see Figure 7.14). This means that Table 750 shows the

28 — AMSTERDAM - FRANKFURT, WIEN and MÜNCHEN

train type / train number / notes	1041 Z	IC 1141 Z	✗	EC 141 ✗	EC 27 ✗	EC 167 ✗	EC 9 ✗	ICE 793 ✗		EC 3 R ✗	ICE 593 ✗		EC 143 ✗	EC 29 ✗	EC 109 ✗	ICE 795 ✗		EC 105 C ✗	ICE 595 ✗		EC 145 ✗	IC 729 ✗	IC 501 ✗	ICE 797 ✗	
Amsterdam CS ...... d.	...	...	...	0700	...	...	...	...	...	0800	...	...	0900	...	...	...	...	1000	...	...	1100	...	...	...	...
Rotterdam CS ...... d.	...	0637			...	...	...	0737	...		...	0837		...	...	...	0937		...	1037		...	...	...	...
Utrecht CS ...... d.	0620	...	0713	0730	...	...	...	0816	0830	...	0913	0930	...	...	...	1016	1030	...	1113	1130	...	...	...	...
Arnhem ...... d.	0704	...	...	0804	...	...	...	...	0904	...	...	1004	...	...	...	...	1104	...	...	1204	...	...	...	...
Emmerich 🚪 ...... d.	0721	0725	...	0829	...	...	...	...	0932	...	...	1029	...	...	...	...	1132	...	...	1229	...	...	...	...
Oberhausen ...... a.	...	0759	...	0858	...	...	...	...	1001	...	...	1058	...	...	...	...	1201	...	...	1258	...	...	...	...
Duisburg ...... a.	...	0805	...	0906	...	...	...	...	1010	...	...	1105	1114	...	...	...	1210	...	...	1305	1314	...	...	...
Düsseldorf Hbf ...... a.	...	0818	...	0918	...	...	...	...	1030	...	...	1118	1127	...	...	...	1230	...	...	1318	1327	...	...	...
Köln Hbf ...... a.	...	0841	...	0941	...	...	...	...	1055	...	...	1141	1152	...	...	...	1255	...	...	1341	1352	...	...	...
Köln Hbf ...... d.	...	...	...	...	0954	1000	...	...	1100	...	...	...	1154	1200	...	...	1300	...	...	1354	1400	...	...	...
Bonn Hbf ...... a.	...	...	...	...	1012	1018	...	...	1118	...	...	...	1212	1218	...	...	1318	...	...	1412	1418	...	...	...
Koblenz ...... a.	...	...	...	...	1044	1050	...	...	1150	...	...	...	1244	1250	...	...	1350	...	...	1444	1450	...	...	...
Mainz ...... a.	...	...	...	...	1137	1144	...	...	1244	...	...	...	1337	1344	...	...	1444	...	...	1537	1544	...	...	...
Frankfurt Flughafen ✈ ...... a.	...	...	...	...	1156		...	...		...	...	...	1356		...	...		...	...	1556		...	...	...
Frankfurt (Main) Hbf ...... a.	...	...	...	...	1208		...	...		...	...	...	1408		...	...		...	...	1608		...	...	...
Würzburg ...... a.	...	...	...	...	1330		...	...		...	...	...	1530		...	...		...	...	1730		...	...	...
Nürnberg ...... a.	...	...	...	...	1428		...	...		...	...	...	1628		...	...		...	...	1828		...	...	...
Regensburg ...... a.	...	...	...	...	1527	1537		...		...	...	...	1727		...	...		...	...	1927		...	...	...
Praha Hlavni 57 ...... a.	...	...	...	...		2012		...		...	...	...			...	...		...	...			...	...	...
Passau 🚪 ...... a.	...	...	...	...	1630			...		...	...	...	1830		...	...		...	...	2038		...	...	...
Linz 🚪 ...... a.	...	...	...	...	1750			...		...	...	...	1950		...	...		...	...			...	...	...
Wien Westbahnhof ...... a.	...	...	...	...	1945			...		...	...	...	2145		...	...		...	...			...	...	...
Mannheim ...... a.	...	...	...	...	...	...	1225	1229	...	1325	1329	...	...	1425	1429	...	...	1525	1529	...	...	1625	1629	...
Stuttgart ...... a.	...	...	...	...	...	...	...	1308	...	...	1408	...	...	...	1508	...	...	...	1608	...	...	...	1708	...
Ulm ...... a.	...	...	...	...	...	...	...	1406	...	...	1506	...	...	...	1606	...	...	...	1706	...	...	...	1806	...
Augsburg ...... a.	...	...	...	...	...	...	...	1447	...	...	1547	...	...	...	1647	...	...	...	1747	...	...	...	1847	...
München Hbf ...... a.	...	...	...	...	...	...	...	1518	...	...	1618	...	...	...	1718	...	...	...	1818	...	...	...	1921	...

A – Sept. 28 - Oct. 17 and Apr. 28 - May 23.
B – Oct. 18 - Apr. 27.
C – BERNER OBERLAND – ⊡ and ✗ Amsterdam - Mannheim (- Interlaken) and v.v.
F – ①-⑥, not Dec. 25, 26, Jan. 1, Apr. 11-13.
J – Sept. 28 - Oct. 18 and Apr. 29 - May 23.
K – Oct. 19 - Apr. 28.
L – DONAUWALZER – 🛏 1,2 cl., ▬ 2 cl. and ⊡ Amsterdam - Wien and v.v.
M – 🛏 1,2 cl., ▬ 2 cl. and ⊡ Amsterdam - München and v.v.
P – 🛏 1,2 cl., ▬ 2 cl. and ⊡ (Dortmund -) Duisburg - Praha and v.v.
R – REMBRANDT – ⊡ (observation car), ⊡ and ✗ Amsterdam - Mannheim (- Chur) and v.v.

S – SCHWEIZ EXPRESS – 🛏 1,2 cl., ▬ 2 cl. and ⊡ Amsterdam - Basel and v.v.
V – Cross-platform connection to/from Amsterdam is made at Duisburg, not Köln.
Y – Daily except ⑥, not Dec. 24,25,31, Apr. 10-12.
Z – ①-⑤ (not Oct. 3, Dec. 20 - Jan. 4, Apr. 10-13, May 1,21).
b – Daily except ⑥, not Dec. 24,25,31, Apr. 10-12.
f – ①-⑥, not Dec. 25, 26, Jan. 1, Apr. 11-13.
✗ – Supplement payable.
* – Classified IR in Germany.

Amsterdam ┼┼┼┼┼┼┼┼┼┼┼┼┼┼┼┼┼┼┼┼┼┼┼┼┼┼┼ Mannheim

FIGURE 7.15
International through service between Amsterdam and Mannheim.
Source: Thomas Cook European Timetable.

connections on this route.

Consider the journey from Amsterdam to Mannheim as an example. The index indicates that schedules for this city pair may be found on Table 28 which shows the international through services. Consider this table (Figure 7.15). Two steps are extremely important. The first is to learn the symbols (which are decoded at the beginning of the book). The second is to read the footnotes denoted by various letters. The footnotes provide information on the particular train, such as whether it is a daily service, the facilities (sleeping cars, couchettes, dining car or snack bar) it offers, and whether it carries through cars to the final destination.

Train numbers are written at the head of each schedule. This information may be followed by the number 2 which designates the second class of service only. If no number appears, then both first and second class service is offered. The top of each schedule also shows letters in bold print (for example Z, R, C) or symbols. These refer to the footnotes and must be read. The schedule from Amsterdam to Mannheim is then displayed. When the itinerary is listed in the left column of the timetable, it is always read from top to bottom. (When a timetable lists the itinerary in the centre and the schedules on either side of this column, the left side is always read from the top to bottom and the right side from the bottom up.) All services operate daily unless otherwise noted. In the middle of the itinerary column there is a small house symbol beside Emmerich. This symbol indicates that Emmerich is the border city where customs officials board the train to check papers and belongings. (Since 1993 when internal customs barriers were eliminated, most of these symbols have been removed from the timetable.) The number 57 is listed after Praha Hlavni (Prague). This number refers to another timetable which provides details of connections available from Prague. If the same table number is shown more than once, there may be alternative services available between these cities.

There are three types of trains listed in the Cook European Timetable. Direct or through trains run from point A to point B. For example, see Table 28 which lists the EC3 train REMBRANDT from Amsterdam to Mannheim (Figure 7.15). The intermediate stops are indicated on the schedule.

However, not all trains operate directly to their destination. Some trains carry coaches for only a portion of the journey. These are known as trains with through cars. Such trains leave from point A and travel to points C or D via point B. At point B one car goes to point C and another goes to point B. For example, Table 88 lists the REMUS which runs from Vienna to Rome and Milan via Venice (Figure 7.16). At Venice one car goes to Rome (train 235H) while the other operates to Milan (train 235J).

A third type of train is the multi-car train which at some points has cars joining the train while at other points cars may separate. For example, Table 71 shows the

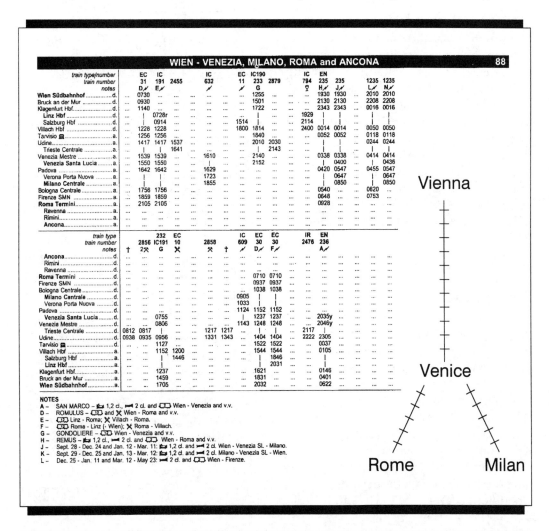

FIGURE 7.16
The REMUS is a train with through cars.
Source: Thomas Cook European Timetable.

WETTERSTEIN which runs from Berlin Zoo to Seefeld in Tirol, Austria (Figure 7.17). Carriages coming from (or destined for) Hamburg join (or leave) the train at Berlin Zoo.

It is not only important to correctly read the timetable but also to alert your clients if they will not be travelling on a direct service. The destination of each coach is usually clearly marked on a plate attached to the outside of the car. Clients should be advised to check the car's destination and to avoid changing seats once they have located the correct place.

The above outlines the basics of reading the Cook European Timetable. Do not be apprehensive to open the book, at least to find an easy schedule. Remember that help is available for complicated itineraries.

European Rail Fares

Over the years, three major ticket categories have been created for European rail transportation; Eurailtariff, Eurailgroup and rail passes (either Eurail passes or national rail passes). Most of the rather complicated national tariff regulations have been standardized so that overseas travellers have almost complete freedom in rail travel. Children's age limits provide an example of this standardization. From four through eleven years of age, children travel at half fare; under four years of age, they travel free of charge.

Eurailtariff

The European railroads and shipping lines participate in a common pricing system for international rail and ferry service within their jurisdiction. Prices for point-to-point transportation are printed in a reference manual known as the Eurailtariff. This manual consists of four sections printed on green, white, yellow and blue paper respectively.

The manual commences with the green section which outlines the general conditions, seat reservation fees and specific regulations concerning the fares listed in the tariff. All fares are listed in U.S. dollars and are guaranteed for the entire calendar year (from January 1 to December 31). However, this guarantee does not apply to any fare increase which results from a devaluation of the U.S. dollar against European currencies. In Canada, fares are converted to Canadian dollars at the rate of exchange (set by the European railroads) in effect at the time the ticket is purchased. Eurailtariff prices include the cost of surcharges required to travel on quality trains such as the EuroCity, TGV and International Intercity. Rail tickets are valid for six months from the first day of validity indicated on the ticket. Children, as noted, travel free or at half fare. There is no half fare on supplements, reservations fees, couchettes and sleeping accommodation. There are some exceptions to these common rules for travel within certain countries.

In addition to their extensive rail network, several European railroads also operate a motorcoach system on scenic routes throughout Europe, the Europabus system. Information may be obtained through the issuing offices. Within Germany, rail tickets are also valid for travel on certain buses operated by German railroads. In Austria, rail tickets are accepted with a surcharge payment on some boats of the Donau Steamship Company. Switzerland allows passengers to substitute travel by lake steamer at no additional charge if the corresponding ticket is issued for an itinerary running alongside the lake.

The part most used by travel counsellors is the white section which lists point-to-point transportation prices for individuals. Cities are displayed in alphabetical order using the local spelling (Praha not Prague, Milano not Milan) just as they are in the Cook European Timetable. Since the price is the same in either direction, information is shown only under the city which comes first in the alphabet. For example, a fare from Heidelberg to Amsterdam can be found only under Amsterdam. The Heidelberg listing shows Amsterdam in italics which refers the reader to the correct heading (Figure 7.18). The map location for each city is noted in the column to the left. To the right of the itinerary section is a column headed "via" which usually indicates the routing cities, some of which are listed in parentheses. For example, Frankfurt has three stations and trains depart from different stations depending on the route and destination. The word in parentheses indicates the departure station. To the right of the routing section are listed four fare columns. Individual one-way fares, designated by a single arrow, are shown first with first class fares appearing in a shaded column. The rows for round trip fares appear to the right of the one-way fares and are marked by a double arrow. The final column gives an approximate time for the relevant journey shown.

Fares for various connections are shown and may be quoted for those journeys. For trips involving several connections simply add the price of each leg of the journey to arrive at a total fare. The total fare, however, is frequently not the total price for the journey. Many routes and trains require seat reservations to which a reservation charge applies. Further, if clients require sleeping accommodation or if they will make certain sea crossings as part of their journey, supplements will apply. All supplements and reservations fees must be added to the rail fares in order to arrive at the correct total cost of the rail transportation. Independently operated trains, such as the *Thalys* mentioned earlier, charge a global price which includes seat reservations, meals and newspapers. Most of them issue a separate ticket and require a supplement. For example, holders of a Eurailpass, a national rail pass or a Eurailtariff ticket must pay a supplement which ranges from $15 to $150. Open tickets are not permitted

The next chapter (the yellow section) lists the supplements applicable to couchette berths and sleeping car beds (Figure 7.19). As well as displaying prices for each of the four categories of accommodation, this section indicates which companies operate the service. Children under the age of ten do not pay a supplement provided they share the bed with an adult or another child under ten who pays the full supplement. Prices are

FIGURE 7.17
The WETTERSTEIN is a multi-car train.
Source: Thomas Cook European Timetable.

BERLIN - ZÜRICH, INNSBRUCK and VERONA   71

For other services from Berlin to Innsbruck and Verona, change at München (Tables 850 and 70); for Dresden - München connections see Table 880.

train type / train number / notes	EC 11	EC 166	IC 813 K	EC 98	D 1283 EN	D 1183 GP	EN 358 M	1548 EN358 M	ICN 1501 L	EC 92
Berlin Zoo ....d.	0538	...	0940	...	...	...	2149	...	2230c	...
Berlin Wannsee ....d.	0550	...	0952	...	2012	2012	2201	...	2257	...
Dresden Hbf.........................d.								2122		
Leipzig ....d.	0738	...	1138	...				2257		
Halle ....d.				...	2234	2234	2359	2359	0043	
Nürnberg Hbf ....d.	1126	...	1526	...						
München Hbf ....a.	1306	1402	1706	1815					0645	0815
Garmisch Partenkirchen..a.	...		1849						...	
Mittenwald ....a.	...		1919n							
Seefeld in Tirol...............a.	...		1940n							
Lindau ....a.	...	1622	...	2022					...	1022
St Gallen ....a.	...	1718	...	2118					...	1118
Basel SBB (= Bad)...........a.	...					0816	0816			
Zürich Hbf ....a.	...	1826	...	2223		0934	0934			1226
Kufstein ....a.	...	...	...	...	0727	0727	...	...	...	...
Innsbruck.........................a.	...	...	...	...	0838	0838	...	...	...	...
Brennero / Brenner ....a.	...	...	...	...	0932	0932	...	...	...	...
Bolzano / Bozen ....a.	...	...	...	...	1116	1116	...	...	...	...
Trento ....a.	...	...	...	...	1212	1212	...	...	...	...
Verona Porta Nuova ....a.	...	...	...	...	1325	1325	...	...	...	...

train type / train number / notes	IC 812 K	EC 167	IC 702	EC 93	ICN 1500 L	EN 359 M	EN 359 M	D 1282 FN	D 1182 HP
Verona Porta Nuova .....d.	...	...	...	...	...	...	...	1530	1600
Trento ....d.	...	...	...	...	...	...	...	1629	1703
Bolzano / Bozen ....d.	...	...	...	...	...	...	...	1748	1748
Brennero / Brenner ......d.	...	...	...	...	...	...	...	1928	1928
Innsbruck......................d.	...	...	...	...	...	...	...	2025	2025
Kufstein ....d.	...	...	...	...	...	...	...	2133	2133
Zürich Hbf.....................d.	...	0933	...	1733	...	1944	1944		
Basel SBB (= Bad)........d.	...	...	...	...	...	2117	2117		
St Gallen ....d.	...	1041	...	1841	...				
Lindau ....d.	...	1137	...	1937	...				
Seefeld in Tirol...............d.	0807r	...	...	...	...				
Mittenwald ....d.	0829r	...	...	...	...				
Garmisch Partenkirchen. d.	0920		...		...				
München Hbf ....d.	1052	1357	1452	2154	2312				
Nürnberg Hbf.................a.	1232		1632	...					
Halle ....a.				...	0453	0514	0514	0659	0659
Leipzig ....a.	1617		2017	...			0632		
Dresden Hbf..................a.				...		0817			
Berlin Wannsee ....a.	1806	2206		0708	0743			0854	0854
Berlin Zoo ....a.	1819	2219		0726c	0801				

E – ⑤ Oct. 3 - 24 and ⑤ Apr. 24 - May 22 (also Oct. 2, Apr. 30, May 20; not Oct. 3, May 1).
F – ⑥ Oct. 4 - 25 and ⑥ Apr. 25 - May 23 (also May 21).
G – ⑤ Jan. 2 - Apr. 17 (also Dec. 19, 23, 25, Apr. 9; not Apr. 10).
H – ⑥ Jan. 3 - Apr. 18 (also Jan. 1).
K – WETTERSTEIN – 🚏 and ✕ (Hamburg -) Berlin - Garmisch [- Seefeld, see notes n/r] and v.v.
L – 🛏 1,2 cl., 🚏 2 cl., 🚏 (reclining) and ✕ Berlin - München and v.v. Special fares payable.
M – *CityNightLine* BERLINER – 🛏 1,2 cl., 🚏 (reclining) and ✕ Berlin and Dresden - Zürich and v.v. Special fares payable.

N – 🚏 2 cl. and 🚏 Berlin - Verona and v.v; 🛏 1,2 cl. Berlin - Bolzano and v.v.
P – 🚏 2 cl. and 🚏 Berlin Wannsee - Verona and v.v.
c – Berlin Charlottenburg.
n – ⑥ Jan. 3 - Apr. 4, also Dec. 20, 23, 26, Apr. 1. On other dates change at Garmisch Partenkirchen, arriving Mittenwald 1951, Seefeld 2009.
r – ⑤ Jan. 10 - Apr. 4, also Jan. 2 - 4, Apr. 13, 18. On other dates depart Seefeld 0742, Mittenwald 0803 and change at Garmisch Partenkirchen.
✗ – Supplement payable.

listed in the same manner as in the white section, that is, supplements are to be found only under the heading which comes first in the alphabet. The final (blue) section of the manual identifies the supplements charged for cabins, berths or reclining seats on ferry or steamship services.

Groups consisting of six or more people travelling together pay a reduced fare which does not include supplements for special trains. Groups consisting of 6-24 fare-paying adults receive a discount of 20 percent on the published fare. Groups of 25 or more fare-paying adults receive a discount of 40 percent. Free transportation is provided for one person if the group consists of 15 to 30 paying passengers. For groups of more than 31 fare paying passengers, one additional person will receive complimentary transportation for each additional group of 15 paying passengers or fraction thereof. Free accommodation is granted to one person for

a group consisting of 15-30 persons paying for accommodation. If the group consists of more than 30 persons paying for accommodation, free accommodation is granted to one person for each additional 30 persons paying for accommodation, or fraction thereof. A reservation fee per person applies for one-way journeys and must be paid by all participants including those travelling free. Special booking conditions apply for groups. Group transportation is restricted or not permitted on certain trains. Railroads are especially suited for carrying large groups and higher fare reductions than those listed in the manual may be granted. Details of these regulations can be obtained by contacting the issuing office. If a special train or a chartered train is ordered, certain minimum requirements must be met. In particular, the organizing railroad levies a minimum charge. Requests for groups should be made in writing to the issuing office. In Canada,

FIGURE 7.18
Typical listing of European rail fares.
Source: Eurailtariff.

Map Carte	Section Relation	via	Individual passengers Voyageurs isolés				Travel Time Temps de parcours
			1 cl	2 cl	1 cl	2 cl	
			US $				hours heures
E 4	**HEIDELBERG HBF**						
	Amsterdam/Amsterdam Schiphol Airport, Baden-Baden, Basel SBB, Bremen, Frankfurt (Main), Frankfurt (M) Flughafen, Hamburg						
E 4	- Karlsruhe	Bruchsal	11	7	22	14	½
D 3	- Koblenz		33	22	66	44	2
D 4	- Luzern	Mannheim—Basel	78	50	146	95	4½
E 3	- Mainz	Darmstadt / Worms	17	11	34	22	1
E 4	- Mannheim		5	3	10	6	¼
E 4	- München Hbf	Stuttgart	65	43	130	86	4
E 4	- Nürnberg	Würzburg / Crailsheim	48	32	96	64	4
C 4	- Paris	Kaiserslautern—Forbach	80	53	160	106	7
E 4	- Rothenburg ob der Tauber	🚌 Würzburg / 🚂 «Road of the Castles»/«Route des Châteaux»	42	28	84	56	3
E 4	- Stuttgart		21	14	42	28	1
E 3	- Wiesbaden	Worms / Darmstadt	18	12	36	24	1½
E 4	- Würzburg Hbf	Osterburken	29	19	58	38	2
E 3	**HELMSTEDT (Gr)**						
	Berlin, Hannover						
E 2	**HELSINGBORG**						
	Göteborg						
E 2	- København		14	9	28	18	1
F 1	- Stockholm	Hässleholm	97	61	194	122	6½
H 1	**HELSINKI**						
	Hamburg, Haparanda (Gr)						
H 1	- Joensuu	Kitee	51	34	98	65	6
H 2	- København[1]	Turku—🚢—Silja Line—Stockholm— Hässleholm—Helsingborg	156	109	309	216	23½

Supplements for couchette coach accommodation

Per person: 1st class US $ 12
2nd class in 6 berth compartment:
with 4 persons US $ 16
with 6 persons US $ 12

Supplements for sleeping car accommodation

The railroad or the sleeping-car company operating the sleeping cars on the sections mentioned below is shown in the column «Operator» with its initials and its code number. «Pool 04» indicates that the section is operated under a pool system by CFL, DB, DSB, FS, NS, OeBB, SBB, SNCB and SNCF.

Suppléments pour voitures-couchettes

Par personne: 1re classe US $ 12
2me classe en compartiment à 6 couchettes:
avec 4 personnes US $ 16
avec 6 personnes US $ 12

Suppléments pour voitures-lits

Le résau de chemin de fer ou la compagnie de voitures-lits qui exploite les voitures-lits circulant sur les parcours indiqués ci-dessous est désigné par ses initiales et son numéro de code. L'indication «Pool 04» signifie que la relation est exploitée sous un régime de pool par les résaux CFL, DB, DSB, FS, NS, OeBB, SBB, SNCB, et SNCF.

from/de	to/à or/ou vice versa	Operator Exploitant	Supplement per person/Supplément par personne			
			Tourist (T3)	Double (T2)	Special	Single
			US $	US $	US $	US $
Algeciras	Madrid[1]	RENFE 71	–	46	–	77
	Madrid[2]	RENFE 71	23	31	–	58
	Madrid[3]	RENFE 71	19	27	–	46
Alicante	Bilbao[2]	RENFE 71	23	31	–	58
	Irún[2]	RENFE 71	23	31	–	58
	Madrid[2]	RENFE 71	23	31	–	58
	Madrid[3]	RENFE 71	19	27	–	46
Almeria	Madrid[1]	RENFE 71	–	46	–	77
	Sevilla[2]	RENFE 71	23	31	–	58
Amsterdam	Chur	Pool 04	36	53	89	125
	Luzern	Pool 04	36	53	89	125
	Milano	Pool 04	36	53	89	125
	München	Pool 04	36	53	89	125
	Zürich	Pool 04	36	53	89	125
Åndalsnes	Oslo	NSB 76	11	22 [6]	–	44
Athènes	Beograd	JZ 72	34	51	–	119
	München	JZ 72	35	82	–	191
Badajoz	Madrid[2]	RENFE 71	23	31	–	58
Bar	Beograd	JZ 72	8	13	–	30
Barcelona	Berne[4,5]	RENFE 71	–	80	–	162
	Berne[2,5]	RENFE 71	34	67	–	143
	Bilbao[1]	RENFE 71	–	46	–	77
	Cartagena[1]	RENFE 71	–	46	–	77
	Coruña[3]	RENFE 71	19	27	–	46
	Gijón[2]	RENFE 71	23	31	–	58
	Irún[1]	RENFE 71	–	46	–	77
	Irún[3]	RENFE 71	19	27	–	46

[1] compartment with shower/[1] compartiment avec douche
[2] with airconditioning/[2] avec climatisation
[3] with partial airconditioning/[3] avec climatisation partielle

FIGURE 7.20
Supplements for sleeping accommodation.
Source: Eurailtariff.

issuing offices are French National Railroads, German Rail and CIT (Italian Railroad).

The prices contained in the manual are applicable if all rules are observed. The manual should be used for information purposes and exact quotations obtained through the issuing offices. Geography is just as important a factor in computing fares as it is in planning itineraries. A detailed map is therefore included with each manual to simplify this matter.

Rail Passes

For clients who have a limited itinerary and for those who just wish to sample European train travel, the point-to-point fares found in the Eurail tariff are the most appropriate products. For those who plan to travel more extensively by rail, however, a rail pass offers better value. Most of Europe's national railroads offer special bargains for travel within their country and some, for example, Britain and France, the Scandinavian nations, and Portugal and Spain cooperate to offer regional passes. Passes are designed to make it easier and more attractive for visitors to travel on the rail network. Travellers planning to visit one country, or at most two, can often save money by using combinations of national rail passes. They also have an option of first or second class travel and in some cases receive additional perks such as additional private railways (Scandinavia and Switzerland), freedom from reservations fees (Italy) and regional coupon books (France). Two types of pass are available; railpasses and flexipasses (Figure 7.20). Railpasses permit the traveller unlimited transportation for a fixed period of time ranging from 15 days to three months. Flexipasses are a relatively recent product and have proved extremely popular in the short time since their introduction to the market. They are based on the fact that many tourists do not wish to spend their entire vacation travelling. A flexipass permits the traveller to tailor travel arrangements to suit individual needs. For example, some flexipasses permit ten days travel in two months, while others allow 15 days travel in the same time span. Users

**FIGURE 7.20
Types of Eurail passes.**

Type of Pass	Class of Service	Validity	Restrictions
Eurailpass	1st	15 consecutive days 21 consecutive days 1 month 2 months 3 months	
Eurail Flexipass	1st	Any 10 or 15 days within 2 months	
Eurail Saverpass	1st	Same as Eurailpass	Two passengers must travel together at all times
Eurail Saver Flexipass	1st	Any 10 or 15 days within 2 months	Two passengers must travel together at all times
Eurail Youthpass	2nd	Same as Eurailpass	Under 26 Years
Eurail Youth Flexipass	2nd	Any 10 or 15 days within 2 months	Under 26 Years

who start their trip between 7:00 p.m. and midnight have their validation continued until the following midnight. Flexipasses allow the holder to stay in one place, rent a car, tour around, or visit countries not included in the pass. For people who want to travel extensively an unlimited travel railpass should be recommended; for those who want to travel selectively advise a flexipass. Holders of rail passes do not generally pay for high-speed surcharges that are levied on point-to-point ticket holders. They pay only for seat reservations where required, sleeping accommodation, and meals aboard the train.

The most popular European rail passes with Canadians are those issued by Eurail and available for travel throughout most of Western Europe. These Eurail passes are, in fact, sold in much greater quantity than are point-to-point rail tickets. Just as national and regional rail passes are suitable for those who wish to travel within a limited geographical area, Eurail passes are appropriate for those who plan a more extensive itinerary.

Eurail is an organization of 17 European railroads which cooperate for marketing purposes by issuing a series of rail passes; Eurailpass, Eurail Saverpass, Eurail Flexipass and Eurail Youthpass. All Eurail passes give the traveller access to a network of over 160,000 km which links countries, cities and smaller towns as well as scenic and historic attractions. All passes must be purchased in advance outside of Europe. The range of passes is designed to meet a variety of tourist needs. They permit tourists to travel in total freedom, stop where they wish, change itinerary at will without any formalities, and take advantage of the frequent train service offered in Europe. Alternatively, tourists can base themselves in a city of their choice and make an unlimited number of different excursions each day.

Eurailpass

The first pass, the Eurailpass, was introduced in 1959 to promote train travel by non-European tourists. This pass provides unlimited travel in first or second class through 17 countries of continental Europe, that is, Austria, Belgium, Denmark, Federal Republic of Germany, Finland, France,

Greece, Hungary, Italy, Luxembourg, Netherlands, Norway, Portugal, Republic of Ireland, Spain, Sweden and Switzerland. The Eurailpass is a single, convenient card which once validated is the key to travel the length and breadth of Europe. Travellers need not stand in line to purchase tickets nor need they be concerned with different currencies. A Eurailpass is effectively a credit card for the European rail system with one difference; everything it offers has already been paid for. Eurailpass holders may choose from any of the many trains, whether the famous EuroCity trains or local trains, running daily throughout the system. Surcharges for travelling on trains such as the EC network are included in the price of a Eurailpass. A choice of Eurailpasses is offered with a validity of 15 days, 21 days, one month, two months and three months. A Eurailpass is also valid for either free travel or substantial reductions on Europabus lines, lake steamers, certain private mountain railroads and several sea crossings.

Eurail Saverpass

The Eurail Saverpass is a relatively recent addition to Eurail's marketing efforts. It is valid for unlimited first class travel for two people travelling together. The Saverpass can be purchased for 15 days, 21 days, one month, two months or three months of travel. The Saverpass permits travel at an even lower rate than with an individual Eurail pass.

Europass

Eurail also offers the Europass which is similar to the Eurail Saverpass. This pass offers a discount for two persons travelling together. It provides unlimited first class travel in Germany, France, Italy, Spain and Switzerland within a two month period. Various options permit clients to choose a pass for travel in any one these countries for a five to 15 day period. Other countries can also be selected at an additional cost. This pass has become extremely popular since its introduction. A Youth Europass, valid for second class travel for those under age 26, is also available.

Eurail Flexipass

A range of flexible passes has also been introduced under the name Eurail Flexipass. Three types of flexipass are available. The Eurail Flexipass is valid for individual first class travel. A Eurail Saver Flexipass, also valid for first class travel, is available for two people travelling together at all times. It is available at a lower price. A Eurail Youth Flexipass offers the same benefits to those aged under 26 but is valid only for second class travel. Travellers can choose a flexipass which permits travel on any 10 days within a two month period, or on any 15 days within a two month period. A flexipass permits travel counsellors to make reservations for their clients in a few selected cities and suggests that they take daily train excursions to the main local sights. Such a recommendation increases customer service by providing a way for clients to avoid packing and unpacking every day. At the same time, commission income increases.

Eurail Youthpass

A special pass, the Eurail Youthpass valid only for second class travel, is available for anyone under age 26. These passes, obtainable with the same validity as the Eurailpass, are accepted by the same railroad networks as the regular Eurailpass in the 17 countries mentioned earlier. Unlike other Eurail passes, however, all supplements for certain express trains must be paid separately. Certain EC trains such as those which offer first class service only, for example, can be boarded with a Eurail Youthpass only if the holder pays the difference between the regular first class and second class fares, plus the applicable supplement.

Combination Passes

Combination passes known as Euraildrive are also available. These passes permit travellers to combine the benefits of a rail flexipass with the freedom of car rental. The result is a completely flexible travel option. All passes follow a similar format. For example, a Euraildrive pass is available which offers unlimited first class rail travel for four days combined with car rental for three days. This option operates on any seven days within a 2 month period. Each Euraildrive pass permits additional days of car rental.

In comparison with point-to-point tickets, rail passes are frequently more economical for travellers, even on a simple round trip journey. In addition, rail passes include extras which must be paid by travellers using point-to-point tickets. The price of these passes, however, does not include extras such as seat reservation fees, charges for couchettes or sleeping car accommodation, meals, or port taxes.

All Eurail passes are sold only outside of Europe. When travellers first use the pass, an attendant enters the holder's passport number on the train ticket. The rail pass will be stamped with the starting and final dates at the same time. Many internal boundaries within Europe were removed in 1993. For travel between countries where there are still border inspections, an attendant collects tickets, passports and customs declarations in the evening so that passengers will not be awakened at the border. These items are returned in the morning when clients receive their wake-up call. Further details on travel by rail and the use of rail passes can be obtained by contacting the appropriate tourist board or the rail company's official representative. Rail Europe, French, German and Italian Rail offices in Canada distribute all European rail passes.

Reservations and Ticketing

Individual seat reservations can be requested for most long distance trains. Some trains, such as the EuroCity service, require special supplements and compulsory reservations. Seat reservations cannot be made for domestic trains in the Benelux countries (Belgium, Netherlands and Luxembourg) and Switzerland. Reservations for trains originating or operating within Eastern European countries, Spain and Portugal must be obtained locally. A nominal fee plus a communication charge is applied to such reservations, including those for Eurail passes. Seat reservations should be obtained for only the initial portions of the itinerary, preferably no more than the first three segments, in case clients decide to change their itinerary. For groups, especially those with over 15 participants, advance reservations are recommended for all trains. Information about restrictions on certain trains or for certain time periods is available at all North American offices of the European railways. Reservations are required for all couchettes and sleepers. Arrangements for all reservations are usually confirmed within two months prior to the travel date.

Although it is not complicated to make a reservation or to request regular Eurailtariff tickets or Eurail passes, the railway office needs precise information to correctly issue a ticket. These procedures are mere recommendations, designed to simplify the work of the rail issuing office and of the travel counsellor. This not only saves money but also gives the railway offices a chance to provide better service. To make a reservation and issue tickets, the issuing office requires the following information.

Eurailtariff (Point-to-point Transportation)

- Reference. State your agency name, reference number and your agency's customer number with the supplier, if known.
- Names. Provide the number of passengers, state their names and give the age of any children in the party.
- Itinerary. Give the routing desired. State the travel date (e.g., Nov. 4 or Nov. 4/5 in case of night travel), the train number and departure time. If these are not known, indicate approximately when the clients wish to leave.
- Class of Service. Request first or second class as desired. For seats or couchettes, state whether smoking or non-smoking is requested. Reservations are assigned on the basis of availability. For sleepers, report the type of accommodation requested. If necessary give the issuing office authorization to cable.

Eurailgroup

- Supply the information as above for individual reservations and in addition provide:
- Group name and reference.
- Name of tour conductor or group leader.
- Total number of participants in group. (A passenger name list will be a more useful reference for the supplier.)
- Ages of passengers under 26 years, if any (for youth group reduction).
- Deposit required depending on size of the group.

Eurail Passes

- Eurail passes are easier to request than point-to-point transportation tickets. Simply provide the following information.
- Reference. The agency's customer number with the supplier, if known.
- Name. Full name (preferably as registered in passport) of all passengers.
- Country of residence.
- Ages of children under 12 years.
- Category of pass requested.

To order a Eurail Youthpass, provide the same information as for any other Eurail pass and state the age of persons under 26 years.

Note that since all European railways are linked by computers, clients can reserve berths on any train in any country at any major train station.

Statistics suggest that sales of all types of Eurail passes account for almost 90 percent of the total sales figure in North America. Only ten percent of the sales through travel agencies are for Eurailtariff and Eurailgroup products which are more cumbersome to plan, sell and request. As more national, regional and combination passes for unlimited railway travel are offered, even this ten percent figure for point-to-point tickets will be reduced. These statistics seem to indicate that rail passes are easy to sell. Eurail passes and Eurailtariff tickets are commissionable to agencies at ten percent. Tickets are readily available from the Canadian offices of the railroads.

Refunds and Cancellations

Refunds are an important part of the railways' customer service and certain rules must be observed. Refunds on point-to-point tickets can be secured for entirely unused as well as partially used tickets. Applications for a refund must be submitted within six months from the last day of the period of validity of the ticket concerned. Since tickets are valid for six months from the date of issue, passengers effectively have one year in which to claim a refund. To receive a refund, travellers must have the ticket properly endorsed by a railway official at the station where the journey was abandoned or altered. The fact that tickets were not punched or do not bear any other control marks does not constitute sufficient proof of their non-use. Advise your clients to secure endorsements for unused tickets while in Europe and also to retain them as they must be attached to the refund application. No refunds are available after one year.

Eurail passes are valid for six months from the date of issue. If unused, a pass must be returned to the issuing office for refund before the first date of validity appearing on the ticket. Travellers have their passes validated at the departure station where they first commence their train journey. Passes can be validated at any train station. Validation is denoted by imprinting with an official stamp and entering the holder's passport number on the pass. Lost or stolen passes which have not been validated are totally nonrefundable. Travellers who lose a validated pass must contact a Eurail Aid office, located in major train stations, to have the pass reissued. In other circumstances these tickets will be considered used in conjunction with the tariff rules, even when they are returned before the validity is expired.

All tickets, including Eurail passes, are subject to a 15 percent cancellation fee which is deducted from the amount to be refunded. The agent's commission, however, is not recalled. Surcharges for seat, couchette and sleeper reservations are subject to cancellation fees even when the reservation is properly cancelled. Cancelled seat and EC reservations are not eligible for a refund. Cancelled couchette reservations are subject to a ten percent cancellation penalty if cancelled prior to departure, otherwise there is no refund. Sleeper reservations are subject to a penalty of 15 percent of the surcharge when cancelled before the departure date of the train, otherwise 50 percent of the surcharge is withheld. There are no refunds for communication fees.

Rail Travel in Britain

Much that has been written about European railroads applies equally to the facilities and services available in Britain. Great Britain is by far the most popular overseas destination for Canadian tourists. Thus it is particularly important that travel counsellors become fully familiar with its rail products. Sources of product information for British rail services are the Thomas Cook European Timetable and the Canadian office of Rail Europe which can provide information and reservations. British rail products are now online and are issued electronically by Rail Europe.

The governement-owned British Rail system was recently privatized into 25 independent organizations, most of which operate regionally. Together, these companies run 15,000 passenger trains daily. Some 1,600 trains are classed as InterCity expresses which provide fast service in modern equipment between major cities and towns in England, Scotland and Wales. Included in this extensive network of services are 70 overnight sleeping car trains linking London and other provincial cities. The InterCity 225 service introduced in 1990, upgraded the excellent quality of the existing high-speed service and uses trains capable of travelling at speeds up to 225 km per hour. This service has reduced travel times considerably. For example, London to Edinburgh, a distance of over 630 km, can be reached in less than five hours. There are no additional charges on these trains, other than seat reservation fees when applicable.

In addition, there is a series of Sprinter Trains that link a number of towns with the InterCity network.

First and second (economy) class services are available. First class cars, provided on all but commuter trains, have a seating arrangement of two-and-one across the aisle. Groups of seats are arranged with a table between them. This arrangement permits the use of wider seats which on modern equipment are adjustable. First class cars are identified by a yellow stripe above the windows on the outside of the coach. Economy class cars have two fixed seats on either side of a centre aisle. Seats are arranged either facing across a table or side-by-side as in a plane. Every car is equipped with a restroom. Restaurant and buffet cars, identified by a red stripe, are available on most InterCity trains.

Sleeper service on overnight trains is available in first and economy class. First class sleepers accommodate one person in a single bed but connecting bedrooms are available. Economy sleepers offer double accommodation with an upper and a lower berth. Both sleepers have private washing facilities. A sleeping berth supplement is charged in addition to the applicable fare. For this supplement, the accommodation provides wall-to-wall carpet, hot and cold running water, towel and soap, a soft mattress and a steward call button. In the morning sleeper patrons are served complimentary biscuits with coffee or tea. Sleeper services operate between London and the main centres in Scotland, the North of England, South Wales and the West of England.

In most cases, advance reservations may be made on Britain's rail services. There are, however, some exceptions to this general rule. No reservations are taken for day services from London King's Cross to Edinburgh, from London Euston to Glasgow, or from London Paddington to

BRITRAIL CLASSIC PASS

	Adults 1st Class	Adults Standard Class	Senior** 1st Class	Youth** Standard Class
8 consecutive days	$ 455	$315	$387	$250
15 consecutive days	$ 703	$485	$597	$389
22 consecutive days	$ 900	$620	$765	$495
1 month	$1045	$720	$888	$579

BRITRAIL FLEXIPASS

	Adults 1st Class	Adults Standard Class	Senior** 1st Class	Youth** Standard Class
Any 4 days in 1 month	$387	$267	$329	$213
Any 8 days in 1 month	$560	$387	$475	$309
Any 15 days in 1 month	$849	$585	$720	–
Any 15 days in 2 month	–	–	–	$469

BRITRAIL PASS 'N DRIVE

Any 6 days (3 rail & 3 car) within 1 month + add'l cor days.

Car Categories	1 Adult 1st Class	Standard	Senior 1st Class
Cat. A – Economy	$510	$425	$469
Cat. E – Compact Automatic	$700	$615	$659
Add'l Adult Rail Supplement	$270	$185	$229

BRITRAIL PARTY PASS‡

Parties of 3 Persons	Adults 1st Class	Adults Standard Class	Youth** Standard Class
Any 4 days in 1 month	$323	$223	$178
Any 8 days in 1 month	$467	$323	$258
Any 15 days in 1 month	$708	$488	–
Any 15 days in 2 months	–	–	$391
8 consecutive days	$379	$263	$208
15 consecutive days	$586	$404	$324
22 consecutive days	$750	$517	$413
1 month	$871	$600	$483

Parties of 4 Persons	Adults 1st Class	Adults Standard Class	Youth** Standard Class
Any 4 days in 1 month	$290	$200	$160
Any 8 days in 1 month	$420	$290	$232
Any 15 days in 1 month	$637	$439	–
Any 15 days in 2 months	–	–	$352
8 consecutive days	$341	$236	$188
15 consecutive days	$527	$364	$292
22 consecutive days	$675	$465	$371
1 month	$784	$540	$434

‡Price per person based on parties of 3 or 4 persons traveling together at all times.

BRITRAIL SENIOR PARTY PASS‡

	Parties of 3 1st Class	Parties of 4 1st Class
Any 4 days in 1 month	$274	$247
Any 8 days in 1 month	$396	$356
Any 15 days in 1 month	$600	$540
8 consecutive days	$323	$290
15 consecutive days	$498	$448
22 consecutive days	$638	$574
1 month	$740	$666

‡Price per person based on parties of 3 or 4 persons traveling together at all times.

FIGURE 7.21
Rates and conditions for BritRail passes.
Source: Rail Europe.

Frequently Asked Questions

Airline Systems

Q *What BritRail products can I issue through my airline computer?*

A BritRail Passes, BritRail Flexipasses, BritRail/Drive, and London Visitor Travelcards ONLY. (You CANNOT ticket the London Extra package, Freedom of Scotland Travelpass, BritFrance, BritIreland, or England/Wales Passes.)

Q *Can these tickets be used for travel in Britain?*

A The AMERICAN AIRLINES or UNITED AIRLINES ticket must be exchanged in Britain prior to travel. (See pages A-6 and A-7 for instructions.)

Q *Can I order other products through my airline computer?*

A Yes. You can send us a message to order tickets, reservations, and literature. Access codes and full details are opposite.

FIGURE 7.22
BritRail passes can be reserved and ticketed using an airline computer reservation system.
Source: BritRail.

Exeter and all points in Cornwall, especially during summer peak weekends. Always enquire about advance booking when ordering tickets.

As with the Eurail tariff, it is generally much less expensive to purchase a rail pass if one is intending to travel to any degree in Britain. Regular fares can be quite expensive. Cheap return fares are available and many are less than twice the price of a one way ticket. The BritRail Pass is similar in concept to the Eurailpass. It is valid for rail travel in Scotland, England and Wales. The pass is not sold in Britain, thus offering sales possibilities to agencies in Canada. First class passes allow unlimited travel ranging from eight days to one month, while standard passes offer economy class travel for the same time periods (Figure 7.21). A Youth Pass for those between the ages of 16

and 25 years gives access to economy class travel and a Senior Citizens Pass provides first class rail travel for those aged 60 or over. Children between the ages of five and 15 travel free if accompanied by an adult paying the full pass price. Additional children can travel by paying half the adult rate. In 1989, BritRail introduced a series of flexipasses which offer unlimited rail travel on any four days or any eight days in one month, and on any 15 days in one or two months. These passes are available for first class or economy travel. Senior, youth and child flexipasses are also offered. All BritRail passes can be booked by telephone or through an airline CRS (see Figure 7.22). As traveller habits change towards shorter trips and spending more time in fewer areas, it is expected that more flexipasses will be introduced. BritRail also offers a combined flexipass and car rental option, as well as BritFrance and BritIreland Railpasses.

In addition, British Rail is associated with a network of Sealink passenger and car ferry services to Ireland, the Channel Islands, and the continent of Europe. There are approximately 20 daily crossings between Britain and France ranging from 1 hour 45 minutes for Dover-Calais to four hours for Newhaven-Dieppe. Sealink also operates ferries to Holland and Belgium in addition to three routes to Ireland and two to the Channel Islands of Jersey and Guernsey. The English Channel crossing can be rather choppy and clients who do not enjoy sea travel should be advised to choose the shortest route. This route allows clients who have purchased a Eurailpass to begin using it as soon as they land on the continent. Some of the most popular services offered by British Rail are the hovercraft services between Dover and Boulogne and Dover and Calais. Crossing time is 35 minutes available at frequent intervals throughout the day. Reservations for car and passenger space on ferry or hovercraft services must be made in advance. Facilities for quick confirmation are available in Canada by making reservations via telex or fax. An answer will normally be received within 24 hours.

Since the completion of the Eurotunnel in 1994, travel time between Britain and continental Europe has been reduced by two hours. Eurostar, the independently operated London to Paris or Brussels service, was introduced to take advantage of this routing. Eventually, Britain's rail services will be linked with the high-speed European network. Rail will therefore offer much stiffer competition for the airlines on journeys between London and many European cities.

Rail Travel Worldwide

Although Canadian travel counsellors will most likely be concerned with domestic and European rail travel, they should have a basic knowledge of railway systems throughout the world. For many countries rail is the principal means of transportation and for some rail is not only the most comfortable but also the safest and most reliable mode. The *Thomas Cook Overseas Timetable* published six times yearly provides details of rail transportation for destinations not shown in the European edition. The relevant national tourist board is also a valuable source of product information on rail services.

It would be helpful for travel counsellors to be familiar with rail systems in South America, Africa and Asia. The largest system in the world is that of Russia which has about 130,000 km of track, one quarter of which is electrified. The Trans-Siberian Railway at almost 10,000 km is the longest continuous route in the world and is in this system. India has over 60,000 km of track in an extensive network. South Africa operates the famous Blue Train, a luxury train running from Pretoria to Capetown. Australia and New Zealand have installed new equipment, improved schedules and personalized services. The Australian Indian Express from Sydney to Perth enjoys a high reputation as a worthwhile experience.

One of the most important services for Canadian travel counsellors is the Bullet Train (or *Shinkansen*) operated by Japanese

National Railways. The first high-speed line opened in 1964 and now links both the northern and southern points with Tokyo. Some of Japan's major cities including Kyoto, Osaka, Kobe and Hiroshima are located along the Shinkansen line. Bullet trains cruise at 210 km per hour on a specially designed track. Such have been the advances that travel time between Tokyo and Osaka, a distance of over 500 km, has been reduced to 3 hours 10 minutes from 6 hours 40 minutes. Part of the reason for this is that the Shinkansen line carries passenger trains only. Bullet Trains are so popular that they now leave Tokyo every 15 minutes between 6:00 a.m. and 9:00 p.m. Generally, 90 Shinkansen trains leave Tokyo daily for the south. The Shinkansen network has been expanded from its original southern line. Two separate lines were extended north from Tokyo, both equipped with tracks that have a sprinkler system to spray heated water to clear snow. The Tohuku Shinkansen began operating to the northeastern part of Honshu, Japan's main island, in June 1982. There are now 28 daily round trips offered. Passengers begin their trip at Tokyo's Uneo Station by taking a relay train that connects to the high-speed line at Omiya. The shuttle service takes about 30 minutes. Total travel time has been reduced to about 2 hours 30 minutes. In November 1982, the Joetsu Shinkansen between Omiya and Niigata, a major coastal city north of Tokyo, was opened. This bullet train operates 21 round trips daily which cut across mountainous country and pass through 23 tunnels including the 22 km Dai-Shimizu Tunnel, the world's longest. Travel time has been reduced to 1 hour 45 minutes from four hours. Further expansion included the massive Seikan underwater tunnel which now links Hokkaido with the mainland.

Japanese high-speed trains provide seating for 1,400 passengers. Windows are placed higher than on European trains and all carriages are air-conditioned. Trains have on-board telephones, buffet cars, and snacks and beverages are sold seat to seat. In addition to the Shinkansen service which operates on dedicated lines, Japan has a national network of super-express trains called Hikari. Japan is also experimenting with a new system of trains which glide over a single rail. Powered by electromagnetism, these magnetic levitation or maglev trains can reach speeds of over 400 km per hour.

In Japan, fares are based on distance travelled. There are additional charges for green cars (former first class), various express services, berths and reserved seating. Tickets are available at the principal offices of the Japan Travel Bureau and Nippon Travel Agency. Up to two pieces of baggage may be taken, free of charge, into cars. Extra baggage up to a limit of 90 kilos may be checked on each passenger ticket. There are, however, size and weight restrictions on each piece.

Specialized Train Services

The market for chartered and specialized train service is growing in many parts of the world. The Venice-Simplon Orient Express was the first to repackage train travel in the luxury form that once was commonplace. Restored in 1982, the Venice-Simplon Orient Express follows the traditional route from London to Venice in surroundings which are likely to remain exceptional. The travel time for this journey is 24 hours each way.

The fare is about the same as first class air fare. A Canadian tour operator (who represents the Orient Express in Canada) purchased the rights to transcontinental train service from VIA Rail to offer a comparable luxury cross-Canada service (the Royal Canadian). Using totally refurbished cars, the Royal Canadian will operate on a route linking Toronto and Vancouver. Shorter trips connect Calgary, Banff and Lake Louise with either Toronto or Vancouver. The train features panorama dome cars, a domed dining car and an outside observation platform. All rooms have telephone, TV, video and private bathrooms with showers. Vegetarian, Japanese, Kosher and low calorie food are available as well as elegant dining. As with other specialized train services, the target market is the luxury traveller. The Royal Scotsman, British Rail's famous steam train originally running from London to Scotland, has been in service since 1985 providing luxury tours of Scotland in renovated carriages from the late Victorian and Edwardian periods. Chartered train service is also growing in the USA where art deco lounge and dining cars can be chartered by groups for meetings and incentive tours. Murder mystery tours have also enjoyed popularity in Canada. With this product, the train journey becomes the scene of a murder mystery which passengers attempt to solve.

Review Questions

1. Give a brief review of the development, growth and decline of rail transportation.

2. Discuss the benefits and disadvantages of train travel for both the traveller and the travel counsellor.

3. Compare the equipment, facilities and services offered on North American passenger trains with that available in Europe.

4. Discuss the various rail passes available in Europe.

5. What information is needed to reserve an individual seat on the TGV from Paris to Lyon?

6. Using a current edition of the Thomas Cook European Timetable, plan the itinerary shown below. For each leg of the journey, provide the train names, numbers, departure and arrival times. Plan the trip so that your clients depart as close as possible to 10:00 a.m. on every occasion. In addition, name the towns where there will be customs formalities.

    - July 7   Amsterdam to Paris by EC service.
    - July 14   Paris to Lyon by TGV.
    - July 16   Lyon to Barcelona by international express.
    - July 20   Barcelona to Madrid by Talgo.
    - July 25   Madrid to Paris by EC overnight service.

References

Eurailtariff. Eurailpass Distribution Centre, P.O. Box 300, Station R, Montreal, Quebec H2S 9Z9.

Forsyth Travel Library, P.O. Box 2975, 9154 West 5th Street, Shawnee Mission, Kansas 66201, USA. This company is a valuable source of railway information, guidebooks, destination videos and cruise material.

Go BritRail. BritRail Travel International offices.

National Railroad Passenger Corporation (Amtrak), 60 Massachusetts Avenue NE, Washington, DC 20002, USA.

Official Railway Guide. International Thomson Transport Press, 424 West 33rd Street, New York, NY 10001, USA.

Saltzman, M.L., and K. Saltzman Muileman. *Eurail Guide*. Eurail Guide Annual, 27540 Pacific Coast Highway, Malibu CA 90265, USA.

Thomas Cook European Timetable. Thomas Cook Limited, Timetable Publishing, P.O. Box 36, Peterborough, PE3 6SB, England or from the Forsyth Travel Library.

Thomas Cook Overseas Timetable. From the above address.

VIA Rail Canada Inc. *RESERVIA Job Aid*. Montreal, 1985.

VIA Rail Canada Inc. *Vocabulary of Passenger Service*. Montreal, 1989.

VIA Rail Canada Inc. *Vocabulary of Ticketing*. Montreal, 1989.

VIA Rail Canada Inc. *VIA Tours Policies and Procedures*. Montreal, 1989.

VIA Rail Canada Inc. *Your Selling Guide*. Montreal.

## Chapter 8

Ground Transportation

Chapter Summary

The chapter begins with a summary of the development of bus transportation and a review of the terminology. Types of buses and their facilities are discussed, followed by an examination of the motorcoach industry in North America and in Europe. The next section considers the components which comprise ground transportation services, that is, sightseeing and transfers. The remainder of the chapter studies the car rental industry. Terminology and sources of product knowledge are reviewed. Rental charges, terms and conditions are examined in some detail. Reservation procedures and client counselling are also outlined. The chapter concludes with a brief review of car leasing and motorhome rental as alternatives to car rental.

Chapter Objectives
After completing this chapter you should be able to:

- Describe the bus industry.

- Use the terminology of the industry.

- Discuss how buses are marketed.

- Describe the sales features of bus travel.

- Discuss the advantages and disadvantages of bus travel.

- Define transfers.

- Arrange transfers and sightseeing.

- Use the terminology of the car rental industry.

- State the benefits to both clients and a travel agency when a rental car is offered.

- Research the best rate for clients.

- Book car rentals.

- Calculate car rental costs including CDW, PAI and taxes.

- Identify additional charges.

- Describe various types of car rental packages.

- Interpret car rental manuals.

- Compare car leasing and car rental.

Bus Transportation

Throughout the nineteenth century horse-drawn buses, descendants of the stagecoach, were the main form of urban transport. Self-propelled buses and trucks, many of them steam driven, were a tiny minority of vehicles. The gasoline engine was not yet powerful enough nor sufficiently reliable to propel heavy vehicles. The development of city railways, particularly the introduction in 1863 of a subway system in London, compelled bus companies to consider changing to powered vehicles. Motorcoaches first appeared in the 1890s and from 1920 on self-propelled buses outnumbered horse-drawn vehicles. Prior to the First World War buses were used primarily for commuter and urban transport but by the 1920s their use was more varied. Town and country bus operators began to run excursions to places of interest. The age of modern bus travel had begun.

It would be difficult to imagine the travel industry without buses. No other vehicle serves the needs of travellers on such an extensive and global scale. Buses provide urban and intercity transport on every continent, offering regular service within and between communities large and small. No other form of transport is as flexible and responsive to passenger demand. Buses provide carriage for everyone, native or tourist. They can operate on a point-to-point schedule or on a charter basis for tours, trips and excursions of all kinds. At airports from Rome to Singapore, buses transport passengers from jets to the city centres and hotels. Buses supply sightseeing services in Mombasa, Moscow, Sydney, Liverpool, Boston, Quebec City and in about five hundred other centres around the globe. No other common passenger carrier can achieve such low operating costs. Fast, cheap and efficient, buses can go where other forms of mass transport cannot.

The terms bus, coach and motorcoach are used interchangeably, however, to avoid semantic confusion the term "bus" is usually applied in the travel trade when a vehicle provides point-to-point transport only. That is, a bus provides scheduled service for individually-ticketed passengers. "Motorcoach" is more commonly used in Britain than "bus". In Canada and the USA, the term "motorcoach" is generally used when the vehicle operates in connection with a tour or package involving a program of sightseeing and accommodation. Bus companies, using basically the same types of vehicles, offer either intercity service or charter and tour operations. Several operators handle both functions. Most travel agents derive little income from the

sale of point-to-point bus tickets. The labour involved in issuing and handling such tickets is often unprofitable when measured against the low fares. There are some notable exceptions, however, especially in smaller centres and towns where appointed ticket agents rather than full service travel agencies do a steady trade in bus tickets to neighbouring cities.

Types of Buses

There are four main types of buses. **City buses** are used for mass transit but rarely for tours. **Minibuses** and vans are employed on shuttle services and sightseeing tours for groups of 15 people or less. **Sightseeing buses** are designed specifically for local tours. These coaches accommodate up to 45 passengers, have large windows and comfortable seats. **Highway coaches** are operated on long distance routes, either for regular transportation, tours or charters. They are comparable in size to sightseeing buses but often have different features and amenities. Modern coaches can be quite spectacular. In addition to standard vehicles, many companies have coaches custom designed to meet the needs of specific markets (Figure 8.1). Most new coaches have air conditioning and heating, reclining seats and individual fresh air controls as well as a modern

FIGURE 8.1
Layout of a custom designed coach.
Reproduced courtesy of Custom Coach Corporation.

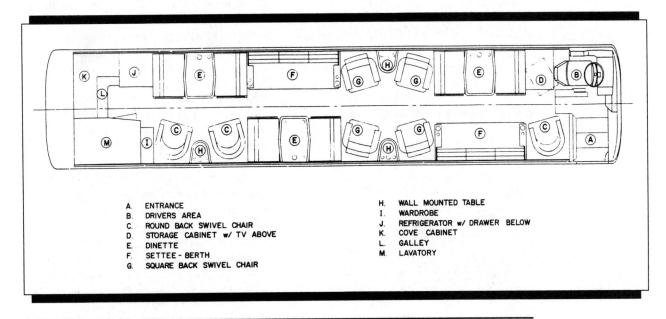

A. ENTRANCE
B. DRIVERS AREA
C. ROUND BACK SWIVEL CHAIR
D. STORAGE CABINET w/ TV ABOVE
E. DINETTE
F. SETTEE - BERTH
G. SQUARE BACK SWIVEL CHAIR

H. WALL MOUNTED TABLE
I. WARDROBE
J. REFRIGERATOR w/ DRAWER BELOW
K. COVE CABINET
L. GALLEY
M. LAVATORY

EDMONTON—CAMROSE—STETTLER—DRUMHELLER

READ DOWN					READ UP		
153	153	SCHEDULE NUMBER	154	154	154		
		Folder No. 3 **734** 4-2-89					
7	X7	FREQUENCY	X71	1	7		
5 30	5 30	Lv ▼EDMONTON, AB 🚍 .... Ar	11 00	11 20	3 50		
5 42	5 42	Edmonton South	↑	D	D		
▮	f	Looma Corner	f	↑	↑		
Via	f	New Sarepta Corner	f	Via	Via		
Wetaskiwin	6 30	Hay Lakes Corner	f	Wetaskiwin	Wetaskiwin		
↓	f	Armena Corner	f				
7 15	▬ 7 00	Ar ▼Camrose 🚍 Lv	9 50	9 50	2 15		
2 00	2 00	Lv Calgary .... (704)GLC Ar	2 30	2 30	7 55		
6 33	6 33	Ar Wetaskiwin Lv	10 30	10 30	3 25		
6 40	6 40	Lv Wetaskiwin .... (732)GLC Ar	10 22	10 22	2 55		
7 15	7 15	Ar Camrose Lv	9 45	9 45	2 15		
7 15	7 15	Lv ▼Camrose 🚍 .... Ar	▬ 9 40	▬ 9 40	▬ 2 00		
f	f	Duhamel Corner	f	f	f		
7 33	7 33	▼New Norway	9 22	9 22	1 35		
② 7 41	② 7 41	Ferintosh	9 14	9 14	1 25		
7 56	7 56	▼Bashaw	8 59	8 59	1 10		
① 8 10	① 8 10	▼Mirror	① 8 45	① 8 45	① 1 00		
f	f	▼Nevis	8 25	8 25	12 45		
f	f	Erskine	8 20	8 20	12 38		
▬ 8 40	▬ 8 40	Ar ▼Stettler 🚍 Lv	8 15	8 15	12 30		
9 05	9 05	Lv ▼Stettler .... (733) Ar	8 00	8 00	▬ 12 25		
11 10	11 10	Ar ▼Consort Lv	6 15	6 15	10 20		
9 00	9 00	Lv ▼Stettler 🚍 .... Ar	8 10	8 10	▬ 12 15		
9 25	9 25	▼Big Valley	7 45	7 45	11 51		
f	f	Rumsey Jct.	f	f	f		
f	f	Rowley Jct.	f	f	f		
f	f	Morrin Jct.	f	f	f		
10 15	10 15	Ar ▼DRUMHELLER, AB 🚍 Lv	7 00	7 00	11 00		

① — Schedule goes into town.
② — Goes in town only to discharge.

©A734-0208wa

FIGURE 8.2
The schedule format used in Russell's Official Canada Bus Guide.
Courtesy of Russell's Guides Inc.

speaker system. Many are equipped with TV monitors, VCRs and stereo headphones. On some intercity services the seating capacity has been reduced to improve leg room and passenger comfort. Double-decker models used for European touring feature sleeping quarters, showers and cooking facilities. In North America, executive coaches can be chartered with leather swivel chairs, sofas, VCR monitors, telephones, fax machines, a full galley featuring a microwave, fridge and freezer, and complete washroom facilities including shower.

Bus Transport in North America

Individual bus routes connect communities across Canada and the USA in a basic intercity network. The system not only provides an important transcontinental public transportation link, it also supplies connections to and within regions not accessible to or serviced by planes or trains. Statistics Canada figures for 1994 reported that over 10 million people travelled by motorcoach on scheduled intercity service in Canada. The Canadian bus industry comprises about fifty operators most of which are privately owned. It is dominated by two companies, Greyhound and Voyageur Colonial, who together carry about half of all intercity passengers. Almost as many passengers travel on charter and tour services as on scheduled routes. Equipment and service are identical for both Canadian and American bus companies. Standard 30, 35, 40 and 45 passenger coaches are used by nearly all companies. Interline agreements allow various companies to provide uninterrupted passenger service both nationally and internationally. Under these interline agreements, ticketing procedures, accounting arrangements and published through fares have been mutually prepared to facilitate passenger service, comfort and convenience.

Bus operators rarely provide tariffs to travel agencies although simple rate sheets are usually distributed to agencies on the route network. Since most bus lines operate regionally, agencies need stock only the published schedules of those lines and routes that they are likely to sell. Agencies which sell a large amount of intercity bus transportation should subscribe to the standard references, *Russell's Official National Motor Coach Guide* and *Russell's Official Canada Bus Guide*. Issued monthly, the former publication provides current schedules and rates for all bus lines throughout North America while the latter gives the same information for all bus services within Canada (see Figure 8.2). Russell's Guides also contain other useful information for travellers planning a trip.

Most travel agencies are not supplied with ticket stock. Unless the travel agency has a large volume of business, tickets are issued as required by the bus company and sent to the agency. Commissions vary between five and ten percent. Where Canadian travel counsellors do sell point-to-point transportation, they will most likely deal with national carriers such as the Greyhound System, Voyageur and the National Travelways Bus System or regional services such as those offered by Ontario Northland. These companies operate regular service using the equipment described above. On intercity services, bus companies compete directly with private cars, rail and air service. On shorter routes of up to 500 km, bus transportation is more economical than other modes and rivals them with respect to travel time. Discount air fares, however, have increased the pressure on the industry which has responded with a number of initiatives. Among these are upgraded onboard services such as refreshments served by attendants, lower fares, concentration on markets not served by rail or air, increased use of target marketing, and the introduction of new services such as airport transfers. Unlimited travel passes such as Greyhound's Ameripass are also available for seven, 15 or 30 day periods within the United States and Canada. These passes are valid from the date of purchase and can be renewed at any time prior to the expiry date.

Bus Transport in Europe

As in North America, each European nation has bus lines which provide a network of well organized and frequent services. Roads and highways are extensive and in good condition. Equipment is modern and well maintained. Many principal tourist routes have air conditioned buses equipped with washrooms and staffed with attendants who serve refreshments enroute.

The European railroads created Europabus in 1951 to complement the extensive rail network. Operating in twelve European countries, Europabus is a consortium of many of the national bus companies. Europabus is a comprehensive motorcoach system with over 110,000 km of scenic routes that also runs special scheduled services for tourists on particularly interesting routes (Figure 8.3). Holders of Eurail passes may travel on these scheduled services for which seats must be reserved. In addition to regular express services throughout Europe, Europabus offers a program of inclusive tours. About 100 all-inclusive tours, roundtrips or line services are available through Europabus. Travel counsellors are more likely to sell Europabus tours rather than European

FIGURE 8.3
Europabus offers scheduled service on many scenic routes.
Courtesy of Europabus.

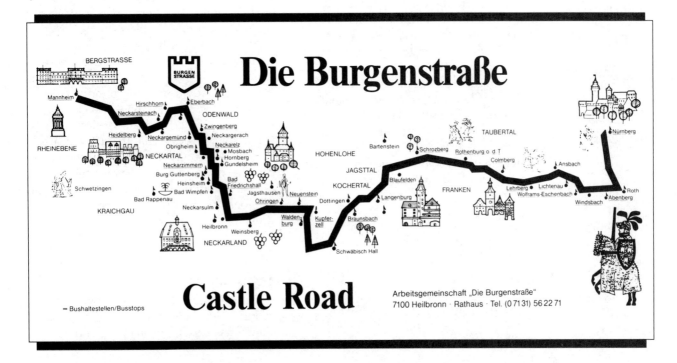

TRANSFERS/FARES — OUTER ISLANDS

SOUTH SEA CRUISES (By Catamaran — ISLAND EXPRESS)	
FARETABLE	PER PERSON RETURN F$
Plantation Resort and Musket Cove (Dicks Place) Bus/Launch connections from/to all Nadi Hotels Launch from Regent Hotel Beach	40 00
Castaway Resort and Club Naitasi Bus/Launch connections from/to all Nadi Hotels Launch from Regent Hotel Beach	43 00
Mana Island Resort Bus/Launch connections from/to all Nadi Hotels Launch from Regent Hotel Beach	46 00
Matamanoa via Mana Island Resort incl speedboat	68 00
Inter-Island transfers	15 00 each sector

FIGURE 8.4
Transfers can be provided by almost any mode of transport. This example quotes net rates in Fiji dollars.
Source: UTC United Touring Fiji.

point-to-point travel. Tours range in length from half day sightseeing excursions to 17 day inclusive tours in Western Europe and Great Britain. Tour literature, timetables and reservatoins for Europabus service can be obtained from the Canadian offices of DER, the German railroad company.

Although long distance bus transportation fills the need for low cost transportation, bus companies have lost market share to airlines and the private car. This loss has occurred even though the industry has improved its product quality and in spite of the fact that it offers a more versatile and convenient service to more communities than any other form of public transport. The industry's largest challenge is to overcome the public's perception that bus travel is slow and uncomfortable.

Ground Transportation

Ground transportation generally comprises two main services; transfers and sightseeing.

Transfers

A transfer is a specific type of transportation service which involves carrying travellers from one type of transportation to another, or from one type of travel service to another (see Figure 8.4). For example, transfer services operate at airports to take passengers from one terminal to another to change aircraft. Another type of airport transfer service shuttles passengers to and from their hotels. Similar transfer services operate at any major transportation terminal, whether bus, rail or cruise ship pier. Transfers are also used to deliver individuals or groups from their hotels to specific attractions. Taxis, limousines, minibuses, motorcoaches and private cars are used to provide transfers. Bus companies are actively involved in the provision of transfer services, either by actually operating the service or by chartering the vehicles. Many hotels and motels offer their guests complimentary shuttle service to and from the airport. In the case of cruise lines, transfers are also performed by tenders, which are small vessels that carry passengers between the cruise ship and the shore.

Receptive services operators, also known as meeting services operators or ground handlers, specialize in providing more than just transfers. Their duties also include greeting arriving passengers, dealing with their luggage and assisting them with customs preliminaries. These services are included in many group tours but are equally important to individuals travelling independently. If travel counsellors order transfer services separately, it is essential that they clearly communicate accurate details of the number of arriving passengers, their arrival and departure times, and the flight numbers or other particulars of the transportation utilized.

Sightseeing

Transfer services do not generally include sightseeing, although the two are sometimes combined since ground transportation companies often operate regular sightseeing tours (Figure 8.5). Others simply charter vehicles to tour companies who actually operate the sightseeing service. Although public transit offers an economical way to explore a city, many tourists do not feel comfortable using this method. Instead, they prefer the city tours and 1-day sightseeing tours offered worldwide in most major and many smaller cities. These tours are typically operated by local companies or by separate divisions of large companies such as Greyhound or American International. Such tours not only acquaint travellers with an area and its attractions, but also offer excellent value for money and are commissionable to travel agencies if booked in advance. These tours should be recommended to any first-time visitor to a city (see Figure 8.6). As well as standard tours offered by coach or minibus, many destinations offer specialty sightseeing tours such as those in horse-drawn buggies, rickshaws or old-fashioned streetcars.

Grayline and American Sightseeing International together account for about 90 percent of the market and are two of the world's largest sightseeing operators. Grayline provides sightseeing tours ranging from three hours to five days in over 200 cities and towns in the USA, Canada, Mexico and most other countries of the world. Grayline sightseeing tours are quite often the only means for foreign visitors to see something of the cultural

aspects of the city they are visiting. Both companies have also expanded into charters and transfer operations. Tariff schedules and other information on ground transportation services are found in the WATA Master-Key, the American Sightseeing International Worldwide Tour Planning Manual, and Grayline Sales and Tour Guide.

The Bus Regulatory Reform Act passed by the US government in 1982 deregulated the American bus industry and ended the requirement of licensing motorcoach tour brokers. Canada's National Transportation Act of 1987 had a similar effect on the Canadian bus industry. Both acts stimulated the growth in the number of travel agencies that operate their own tours. Canadian agencies with wholesaler licenses may create tours by chartering buses and booking individual components of the tour. After adding a mark-up, these tours can be marketed directly to the public. The result is that charter and tour operations is the fastest growing segment of the bus industry. Tours will be discussed in detail in Chapter 11.

Car Rental

The vast majority of domestic tourists travel by private car. This in turn has stimulated tourism by creating a need for services along tourist routes. A

FIGURE 8.5
Many ground transportation companies operate both transfer and sightseeing services.
Courtesy of American Sightseeing International.

MADEIRA – FUNCHAL

TRANSFERS – NET rates per person including assistance and porterage.

	FIT's BY TAXI			GROUPS		
	1	2	3	11-19	20-29	30 Up
From the Airport to Hotels In Funchal (or v.v.)...	$37.00	$18.50	$16.00	$14.50	$13.60	$11.20

SIGHTSEEING – less 10% commission – Group Tours – NET per person	Regular Tours			GROUPS		
		15-19	20-24	25-29	30-34	35 Up
AS/1F – CITY TOUR – 8:45 a.m. Mon. (half day)	$18.00	$20.00	$15.20	$12.40	$10.80	$ 9.60
AS/2F – EIRA DO SERRADO/MONTE (toboggan ride) – 2:00 p.m., Mon., Wed. (half day)	28.00	34.40	28.00	24.40	21.60	20.00
AS/3F – PORTO MONIZ – 8:00 a.m., Tue., Fri. (full day with lunch)	44.00	64.40	50.00	41.60	36.00	32.40
AS/4F – EAST TOUR-SANTANA – 9:00 a.m., Thu., Sun. (full day with lunch)	41.50	58.40	45.60	38.00	33.20	29.60
AS/5F – NIGHT TOUR – 7:30 p.m., Wed. (4 ½ hours with dinner)	32.00	38.80	32.80	29.60	27.20	25.60

comprehensive support system, including gas stations, motels and fast food outlets, has emerged to meet the needs of these automobile travellers. This automobile infrastructure also serves the car rental industry whose success is closely related to the increased number of tourists travelling by plane who wish a car on arrival.

Although cars were first rented in the years following World War I, the industry did not really start until the 1940s. It grew rapidly and by the late 1950s car rental companies had outlets at all major airports. Today it is a global industry. Worldwide car rental sales in 1988 exceeded US$12 billion, of which two-thirds is generated by car rental desks at airports. North America accounts for half of all car rentals while Europe contributes 30 percent of demand. Hertz, Avis, Budget and National (which is affiliated with Tilden in Canada and Europcar in Europe) have outlets in over 100 countries and dominate the international market. Several smaller companies challenge these four in various local markets. Rental companies can therefore be found on

FIGURE 8.6
Ground operators often feature a variety of sightseeing tours.
Source: Vienna Sightseeing Tours.

Nr.	Tour		Abfahrt Departure 出発時間	Dauer Duration 所要時間	Preis in öS Price in öS 大人料金	Kinder Children 子供
1	Große Stadtrundfahrt / Grand City Tour	täglich daily	9.30, 10.30 h 14.30 h	3 h	300,–	110,–
12	Wien informativ / Vienna – getting acquainted — Abfahrtsstelle Dep. point ❶	täglich daily	10.30 h 11.45 h 15 h 16.30 h	1¼ h	160,–	60,–
31	Wiener Potpourri / Vienna Potpourri — Oper Dep. point	täglich daily	10.00 h 13.30 h	3 h	220,–	60,–
2	Spanische Reitschule / Spanish Riding School	Di – Sa Tu – Sat	9.30 h	3 h	380,–	110,–
21	Wiener Sängerknaben / Vienna Boys' Choir	Sonntag Sunday	8.30 h	3 h	*250,–	110,–
2 Sp.	Kurzvorführung Spanische Reitschule / Short Performance Spanish Riding School	Samstag Saturday	8.30 h	3 h	*250,–	110,–
22	Galavorführung Spanische Reitschule / Gala-Performance Spanish Riding School	Sonntag Sunday	8.30 h	3 h	*250,–	110,–
25	Galavorführung Spanische Reitschule / Gala-Performance Spanish Riding School	Mittwoch Wednesday	18.30 h	5 h	*250,–	110,–
	* Die Reitschul- und Sängerknabenkarten sind zusätzlich im Bus zu beahlen. – The tickets for the Spanish Riding School or the Vienna Boys' Choir are to be paid additionally on the bus.					
3	Panoramatour mit Donau / Panoramatour with Danube	täglich daily	9.30 h 14.30 h	4 h	370,–	110,–
33	Panorama- – Joh.-Strauß-Walzerkonzert / Tour – conc. w. Waltzes by Joh. Strauss	Di–Sa Tu–Sat	14.30 h	8 h	*560,–	220,–
4	Wienerwald – Mayerling / Vienna Woods – Mayerling	täglich daily	9.30 h 14.30 h	4 h	370,–	110,–
41	Operette in der Kaiserstadt Baden ❸ / excl. Theaterkarte/excl. Theatre ticket	Juli–Sep., Di–Do July–Sep., Tu–Sun	18 h	ca.5 h	*160,–	–
44	Wienerwald – Operette *exkl. Theaterkarte / Vienna Woods – Operette *excl. Theatreticket	Juli–Sep., Di–Do July–Sep., Tu–Sun	14.30 h	8 h	*560,–	220,–
5	Beleuchtetes Wien / Illuminated Vienna	tägl. Mai–Okt. daily May–Oct.	20.00 h	3½ h	380,–	110,–
6	Wiener Serenade – Grinzing / Viennese Serenade – Grinzing	täglich daily	20.00 h	4 h	620,–	330,–
7	Wiener Serenade – Nachtklub / Viennese Serenade – Nigth Club	täglich daily	20.00 h	5 h	850,–	–
8	Romantisches Donautal – Wachau / Romantic Danube Vailley – Wachau	täglich daily	9.30 h	8 h	850,–	440,–
10	Pusztatour / Pusztatour	Mo, Mi, Fr, So Mo, Wed, Fr, Sun	9.30 h	8 h	850,–	440,–
11	Ausflug in die Alpen / Alps and Nature Tour	Di, Do, Sa Tu, Th, Sat	9.30 h	8 h	850,–	440,–
13	Salzburg – Festpielstadt / Salzburg – Festival Town	Di, Do, Sa Tu, Th, Sat	7.30 h	1 Tag day	1500,–	880,–
17	Budapest informativ / Budapest – getting acquainted	täglich daily	7.00 h	1 Tag day	1290,–	660,–
30	City Tour in japanisch / Abfahrt Oper ❷	tägl. April–Okt. jed. Sam. Nov.–März	13.30 h	4 h	400,–	250,–
40	Wienerwald in japanisch	täglich April–Okt.	14.00 h	4 h	550,–	400,–

FIGURE 8.7
Car rental
combined with a
rail pass gives
clients maximum
flexibility.
Source: BritRail.

BRITRAIL/DRIVE

Canadian Dollars. Prices Effective Through 12/31/95. The package price applies when one person travels. Each additional person pays the supplement shown below; children (5-15) pay half the adult supplement.

Group/ Typical Car	Class of Rail Travel	3 day BritRail Flexipass plus 3 days car rental within 1 month		6 day BritRail Flexipass plus 7 days car rental within 1 month	
		Adult	Senior Citizen (60+)	Adult	Senior Citizen (60+)
MANUAL TRANSMISSION					
Economy	Standard	$319	$305	$597	$574
2 door/4 seat	First	364	350	689	654
Compact	Standard	340	325	645	625
4 door/5 seat	First	385	370	739	705
Intermediate	Standard	375	361	728	704
4 door/5 seat	First	420	406	819	784
AUTOMATIC TRANSMISSION (Automatics not available at all locations. Please call Hertz prior to departure for details)					
Intermediate	Standard	410	396	760	745
4 door/4 seat	First	455	440	835	805
Full Size	Standard	438	424	874	851
4 door/4 seat	First	483	469	966	931
Additional Adult	Standard	175	161	255	229
Rail Supplement	First	225	209	352	314

Additional Car Rental Days are available: Please inquire for details.

every continent and even on remote islands. Cars may be booked in a matter of seconds through airline computer systems or international computer networks established by the principal rental companies. Even if the firm is not a worldwide chain it is probably represented in major cities by a representative company or wholesaler.

Sales Features

The key sales features of rental cars are their flexibility and independence. These characteristics cannot be matched by airlines, trains or motorcoaches. Travellers who rent a car have total control over their departure times, their route and the stops they make. This versatility permits drivers to reach almost any destination and to change itineraries at will. In addition, cars permit their occupants to easily carry baggage and

equipment. Car rental offers unequalled freedom but can be costly, especially for single travellers. For three or more persons travelling together, however, car rental can be an economical means of travel. One disadvantage of car rental is that rental charges apply whether or not the car is being used. Clients who intend to rent cars should be cautioned to use the car as much as possible. Most people, however, do not wish to spend their entire vacation driving. Car rental companies have responded to this need by offering car rentals in conjunction with rail flexipasses. This arrangement permits tourists to travel to a few cities by rail, stop at each destination for a few days and make local excursions by rental car (see Figure 8.7). Car rental packages are most popular in places with well-developed highways and where a great deal can be seen in a relatively small area. Cars are also required by FIT travellers in more remote areas, such as in South and

Central America or Africa, where there may be no other convenient mode of local transport. Car rental is popular with tourists worldwide but the majority of rental income is produced by business travellers. Business travellers often have no choice; a car may be essential at the destination. Many business travellers frequently combine a business trip with a short vacation and use rental cars for these combination trips.

Unlike some other segments of the travel industry, the majority of car rental sales are made through rental companies dealing directly with their clients. The main distribution points are car rental desks at airports and downtown ticket offices. Car rental companies also work closely with other travel industry organizations. Tour companies often include a car as an option or as one component of a tour (Figure 8.8). Such fly/drive holidays are sold through travel agencies. Car rental firms also cooperate with airlines in marketing fly/drive programs. Some car rental companies are affiliated with airline frequent flyer programs. Members of the program can earn mileage points by renting a vehicle from a company associated with the airline's plan. Hotel chains and rental firms offer joint weekend packages at reduced rates to encourage business during slower periods. Hotels reduce the nightly rate and the car is offered at a weekend rate.

Car rental sales can significantly increase a travel agency's income. A commission rate of 10-15 percent is standard while commissions in excess of 20 percent can be easily attained with overrides. Although car rental commissions generate substantial revenue for travel agencies, their significance is in the fact that they represent a source of additional income. Customers rarely contact a travel agency if their only need is a rental car. They would typically approach a rental firm directly for that type of business. Consumers do, however, purchase plane tickets, hotel rooms and tour packages from travel agencies. When that order has been filled, an opportunity to upgrade the sale by offering the client a rental car still remains. Rental income therefore contributes additional revenue to an agency. Major car rental companies may earn half of their income from travel agencies. The relationship is particularly lucrative for both parties in the area of commercial accounts where travel agencies can provide a steady source of business clients for car firms. Many business travellers book a flight through a travel agency but do not necessarily think of reserving a car at the same time. Too many agencies and counsellors fail to ask

FIGURE 8.8
Tour companies often include a car as one component of a tour.
Source: Air Canada Vacations/Budget.

BUDGET OPTIONAL CAR RENTAL IN FLORIDA
FOR AIR ONLY PASSENGERS
(prices per car in Cdn $)

TYPE OF CAR	Economy (ECAR)	Inter-mediate (ICAR)	Full-size (SCAR)	Luxury (LCAR)	Minivan (MCAR)
Daily	22	34	44	63	57
Weekly	110	170	219	300	285

INCLUDED
- Unlimited Mileage
- Primary liability insurance (US $10,000 per person/US $20,000 per occurrence/US $10,000 property damage)
- No drop-off charges between participating Florida airport locations.
- Automatic transmission, air conditioning, radio.

NOT INCLUDED
- Optional Loss Damage Waiver (LDW) can be purchased at the time of rental for approximately US $12.98 per day.
- State-imposed taxes and surcharges.
- Refueling.
- Optional personal accident insurance, personal effects coverage and supplemental liability insurance.
- Infant car seat. Approximately US $5 per day, deposit required.

their clients, whether business or pleasure, if they require a car and thus pass up an opportunity to earn extra commission and improve customer satisfaction.

To properly service clients, counsellors need to know the products sold by the various rental companies. Some firms specialize in Ford vehicles, others use GM or Chrysler. Some can provide a sports car or a luxury limousine while others may be able to offer a vehicle equipped with hand controls for a handicapped client. The services as well as the equipment vary. Some rental companies supply better maps and driver information, some offer car phones or other extras, and some are connected with frequent flyer programs. Smaller dealers or discount companies should not be ignored. These firms offer lower rates but are usually not located at airports. Most off-airport companies, however, provide free transportation from the airport to their location. The cost of leasing space at an airport must be included when determining the rental fee and therefore the rate quoted by the major companies can be quite expensive. Although consumers pay a higher price than for cars from rental companies with no airport location, they benefit from the convenience of collecting their vehicle at the airport. In addition to product knowledge of the rental companies, counsellors must be able to advise their clients on the driving conditions at the destination. Sometimes the best advice might be that the client use public transport. For example, large cities such as London and Paris are congested and have good public transit systems. At other destinations, there may be no viable alternative to a car.

Car rental rates can be found in airline computer systems and in the brochures and directories supplied by car rental companies. The information in the computer system is likely to be the most current. All major car rental companies issue a worldwide directory which outlines the cars and the terms and conditions available (Figure 8.9). In addition, brochures are regularly made available to all travel agencies from car

rental companies. Travel counsellors should become familiar with these materials, not only for potential bookings in Canada and the United States but also for Europe and other overseas destinations. Car rental rates vary depending on the location and competition and frequently change. Counsellor should check the rates of all major companies unless their clients instruct them to book with a particular company.

GREECE (CORFU)

The information in this section is provided as a guideline. Full details are available from the:

● **RESERVATION OFFICE**

Telephone: 0661-30787   Telex: 332131

CAR MAKE GRP MODEL (or similar)	DESCRIPTION
A . . .Suzuki Alto	4DR, 4S, L5, MAN
Subaru 600	4DR, 4S, L5, MAN
B . . .Nissan Cherry	4DR, 4S, L7, MAN
C . . .Nissan Sunny 1300	4DR, 5S, L14, MAN
F . . .Suzuki Jeep 1000 Conv.	4DR, 4S, L18, MAN
G . . .Honda Civic	4DR, 4S, L7, AUT
H . . .Fiat Minibus	4DR, 6S, L33, MAN

The following information provides additions or exceptions to the general information section contained at the front of this directory.

Age: Minimum is 21 for groups A-C; minimum 25 for Groups F-H. Maximum none.

Tax: 16%.

Special Equipment: Baby seats, luggage racks and snow chains are available.

Special Services: Delivery/collection service is available.

One-Way: Vehicles are not allowed to leave the island unless confirmed by Avis.

Credit Identification: Prepayments made in foreign currency are refundable in Drachma only.

LOCATIONS

● **CORFU**
Address: International Airport **CFU/4277**
Telephone: 0661-32565
Telex: 332131
Hours: 0700-2200 Mo-Su

Address: 31 Alexandras Ave **CF1/4278**
Telephone: 0661-38820
Telex: 332131
Hours: 0800-1500, 1700-2000 Mo-Su

FIGURE 8.9
Major car rental firms publish a worldwide directory of services and locations.
Source: Avis.

Qualifying Car Renters

All rental companies set the terms and conditions under which they will rent vehicles to the public (see Figure 8.10). These restrictions form the basis for counsellors to quality their clients. The first requirement is that the renter have a valid driver's license. Counsellors should check the expiry date to ensure that it is valid for the duration of the rental. Some countries also demand that renters hold an international driving permit. A second limitation imposed is the age of the driver. Companies usually set both a minimum and a maximum age requirement. In some areas drivers can be as young as 21 while in other areas those under 25 cannot rent cars. Many companies also impose a maximum age

restriction of 65. All rental companies insist on some form of credit identification such as a credit card. This does not imply that the final payment must be made by credit card; the rental industry readily accepts cash at termination. Credit card holders, however, have had their employment, home address and credit references verified by the company issuing the card. By verifying the card a car rental company can entrust a valuable vehicle to the renter with reasonable assurances that it will be returned. A cash deposit of even $500 is inadequate if character references are not available. Some rental companies also impose geographic restrictions which limit the rental to particular states or countries.

FIGURE 8.10
All companies clearly identify their rental conditions.
Source: Budget rent a car.

Terms and Conditions

- Rates are based on 1,050 kilometers per week and 150 kilometers on additional days. Any kilometers used over this allowance will be calculated at 14¢ per kilometer.
- Luxury and Minivans include 700 kilometers per week and 100 kilometers on extra days. Any kilometers over this allowance will be calculated at 20¢ per kilometer.
- Rates are guaranteed in Canadian dollars from November 1, 1989 to March 31, 1990
- Rates do not include Loss Damage Waiver, Personal Accident Insurance, local taxes or refuelling services.
- Rates based on returning car to renting location. No one way rentals allowed.
- Car must be reserved at least 24 hours prior to time of rental.
- Rentals are for a minimum of five (5) days, no maximum. See chart for extra day rates.
- Ski racks, baby seats, and air conditioning are available at most major airport locations for a nominal charge, if requested at time of reservation.
- Driver must meet local age and credit requirements and present a valid driver's license at start of rental.
- Payment may be made locally by major credit cards. Cash/travellers' cheques accepted at most locations subject to local cash requirements and will necessitate a cash deposit. Prepayment may be made by hand delivered MCO only.
- "Budget Plan Canada" is available at the following major airports and many other participating Canadian locations: Victoria, Vancouver, Calgary, Edmonton, Saskatoon, Winnipeg, Toronto, Ottawa, Montreal, Quebec City, Halifax and St. John's.

Car Rental Charges

Counsellors must always make sure that their clients are aware of what is included in the price of a car rental and which charges must be paid by the client when the car is collected or returned. Car rental rates vary according to the size and type of vehicle and the rental duration (Figure 8.11). Cars may be classified according to size, such as economy, small, medium and large, or according to type, for example subcompact, compact, standard, deluxe and station wagon. Regular rates are quoted on a daily and a weekly basis. Special rates are those which offer a discount for weekends, holidays or other packages. Lower corporate rates are offered to companies with a high rental volume. Rental rates do not include gasoline, local taxes or charges for extra services. Commission is earned on the rental price only. Taxes are non-commissionable. Depending on their nature, some extra services are commissionable.

Cars are rented under one of three mileage systems; a two-tier system, base mileage included, and unlimited mileage. The two-tier system charges the renter a given amount per mile or kilometre driven up to a specified limit known as the cap. Mileage incurred beyond the cap is charged at a higher rate. The base mileage included system is a variation on the two-tier system. Here, a given distance is included free of charge in the rental price. Mileage driven beyond this cap is charged at a specific rate. The third option is the unlimited mileage plan which provides the client with a rental rate which includes mileage; no charges are added for distance driven. This plan offers clients even more flexibility and independence as it is less expensive than rentals based on time and distance. Car rental has consequently become easier for counsellors to sell.

Many car rental firms include a full tank of gas in the price of the vehicle. If the tank is not full when the client returns the car, the rental company will fill the tank and add a fuel charge to the rental agreement. This fill-up is usually charged at a premium rate. Other companies rent with a specific amount of gasoline in the car and it is the client's responsibility to ensure that the vehicle has sufficient gas. For such rentals there is no additional fuel charge when the car is returned.

All car rental fees include third-party liability insurance covering death or injury to others or damage to another's property. Each car is insured for up to $1,000,000 of property damage and public liability. This insurance, however, does not provide renters with coverage for personal injury. Should they wish such protection, clients may purchase optional security in the form of Personal Accident Insurance (PAI). PAI covers passengers and the driver for costs associated with injuries incurred in an accident. It is assessed at a daily rate which can reach $5 per day. Renters involved in an accident must pay a deductible amount towards repairs to the vehicle. This collision deductible varies from $200 to $1,000. Clients may, however, purchase Collision Damage Waiver (CDW) to avoid such charges. CDW absolves the client of financial responsibility if a car is returned damaged (Figure 8.12). It is not insurance, however, as the car rental industry is not licensed to sell insurance. In addition, CDW may not cover the client for damage caused by fire or theft.

For these reasons, CDW has come under attack. Some states in the USA have prohibited its sale and other jurisdictions are considering this measure. Car rental companies have resisted this action as CDW is a profitable product line. The price of CDW has increased over the years and can be as high as $15 per day.

As fees for CDW have risen, the number of customers purchasing it has fallen. Travellers currently have several options concerning risk of damage to a rented car. They can personally accept the risk or they can purchase CDW. Alternatively, they can pass on the risk to their personal car insurance. (Many personal car policies offer coverage of non-owned cars at a small annual premium, likely for less than the cost of the daily rate for CDW.) A fourth choice is to pay for the rental using a premium credit card which offers card holders free primary car rental collision coverage. People who rent a car on business have two further options. They can pass the risk of damage to their employer or to the employer's insurer.

For some companies PAI and CDW are

FIGURE 8.11
Car rental rates vary according to a number of factors such as rental category, duration and mileage system.
Source: UTC United Touring Fiji.

SELF DRIVE CARS

CAR RENTAL RATES		TIME AND KILOMETRES			UNLIMITED KILOMETRES	
Less 20% commission total charge plus 8% Tax						
MODELS	GRP	PER KM FS	PER DAY FS	PER DAY FS	PER DAY FS	PER WEEK FS
DAIHATSU Charade Sedan 4 door **SUZUKI** Sedan 4 door	1	.19	19.00	114.00	56.00	300.00
NISSAN Sunny 1300 S/Wagon	2	.26	26.00	156.00	60.00	330.00
NISSAN Bluebird S/Wagon (air-conditioned) Sunny 1500 S/Wagon (air-conditioned)	3	.40	40.00	240.00	88.00	480.00
TOYOTA Cressida S/Wagon (air-conditioned)	4	.47	47.00	282.00	96.00	520.00
NOTE: All Rates are subject to change.						

Dec. 16/89 - Dec. 15/90* Prices are per vehicle, CDN$		ONE ISLAND				ISLAND HOPPING/2 OR MORE ISLANDS			
		Basic - rental only (NALAH)		Carefree Special** (NALHI)		Basic - rental only (NALIR)		Carefree Special** (NALIH)	
GROUP/VEHICLE (ALAMH)		PER WEEK	EXTRA DAY	PER WEEK	EXTRA DAY	PER WEEK	EXTRA DAY	PER WEEK	EXTRA DAY
EC	2-dr. Economy	99	31	185	44	175	25	259	37
E4	4-dr. Economy	114	34	197	46	189	27	280	40
CC	2-dr. Compact	114	34	197	46	189	27	280	40
C4	4-dr. Compact	126	36	210	49	210	30	294	42
IC	2-dr. Intermediate	152	41	235	54	252	36	343	49
I4	4-dr. Intermediate	164	44	248	56	273	39	357	51
IW	5 passenger wagon	266	53	350	65	329	47	420	60
SC	2-dr. Standard	241	50	324	64	294	42	385	55
S4	4-dr. Standard	252	53	337	67	315	45	406	58

*Dec. 20-31 89 add $13 per week $3 extra day   **incl CDW, PAI, EP

RENTAL INFORMATION

Location: Honolulu airport — off-airport. Courtesy bus picks up clients from baggage claims area for transportation to rental location nearby. Airport rental counters are located in Hilo and Kailua-Kona on the Big Island; Kahului and Kaanapali (west Maui) on Maui; Lihue on Kauai and in the heart of Waikiki.
Driver's Age: 21 years.
Surcharge for drivers under 25 years, per day: US$ 6.
Surcharge for additional driver, per day: US$ 2.50
Tax: 6%.
Airport fee: 55¢ per rental in Honolulu.
Customer deposit requirements: US$ 200 per week or major credit card.
Refuelling service charge: Vehicles are supplied with a full tank of gasoline. Renters are requested to return the tank full or will be charged for the amount needed to refill the tank at the end of the rental.
Collision Damage Waiver (CDW), cost per day: (unless Carefree Special purchased)

Groups EC, EC $10.99
CC, IC, SC $11.99
All other groups $12.99
CDW coverage: Relieves the renter of financial responsibility for damage to the vehicle while in the renter's possession. CDW is not insurance and may be voided by the car rental company under certain circumstances — including impaired or reckless driving and the operation of the vehicle by unauthorized drivers. If CDW is declined, the renter is responsible for the total cost of all damages regardless of faults. There is no deductible liability.
Personal Accident Insurance (PAI), cost per day: US$ 3.00
PAI coverage: medical — US$ 550 per person
accidental death, primary driver — US$ 15,000
accidental death, passenger — US$ 5,000
Third Party Liability: Coverage is primary at the minimum

required by the state of Hawaii — US$ 25,000 per person
— US$ 10,000 property damage
Fire and theft: The purchase of CDW relieves the renter of financial responsibility for damages due to fire or theft.
Extended protection (EP), cost per day: US$ 5.99
EP coverage: Raises the total limit of liability protection and includes uninsured motorists coverage up to US$ 1,000,000.
Personal effect coverage (PEC), per day: US$ 1.50.
PEC coverage: Protects renter's personal belongings (most items) from loss or damage caused by theft, fire, explosion, lightning or accident to the rental car for most items up to $1,000 per person or per piece of luggage.
One-way rentals either direction: Hilo-Kona: US$ 30; Honolulu Airport-Waikiki: US$ 15. Available for group C and larger.
Credit cards accepted: American Express, Carte Blanche, Diner's Club, Mastercard and Visa.
The purchase of CDW, PAI, EP, PEC is optional.

FIGURE 8.12
Car rental rates and information always identify CDW and PAI charges and terms.
Source: Holiday House.

compulsory while others view them as optional charges. Travel agencies do not earn commission from the sale of PAI and CDW. Some travel insurance companies have therefore entered the market and now offer a collision insurance program commissionable to agencies. If CDW is abolished as threatened, rental companies will spread the cost of accidental damage to vehicles among all renters and rates will rise. Because of the controversy over CDW and the confusion among renters faced with a host of additional charges, many companies have voluntarily eliminated CDW, PAI and other supplements and promote one all-inclusive price to their customers. This strategy leads to a higher advertised price but the actual rental rate tends to drop because there are no add-ons. These all-inclusive rates are popular with travel counsellors as they are easier to sell, clients are less confused, and the total amount is commissionable and therefore commissions increase.

Another option which has increased the client's flexibility and the product's saleability is the introduction of one-way rentals or "rent it here - leave it there" opportunities. Some companies or locations require the payment of a drop-off charge for this privilege. Depending on the destination, this service is sometimes included in the rental price (Figure 8.13). Like insurance waivers and taxes, drop-off charges are generally paid locally by the client and are non-commissionable.

Reservation Procedures

Car rental reservations may be quickly and easily made in several ways. Automated travel agencies can book through an airline computer system. Counsellors who work in non-automated agencies can book a car through an airline when calling to request a client's airline seat. Alternatively, counsellors can telephone the car company's reservations centre directly using a toll-free number. If the car rental is part of a tour package, the vehicle can be reserved by contacting the tour company. The first step is to check the availability. For this, travel counsellors must initially identify themselves and their agency and then supply the following information.

- Destination and specific location for the car pick-up (i.e., airport or downtown).
- Drop-off location if it is different from the pick-up point.
- Category of vehicle.
- Duration of rental, that is, the arrival and departure dates.
- Special equipment or client requests such as roof rack or handicapped driver vehicle.

The reservations centre will be able to quote a rental rate from this information. If a suitable car is available, travel counsellors can confirm the reservation by providing:

- Client's name.
- Carrier, flight number and arrival time. (This is provided in case the flight is late and is particularly important where the airport has more than one terminal.)
- Form of payment.
- IATA number for commission payment.

The car rental reservations agent will assign a reservation confirmation or identification number which the counsellor should record on the client file. Counsellors should also note the reservationist's name on the file. The confirmation number is used to retrieve the reservation if a change, cancellation or commission inquiry is necessary. Before

FIGURE 8.13
One way rental charges vary depending on the destination.
Source: Avis Rent-a-Car.

SWITZERLAND Groups A to I.K	FRANCE Groups G, B to E	SPAIN Groups B,C,D,F,H	HOLLAND Groups A to I	DENMARK Groups A to I	ITALY Groups A to F	GERMANY Groups A to F,H,N	BELGIUM All Car Groups	AUSTRIA Groups B to E	All Car Groups	CURRENCY	
SFR	FFR	PTS	DFL	USD	LIT	DMK	BFR	AUS		CURRENCY	
150	927.89	20,000	600	76	210,000	FREE	7,000	FREE		VIENNA	
150	390.16	20,000	600	76	FREE	300	7,000	900		ROME/NAPLES	
FREE	FREE	20,000	600	38	FREE	120	7,000	FREE		MILAN	
150	FREE	20,000	FREE	38	320,000	FREE	FREE	1,350		BRUSSELS/OSTENDE	
FREE	FREE	20,000	300	38	120,000	FREE	3,600	FREE		MUNICH	
FREE	FREE	20,000	150	38	210,000	FREE	FREE	FREE		FRANKFURT	
150	390.16	20,000	150	38	320,000	FREE	FREE	900		HAMBURG/COLOGNE	
150	927.89	20,000	600	FREE	640,000	120	7,000	1,350		COPENHAGEN	
150	375	20,000	FREE	38	320,000	FREE	FREE	1,350		AMSTERDAM	
FREE	FREE	20,000	150	38	210,000	120	FREE	1,350		PARIS	
FREE	FREE	13,000	600	76	120,000	300	7,000	900		NICE	
FREE	FREE	13,000	300	38	120,000	FREE	7,000	FREE		ZURICH/GENEVA/BASEL	

RENTING COUNTRY

RETURNING COUNTRY

ending contact, counsellors should reconfirm the rental rate, ensuring that they have recorded any applicable charges for drop-off privileges or other requests. The car company may send the agency a voucher which identifies the details of the reservation and the confirmation number. This voucher is given to the client who presents it when picking up the car. Counsellors sometimes use an MCO to prepay the rental. The travel counsellor will also complete an agency confirmation slip for the agency's records. A copy of this slip will be given to the client if a car rental company voucher is not available.

Most rental companies have computerized reservations offices. Automated reservations systems make car rental bookings easier and permit rental firms to offer improved service to their clients. Some firms have developed comprehensive client records for regular business customers. By retaining a description of client information, such as standard reservations data and car preferences, car rental companies can more quickly and efficiently service their clients. Some companies provide express service for these regular clients. Express service allows renters to bypass the rental counter and proceed directly to a courtesy bus which takes them to their car.

Client Advice

It is the counsellor's responsibility to ensure that clients understand the conditions under which they rent a car. Car rentals are usually paid on completion of the rental period. Cars rented as part of a tour package are the exception to this rule and are prepaid. Clients should be clear on which services are included in the rental fee and those which must be paid on returning the vehicle. In addition to PAI and CDW, which may be optional, there will be local taxes and perhaps some additional charges associated with the mileage plan selected. Drop-off charges should also be explained. If clients wish to rent a car in

Paris, drive through Europe and leave the car at a Rome airport before returning home, they will usually understand that the car company must return the vehicle to Paris and that this operation has a cost factor. This charge may be less cheerfully accepted if it applies to a car picked up at the airport and left at a hotel in the same city. Drop-off charges are often waived on routes where there is a large volume of traffic. Clients should be encouraged to read the rental contract carefully to ensure they understand the conditions relating to insurance coverage, mileage charges, rental duration and gas level. Counsellors should advise their clients to inspect the car for minor scratches and dents before leaving the rental area. Renters should return the vehicle sufficiently in advance of their flight departure to allow for time to examine the rental bill for errors.

Some general advice from a counsellor can also help clients to gain the most enjoyment from a car rental. It is most important that counsellors correctly match the vehicle with the needs of the renter, particularly for pleasure travellers. Counsellors must know the number of passengers and the amount of luggage which will be carried in order to advise a suitable car. If the clients are touring, a crowded vehicle will soon bring disharmony to the trip. Touring clients will increase their pleasure if they pace the itinerary so that they do not rush or spend the whole vacation driving. If they are travelling independently, they should book at least some overnight stops in advance. This not only eliminates the necessity of wasting vacation time searching for accommodation but also increases a counsellor's commission income. Similarly, a planned itinerary will highlight any pitfalls in the routing such as off-season ferry closures. Clients will also have more fun if they do not attempt city sightseeing by self-drive car. Clients intending to drive in Europe should be aware that European cars are smaller, may have less luggage space and are subject to additional charges for automatic transmission and air conditioning. The least expensive model may not always be the best choice. Transatlantic travellers should be cautioned against picking up a car upon arrival in Europe. Counsellors should also routinely point out the different driving practices, different laws and unfamiliar signs. Speed limits vary from one country to another. Britons drive on the left side of the road and use different terminology such as "boot" and "petrol".

Most car rental companies have fly/drive tour packages to Florida, California and parts of Canada. These packages combine the speed of air travel to the destination with the convenience, comfort and flexibility of a car upon arrival at the airport. These packages usually include a mileage allowance in the tour price. Fly/drive packages have been so popular that they have created an expectation among travellers that a car will be available at the destination. If a vehicle is not included in the tour a traveller will often rent locally. Counsellors should therefore never pass up an opportunity to enquire whether a client would like a car at the destination. All rental firms have sales offices which will assist counsellors to learn the rental business.

Car Leasing

Clients who require a car for more than two weeks should consider car leasing. Car leases are subject to different terms and conditions than rentals and vary from one company to another. Car leases are not subject to taxes and they often include automobile and personal insurance in the price. For longer driving periods they offer clients a substantial saving.

Motorhomes and Specialty Vehicles

The recent growth in popularity of recreational vehicles (RVs), campers and motorhomes has widened the market for rental opportunities. In addition, specialty vehicles such as sports cars and four-wheel drive machines have become more common. Campers offer sleeping accommodation for four to eight people while motorhomes generally sleep four or five persons (Figure 8.14). These vehicles permit tourists to vacation together at a fairly low cost. The rental price includes all bedding, cooking equipment and dishes thus reducing a group's accommodation and eating expenses. Motorhomes are rented under similar mileage systems and charges as cars. Terms and conditions are also similar (Figure 8.15). The growth in this type of travel has fostered a parallel growth in campgrounds with suitable facilities.

FIGURE 8.14
Motorhomes offer a variety of facilities and arrangements.
Source: Pathfinder Vacations.

FLOOR PLAN COMFORT ... GUARANTEED!

All motorhomes are fully equipped like no other ...

Automatic Transmission • Tilt & Power Steering • Cruise Control • Power Brakes
Dual Batteries • Fresh Water Tank • Waste Water Tanks • 110 Volt Converter
Stove • Refrigerator & Freezer • Forced Air Furnace • AM/FM Cassette Stereo
Radial Tires • Dual Wheels • Sunscreen Glass • And many more conveniences ...

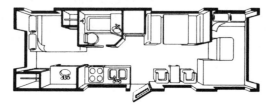

B Luxury
26'/27 ' Motorhome
• sleeps 5/6
• bathtub
• dash air
• roof air

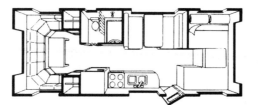

B Deluxe
24/25' Motorhome
• sleeps 5/6
• dash air
• roof air

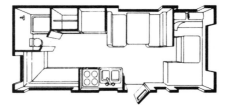

B Midsize
22/23' Motorhome
• sleeps 4/5
• dash air
• roof air

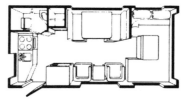

B Compact
19/20' Motorhome
• sleeps 3/4
• dash air
• roof air

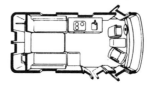

C Camper Van
• sleeps 2
• portable toilet
• dash air

RENTAL CONDITIONS AND POLICIES

Reservation Deposit
$200.00 reservation deposit is required at time of booking to hold and confirm reservation. The reservation deposit is non-refundable but will be credited towards the rental charges.

Payments
Final payment of rental invoice is due 15 days prior to departure date. If payment is not received by due date, the reservation will be subject to cancellation. The following credit cards are accepted for payment: VISA, Mastercard, American Express, Diners Club and EnROUTE.

Cancellation Charges
From time of booking until 15 days prior to departure date the cancellation charge is $200.00 (reservation deposit). Cancellation 14 days or less prior to departure date requires full payment of one week's rental fee.

Minimum Rental Period
The minimum rental period is 7 days. For oneway rentals the minimum rental period is 14 days.

Early Refunds
No refunds will be made for return of rented vehicle prior to the date indicated and agreed upon on the rental contract.

Late Returns
All rental vehicles have to be returned no later than 11:00 AM on the last rental day. Penalty for late return is $25.00/hr.

Driver Requirements
The minimum age for qualified drivers is 21 years. Driver must be in possession of a valid driver's license.

Transfers
Transfers will be provided free of charge between downtown hotels and rental stations in Calgary and Edmonton (no airport transfers). In Vancouver courtesy transportation will be provided between airport or downtown hotels and rental station. Clients are asked to contact the local rental station to arrange for transfer time.

Office Hours
Rental centres are open for pick-up from 9:00 AM - 3:00 PM Monday through Saturday. All rental offices are closed on Sundays and public holidays.

Taxes
There is no sales tax in Alberta.
All rentals originating in Vancouver are subject to British Columbia provincial sales tax (6% at time of printing).

Insurance and Waiver Options
Insurance coverage of $1,000,000 public liability/property damage as well as $1,500 deductible collision insurance is included in the basic rental rate.
Two options to reduce the deductible amounts are available:
1. CDW - Collision Damage Waiver is available for $8.00 per day. CDW reduces the renter's liability to $250.00 per occurrence for accidents with other vehicles on public roads. Damage to roof, undercarriage and interior of vehicles is not covered by CDW.

2. VIP - The VIP insurance option is available for $14.00 per day and includes CDW coverage. VIP reduces renter's liability to $100.00 per occurrence and includes the following: accidental collision including roof, overhead and undercarriage. Exceptions: damages as a result of customer intent, gross negligence, contract violations or driving in height restricted areas are not covered. The windshield is fully covered: no deductible at all.
Also included with VIP coverage are all necessary expenses in the event of a mechanical breakdown requiring the motorhome to be repaired for more than 12 hours.
Please read the insurance restriction clauses as supplied by the rental stations.

Security Deposit
At time of pick up of the rental vehicle, the client is required to leave a security deposit which is refundable if the rental vehicle is returned in original condition:
$1,500 with basic insurance
$250 with CDW
$100 with VIP/CDW
Security deposits are accepted by means of credit cards or traveller cheques.

Convenience Kits
The following housekeeping items are available as "Convenience Kits" for a one-time charge of $35.00 per kit. Some items are per person, others are per vehicle:

Per Person:	Sleeping bag	Cutlery
	Pillow/pillow case	Dishes
	2 towels	Cup/saucer
	Bed sheet	
Per Vehicle:	Set of pots	Waste basket
	Frying pan	Bucket
	Kettle	Broom/dust pan
	Mixing bowls	Clothes hangers
	Coffee pot/filter	Flashlight
	Juice container	Small tool set
	2 Tea towels	Can/bottle opener

All motorhomes are equipped with water hose, sewer hose, 110-Volt adaptor and operator's manual.

Optional items available at reasonable rates are: lawn chairs, axes, toaster, baby seats, toilet chemicals, etc.

Travel Restrictions
No motorhomes are allowed to travel to Alaska, Yukon and N.W.T. Travel on Cassiar, Liard, Dalton and Dempster Highways is also prohibited. The following exception applies: B3/20-21 ft. motorhomes are allowed to travel to the above mentioned areas subject to a $400.00 "Northern Travel Surcharge". Some restrictions apply - please inquire at time of booking. All vehicles are restricted from operating in Death Valley between May 15 - Sept. 15. No vehicles are allowed into Mexico.

Responsibility
5 Star is not responsible for hotel charges, car rental or any other incidental or consequential cost in the event of a breakdown. Liability is expressly limited to the schedule of daily rental rates.

Currency
All rates and charges are quoted in Canadian dollars.

FIGURE 8.15
Terms and conditions for motorhome rental are similar to those for a car rental.
Source: 5 Star.

Review Questions

1. Describe the various categories of coach equipment available and discuss the types of service that each would be used for.

2. Discuss the sales features, advantages and disadvantages of travelling by motorcoach.

3. What services does the term ground transportation include?

4. Outline the key sales features of car rental.

5. Discuss the demands which car rental companies impose on potential renters.

6. What advice concerning car rental terms and conditions should a counsellor review with a client?

7. List the information required to make a car rental reservation.

References

Canadian Bus Association, 601-170 Metcalfe Street, Ottawa, Ontario K2P 1P3, Telephone (613) 238-1800.

Europabus information from DER, German Rail.

Gray Line Official Sightseeing Tariff, Gray Line Sightseeing Association, 350 Fifth Avenue, Room 1409, New York, NY 10018, USA.

Russell's Official Canada Bus Guide, Russell's Guides, Inc., P.O. Box 278, 834 Third Avenue S.E., Cedar Rapids, IA 52406, USA, Telephone (319) 364-6138.

Russell's Official National Motor Coach Guide, available from the above address.

WATA Master-Key, World Association of Travel Agencies, 37 quai Wilson, P.O. Box 852, 1211 Geneva 1, Switzerland.

Worldwide Tour Planning Manual, American Sightseeing International, 309 Fifth Avenue, New York, NY 10016, USA.

## Chapter 9

Accommodation

Chapter Summary

This chapter examines the hospitality industry. Following a brief introduction to the sector's development, categories of hotels are reviewed. The role of hotel representatives is considered. The chapter continues with a discussion of hotel grading systems, sources of product knowledge and methods of evaluating accommodation. Common hotel terms and abbreviations are presented. Room rates, hotel services, booking and payment procedures, and commission arrangements are then studied. The chapter concludes with a survey of the timeshare industry.

Chapter Objectives
After completing this chapter you should be able to:

- Define and use terms in the accommodation, representative and food service industries.

- Identify and describe different types of accommodation.

- Distinguish between various categories of resorts.

- Differentiate between various types of ownership and management control.

- List and describe the functions of hotel departments.

- Interpret WTO and other classification systems for accommodation.

- Interpret room classifications and meal plans.

- Evaluate and recommend hotels for clients.

- Complete a hotel assessment form.

- Make a hotel reservation and issue appropriate documentation.

- Discuss the concept of overbooking and guaranteed reservations. Explain the various procedures used by travel agents in handling hotel reservations.

- Discuss the hotel industry's pricing structure.

- Differentiate between gross and net charges.

- Use industry references to calculate the appropriate rate for accommodation.

- Discuss forms of resort timesharing.

History and Background

In an earlier time, when the human race lived a nomadic lifestyle, people took their possessions with them when they moved. As civilization progressed, human settlements became more permanent. Not all travellers, however, were nomads or hunters and for such people it was both inconvenient and impractical to carry unnecessary equipment. Inns and hostels designed to provide food and shelter for weary travellers and pilgrims have existed in various forms since Biblical times, although these were primitive refuges compared with today's hotels. Even during the Middle Ages, when travelling was a rare and risky proposition, pilgrims could be certain of finding some type of accommodation along the way. The modern practice of innkeeping, like other segments of the tourism industry, however, had its roots in the Industrial Revolution of the late eighteenth century. In those days English coaching inns were famous as way stations where traveller and horse could be fed and bedded. As mechanization spread and railways developed, hotels sprang up to serve the needs of disembarking passengers. Many hotels were constructed at city centre railway stations and at resorts located at the terminus of various railway lines. The rail companies encouraged this development and were frequently the builders and operators of these establishments. During the early to middle nineteenth century, deluxe hotels opened in the capitals of Europe. These hotels catered to members of the British aristocracy taking the "Grand Tour" of the Continent. To make their guests feel at home, hotel owners often included at least one English word in their hotel's name. Even today, there are many hotels named Bristol in Europe.

Social legislation, introduced in many countries during the 1920s and 1930s, made paid holidays for workers mandatory and had a considerable impact on the expansion and growth of the hospitality industry. Until the Depression of the 1930s much of the growth was in grand luxury hotels, such as the Ritz in Paris and the Plaza in New York City. Most travellers were those who had the time and money to indulge in the pastime. As a result, people generally travelled in luxury and stayed a long time. Hotel construction in North America grew steadily with the economy during the first half of the present century. At the same time tourism leapfrogged ahead to its present enormous size. With the increasing number of cars came highway construction. As a direct result a new phase of construction brought motor hotels and motels. The concept of standardized hotel chains such as Holiday Inn emerged during the 1950s. By then hotels were changing to a middle standard and were designed for mass appeal rather than class appeal. Large modern hotels began to develop during the 1960s as the jet age stimulated both tourism and business travel. The growth of chains and franchises coincided with this expansion.

The growth of hotels has generally reflected the development of tourism. The strongest link, however, has been between the dominant form of transport and the design and location of hotels. Prior to the Industrial Revolution, stagecoaches stopped at coaching inns in England and at similar route stops in the USA and Europe. As trains became the major transport force in the late nineteenth and early twentieth centuries, hotels were constructed at or near stations to serve the needs of these travellers. The middle of this century saw the growth of automobile and road transport and a similar increase in motels and hotels located at or near highway intersections. More recently, the airplane has dominated the travel industry and hotel growth has been primarily near airports on major airline routes.

Importance of the Hospitality Industry

The hospitality industry is one of the most important components in travel and tourism. Tourist transportation is certainly essential to this enterprise, however, hotels and resorts provide tourists with accommodation, meals and entertainment at the destination. Hotels and resorts serve as a place for rest, relaxation, recreation, as a social centre and as a base of operation. About nine million hotel rooms are available worldwide. Although resorts represent only 12 percent of this total they generate one quarter of the sector's income.

The hotel is the most important part of a client's vacation, not only because it represents the largest proportion of the cost but also because it is the tourist's home during a holiday. Selecting appropriate accommodation to match a client's tastes and budget therefore requires considerable attention and research. Too often, holiday plans are ruined and clients lost as future customers through a careless hotel recommendation. Tourists will accept and tolerate transportation arrangements that are less than ideal; they may make allowances for a careless slip-up in itineraries or wrong information; but they are absolutely unforgiving when the accommodation proves to be less than their expectations. Since client expectations can be unrealistic, counsellors must be able to give an accurate picture of the accommodation selected.

Hotel Ownership

Several forms of ownership are observed in the hospitality industry. Hotels can be owned and managed by the same company which may be part of a hotel chain or an individual corporation. Joint ventures and franchises are also found. Some hotels are operated under a management contract in which a company runs the hotel for a fee and/or a percentage of the gross revenue. The hotel industry has in recent years been characterized by mergers and takeovers. Consolidation has occurred in a similar manner to that observed in the airline and travel agency sectors. Where construction and labour costs are high, efficient and profitable management of hotels and resorts can be achieved only by large corporations such as chain operations. Purchasing can be done in bulk and capital requirements can be more readily satisfied when economies of scale can be practised. One result is that there are few remaining hotel organizations that concentrate on just one segment of the travel market. Continued growth in hotel construction and resort development is predicted with a focus on specialized markets, particularly full-service luxury establishments and no-frills budget properties.

Types of Hotels

Hotels can be classified in a number of ways. They may be categorized according to size, the type of ownership or by their location, such as city, suburban, airport, highway and resort. They may simply be grouped according to price, for example, budget or economy, standard and deluxe. A basic classification, however, is by the type of guest; commercial or resort. Each has certain distinctive features which place them in that category. Commercial and resort hotels can be further subdivided.

Commercial Hotels

Commercial hotels are targeted at individuals travelling on business and at tourists staying for a short time in the course of a longer itinerary. Tourists on escorted tours and those with limited time generally stay in commercial hotels. These hotels are located in urban centres and can be found in wide variety in all major cities and tourist centres. Commercial hotels are typically located on main transportation routes and at points where people gather, for example, city centres, shopping areas and downtown districts. Older commercial hotels are usually centrally located. As such, they serve as excellent sightseeing and excursion centres for tourists. New hotels are often found near airports or at major expressway intersections.

Commercial hotels offer a wide variety of accommodation and facilities. They range from budget level to extremely expensive, and vary from old but impressive hotels like the Empress in Victoria or the Palmer House in Chicago to the modern and distinctive Chateau Champlain in Montreal or the Prince in Toronto. Many European hotels are older and smaller than North American hotels. Frequently, however, they provide superior service and accommodation. Typical North American commercial hotel rooms have standard furniture and are equipped with telephone, private bath, radio, TV and air conditioning. The rooms vary in size from accommodation for one or two guests to fully equipped suites with several rooms and expensive furnishings. A commercial hotel usually has a coffee shop, popularly priced menus and one or more dining rooms with a more formal atmosphere. There is generally at least one cocktail lounge with some form of entertainment. Larger hotels often provide first class entertainment. Commercial hotels frequently have specialty shops on the premises. There may be clothing stores, bookstores, gift shops or art galleries. Modern hotels may be connected to shopping malls. As part of their service, commercial hotels provide laundry, cleaning, pressing and other valet services as well as barber shops, beauty salons, airline ticket offices, and frequently a nightclub.

Counsellors should be aware of the limitations of some older commercial hotels. This is particularly so when arranging bookings at older hotels in Europe where not every room is equipped with a private bathroom. Such hotels frequently have washroom facilities on each level which must be shared by all guests on that floor. Further, there may be no air conditioning. Today, when such amenities are taken for granted in North America, it is most important that travel counsellors make absolutely certain that either or both of these features are available before proceeding with a booking.

Many travel agencies handle accommodation requirements for salespeople who require sample rooms at centrally-located commercial hotels. A sample room does not necessarily contain sleeping facilities. It will, however, have display racks, shelves and tables which enable salespeople to exhibit their wares to prospective clients.

Resort Hotels

Resort hotels cater to vacationers and recreation-minded people. They are usually located away from major cities in areas popular for their natural attraction and recreation facilities. They are often isolated but in many cases are close to centres where rail or air travel connections can be made.

Guests usually stay for between one and four weeks at resorts, although in recent years there has been growth in the market for long weekend visits. The accommodation, recreation facilities and services found at a resort hotel are

therefore designed for tourists visiting for an extended period of time, certainly much longer than in the average commercial hotel. To meet guests' needs, a typical resort hotel can provide a complete vacation package entirely on its own premises; they offer both foodservice and entertainment facilities. There is usually at least one restaurant on the premises and a variety of recreational outlets, in addition to cocktail lounges and nightclubs at larger resorts. Resorts must also provide attractive, comfortable accommodation. Room appointments and hotel facilities are generally more luxurious than in an average commercial hotel, in part because of the lower land, construction and labour costs associated with resorts. Rooms are larger and equipped with such special features as full size bathrooms, small refrigerators and balconies.

Resorts are designed for rest and relaxation. They can be subdivided into at least four seasonal categories; summer resorts, winter cold resorts, winter warm resorts and year-round resorts.

- **Summer resorts** are located in regions that have warm summer climates and good transportation connections. The activities offered are based on the surrounding natural environment which usually takes advantage of nearby lakes, mountains or oceans. Recreational pursuits are based on the outdoors and tend to focus on water sports or land activities such as golf and tennis. Popular summer resort areas in Canada are the Maritimes and Muskoka.
- **Winter cold resorts** emphasize winter sports such as skiing and are therefore typically situated in mountainous regions, for example, in Switzerland, the Laurentians and the Rockies. To be successful, winter cold resorts should receive snow for about four months of the year. Some winter cold resorts are located in areas where the climate and topography also allow them to be summer resorts. For example, Banff has excellent summer and winter facilities and conditions.

FIGURE 9.1
Hotels and resorts
feature different
types of rooms
and facilities.
Source: Sheraton.

Portugal (Cont'd)

LISBON
LISBOA SHERATON HOTEL & TOWERS

LISBOA SHERATON TOWERS **366**
Rua Latino Coelho 1, 1097 Lisboa-CODEX   HOTEL SCI
☎ (351) 1-57-57-57   Telex: 12774 SHERCO P
FAX: (351) (1) 547164   Cable: SHERACO LISBOA
85 Rms and Suites on Top 6 Floors of Lisboa Sheraton Hotel.
All Rooms Overlook Lisbon, Separate Guest Registration, Comp
Amenities, Newspaper, Mini-Bars, Towers Lounge. Secretarial
Services Available, All Lisboa Sheraton Hotel Facilities Avail-
able, 4 Non-Smoking Rms Avail.
Portugese Escudos
1 P.   28.000   2 P.   31.000
Suites   50.000- 80.000
Rates Include Buffet Breakfast and All Presently Applicable
Taxes.

LISBOA SHERATON HOTEL **292**
Rua Latino Coelho 1, 1097 Lisboa-CODEX   HOTEL SCI
☎ (351) 1-57-57-57   Telex: 12774 SHERCO P
Cable: SHERACO LISBOA FAX: (351) (1) 547164
300 Rms and Suites, Dntwn, nr Edward VII Park, St. George
Castle, Alfama District, Tower of Belem, Bus-Shop-Tour Areas.
Arpt 4 Mi, Limo Avail. 2 Rests, 2 Bars, 7 Mtg Rms Accom 15-
500 and Panorama Roof-Banquet Room Overlooking Heart of
Lisbon. Free Prkng, Outdr Htd Pool, Sauna, Hlth Club, Pets, 8
Non-Smoking Rms Avail, Disabled Facilities Avail.
Portugese Escudos
1 P.   22.000   2 P.   25.000
Suites   50.000- 80.000
Rates Include Buffet Breakfast and All Presently Applicable
Taxes.

PORTO
PORTO SHERATON HOTEL **461**
Av. da Boavista, 1269   HOTEL SCI
Porto, Portugal 4100 PORTO
☎ 668822   Telex: 22723 SHERPO P
FAX: (351) (2) 691467
253 Rms, Incl 2 Pres Suites & 15 Executive Suites, Loc in
Financial District, Pedras Rubras Arpt 10 Mi. All Rms with
Color TV/Video, Direct Dial Tel, Mini Bar, 24 Hr Rm Svc. Health
Club, Indr Pool, Squash Crt, Beauty/Barber Shop. Rest, Bars,
Conf/Banquet Rms Accom up to 300. Near Port Wine Cellars,
Beaches. Disabled Facs Avail, 17 Non-Smoking Rms Avail.
Portuguese Escudos
1 P.   16.000- 22.000   2 P.   18.000- 24.000
Suites 35.000- 66.000
Above Rates inc. Continental Breakfast in Restaurant and All
Presently Applicable Taxes.

Spain

PALMA de MAJORCA
SON VIDA SHERATON HOTEL

Urbanization Son Vida, Palma de   RESORT SCI
Majorca, Balearic Islands
☎ (71) 79.00.00   Telex: 68651 SVIDAE
FAX: (71) 79.00.17
171 Rms, Resort Htl, 11 Mi from Palma Arpt, Pool Bar/Bbq,
Rest, Lounge, Outdr Pool, Tennis, Golf, Mtg Rms Accom to 150,
Health Center with Sauna, Turkish Bath, Massage, Gymna-
sium, and Covered Pool with Whirlpool, M.A.P Rates Avail at
$48 Per Person Per Day, 2 Non-smoking Rms Avail.
U.S. Dollars

	Jan. 1-Feb. 28		Jul. 16-Oct. 31
1 P.	$75.00- $100.00	1 P.	$117.00- $146.00
2 P.	93.00- 124.00	2 P.	142.00- 183.00
Suites	200.00- 292.00	Suites	292.00
	Mar. 1-Jul. 15		**Nov. 1-Dec. 31**
1 P.	$100.00- $133.00	1 P.	$83.00- $117.00
2 P.	125.00- 167.00	2 P.	108.00- 142.00
Suites	250.00	Suites	250.00

15% Service Charge Included in Rates, 12% Government Tax Not
Included in Rates.

- **Winter warm resorts** provide the most commonly recognized picture of Canadian tourists; that of people escaping from the harsh northern winter. Most of these resorts are located in the southern United States and the tropics. Mexico, the Caribbean and Hawaii are extremely popular with Canadian tourists. The main attraction of these resorts is the warm climate. Depending on their location, they concentrate on either beach and water sports or golf and tennis, although some resorts feature all these activities.

- **Year-round resorts** require one of two climatic types; tropical conditions which effectively provide a year-long summer, or cold winters and hot summers. Hawaii and the Caribbean are typical tropical resort areas while many parts of the Rockies have both the climate and the facilities to provide different vacation experiences throughout the year.

At one time almost all resorts operated on a strictly seasonal basis and closed during the off season. Today, however, the quest for economic efficiency has promoted the year-round operation of most resorts. Resorts employ several strategies to counteract the drop in occupancy during the off season when the climate is less favourable. They may lower rates, create special promotions and diversify into new markets such as meetings, conventions and incentive groups which are traditional markets for commercial properties. It should also be noted that because the climate in the southern hemisphere is the reverse of that in the northern hemisphere, a seasonal resort can always be found to meet any need. Spring in one hemisphere is fall in the other, just as winter and summer are reversed. An avid skier can therefore indulge that passion just as well by visiting Chile or New Zealand in July as by travelling to Whistler in February.

There are also many resorts that appeal to special interests. Dude ranches, common in Arizona and Alberta, promote a western, informal atmosphere and offer typically western recreation such as horseback riding, camping, guided trail riding, chuck wagon dinners and rodeos. Health spas, especially popular in Europe, are located near natural mineral springs or other reputedly beneficial elements. Tourists patronize such resorts primarily for their health benefits. Special baths are featured as well as massage, sun lamp treatment, nutrition and health-restoring activities. Outdoor recreational equipment is commonly provided. Health spas can offer supervised exercise programs and special diets catered to meet guests' particular needs. Youth hostels, Irish Castles, Villas and Spanish *Paradores* are some other types of accommodation that travel counsellors may be asked to book for clients. Many people are looking for a different experience and counsellors therefore need to know all forms of the product.

Specialization

Perhaps the clearest trend in the hotel industry is the spread of specialization or niche marketing. At one time, commercial hotels were confined to city centres near railroad stations and resort properties were located in remote areas. The former catered to business people and the latter served tourists. As the travel industry expanded, its marketing became more sophisticated. The use of market segmentation as a selling technique led to the development of specialized hotels to meet the needs of different markets. A simple example is the division of recognized hotel chains into separate budget, moderate and deluxe segments. For example, the Ramada chain operates Ramada Inn (budget), Ramada Hotel (moderate) and Ramada Renaissance (deluxe) properties. Holiday Corporation has also embraced this concept but it has chosen to develop budget properties under a separate name, Hampton Inn, to distinguish them from the mid-priced Holiday Inn. The same company has also targeted the upscale market using both techniques; the Holiday Inn Crown Plaza and Embassy Suites. Other chains concentrate on just one segment of the market, for example, no-frills, budget type of accommodation. However,

specialization in just one market segment is more likely at the higher end in chains such as Hilton, Four Seasons and Omni. Budget organizations have tended to expand into moderate and luxury markets. Some companies have reacted to the changing marketplace by offering different types of accommodation within the same property (Figure 9.2). For example, separate floors may be assigned to non-smokers, to executive clients (with extra services and luxury rates), or to any other segment which the hotel wishes to attract. Other recent trends in the hospitality sector are condominium hotels and all-suite hotels. Although the first all-suite hotel opened in Texas in 1961, this segment expanded most during the 1980s aided by the increased number of female business travellers who do not wish to hold meetings in a bedroom. Even within the various segments, sub-markets continue to develop. For example, all-suite hotels are now available in economy, mid-priced, luxury and full-service versions. Holiday Corporation has developed extended stay properties under the name Homewood Suites, and mega-resorts combine business and resort facilities.

A further development in the hospitality sector is the increased variety and sophistication of services available. Some hotels now use computer-coded plastic cards in place of cumbersome pass keys. Computerized front desks and check-in/check-out systems are common. The automation of room inventory and supplies is becoming standard and many hotels now have automated individual client files. For example, telephone calls, movie rentals, and room service orders can be automatically recorded on the client's folio. Another trend among hotels is to offer a particular range of services corresponding to the specific market being targeted. At one extreme there are no-frills properties which offer accommodation but no other facilities, such as restaurants or swimming pools. At the other extreme, guests are provided with luxurious toiletries, bathrobes, oversized towels, hair dryers, bathroom televisions, in-room cable movies, complimentary breakfasts and free newspapers. Modern commercial hotels now feature business centres with secretarial services and fax machines. Frequent guest programs have also been created in an attempt to enhance brand loyalty. Such programs have created additional weekend business. Some frequent guest programs are associated with airline frequent flyer plans. However, as with airlines, costs have escalated and some chains have dropped these schemes.

person operations or international organizations with a network of sales offices in major world centres. They are appointed by hotels or resorts to handle sales, promotion and reservations for their client properties. The representative business originated because many hotels needed a distribution system to perform these functions in areas where it was not feasible for them to open their own sales offices. Representative firms originally dealt only with hotels, but today they represent resorts, attractions, tour companies, cruise lines, car rental firms, airlines and tourist boards. All representative companies function in much the same manner and meet similar client needs. Hotel representatives can provide their clients with the following advantages:

FIGURE 9.2
Some hotels target different markets within the same property.
Source: York-Hannover Hotels.

Hotel Representatives

Hotel representatives are independent commercial enterprises. They may be one-

Introducing a hotel that matches your style.

The Skyline Airport Tower & Hotel, a whole new dimension in accommodation.
Whether it's Corporate Class, First-Class or Economy Class, we can match your style.
Our enclosed hospitality complex offers you every comfort imaginable.
Choice of accommodation. Superb dining and entertainment. Indoor shopping mall with
30 stores. Two cinemas. A complete fitness club. Convention space for up to 4,500.
With a personality all of its own The Skyline Airport Tower & Hotel matches your style.

ECONOMY CLASS
FROM **$64.00** PER NIGHT

For value priced accommodation with all of the amenities of a first-class hotel choose Economy Class in The Hotel.

FIRST-CLASS
FROM **$89.00** PER NIGHT

For the traveller who desires superior accommodation at a reasonable rate choose First-Class in The Tower.

CORPORATE CLASS
FROM **$119.00** PER NIGHT

Receive continental breakfast, private lounge, bathrobe and more when you upgrade to Corporate Class in The Tower.

- **Economy**. The cost of running and staffing a local sales office in several areas is prohibitive for many companies. Small companies do not have the resources to pay rent, acquire equipment and hire staff in all the locations that might represent business potential. It is less expensive to contract for the services of a representative.

- **Industry Knowledge**. A good representative knows the local travel industry, which companies are active, their potential and specialties, and can evaluate the market for its clients. A hotel is unlikely to know one agency from another in a distant location, even by making frequent promotional trips to the area. A representative who is a member of the local community has this knowledge and can stay current with personnel, changes and trends.

- **Constant Presence**. A representative's presence in a market area means that the client is represented at all relevant industry seminars, trade shows and presentations. This maintains awareness of the client's product in the market.

- **Promotional Advice**. Representative companies' knowledge of the local market permit them to advise their clients on direct mail, advertising and other promotional strategies.

Many representatives specialize in particular products, such as a specific region or a certain calibre of property. Most representative companies are owned by industry veterans, as extensive knowledge of the local market is essential to promote their clients' interests. A representative company's image is especially significant as it reflects its style and by extension, that of its clients. Both parties therefore choose their partners carefully.

Hotel representatives have become a vital link in the chain between hotels and their guests. Their objectives are to keep their client's properties filled with visitors, including individuals, groups, meetings and conventions, and to keep retail travel agencies, tour companies and carriers notified of the rates, features and amenities of those properties. Large companies operate separate reservations and sales departments and may have a computer system to check availability and confirm reservations. Smaller companies use a variety of manual control systems for these functions and may have one person handling both sales and reservations. Most companies install toll-free lines for out-of-town agencies. In addition to the marketing functions described earlier, hotel representatives make personal sales calls on the agencies and others likely to produce business for their clients. Many also attend travel industry functions on behalf of their clients and some run a booth at these events. Others organize inspection trips and familiarization tours for travel counsellors.

Each week, representatives who are not linked by computer with their client's property receive "sell and report" charts from the hotel. These charts show the hotel's room reservation status (its inventory) for the next few months, the number of rooms available in each price range, any closed out dates, and dates when rooms are "on request". This permits hotel representatives to sell with complete confidence provided that all representatives keep their charts current. Hotels must be advised immediately a room is sold otherwise overbooking can occur. In practice, major representatives are in daily communication with many of the properties they represent.

Hotel representatives earn income from two sources; retainers and commissions. Some hotels sign a contract to pay their representatives a monthly or annual fee to cover their overhead, time, expertise and promotional costs. The size of the retainer is negotiated between the representative and the client. The amount depends on the size and importance of the market area, the service desired, the size and reputation of each party, and their negotiating skills. Alternatively, some companies prefer to work on the basis of a commission on the number of reservations handled. Ten percent is the standard commission although this varies

Hotel Terminology

The hospitality industry employs a number of standard terms and abbreviations to distinguish the features of the business. A brief review of the most common terms is provided below.

Accommodation

Adjoining Rooms.	Two or more hotel bedrooms immediately adjacent to each other but without private connecting doors.
Connecting Rooms.	Two or more hotel bedrooms immediately adjacent to each other with a private door between them. This permits access from one to the other without having to use the public hallway.
Double: DWB (double with bath). *one bed*	A room with a double bed meant for occupancy by two persons. It can also serve as a single.
Double-Double: DDWB (double double with bath).	A room with two double beds sometimes called a family room or twin-double.
Efficiency Unit. *Kitchenette.*	A room containing kitchen facilities so that guests may store, prepare, cook and serve meals for themselves.
Hospitality Room. *charters (late flights) leave carry on there.*	A hotel room used to entertain guests and for receptions arranged for tour members, convention delegates or meeting participants. It generally contains a bar, seating and occasional tables. A hospitality suite has a connecting bedroom.
Junior Suite.	A large room separated into an entertainment area and a sleeping area.
Penthouse Suite.	This suite opens to the roof.
Quad.	A room for occupancy by four persons.
Sample Room.	A room used by salespeople to display merchandise or set up exhibits.
Single: SWB (single with bath). *one bed*	A room with one bed intended for occupancy by one person. A single often contains a double bed or one larger.
Studio.	A room with a foldaway bed or a couch that converts into a bed. A studio can be used as a living room as well as a bedroom.
Suite.	Hotel accommodation consisting of one or more bedrooms plus a living room. A suite may also contain a wet bar, a small kitchen and other facilities. It is often the best room in the hotel.
Triple.	A room meant for occupancy by three persons.
Twin: TWB (twin with bath).	A room containing two single beds for occupancy by two persons.

Other Terms

Check-in.	This term describes guest registration upon arrival at a hotel. It is usually required by law as well as for the hotel's own records.
Check-out Time.	The latest hour by which a hotel guest is required to vacate the room and pay all charges. Check-out times vary from late morning to mid-afternoon.
Day Rate. *for the day.*	A special low room rate for accommodation used during the day from approximately 8:00 a.m. to 6:00 p.m. It is the rate charged for a sample room.
Deposit.	Payment made in advance on behalf of a guest to ensure that the room will be held regardless of the time of the guest's arrival. Deposit amounts, cancellation and refund requirements vary widely depending on hotel policy and the season of the year. These must always be verified in advance.
Extra Person Charge.	The charge for an additional person in a room.
Folio.	An invoice which shows the total cost, including the room rate and incidentals, incurred by a client.
Garni.	A term applied to European hotels which have no dining room or restaurant services. They may, however, offer continental breakfast.
Guaranteed Payment Reservation. *for late arrival.*	A reserved room for which payment is guaranteed by the guest whether or not it is used.
Incidentals.	The additional charges, such as phone calls, bar bills, laundry and room service, on a guest's folio.
Master Account.	A bill of all group charges prearranged between a hotel and the convener or group leader. It is the total bill for all accommodation, meeting rooms, receptions and other services arranged in advance. It does not include incidentals which are charged on the individual group member's folio.
Pension.	A French word widely used in Europe to denote a guest house or boarding house.
Pre-Registration.	This term indicates that room assignment and registration was completed prior to the guest's arrival. It is often used for tour groups and convention delegates to save time at check-in.
Rack Card.	A sheet inserted in hotel brochures which gives the rack rate. In Europe this is known as a tariff sheet.
Rack Rate. *most expensive rate for room. look for a bed*	The published official retail tariff rate established by a hotel. This is the maximum rate charged for the room (depending on the number of occupants) and differs from the net rate or any special rates offered by a hotel.
Rollaway Bed.	A bed which can be provided for an extra person in a room. Some hotels charge for a rollaway bed in addition to the extra person charge. Others charge only for the extra person.
Run of the House. *(ROH) don't know where it is.*	A special hotel rate offered to groups. It is a flat rate for each room regardless of its location.
Service Charge.	A fee added to a hotel bill (usually between ten and 15 percent of the total) assessed as a gratuity for staff.

FIGURE 9.3 Hotel terminology.

according to individual agreements and bonus arrangements. Some representatives collect revenue from both retainers and commissions. Since the hotels pay these charges directly to their representatives, a representative company's services are free of charges to travel agencies. Travel agencies that deal with hotel representatives are assured of a fast and efficient response to requests for room availability for proposed bookings, rapid confirmation of reservations, supplies of hotel literature and current information on the hotel's rates. Some well-known independent hotel representatives presently serving Canadian travel agencies are Keith Cooke & Associates, Robert Reid Associates and Utell International.

Grading of Hotels and Resorts

One of the most difficult requests made of a travel counsellor is to recommend a hotel for a client. Not only does accommodation have an emotional and perceptual impact on clients, but there is no single source that categorizes and rates hotels for travel counsellors. Furthermore, there are so many properties offering such a range of styles, standards and services that it is impossible for even an experienced and widely-travelled counsellor to be familiar with all of them.

Over 100 different methods are currently used to classify hotels. Most of

FIGURE 9.4
Some hotel personnel.

Hotel Personnel

General Manager.	Supervises all activities within a hotel. Responsible for the coordination of all departments.
Resident Manager.	Takes over when the GM is absent. Usually handles special duties assigned by the manager.
Assistant Manager.	Assists General and Resident Managers in discharging their duties. Performs specific assignments on their orders.
Front Office Manager.	Acts as liaison between guests and the hotel for reservations, registration and information.
Director of Sales. _deal first with._	Sells convention facilities for meetings, banquets and receptions.
Conventions Manager.	Supervises and sells convention facilities.
Maitre d'Hôte.	Supervises the service of the public dining and banquet rooms.
Catering Manager.	Sells banquets and supervises banquet service.
Steward.	Purchases or supervises the food and beverages for a hotel.
Executive Housekeeper.	Supervises all housekeeping personnel. In charge of renovations and the purchasing of housekeeping supplies.
Assistant Housekeeper.	Supervises the work of maids and housemen in assigned areas.
Concierge.	In many hotels, the superintendent of minor guest services and amenities such as obtaining theatre and concert tickets, mailing letters, arranging local sightseeing or car rental. May sometimes be called a porter in North America.

Luxury Class (often called luxe or deluxe in Europe). These are hotels of great luxury, comprising arrangements available for first class, plus:

    a. High class public rooms, very big hall, reception and reading rooms;
    b. A number of apartments with private rooms (suites);
    c. Spacious rooms, well decorated and elegantly furnished;
    d. At least 75% of the suites or rooms with complete private bathrooms (tub and shower combined) and 25% with washrooms with shower and WC (water closet and toilet);
    e. Equipment and general appointments of the most modern standards;
    f. Outdoor or indoor swimming pool according to climatic conditions.

First Class. Hotels of very great comfort, comprising the installations found in second class, plus:

    a. Spacious public rooms;
    b. Apartments with private sitting room (suites);
    c. Spacious bedrooms appointed with high class furniture of good taste;
    d. At least 60% of the rooms with complete bathrooms (tub and shower combined);
    e. The remaining 40% of the rooms with washrooms with shower and WC;
    f. Adequate reception service, cashier, doorman, dining room.

Second Class. Hotels of great comfort, comprising the arrangements provided for third class, and also:

    a. Reception hall and reading room; the reading room or lounge should be separate from the bar and users should not be obliged to buy a drink;
    b. Spacious rooms, appointed with decor and furnishings of high quality;
    c. Soundproof arrangements;
    d. At least 25% of the rooms with complete private bathrooms (tub and shower combined);
    e. At least 75% of the rooms with washrooms with WC (washbasin, bidet, toilet);
    f. Telephone with outside connections in at least 50% of the rooms;
    g. High class general appointments, especially sanitary fixtures;
    h. Qualified and trained staff.

Third Class. Hotels of good comfort, comprising the arrangements provided for fourth class, plus:

    a. An elevator for at least three floors;
    b. 40% of the rooms with washrooms with WC (washbasin, bidet, toilet);
    c. All remaining rooms with bidets with running water;
    d. Carpets in the public rooms;
    e. House switchboard with internal telephone service in rooms;
    f. Telephones with outside connection in some rooms and at least one phone per floor;
    g. A common bathroom or shower for ten rooms and at least one per floor;
    h. Reception service.

Fourth Class. Hotels of average comfort and with at least ten rooms comprising the following:

    a. Common premises including a lounge or sitting rooms available to guests or lobby with necessary appointments;
    b. Central heating or automatic heating;
    c. Telephone booth at the disposal of guests;
    d. Bright and well appointed rooms which should have either shutters or thick double curtains, fitted with furniture of good quality and carpets or bedside rugs; complete and modern electrical equipment consisting of three lights with separate switches for ceiling, bed and washbasin;
    e. Hot and cold running water in all rooms;
    f. At least 50% of the rooms with a bidet and running water;
    g. 25% of the rooms with washrooms made up of fixed installations or private shower; these washrooms should be rooms adjoining the bedrooms but quite distinct from them;
    h. A common bathroom or shower for 15 rooms in transient hotels; in residential hotels a common bath or shower room for each seven bedrooms;
    i. A common WC for five rooms and at least two on each floor, one for ladies and the other for gentlemen;
    j. Sanitary fittings of good quality and in perfect state;
    k. Breakfast service in rooms;
    l. Separate hotel entrance in case the premises also includes a bar or public house.

FIGURE 9.5
The WTO hotel classification system.

CAMP SPRINGS, MD.   AC 301
NEAREST AIR SERVICE WASHINGTON, DC. - NATIONAL, DCA, 13 MI. SE; WASHINGTON DULLES INTL., IAD, 37 MI. SE **ADDITIONAL** BALTIMORE, BWI, 35 MI. SW.
FOR HOTELS/MOTELS, SEE WASHINGTON, DC. (SUBURBAN CATEGORY).
CAMP VERDE, AZ.   AC 602
NEAREST AIR SERVICE PRESCOTT, PRC, 45 MI. SE **ADDITIONAL** FLAGSTAFF, FLG, 55 MI. SW. SERVICE ALSO AVAILABLE THROUGH PHOENIX, PHX, 95 MI. NE
○━ HOTEL/MOTEL (Downtown and other)
BEST WESTERN CLIFF CASTLE LODGE, BOX 3430
NP $45 UP ® ✴ ■   567-6611   ①BW   ZIP: 86322
CANADIAN, TX.   AC 806
NEAREST AIR SERVICE AMARILLO, AMA, 100 MI. NE
CANAJOHARIE, NY.   AC 518
NEAREST AIR SERVICE ALBANY, ALB, 50 MI. NW.
○━ HOTEL/MOTEL (Downtown and other)
MOHAWK MOTOR LODGE, E. GRAND ST., BOX 130 (PALATINE BRIDGE)
* $36-50 ®   673-3233   ZIP: 13428
CANAL FULTON, OH.   AC 216
NEAREST AIR SERVICE AKRON, CAK, 9 MI. W.
CANAL WINCHESTER, OH.   AC 614
NEAREST AIR SERVICE COLUMBUS, CMH, 20 MI. SE
CANANDAIGUA, NY.   AC 716
NEAREST AIR SERVICE ROCHESTER, ROC, 33 MI. SE
○━ HOTEL/MOTEL (Downtown and other)
BEST WESTERN SUNRISE HILL INN, 6108 LOOMIS RD. (FARMINGTON)
  $46-53 ■   924-2131   ①BW   ZIP: 14425
BUDGET HOST HERITAGE MOTOR INN, RTE. 5 & 20E
* $32-36 © ■   394-6170   ZIP: 14424
ECONO LODGE, 170 EASTERN BLVD.
** $35-39 ® ✴ ■   394-9000   ①ECO   ZIP: 14424
KELLOGG'S PAN-TREE MOTOR INN, 130 LAKE SHORE DR. (OPEN APR-OCT)
** $42 UP ✴ ■   394-3909   ZIP: 14424
SHERATON CANANDAIGUA INN, 770 S. MAIN ST.
*** $39-65 ® ✴ ■   394-7800   ①SHR   ZIP: 14424

CANTON, OH. ✈   AC 216
SERVED THROUGH AKRON, CAK, 10 MI. N.

AIRPORT GROUND TRANS.	PHONE	SVC.	AREA SERVED
AMERICAN LIMO SVC	221-9330	NS	CLEVELAND
CAREY LIMOUSINE	253-6743	NS	DOWNTOWN & SUBURBS
HOPKIN'S ARPT. LIMO	494-0405	S,NS	METRO AREA, AKRON; CLEVELAND/HOPKINS ARPT

OTHER CARRIER OFFICES	RES. PHONE	LOCATION
AMERICAN	SEE DIAL 800	AIRPORT TERMINAL
DELTA CONNECTION - COMAIR	SEE DIAL 800	AIRPORT TERMINAL
EASTERN	454-8899	AIRPORT TERMINAL
UNITED	453-8201	AIRPORT TERMINAL
UNITED EXPRESS - AIR WISCONSIN	453-8201	SEE UNITED
USAIR	499-5154	AIRPORT TERMINAL
USAIR EXPRESS	SEE DIAL 800	AIRPORT TERMINAL

ADDITIONAL CLEVELAND - CUYAHOGA COUNTY, CGF, 52 MI. S; BURKE-LAKEFRONT, BKL, 56 MI. SE; HOPKINS INTERNATIONAL, CLE, 59 MI. SE
○━ HOTEL/MOTEL (Downtown and other)
COUNTRY HEARTH INNS, 4475 EVERHARD RD. NW
  $44-80 ®   494-6360   ①COU   ZIP: 44718
HAMPTON INN, 5335 BROADMOOR CIRCLE
** $40-49 ① ® ■   492-0151   ①HMT   ZIP: 44720
HILTON NEWMARKET-CANTON, 320 MARKET AVE. S
*** $49-88 ® ✴ ■®   454-5000   ①HIL   ZIP: 44702
KNIGHTS INN-CANTON-NORTH, 3950 CONVENIENCE CIRCLE NW
* $31 UP ® ■   492-5030   ①KNI   ZIP: 44718
PARKE HOTEL, 4343 EVERHARD RD. NW
  $57-70 ® ■℗   499-9410   ZIP: 44718
REPS: UT①
RED ROOF INN, EVERHARD RD. AT I-77
* $32-44   499-1970   ①RER   ZIP: 44720
SHERATON BELDEN INN, 4375 METRO CIRCLE NW
*** $72-86 ® ✴ ■   494-6494   ①SHR   ZIP: 44720
SIGNATURE INN-CANTON, 5345 BROADMOOR CIRCLE NW
NP $45-51 ® ✴ ■   492-1331   ①SIG   ZIP: 44709

Hotel Information/Facilities
👥 — AH&MA Member
NP — New Property
RP — Renovated Property
■ — 10% or more commission
℗ — Free Airport Pick-up
① — Toll-Free Number Available (see Hotel/Motel Reservations Directory)
✴ — Rooms for Handicapped
Reps — Hotel Representatives
Note: Hotel/Motel room rate ranges are for guideline purposes only. Always confirm rates when booking reservations. Also see preceding/following pages for additional Symbols and Abbreviations.

Hotel Rate Plans
Ⓐ — American Plan
Ⓒ — Continental Plan
Ⓜ — Modified American Plan
Ⓟ — Additional Rate Plans

Mobil® Travel Guide Ratings
★ — Good, better than average
★★ — Very Good
★★★ — Excellent
★★★★ — Outstanding
★★★★★ — One of the Best in the Country
NR — Listed, but not yet rated
SR — Scheduled for Reinspection

these systems employ three interrelated criteria to assess a property; type of clientele, price and service. The type of clientele (either transient, long-stay or corporate) determines the services offered by a hotel. To a large extent, the cost of a hotel's rooms determines its market segment and type of clientele. The class of service is directly related to the other two factors. Most rating systems compare hotels of the same type and assess their facilities and the service they offer. One problem, however, is that rating systems have not responded to changes in the hospitality sector such as market segmentation. Thus large convention hotels are often measured by the same standards as more transient properties. Similarly, all-suite hotels were not widespread until the mid-1980s. Such properties have different layouts and services from traditional hotels and therefore cannot be measured by the same standards as other properties.

Many countries have a government rating system based on regular inspections to ensure that hotels maintain their standards. Different governments, however, apply various standards and definitions to the task. Travel counsellors

soon discover that a hotel considered deluxe in one country often compares with first or second class hotels in another. For example, in France a one-star property is considered plain but fairly comfortable whereas the same rating in North America could be unacceptable. Thus if tourists accustomed to second class hotels in their own country select second class hotels in a foreign country, they may find the accommodation far below their accustomed standard. The World Tourism Organization (WTO) has attempted to resolve the confusion with the development and promotion of a uniform hotel classification system, recognized internationally and accepted by all countries concerned with the reception and accommodation of tourists. About fifty nations have adopted some or all of the WTO classification standards. The WTO system, which recommends grading hotels according to five categories, is reproduced for reference (Figure 9.5). However, even worldwide organizations set different standards. The World Association of Travel Agents (WATA), for example, uses four categories (deluxe, first class, standard and economy) which range from 5-star to 2-star.

FIGURE 9.6
Listings in the North American edition of the OAG Travel Planner reflect the Mobil rating system. Other editions contain local ratings.
Reprinted by special permission from the Winter 1989 issue of the North American Edition OAG Travel Planner Hotel & Motel RedBook. Copyright© 1990, Official Airlines Guides, Inc. All rights reserved.

FIGURE 9.7
Typical listings in the OHG.
Courtesy of the Official Hotel Guide.

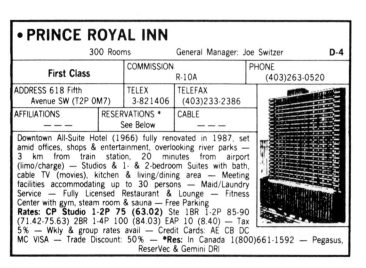

In North America, many hotels are graded by the American Automobile Association (AAA) which conforms to the WTO categories. The Mobil Star system is the most comprehensive in the USA but it is designed to cater to automobile travellers. Mobil uses three categories of accommodation; hotels, motels and resorts. With so many different examples in each category it is hard to accurately rate each type. The Zagat Hotel Survey assesses only luxury properties in the USA and therefore is limited. All evaluations are based on physical structure, furnishing, maintenance, housekeeping, overall service and food service. Hoteliers claim that guidelines for these categories are often vague and not shown to them. They contend that little things such as hot coffee in the rooms and umbrellas when it rains make a difference between a four-star and five-star property.

Several references can help counsellors to develop a sound basis for making hotel recommendations. The following publications are widely used in the Canadian travel trade. No single publication can adequately serve to provide information about every hotel or resort property. Travel agencies therefore require a wide selection of material to help counsellors obtain a complete perspective on properties being considered. Three different editions of the *OAG Travel Planner Hotel and Motel RedBook*, each issued quarterly, cover North America, Europe and Pacific Asia. This reference is the official directory of the American Hotel and Motel Association (AHMA) whose members must meet standards set by the organization. The North American OAG Travel Planner uses the Mobil rating guide and list hotels alphabetically by city (Figure 9.6). Other editions quote government rating systems where they are used. The publication indicates a property's price and location and describes a variety of destination and

NA
Asia Pacific
Europe

transportation information. The *Official Hotel Guide* (OHG) is a reference in three bound volumes that is updated once a year. It assesses almost 30,000 properties worldwide and includes property descriptions, rates, commission information and hotel representatives (Figure 9.7). The OHG also includes

PRINCE ROYAL INN

Your best choice in CALGARY for:

☑ **ALL SUITE ACCOMMODATION**

☑ **VALUE** — studio, one and two bedroom suites available.
— daily weekly and monthly rates available

☑ **LOCATION** — heart of downtown Calgary, walking distance to river parks, major downtown office buildings and shopping.

BUSINESS — corporate and government rates available.

PLEASURE — Galeano's Restaurant and Lounge
— outdoor roof top garden, health club, all on premises

toll free in Canada
1-800-661-1592

618 - 5th Avenue S.W., Calgary, Alberta T2P 0M7
Telephone (403) 263-0520   Fax (403) 233-2386

CALGARY (Listings Continued from Page 10)

● **MARLBOROUGH INN CALGARY** 250 R ⒺCND SWB $80-90, D/TWB $90 (STI)(UI)(VRS)
1316 33 St NE, T2A 6B6, Tel: 403-248-8888, 800-661-1464, Fax 403-248-0749 ①
See Advertisement This Page

● The Palliser 405 R ⒺSWB CND $115 up, DWB CND $130 up (CPH)(IC)(UI)(WG) ....R P Thompson
133 Ninth Ave SW, T2P 2M3, Tel: 403-262-1234, Tx: 03822512, Fax 403-260-1260 AE MC VS

● Parkview Inn 44 R ⒺSWB/DWB CND $31-49, TWB CND $36-58 ....Alnoor Lakhani, Mgr
3630 Macleod Trail S, T2G 2P9, Tel: 403-243-4651 AE MC VS

● Plum Tree Inn 75 R CND SWB $32.95-$36.95, D/TWB $39.95-$43.95 ....Nizar Mohamed, Mgr
1947 18th Ave, NE, T2E 7T8, Tel: 403-250-5015, Tx: 822008, Fax 403-277-2623 AE MC VS

● **PORT O'CALL INN** 200 R ⒺDWB $79.95, DDWB $81.95 (VRS)
1935 McKnight Blvd, NE, T2E 6V4, Tel: 403-291-4600, 800-661-1161 ①①℗⑤
See Advertisement Preceding Page

● **PRINCE ROYAL INN** 300 U ⒸCND Studio $65, 1 Bdrm $75, 2 Bdrm $95 (LRI)
618 5th Ave, SW, T2P 0M7, Tel: 403-263-0520, Tx: 03821406, Fax 403-233-2386 AE MC VS
See Advertisement Preceding Page and Map Page 12

FIGURE 9.8
Standard listings in the Hotel and Travel Index are brief, however, properties may also advertise to raise their visibility.
Source: Hotel and Travel Index.

online:

details of recreational activities and maps of various geographical areas. The *Hotel and Travel Index*, a quarterly publication, does not attempt to evaluate or describe properties. Rather, it contains a complete listing of all hotel and motel systems in North America as well as larger individual resorts and hotels worldwide (Figure 9.8). Nevertheless, the Hotel and Travel Index is an extremely valuable reference which indicates room and commission rates, hotel representatives and other useful reservation information. In addition to the 45,000 properties recorded in it, the Hotel and Travel Index offers destination maps and information, and lists applicable local taxes and air services. Properties are listed geographically by region and alphabetically by country and city. A useful source of information is the ABC Star Service, a looseleaf binder which describes over 8,000 properties. Many evaluations are based on assessments conducted by travel counsellors and as such provide a unique perspective on hotel standards (Figure 9.9). In addition, a well-stocked travel agency will have directories and brochures from major hotel chains. This literature is provided free of charge and detail rates, facilities, site locations and other useful information. Most tourist offices also publish and distribute guidebooks and manuals which list all hotels, pensions, guest houses and spas within the country. In some cases the properties listed are graded for quality. For travel within

online:

FIGURE 9.9
The ABC Star Service contains descriptive evaluations of hotels.
Courtesy of the Reed Travel Group.

Western Europe, especially by car, the Michelin Guides provide useful information and gradings for motels, hotels and restaurants in smaller cities and towns. Independent hotel representatives will also supply lists and manuals describing the properties they represent.

There is so much information on accommodation, much of it conflicting, that counsellors need to develop their own methods for assessing properties and facilities. Experienced counsellors combine evaluations from several sources to build a complete picture of the property. Whenever possible these assessments should be augmented by the counsellor's personal inspection. Specific knowledge of a property is invaluable. This enables a counsellor to recommend or disregard, as the case may be, the features of hotels and resorts visited. Such visits enable counsellors to become aware of the prevailing standards in the country and the property, and to relate these to the tastes of their clients. Hotel and resort standards, however, can decline and personal knowledge must be maintained and updated. A single visit cannot guarantee that a property will always have a favourable recommendation. Hotel owners may try to decrease high operating costs by cutting staff, firing a famous chef, reducing room service or maid service, or closing entertainment facilities.

A travel counsellor's challenge is to develop a method for researching and rating hotels. As a first step, counsellors must identify their clients' needs and interests to help direct the research phase. Matching of client's needs with an appropriate property refers not only to a counsellor's knowledge of the client, but also to the particular situation. For example, if a client is visiting Europe in the spring, a counsellor need not spend time searching for a hotel with air conditioning. At the same time, the client will be saved unnecessary expense. The search should begin by consulting standard hotel guides such as the OHG. These will help identify the preferred properties and locations which of course

RESIDENCE CHAMPS-ELYSEES, 92 Rue de la Boetie, is a true first-class property that is notable for the ultramodern manner in which its old building was converted. Glass and chrome lobby is splashed with colors, and lounge is designed like an art gallery. Only breakfast is served. Bar and sauna are on the drawing board. All guest rooms have been redone in upbeat eclectic style and are up to uniformly high standards. Mattresses, seating, and TVs are new. Units are equipped with fabric wall coverings, large closets, color TVs, minibars, direct-dial phones, ample, well-lit workspace, and small, modern marbled baths with robes and hairdryers; street-side rooms have balconies. Court units overlook modest garden, which is overgrown. Maintenance and housekeeping are excellent. Refined, attentive staff speaks good English. Families are made especially welcome. 85 rooms. $115-$135 single, $135-$149 double. Evelynne Rieger, mgr. (CC) Phone 43-599615. Telex 650695.

depend on the reasons for the client's trip. No matter how good the rating system, however, there must be a description of the property to help counsellors make an intelligent decision. Many hotel guides name the hotel's representative who can expand on the information in the guide. Some representatives may have visited the destination and can describe the particular hotel. All can process reservations. Individual hotel brochures may supply additional information on facilities, rates, locations and services. Major hotel chains distribute directories of their properties. Tourist boards can also assist with research. Although they will assist by providing information on locations and facilities, tourist boards rarely make recommendations or take reservations. Counsellors should also consult airline computer systems which can help them to plan itineraries and make reservations. Once various hotels have been researched for their suitability in terms of price, location and facilities, the task becomes one of selecting the most appropriate property to meet the client's needs. Counsellors must frequently recommend hotels that neither they nor their co-workers have visited. In such cases, the above sources and a counsellor's ability to interpret them provide the basis for the suggestions made.

Checklist for Quality

During personal travels or familiarization tours, counsellors have an opportunity to visit local properties to determine their suitability for various clients. One aircraft is much like another but hotels differ even if they have similar designs, furniture and facilities. The quality of a hotel is highly dependent on the staff who run it and thus they can truly be assessed only by personal inspection (see Figure 9.10). Even so, counsellors must be aware that staff and ownership change. The checklist below is a useful basis for evaluating a property. Counsellors may wish to expand on the information provided to build a

personalized hotel file. Many counsellors carry the relevant reference pages from brochures and hotel guides such as the OHG when they conduct a hotel inspection. Features can be highlighted and notes made on such materials. Some counsellors find it helpful to take their own photographs of the aspects that interest them rather than relying on the publicity material provided.

Location

The first item to check is the property's location. Pleasure travellers prefer hotels that are located in a safe area, close to shops, entertainment, restaurants, beaches, museums and art galleries. It should also have convenient access to transportation services such as the airport, taxis and public transit. Business travellers require their hotels to be near or easily accessible to their appointments. Depending on the client's schedule, airport hotels may be more convenient than downtown commercial properties.

Physical Condition

First impressions are important. A hotel need not be new but it should be well maintained and have an attractive appearance. Note whether the exterior needs painting and whether the grounds are carefully tended. Enter the lobby area and record your impressions of the lighting, furnishings, front desk area and guest mix. Check for elevators and ramps to determine whether the hotel and its facilities are accessible to handicapped travellers. Move on to inspect the guest rooms and observe their physical condition. Is the general impression clean or shabby, spacious or small? Do bedrooms need to be painted or redecorated? Are drapes, bedspreads and windows clean? Are walls soundproof? Is the room well maintained, for example, do all lights work? Do taps drip? Is the air conditioning in working order?

Room Equipment and Housekeeping

Check the standard features to ensure that rooms are equipped with a telephone, radio, TV and reading lights.

Does the room contain an ice bucket, a room service menu and writing materials? Note whether there are sufficient clothes hangers, luggage racks, waste baskets and drinking glasses. Investigate the little things. Is the tissue container filled? Are bathroom mirrors and tiles clean and is there an ample supply of towels, washcloths and soap?

Amenities and Services

Investigate the property's amenities and services. Is there a nightclub? Does the bar have entertainment? Check the coffee shop and restaurant menus for price and selection. Can guests obtain laundry and dry cleaning service, room service and safety deposit boxes? If there is a swimming pool, are free towels available? Does the lobby have a newsstand or gift shop and is information on sightseeing, local entertainment and shopping posted? A suitable hotel is well managed and there is good communication between its various departments. Note whether the staff

FIGURE 9.10
Sample hotel assessment form.

LOCATION:

Hotel Name: _____

Address: _____ Telephone: _____

Contact: _____ Position: _____

Type of Hotel: _____ Location: _____

Number of Rooms: _____ Type/Quality of Rooms: _____

PHYSICAL CONDITION:

Exterior: _____

Grounds: _____

Public Areas: _____

Rooms: _____

Disabled Accessibility: _____

ROOM EQUIPMENT/HOUSEKEEPING:

_____
_____
_____

HOTEL AMENITIES/FACILITIES:

_____
_____
_____

SERVICE QUALITY: _____

GUEST MIX: _____

HOTEL RATING/COMMENTS: _____
_____
_____

appear to be helpful and courteous or aloof and indifferent. Is luggage delivered to a guest's room shortly after registering? Is room service prompt? Is wake-up service available? Try to determine the housekeeping routine. Are rooms made up by check-out time? Is the bed linen changed frequently? Commercial clients may need access to secretarial services and office equipment. Check whether the hotel has a business centre for such travellers.

Guest Mix

Perhaps the most crucial area for a travel counsellor to examine is the guest mix at a property. Each hotel and resort attracts a different type of clientele. Some properties direct their marketing strategies to group business, conventions and tours. Others try to strike a balance between individual guest bookings and large groups. Still others, usually smaller properties, feel best equipped to serve individual travellers. Travel counsellors must try to match their clients to a property's size, type and guest profile.

Most hoteliers find group business to be profitable. Groups offer maximum room occupancy and a higher utilization of other revenue-producing services such as bars, dining rooms and hospitality suites. Many travellers, however, choose to travel independently to avoid such crowds. It is understandable that a couple might resent the idea of staying at a property where a large convention is being held. Another aspect of guest mix to consider is the suitability of the property to the tastes, attitudes and age levels of one's clients. For example, it is unlikely that an elderly couple would enjoy staying at a resort which caters largely to a younger crowd and which has a rock group performing in the discotheque until 5:00 a.m. For similar reasons, a young couple with small children would feel uncomfortable in a resort which emphasizes formality and has no recreational facilities or menus for children. In the same way, if a couple wishes to "get away from it all", a resort that encourages participation and group activities should not be recommended

simply because the clients share the same age group and income bracket as the other guests.

Rates and Charges

Room rates are generally quoted in one of three ways; on a per room basis, as a cost per person per night, or the price for two people sharing (double occupancy). Prices tend to be shown in either local currency or in U.S. dollars. Three main factors influence the rack rates charged by a hotel. The chief considerations are the nature of the hotel, the features of the room and the characteristics of the guest's stay. The location of the hotel is extremely important. Clients at a resort hotel can expect to pay more for a room in a beachfront property than for one which is a ten minute walk from the ocean. Similarly, a business person would generally pay more for a city centre hotel than for a suburban property. If a hotel is isolated, the rates will be higher than if competing properties also operate in the area. The quality of the hotel and special features such as 24 hour room service, swimming pool and gym also influence rack rates.

Not only must one expect to pay more for luxury accommodation than for first class, but even within a given category room rates vary depending on the location, size, facilities and amenities of the individual room. For example, an oceanfront room with balcony will cost more than a comparable room located on the land side of a hotel. Rooms situated on upper floors offer clients a better view and those far from elevators and public areas are quieter. Guests can therefore expect to pay more for them. Similarly, a corner suite will have a higher tariff than a studio room located above the kitchens. Since room rates are partly based on construction and maintenance costs, larger rooms will cost more than similar but smaller accommodation. The room facilities and number of occupants also influence the price charged. A single room with shower may be priced at $45

PRINCE ROYAL INN

CALGARY'S ALL SUITE HOTEL

618 - 5th Avenue S.W., Calgary, Alberta T2P 0M7

Telephone (403) 263-0520   Fax (403) 298-4888

DAILY RATES
(1990)

	RACK	CORP.	W/E
Studio Suite single or double	$75.00	$59.00	$45.00
One Bedroom Suite single or double	$85.00	$69.00	$45.00
Two Bedroom Suite up to 4 persons	$105.00	$89.00	$65.00
Additional person sharing suite	$10.00	$10.00	$10.00
Children 14 years and under		No Charge	
Roll-a-way/Hide-a-bed charge		$10.00	
Playpens		No Charge	

Rates are subject to a 5% Provincial Tax.

All Rates are in Canadian Funds.

(Sorry, No Pets)

Weekly and Monthly Extended Stay Rates
Available Upon Request

For meeting rooms and Group Rates,
Please Contact our Sales Department.

FIGURE 9.11
Room rates depend on a number of factors.
Source: Prince Royal Inn.

factors which can influence room rates. Room costs also vary depending on the time and duration of a guest's stay. Hotels and resorts charge by the number of nights that the guest occupies the room, although weekly rates may be less than daily rates. In many instances, room rates and other charges fluctuate with demand. For example, commercial properties are busiest during the regular working week. Many, therefore offer reduced weekend rates to increase occupancy during their low demand phase (Figure 9.11). European hotel rates are generally higher in summer, the season of high demand, whereas the opposite occurs in the Caribbean, Mexico, Florida and other warm winter areas. Winter is the high season in such destinations and consequently hotel prices are higher at that time. Rates generally drop by ten to fifteen percent or more to attract guests during the summer off season. The room rate also depends on whether it includes meals and, if so, the particular meal plan selected. Meal plans are discussed later in this chapter.

Some authorities demand that rack rates be posted, usually on the inside of the entrance door to each guest room. Hotels, like airlines however, have a graduated pricing structure and therefore the rack rate is not always the price charged. All hotels have a rack rate which represents the official published price for a room but discounted rates are offered to certain groups of clients. For example, a commercial hotel may reduce its prices on weekends, a resort may drop the rack rate during particular seasons and tour groups may be offered a flat rate (run of the house). Hotels also have lower rates for travel industry employees, convention delegates, families and various other groups. The hospitality industry uses a graduated pricing structure because hotels have a very high break-even point and a hotel room is an extremely perishable product. To be profitable, hotels must maintain a high occupancy rate and a tiered pricing system is one method employed to achieve this.

Several hotel and resort tariffs are reproduced in this chapter. These list

per night whereas a single with bathtub may cost $50. However, if these rooms are occupied by two persons the rates might be $60 and $70, respectively. More luxurious decor or furniture, colour TV and air conditioning are some other room rates, meal prices and other charges. A comparison of the sample tariffs will reveal that while the essential information is the same, each hotel brochure has a different layout (Figure 9.12). Rarely does one find two hotel rate sheets or tariffs that look exactly alike. This is quite unlike the airline industry whose tariffs have a standardized worldwide format to reduce the possibility of error in quoting and calculating fares. Note that hotel rates are often quoted in local currency. Some rates are "gross" (inclusive of an agency's commission) while others are "net" (no commission included). Some properties list double room rates as a total for the room while others quote them on a "half-twin" or "per person double occupancy" basis. Some tariffs list double rates as the

FIGURE 9.12
Hotels print their rack cards in a number of formats.

RATES
Valid from Dec. 15, 1989 through Dec. 14, 1990

AIR CONDITIONED ROOMS

Single	$ 55.00
Double	$ 65.00
Triple	$ 75.00
Suite	$ 90.00
Presidential Suite	$115.00

NON-AIRCONDITIONED ROOMS

Single	$45.00
Double	$55.00
Triple	$59.00

Children under 12 sharing room
with their parents complimentary.

*Rates do not include tax (13.3%)

Agency Commision 10%.
Service charge: $1.00 per person covering
baggage handling in/out.
$0.50 per person per day for chambermaids

MEAL PLAN NET PRICES

Continental Breakfast	$ 3.50
American Breakfast	$ 5.00
MAP	$16.00

*Meals do not include tax (20%)
Number of rooms: 350.
6 meeting rooms.
Convention Facilities: Accommodation from 20
to 1.000 persons.
Location: 2 miles from downtown San José.
Facilities: Shuttle bus to and from downtown
daily from 8:15 a.m. till 11:15 p.m. Two
lighten tennis courts, swimming pool, night club,
restaurant, cafeteria and casino (black jack only).
Rent-a-Car , Sauna, Beauty Parlor.
*Quoted in U.S. Dollars.

THE STAFFORD
DAILY ROOM RATES

Single Room with private bathroom	£135.65
Double Room (queen-size bed) with private bathroom	£147.83
Twin Room (2 beds) with private bathroom **Double Room** (king-size bed) with private bathroom	£165.22
Suite of Rooms sitting room, double or twin room and private bathroom	from £195.65

V.A.T. is added to the amount at the prevailing rate.

MEALS
(inclusive of 15% Service Charge and 15% V.A.T.)

Early Tea	£1.85
Breakfast, Continental	£6.75
Breakfast, English	£10.00
Lunch in restaurant	Table d'Hôte £20.00 and à la Carte
Dinner in restaurant	Table d'Hôte £25.50 and à la Carte

The terms quoted are subject to revision without notice.

THE STAFFORD HOTEL
St. James's Place
London SW1A 1NJ
Telephone: 01-493-0111 (10 lines)
Telex: 28602 Stafrd G
Cables: Staforotel London
Fax: 01-493-7121

A PRESTIGE HOTEL

CUNARD
HOTELS·RESORTS

total for two persons but define meal rates on a per person basis. Others show rates for individual bookings and groups on one sheet. Local taxes, Value Added Taxes (VAT) in Europe, and service charges are also listed. This confusing mixture of terms, rates and currencies tends to increase the possibility of error.

Deposits

Hotels usually require a deposit to ensure that the accommodation reserved will be held for the guest. Each company sets its own policy regarding deposits and the payment of a refund in the event of cancellation. Travel counsellors must ensure that both they and their clients are aware of these procedures. For example, to confirm bookings during the winter months, member properties of the Caribbean Hotel Association require that a deposit of three nights' accommodation be received by a specific date. Commercial or city hotels usually demand a deposit if the guest will arrive after 6:00 p.m. It is the agency's responsibility to collect the appropriate deposit and forward it to the hotel. Commission is not deducted from a deposit. Clients should be advised to inform the hotel of any delays or cancellations they encounter en route. Failure to follow this advice may result in the property considering the client to be a "no show". This conclusion permits the hotel to re-sell the room or to withhold refund of part or all of the deposit as a cancellation fee for revenue lost through the non-sale of the room. One way to avoid this problem is to quote a credit card number when making a booking. This ensures that the hotel will be paid. The hotel will then provide a "guaranteed reservation" which means that the room will be held until the client arrives.

Service Charges and Taxes

Many hotels apply service charges and taxes to the rack rate and, in some cases, to other items such as meals. Agency commission is never paid on either of these fees. Service charges represent gratuities to be paid to the hotel's staff and typically amount to between 10 and 15 percent of the hotel bill. This practice is common in Europe and in many other parts of the world. When service charges are added, the client is relieved of the necessity of tipping the hotel's personnel (except the concierge and porters). Government taxes must be considered when calculating the total cost of a client's hotel stay. In some countries, most notably in Europe, state taxes and town taxes may be added to the room rate in addition to a national tax. These taxes may apply only to the room cost or to both rooms and meals. Counsellors need to note whether the rates they quote include service charges and taxes or whether these items must be added to the published rates. Examples of both tariffs may be seen in this text. If the hotel does not apply service charges, it is the guest's responsibility to pay gratuities locally.

Food Service and Meal Plans

Most hotels and practically all resorts offer meal service. The cuisine prepared by the kitchen is often one of the highlights of a guest's stay at a hotel or resort. Some of the world's finest dining rooms are operated in conjunction with hotels, and clients should be made aware of the fare available at their destination. Most commercial hotels operate at least one dining room and a coffee shop. Those which do not have such facilities tend to be budget or no-frills properties. Commercial hotels do not as a rule include meals in their room rates. This is known as European Plan (EP). Ironically, European hotels are an exception to this rule and usually include a traditional continental breakfast in the room price. Most resorts include meals in their published rates and offer either American

Plan (three meals daily) or Modified American Plan (two meals daily). Resorts which include meal service are usually located far from large cities or cosmopolitan centres. For example, hotels in the Caribbean generally include meal service in the tariff. Regardless of whether a hotel bases its rates on the room or the number of occupants, meal prices are almost always published on a per person basis. Counsellors must therefore be alert to these differences when preparing budget recommendations or costing itineraries for clients. A description of the most commonly used terms and abbreviations for hotel meals plans is shown in Figure 9.13.

Booking Procedures

After recommending a suitable property, travel counsellors can then use one of several methods to make their client's reservation. They can contact the hotel's reservations department directly, most likely by using a toll-free telephone line. Many hotels and resorts have a Wide Area Telephone Service (WATS) line (an 800 number) and accept long distance calls for reservations without charge. All reference manuals publish these numbers to encourage and simplify booking procedures. Large hotel chains such as Hilton, Westin, Sheraton and Holiday Inn have computer systems which show space availability and can confirm

FIGURE 9.13
Hotel meal plans.

Hotel Meal Plans

À la carte.	A menu from which items are selected and paid for individually. Compare with table d'hôte.
American Plan: AP.	A hotel rate that includes accommodation plus three meals (breakfast, lunch and dinner) daily. This plan is often used by resort hotels where no alternative dining facilities may be available. Meals are normally table d'hôte. American Plan is sometimes known as Full Pension or Full Board in Europe.
Bermuda Plan: BP.	A hotel rate that includes accommodation and a full English or American type of breakfast. Bed and breakfast establishments usually offer the Bermuda Plan. It is common in Bermuda and in some other places.
Continental Breakfast.	A light breakfast consisting of a beverage (tea or coffee) served with bread, butter and jam. A North American version may offer coffee, juice and a pastry. It is most often offered by European hotels where the room rate frequently includes a European or continental type of breakfast.
Continental Plan: CP.	A hotel rate that includes accommodation and a continental breakfast.
European Plan: EP.	A hotel rate that includes sleeping accommodation only. There are no meals included. This plan is the most common rate quoted by North American hotels.
Modified American Plan: MAP.	A hotel rate that includes accommodation plus two meals. Typically, the meals are breakfast and one other meal (either dinner or lunch but not both). This plan is often used by resorts. it is also known as Demi-Pension, Half Board or Half-Pension in Europe.
Table d'Hôte.	A full course meal served at a fixed price with no alternative selections available on the menu.

[handwritten annotations: "no meals" under European Plan; "breakfast + dinner" under Modified American Plan; "sometimes there is a selection." below Table d'Hôte; "a-la-carte - order what you want"; "Quebec & France Table d'Hôte"]

bookings worldwide. Alternatively, counsellors can use the services of a hotel representative (who may be linked with a hotel's computer reservation system) and again they will probably use the telephone. A third option is to book the hotel room through an airline. Airline computer systems have reservations capability for many hotels and resorts. Counsellors can make both flight and hotel reservations by accessing the information directly through a computer or with one call to the airline. The procedure selected depends on the particular hotel and the ease of booking. Prior to making a reservation, counsellors generally observe the following procedure to learn whether the required space is available.

- Give the agency's name, its location and the counsellor's name. If booking through an airline CRS the agency's IATA number would also be supplied. Some hotels and representatives use the agency's IATA number as a reference while others provide the agency with its own identification number.
- State the destination and request the hotel by name. If the property is part of a chain or franchise also identify its location as there may be more than one hotel by that name in the city. Give the arrival date, the number of nights requested and the type of room desired.

The reservation agent will check availability, confirm the space and quote a room rate. The following booking information must then be accurately transmitted.

- State the client's full name and give the ages of any children in the party. This is important as rates for children vary depending on age. If there are special requests such as an oceanfront room, the ground floor or a rollaway bed, they are requested at this time. Meal plans should also be mentioned.
- The date, time and means of arrival are reported. If the guest will arrive by air, state the flight number so that the hotel will hold the accommodation if the

flight is delayed. A hotel's day almost universally begins at 6:00 a.m. local time. However, occupancy of reserved space cannot be guaranteed until the previous occupant has departed in accordance with the hotel's check-out time. Although check-out times vary, guests must usually vacate their rooms between 11:00 a.m. and 3:00 p.m. If a client is likely to arrive in the evening, a counsellor can request a "6:00 p.m. hold" or can ask the hotel to guarantee the room.

- Repeat the number of nights requested for the client and give the departure date. Confirm the type of accommodation desired, the deposit required and the option date. Verify the rate and the applicable taxes and service charges.
- Reiterate the agency information and identify the counsellor who is making the booking. Confirm the reservation agent's name and record the confirmation number on the client file.

Some hotels and representatives send the travel agency a written confirmation of the reservation while others supply these only on request. A confirmation voucher records all the details of the reservation and must include the confirmation number provided by the hotel as its reference number for the reservation. If a confirmation is received, check the information against that recorded on the client file. Counsellors should give their clients the voucher to present to the hotel on arrival. One copy of the voucher is always kept in the client file and another retained in an agency file for commission and accounting purposes. Travel agencies issue their own confirmation voucher if a hotel or its representative does not supply one. A copy of this voucher is given to the client to present to the hotel. Again, copies are kept for record-keeping.

Group Bookings

Group reservations, whether as part of a tour, a business meeting or a convention, can be a lucrative source of income for a travel agency. However, these bookings require meticulous attention to detail to ensure the needs of each group member are satisfied. Groups who travel together usually share a common interest other than the trip. For example, an insurance company might organize a meeting for its salespeople, lawyers might attend a legal convention, opera lovers might participate in a tour of the great opera houses of Europe, or business people might travel to Asia to seek investment opportunities. Group needs and requirements are often quite distinct from those of individual travellers.

Advance planning and careful costing are the keys to success in handling group business. Six to nine months' lead time is standard for a group reservation, although larger groups generally need one to three years' advance planning and booking. Too often, group bookings are carelessly costed, small items are overlooked and the accounting function becomes inaccurate. An inclusive, day-by-day record should be kept of all costs. This can be easily achieved by using a costing format similar to that described in Chapter 10. By following these procedures counsellors can ensure that the many details associated with group travel will be well managed and smoothly integrated.

Each property sets its own policies concerning group rates (Figure 9.14). Some hotels offer a discounted rate for parties of fifteen or more people travelling together who arrive and depart as a group. Others base the group rate on the number of rooms booked rather than on the number of people in the group. Group rates are generally quoted as net prices, a cost that does not include agency commission. It is the counsellor's responsibility to add an appropriate amount to cover expenses and to provide for a profit. Once the applicable room rate has been determined, the counsellor in consultation with the group leader establishes the other services needed during the group's stay. These costs are added to the room charges. For example,

groups typically request a welcome cocktail reception, special meals such as a farewell dinner or business luncheon, and porterage. Conventions and other large groups may want special meeting rooms, hospitality suites, banquets, movie projectors and other equipment, original entertainment and an "open bar" reception. These requirements are the subject of negotiation between the counsellor and the hotel. In addition to the cost for rooms and special requests, service charges and local taxes may apply. The total for all rooms, additional charges and taxes for group bookings is fully prepaid to the travel agency. Groups receive written confirmations and quotations for everything requested.

Group reservations must be made through a hotel's group sales department. All hotels require a rooming list which indicates the group member's names, passport numbers and rooming arrangements. Counsellors should send the hotel a rooming list with the written booking. If this is not possible, the rooming list should be forwarded at least two weeks before the group's arrival date. The hotel should also be advised of the type of group (business meeting, convention, social organization) and any special requests (hospitality suite, meeting room, equipment). Travel counsellors arranging group reservations will most likely deal with the Sales Manager, the Director of Sales or the Catering Manager. These individuals will verify the availability of the requested rooms, confirm the reservations, arrange special meals and services, and establish the deposit and final payment requirements. Final payment for the services requested is a matter of individual hotel policy. Most hotels require full payment in advance of a group's arrival. Actual room reservations are made with the Front Office Manager or assistant who should also receive the rooming list. Convention hotels such as the Royal York, the Sheraton Centre, and the Westin Harbour Castle in Toronto, have a Conventions Manager who handles all arrangements for larger groups.

FIGURE 9.14
Each property sets its own group rate policy.

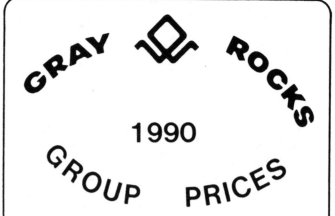

GRAY ROCKS

1990

GROUP PRICES

85$
per person, per night, double occupancy

115$
per person, per night, single occupancy

Rates are applicable to any type of accommodation
within the Inn and/or Le Château

From April 15th
to May 18th, 1990

From October 8th
to November 21st, 1990

Including:
- 1 complimentary per 25 persons
- 3 meals from our regular Table d'Hôte menu
- 2 coffee breaks
- Use of meeting rooms/audio-visual aids
- Free transportation on Hotel property
- Access to Le Spa (indoor pool, whirlpools, sauna, fitness equipment)
- Tax and service charges

Reserve now:

Jocelyne Levert

ou

Karim Mouldi
Group-Sales Managers

NOTE TO TRAVEL AGENTS:
THE ABOVE RATES ARE NET

Saint-Jovite	(819) 425-2771
Montreal	(514) 861-0187
Fax	(819) 425-3006

Before committing either themselves or their prospective clients, counsellors will wish to make certain that the property under consideration meets the group's expectations for quality, service and location. This is especially important in cases where neither the travel counsellor nor the group organizer have personal experience of the hotel. In such instances, a personal inspection of the hotel and its facilities is strongly recommended. Counsellors can use a variation of the checklist described earlier to assess the property. A modest investment of time and travel expenses will help assure the group's satisfaction. Future business from the group, or from other clients purchasing the same tour itinerary, may depend on this research. Most hotel Sales Managers, when made aware of the size and scope of the potential group booking, readily approve a two or three day visit to the property either as its guest or at a substantial trade discount.

Checking In and Checking Out

Travel counsellors concerned with their clients' comfort will attempt to plan itineraries so that check-in and check-out arrangements are convenient. A client's arrival should be timed to coincide with the hotel's regular check-out time. This is especially important where clients have made a long air journey and will wish to rest or sleep as soon as possible after arrival at the destination. For example, most eastbound transatlantic flights from North America to Europe are overnight. They arrive at a morning hour which is generally much earlier than the check-out times of most hotels. Clients who are already tired will therefore be forced to wait in the hotel's lobby until a room is ready. Many hotels ensure that rooms are free for transatlantic arrivals but counsellors must ascertain this before advising their clients. The only way to assure immediate access to a room is to reserve the accommodation for the

evening prior to actual arrival. Although the clients must then pay for an extra night without occupying the room, many will accept this arrangement when the extra convenience and comfort are pointed out.

Check-out times also affect clients. Rooms must be vacated in sufficient time to prepare them for newly arriving guests. A thoughtful travel counsellor will try to plan departure arrangements that coincide with the hotel's check-out time. For example, if the check-out time is 3:00 p.m., a flight departing at 5:00 p.m. will be more convenient than one leaving at 10:30 p.m. Alternatively, a client may prefer to leave earlier and board a 2:00 p.m. flight instead of waiting for the 5:00 p.m. departure. Counsellors should remind their clients that check-out time refers specifically to the time by which a room must be vacated and the account settled. It does not oblige guests to leave the hotel premises. If a hotel's check-out time is 11:00 a.m. but the guests' departing flight is not until 6:00 p.m., they can leave their bags with the porter and use the hotel's facilities such as the bar, lounges, dining room, coffee shop or swimming pool. Hotels that are not fully booked will sometimes at no extra charge extend a guest's check-out time for two hours provided that the room has not been rented for that day. The client, however, must request this late check-out privilege on the morning of departure. Counsellors who are dealing with a group booking can suggest that the group retain one room where baggage can be stored for the day or until departure time. Alternatively, a late check-out can be arranged for a portion of the rate. Hotels and resorts usually require that their guests observe the posted check-out times, especially during peak periods. Failure to do so may mean that the guest is billed for a further day or half-day.

Commission Arrangements

In common retail practice, the travel agency collects the full cost of a client's hotel stay, including local taxes, service charges and meals. This amount less commission is forwarded to the hotel. If a client chooses to prepay a deposit only, rather than the cost of the entire stay, the agency will forward this amount to the hotel. The hotel then calculates the commission due only after the client has paid and departed. Many hotels mail a commission cheque to the travel agency shortly after its clients leave the hotel. Others issue commission cheques once or twice monthly. Commission is earned only on the sale of rooms and meals. It is never paid on taxes or service charges. Prepayment of hotel bills benefits both the client and the agency. For the client, a sizeable (and often the largest) part of the trip cost has been prepaid. This reduces the need to budget while on vacation. The only additional costs will be for the incidentals purchased, such as the bar bill, room service, telephone calls and laundry. Prepayment also reduces accounts receivables and extra record keeping for the travel agency.

Commission from hotel and resort bookings can provide a sizeable and steady income for travel agencies. The standard rate of commission is ten percent of the room rate, however, many European hotels pay only 8 1/2 percent or less. Meal plans such as AP or MAP are also commissionable, usually at ten per-cent. Hotels in some resort areas, Florida for example, occasionally pay 12 to 15 percent as an off-season inducement, or offer the higher rate as an override when a certain number of bookings has been reached. Generally, prices for groups are quoted on a net basis although some hotels pay a five percent commission on groups and conventions.

A travel agency will occasionally not receive its commission payment from a hotel. Such occurrences underline the importance of careful record-keeping and auditing of each booking. As discussed, a copy of the confirmation voucher or reservation coupon which is given to the client as proof of the reservation is the most accurate way of monitoring commissions due. Non-payment of commission is most commonly caused by oversight or carelessness on the part of the hotel's accounting department. Sometimes non-payment occurs when a property changes ownership and the new owner is unwilling to assume the liabilities or obligations of the former owner. Occasionally, when dealing with hotels in Europe, South America or Asia, prevailing currency regulations may make it unlawful to export currency, particularly dollars. These restrictions prevent hotels from mailing travel agencies their commissions. As an alternative, most hotels will send the agency a credit note for the equivalent value of the commission due. This credit can then be applied as a deposit on future bookings. There are also a few properties that do not honour their trade obligations to travel agencies and make no commission payments whatever. This is a grievance which disturbs the agency community. There is little hope of redress for there is no government body or trade organization in the hospitality industry which regulates, codifies and adjudicates relationships between travel agencies and hotels. IATA acts as a regulatory body which manages relations between member airlines and appointed travel agencies by means of Sales Agency Contracts. No similar formal agreements or certificates of appointment are required for travel agencies to do business with hotels or resorts. An agency's only recourse for non-payment of commission is to learn from the experience and to inform colleagues of the particular hotel's policy.

The Hotel Clearing Corporation (HCC), a clearinghouse for the collection and payment of hotel commissions, was formed in 1992 to help ensure that agencies receive their hotel commissions. Every month the HCC issues each member travel agency with a cheque to cover all commssions due from participating hotels. Agencies also receive a monthly management report which analyzes their hotel sales. In return, agencies pay a membership fee plus a percentage of their annual commissions to the HCC.

Business Relations

Relations between travel agencies and the hospitality sector range from warm, cordial and cooperative to cold, bitter and even hostile. Travel agents accuse some properties of overbooking, failure to provide promised reservations, dirty rooms and non-payment of commissions. Hotel managers on the other hand fault travel agencies for failing to observe even the simplest regulations and procedures meant to facilitate business and ensure a guest's welfare. The income potential from hotel and resort bookings is considerable. It is foolish for either party to jeopardize what should be a good business relationship by careless practice or unprofessional conduct.

The fact that no rules govern business practices between agencies and hotels makes it both easy and difficult for a travel counsellor to book accommodation. Easy, because there are no regulations which must be obeyed and no penalties imposed; difficult, because there is a danger of making unilateral decisions and following practices which might damage good business relations and which might be detrimental to the comfort and pleasure of clients. Counsellors can do much to further genuinely good business relations by complying with the following easily understood guidelines. At the same time they will assure that their clients' needs and interests are considered.

- Adhere to deposit specifications as laid down by the hotel.
- Observe option dates for accommodation.
- Release unsold or unwanted accommodation promptly so that the hotel may resell it.
- Communicate the client's requests clearly and accurately to the hotel.

- Describe the accommodation reserved factually for the client.
- Provide the hotel with rooming lists for group bookings when required. Specify last minute additions in writing at least 48 hours in advance. (At such short notice, changes would usually by transmitted by fax.)
- Make final payments as specified in the agreement, or upon receipt of billing from the hotel. Settle all accounts without delay.
- Follow hotel check-in and check-out times. Notify the hotel of changes.

Timesharing

Timesharing (or interval ownership) is a relatively recent phenomenon in the accommodation sector. The concept for resort timesharing is reputed to have originated in France during the 1960s. A hotelier having trouble with cash flow and seasonal occupancy noted that many guests were repeat customers who usually returned at the same time each year. The owner offered these clients the opportunity to "buy" their rooms for that specified time; for a fixed price paid in advance, they could own their accommodation for a given number of weeks per year for the rest of their lives. The idea was successful and the industry developed from that point. Resort timesharing reached the USA in the early 1970s and after a slow start hit its stride around 1978. The industry in the USA currently exceeds $4 billion and continues to grow.

Perhaps the easiest explanation is to view timesharing as a way for individuals to prepay at today's prices their future hotel accommodation for many years to come. By permitting buyers to own or have occupancy rights at a resort for a portion of the price of the entire unit, timeshare offers purchasers a hedge against inflation. Timeshare has been implemented in hotels, motels, condominiums, residential homes, campgrounds and even boats and yachts. There are two basic categories of timeshare, ownership and non-ownership (or right to use), although a number of variations exist.

Timeshare Options

- **Fee Simple**. A purchaser buys a particular unit for specific dates and receives title (or deed) for that period. Ownership is for life. Purchasers can use the accommodation, lend it, rent it or leave it to their children.
- **Right to Use**. A buyer acquires a specific unit for certain dates for a predetermined number of years. In effect, the purchaser leases the unit(s) for that period of time. During that time purchasers are entitled to use the accommodation, lend it, rent it or sell the number of years remaining on the lease. At the end of the agreed time, the unit reverts to the original owner (i.e., to the resort). This is a cost-effective arrangement. For example, a one bedroom apartment with a one-time price of $6,000 for a 40 year right to use agreement, costs on average $150 per week. Thus accommodation at a luxury resort for a unit that can sleep four costs only $37.50 per person per week.

Within these two categories are further variables.

- **Floating Time**. Purchasers are entitled to accommodation during a specific season. They can reserve any time in that season provided that space is available.
- **Split Week**. Purchasers may divide their access period. For example, if they buy a week they may use three days at a certain time and the remaining four days on another occasion. A resort must offer floating time for this option to be available. Split weeks are becoming quite common at urban resorts in larger cities like New Orleans and San Francisco. They are also offered at some vacation resorts during low season.

As the timeshare industry becomes

more sophisticated, further choice can be expected.

Consider one unit in a resort hotel which can be purchased in multiples of one week. Most resorts offer that unit for sale for 50 weeks of the year. (Two weeks are put aside for general maintenance, usually one week in the spring and one in the fall.) The 50 weeks are divided into seasons: high season is the most popular time and has the largest demand; low season is the least desirable time; and shoulder (or swing) season lies somewhere in between. High season accommodation is the most expensive, shoulder season costs less, and low season rates are the least expensive. Seasons vary according to the nature of the resort. For example, late January through the middle of March is usually high season at a ski resort, whereas April is often called a "mud" month and is generally low season. Sun destinations like Florida, the Caribbean and Mexico have a similar seasonal pattern.

Now consider a couple that vacations in Florida for two weeks each February. Instead of making reservations at ever-increasing rates each year, they might decide to buy the last two weeks in February at a timeshare resort. They will pay a one-time fixed price which allows them use of the property for those two weeks every year, possibly for the rest of their lives. Once they have paid the initial charge, they pay only an annual maintenance fee. This fee can be compared to the service charges and taxes payable at hotels. It covers such items as insurance, repairs, property maintenance, management of the facility, and replacement of furniture, appliances and equipment as they wear out (but usually at least every 5 years).

Timeshare owners are under no obligation to use the accommodation so they have substantial flexibility. For example, if the couple decides not to travel to Florida one year they have several options. Since they have paid for the right to use those weeks, they could let friends stay at the property. They could also rent the two weeks to someone else, either on their own or with the help of the resort. A third alternative is that they could exchange their weeks. Timeshare buyers who wish to swap accommodation can call an exchange network. (Most timeshare resorts belong to an exchange network.) The two largest are RCI (Resort Condominiums International) and II (Interval International), each with over 1,000 member resorts around the world. Exchange companies are not resort developers or management companies. They are accommodation reservation firms that help timeshare owners exchange their timeshare accommodation for a timeshare somewhere else. Each resort pays an initial membership fee to join an exchange network and have the property listed. Individual timeshare owners are generally charged an annual membership fee and must pay the network company each time an exchange is made. They are sometimes charged an initial membership fee. An exchange network is similar to a bank in its operation. Timeshare owners deposit their accommodation into the exchange network and in return are entitled to withdraw an equivalent at some other resort. The exchanges do not necessarily occur on a one-to-one basis. That is, an owner of a unit in Florida who desires a vacation in Las Vegas does not always find someone in Las Vegas who wishes an exchange to Florida. It may be that the owner of the Las Vegas unit wants an exchange in Canada, while someone in Canada wants to visit Hawaii, a purchaser in Hawaii seeks accommodation in England, and someone in England wishes to holiday in Florida. Exchange companies have sophisticated computers to match such requests. Owners can exchange time periods as well as destinations. There are, however, certain considerations relating to equivalent value, flexibility and demand. The owner of a low season week at one resort cannot request a high season or shoulder week at another resort. The reverse, however, is permitted; someone who owns a high week can request a shoulder or low week at another resort. In general, exchanges occur between like

seasons. Similarly, the accommodation must be comparable. Someone who owns a studio or efficiency unit at one resort cannot request a two bedroom unit at another resort. The reverse is again permitted; the owner of a two bedroom unit can request a one bedroom or studio unit at another resort. The more flexible owners are in their requests, the more likely that an exchange will be confirmed. An individual who insists on the first two weeks of March in Acapulco will have more difficulty than someone requesting any two weeks in February or March anywhere in Mexico. More popular resorts and time periods are easier to exchange.

When someone buys a unit at a timeshare resort, the accommodation is usually deluxe and there are always many amenities and facilities available. Unit prices vary according to their size and quality. Timeshare units are always fully furnished and have equipment and supplies for a specific number of people. For example, a studio sleeps two people and will therefore be equipped with table settings, glasses, cutlery, pots, pans, towels and other necessities for at least two. Similarly, a one bedroom unit typically sleeps four, so it will be outfitted for at least that number. Timeshare units also have a fridge and stove and there will frequently be a washer and dryer and perhaps a dishwasher. The accessories considerably exceed those provided in a standard hotel room. The extent of the facilities available depends on the type of resort and its location, but they are always extensive and varied.

Some travel counsellors feel threatened by the timeshare industry and prefer to ignore it, probably hoping that by doing so it will disappear. This is unlikely to happen in such a large and growing industry. Travel counsellors must therefore find ways to take advantage of this business. Most timeshare resorts pay at least a referral fee to travel counsellors who send clients who ultimately buy a unit.

Consider the following figures. A hotel room at $80 per night for seven nights costs $560. If the hotel pays ten percent commission, a counsellor will earn $56 from a booking (and perhaps the client will book through the agency again). However, if one assumes that an average timeshare unit costs $6,000 (they vary from $2,500 to over $20,000) and that the company pays a five percent referral fee, counsellors will earn $300 from the sale. (If a client buys more than one week, the referral fee is paid on the total amount.) The resort will advise the agency of the dates purchased. This information is an ongoing sales lead. Each year the agency can contact the client in plenty of time to offer the best available airfare to the destination. When the client is ready to start exchanging to other resorts and to travel further afield, the counsellor can continue to provide service. Such travel arrangements are not limited to air fare but also include car rental, sightseeing trips and insurance. Research indicates that timeshare owners are prepared to spend more money, to travel further, and to see and do more since they need not worry about accommodation costs. Involvement in this type of business means that travel counsellors must be more organized and do more follow-up, however, the potential income from a timeshare owner is considerable. Since the timeshare industry is here to stay, counsellors should learn all they can about this new partner in the travel and tourism industry.

Review Questions

1. Discuss the development of and current issues in the accommodation sector.

2. Describe the various categories of accommodation.

3. Why is it important for travel counsellors to develop a personal method for evaluating hotel and resort properties? What should be included in such an assessment?

4. Why does friction sometimes exist between hoteliers and travel agencies?

5. Describe the forms of timeshare available.

References

ABC Star Service Reports, ABC International, 131 Clarendon Street, Boston, MA 02116, USA.

Consolidated Tour Manual (CTM), 11510 NE 2nd Avenue, Miami, FL 33161, USA.

Hotel and Travel Index, 500 Plaza Drive, Secaucus, NJ 07096, USA.

National Timesharing Council, 1000 16th Street NW, Washington, DC 20036, USA.

OAG Travel Planner Hotel and Motel RedBook. Official Airline Guides, 2000 Clearwater Drive, Oakbrook, IL 60521, USA.

Official Hotel Guide (OHG). 500 Plaza Drive, Secaucus, NJ 07096, USA.

WATA Master-Key, World Association of Travel Agencies, 37 quai Wilson, 1211 Geneva 1, Switzerland.

World Tourism Organization, Capitan Haya 42, 28020 Madrid, Spain.

## Chapter 10

Tours

Chapter Summary

This chapter describes how the skills counsellors develop in each segment of the travel industry can be applied to create the most common vacation arrangement, a tour. Tour terminology, components and categories are described. The two main types of tours, FITs and ITCs, and the two main types of tour companies, wholesalers and tour operators, are examined in detail. In each area, relevant references, costing procedures, advantages and disadvantages are studied. Tour development and the evaluation of tour products are also reviewed.

Chapter Objectives
After completing this chapter you should be able to:

- Provide a brief history of tour development.

- Define and correctly use tour terminology.

- Describe various categories and types of tours.

- Identify the key sales features of various tours.

- Distinguish between tour operators and tour wholesalers.

- Describe a tour escort's functions and responsibilities.

- Distinguish between inbound and outbound tour operators.

- Describe how tour operators research, plan, cost, and promote tour packages.

- Discuss negotiations between tour operators and their suppliers.

- Describe the relationship between contracts, negotiations and brochure development.

- Discuss and interpret confidential tariffs.

- Plan and cost independent, group and package tours.

- Interpret tour brochures.

- Evaluate tour products using a checklist.

- Book tours for clients.

- Describe the use of tour orders and vouchers.

- Discuss the advantages and disadvantages of various types of tours.

Tours

This text has thus far examined the client and the various segments of the travel industry. Each element has been discussed somewhat in isolation. Although many clients call on a travel agency to simply buy a plane ticket or book a hotel room, most order more than one service to complete their desired travel arrangements. The standard arrangement is a complete tour.

Tours have been defined as:

The services on a tourist's itinerary, usually consisting of but not limited to, transportation, accommodation, transfers and sightseeing in one or more countries, geographical regions or cities. The services are entirely reserved or contracted for in advance by a travel agent, a tour wholesaler or a tour operator and are fully prepaid by the tourist.

Tours follow a prearranged itinerary and can be planned and operated either for independent travellers or for groups. They may be as simple as three nights' hotel accommodation and round trip transfers between the airport and hotel, or they can be as thorough as a multi-country extended itinerary. Tours can be designed around one mode of transportation, such as a motorcoach, or they can use several forms of transport. Air/sea tours are an example of an intermodal tour which combines air transportation, cruise passage and coach transfers between the airport and pier.

Previous chapters investigated how travel counsellors can research and book the individual travel components that comprise a tour. This was the only method of creating a tour in the early years of the travel industry until the 1960s. This arrangement was known as an independent tour. More accurately, there were two types of independent tours; FIT (foreign independent tour) and DIT (domestic independent tour). Today, however, many industry personnel make no distinction between foreign and domestic independent tours; they describe all such tours as FITs, that is, fully independent tours. Counsellors will encounter both meanings for these terms.

The selling, handling and marketing of tours has become a major industry within the larger structure of tourism. Tour transactions annually contribute millions of dollars to retail and wholesale travel businesses, airlines, hotels and resorts. Sales and marketing strategies for most major airlines, many hotels and numerous resorts are built on the public's unqualified acceptance of tours. Tour sales are often the largest single source of income and profit for a retail travel agency. Travel counsellors must therefore become thoroughly acquainted with as many current tour products as possible. They must learn to assess the companies which design and operate tours, as well as the products they create. Some agencies may sell preferred suppliers or have other policies regarding which products are sold. Some agencies and wholesalers specialize in specific destination areas or in types of travel, for example, seniors citizens or adventure travel. However, such policies do not relieve counsellors from their responsibility for product knowledge. They must become familiar with this merchandise to successfully sell it to the public.

Employees of the wholesale travel companies that construct tours from the various components require similar abilities. For them, painstaking research and meticulous attention to detail are essential. These are necessary to properly integrate and coordinate the tour elements. Tour marketing demands a thorough knowledge of local and world conditions, particularly if tour programs are conducted on a large scale.

Types of Tours

Readers need only glance at the racks of brochures and folders displayed in any travel agency or airline ticket office to realize that tours are available in a bewildering profusion of numbers, variety and content (Figure 10.1). Tours can be simple, for example, a weekend trip to Montreal including air fare, hotel accommodation and a visit to a nightclub. Or they can be as complex as a round-the-world itinerary involving travel and sightseeing programs in thirty countries, accommodation at a different hotel for each of perhaps sixty nights, entertainment, meals, and transportation by land, sea and air. Tours may be prepackaged and widely advertised in a brochure, as are many group tours. Alternatively, they may be tailored to an individual client's tastes and wishes as an FIT.

Tours have two major classifications, each of which overlaps. They can be categorized as individual or group tours, or they can be described in terms of independent and packaged tours. Individuals can choose to travel independently or they can purchase prepackaged tour arrangements. Similarly, groups can decide to travel unaccompanied (independent group

FIGURE 10.1
Tours can be designed to appeal to almost any interest.

tours) or attended by a guide or leader (escorted group tours). In general, independent tours are assembled by travel counsellors, sometimes assisted by a wholesale travel company. Group tours, on the other hand, are constructed almost exclusively by tour operators. Within these basic types, tours can be further classified in a number of overlapping categories. For example, the following description identifies eight tour classifications. However, this number could easily be increased or reduced according to the particular definitions applied.

The Tour Components

The variety of travel products available means that the choice of tour components is virtually limitless. Some popular types of tours classified in this manner are fly/drive tours, fly/cruise tours, land-only tours consisting of accommodation and meals, all-inclusive tours, special events tours such as those associated with the Olympic Games, special interest tours such as historical tours, and escorted tours.

The Target Market

Incentive groups, conventions and meetings, clubs and associations, families, and special interest groups are just some of the many markets targeted by tour designers.

The Tour Length and Timing

Many tours are planned for a specific duration to fit standard vacation patterns, such as one or two weeks. Others are based on a shorter period, such as a weekend. The fastest growing segment is for 4-day mini-vacations. Many tours are designed around particular seasons or events such as Christmas, Labour Day, and pre- and post-convention tours. Some tours are offered only in a particular season while others are designed to attract tourists during off-peak times.

The Tour Destination or Arrangements

Many tours are planned around specific destinations. Others are based on particular arrangements such as independent tours, group tours or charter tours.

The Tour Purpose

Tours are designed to meet particular client interests or needs and as such are as varied as those interests. Chapter 3 reviewed some reasons why people travel. Tour planners develop tours intended to meet those needs. Some of the interests for which such tours are planned are:

- **Relaxation**: Holiday tours or stay-put holidays are designed with little sightseeing or activity other than simply lying on a beach, relaxing, and eating good food.
- **Scenery**: Some of the most popular tours are those to view fall foliage in North America, the mountains of the European Alps, or the spectacular Grand Canyon.
- **Education and Learning**: Historical and cultural activities, such as music and art tours, are among the many tours planned to meet tourists' needs for intellectual stimulation. The Edinburgh Festival in August, or the Mozart Festival held in Salzburg every June are typical examples. Other tours are more personal such as those designed to explore one's ethnic roots.
- **Religion**: Religious tours (or pilgrimages) have been a basic reason for travel almost since the beginning of time. Tours to the Holy Land for Christians during Christmas and Easter, and for Jews during High Holy Days, remain popular. Others attend the Catholic shrines of Europe such as Fatima and Lourdes, some visit Rome during the Holy Year held every 25 years, and many travel to the Passion Plays held in Oberammergau, Germany every ten years.
- **Adventure**: As tastes change and lifestyles become more active, tours are introduced to appeal to the traveller's sense of adventure. Typical examples are trekking in Nepal, jungle safaris to Borneo, and river rafting in the Grand Canyon.

- **Sports and Recreation**: These tours identify with favourite traveller activities, either as a participant or a spectator. For example, tours are available to Switzerland, Western Canada and Colorado for skiing, to Florida, Scotland and Bermuda for golf, Nassau for tennis, to the Bahamas and Cayman Islands for scuba diving, and to Mexico, the Bahamas and Florida for deep sea fishing. Spectators can travel to the Kentucky Derby, the Indy 500 race, the Rose Bowl Football game, the Olympic Games, the Commonwealth Games, and the World Cup Soccer Tournament.
- **Special Interests**: Tours for specialized purposes can be constructed and marketed to appeal to almost every taste and desire. Students can make exchange visits, farmers can take agricultural study tours, camera fans can go on East African photographic safaris, naturalists can cruise the Galapagos Islands or view whales off Baja California, and wine lovers can visit vineyards in France. Special interest tours are limited only by one's imagination.

Special Needs Tours

As the tour market has grown, an increasing number of market niches have developed. Tours designed for tourists with special needs, such as travellers with disabilities or senior citizens, is a growing segment.

Incentive Tours

These are specialized tours which are generally created for employees of medium to large corporations. Incentive tours attempt to foster increased sales or productivity by offering travel as a reward for achieving a company's goals. Depending on the company's objectives, incentive programs can also be devised to produce benefits such as reduced absenteeism or a lower accident rate. The incentive tour market is one of the tour industry's fastest growing sectors.

General Interest Tours

Within this extremely broad classification are those tours which are assembled and marketed for their wide appeal. These are usually directed to first-time visitors to a destination. Examples of such products are the London Show Tours, Rhine Cruises, Capitals of Europe Tours, and California Tours.

General Advantages of Tours

Tours represent a major source of income for most Canadian travel agencies. Each type of tour has its own merit and within each category are found a variety of tours from which clients may choose. Travellers faced with this choice can be helped with advice and guidance from a travel counsellor. Although individual tours have considerable differences, two key sales features are common to all; convenience and prepayment.

Convenience

All essential elements in a holiday are prearranged. Reservations for hotels and other services are confirmed in advance, as are arrangements for baggage handling, transfers and sightseeing. Clients need not waste time waiting for transportation at airports and hotels, and visits to points of interest are assured.

Prepayment

The prepaid nature of tours offers convenience for clients, travel agencies and suppliers. It is easier for clients to accurately budget for their trip. They need not worry about buying foreign currencies to pay for their vacation, and there is less likelihood that they will run out of money while away from home.

In addition to convenience and prepayment, prepackaged tours for groups offer some further benefits to both travellers and travel agencies:

- **Companionship**. Tours, particularly group tours, allow clients to meet and travel with people of similar tastes and interests.

- **Economy**. Special rates often apply which may make these tours more economical for travellers.
- **Convenience and Time Saving**. After clients select a tour, reservations are easily confirmed by a single contact with the tour company or the airline's tour department. Counsellors are relieved of the need to separately request each component desired. This also eliminates the laborious job of arranging individual deposit payments and final settlements for each item on the itinerary.
- **Higher Commissions**. Package tours earn a standard rate of ten percent commission and many tour companies offer a scale of incentive payments reaching 17 percent for increased sales volumes. One commission is paid on all tour components, with the exception of taxes and service charges. Since the price of a package tour includes items such as meals and activities which independent travellers do not generally purchase from a travel agency, the dollar value and therefore the commission earned is frequently higher.

No matter which type of tour is chosen, there is a basic distinction between independent tours and those designed for groups. Each has particular benefits and drawbacks, and each must be researched and arranged by travel counsellors in a different manner. The remainder of this chapter examines these differences.

Tour Wholesalers and Tour Operators

The tour industry is among the simplest and, at the same time, among the most complex sectors of the travel industry. It is simple because tours are a product which both consumers and travel counsellors understand. Most people can name several large tour companies and perhaps even list some of their products. It is complex because much of the terminology is used interchangeably and tours involve many different types of arrangements with various suppliers. The use of the term "independent" to describe a type of individual tour and a type of group tour is just one example. The terms "tour wholesaler" and "tour operator" are similarly confused in the travel industry. The following discussion attempts to distinguish between them.

Both tour wholesalers and tour operators offer services on a wholesale basis to travel agencies. In theory, neither deals directly with the public. Traditionally, tour wholesalers were representatives (or brokers) for other travel suppliers such as hotels. They acted as middlemen between suppliers and travel agencies. Thus tour wholesalers did not purchase tour components until they received a request from a travel counsellor to do so on behalf of a client. Tour wholesalers still fulfill this role when travel counsellors seek their assistance to construct independent tours.

Tour operators emerged in the late 1960s as a result of changing conditions. In contrast to wholesalers, tour operators took the tour development process one stage further. They actually purchased tour components in advance, combined them into a single entity (a tour package), and sold the package to consumers through retail travel agencies. Since tour operators had already committed to pay for the tour components, they were at risk if the public failed to purchase their products.

At one time these distinctions were clear. Today, however, the functions overlap. There are tour wholesalers who package tours and thus are technically tour operators. Moreover, there are tour operators who represent other suppliers, particularly cruise lines and motorcoach companies, and so act as wholesalers. Travel wholesalers and tour operators are therefore evolving into a single form. Some tour operators retail their products direct to the public, bypassing the retail travel agency. To further complicate matters, some retail travel agencies act as wholesalers by creating and selling tours. The differences have become blurred and the terms tour wholesaler and tour operator are often used interchangeably. To clarify the discussion, this text retains the original distinction between tour wholesalers and tour operators. The term wholesaler is used when discussing independent tours planned by travel counsellors while tour operator is used in relation to prepackaged tours.

The major difference between tour wholesalers and tour operators is **financial risk**. This difference has influenced how each tends to approach marketing. Generally, tour wholesalers advertise to the travel trade; they try to convince travel agents to sell the products they represent. Tour operators, on the other hand, usually direct their promotions to consumers; they attempt to persuade travellers to buy their packages through travel agencies. The former focuses on industry sales while the latter concentrates on consumer purchasing.

Independent Tours: The Original Tour

This discussion begins with independent tours not because they comprise the largest portion of the tour industry or are the most popular but simply because historically, independent tours preceded prepackaged tour groups. Though the market for package tours is a large and steady one, some travellers feel that travelling on a group basis restricts their individual mobility. Independent tours offer such travellers the flexibility and freedom of movement they seek. Independent tours are typically referred to in the trade as FITs, although the term DIT is still occasionally used to distinguish domestic from foreign travel.

For the most part, independent tours are arranged by travel counsellors, although at times they are planned by wholesalers. Independent tours should not be confused with independent travellers, who make their own arrangements for each part of their itinerary. For example, independent travellers may purchase airline tickets directly from an airline and may (or not) make other arrangements before travelling to a destination. At the destination, they arrange accommodation and other services as necessary throughout their journey. Thus they make no use of the professional coordinating services which a travel counsellor can provide. By contrast, independent tours are arranged in advance by travel counsellors or tour wholesalers to meet the specific tastes and requirements of their clients. In most travel agencies, senior personnel are responsible for planning and costing independent tours. Junior counsellors should, however, understand the procedures involved and should be able to cost a simple FIT. No matter whether a counsellor personally constructs and costs an independent tour or uses the services of a wholesaler for this purpose, the references and procedures are similar. The references relating to transportation, accommodation, and other travel services have been examined earlier and thus will not generally be discussed here.

At one time, independent tours were considerably more expensive than prepackaged vacations but deregulation has promoted lower cost scheduled air fares and has reduced the limitations on their use. The result is that many independent itineraries are now competitive with tours arranged by tour companies. However, it is essential that calculations be verified to ensure quotes are correct. Although independent tours take longer to arrange and require greater expertise, separate commissions are earned from each tour component booked. In addition, if a counsellor constructs an independent tour by combining an air fare with an approved package of land arrangements, the commission on the sale of the airline ticket is higher than if only the air transportation had been sold.

The simplest type of independent tour to organize is one which combines transportation with an available package of land-based tour arrangements (Figure 10.2). For example, an inexpensive charter or excursion air fare may be combined with a land package available at the destination. Some travellers, however, do not wish to be confined to a fixed timetable or itinerary. A combination of hotels, car rentals and perhaps rail passes, however, would allow them to organize their own time. Depending on the destination, duration and client's interests, a counsellor may be able to assemble a tour from a range of inexpensive options or may have little choice but to select regular air fares and full price accommodation. To successfully create independent tours, counsellors must therefore be able to construct and cost itineraries based on the supplier references discussed in earlier chapters. Such independent tours challenge counsellors to apply and combine their skills in different segments of the industry. By so doing, they create another travel product, a tour.

Independent Air Tours

The simplest type of independent tour was described as one which combines transportation with an existing package of land arrangements. Both IATA and the ATA support this type of tour, and at the same time encourage air travel, by approving tours which meet certain criteria. Passengers booking such approved tours are eligible to purchase a promotional air fare which is sold only in conjunction with these tours. These air fares are known as IT (inclusive tour) fares. Individuals who purchase approved tours are eligible to buy IIT (individual inclusive tour) fares, while those travelling in groups are eligible for GIT (group inclusive tour) fares. As discussed in Chapter 6, groups also have access to other tour basing fares.

IATA airlines offer a number of IIT fares in connection with IATA approved tours. For destinations in the Pacific area, the Caribbean, the Bahamas and Bermuda, these fares have a lower price than 21-day excursion fares. Similarly, ATA carriers follow the principle of offering special, lower than regular or

excursion fares to those passengers travelling on holidays and purchasing approved tour arrangements. Thus there are IIT fares between many points within Canada, and between many points in Canada and the USA including Hawaii. Counsellors must examine and follow the rules and regulations applicable to promotional IT fares to ensure that prospective clients can in fact travel at the cheaper rate.

Requirements for IATA Approval

IATA designates an inclusive tour as a prearranged round or circle trip journey which includes a combination of air travel and land arrangements (other than those solely public transportation) which is designed to encourage air travel. In addition, the association defines an inclusive tour fare as a fare specifically established for the use of inclusive tours and which conforms to certain minimum standards specified in Standard Condition C of the Air Tariff. To earn IATA's approval, and thus be eligible to use an IT fare, an inclusive tour must therefore meet or exceed the criteria set out in Standard Condition C. These requirements generally consist of:

---

17 Romantic Germany
7 Days (tour code: 6TT1A)

including the OBERAMMERGAU PASSION PLAY
Frankfurt to Frankfurt
Sundays, May 27 to September 16
Highlights:
Frankfurt – Rüdesheim – Rhine river cruise – Heidelberg (1 N) – Baden-Baden – Black Forest – Lindau (1 N) – Lake Constance – Neuschwanstein castle – Oberammergau or area (2 N) – Oberammergau Passion Play – Munich (1 N) – Romantic Road – Rothenburg (1 N) – Frankfurt

Rates in Canadian Dollars per Person		
Twin	$1427	Start: 09:00h - 09:30h End: 18:00h
Single	1637	

"Oktoberfest" supplement for departure Sep 16: add $120

Meals Included: 6 breakfasts & 6 dinners, wine sampling party
Accommodation: first class and deluxe hotels (except in Oberammergau or area, where a certain category cannot be guaranteed.)

FIGURE 10.2
A simple FIT can be constructed by combining an air fare with an existing package of land arrangements such as this.
Source: DER Tours.

- Round trip or circle trip transportation wholly or partly over the lines of one or more IATA members.
- Sleeping accommodation.
- An additional feature such as transfers, motorcoach trip, sightseeing, or car rental.
- An inclusive tour code which must be shown on the tour literature and the passenger's ticket.

The specific details concerning the length and type of accommodation, and the type of additional features required for approval, vary depending on the IATA traffic conference area where the tour commences. In addition to defining the ingredients required for land arrangements, IATA sets the minimum tour cost and monitors the contents of tour literature. For example, the brochure must identify each tour with an IT code number (assigned by the sponsoring airline), and must include the tour operator's name and a description of the tour.

Requirements for ATA Approval

The Air Transport Association of America has established similar categories of approved air tours as IATA. The ATA's definitions and requirements for inclusive tours are similar to those of IATA. These criteria are stated in the General Provisions section of the ATPCO and consist of air transportation, accommodation and at least one additional feature. The ATA also assigns similar conditions as IATA for tour literature. For example, ATA approved tours must clearly identify and list all prepaid features, including the names of hotels/motels offered on the tour, must quote the cost of each tour, and must show the validity dates. However, IT tour numbers are no longer mandatory for domestic tours approved by the ATA.

Retail counsellors can reasonably assume that the tours described in their agency's brochures have already been approved by either IATA or ATA. Nevertheless, there are some aspects of approved tours which demand a counsellor's close attention. For

counsellors employed by tour companies, it is essential that the tour products comply with the definitions and regulations described above. Those involved in tour design must be aware of the regulations before submitting an application for approval to a member airline of either IATA or ATA.

Counsellors who sell tours associated with IT fares earn commission from both the airline and the tour company. However, to collect commission on the air fare, all tickets must be marked with the IT tour code in the appropriate Tour Code box. Although still available, this type of approved tour has become increasingly rare in Canada. The IT tour number must be clearly indicated in the wholesaler's brochure (Figure 10.3) and will have the format shown below:

IT0AC1AT10

A package with such a tour number means that it has been approved by IATA or the ATA and therefore meets its criteria. The tour number can be decoded as follows:

IT   Inclusive tour.

0   The final digit of the year in which the tour was approved (in this case, 1990).

AC   The code of the sponsoring carrier (in this case, Air Canada).

1   The IATA traffic conference in which the tour can be sold (in this case, Area #1).

AT10 The tour operator's identity number for the particular tour. Carriers are allotted up to eight characters for this identifier but need not use them all.

Constructing Independent Tours

Independent tours are constructed by combining various components to create travel arrangements that suit the needs of

IT8NW1HEW1

Hongkong Experience®

An 8-day tour program to the celebrated shoppers' paradise

TOUR FARES:

$870.00*	$950.00*	$1160.00*
(Honolulu)	(West Coast)	(East Coast)

YEAR-ROUND WEEKLY DEPARTURES ON THURSDAYS

TOUR FARE INCLUDES:

☐ Round-trip economy class air transportation via Northwest's wide-body 747 jetliner.

☐ Six nights' elegant accommodations based on double occupancy.

☐ Attentive transfers between Kai Tak International Airport and your hotel, including all tips for porters and bellhop services.

☐ Afternoon guided tour of Hong Kong Island by deluxe air-conditioned motorcoach.

☐ Services of courteous and competent English-speaking representatives and knowledgeable tour guides.

☐ Hotel taxes and gratuities.

HOTEL	R T	TOUR FARE				
		JAN 01-FEB 21	FEB 22-MAR 24	MAR 25-MAY 31	JUN 01-AUG 24 DEC 01-DEC 13	AUG 25-NOV 30 DEC 14-DEC 31
GRAND TOWER LEE GARDENS	HNL	$ 870	$ 910	$1070	$1150	$1160
	WC	$ 950	$ 990	$1150	$1150	$1240
	EC	$1160	$1200	$1360	$1360	$1450
	SS	$ 250	$ 290	$ 300	$ 250	$ 380
SHERATON HILTON	HNL	$ 970	$1070	$1200	$1250	$1290
	WC	$1050	$1150	$1280	$1250	$1370
	EC	$1260	$1360	$1490	$1460	$1580
	SS	$ 350	$ 430	$ 440	$ 350	$ 500

* Tour fare is based on per person double occupancy at Grand Tower or Lee Gardens for departures in from January 1 to February 21. For departures in other months and/or use of other deluxe hotels, please refer to the above chart for tour fares, which are subject to change without notice.

R/T = ROUND TRIP   HNL = HONOLULU   WC = WEST COAST   EC = EAST COAST
SS = SINGLE SUPPLEMENT

Note: Tour fare does not include $3.00 U.S. Transportation Tax, $10.00 U.S. Federal Inspection Fee and approximately $14.00 International Embarkation Tax for HONG KONG.

FIGURE 10.3
An example of an approved tour. Note the IT number.
Source: Pacific Delight Tours/Northwest Airlines.

UTAH
SKI/WINTER SPORTS 1989-90

SNOWBIRD SKI AND SUMMER RESORT
CALL RE: WEEKEND AND SPA PACKAGES
2/3/5/8 DAYS — 1/2/4/7 NIGHTS

SNOWBIRD SKI AND SUMMER RESORT
TOUR: ITCTM-SBSKI2/3/5/8

Snowbird is one of the most accessible resorts in the U.S. only 31 miles from Salt Lake International (40 minutes), morning flights can get guests here early enough for them to enjoy a full, half day of skiing. Gentle boulevards, steep chutes, and wide-cut trails wind their way through snow-covered pines. This mountain was made for skiing. Snowbird averages over 500″ of snowfall a year, blanketing all 2,100 acres of glorious ski slopes; 20% beginner, 30% intermediate and 50% advanced. Over 3,100 vertical feet from top to bottom means there's a lot of mountain to ski. Kids under 13 ski FREE when lodging in their parents room at a nightly rate. Seniors 70+ ski free.

The Cliff Lodge has 532 guest rooms, state of the art conference facilities and a complete health and beauty spa. There are 368 beautiful condominium units in adjacent buildings. The resort has 15 restaurants, private clubs and lounges, some offering live entertainment. Located in the Wasatch Nat'l. Forest.

Base Elevation: 7,900 feet.
Peak Elevation: 11,000 feet.

NIGHTLY RATES EFFECTIVE: As Indicated

Hotel	Accommo-dations	Early/Late Season 11/21-12/23/89 4/15-4/30/90	Value Season 1/2-1/20/90 3/25-4/14/90	Peak Season 12/24/89-1/1/90 1/21-3/24/90	Occupancy
THE CLIFF LODGE	North Bedroom	88.00	129.00	159.00	1-4
	South Bedroom	88.00	149.00	179.00	1-4
	Deluxe Bedroom	139.00	219.00	259.00	1-2
LODGE AT SNOWBIRD	Bedroom	69.00	119.00	149.00	1-4
THE INN	Efficiency/Studio	74.00	130.00	160.00	1-2
IRON BLOSAM LODGE	Studio Loft/1 Bdrm. Condo.	143.00	260.00	320.00	1-6
	1 Bdrm. Condo. w/Loft	212.00	390.00	480.00	1-8

*Restrictions may apply.   Rates and dates are subject to change without notice.

COMMISSIONABLE OPTIONS, ADD TO BASIC PACKAGE PRICE:
To Bonafide Travel Agents at 10%.

INTERLINE/TRAVEL AGENCY PERSONNEL DISCOUNT:
20% savings, space available, bedrooms only, any property.

DEPOSIT/CANCELLATION/REFUND/NO SHOW PENALTY POLICY:
Two nights' lodging is due within 10 days of a reservation request. To guarantee space, full payment is due 30 days prior to arrival. If payment is not received, the space is released and the deposit retained until the original arrival date, then refunded less $25.00 per room. Full payment is required on any booking received within 30 days of arrival date. CANCELLATION FEE: $25.00 per room for space released more than 30 days before arrival; two nights' lodging on space released 29-15 days before arrival; and full payment if cancelled within 14 days of arrival. MINIMUM STAY REQUIREMENTS: Value Season - 3 night minimum at all properties if a Friday or Saturday night is included. Peak Season - 4 night minimum at The Cliff Lodge. (Shorter weekend stays, booked 30 days in advance, are available at a higher rate.). 1-night minimum at the Condominium Lodges (Saturday or Sunday arrivals).

TICKETING INFORMATION

TOUR ORDER:
1. Present to (line 1) — Pull, void and attach to auditor's coupon.
2. Present to (line 2) — SNOWBIRD SKI AND SUMMER RESORT.
3. Present to (line 3) — Pull, void and attach to auditor's coupon.
4. Present to (line 4) — Pull, void and attach to auditor's coupon.

TOUR OPERATOR: SNOWBIRD SKI AND SUMMER RESORT, Snowbird, UT 84092. Telephone: General Information (801) 742-2222; Reservations: Local (801) 532-1700, Out of State (800) 453-3000; Group and Conference Sales (800) 882-4766. Telex: 910-240-0389-SNOWBIRD UT USA. Telefax: (801) 742-2150.

FIGURE 10.4 CTM listings include much useful information. *Courtesy of the Consolidated Tour Manual.*

the particular client. The air component is obtained by consulting the appropriate tariff for IT or excursion fares, or by researching charter fares available from carriers or tour operators. IT fares can be offered only to clients who book approved tours. Brochures for some approved tours are available to both travel agencies and consumers. Other approved tours are published only in travel industry manuals known as confidential tariffs. The best known confidential tariff is the *Consolidated Tour Manual* (CTM) which was briefly described in Chapter 8. Excursion or charter fares, on the other hand, can be combined with land arrangements obtained from any industry reference (except approved tour sources, of course). Counsellors can contact suppliers directly using standard industry references such as the OAG Travel Planners, directories, and other sources discussed in earlier chapters, or they can use the services of a wholesaler.

Consolidated Tour Manual

The CTM is a tour sales manual published by ATA member airlines and major tour operators. It lists a variety of tours which meet both the tour component and the tour brochure specifications for advertised air tours discussed above. Most of the arrangements cited are not tours in the usual sense but are packages of individual cities or events for independent travellers. The CTM is useful when hotel rooms are otherwise unavailable. The manual provides both prices and selling instructions for tour components within the USA, Canada, Mexico, Central America and the Caribbean (Figure 10.4). It also contains selected city and area maps, and information on some of the hotels utilized on the tour packages. Three issues of the CTM are produced each year; an all-year edition, a ski/winter season (November-May) issue, and a summer season (June-October) issue. The CTM is provided free of charge to all travel agencies holding an ATA appointment.

Reservations for any tour listed in the CTM are readily obtained by contacting the carrier that performs the initial air transportation. Upon receiving confirmation from the airline, travel counsellors issue a standard tour order using the carrier's CIP as described in Chapter 6. A tour order should be completed to reserve any IT tour. (The CTM provides complete instructions on how to issue this document.) A tour order form is, in effect, a confirmation and receipt for payment of tour arrangements. Clients simply present the tour order at the first point of contact with the tour company at the destination. In return, clients receive a complete set of vouchers or coupons supplied by the operators of the services requested. Each supplier provides a voucher or coupon which clients present as the service is rendered.

Confidential Tariffs

The CTM is the most familiar and useful confidential tariff for domestic tour arrangements. Confidential tariffs are quite commonly issued by tour companies in Europe where the reception and handling of tourists has long been regarded as a highly specialized occupation. A regular influx of independent tourists has also fostered their distribution and use. Confidential tariffs, however, are a worldwide phenomenon and their numbers are constantly growing to keep pace with the increase in FIT traffic to more exotic destinations.

Confidential tariffs do not follow a standard format as airline tariffs do. Some tariffs show prices in dollars; others indicate costs in local currency. Many references publish the charges for services as gross prices which include the agent's commission; others show net prices to which the counsellor must add a mark-up before collecting from the client. Still others mix net and gross prices, quoting net prices for some services (e.g., transfers) and gross prices for others (e.g., sightseeing tours). Further, some show prices on a per person basis, some quote on a group basis, and others mix them. All have varying terms and conditions for doing business. Care must therefore be

WORLD ASSOCIATION OF TRAVEL AGENCIES

WATA – AREA
AREA TRAVEL AGENCY LTD
ALEKSANTERINKATU 8 - 15110 LAHTI 11 — FINLAND

PHONE : 18-525711 — TELEX : 16242 — TELEFAX 18-525720
Office open from 8.30 a.m. to 5.00 p.m. Saturday closed

Office Manager : Mr. Juhani KALLIOINEN

FINLAND — LAHTI

LOCAL ARRANGEMENTS - 1989

CURRENCY : Finnish marks
1 US $ = FIM 4:40 (July 88)

CONFIDENTIAL TARIFF FOR TRAVEL AGENCIES

1. INTERPRETER : ASSISTANCE ONLY	1 to 3	Any add person	Party of 15 or more per person
	200:—	80:—	30:—

2. PORTERAGE

	For 2 pieces	Any add. piece
When in relation with transfers : included (see 3. Transfers) When **assistance only** is required : At airport HKI-VANTAA, station, bus or air terminal	18:—	10:—
At hotels it is not advisable to include tip to porters for individuals For groups, however, from bus to room or vice versa, per piece	12:—	

3. TRANSFERS

Including interpreter meeting and assistance, accompanying clients, porterage and transportation of two pieces hand luggage per person between hotels and points indicated below or vice versa.
Tip to driver included. (Tip to hotel porters not included.)

1. **Individual clients : per person**

	1	2	3	4
a) Station				
On foot to nearby hotel (to be clearly stated on voucher)	220:—	125:—	95:—	75:—
By taxi cab	235:—	120:—	80:—	60:—
b) Airport				
By taxi cab	765:—	390:—	260:—	200:—
Helsinki-Vantaa airport, about 102 km from Lahti.				

2. **Groups : per person**

	7-14	15 to 19	20 to 30	31 and upwards
a) Station, bus terminal				
On foot to nearby hotel (to be clearly stated on voucher)	32:—	15:—	11:—	7:—
By motorcoach	75:—	35:—	26:—	17:—
b) Airport				
By motorcoach	260:—	120:—	90:—	60:—

4. RESERVATIONS

	Individuals per person	Party of 15 or more per person
Reserved seats on trains (tickets and agency fee)	45:—	25:—
Agency fee only for : hotels (see also the page "General Information")	40:—	10:—
Take note that possible telephone calls or cables will be charged in addition.		

5. OFFICIAL GUIDE

	mo - fr	sa - su
Per hour	126:—	196:—
Full day (lunch not included)	510:—	870:—
Night : supplement 50 %.		

6. ENTRANCE FEES (for parties using own car or coach) · · · · · approx. 10:—

7. SIGHTSEEING (within city limit)

	Adults	Children
Lahti sightseeing : departure at 5.15 p.m. on Wednesdays, 2.15 p.m. on Saturdays, June 1 - August 31. Duration 2 hours	20:—	10:—

8. EXCURSIONS (outside city limits, up to one day, no overnight)

	Adults	Children
Lake cruise on lake Vesijärvi : departure 7.30 p.m., Wednesdays, Fridays and Sundays, June - August. Duration 3½ hours	65:—	35:—

9. TOURS — See Helsinki tariff.

10. CHAUFFEUR DRIVEN CAR HIRE — Taxi cars available only, phone 170.

11. SELF DRIVE — Hertz, Europcar, Interrent, Budget.

12. MOTORCOACH HIRE — On request.

13. MISCELLANEOUS — See Helsinki tariff.

14. REMARKS
All rates are subject to change without further notice.

ALL PRICES ARE NET

FIGURE 10.5
The WATA Master-Key is a useful confidential tariff whose listings are described under 14 headings.
Courtesy of The World Association of Travel Agencies.

taken when quoting prices and deposit requirements. In most cases, the tariff clearly indicates the type of charge; net or gross, per person or per unit, individual or group (see Figure 10.5). It is the counsellor's responsibility to carefully read the tariffs.

Tour company confidential tariffs provide information on a range of services. Since many of these tour companies are ground handlers, the tariffs typically include details of transfers and sightseeing arrangements. Some tour companies also arrange accommodation.

Transfers

Tour companies arrange transportation for their clients between the airport, railway station or pier and their hotel. Counsellors must inform the tour company of the date and specific means of the passenger's arrival in the city where the transfer service is to be performed. Some tour companies include baggage handling charges (porterage) in the transfer charges. This should always be verified. Transfers are almost always provided in a tour because of the convenience and time-saving benefits to passengers.

Sightseeing

Most visitors wish to view or experience some aspects of the history, scenery or culture of a destination. Tour companies create various sightseeing programs to meet these needs and print the details in confidential tariffs. Tours range from half-day (usually three hours) and full-day city tours, including visits to local museums or historical monuments, to longer excursions of from three to five days. Entrance fees to museums, art galleries and other attractions are usually included in the price of the sightseeing program.

Most large cities offer sightseeing tours by motorcoach. Tours usually commence at a fixed time from a central departure point, such as the main train station. In some cities passengers must make their own way to the tour departure area whereas at other destinations ground handlers transfer clients between their hotels and a central distribution point as part of the tour price. Private car sightseeing, though more expensive than by motorcoach, offers the convenience of pick-up and return to the client's hotel and the opportunity to customize a tour to the client's wishes.

Local tour operators must, by the very

FIGURE 10.6 Tourist boards publish confidential tariffs for industry use. *Source: Holland Travel Trade Guide 1990.*

Hotel name classification	Address, telephone telex, fax	Representative code	Max. capacity of beds	Group prices per room from-to	Minimum group size	Commission % for individual booking
Cok Superior Tourist Class Hotel **Classification in 1990**	Koninginneweg 34-36 1075 CZ Amsterdam Tel.: 020-6646111, Tlx.: 11679 Fax: 020-6645304	**UT**	100	Dfl 200 - –	15	10
Crest Hotel *****	De Boelelaan 2 1083 HJ Amsterdam Tel.: 020-462300, Tlx.: 13647 Fax: 020-464790	**CH, UT**	520	Dfl 140 - Dfl 240	15	8
Hotel Dikker & Thijs (AH 2) ****	Prinsengracht 444 1017 KE Amsterdam Tel.: 020-267721, Tlx.: 13161 Fax: 020-258986				–	8
Doelen Crest (AG 6) **Hotel** ****	Nieuwe Doelenstraat 24 1012 CP Amsterdam Tel.: 020-220722, Tlx.: 14399 Fax: 020-221084				15	0

The Best of Holland
Sightseeing tour to Amsterdam, Enkhuizen, Harderwijk, Apeldoorn, Gouda and The Hague.
2 days; April 17-Sep 25; every Mon 8:30a.m.; dep. Amsterdam Hilton Hotel.
Price: Dfl. 495 p.p.; 10% commission; (min. 25 pers.).
Tour Operator: **Van Wijk European Tour Operators and Incentive Travel Bureau.**

nature of their business, be experts on the destination's tourist attractions. The success of their efforts and services is critical to a client's pleasure and enjoyment of a holiday. Tour operators can make reservations for hotels, car rentals, and for local theatrical attractions (such as London theatrical productions), festivals (Edinburgh Music and Art Festival), and nightclubs (the Lido in Paris). Information on many of these services can be found in confidential tariffs supplied by tourist boards (Figure 10.6).

Role of Tour Wholesalers

The USA is the major leisure market for Canadian tourists. Prior to the introduction of jet airline service in the late 1950s, the majority travelled by automobile; they drove in their own cars and found accommodation along the way. Few travellers could afford the time or money necessary for overseas travel to Europe or more distant destinations. A sizable minority, however, visited Bermuda, the Bahamas and the Caribbean. It was neither possible to drive to these island destinations, nor simple to find accommodation on arrival. Wholesale travel companies emerged to fill the need for reliable accommodation. Wholesalers accomplished this by signing contracts to act as Canadian representatives for the hotel associations in these areas. Under these agreements, the wholesaler consented to promote all hotels at the destination equally, produce promotional materials listing all rack rates, and deposit a bond or letter of credit to the association to cover the wholesaler's financial liability. This bond ensured that vouchers or coupons issued by wholesalers for room bookings would be honoured. Wholesalers today still operate in the same manner in these locations.

Wholesalers have extended their services beyond representing a few hotel associations. Tour wholesalers now count hotels, airlines, cruise lines, car rental companies and ground handlers among

their clients. They also construct tours for retail agencies. Wholesalers, however, create a tour only after an agency requests it; they make no financial commitments to their suppliers until a booking has been requested by a travel agency. Many wholesalers sell to the mass market by promoting popular destinations. Others cater to specific market segments while some specialize by destination or transportation used.

Benefits of Dealing with Wholesalers

Travel counsellors find that dealing with a tour wholesaler offers several benefits.

Ease of Booking

Once clients have made a decision, counsellors need only contact an appropriate local wholesaler who will make the reservation with the hotel, car rental company, or other supplier. Depending on availability, wholesalers can usually confirm the arrangements within hours. Agencies are relieved of costly communications charges and lengthy correspondence.

Deposit

Travel counsellors must send a deposit to the wholesaler at the time a booking is made. This again reduces the communication time needed and removes the chance that deposits will be lost in the mail in a foreign country.

Final Payment

Travel counsellors send the balance of the payment to the wholesaler, usually 30 to 42 days before departure. Clients are freed from the need to pay suppliers at the destination which eliminates the possibility of overcharging. This procedure reduces the number of client complaints to travel agencies.

Commission

When counsellors book directly with suppliers, it can be several months before commission is received. Further, the commission earned from a direct booking with a supplier may be less than ten percent. When bookings are made through a wholesaler, however, it is the wholesaler who is responsible for paying the agency's commission, not the supplier. This means that commission can be deducted from the final payment and retained by the agency. Wholesalers generally earn 15 percent commission from their suppliers. They pass on ten percent to retailers and retain five percent to cover overheads.

Reduced Costs

The rates available through wholesalers are generally the same as those available from suppliers. Agencies save money, however, by eliminating costly phone calls, faxes or telexes, and time-consuming correspondence to numerous suppliers. Wholesalers are contacted directly, usually through a toll-free line for out-of-town businesses. All costs associated with making a booking (e.g., phone calls and correspondence) are absorbed by the wholesaler who pays for them from the five percent commission retained.

Accurate Product Knowledge

Wholesalers assume responsibility for the products they represent. Just as suppliers know their products better than do travel counsellors, so too do wholesalers. Larger wholesale companies have specialists trained in specific suppliers and destinations.

Promotion

Wholesalers produce catalogues or brochures listing the products they represent. These are distributed to travel agencies for use with their clients. Consumers thus have access to descriptions of the products, their rates and the amenities available. This simplifies the selection procedure and helps them choose the ingredients for their vacation. Wholesalers also employ sales representatives to visit travel counsellors and educate them on their services.

Quality Control

Wholesalers monitor their products to ensure they achieve the standards claimed. Problems arising between consumers and suppliers are generally handled by the wholesaler.

Costing System for Independent Tours

Travel counsellors who construct FITs can minimize the possibility of calculation errors by using a costing system. A costing system is a daily listing of every component arranged for a client and for which the travel counsellor must collect payment (see Figure 10.7). Costing systems vary from one agency to another but a dependable system identifies the client's name and currency used, followed by a chronological listing which states the date the service is needed, the name of the supplier, particulars of the service and its cost, either net or gross. Certain itineraries will have both net and gross costs. The costing system will therefore show two columns; one for net rates and one for gross rates. After the net column has been totalled, it will be marked-up from ten to 30 percent depending on the time required to arrange the tour and the policy of the individual travel agency. The marked-up net column and the gross column are then added together. This total is the amount collected from the client.

Confidential tariffs indicate the currency used to price the services. This is frequently the local currency, although a "standard" currency such as U.S. dollars may also be used. It is recommended that counsellors always cost a tour using the currency identified in the tariff. If local currency is quoted, then it should be used and clearly noted in the calculation. Many countries stipulate that payments to suppliers be made in local currency. Even where this is not the case, fluctuating exchange rates make it risky to quote prices in anything other than the currency mentioned.

A proper costing system ensures clear

CLIENT'S NAME: Mr. E Jones   CURRENCY: Pounds Sterling (GBP)

Date	Name of Supplier	Service Provided	Prepaid Cost Per Person	
			Net	Gross
June 5	Supertravel Ltd.	Transfer: Heathrow/Hotel	3.50	
	London: Tara Hotel	1/2 TWB	37.50	
		VAT	3.75	
June 6	Supertravel Ltd.	Full day sightseeing tour: London at Leisure		15.00
	London: Tara Hotel	1/2 TWB	37.50	
		VAT	3.75	
June 7	Royal Tours	Half day sightseeing tour: Windsor Castle	8.50	
	London: Tara Hotel	1/2 TWB	37.50	
		VAT	3.75	
June 8-10	Heritage Tours	3-day, 2-night tour: Stately Homes of S.W. England		220.00
June 10	London: Tara Hotel	1/2 TWB	37.50	
		VAT	3.75	
June 11	Supertravel Ltd.	Transfer: Hotel/Heathrow	3.50	
		Subtotals	180.50	235.00
		Plus agency mark up (10%)	18.05	
				198.55
		TOTAL DUE FROM CLIENT	**GBP**	**433.55**

FIGURE 10.7
Sample FIT costing system.

and accurate record-keeping whether the services involved are for one day or for an extended tour. A reliable system identifies each item sold to a client as part of a tour, including service charges, local taxes, profit mark-ups and overhead charges. A good costing system is sufficiently flexible to permit all component costs to be shown as net or gross charges in any currency. Following these guidelines for a costing system minimizes under-collection and assures that each supplier will receive proper compensation for the services provided. When clients cancel, a costing system provides an accurate record which assists counsellors to promptly determine the refund due, whether the cancellation is for some of the services or for the entire tour. Retail agencies find that a costing system is particularly useful for determining prepaid hotel charges for any number of nights' accommodation. It is also a convenient and practical method to cost itineraries for journeys of any length or to any destination.

Booking Independent Tours

As mentioned, tours may be booked independently and directly by travellers. They can make arrangements prior to departure by contacting each supplier to reserve the various tour components. This is a time-consuming process which may involve phone calls, letters and personal visits to several suppliers for each element in the tour. Travellers are responsible for sending deposits, making payments, planning the itinerary, and ensuring that their documentation is in order. The process can be awkward and costly. Not only must such tourists cover all communications charges, but they are unlikely to have access to group rates. There may also be hidden costs and problems with suppliers. Many travellers therefore find that it pays to use the services of a travel counsellor who can advise them on itinerary planning and can book the tour components.

An independent tour may require only that counsellors make a reservation for transportation to the chosen destination and guide clients in the selection of an appropriate ground package from a local tour company. However, given the number of tour companies, the variety of air fares available, and the speed with which both can change, travel counsellors can assist with even this simple task. For more complex tours, travel counsellors need expertise and experience in planning and costing independent tours as well as knowledge of current rates, timetables and products available. Each tour component may require extensive research and a separate reservation. Travel counsellors who lack these abilities can use the services of a wholesaler to organize the tour and book the various components.

Advantages of Independent Tours

Independent touring allows travellers complete flexibility and freedom to devise a trip to meet their particular needs. It permits them to choose destinations, dates, duration, and particular components to suit their special tastes, preferences and interests. They are responsible for setting and following their own itineraries, and for selecting the types of transportation and hotels they favour. They are therefore free of the restrictions imposed by group travel.

Disadvantages of Independent Tours

All plans for an FIT are prearranged and prepaid in full through a travel agency in the same manner as other types of travel. The result is a holiday which is tailored to the client's own specifications and inclinations. However, travelling on an independent tour basis does have some disadvantages. Clients are generally unable to take advantage of special air fares or hotel rates which apply to group tours. Similarly, they will not be able to call upon the services of a tour company's escort or representative if needed.

Planning an independent tour usually requires more discussion and counselling between the prospective client and the counsellor. Counsellors must make use of a wide variety of trade reference sources. Since no one publication deals with the many parts of an independent tour, counsellors must consult airline guides, timetables for bus and rail travel, hotel manuals, air fare tariffs, confidential tariffs, maps, destination resources, and other references described. They must then coordinate and integrate the essential components, taking care that each is accurately timed to fit with the connecting services. Finally, the total cost must be calculated.

Travel counsellors who do not possess the time or expertise to construct independent tours will contact a tour wholesaler to plan and cost an itinerary for their client's consideration. Such an itinerary may cost more than if produced by the travel counsellor since the wholesaler must add a profit mark-up to cover time and expertise. However, counsellors, too, often add a fee for their services on independent tours. All services used on independent tours are based on typical industry tariffs. Clients may be unable to save money by using lower group tariffs or GIT air fares. As a result, independent tours may be more costly than group tours.

As a general rule, the greatest market potential for independent tours is with experienced travellers, with those whose travel tastes are somewhat more sophisticated, those who do not care for group travel, and those who like to personalize their travel plans. However, business travellers as well as tourists are a source of clients for independent tours. These travellers sometimes wish to combine sightseeing with a business trip, if they have time to extend their stay.

Group Tours

The second category of tours is group tours. Group tours are organized on the basis of a predetermined number of passengers travelling together, usually a minimum of 15 people. Group tours also impose a maximum limit, usually based on the capacity of the primary form of transportation. For example, motorcoach tours restrict the number of people in the party to the number of seats available on the motorcoach. Group tours were originally available only to members of authentic groups, that is, the group had to be an established association with a common interest. Today, however, the distinction between independent tours and group tours is in their costing. Even though many group tours may be purchased by individuals, they are costed on the basis of a predetermined participation rate. Group tours therefore exhibit certain characteristics in common with independent tours. In general, group tours are created by tour operators whereas independent tours are constructed by travel counsellors, either alone or in conjunction with tour wholesalers.

Group tours can be arranged as ground (or land) packages or as inclusive tours. These may be fully escorted, partially escorted, or unescorted (independent). Typically, group tours follow a prearranged itinerary which has been planned months, and sometimes years, in advance.

Ground Package or Land Package

These tours contain a prearranged portion (e.g., accommodation for seven nights plus car rental) which is offered to groups at a specified price. As discussed earlier, tour companies may seek IATA or ATA approval for the land package and thereby arrange for an airline to offer a special fare to the group. Travel counsellors book such tours for their clients through the tour company and then separately reserve transportation (using the special fare) through the airline. Commission is earned on both the tour and the air fare. For various reasons, some ground packages may not be approved by either airline conference. These tours are also reserved through the tour operator but if air transportation is required counsellors must conduct their own research to find the best fare for their clients; no special air fare is associated with the package. Counsellors will again earn separate commissions from the airline and the tour operator.

Inclusive Tours

An inclusive or package tour is a tour for a predetermined number of days which includes a fixed combination of travel services and features. It is offered for sale at a set price. The components have been carefully integrated, and are planned, marketed and managed by tour operators. Package tours are both group tours and individual tours. They are group tours in that components are purchased in bulk based on a given number of people travelling together. They are individual tours, however, in that they are sold to clients on an individual basis. Package tours are sold primarily through retail travel agencies which earn commission, based on the set price of the tour, only from the tour operator.

Package tours are combinations of travel services which typically consist of one or more forms of transportation, accommodation, meals, attractions and events (including sightseeing and admissions), and extras (including transfers, baggage handling, tips and taxes, tour guide or representative services, travel bags, discount coupons). **Inclusive Tour Charters** (ITCs) have not only become the most popular type of group package tour, but they also enjoy the largest sales volume of any type of tour. The minimum components of an ITC are charter air transportation, transfers and accommodation. Frequently, however, additional components are added in the same way as for tours using other forms of transportation (Figure 10.8).

All package tours are designed to cater to a variety of specific destinations, markets or interests. Tour operators continually refine and develop the product to extend its marketability. All-inclusive packages are one of the most recent examples of this process. The concept of all-inclusive resorts was introduced in Majorca around 1950. Since then they have grown in popularity with both consumers and travel counsellors. Originally, the concept focused on the resort and denoted one place. Today the term also signifies one price. Several companies have now added themes to the idea. All-inclusive resorts provide three meals daily, snacks, drinks, entertainment, water and land sports, luxury accommodation, and no tipping in a one-price package. They are easy to sell and offer high commission. These packages appeal to all age ranges, occupations and interests.

Motorcoach Tours

Many tours are based at a specific resort or destination and involve no other travel. These are known as stay-put vacations. Another type consists of a more literal tour arrangement where tourists travel from place to place. Motorcoach tours fall into this category. The increase in airline routes and the growth in excursion and promotional air fares has helped to promote motorcoach tour programs. Several tour companies now offer air/bus tours which include an escorted motorcoach tour and hotel package at the destination. Coach tours vary in length from one day to one month. Other companies, most notably the Gray Line, specialize in sightseeing tours ranging from three hours to five days. These tours are frequently the only way for a visitor to view something of the cultural aspects of the region.

Preplanned motorcoach tours are extremely popular in Canada, the United States and Europe. The Bus Regulatory Reform Act which deregulated the American bus industry in 1982 ended the requirement that motorcoach tour brokers be licensed. This greatly increased the number of American travel agents operating their own tours. Canadian agencies with wholesaler licenses may also create tours by chartering buses and booking the individual components of the tour. After adding a mark-up, these tours can be marketed to the public. The size of the group is determined by the capacity of the motorcoach. Normal full size coaches have about 48 seats but this number varies depending on the space taken up by the vehicle's amenities.

Motorcoach tours appeal to all age groups. Seniors value the total care and convenience they provide. Younger people and first-time travellers appreciate motorcoach tours for the variety of destinations they embrace. Coach tours are available in a range of prices, depending on the accommodation selected as part of the package. Most coach tour clients prefer the convenience of a completely preplanned trip and choose to let someone else do the driving.

FIGURE 10.8
ITCs have become the most popular type of tour.
Source: Sunquest Vacations.

Sunquest JAMAICA
MONTEGO BAY, OCHO RIOS, NEGRIL

YOUR HOLIDAY INCLUDES:
- Roundtrip flight from Toronto
- Complimentary in-flight meals and bar service
- Sunquest airport greeting upon arrival
- Transfers to & from hotel (except air only)
- Accommodation as selected
- Welcome orientation briefing
- Services of a Sunquest representative

Not included: Taxes and Service Charges as indicated on price chart, payable with final payment.

Resort	SEAWIND BEACH RESORT																TRELAWNY BEACH								FOR SAT/SUN FLIGHTS ADD
Accommodation	Tower Room												1 Bedroom				Hotel Room								
Meal plan	Breakfast Daily												No Meals				Breakfast & Dinner Daily								
No. of nights	3 (Thurs)			4 (Sun)			7 (Th,Fr,Mo)			14 (Th,Fr,Mo)			7 (Th,Fr,Mo)		14 (Th,Fr,Mo)		3 (Thurs)		4 (Sun)		7 (Th,Fr,Mo)		14 (Th,Fr,Mo)		
People sharing	1	2	3/4	1	2	3/4	1	2	3/4	1	2	3/4	2	3/4	2	3/4	2	3	2	3	2	3	2	3	
Oct 04 - Oct 31	469	369	349	579	449	429	789	569	519	1249	799	719	649	529	969	729	429	419	529	499	649	599	1049	929	40
Nov 01 - Nov 28	469	369	349	579	449	429	789	569	519	1249	799	719	649	529	969	729	449	429	549	529	719	659	1159	1049	40
Nov 29 - Dec 12	449	349	329	559	429	399	769	519	479	1229	769	669	589	479	939	689	449	429	539	519	699	639	1149	1029	40
Dec 13 - Dec 19	449	349	329	559	429	399	769	519	479	1599	969	839	629	489	1129	799	449	429	539	519	699	639	1449	1299	40
Dec 20 - Dec 26	629	469	459	859	639	619	1299	919	889	2039	1299	1229	999	829	1469	1129	629	599	849	799	1229	1149	1969	1799	40
Dec 27 - Jan 02	719	549	529	739	539	519	1259	899	869	1819	1119	1069	989	819	1299	969	699	659	729	729	1229	1149	1799	1639	40
Jan 03 - Jan 30	569	419	399	719	529	499	989	649	619	1719	999	969	739	579	1199	879	569	539	719	679	949	879	1649	1499	40
Jan 31 - Mar 06	649	499	479	829	599	579	1179	799	769	1969	1199	1129	889	699	1369	1019	649	619	819	769	1099	1029	1859	1699	40
Mar 07 - Mar 13	649	499	479	859	649	629	1299	919	889	1969	1199	1129	999	829	1369	1019	649	619	849	799	1229	1149	1859	1699	40
Mar 14 - Mar 20	649	499	479	829	599	579	1179	799	769	1969	1199	1129	889	699	1369	1019	649	619	819	769	1099	1029	1859	1699	40
Mar 21 - Apr 10	639	479	469	829	579	559	1079	699	669	1699	899	969	829	669	1229	929	619	599	799	749	1069	989	1799	1599	40
Apr 11 - Apr 17	499	399	389	649	549	499	879	629	579	1399	879	789	729	589	1099	819	619	599	669	629	949	879	1419	1289	40
Apr 18 - May 29	489	389	369	599	479	459	799	559	499	1299	819	699	649	519	999	749	499	469	619	579	749	689	1219	1099	40
May 30 - Jun 26	449	359	339	569	439	419	739	519	469	1199	759	659	599	479	919	679	449	429	569	539	699	639	1179	1059	40
Upgrade A - Add	40	20	-	50	30	-	90	50	-	180	100	-	-	-	-	-	40	30	50	40	80	60	160	120	-
Tax & Service	115	115	115	115	115	115	115	115	115	145	145	145	115	115	145	145	125	125	125	125	165	165	205	205	-

Motorcoach tour operators are however, expanding their product range to appeal to a more varied clientele.

Motorcoaches were once perceived as being uncomfortable and only for the older generation or those who could not afford other transportation. The seating on modern equipment, however, is often more comfortable than on a train or plane and most coaches have washroom facilities. Services have been improved and many companies offer meals, drinks and entertainment services on board. The traditional image of coach tours is one of ten countries in seven days but this too is changing. Shorter tours from a home base are now marketed to those who do not wish to spend all their time travelling. These tours accommodate passengers in one or two central locations (say Munich and Vienna). From these bases passengers take short trips to surrounding attractions. Travellers have the opportunity for a more in-depth experience and do not have to repeatedly pack and unpack.

Motorcoach tours are marketed as all-inclusive vacations that incorporate everything in the price except personal expenses (Figure 10.9). Transportation is provided. Accommodation and most meals are arranged, reserved and paid for in advance. Sightseeing is planned so that the most interesting sights, attractions and places of interest are seen within the time available. Many coach tours are accompanied by experienced tour escorts who monitor the complete vacation. Longer tours through one or more countries may be operated by local, national or international companies. Their products and performance range in quality in much the same way as do tours based on other modes of transport and they can be assessed in a similar fashion. That is, the accommodation generally determines the cost and quality of the tour. Other factors that help counsellors to assess their quality are the service, facilities and coaches used. The calibre and experience of the guides employed are also critical.

Advantages of Motorcoach Tours

Motorcoach tours have several distinct selling features. Since coaches can travel virtually anywhere, these tours provide extreme accessibility. This permits them to include a variety of attractions and a number of destinations in a short time. Their accessability also extends to disabled travellers. Each company may carry one disabled person per tour. This is often the only practical method for such clients to see a destination. The all-inclusive price offers economy and value for money. Coach tours are convenient since door-to-door service is provided and someone else does the planning, organizing, driving and baggage handling. These tours offer continuous sightseeing, an educational aspect and a strong social component which create a total experience.

Disadvantages of Motorcoach Tours

The main disadvantage of motorcoach tours is the perception that they are for senior citizens. Coach tours are also criticized for the length of time spent travelling and the inflexibility of the tour arrangements. The tour companies have, however, attempted to overcome these drawbacks as discussed earlier.

Escorted Tours

Escorted tours are also known as conducted tours and guided tours. They are true group tours in that they require a predetermined number of people to travel together, usually governed as before by the capacity of the featured mode of transportation. An escorted tour follows a prearranged itinerary which has been planned in advance. Every aspect of the tour, the itinerary, location and duration of stay in each place, the dates, times and forms of transportation, and the accommodation, are organized and reserved months or years in advance. A participant in an escorted or group tour cannot deviate from the planned itinerary, and must travel at the same time, to the same destination, and in the same manner as the other tour members. Some escorted tours are set up such that clients may join the tour either in their home town or at the first overnight stop on the tour. For example, Horizon Holidays offers a tour of Northwest Canada which can be joined in Toronto or in Edmonton. Clients who begin the tour in Toronto have the return air fare from Toronto to Edmonton included in the price of the tour. Those who prefer to join the tour in Edmonton can have their travel arrangements made by a counsellor and pay a lower tour cost which reflects this fact. An escorted tour can use a single mode of transportation, such as a 7-day motorcoach tour of New England, or several modes. For example, an intermodal tour of Western Canada could consist of a flight from Toronto to Edmonton, motorcoach through the Rockies, ferry between Vancouver and Victoria, and return from Vancouver to Toronto by train.

FIGURE 10.9
Escorted motorcoach tours are designed to include a variety of features and meet many interests.
Source: Trentway Tours.

Nashville

INCLUDED IN PRICE:

• **TRENTWAY VALUE PAK** • 4 nights accommodation • Guided tour of Nashville • Country Music Hall of Fame • Opryland, U.S.A. • Reserved seat to The Grand Ole Opry • Twitty City • Barbara Mandrell Museum

Smoking is NOT permitted on coach.

Tour No.	Departs	Returns
98106	Mar 23	Mar 27
08101	May 18	May 22
08102	Jun 29	Jul 3
08103	Aug 3	Aug 7
08104	Aug 31	Sep 4
08105	Oct 5	Oct 9

Cost Per Person

Four to a room	$385.00
Three to a room	$405.00
Two to a room	$450.00
Single room	$570.00

Comprehensive Insurance Package $26.00 per person. Includes Hospital, Medical, Cancellation, Accident and Baggage insurance.

TRENTWAY VALUE PAK

The tremendous Trentway value continues with every Trentway Tours offered. Consider all of these inclusive features that we include on each and every Trentway Tour:

- **Transportation by deluxe air conditioned motorcoach with washroom facilities**
- **Services of an experienced driver and escort**
- **Baggage handling (one piece per person)**
- **Tax and gratuities on any included meals**
- **U.S. exchange on included items**
- **Trentway Tours' services in contracting the travel services, organizing the trip, and hiring and training the escorts and drivers and other such administrative tasks.**
- **PRICE GUARANTEE**

The principal characteristic of an escorted tour, however, is that the group is accompanied by a tour escort, tour conductor or tour leader. A variety of escorted tours have been developed to meet the needs of tour operators and their clients. Some escorted tours are accompanied by an escort from the client's gateway city, through the complete itinerary, to the return to the gateway city at the conclusion. Here, the escort is entirely responsible for the group arrangements throughout the tour. Other escorted tours include the services of an escort only after the group arrives in the country where land arrangements for the tour commence. These are commonly called hosted tours. A third type of escorted tour employs a different escort for each country or city through which the tour passes. Occasionally local guides are also hired to join a tour at specific points to enhance the tour's attractions and points of interest. Guides in residence at specific attractions are called site guides.

Many countries strictly control the quality of guides or escorts and recognize tour guiding as a profession. Those who seek to enter it often require specific educational qualifications and proficiency in languages. Tour guides are frequently students of history, architecture, archaeology, or other related fields, and are regarded as specialists in their particular topic. Several countries license as tour escorts only those who successfully complete an approved training course. Tour operators make use of these well-qualified people who are knowledgeable in the tourist attractions and culture of their native country. Furthermore, tour escorts are experienced travellers who are familiar with the tour itinerary and places visited. The presence of a tour escort familiar with the local language, customs and currency regulations is comforting for first-time travellers who might not otherwise have the courage to travel abroad. A guide's specialized knowledge and experience often increase the group's enjoyment of a tour.

Escorted tours are performed by tour operators on a series of regular departure dates, either weekly, monthly or seasonally. They are sold at one all-inclusive price based on transportation, transfers and accommodation at a special group rate. Tour operators calculate the per person selling price by totalling these costs, plus selling costs (such as travel agent's commission and advertising), then adding a profit mark-up. The total is often less expensive than for the same tour taken independently.

The two main features of an escorted or group tour are that the entire itinerary is prearranged by the tour operator with no deviation possible, and that the complete tour is prepaid by the client with no refund available for unused components.

Tour Escort Functions

Tour escorts have a number of responsibilities in addition to accompanying a tour. Their main duties are the payment of bills and gratuities, the handling of all tickets and documents, ensuring that all tour members are comfortably lodged, and monitoring baggage handling. They also coordinate and maintain the tour and sightseeing schedules, anticipate and solve problems, assign rooms, ensure rooms are ready, and act as a host and counsellor for shopping, dining, attractions and personal problems. Tour escorts require special characteristics to meet these challenges. Common sense, adaptability, a cooperative approach, patience, a sense of humour, firmness and leadership are particularly useful.

Tour Escort Binder

Travel counsellors are sometimes given the opportunity to escort a group tour. A comprehensive tour binder is a necessary reference for those with the attributes and inclination to act as a tour leader. The following information will help prospective escorts create a suitable guide. The material is more readily retrieved if stored in three-ring binders. The number required depends on the complexity of the tour and how much talking the escort expects to do. Binders will be necessary for historical and cultural information, for anecdotes, and as a working notebook. The latter is vital as it contains details of the specific tour arrangements. It should contain at least the following items.

- **Passenger List**. A basic list includes each passenger's name and address. Passport numbers, notes on general health, next of kin, and similar details may be added. Several copies of the passenger list should be made.
- **Rooming Lists**. Type the name of each hotel on separate copies of the passenger list. As the group arrives at each property, note the room assigned to each client.
- **Baggage Lists**. Use a copy of the passenger list to record the number of bags each member checks when moving from one stop to another.
- **List of Contact Persons**. For each destination or stop, prepare a list of useful contacts such as airline or cruise personnel, tour operator/motorcoach company contacts, embassy staff and hotel managers. Each name should include title, address and telephone number. Try to develop a complete list of everyone who might be helpful, especially in the event of an emergency.
- **Confirmations**. Carry copies of documents provided by suppliers to confirm hotel, restaurant or theatre reservations.
- **Detailed Itinerary**. Prepare an hour-by-hour breakdown of the itinerary. This can be used to note individuals you must contact.
- **Report Forms**. Keep a diary of daily events to record problems with passengers, missed connections, altered itineraries, supplemental hotel and restaurant charges, and similar events. This is used as the basis for reports to the tour operator. There should also be an expense sheet to monitor money you spend en route.
- **Trip Brochures**. Carry extra copies of the tour brochure for distribution to clients and to note any changes or comments.
- **Miscellaneous**. Extra copies of

everything from passenger lists to itineraries will prove useful. Information on passengers' birthdays or anniversaries should also be gathered, if possible.

Advantages of Escorted Tours

Passengers choose escorted tours because they provide freedom from hassles and decision making. Every detail is preplanned and a tour demands nothing from travellers other than their presence. Escorted tours save time by ensuring that tourists avoid wrong turns, poor hotels and attractions which are closed for holidays or other reasons. They also provide the companionship of people with similar interests.

Escorted tours find their widest appeal among first-time travellers, among tourists who wish to visit an area where language and customs are different from their home country, and among those who appreciate the convenience of travelling under the guidance of a tour escort responsible for the operation of the tour.

Role of Tour Operators

Modern mass tourism had its origins in the aftermath of the Second World War. This was a period of rising affluence and increasing leisure time. The post-war years also left a surplus of aircraft and of trained pilots. Many pilots took advantage of these conditions and formed airlines, sometimes operating with only one aircraft. Later technological developments, such as the introduction of jet aircraft, further contributed to the growth of the travel industry. Gradually, a new type of wholesaler emerged to deal with the changing situation.

Until the late 1950s, travel wholesalers acted almost exclusively as representatives for travel suppliers. By 1960, however, European tour companies had developed the concept of an inclusive tour consisting of transportation, accommodation and other services. The first tour packages soon followed and tour operators, as they are now known, appeared. These European operators chartered aircraft and bought hotel space in bulk. By combining these elements with transfers between airport and hotel, they created a tour package or Inclusive Tour Charter (ITC). By the mid-1960s, Canadian tour companies were exploring the European example and in 1967 the first Canadian ITC program began operating. Since the early 1970s this type of tour has enjoyed phenomenal growth, development and consumer acceptance. ITCs combine low price and dependability with a regular frequency of service to high demand holiday destinations. ITCs have also been used to develop service to destinations which do not have scheduled service. One advantage of ITCs to such "new" destinations is that sometimes an ITC is the only way to reach the destination.

A tour operator is a principal (or supplier) that contracts with other suppliers and pays a negotiated price. Tour operators sell their products through travel agencies to whom they pay a commission. The principal (or tour operator) is responsible for the success or failure of a tour's operation and sales. Although most tour operators also hold a retail license, they do not generally sell directly to the public. To be successful, tour operators must develop and maintain a cooperative relationship with their suppliers (the airlines, hoteliers and local ground handlers) and their distributors (retail travel agencies). This is a sensitive alliance demanding care and attention.

Tour operators typically specialize in one of two areas, the inbound market or the outbound market. **Inbound tour companies** are based and operate tours within the same country. They offer tours to incoming visitors to a specific city, area or country. Sometimes they are called local operators. Local operators create tours, perform various tour services and subcontract their services. They arrange flights, accommodation, airport transfers, sightseeing and transportation. A local operator may be a bus company, a government tourist office or, more frequently, a local retail travel agency that in turn subcontracts many of the services needed. Retail travel agencies can obtain reservations for FIT tour components through a local tour operator.

Outbound tour operators are companies based in one country which create and market tours offered in another country. They concentrate on sending tourists to international destinations. Sunquest, Fiesta and American Express are just some of the many well-known outbound tour operators in Canada who create a variety of tour products and market them through retail agencies. Outbound tour operators frequently use local inbound operators to perform the services at the destination. For example, a Canadian tour operator offering a motorcoach tour of Europe will charter the motorcoaches from a European local operator.

Tour operators construct tours prior to their sale. They must therefore buy all the tour components before the start of the year or season. This entails legal contracts with and financial commitments to suppliers before any tours are sold. Tour operators are financially at risk if their tours do not sell. The tour arrangements are based on groups, although they are intended for sale to individuals. Tour operators contract for the tour components in bulk and this enables them to offer package tours at a low price. Once the tour components are purchased they are packaged as Inclusive Tour Charters (ITCs). ITC packages are granted Canadian government approval in this form and therefore do not require an IT code number.

Tour operators try to generate repeat business and utilize media advertising to target potential tourists and prospective retailers. Consumer advertising attempts to stimulate interest in the tour and is inclined to be more dazzling. Trade advertisements feature tour descriptions and details of how counsellors can book a tour. The message generally emphasizes how agents can satisfy clients and earn income by selling the tour. Advertisements often include a coupon so that counsellors may order brochures, posters and other sales aids.

As the tour business becomes more competitive, and as the consumer market becomes more segmented, tour operators have become increasingly inventive. Tour packages have become more specific and narrowly targeted to meet these trends. Selling a tour based on a theme (for example, architecture, wine-tasting or sports) is just one method used to market the product. Theme vacations are popular because people enjoy travelling with those who share their interests. They also provide companionship, safety, conversation, and an opportunity to make new acquaintances. Tours with a theme attract travellers with a common interest and are easier to sell. The only way to tell whether they will sell, however, is to package the tour and try to sell it. This entails a high degree of risk. Tour operators must continuously search for new destinations and new product lines to keep up with changes in the marketplace.

Creation of an ITC Program

There are four main stages in creation of a tour package: planning; costing; brochure production; and promotion. During the preliminary phase, tour operators research the destination and the consumer market, plan the tour elements, and negotiate with suppliers. The costing of a package tour is a complex process requiring skill and experience. Tour operators must estimate a selling price which will be attractive to consumers, match or better that of their competitors, and still generate sufficient income to cover costs and allow for a profit. Brochure production is equally demanding. Not only are brochures costly, but they must entice consumers and yet be simple to understand. At the same time they must contain everything necessary for travel counsellors to use them as references and sales tools. The final stage in the development of a tour program is its promotion through media advertising to the travel trade and consumers, and familiarization for counsellors.

Tour packages require a lengthy planning period in order to avoid mistakes and overcome unexpected difficulties. Tour planners begin the process by studying the target market to learn its preferences in terms of attractions and services. Tours must be planned with suitable pacing, balance and variety to fit the needs of the segment selected. Individual tour elements must be consistent in quality and the package should be priced to give value for money. Most planners build packages around one or more attractions. These act as tourism generators and persuade consumers to purchase the tour. The destination must have adequate infrastructure and be accessible. Tour operators usually pick popular destinations on main transportation routes. Tour packages, however, have also been responsible for opening new markets such as Venezuela and the Dominican Republic. Packages usually contain one or more bonus features which those who buy the components separately cannot receive (Figure 10.10). Another characteristic of tour packages is their relatively short season. To successfully overcome these conditions, tour packagers must possess or develop the ability to anticipate future trends.

Once a tour operator has chosen a destination and researched the potential Canadian market for the product, work commences on assembling the program's assorted components. The process involves a series of negotiations with the suppliers of the services.

Negotiations with Airlines

Tour operators generally secure transportation arrangements for a tour before contracting for any other components. An operator may choose to charter an entire aircraft, purchase a certain number of seats (minimum 20) on board an already chartered aircraft, or purchase CBIT seats on a scheduled flight. (See Chapter 6. This is considered a mini-charter since a certain number of seats are available at charter fares on scheduled flights.)

When a tour operator decides to use GIT or CBIT fares, negotiations centre on the number of seats being purchased. If a tour operator is planning to charter an entire aircraft for a season, however, the discussions are more complex. The operator must negotiate a suitable contract with an airline to charter aircraft at a specified price for a series of flights between Canada and the chosen destination. Depending on traffic demands and the destination's potential, a charter contract will be arranged for a year or on a seasonal basis, say from December to April. Aircraft can be chartered either "wet" (with fuel included) or "dry" (without fuel). If the carrier supplies a crew, their cost will be included in the quote. Most charters are based on a cost per mile and/or a cost per hour. A one-way charter can cost as much as a round trip since the operator must return the equipment to its home base. Scheduling therefore becomes an important factor. The airline and tour operator develop a flight schedule based on government tour regulations and the tour operator's research of the market potential for the selected destination. The carrier usually operates the required flight series between the origin in Canada and the destination on a back-to-back basis. On this basis, only the first flight returning to Canada and last flight out from Canada carry no passengers and are non-revenue trips. The second and all succeeding flights in the program not only carry passengers to the destination, but also collect and return to Canada those passengers who travelled to the destination on the previous trip. A flight that carries passengers is called a **live** flight. A flight which carries no passengers and is paid for by the tour operator is called a **ferry** flight. A similar non-revenue flight paid for by the air carrier to position the aircraft for a revenue-producing flight is called a **deadhead**. Back-to-back shuttle operation means that the chartered aircraft earns at

least some revenue on all trips.

The price that an airline can charge to perform charter services is ratified by the NTA. During negotiations, a tour operator must consider several variables which affect the saleability of an ITC program. For example, flights timed to depart at say 5:00 p.m. on a Friday afternoon have greater sales appeal than those scheduled for departure at 3:00 a.m. on a Sunday morning. Arrival time at the destination is an equally important sales factor. The arrival time also has operational implications. For example, it would be difficult or impossible for clients arriving at say 4:00 a.m. to check into a hotel or gain customs clearance. The technical capabilities of the aircraft are a further consideration. Where possible, an operator prefers to charter an aircraft with sufficient range for a non-

---

Included Features!

- Return air transportation from Toronto to Cancun
- Inflight meals with wine, cash bar available
- Transfers & baggage handling
- Accommodation
- All hotel taxes & service charges
- 3 buffet-style meals daily & snacks (5 buffet-style & 2 à la carte dinners weekly)
- All drinks (house wine, domestic beer & international brand cocktails) 11am to 1am
- Introductory scuba lesson in pool
- Snorkelling
- Sunfish sailing with group instruction
- Tennis
- Bicycles, volleyball & aerobics
- Daily activities
- Nightly entertainment theme nights & dancing
- Representative service

Not Included

- Departure taxes as shown
- Travel insurance (page 75)

Available at extra charge
- Scuba diving
- Golf

FIGURE 10.10
Tour planners usually build several features into an ITC program.
Source: Adventure/Fiesta.

stop flight to the destination. A fuel stop en route is inconvenient to passengers and increases the cost of the flight as aircraft are subject to landing charges and other costs. Another aspect of program saleability is whether the anticipated traffic is sufficient for the number of seats contracted on the aircraft. Tour operators must try to balance the capacity and range of the aircraft with the number of seats contracted. Charter agreements specify that a tour operator must pay for all seats contracted, regardless of whether or not they are occupied. Tour operators need not charter every seat on an aircraft but current regulations demand that they purchase a minimum of 20 seats on the plane to be eligible for ITC approval.

Charter arrangements pose the greatest degree of risk for a tour operator. When an airline is chartered, the tour operator commits to a certain number of seats on all flights for which the aircraft is chartered. If the tour operator cannot sell these seats, it is still financially liable for them and the airline must still be paid. To reduce their financial risk, tour operators often purchase seats on a CBIT or GIT basis during the low season or when introducing a new program.

Airlines Owned by Tour Operators

Deregulation has liberalized the rules surrounding the sale of airline tickets but has not seriously influenced the types of air fares available to tour operators. The easing of restrictions has, however, increased tour operator concerns regarding security of supply and competitiveness.

Each of Canada's two major airlines offers its own tours and, in addition, owns a tour operating company. This organizational structure permits the airlines to operate in a more flexible manner than independent tour operators. For example, these airlines may choose to offer seats first to their subsidiary tour operating company rather than to an independent tour company. Or they may choose to run their own tours or charters. Competing demand for these air seats limits an independent tour operator's

security of air transportation. Airlines may further threaten tour operators by offering preferential contract arrangements, better rates and/or a wider selection of equipment to their tour division that are not available to competing tour operators. The airline subsidiary may then be able to offer packages at a lower price than its competitors.

Deregulation has also eased the requirements to acquire an airline operating license. A company must now only show itself to be "fit, willing and able" to operate to receive a license from the NTA. Some tour operators have been prompted by these permissive regulations to enter the airline business. Several have formed airlines with the sole purpose of assuring air transportation for their charter and package tour passengers. These airlines have no interest in offering scheduled service and are unlikely to do so in the foreseeable future. The parent tour companies are, however, determined to remain competitive in the tour industry. By creating its own airline, a tour operator guarantees its seat supply. This year-round commitment for aircraft also permits tour operators to schedule flights that best suit their own needs and eliminates the necessity of working around an airline's priorities.

Negotiations with Airline Catering Companies

Once negotiations with the airline have been completed, the appropriate fare basis chosen, the charter (or other) contract signed, and the flight schedule determined, the next step in the process is selection of the in-flight meals and beverages to be offered. Tour company buyers negotiate these items with airline catering companies. A tour operator that owns its own airline has more control over the in-flight services and how they are presented. This allows it to more clearly create a distinctive image or style for its products. Tour operators that charter from an airline must make similar decisions but may have less choice. Vacationers on all package tours receive some type of in-flight food and/or beverage, even on flights of short duration. The particulars are decided by the tour operator to match the goals of the tour program.

Soft drinks, coffee and tea are available free of charge on both scheduled and charter flights. Alcoholic beverages are served on longer flights, although this may depend on whether the destination is domestic or international. Domestic flights are more likely to have restrictions on the free distribution or sale of alcohol. A tour operator's main goal is to ensure that its clients enjoy themselves. Most charters and package tour flights therefore serve complimentary alcoholic beverages to passengers. This service is considered part of the package; the holiday begins when a passenger boards the aircraft.

The choice of suitable in-flight meals is a more complex decision. Again, as part of the package and to reinforce a feeling of "special treatment", clients are usually served a light snack, even on short flights. Longer flights necessitate a complete meal and perhaps other snacks which demand more care and planning. Lunches are usually restricted to a fixed menu but a choice of two entrées is quite common for dinner. Tour operators usually offer any two of a meat dish, a chicken dish and a fish dish. Clients with special needs or tastes, such as kosher or vegetarian, can be accommodated if requests are made in advance.

The style of service reflects the image of the airline and the tour company which has selected it. Tour operators usually consider the quality of items such as chinaware, tableware and linen when making their final decision on air service.

Negotiations with Hoteliers

After a tour operator has signed a charter contract with the selected airline and arranged the flight schedule, attention is turned to the accommodation component of the program. This is the single most important part of a package tour. Accommodation not only has the largest influence on the final selling price of the package, but it also has the greatest impact on the consumer. Tourists may accept an untidy aircraft or less than perfect service from flight attendants, but they will neither forgive nor forget a substandard hotel. The choice of hotels therefore becomes critical to the success of a tour program.

Typically, land arrangements are made by direct negotiations between the operator and hotel(s) at the destination. This begins with a personal inspection by the operator of the standards and facilities offered at various hotels. As ITCs are targeted at pleasure travellers, a variety of amenities is considered a top priority. Buyers from the tour operator will examine the quality and mix of features such as swimming pools, beaches, entertainment, dining rooms and bars, and air conditioning, as well as the standard of rooms and facilities. The particulars will depend on the operator's target market for the tour program. The tour operator then negotiates a contract with the selected hotel(s) based on a special net rate per room. This net rate is only one element in a number of net costs which are ultimately combined and marked up into a selling price. The number and blend of rooms (singles, doubles, twins, triples or quads) purchased for each departure in the program is based on the anticipated traffic. The net rate charged to tour operators is considerably less than the rack rate since the accommodation is purchased in bulk. The cost of each room, however, varies according to the following factors.

Standard and Type of Accommodation

A room's quality, size and facilities typically governs its price level. A deluxe room generally costs more than a standard room. However, a buyer can normally negotiate a better rate if the property is new or if the operator has not previously used it. Similarly, a double room generally costs more than a single (although the per person cost for a single may be higher). Rooms with added features such as a balcony, air conditioning, or an ocean view raise the price. In the same way, hotels with amenities such as tennis courts and swimming pools may charge more for a room.

Seasonal Demand and Economy

Travel products are subject to the same law of supply and demand as other items. Tour operators who purchase accommodation for the low season or other "slack" time can therefore negotiate a better price. Similarly, if the local economy is in poor condition or if the destination needs to gain (or regain) market share, a better room rate can be arranged. The reasons for the lack of demand may differ but the financial effects are the same.

Buying Power of the Tour Operator

When tour operators contract for airline seats, the larger the number they purchase, the lower the price they can negotiate. A similar rule applies to accommodation. Since tour operators buy in bulk, they expect the room rate to fall as the quantity bought increases. Similarly, the longer the duration of the agreement, the lower the price anticipated. For example, if a tour operator wishes to secure all rooms for a full year covering both high and low seasons, a better rate can be demanded. This arrangement produces a double benefit for the tour operator. In addition to a lower price, the tour operator gains an exclusive service which it can market. Such full season contracts, however, carry a greater risk which the tour operator must consider. Hotels must also evaluate this arrangement which assures them full occupancy at a lower rate but means they have no rooms to rent at the full price should there be a demand.

Past Performance

The tour operator's past performance at the destination and its business history with the hotelier have an effect on the room rate that can be negotiated. Repeat business and fair negotiations generally bring more favourable rates.

Meal Plans

The choice of meals and meal plans is similar to the decisions faced with airline catering companies but is more complex. Negotiations concern the number, variety and type of meals to be included in the package. Many variations from standard meal plans are available. For example, a tour may include seven breakfasts and four dinners, an arrangement which permits flexibility and does not follow a standard meal plan. Decisions must also be taken on whether clients have a choice of dishes or are served from a table d'hôte, how often a particular item such as chicken is served for dinner, the meal preparation (spicy or bland) and the style (buffet or table service). Tour operators are guided by their research into the tastes and budget of their target markets. For example, patrons of deluxe tours are generally offered a wider choice of meals (perhaps à la carte) and may have a dine-around plan which permits meals to be taken in a variety of restaurants.

Negotiations with Local Tour Companies

A local tour or transport company at the destination will be approached to perform round trip transfers between the airport and hotels. Passengers' luggage is picked up and delivered to the hotels as part of these arrangements. The local tour company (known as a ground handler) may also be asked to handle sightseeing trips and other special features included in the package.

Contracts

At the conclusion of each set of negotiations, the tour operator signs a contract with the supplier of the service. Tour operators and suppliers base many contracts on U.S. dollars rather than local currency to minimize the risk of value fluctuations. Contracts legally bind the tour operator to certain financial risks and payment dates. It is these advance payment dates which determine the deposit and final payment requirements that appear in the terms and conditions section of a tour brochure (Figure 10.11).

Representatives

Tour operators may hire a local representative to monitor their interests at the destination. Many tour operators prefer to send a Canadian-trained representative to the destination, provided it is permitted by local regulations. Representatives ensure that a tour operator's clients are well treated during their stay, and that they receive all services and facilities promised.

Costing an ITC Package

Once the airline, hotel and local transportation arrangements have been finalized, a tour operator must then cost the package that will be offered to the public. This is a process which requires skill, experience and foresight.

The costing of air seats is based on anticipated **load factor**. This is the tour operator's estimate of how many of the seats purchased will actually be bought by travellers. It is impossible to expect every flight to be full. However, a price has been negotiated for all airline seats and so the cost of any unoccupied seats must be borne by the passengers who actually travel. For example, if a tour operator buys 1000 seats over a given season but sells only 850, the actual load factor will be 85 percent. The underload on these seats is therefore 15 percent. To remain profitable, a tour operator must ensure that the money collected from those travelling covers the cost of all the seats contracted. This is achieved by dividing the cost of the unsold seats

HOW TO BOOK YOUR SUNQUEST VACATION:

Call a travel agent to make your immediate reservation. Full payment or a deposit is due at time of booking as follows:
- Airfare: $50 per person.
- Coach tours, driving tours, golf tours: $100 per person per tour.
- Hotel accommodation: 1 night's rate stay per person per hotel.
- Car rental: $50 per car.
- Other: $50 per person.

On all of the above, Sunquest travel insurance is recommended and must be paid for at time of booking. No reservation will be confirmed to your travel agent until this payment is received by Sunquest. When Sunquest's indemnity "Travel Payment Protection" outside of Ontario or British Columbia is purchased, the premium must be sent with this payment for your trip.

Credit Card Bookings: Your authorization to use your Credit Card number for deposit and/or final payment indicates your compliance with our booking terms and conditions, whether or not you have actually signed the appropriate draft. Verbal authorization of the use of your Credit Card confirms your reservation.

Full and Final Payment: Full and final payment on all bookings is required no later than 45 days prior to flight departure. Sunquest reserves the right to cancel any booking for which full payment has not been received 45 days prior to departure.

Cancellation Charges: Unless otherwise indicated, cancellation charges depend on the length of time prior to the departure that written notice is received.

Cancellation charges	36 days & prior	35 to 30 days	29 to 22 days	21 days to departure
Air only	Deposit	50%	75%	100%
Coach tours	Deposit	50%	75%	100%
Driving tours	Deposit	50%	75%	100%
Golfing tours	Deposit	50%	75%	100%
Hotel accommodation	Deposit	*50%	*75%	100%
Car rental	Deposit	Deposit	Deposit	Deposit
Other	Deposit	Deposit	Deposit	100%

All above percentages are of total price, which includes all taxes and service charges with the exception of those marked with an asterisk (*), in which case the cancellation charges are the greater of the percentage of the total price or the deposit.

Passengers are requested to notify Sunquest in writing of their intention to cancel. The applicable notification date will be the date written notice is received by Sunquest.

FIGURE 10.11
Tour operator terms and conditions are partly determined by the contracts negotiated with their suppliers.
Source: Sunquest Vacations.

among paying passengers. The higher the load factor the lower will be the cost assigned to the air component. Tour operators typically estimate the load factor by researching statistics from past tours, analyzing the market, and evaluating the competition. A figure between 85 and 95 percent is common for the anticipated load factor on ITCs. The tour operator's experience and judgment become critical in this process. For example, statistics from past tours may favour the use of a relatively low load factor. However, the operator may increase this percentage to lower the price and promote better sales. Alternatively, experience may suggest a high load factor but the operator may reduce it to raise the price and improve the profit margin.

The following example more fully illustrates the costing of an aircraft. Consider a quote of $16,000 per flight for a series of ten flights using a Boeing 737 aircraft from Toronto to Nassau. The total contract cost for the ten flights is therefore $160,000. The seating capacity of a Boeing 737 is 120 seats which produces a total available seating capacity of 1200 for ten flights.

If the tour operator assumes a 100 percent load factor, the air seat cost would be $160,000 divided by 1200 passengers; a per seat cost of just over $133. More realistically, the tour operator would consider that an average load of 85 percent is likely. The total number of passengers expected will therefore be 1020. The air seat cost is again determined by dividing $160,000 by 1020 passengers. This provides an air component seat cost of $156.86. By comparing the cost at 100 percent occupancy with the higher figure at 85 percent it can be seen that the tour operator builds in a reserve factor for unused seats. If a load factor in excess of 85 percent is achieved, the tour operator will have a higher profit. By the same token, if the load factor is less than 85 percent the cost per seat will increase and the results will be less satisfactory. If the load factor drops to 50 percent the tour operator will suffer a severe loss on the flight.

It is clear that an ITC operator must

cost air transportation at a realistic load factor if the estimate is to be valid. Once this has been determined, the cost of hotel accommodation, meal plans, transfers, and any included excursions or extras, is calculated. Tour operators usually provide clients with a beach bag and a tour wallet and these costs must be added when developing the package price. A number of other expenses such as the cost of advertising, brochure production and travel agency commission are direct costs incurred by tour operators to sell their products. Airport dispatch, documentation, credit card commissions and refunds must also be entered in the equation. After all component costs have been added, the tour operator adds a margin to cover overhead and profit. The profit figure is dependent upon first achieving the anticipated load factor on which the air transportation cost is based.

The calculation can be quite complex. For example, a tour operator may charter buses to perform transfers and sightseeing. The cost of a bus depends on its capacity and the number of occupants, just as the cost of airline transportation is based on the size and occupancy of the aircraft. Similarly, if a driver must wait for the group at an attraction an hourly waiting charge is added to charter price. Sometimes tour operators lease hotel accommodation and again this cost is based on the occupancy level anticipated.

To cost a package, a tour operator needs to know more than just the price of each tour component. The number of people likely to purchase the tour must be estimated. As a general rule, the more persons on a tour, the lower will be the cost to the consumer. All tours have certain fixed costs and certain variable costs. Since the fixed costs associated with any given tour are distributed among all participants, the larger the number who take the tour the lower the individual cost. For example, a tour escort's payment is a fixed cost. If a tour escort is paid $400 to accompany a group of ten passengers, each person must be charged $40 to cover the cost of the guide. If, however, 40 people buy the tour, the per person charge for the escort's service is reduced

A tour operator has developed a 7-night tour program to Montego Bay, Jamaica. The program will operate weekly from Toronto for ten weeks on a back-to-back schedule. The following components have been negotiated:

- Air: A Boeing 737 with a capacity of 115 seats has been chartered at a cost of CAD 17,500 for live/live flights and CAD 15,800 for live/ferry flights. (Airlines charge less for a ferry charter since their overhead, such as flight attendant service, is lower.)

- Accommodation: Seven nights at the Holiday Inn, Montego Bay @ USD 30.00 per person per night. Hotel taxes, gratuities and service charges (TGSC) are USD 50.00 per person for the week.

- Transfers between the airport and Holiday Inn are USD 20.00 per person return.

- Sightseeing: The tour includes a visit to Rose Hall Great House at a cost of USD 12.00 per person.

- Miscellaneous: The tour operator's overhead mark-up to cover costs such as profit, administration, baggage tags, beach bag and the like is ten percent. Travel agency commission is 12 percent and the anticipated load factor is 90 percent. USD 1.00 = CAD 1.35

Air Cost Calculation

Cost of live/ferry charter	= CAD 15,800	
Cost for the series (2 RT charters)		= CAD 31,600
Cost of live/live charter	= CAD 17,500	
Cost for the series (9 RT charters)		= CAD 157,500
Total air cost		= CAD 189,100 Capacity of Boeing 737 = 115

Since two of the 11 charters are live/ferry flights, the total number of passengers which could be carried is equivalent to ten live/live flights. At 100 percent load factor the plane would carry 115 x 10 = 1150 passengers. The per passenger air cost is found by dividing the total air cost (CAD 189,100) by the total number of passengers (1150). The per passenger air cost at total capacity = $164.43.
At an anticipated load factor of 90 percent, the plane would carry 115 x 10 x 0.9 = 1035 passengers. At this load factor the per passenger air cost is $182.70.
The air reserve at 90 percent load factor therefore adds $18.27 ($182.70 - $164.43) to the selling price of the air seat.

Ground Package Cost Calculation

Accommodation 7 nights @ USD 30.00	= USD 210.00	
Conversion to CAD @ 1.35		= CAD 283.50
Hotel taxes and service charges	= USD 50.00	
TGSC Conversion to CAD @ 1.35		= CAD 67.50
Transfers (Round Trip)	= USD 20.00	= CAD 27.00
Sightseeing	= USD 12.00	= CAD 16.20
Total Ground Cost		= CAD 394.20

Air: 100 percent basis	$164.43		**Final Selling Price Calculation**	
Air Reserve (90 percent load factor)	18.27			
Total Ground Cost	394.20		Proposed Selling Price	$799.00
Subtotal	$576.90		Less: TGSC (not eligible for commission)	67.50
Overhead (10 percent)	64.10		Commissionable Package Price	$731.50
Total Net Cost	$641.00		Less: Travel Agency Commission (12 percent)	87.78
Agency Commission (12 percent)	87.41 (approx.)		Tour Operator's Net Income	$643.72
TGSC (commission is never paid on this)	67.50		Less: Total Net Cost	641.00
Total	**$795.91**		Tour Operator "cushion"/additional profit	$ 2.72
Proposed Selling Price	**$799.00**		**Final Selling Price**	**$849.00**

The tour operator based the costing on an anticipated load factor of 90 percent. If the load factor should fall to 80 percent, the total number of passengers carried would drop to 920 and the per passenger seat cost would rise to $205.54. Compared with the cost at 100 percent load factor ($164.43), this would add $41.11 to the price of the air seat rather than the $18.27 used in the calculation. The difference between the two air reserve figures is $22.84. The tour operator therefore decides that the cushion ($2.72) is too low and raises the final selling price to $849.00.

FIGURE 10.12
Example of a simple ITC price calculation.

to $10. In this example, transportation is a variable cost. The smaller group could tour in a minibus whereas a tour coach would be necessary for the 40 passengers.

Some costs associated with tour escorts or destination representatives, such as transport and accommodation, are often partially or totally absorbed by suppliers. For example, an airline might provide a free ticket for the escort provided that a minimum group size is reached. Similarly, hotels may grant complimentary accommodation and/or meals. Most tour operators consider tour escorts and destination representatives as a cost rather than as a profit area as their primary function is to offer a service to clients. Thus salary and miscellaneous expenses (telephone, fax, telex, complimentary drinks and the like) are generally covered by the tour operator.

In much the same way that the price of any given tour depends on the number of participants, the price of all tours in a tour operator's program is affected by the total number of clients who purchase tours in a given year. Thus part of a traveller's tour cost covers the tour operator's general fixed costs, such as rent and salaries, that apply no matter which tour a client purchases. This cost varies from year to year (or from season to season) and is usually set at the beginning of the year based on a projection of the operator's expected volume for the period in question.

Package tours are planned and preliminary costing done several months and sometimes years before departure. The actual published selling price varies, depending on the inflation rate, currency fluctuations, surcharges and the season.

During the course of an ITC program, tour operators have obligations to the suppliers that perform their services. A regular system of reporting sales, releasing unwanted accommodation, and sending rooming lists and passenger manifests constantly occurs behind the scenes in a tour operator's office. Tour operators frequently pay for accommodation in advance to guarantee that it will be available. Further, National Transportation Agency regulations require tour operators to pre-pay the airline for transportation services to be performed. It has been estimated that air transportation comprises approximately 35 percent of a tour's package price, 40 percent covers hotels and transfers, and 15 percent is commission to travel agencies. An operator's overhead and profit margin account for only ten percent. Even though these figures vary according to the company and the program, the amount available to cover overhead and profit is remarkably low. ITC operators rely on sales volume to make a profit. One major Toronto operator feels that a tour is profitable if it contributes $50 per seat sold to overhead and profit.

Tour operators run their programs on a risk basis, a fact which differentiates tour operations and other wholesale activities in the travel industry. A tour operator who does not achieve sufficient passengers on any given flight may well face a severe loss on the operation. When insufficient advance bookings are made, operators may consolidate tours by cancelling some flights and sharing space on other charters. However, this can be expensive as the air component is part of a prearranged contract which generally has financial penalties. Another option is to increase promotional activities, but this is a further expense to carry. The operator's costing and forecasting expertise are therefore particularly important.

Surcharges

In recent years, two additional factors have become major considerations when tour operators cost their packages; currency fluctuations and fuel costs.

At one time, the world currency system was fairly stable and most major currencies did not suddenly or substantially change in value. The market today, however, is more volatile and currencies can vary widely in a short period. These fluctuations affect tour operators who must consider the exchange rate when costing a package.

For example, if the Canadian dollar retains it value, the calculation will be accurate. If the Canadian dollar increases in value, tour operator profits will increase. If the Canadian dollar decreases in value, however, profits will drop correspondingly. Tour operators must then decide how much of a decline in profit they are willing to absorb before passing on the extra cost to their clients. Competition with other operators and with other destinations are factors which influence this decision. If a tour operator decides to pass on some or all of the costs associated with currency fluctuations, the increase takes the form of a surcharge. The tour operator would advise travel agencies that due to the devalued dollar the cost of the package has been increased by a specified amount. Agents must collect this surcharge from clients who are usually given the option of cancelling without penalty if they decide against paying the additional amount. Consumers in Ontario can legally cancel without penalty if the surcharge exceeds a specified percentage of the tour price (see Figure 10.13). Clients must not only decide whether to pay the surcharge but they must also consider the implications of a devalued dollar at the destination.

The second factor affecting tour costing is the price of aviation fuel which makes up about 15 percent of an airline's expenses. When an airline quotes a tour operator for the cost of a charter flight, fuel costs are included in the rate. A factor is built into this estimate to allow for an increase in fuel costs. If fuel costs rise more than anticipated (and/or more frequently than expected), the cost of operating the charter will climb and airlines will relay this added cost to tour operators. Tour operators must decide whether to absorb this extra cost or in turn transfer it to their clients. If passed on, tour operators advise travel agencies to collect a specified fuel surcharge from their clients. Again, clients in Ontario may cancel without penalty if the surcharge exceeds a specified percentage of the tour price. Some tour operators attempt to stabilize currency costs by buying "futures", that is, they agree to buy

INCREASE IN PACKAGE PRICE: The prices are based on all fixed costs relating to the package price. These cost depend on fuel, rates of exchange land cost and other factors. In the event that these costs increase, SERENA HOLIDAYS reserves the right to increase the package prices, these include car rental, ground transportation, air fare and hotel cost. Should the prices increase be greater than 7% the passenger has the right to cancel the trip with full refund. Every effort will be made to advise your preferred Travel Agent of any price increase at lease 15 days prior to your date of departure. These increases can be avoided under SERENA HOLIDAYS PRICE GUARANTEE.

currency on a future given date at a fixed rate (see Figure 10.14). If the currency has increased in value the tour operators gain in the transaction; if it has decreased they will lose. In either case, tour operators know exactly what the currency will cost and so can budget accordingly.

It demands skill and experience to anticipate currency exchange rates and fuel price increases, just as it does to predict load factors, changing trends and the popularity of destinations. If a tour operator builds too much of a protective base into the package cost, the price will be too high and it will lose business to competitors. If there is insufficient protection in the package price, the operator will either make no profit at all or will be obliged to impose surcharges which may cause travel agencies and consumers to lose confidence in the tour company. Legislation in Ontario has attempted to make tour operators more careful in their predictions. Travel counsellors also have an important role to

FIGURE 10.13
Tour operators state their surcharge policy in the terms and conditions section of their brochures.
Source: Serena Holidays.

FIGURE 10.14
Tour operators sometimes try to minimize the effect of currency fluctuations by buying futures.
Source: The Globe and Mail.

CANADIAN DOLLAR FORWARDS

$ to buy one	1 month	2 months	3 months	6 months	1 year
U.S. dollar	1.2581	1.2611	1.2640	1.2727	1.2900
British pound	1.7796	1.7790	1.7791	1.7820	1.7935
German mark	0.7537	0.7522	0.7509	0.7488	0.7493
Japanese yen	0.010413	0.010438	0.010462	0.010541	0.010724
Swiss franc	0.8148	0.8151	0.8155	0.8178	0.8259
French franc	0.2221	0.2210	0.2199	0.2179	0.2167
Dutch guilder	0.6700	0.6688	0.6679	0.6661	0.6667
Italian lira	0.000809	0.000805	0.000802	0.000793	0.000778

play in this area. Counsellors should know which tour operators have a good track record, are reliable and do not abuse the imposition of surcharges.

ITC Regulations

After tour operators conclude the contractual and costing processes, they must obtain approval from the National Transportation Agency to operate the packaged tour. As the first step, a tour operator must apply to the airline which will perform the transportation services. The airline, in turn, submits the tour operator's application together with its own application to the NTA. This should be done at least 15 days prior to the start of the proposed ITC program. A tour operator may not advertise or promote an ITC program until NTA approval has been granted.

The NTA's regulations on tour operations change according to existing needs and conditions. The rules have become progressively less restrictive since 1988 when the federal government implemented its policy on transportation deregulation. Submission procedures have also been simplified. Tour operators need only file once per year (rather than for every program) and need not supply all documentation.

Once approval for the program has been granted, a tour operator may then promote the program to the public. The

FIGURE 10.15
British Airways has sponsored London theatre tours for many years.
Source: British Airways Holidays.

London ShowTours Feature:

- 3 or 6 nights accommodation in a room with private bath (Regent Palace has shared facilities; St. Giles has private shower)

- Continental breakfast daily

- Service charges and taxes

- Standard Applause Theatre Pass† (1 pass for 3 night Mini ShowTour and 2 passes for 6 night ShowTour) to your choice of play or musical. Choose a show from our list for selected matinée and evening performances (subject to availability for shows Mon-Thurs and Saturday matinées). On the

day of the performance, exchange your Applause Theatre Pass at the theatre box office for your ticket.

- 1 Applause Backstage Tour Pass which includes admission to the Theatre Museum or a backstage tour of either the National Theatre or the Royal Theatre Drury Lane.

- A Walk of Theatreland – with an illustrated map you can take a fascinating self-guided tour through London's historic theatre district (1 map per booking).

- A three-course pre-theatre dinner at your choice of 11 fine specialty restaurants (for 6 night ShowTour only).

3 NIGHT SHOWTOUR

HOTEL	CODE	Apr 1-July 5/98		Jul 6-Aug 31/98		Sept 1-Oct 31/98 Dec 10-26/98**		Nov 1-Dec 9/98		Dec 27/98-Feb 28/99		Mar 1-31/99**	
		TWIN	SGL	TWIN	SGL	TWIN	SGL	TWIN	SGL	TWIN	SGL	TWIN	SGL
Tavistock	XX7145	159	309	189	339	189	349	69	219	29	179	59	209
Royal National	XX7116	159	309	189	339	189	349	69	219	29	179	59	209
Regent Palace	XX7113	159	239	219	299	189	269	98	179	79	169	119	199
President	XX7097	189	339	209	359	219	369	89	249	59	209	89	239
Phoenix	XX2971	209	319	239	349	239	349	119	229	99	199	129	229
Plaza on Hyde Park	XX7152	259	479	299	499	289	499	179	379	139	329	189	369
St. Giles	XX7023	269	459	289	519	289	489	179	399	159	399	189	429
Forum	XX7033	319	659	349	659	349	679	229	539	199	479	229	509
Strand Palace	XX7126	379	589	419	699	409	619	309	579	239	519	329	609
Mount Royal	XX7729	439	919	479	939	469	949	359	819	319	729	369	809
Park Lane	XX7093	529	1029	559	1029	559	1059	439	909	399	819	489	959
Langham Hilton	XX7157	709	1279	709	1259	739	1309	589	1139	579	1129	669	1199

Triple, quad and child rates also available. Please contact your travel agent or British Airways Holidays.
To help you in the selection of your hotels, turn to pages 23-26.
*** Please see page 71 for some very important details about London ShowTour and Christmas and March Break surcharges.*

most widely used promotional medium is an illustrated brochure or catalogue which is distributed locally, regionally or nationally through the retail travel agency network. Even here, a tour operator is subject to government control as all advertisements and brochures must state the name of the participating carrier, the period during which the program operates, and the items specifically included in the entire package. In Ontario, government legislation strictly controls the contents of a tour brochure and how the tour may be advertised.

Airline Promotion of Tours

The world's airlines recognize the importance of encouraging pleasure travel. This enables them to expand their markets and fill their plane seats. Airlines therefore actively promote tours (see Figure 10.15). Today, one rarely encounters a tour brochure that is not sponsored, endorsed or promoted in some fashion by an airline. Indeed, some tours are co-sponsored by two or more carriers. Many airlines construct and run their own tours. These packages are available only to clients flying the particular airline. For example, a client cannot fly Air Canada to Los Angeles and book an American Airlines Fly/Drive package. If the tour is created by a wholesaler, however, clients may select any airline and any airline will book the tour for the client.

An airline's prime objective is to sell transportation over its routes. As one method of achieving this goal, however, airlines help travel counsellors to sell tours. For example, the sales message promoted in most carriers' advertising campaigns is not simply "buy a ticket and fly with us". Instead, the theme directs its appeal to the pleasures, delights and wonders the buyer will enjoy on arrival at the plane's destination. In other words, emphasis is placed on the benefits to be derived at the end of the journey rather than on the plane ride. Many airlines have a tour desk or tour department to promote tours and simplify their

purchase. An airline's tour department confirms reservations for the carrier's tours. Travel agencies can often obtain confirmation of flight reservations and an accompanying tour in one phone call or computer contact with the selling airline. Further, airlines will frequently distribute a wholesaler's brochures to district sales offices and travel agencies throughout their route system. Some airlines also pay part of the printing costs of brochures published by wholesalers.

Tour Brochures

Tour brochures are the principal sales tool used by tour operators. Travel agency shelves are stocked with a seemingly endless array of colourful, dazzling and enticing brochures. Each destination seems more appealing than another and the choice seems limitless. It is a counsellor's job to help consumers distinguish between destinations and suppliers, to interpret and translate a brochure's sales jargon, and to calculate the product's selling price. This requires that counsellors quickly and accurately find the relevant information, so that a sales dialogue can begin.

As a tour operator's prime sales piece, brochures try to persuade potential consumers to make a buying decision. However, brochures are also used by counsellors as references to sell tours to their clients. As such, they must contain the information necessary to sell the product. This dual purpose means that counsellors must learn to delve beyond the glamour of a brochure's promotional message for the essential selling features of the tour.

How to Read a Tour Brochure

Tour brochures do not follow a standardized format, size or layout. Their style and design, however, tends to have a similar pattern. Brochures are designed to systematically guide prospective consumers through a series of stages leading to a purchase decision. First, an eye-catching cover attracts consumers to the product. A cover usually shows the

FIGURE 10.16
Tour brochures
include validity
dates and proof of
the operator's legal
status.
*Source: Sunquest
Vacations.*

Government Approval: All Inclusive Tour Charter
holidays and ABC flights are operated pursuant to
the rules of the National Transportation Agency and
have been approved by the Agency on behalf of
Sunquest Vacations Limited.

Miscellaneous.
Sunquest Vacations Limited
Ontario Licence No. 1173980
Prices contained in this brochure are valid for
departures from April 1, 1990 to October 31, 1990.
This brochure supercedes all previous brochures.
Sunquest Magazines:
Published by Sunquest Vacations Limited
130 Merton Street, Toronto, Ontario,
Canada M4S 1A4

company name and logo, a list of
destinations, and the brochure's period of
validity. Since dates, prices and products
change, brochures are printed for each
season (see Figure 10.16). Counsellors
must maintain brochure racks to ensure
that only current tour products are
displayed. A brochure's initial pages
generally contain an index followed by a
promotional section describing the
quality of the suppliers, a summary of
special features and the company
philosophy. The central portion of a
brochure describes the tour program,
arranged by destination. Each section
provides necessary details on the
destination and tours. Rates are usually
listed beside the descriptions of the hotels
and tour components. Travel tips and
tour restrictions (the terms and
conditions) are displayed towards the
back of the brochure.

All brochures from reputable
companies clearly describe the
transportation, hotels, meals, transfers
and sightseeing that form the tour. They
state whether taxes, tips, entrance fees
and other charges are included in the tour
price. Information on baggage
restrictions, health and documentation
requirements is provided, and the
company's prices and policies listed.

The vast array of tour brochures can be
bewildering to junior travel counsellors
who must assess and interpret them.
Travel counsellors need to be familiar
with as many different tour brochures as
possible so that they may properly advise
their clients on the travel products sold
by the agency. This task is simplified by
some agencies which restrict their tour
offerings to a few preferred suppliers.
Other agencies give counsellors more
control over the products they sell. In
either case, counsellors must first become
familiar with the products displayed in
the agency. Tour brochures cannot
answer questions or amplify details; this
is a travel counsellor's function.
Brochures should be regraded as tools to
aid the sales process.

Select a few brochures and flip through
them to become acquainted with the
location and style of the main sections
described above. Notice where each
section appears in the brochure and try to
find selected items such as hotel ratings,
validity and departure dates, prices or
additional charges. It will quickly become
apparent which brochures are well
organized and easy to use. Now select
one tour product or destination and
review it more closely. Does it provide
the information you need to answer client
questions and make a sale? Is there an
itinerary? Are the facilities described and
rated? Does the price show what is
included in the tour, and are taxes and
service charges clearly identified? Do
hotel rates differ on different departure
days and for different numbers of
occupants? Rates are usually shown as a
per person charge based on two people
sharing a room. Note the charges applied
for deviations from this arrangement. For
example, is there a supplement for clients
travelling alone, and do three or four
persons sharing a room qualify for a
reduction or an addition to the standard
rate? Some taxes and service charges are
prepaid to the travel agency while others,
certain departure taxes for example, are
paid by clients at the destination. Read
the fine print at the bottom of the rate
chart so that clients can be advised
appropriately.

The rates charged for various tours are
an indication of their quality. The
language used to describe a tour's
features also gives a clue as to what can
be expected. Counsellors who learn to
translate brochure descriptions can help

to make their clients' expectations more realistic. For example, a "secluded" resort may be quite isolated from other amenities and clients may have difficulty in travelling to the local attractions. Similarly, a "lively" hotel may cater to a younger clientele. Brochure photographs are chosen to reflect the product in its most favourable light and help identify the type of clientele being targeted. Most tour operators try to describe their products accurately to prevent charges of false advertising and to ensure that clients are not disappointed. However, tour

FIGURE 10.17
All tour brochures specify the operator's policies and restrictions.
Source: British Airways Holidays.

TERMS & CONDITIONS

HOW TO BOOK
Call your local travel agent or British Airways at 1 800 AIRWAYS.

RESERVATIONS & PAYMENTS
Full payment is required 7 days after booking or 30 days prior to departure, whichever is earlier. Minimum and maximum stay is determined by the rules of British Airways' lowest published apex fare. For stays less than 7 days: Saturday night minimum applies. All travel must be completed by July 7, 1995. Infants pay 10% of the applicable price.

CANCELLATION FEES
No refunds.

WEEKEND SURCHARGES
Add $30 to price when departure is on Fri./Sat. Add $30 to fare when return flight is on Sat./Sun.

CHANGES
Once payment has been made, no changes permitted.

DOCUMENTS
Approximately 21 days before departure, provided full payment has been received, your airline ticket, hotel voucher, transfers and other extras will be mailed. All other items included in your package will be given at the hotel in a "Welcome Packet". Byways of Britain "Welcome Packets" must be obtained at the British Airways Welcome Desk located in the Arrivals Hall, Heathrow Terminal 4. All vouchers are British Airways Holidays documents and serve as both confirmation and exchange documentation. It is essential that you take these documents with you. If for some reason you do not have your hotel/car voucher, you will be requested to make full payment directly to the hotel/Hertz upon arrival. There are no refunds for unused vouchers/portions of a programme.

PASSPORTS & VISAS
You must ensure that prior to the start of your flight/vacation, you possess a valid passport and all relevant visas and/or entry permits appropriate to all countries you will visit. (Failure will result in the forfeit of travel arrangements and monies paid.)

FREE BAGGAGE ALLOWANCE
On flights to/from Canada: Two bags per person plus one carry-on bag. Baggage allowances are subject to change, check with British Airways for up-to-date information. *Baggage insurance is recommended.*

AIRPORT TRANSFERS
In London, the transfers are provided by Hotelink. Departures are grouped according to flight arrival time and hotel to minimize airport wait time and number of stops before reaching your hotel. In Paris, the transfer is via the Air France bus into city centre.

CLAIMS
All claims of any nature must be made in writing within 30 days of the return flight to British Airways, Customer Relations, 4120 Yonge Street, Suite 100, North York, Ontario M2P 2B8. Baggage claims must be made before leaving the airport. Claims will not be honored after such time.

NOT INCLUDED
Canadian international departure tax, U.K. departure tax and Paris airport tax. Also not included are passport and visa fees; laundry; food and beverages not mentioned and items of a personal nature. Costs for excursions, city sightseeing, entrance fees, local guides and transfers are excluded unless otherwise noted. Frequent Traveller mileage may be earned. Award Travel may not be redeemed in conjunction with this offer. Industry, seniors, Privileged Traveller, and children discounts are not permitted.

CAR RENTAL
Price does not include fuel, oil, parking and tolls. A refundable fuel deposit is required to cover the cost of a tank at the beginning of your rental. The minimum driver rental age is 21 and 23 for the Mondeo or Scorpio. All drivers must hold a driver's licence that has been valid at least one year. There is an extra charge of £2 per day plus Value Added Tax for each additional driver payable to Hertz.

RESPONSIBILITY
The hotels and other suppliers providing services are independent contractors. British Airways Holidays or its affiliates are not responsible for the negligent acts and/or omissions of these independent contractors, their employees, agents, servants or representatives. British Airways Holidays gives notice that in issuing tickets and coupons for travel conveyance or transport by any means, and in making arrangements for hotels or other accommodation, it is acting not as a principal but as an agent only for the companies, corporations or persons providing or offering the means of travel, conveyance or transport and accommodation and accordingly that British Airways Holidays will accept no responsibility or liability in respect of either person or property for any loss, damage, injury, accident, delay or irregularity however occasioned, sustained or suffered in or during any package, journey, trip or tour, or in the carrying out of any arrangements booked by or through them, and notwithstanding that their principal may be a foreign company, corporation or person that, British Airways Holidays is not acting as agent for the passengers effecting the bookings. British Airways, as an international air carrier, is subject to international conventions limiting its liability; the limitations of liability are contained on the reverse side of your airline ticket and form part of the terms and conditions hereof.

TRAVEL AGENT INFORMATION
From Toronto: (416) 250-1350; outside Toronto: 1-800-668-1050; from British Columbia: 1-800-668-1070.

Prices are subject to change without notice and are guaranteed at time of deposit. Please reconfirm fare with a reservation agent, no later than 7 days after booking or 30 days prior to departure, whichever is earlier. The M.C.O. number must be called in *and* also forwarded to British Airways (please see below). *Upon receipt of M.C.O., travel documents, including air tickets, will be mailed by British Airways Holidays approximately 21 days prior to departure.*

Payments may be made by M.C.O. M.C.O. payments can only be validated on a British Airways plate. (Note: do not take commission on taxes.) Please remit coupon #1 of the M.C.O. All payments must be sent to British Airways Holidays, Value Plus Ticketing, 4120 Yonge Street, Suite 100, North York, Ontario M2P 2B8.

brochures are an operator's most powerful sales tool and must be treated as such.

The terms and conditions section describes the tour operator's policies and restrictions (Figure 10.17). It advises how to book tours and specifies dates when deposits and final payments are due. Note the deposit amount. Some operators require a flat fee while others request a percentage of the selling price. Cancellation penalties and fees for changing a reservation are also outlined in this section.

Several tour operators may use the same properties at a destination. Their tours may even visit the same attractions and include similar features. The prices, however, may vary considerably. This discrepancy must be explained to clients who may not be aware of the different room locations, meal plans, and carriers used by each operator. Clients will look to a counsellor for advice in making their choice. Review brochures from different operators offering similar products and note the selling features you would use. For example, one operator may offer bonus features such as a free rental car or a discount for early bookings. Some clients may prefer a particular airline or plane, and most prefer nonstop flights. Note whether there is a stopover plan for clients who must travel a long distance to the airport or who have an early morning departure. Clients who must travel to reach the starting point of the tour generally have at least two options. If a tour commences in Toronto, for example, a tour operator's brochure may show supplements or list prices for packages purchased from say, Windsor or Ottawa. These higher prices will reflect add-on fares required to fly clients to Toronto. Travel counsellors with clients in these locations will earn commission based on the higher brochure price which includes the add-on fare. Some packages list prices only from the tour's starting point and clients must purchase an additional air fare to reach the tour gateway. Counsellors then earn commission on transportation to and from the gateway. This commission is paid separately to the travel agency by the transportation company. The majority of tour operators also promote travel insurance. Compare the insurance offered by each operator with the coverage available from a travel insurance company.

Recommending a Tour

Whether a tour is planned as a group package or an independent trip, by a counsellor or a tour operator, the primary factor is the client's needs and comfort. The first step in recommending a tour is to determine the type of travel experience desired by the client. Counsellors then choose brochures from companies that sell such products and compare packages to determine which offers the best value. A major factor in deciding which company to sell is the tour operator's reputation. A profile form (Figure 10.18) can be developed to help counsellors assess tour companies and their products. Counsellors make recommendations to their clients but they rely on the tour operator to actually provide the services. Some agencies sell only from a list of preferred suppliers. Other agencies consider that evaluating the product is part of a counsellor's job. Some counsellors regard the tour company's experience in the industry and to the destination as the prime factor. Other indicators are its reputation with colleagues and its membership in professional associations such as CATO, ACTA and the USTOA. An operator's suppliers can act as a guide to its quality. For example, does it use a reputable airline or an unknown company? Counsellors can also learn from industry reports in trade publications.

Several factors can guide counsellors in suggesting a particular tour. The client's convenience is one element. For example, nonstop flights are more convenient than connecting flights, as are certain days or times of departure and arrival. Similarly, hotels close to the beach and attractions are more convenient than those which are isolated. (However, the client may desire privacy and this might outweigh other considerations.) Within reason most people are concerned with value rather

COMPANY PROFILE:

Company Name: _____

Tour Operator: _____ Tour Wholesaler: _____

Types of Tours: _____
_____

Tour Lengths: _____

Destinations Served: _____
_____

Airlines/Aircraft Used: _____

Hotel Rating System: _____

Special Needs: _____

Car Rentals: _____

Other Services: _____

Destination Reps/Escorts: _____

Association Memberships: _____

Brochure Comments: _____
_____

POLICIES:

Res/Payment Procedures: _____

Changes: _____

Cancellations: _____

Taxes and Service Charges: _____

Children/Infant Rates: _____

Insurance Offered: _____

Commission: _____

Other: _____

ADMIN:

Direct Reservations: Yes _____ No _____

Res: Telephone #: _____

Airline CRS: _____

Sales Rep's Name: _____

Telephone #: _____

FIGURE 10.18
Sample tour company profile form.
Courtesy of Dorothy Chase CTC.

ITC COSTING FORM   Name: _____
                                                  Date: _____

CLIENT: _____

1 - DEPARTURE: ex: _____ Date: _____ Supplier: _____
     Tour Operator: _____ ex: _____ Destination: _____
     Duration: _____ Property: _____
     Type of Accommodation: _____
     # of adults _____ # of children _____ # of infants _____

     Package: _____ @ _____ = _____
                       _____ @ _____ = _____
                       _____ @ _____ = _____
                       _____ @ _____ = _____   _____

2 - EXTRAS:
     Air   _____ @ _____ = _____
     Meal Plan   _____ @ _____ = _____
     Car Rental   _____ @ _____ = _____
     Supplements   _____ @ _____ = _____
     Overnights   _____ @ _____ = _____
                       _____ @ _____ = _____   _____

3 - INSURANCES:
     _____   _____ @ _____ = _____
     _____   _____ @ _____ = _____
     _____   _____ @ _____ = _____
     _____   _____ @ _____ = _____   _____

4 - TAXES:
     Canadian Dep.   _____ @ _____ = _____
     Destination Dep. _____ @ _____ = _____
     Hotel Tax & SC   _____ @ _____ = _____
                       _____ @ _____ = _____
     All Inclusive   _____ @ _____ = _____   _____

                                          TOTAL   _____

FIGURE 10.19
Sample ITC costing form.
Courtesy of Dorothy Chase CTC.

ITC COSTING FORM

CLIENT: _____

5 - DEPOSIT: _____ @ _____ = _____
_____ @ _____ = _____

   DEPOSIT DUE DATE: _____ (weeks prior)

6 - **FINAL PAYMENT: Owing from client to agency:**
   Total Cost: _____
   Less Deposit: _____
   = Balance Owing: _____

   FINAL PAYMENT DUE DATE: _____ (weeks prior)

7 - **FINAL REMITTANCE TO TOUR OPERATOR by agency:**
   Balance: _____
   Less Commission: _____   (10% of Total Cost of
   Net Remittance: _____   commissionable portions)

8 - **Note other costs your client will pay for directly:**

   In Canada:

   Abroad:

   Note amount of commission due your agency from these direct costs:

FIGURE 10.19

than price. The traveller must know exactly what is included in the price (and, by extension, what is excluded) and must perceive value for money or the proposed trip will be unacceptable. Tours offering better value for money may not necessarily be the least expensive but will ultimately offer the most appeal. Counsellors can compare equivalent packages by calculating the tour price including taxes, service charges and supplements. Figure 10.19 is a sample ITC costing form which counsellors may find useful for calculating tour prices. The itinerary should be consulted and the schedule noted. Assess the pacing of the tour and its convenience in relation to the client's needs and capabilities. Are cities visited or merely driven through? Note the amount of time spent travelling and the proportion devoted to free time and walking. Hotel descriptions, their facilities and ratings should be evaluated. Hotel and room locations are particularly important to most clients. Ocean front rooms are not the same as ocean view rooms (which let clients see the ocean but are usually on a side away from the beach.) Meal plans differ so that the number of meals and the choice of dishes (a la carte or table d'hôte) varies. Departure arrangements affect the cost and convenience. Midweek departures are usually less expensive than those on a weekend; seasonal rates may be lower if your client can travel one week earlier or later. Hidden costs should also be considered. There may be additional charges for certain activities. Taxes and service charges may not be included in the price. Selling conditions may vary. Some operators have liberal change and cancellation requirements while others are restrictive. If clients are purchasing an independent package, check whether the services of a local host are included. Note that fly/drive packages should not be recommended for most international travel unless the client knows the language and driving conditions at the destination or is revisiting an area.

Product Analysis

This chapter has reviewed some of the seemingly limitless number of holiday options from which travellers may choose. The foregoing discussion has suggested ways to interpret brochures and assess tour operators and their products. The tour product checklist (Figure 10.20) summarizes these considerations. It may help simplify the evaluation procedure and assist counsellors to compare the quality of services offered. Use of a suitable checklist will help counsellors improve their ability to read tour brochures and develop skill in identifying worthwhile and desirable sales features, such as unusual or outstanding entertainment, good quality hotels and convenient departure times. It will reveal possible flaws in a product, such as poor quality hotels, insufficient leisure time or unfair pricing, and it will encourage counsellors to become price-conscious, thereby developing the ability to judge good value from among a variety of products. A checklist, however, will only benefit counsellors who have previously learned to assess each category of tour component.

Making a Tour Reservation

The products of major tour companies can be booked through an airline CRS using special programs such as LeisureLink (Galileo Canada) or DirecTours (Sabre). Tour companies report that over half of their bookings are now made in this manner. When the CRS is "down", or if the agency is not automated, counsellors can make a manual reservation by following the procedures described below.

Travel counsellors dealing with a tour operator or wholesaler will call the company's reservations department to make a booking. Counsellors first identify themselves and their agency. Depending on the client's needs, counsellors will request availability for the appropriate tour or tour components. Counsellors must supply the reservations sales agent with the following information to complete the reservation:

* Name of travel counsellor.
* Name of travel agency.
* Travel agency code or ID number if the system is computerized.

- Number, names and home phone numbers of clients.
- Client address if travelling on an ABC.
- Destination or Tour Number.
- Departure date and duration.
- Choice of hotel and type of accommodation.
- Request for cancellation/personal insurance if selecting the tour company's option.
- Number of children travelling and their ages.
- Any special requirements, e.g., crib in room, skycot, special meals, assistance for disabled clients.

Confirm the rates and other costs such as taxes, service charges and departure taxes. At the same time, confirm the company's option policies and payment dates. If space is available and is confirmed, the reservationist will provide a confirmation number (also called a file number, tour number or locator number) for the counsellor's future reference. This number should be noted on the client file together with the booking date and the name of the reservations agent.

When space is available in all categories and for all dates, a tour operator describes this as a **free sale** situation. Counsellors may also find that some categories or tour dates offer a limited choice. Reservations agents generally attempt to switch sell when the requested product is unavailable. They may offer a choice such as another departure date, a different destination, another tour, or an alternative hotel. If an acceptable alternative is not available, clients may be put on a waiting list. If a booking is cancelled, the tour operator will contact the agency and offer the space. Waitlisting is seldom used by tour operators because counsellors can usually find alternative space immediately from another tour company.

Some tour companies offer counsellors an option period of from one to seven days for any reservation made. The counsellor must confirm the booking by sending a deposit (and cancellation insurance, if applicable) within the option period, otherwise the wholesaler will release the space for sale. The use of options depends on the proximity of the travel date. For example, any tour or tour component reserved within 42 days of departure usually requires full payment by the option date. A booking within the final payment period is called a late booking.

Making Payments

Deposits are collected and sent to the tour operator who in turn forwards a client confirmation to the agency. Once the confirmation is received, the client should be reminded of the date the balance is due. Counsellors can note this date in their desk calendar or CRT to remind them to contact their client in time to make the final payment. Most tour companies have computerized inventory control systems which automatically cancel reservations if payment is not received by the specified option date. Counsellors must therefore contact the operator if payment will be late. Clients who change a booking are generally charged an administration fee by the tour operator which ranges from $25 to $40.

When the client has paid in full for the tour, the travel counsellor calculates the commission and deducts this amount. The commission is retained by the agency and the balance is forwarded to the tour operator as the final payment. After the final payment has been received, the tour operator will issue the appropriate tour documents and forward them to agency. Depending on the type of tour, the tour operator may issue all documents. Alternatively, the operator may issue some documents while the counsellor issues air tickets. It is the counsellor's responsibility to check the documentation for errors and omissions.

Many tour operators now have computer software which simplifies the booking and payment process for counsellors. Some of these products allow agents to have direct access to the tour operator's private network through an airline CRS.

1. **Is the tour approved?** If so, an independent tour will have an IT code number printed above the itinerary which denotes approval by IATA or the ATA. (IT numbers are no longer mandatory for domestic tours.) The IT code number appears as an alphanumeric designation such as IT9CP1MTA7. Approved tours usually entitle clients to purchase a special promotional air fare. Depending on the destination, a travel counsellor may also receive an override commission on the air fare.

   ITC packages do not require an IT code number. Such tours are approved by the NTA and are not subject to IATA or ATA requirements. NTA approval will be indicated in the contract or conditions section of the tour brochure.

2. **Period of Validity.** A tour's validity dates must be included in the brochure. These dates are often printed on the front cover, although sometimes they appear in the rate chart. The dates identify the period during which the brochure's tours and prices apply. It is important to check validity to ensure that the correct price is charged for a tour and that it still operates. Outdated brochures should be discarded.

3. **Who is the tour operator?** Does the tour operator have a good reputation in the industry? Consult with the agency manager and colleagues concerning their experience with the company. Are reservations confirmed and refund adjustments made promptly? Have clients complained about the quality of the components? Is the tour operator well known through consumer advertising? Does it have an established "brand" name?

   Counsellors must inform clients of the name of the company offering the tour. This is printed in the responsibility clause of the terms and conditions section of the brochure. Further, counsellors must ensure that clients understand that their contract is with the tour operator, not between the agency and the client. This is a legal requirement known as disclosure of the principal. When services are not performed as advertised, travellers often blame the counsellor even though their dispute is with the tour operator. For this reason, it is essential to deal only with companies which have earned the counsellor's trust and respect.

4. **Price.** Is the product fairly priced for the features it includes? How does the price compare with similar products? Are those items which are included in the price clearly stated? Are the items which are not included also shown? Inclusions and exclusions will be stated on the rates page, in the general conditions section of the brochure, and sometimes in both areas. Note that "optional" tours are not included in a quoted price. "Seeing" an attraction is not the same as "visiting" an attraction; "ocean front room" is not the same as "ocean view room". Are admission prices included? Is transportation supplied between sightseeing attractions? Price does not usually include taxes and service charges which must be added. Similarly, there may be supplements for travel on weekends or during high season. Note whether the published price is in Canadian or U.S. dollars and whether it includes air fare from the client's city, a gateway city, or is for land arrangements only (in which case clients must purchase air transportation separately).

   Almost all Canadian tour operators publish per person prices, generally based on double occupancy. However, the price might be based on single, twin, or triple occupancy. Single travellers are frequently charged a supplement to the existing per person twin or double rate, whereas additional occupants in a room usually qualify for a reduction from this rate. Tour operators generally price their products in two parts; the tour cost, and the service charges (TGSC - taxes, gratuities, service charges). Since operators want the tour price to be as low and competitive as possible, the TGSC figure is often quoted in smaller type as a separate item to be added to the tour price. This confuses clients; consumer organizations frequently ask that brochures show only one price which includes all taxes and charges. Note that commission to travel agents is never paid on TGSC. Their commissions are based on the tour price.

   As well as the absolute price, the price per diem (per day) will help measure the value of the tour. The daily rate is ascertained by dividing the total price by the number of nights on the tour since accommodation is always based on this factor. For example, an 8-day, 7-night tour priced at $840 would have a per diem of $120.

5. **What air fare is quoted?** Is it a regular fare without restrictions, or an excursion or promotional fare which have conditions? Is the fare correct and currently available? Who is responsible for issuing the ticket, the tour operator or the selling agency? Is the air fare included in the price of the tour?

6. **Who is the sponsoring carrier?** Is an allotment of reserved seats held for the tour operator? If the client or counsellor wishes, can another airline be selected?

7. **Departure Dates.** When does the tour leave? Every Sunday? Once a month? Only on specified dates? What is the gateway city? Toronto? Montreal? New York City? Is there an add-on fare? How convenient are the arrangements for the client?

8. **Type of Tour.** Is the tour fully escorted from the gateway city to its return? Are tour members met on arrival by an escort at the destination? Are passengers met in each city or country by a local host only for transfer purposes? Is the tour entirely independent?

9. **Hotels/Resorts.** What is the quality of the accommodation? Is it deluxe, first class or second class? Are private bathrooms specified? How is the property rated by standard references? What is its reputation with agency colleagues and clients?

10. **Meals.** Which meal plan is offered? If the tour includes breakfast only is this a continental breakfast or a full breakfast? Are the meals table d'hôte or à la carte? Tea and coffee are not included in meal prices on many European tours; does the brochure clarify this? Are gratuities for meal services included? If dinners are included in the price must clients pay a supplement if steak or lobster is ordered?

11. **Itinerary.** Are the places visited suitable for the client's tastes and interests? Is the itinerary followed too tedious or too strenuous? Is too much time spent visiting places of little interest? Is there sufficient time for rest, shopping and leisure activities?

12. **Terms and Conditions.** What is the operator's policy on deposits, final payment, refunds and cancellations?

FIGURE 10.20
Tour product checklist.

Tour Operator Documentation

When a tour reservation is made, the tour company's reservations department notifies their accounting department which prepares an invoice for the travel agency. The invoice gives full particulars of the booking, the amount required for final payment and the due date (which is usually six weeks or 42 days prior to departure). After the tour operator's ticketing department has been informed that payment has been received, it sends tickets and vouchers to the travel agency (approximately 20 to 35 days prior to departure). For reservations made less than 14 days before departure, the documents are delivered to the travel agency by courier or are handed to the passenger at the time of departure.

Tour operator documents are placed in a ticket wallet which the travel counsellor checks and gives to the client. The wallets contain all relevant travel information for the trip and, depending on the tour or components purchased, consist of the items noted below. Counsellors must always verify that these documents are complete and correct. Counsellors in Ontario are responsible for ensuring that clients receive accurate information.

Tickets and/or Vouchers

Tickets are exchanged for transportation whereas vouchers may be exchanged for transportation or services. Land vouchers cover hotels, car rentals, and included extras such as food and beverage, sightseeing and special activities (Figure 10.21). Sometimes a tour operator issues transportation exchange vouchers instead of the airline tickets. Passengers simply exchange these vouchers for a proper ticket at the departure check-in. Tour operators use these vouchers for various reasons. For example, there may be impending flight changes and rather than having to reissue airline tickets they may decide to issue exchange vouchers. Some tour operators are concerned that passengers may lose their tickets; vouchers are more easily replaced. Clients sometimes purchase packages considerably in advance of the departure date. The operator may not yet have confirmed travelling times, thus proper transportation documents cannot be issued and vouchers are substituted.

FIGURE 10.21
Tour operators often include vouchers for accommodation, transportation or other services in their document-ation.
Source: Sunquest Vacations.

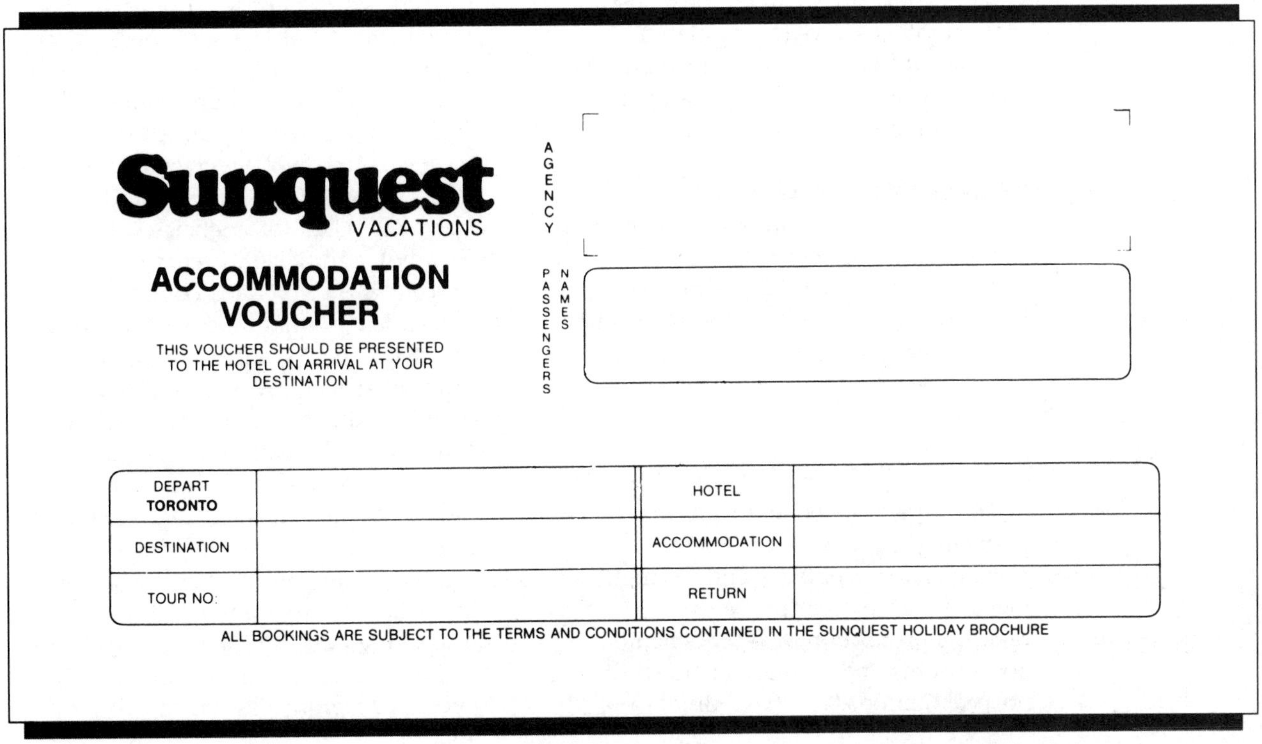

ACCOMMODATION VOUCHER

THIS VOUCHER SHOULD BE PRESENTED TO THE HOTEL ON ARRIVAL AT YOUR DESTINATION

DEPART **TORONTO**		HOTEL	
DESTINATION		ACCOMMODATION	
TOUR NO:		RETURN	

ALL BOOKINGS ARE SUBJECT TO THE TERMS AND CONDITIONS CONTAINED IN THE SUNQUEST HOLIDAY BROCHURE

Itinerary

Every ticket wallet contains a complete summary of the tour from the departure point through to the conclusion of the tour. The contents vary according to the tour and company but generally include:

- Client's name, address and telephone number.
- Passenger's account, docket and file number.
- Transportation company's name(s) and flight number(s).
- Gateway and departure location (i.e., terminal number).
- Arrival and departure times.
- Hotel name and type of accommodation.
- Tour number.
- Cruise line, ship name and cabin number.
- Travel agent's name and address.
- Company phone numbers in departure city and at destination so that clients can reconfirm transportation arrangements.

Miscellaneous Items

Most ticket wallets include travel information such as currency, customs and immigration regulations, hints on what to pack, the weather, local customs and activities, duty-free regulations, tipping, and luggage tags which are often colour coded since baggage handlers at the destination may not read English.

Changes and/or Updates

Tour operators include information on changes to the itinerary or program, such as increased service charges and taxes, fuel surcharges, and changes in currency or customs regulations.

Advantages of Package Tours

Tour operators benefit from the popularity of package tours with consumers. The public's endorsement helps operators to improve sales volume, raise the proportion of repeat clientele, boost profits and increase business during off-peak periods. The flexibility of the package concept allows operators to target many specific markets, and permits them to test new products and ideas to attract fresh markets.

Agency Advantages

Package tours also offer travel agents several advantages. These products combine the low prices associated with group tours with many attributes of individual tours. The shared characteristics permit package tours to appeal to both group and individual travellers. Their popularity has several distinctive sales features.

- **Easy to Sell**. One contact with the operator by phone or computer can immediately confirm all arrangements for an entire package. There is no need to contact each supplier to check space availability and make reservations.
- **Minimum of Paperwork**. Package tours demand less time, paperwork and communications costs than FITs. Individual dealings with several suppliers to send deposits, request services or issue documents are unnecessary. All components are handled by a tour operator who assembles the itinerary and documentation for delivery by the travel counsellor to the client.
- **Economical Promotion**. Tour operators print their own brochures and conduct their own advertising campaigns at little cost to travel agencies. These sales tools are widely distributed and help to "pre-sell" ITCs for agencies.
- **Steady Commission Income**. Ten percent is the standard commission. Override commission can be earned on increased sales volume and operators offer other incentives to stimulate bookings during seasonal recessions.
- **Immediate Reward**. Travel agencies deduct commission from the final payment before forwarding it to the tour operator. There is no delay in receiving compensation from suppliers in remote destinations.
- **Maximize Earnings**. Tours often include items such as meals, special events and gratuities which

independent travellers typically pay at the destination. Their inclusion in the tour price permits counsellors to earn commission on these items.

- **Repeat Business**. High public acceptance of the ITC products of reputable operators generates repeat business.
- **Flexible Product**. Package tours are now well established. Clients can choose from a large variety, designed to meet almost every taste and budget.

Consumer Advantages

Package tours not only benefit operators and agencies, they also have several advantages for consumers.

- **Prearranged**. Travellers know what they are paying for as all tour components are arranged and paid for in advance. Travellers need not be concerned about arriving at a destination to find that no accommodation is available.
- **Easy to Purchase and Budget**. A package has an all-inclusive price which is prepaid to the travel agency. Travellers can thus budget more easily. This concept has been extended; tour operators now offer all-inclusive tour packages that include meals, drinks, activities and tips.
- **Economical**. Bulk buying by tour operators provides consumers with a lower cost package than if the same components were purchased on an individual basis. The deregulation of air fares has affected this factor and an FIT may sometimes be less expensive than a similar package tour. However, tourists on packages gain extra benefits such as the services of a destination representative.
- **Route Convenience**. Most tour packages are operated to popular destinations, such as Florida, Mexico and the Caribbean. The use of direct or nonstop flights enhances this convenience. In addition, departures are generally once or twice weekly according to the season and demand.
- **Carefree**. Advance arrangements are made for the convenience of travellers.

Most tours include transfers which save travellers time and trouble. Tours may also be escorted. Escorted tours offer additional reassurance for first-time travellers who can rely on the escort's specialized knowledge and experience. If tours are not escorted, clients always have access to a resource person (either a local host or the tour operator's representative) who can assist them at the destination.

- **Assured Entrance**. Tour operators make block purchases of tickets for attractions and events, some of which can be obtained only by purchasing a package tour. Tours can therefore ensure that clients secure accommodation at the location and tickets for special events such as the Passion Play or the Olympics. Some countries restrict entry for individual travellers and permit only those on prepaid tour packages to visit.
- **Reliability and Quality**. Consumers know that arrangements and facilities have been verified by the tour operators. The companies' experience and research assures that tours visit the most popular and worthwhile attractions and activities.
- **Variety and Flexibility**. Many specialized interests can be met through tour packages.

Disadvantages of Package Tours

Although the benefits of package tours for travel agencies cannot be denied, these products also have some drawbacks for a counsellor.

Agency Disadvantages

- **Dependence on Tour Operator Integrity**. Travel counsellors must rely on the integrity of the tour operator. They depend on the tour operator's ability to operate and control the product at a level of quality and standard of service which will be acceptable to their clients.

- **Loss of Identity**. As all components are reserved by and under the control of the tour operator, the travel agency loses its identity with suppliers.
- **Lower Commission**. Since tour operators buy tour components in bulk, the cost of a tour package may be lower than if a counsellor constructed an FIT composed of similar elements. The commission per passenger may therefore be lower.

Consumer Disadvantages

Although package tours are popular and have many advantages for consumers, there are some negative aspects associated with these products. Travel counsellors must be aware of both the positive and negative factors which influence their public acceptability.

- **Inflexibility**. Clients are locked into particular travel arrangements. They cannot curtail or extend their vacation except under extreme circumstances such as illness. They cannot, for example, return after four days to keep an important appointment, nor remain longer because they are enjoying the program. The choice of destinations and hotels is restricted to those offered on a tour program. ITCs operate to a limited number of destinations, usually the most popular, and are not available to other areas. Similarly, travellers may not select from any other hotel at the destination, only from those offered in the package. Substitutions are generally prohibited. Most tour operators permit clients to change accommodation if the hotel booked for them is unsuitable; however, the hotel must be in an equivalent category. This practice is not always possible as there may be no equivalents or the alternate hotel may already be fully booked. Naturally, clients who change to a hotel in a higher rated category must pay the difference in price. Tour operators do not publicize or encourage changes at the destination; these are generally considered to be public relations exercises rather than company policy.

Many of the criticisms discussed above can be overcome if counsellors know their products, their suppliers and their clients. The large number of ITC options available makes it easier for counsellors to match different client types, needs and travel products.

Review Questions

1. Name the three broad classifications of tours and discuss the elements that comprise each type of tour.

2. Explain the development of tour wholesalers and tour operators.

3. Describe the stages in the preparation of a package tour.

4. Compare the benefits and disadvantages of FITs and ITCs for consumers.

5. What qualities are required by a tour escort? Give an example of how each quality would be useful on an escorted motorcoach tour.

Review Assignments

1. Make a catalogue, according to destination, of all current ITC programs operating from your city or nearest departure point. The catalogue should show base price, days of operation and period of validity for each program. It should also show the features included in the base price.

2. Use local tourist attractions to plan a 3-day motorcoach inbound tour with two nights' accommodation. Create a tour escort's binder for this tour.

References

Canadian Association of Tour Operators, 70 University Avenue, Suite 250, Toronto, Ontario M5J 2M4, Tel: (416) 348-9083, Fax: (416) 977-2895.

Consolidated Tour Manual (CTM), 11510 N.E. Second Avenue, Miami, FL 33161.

Gray Line Official Sightseeing Tariff, Gray Line Sightseeing Association, Inc., 350 Fifth Avenue, Room 1409, New York, NY 10018.

National Tour Association, 546 East Main Street, P.O. Box 3071, Lexington, KY 40596-3071.

United States Tour Operators Association (USTOA), 211 East 51st Street, Suite 12B, New York, NY 10022, Telephone (212) 944-5727.

WATA Master-Key, World Association of Travel Agencies, 37 quai Wilson, P.O. Box 852, 1211 Geneva 1, Switzerland.

Worldwide Tour Planning Manual, American Sightseeing International, 309 Fifth Avenue, New York, NY 10016.

## Chapter 11

Cruises

Chapter Summary

This chapter examines the growth and development of the cruise industry. Standard references and cruise brochures are explored as sources of product knowledge which are used to assess the features and quality of a cruise. Since cruises are marketed as floating hotels and all-inclusive vacations which compete with tour packages, the daily cost of each is proposed as a valid means of comparing the two types of vacation. Selling features, and the skills required to read deck plans and interpret brochures are also reviewed. Following a summary of the benefits and disadvantages of cruises, reservations and ticketing procedures are highlighted. Other types of marine transportation are also examined and a glossary of common nautical terminology is provided.

Chapter Objectives
After completing this chapter you should be able to:

- Use nautical terminology.

- Describe the various categories of water transportation.

- Discuss the development of the cruise industry.

- Describe how cruises are marketed.

- Identify sources of product knowledge for cruises.

- Interpret deck plans and cruise brochures.

- Assess the quality of a cruise ship by calculating the space ratio and the passenger-crew ratio.

- Use a cruise brochure as a selling tool.

- Compare the value of a package tour vacation and a cruise using a per diem analysis.

- State the selling features of a cruise holiday.

- Summarize the advantages and disadvantages of cruise vacations.

- Cost and book a cruise.

The Cruise Industry

Although ferries and a few other ships provide point-to-point marine transportation, most travel counsellors do not sell much of this type of travel. Their main source of income from sea-going vessels is from the sale of cruises. Some might argue that cruise ships provide such transportation, however, cruises are not sold in this fashion. When counsellors sell transportation, they emphasize service, route and schedule convenience, and travel time. When they sell cruises, however, they stress the experience of cruising, the value for money, and the all-inclusive nature of the product. In fact, a cruise vacation's selling features more closely resemble those of a resort holiday than a means of travel. Many cruise lines market their products as destinations in themselves; others compare a cruise with a vacation at a luxury hotel or resort.

The variety of cruises and cruise ships on the market is almost as large as the range of package tours available. Cruises are packaged as all-inclusive vacations for different target markets, such as pleasure travellers, special interest groups, the meetings and conventions market, or incentive groups. A cruise vessel can be a chartered yacht for a dozen friends or an ocean-going passenger liner with a capacity of 2500 and a crew of 750. Counsellors must therefore be familiar with the different cruise lines, their ships and cruise products to correctly match them with their clients' needs. This chapter focuses on these topics and on the features and selling techniques developed to merchandise this unique travel product.

History of Cruising

Until the development of the steam engine and its application to shipping, ocean travel was predominantly based on trade and trade routes. The introduction of steamships on the transatlantic route reduced travel time and brought ocean travel to a larger group. After 1900, steamship travel gained wide acceptance and by the 1920s it reached the peak of its popularity. Well-known companies such as Cunard, White Star, Canadian Pacific and French Line provided regular line service from their home ports in Britain and continental Europe to New York, Boston, Halifax and Montreal. National pride and prestige were as much tied to the vessels crossing the North Atlantic as are today's national airlines. Famous ships, such as the *Aquitania*, *Ile de France*, *Queen Mary* and *Normandie* were household words. Though frequently still referred to as "steamships", today's passenger vessels are fuelled by oil and driven by diesel engines.

At its peak ocean travel and cruising were restricted to two groups; those with the time and money to enjoy them, and immigrants to Canada, Australia and the USA. Marketing during the first quarter of this century was therefore directed only to those who could afford luxury accommodation. Transatlantic ocean travel suffered during the depression years but after World War II showed signs of regaining its former prominence. The resurgence was brief. Transatlantic jet flights were introduced in the late 1950s and passenger travel by sea dramatically declined. By 1969 only 250,000 passengers sailed across the Atlantic while air traffic on this route numbered six million travellers. The travelling public had overwhelmingly rejected ocean travel in favour of the convenience of travel by jet. Faced with this irresistible evidence, the ship lines changed their sales strategies. In a world with a mania for speed and the saving of time, it was folly to try to convince people to spend five days on an ocean voyage which could be accomplished in a few hours by air. Rather than trying to compete with the airlines in providing point-to-point transportation, the ship lines concentrated on developing the cruise market.

The Growth of Cruising

Ship travel, rather than fading in the face of jet competition, developed steadily from the mid-1960s. Ironically, this growth was prompted by the very success of the airplane which hastened the collapse of most transoceanic passenger service. Even before jets were in service, Europeans were travelling to the Mediterranean by plane to join local cruises. Today, air/cruise combinations are the most common cruise packages sold in Canada (Figure 11.1).

Although a few of the traditional shipping companies, such as Cunard, have successfully changed from providing point-to-point service to offering cruises, most current cruise lines were formed since the late 1960s. The cruise industry has, however, experienced the same type of consolidation in recent years as other segments of the travel industry. There are now fewer owners than during the early 1980s when substantial expansion occurred. Consolidation permits a cruise line to make economies of scale and to promote a range of vessels appealing to different markets.

The cruise industry's trade group, Cruise Lines International Association (CLIA), consists of about 24 major cruise lines operating about 110 ships off North America. CLIA member lines carried 895,000 passengers in 1977. Since then, the number of cruise passengers has increased by an average of about eight percent a year and by 1997 CLIA members carried over 5 million passengers (200,000 from Canada). Today, the cruise industry is one of the fastest growing segments in the travel industry. To meet this rising demand, the number of cruise ships more than doubled during the 1980s. New construction and the refurbishing of older vessels has continued in the 1990s. Some ships were enlarged by creating a "stretched" version through a process similar to that used for

FIGURE 11.1
Most cruises
include return
airfare to the port
of embarkation or
offer it as an
option to
passengers.
*Source: Sunquest
Vacations.*

CRUISE FROM 8 TO 19 NIGHTS

Our cruise takes 20 days (or 19 nights) from beginning to end. You have the option to select one of three different segments of the cruise including the entire cruise. Simply decide how long you want to cruise, what you'd like to see and what dates you'd like to travel.

Cruise	Embark	Disembark	No. of Nights
1.	Puerto Plata	Barbados	8
2.	Puerto Plata	Barcelona	19
3.	Barbados	Barcelona	11

EACH PACKAGE INCLUDES:

- Flights to/from Toronto via Skyservice.
- Transfer to and from the ship.
- Shipboard accommodation.
- Four grand meals a day... plus snacks.
- All shipboard entertainment.
- All shipboard gratuities.

Note: Each package price includes flight from Toronto to your port of embarkation and your flight from your port of disembarkation back to Toronto.

PREMIER CLASS... JUST $200 MORE

Barcelona to Toronto.

Skyservice's new wide-body Airbus 330 has a segregated cabin up front accommodating 32 luxurious spacious seats offering superior comfort, wide seats, more reclining room and 2-3-2 abreast seating.

luxury limousines. The vessels were cut in half and a new section was added to increase the passenger capacity. Cruise lines plan to add 35 more ships to the fleet by the end of the decade. Most of these will be "superliners" carrying 2000 passengers or more, and some will have a capacity in excess of 3000 passengers.

The revival of ocean travel did not come about merely by willing it so. It was supported by the favourable economic climate of the 1960s and 1970s, a time of rising financial expectations, increased leisure time and discretionary income for many North Americans. Equally important was the change in marketing which emphasized the traditional and luxurious shipboard environment. Cruise lines have attempted to maintain the legendary grandeur and elegance associated with the luxury ocean liners from which cruise ships are descended. This theme has been adapted and extended so that cruises are marketed as an ocean voyage aboard a luxury isolated resort. Passengers can enjoy an environment of unparalleled luxury while being entertained, wined and dined. During the voyage the ship visits a number of exotic ports on the cruise itinerary.

A cruise might be simply defined as sailing from place to place for pleasure. The most popular cruising area is the Caribbean Sea and the waters of the mid-Atlantic between south Florida and the Bahamas. Cruises have become commonplace in the Mediterranean, the fjords of Norway, on transcanal journeys between the Pacific and Atlantic, in Asia, and through the Alaska Passage. A wide selection of cruises ranging from three days to three weeks is available in these areas.

The cruise industry depends heavily on travel counsellors to sell its product. About 95 percent of all cruise bookings are made through travel agencies. The current renaissance of ocean travel in the form of cruising can be a significant source of income for travel agencies. Given that the 1993 gross revenue for CLIA member lines was over US$5 billion, the potential annual commission to travel agencies is considerable. This market is expected to continue growing because the romance and glamour associated with ship travel and life at sea have never lost their appeal despite the increasing number of vacationers who travel by jet. CLIA produces reference material, such as the *CLIA Cruise Manual*, offers training seminars across North America, and produces sales training videos and other educational materials to help travel counsellors gain a share of the cruise market.

Types of Cruises

Cruises are typically classified by their duration as the length of a cruise is a major factor in its cost. This method identifies four main types of cruise: short, intermediate, long and point-to-point voyages.

Short Cruises

These cruises are defined as those which extend from three days to two weeks. The brief period suits the vacation schedules of most people. Such cruises are marketed to appeal to travellers who are budget-conscious or are first-time cruise clients. One-day "cruises to nowhere" and mini-vacations of two to four days are becoming increasingly popular with travellers who wish to take a short break or sample a cruise lifestyle. Caribbean, Mexican and Alaskan cruises comprise the majority of cruises in this segment.

Intermediate Cruises

Such cruises typically last from 15 to 24 days. These cruises appeal to travellers with more time and money to spend on a cruise, and to those who enjoy the cruise lifestyle. Typical itineraries are cruises to the major islands of the Caribbean, coast-to-coast voyages through the Panama Canal, cruises to Hawaii from the west coast, and to the Canadian Seaboard from the east coast.

Long Cruises

These are cruises which take more than 25 days. These cruises attract up-market clients who can afford both the time and money necessary. World cruises, and cruises from the United States to Scandinavia, the Mediterranean Sea or the South Pacific are typical long cruises.

In general, longer cruises have an older clientele while short cruises to nearby ports tend to attract younger passengers. Although longer cruises cost more, passengers on a short cruise spend more per day than those on a longer cruise.

Point-to-Point Voyages

Although much reduced in number, transatlantic crossings are considered by some people to be short cruises as they are directed to a similar clientele. This service, however, is offered only during the spring and summer months from New York and Montreal to Britain and continental Europe. Transatlantic sailings are generally not scheduled during the winter months. Point-to-point cruises are also sold as segments of longer world cruises. Passengers on such voyages combine an open jaw air fare with a cruise segment to create an individual package.

Occasional transatlantic crossings are available as part of a world cruise itinerary or when a ship is being repositioned. At the end of a summer season, for example, a ship cruising the Mediterranean may cross the Atlantic to take up position for cruise services in the warmer waters of the Caribbean during the winter months. Similarly, a ship cruising the Caribbean may be transferred at the end of the winter to begin cruising in other areas for the spring, summer and fall schedule. At the end of the season, the ships generally return to their home port for maintenance in preparation for a repeat of the cycle. All such point-to-point voyages, when ships are being rescheduled, are repositioning cruises and are marketed as special cruises.

Other Types of Marine Transportation

Counsellors may have an opportunity to sell some other types of marine transportation.

Freighters

Freighters transport cargo around the world, often visiting ports off the regular tourist path which are never frequented by cruise ships. The possibility of sailing on such vessels appeals to travellers who want something out of the ordinary. Prospective passengers need more than curiosity, however. They must have the time and flexibility to travel according to a freighter's schedule which can be rather erratic. Freighters do not have regularly scheduled sailing dates. The voyage may also be delayed to load or discharge cargo, unscheduled stops and changes in route may be made, and freighters often sail at short notice. Travellers who can adapt to this uncertainty find that freighter accommodation is usually quite comfortable and prices are generally lower than on cruise ships.

Most freight-carrying vessels have accommodation for a limited number of passengers. Maritime law stipulates that ships with more than 12 passengers must have a doctor aboard. For this reason there is usually accommodation for no more than 12 passengers, though there are some notable exceptions to this

FIGURE 11.2
Freighters have limited accommodation and most have age restrictions, however, they do offer an alternative to clients.
Courtesy of Ford's Freighter Travel Guide.

FREIGHTER TRAVEL — FROM NORTH AMERICAN PORTS

Listing No. 13

EUROPE

From the U.S. Gulf, East Coast and Canadian ports, sailing to first port Europe, usually in the Antwerp/Hamburg Range. These vessels, of various foreign flagship registry carry 9 to 12 passengers. Length of voyage is approximately 12 to 15 days. The ships in this service are "tramps" or "unscheduled freighters" and short notice of their arrival is received. As soon as it is known that a vessel will call in the area, the waiting list is offered in date order of request. Deposits are not accepted until a firm offer is made. Passengers who have reached the age of 75 are not accepted. Automobiles, household goods, etc. are not carried. The majority of these vessels are air-conditioned and normally have swimming pools. Bookings cannot be made through travel agents. See below.

Passenger Fares: One-way, per person **from Gulf ports** — in double cabin $540.00, in single cabin $590.00; **from East Coast and Canadian ports** — in double cabin $500, in single cabin $550. Children under 12 years, half-fare.

EGON OLDENDORFF, Postbox 21 35, D-2400 Lubeck 1, West Germany — Tel: 451-1500-0 — Telex: 026411 — Telegrams: NORDREEDER: Agents for bookings Eastbound — Norton, Lilly International, Inc., 245 Monticello Arcade, Norfolk, VA 23510 — Tel: (804) 622-7035 - Ask for Passenger Bookings.

generality. Rather than incurring the expense of an onboard doctor, freighters will dock at the nearest port if a passenger or crew member becomes seriously ill. Many freighter companies therefore restrict passengers to those under the age of 60 years, unless a medical certificate is presented to clear the passenger for freighter travel.

Passenger freighters offer a limited number of sales opportunities to travel counsellors (see Figure 11.2). Potential clients are those who truly enjoy ocean travel, and those who seek a peaceful voyage without the entertainment, recreation, or extensive dining facilities found on cruise ships. Clients also need the time and flexibility to comply with freighter schedules and operations.

Ferries

Ferries provide important transport links in almost every coastal region. In many parts of the world they present travellers with an alternative to other transportation modes and for some destinations, such as the Greek islands, they may be the only realistic way to travel. The ships may be fairly small craft or they can rival some cruise ships in size. Ferry trips can be part of a city's commuter service, as is the Hong Kong to Kowloon crossing, or they can be international ocean voyages providing passenger accommodation and carrying vehicles, such as the passage between Esbjerg in Denmark and Harwich in England. Since ferry journeys typically take less than one day, passengers often have the choice of booking a cabin or travelling on deck (Figure 11.3).

Travel counsellors may occasionally be asked to arrange and reserve ferry connections for their clients. The most commonly requested arrangements are likely to be for ferry services operating from either of Canada's coasts and for European services. Counsellors should be familiar with cross-channel ferries from Britain to Scandinavia, Ireland, France and Holland, and with the European ferries on which clients holding a Eurail pass may travel. In addition to the routes, schedules and fares, counsellor product

knowledge should include the type of vessel used. The cross-channel hovercraft service and Copenhagen to Malmo by hydrofoil are particularly popular.

Other Types of Vessels

Sailing on smaller vessels is growing in popularity and for some clients it rivals a voyage on a cruise liner. Several types of craft have been developed to appeal to different market segments. Cruising on sailing ships, some of which can accommodate up to 150 passengers, is a recent development. Yachts can be chartered, with or without the services of a crew. Houseboat rentals are increasingly available. Houseboats in Kashmir are used simply for accommodation whereas in Ontario's Trent Canal system they are rented by groups who wish to travel the waterway.

River Cruises and Canal Barges

Perhaps the largest of these cruise niches is the market for river cruises and barge trips on canals. Cruising the Mississippi River on a replica of a paddle-powered riverboat is a popular pastime. These two or three day trips offer scenery, casino gambling and entertainment. River cruises on the Rhine and Danube in Europe offer spectacular views and the chance to stop along the way. For those seeking a more exotic trip, cruises on the Nile and Amazon are available. Canal trips on barges in England and France are gaining acceptance from those who wish something different. France, in particular, has developed this market to tie in with visits to vineyards so that passengers can taste wines along the way.

The vessels used for these trips are necessarily smaller and have fewer facilities than their ocean-going cousins (see Figure 11.4). Their main selling feature is the scenery. Passengers therefore do not need the variety of on-board distractions found on larger ships.

PASSENGER FARES HELSINKI–STOCKHOLM AND TURKU–MARIEHAMN–STOCKHOLM

Regular fare: Day service — Currency CAD

	Turku-Stockholm or v.v. May 1, 1989-April 30, 1990				Turku-Mariehamn or v.v. May 1, 1989-April 30, 1990				Stockholm-Mariehamn or v.v. May 1, 1989-April 30, 1990			
Passage	Adults	Youth 12-17 yrs Senior citizens Students	Children 0-11 yrs	Groups, Families	Adults	Youth 12-17 yrs Senior citizens Students	Children 0-11 yrs	Groups, Families	Adults	Youth 12-17 yrs Senior citizens Students	Children 0-11 yrs	Groups, Families
fare	45	23	0	34	30	15	0	22	16	8	0	12
C4	54	32	9	43	39	24	9	31	25	17	9	21
C3	57	35	12	46	42	27	12	34	28	20	12	24
D/C2	63	41	18	52	48	33	18	40	34	26	18	30
D/C1	81	59	36	70	66	51	36	58	52	44	36	48
B4	59	37	14	48	41	26	11	33	27	19	11	23
B3	63	41	18	52	44	29	14	36	30	22	14	26
B2	72	50	27	61	52	37	22	44	38	30	22	34
B1	99	77	54	88	74	59	44	66	60	52	44	56
A4	60	38	15	49	44	29	14	36	30	22	14	26
A3	65	43	20	54	48	33	18	40	34	26	18	30
A2	75	53	30	64	58	43	28	50	44	36	28	40
A1	105	83	60	94	86	71	56	78	72	64	56	68
F4	63	41	18	52	46	31	16	38	32	24	16	28
E/F3	69	47	24	58	51	36	21	43	37	29	21	33
E/F2	81	59	36	70	62	47	32	54	48	40	32	44
E/F1	119	97	74	108	94	79	64	86	80	72	64	76
L3	80	58	35	69	54	39	24	46	40	32	24	36
L2	99	77	54	88	66	51	36	58	52	44	36	48
L1	150	128	105	139	102	87	72	94	88	80	72	84

Regular fare: Night service — Currency CAD

	Helsinki-Stockholm or v.v. May 1, 1989-April 30, 1990				Turku-Stockholm or v.v. May 1, 1989-April 30, 1990			
Passage	Adults	Youth 12-17 yrs Senior citizens Students	Children 0-11 yrs	Groups, Families	Adults	Youth 12-17 yrs Senior citizens Students	Children 0-11 yrs	Groups, Families
fare	69	34	0	52	45	23	0	34
C4	95	60	26	78	63	41	18	52
C3	103	68	34	86	69	47	24	58
D/C2	120	85	51	103	81	59	36	70
D/C1	171	136	102	154	119	97	74	108
B4	102	67	33	85	72	50	27	61
B3	113	78	44	96	81	59	36	70
B2	135	100	66	118	99	77	54	88
B1	201	166	132	184	153	131	108	142
A4	110	75	41	93	75	53	30	64
A3	123	88	54	106	85	63	40	74
A2	150	115	81	133	105	83	60	94
A1	231	196	162	214	165	143	120	154
F4	122	87	53	105	81	59	36	70
E/F3	139	104	70	122	93	71	48	82
E/F2	174	139	105	157	117	95	72	106
E/F1	269	234	200	252	189	167	144	178
L3	–	–	–	–	115	93	70	104
L2	199	164	130	182	150	128	105	139
L1	329	294	260	312	255	233	210	244

C4=4 persons in same cabin, C3=3 persons in same cabin, C2=2 persons in same cabin, C1=whole cabin for one person, B4=4 persons in same cabin, etc.
Price for children is only valid for family trips on condition they travel in same cabin with parents or guardians.

Early bird special
A bunk bed in the Sleep-in compartment is included only when reserved separately. It's smart to book your reservation in good time if traveling without cabin on Silja's night voyages.

Discounts
Children 0-11 yrs travel free of charge without own bed in cabin. To reserve own cabin bed: see prices in the table above.
Youth 12-17 yrs pay according to fares in "Youth 12-17 yrs" column.
Students and Senior citizens get special discounts. Check fares in "Youth 12-17 yrs" column.
Eurail and Eurail Youth passes entitle bearers to free passage on Silja Line. Silja Line is the official carrier for holders of Eurail passes between Finland and Sweden.
Groups of at least 10 persons travel on group discount. Every 16th group member travels free of charge in the price category in which the majority travels. The group travels on a joint ticket.

Families are entitled to discounts when at least three family members travel together. Included are families with children under 21. At least one parent must be present. See fares in "Group/Family" and "Youth 12-17 yrs" columns.

Prices of cars, trailers, campers, vans, small trucks, buses and motorcycles are available upon request. Bicycles and mopeds are transported free of charge on car deck.

Discounts can only be applied when booking your trip. They are not available for special cruises and package tours. And discounts cannot be combined in any way.

Meal prices May 1, 1989 - April 30, 1990   CAD

	Lunch/dinner coupon	Breakfast coupon
Adults	19,-	9,-
Children 6-11 yrs	10,-	5,-

The meal coupons are valid in all restaurants onboard. They cover the smorgasbord price. Meals are free of charge for children under 6.

FIGURE 11.3
Many ferries offer passengers a choice of booking a cabin or transportation only. Group discounts and free passage for Eurail pass holders are a common feature of European ferries.
Source: Silja Line.

ITINERARY NO. 1
Grand Europe Cruise
Basel to Amsterdam
5 days / 4 nights / 4 countries / 8 ports

This cruise covers the entire navigable part of the Rhine, from Switzerland through France and Germany to Holland. Castles and fortresses perch on the slopes that rise on either side of the majestic river and ports of call include sophisticated cities and picturesque wine villages. A shore excursion to romantic Heidelberg visits the castle and quaint byways of the "Student Prince" city.

Cruise Fares in CAN-$
Per adult double occupancy. Single supplement 25%.

Cabin category	until May 31st	from June 1st
A 1 Lorelei Deck	945	1,180
A 1 Rhineland Deck	840	1,050
A 2	760	950

Embarkation
Every Thursday from April 27 to October 19, 1989

Itinerary

Day	Port	Arrive	Depart
Thu.	Basel (Switzerland) Embarkation any time after 7 pm. Sumptuous buffet on board between 7:30 pm and 9:30 pm.		
Fri.	Basel	–	6:00 am
	Strasbourg (France)	3:00 pm	–
Sat.	Strasbourg	–	3:00 am
	Speyer (Germany)	8:20 am	8:30 am
	Gernsheim	11:50 am	12 noon
	Bacharach	4:00 pm	5:15 pm
	Boppard	6:30 pm	
Sun.	Boppard	–	5:30 am
	Bonn	9:30 am	1:15 pm
	Cologne	3:00 pm	6:00 pm
	Düsseldorf	8:30 pm	–
Mon.	Düsseldorf	–	3:30 am
	Amsterdam (Holland)	4:00 pm	–

▶ Arrival and departure times are approximate and subject to change ◀

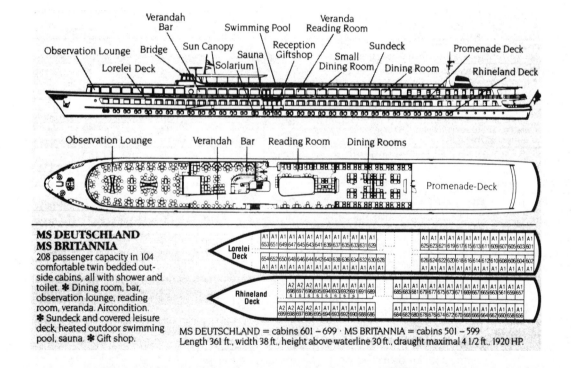

MS DEUTSCHLAND
MS BRITANNIA

208 passenger capacity in 104 comfortable twin bedded outside cabins, all with shower and toilet. ❋ Dining room, bar, observation lounge, reading room, veranda. Aircondition. ❋ Sundeck and covered leisure deck, heated outdoor swimming pool, sauna. ❋ Gift shop.

MS DEUTSCHLAND = cabins 601 – 699 · MS BRITANNIA = cabins 501 – 599
Length 361 ft., width 38 ft., height above waterline 30 ft., draught maximal 4 1/2 ft., 1920 HP.

FIGURE 11.4
River cruises use smaller vessels.
Source: KD German Rhine Line.

Cruise Ships

Cruise ships vary considerably in their size, design and features. Unlike aircraft, buses and cars, ships are not mass-produced but instead are commissioned by shipping lines to specific requirements. There are rarely duplicate cruise ships. Even within a given fleet, identical ships are the exception rather than the rule. It is this individual nature that endows each ship with a unique personality. Despite the highly distinct design of passenger ships, certain features are common to all. Travel counsellors can become familiar with these features and facilities by studying the references and deck plans discussed in this chapter.

As the cruise industry has grown, so too has the size of the average cruise ship. Most vessels are currently constructed to have a capacity of about 2000 passengers. However, even these huge ships may be dwarfed by the giants (with accommodation for 3500 to 5000 passengers) planned for the future. A larger size produces economies of scale for the companies. They are better able to afford top quality entertainment and cuisine on larger vessels and can build in features such as health spas and gyms to meet the needs of current passengers. There are also, however, the risks of overcapacity and of marketing such large vessels.

A typical passenger liner consists of three to twelve decks. The uppermost or top decks (often called the sun or boat decks) are designed for recreation and do not usually contain passenger cabins. They are used for sports, sunning or other outdoor activities which would disturb passengers in nearby cabins. Below the sun decks are one or more promenade decks (often glass-enclosed to permit strolling in inclement weather). Public rooms such as bars, lounges or theatre, and outdoor swimming pools are usually located on the promenade deck. Decks devoted exclusively to passenger cabins are situated below the promenade deck (Figure 11.5).

Clients on a package tour often consider their hotel room to be the most important factor in their enjoyment of a vacation. Although cruises are not sold on the merits of a cabin (sometimes called a stateroom), accommodation is important to passengers. Clients should, however, understand that most cabins are designed as sleeping accommodation only. Space on a ship is highly prized and cruise lines try to create as many cabins as can be comfortably placed in the space available. Although cabins provide comfortable, and sometimes quite luxurious, accommodation they are not generally large (see Figure 11.6). Each cabin is generally air conditioned and equipped with a private bathroom consisting of a washbasin, toilet and shower. Larger cabins or suites may have a tub bath and shower. Some older vessels may have cabins without private bathrooms, however, most of these ships have been refurbished or removed from cruise service. Newer ships built exclusively for cruising may have all cabins "outside"; that is, one wall forms part of the ship's hull and has a porthole or window. Older vessels generally have a porthole; outside cabins on newer vessels and larger suites may have a picture window. Many ships have both outside and inside cabins. Inside cabins have four interior partitions with no portholes and therefore no natural light.

Cruise ships share many characteristics with hotels and resorts in that guests are housed, fed, and entertained. Because they do not have the option of leaving, guests are more likely to be critical as a cruise continues. The size of a cruise ship and its cabins, however, depends upon its target market. Ideally, a ship should be booked to capacity. However, some people may find a ship too large and impersonal while another may consider it too small.

Classes of Service

Early passenger liners operated three classes of service; first, tourist and steerage. Each class was confined to special areas in the ship and dining rooms, lounges, ballrooms and sections of

ISLAND/PACIFIC PRINCESS

626 passengers. 20,000 gross tons. 550 ft. in length. Cruising speed 20 knots. Fully stabilized. British registered.

All first-class cabins with private facilities, multichannel music system, telephones, individually-controlled air conditioning.

Room Type	Deck	Description
A	Promenade	Outside Deluxe Suites
B	Promenade	Outside Deluxe Suites
C	Promenade	Outside Deluxe Singles
D	Promenade	Outside Deluxe Rooms
E	Promenade	Inside Deluxe Rooms
F	Aloha	Outside Twin Rooms
G	Fiesta	Outside Twin Rooms
H	Coral	Outside Twin Rooms
J	Aloha	Inside Twin Rooms
K	Fiesta	Inside Twin Rooms

FIGURE 11.5
The top decks on a cruise ship do not usually contain passenger cabins. Note that deluxe accommodation is generally on a higher deck than standard cabins.
Courtesy of Ford's Deck Plan Guide.

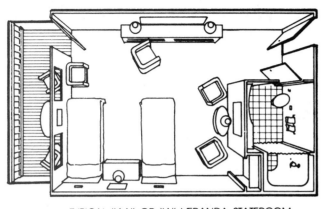

TYPICAL "AA" OR "A" VERANDA STATEROOM
CRUISE VESSEL "NEW ORLEANS"

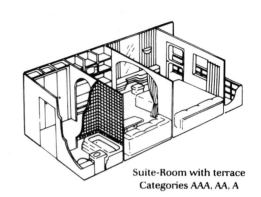

Suite-Room with terrace
Categories AAA, AA, A

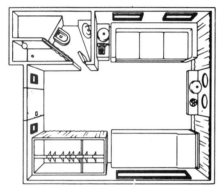

Standard Stateroom with sofa and folding lower bed

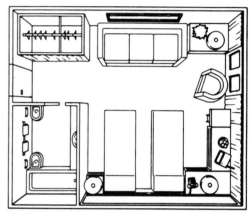

Typical Deluxe (Grade A) Stateroom

FIGURE 11.6
Passenger cabins may be quite comfortable and have a variety of features, however, space is always at a premium.
Reproduced from the CLIA Cruise Manual. Courtesy of CLIA.

the open decks were segregated. First class cabins were luxurious, well equipped, were larger and had choice locations on the ship. Public rooms in first class were spacious and luxuriously appointed. Although tourist class was less luxurious than first, it was still quite comfortable. Passengers in the steerage section were confined to the lower decks and were usually immigrants on an inexpensive or subsidized fare. Regardless of variations in accommodation, all passengers in a given class shared the same privileges and menus. Steerage class has disappeared but some companies operating point-to-point or ferry schedules still offer a two-class system. This permits them to create a wider range of fares on the same ship (apart from the scale of fares for different

cabins within the same class). In contrast, today's cruise ships (with few exceptions) offer only one class of service. This is generally recognized as first class quality. Single class ships give all passengers full access to all facilities, equal service, and a common standard throughout the ship.

Several factors affect the service on board a cruise ship and a client's perception of it. Standard references provide information which can help counsellors advise clients what to expect. The *OAG Worldwide Cruise and Shipline Guide* and the *CLIA Cruise Manual*, for example, publish ship profiles which list the registry and nationality of cruise ships. Many cruise ships fly a flag of convenience which means that the ship is registered in one country but flies the flag of another. This scheme is used to reduce a company's labour costs and taxes. Thus an American-owned vessel may be registered in Liberia. The crew's nationality, however, is a more significant indicator of service than the ship's registry. In some cases, the two may be the same. For example, the Odysseus is registered in Greece and carries a Greek crew (Figure 11.7). This information tells a counsellor what type of cuisine (Greek) can be expected on board. On the other hand, the Fantasy is registered in Liberia but has an international crew which implies the type of food that will be served.

Another measure of service is the size of the vessel. Generally, the larger a ship the more facilities and amenities it has. When clients ask how large a ship is, they are really asking whether the ship is stable, whether there is enough space, and whether they will feel cramped. An awareness of a ship's tonnage and the meaning of this term is therefore important. Passenger ships are measured by their Gross Registered Tonnage (GRT). This measurement has nothing to do with a ship's weight. The GRT is the volume (cubic footage) occupied by passenger accommodation, public areas and service areas; it is a measure of the space passengers can use on board and which generate revenue on a cruise ship. By comparing this volume with the passenger capacity, counsellors can give clients an idea of a ship's spaciousness and comfort. One Gross Registered Ton is equal to 100 cubic feet. The volume of passenger space in a ship can therefore be calculated by multiplying its GRT by 100. A ship's GRT, passenger capacity and crew size are published in several industry references, including the *OAG World Cruise and Shipline Guide* and the *CLIA Cruise Manual*. Counsellors can use these figures to calculate two ratios which provide important assessments of a cruise ship's quality, the space ratio and the passenger/crew ratio.

Space Ratio

The space ratio measures how much room passengers have on a ship. It is calculated by dividing a ship's Gross Registered Tonnage by its maximum

PROFILE

Name	MTS Odysseus
Company	R.O.C.
Originally Built	1962
Rebuilt/Refurbished	1995
Formerly Named	Aquamarine
Country of Registry	Greece
Speed	17 knots
Normal Crew Size	200
Nationality of Crew	
Officers	Greek
Hotel Staff	Greek
Telephone	1130652
TELEX A-BACK	802-1130652

SIZE/CAPACITY

Tonnage	12,000
Length	483 feet
Beam	61 feet
Total Capacity (incl. uppers)	485
Normal Cruise Cap. (basis 2)	400

ACCOMMODATIONS

Type	No. Outside	No. Inside
Deluxe	2	
W/2 Lowers	143	27
Double Bed	10	1
Upper and Lower	10	5
W/3 Lowers	12	
2 Lowers & 1 Upper	6	5
2 Lowers & 2 Uppers		5
Total	183	43
Total Cabins	226	

passenger capacity. Thus if the GRT of a ship is 20,000 tons and her passenger capacity is 400, the GRT per passenger will be 50. Since 1GRT = 100 cubic feet, a space ratio of 50 translates into 5,000 cubic feet per passenger. The larger this ratio, the more space passengers have on board. Most cruise ships currently in service have a space ratio of about 25 while newer vessels which are custom-designed for today's market often have a space ratio over 40.

FIGURE 11.7
Part of a ship profile typical of the listings in the CLIA Cruise Manual.
Courtesy of CLIA.

Passenger/Crew Ratio

A ship's passenger/crew ratio is also an excellent measure of the service to be expected on board. It is simply the passenger capacity divided by the size of the crew. The lower this ratio, the better the service is likely to be. Most cruise ships have a ratio of about 2.0, or one crew member for every two passengers. Modern ships designed for the luxury market may have a ratio as low as 1.5 while those designed for budget cruises may approach or exceed 3.0. Depending on the crew's supervision and training, this ratio indicates the quality of service a passenger can expect on board.

FIGURE 11.8
Meals on board ship are often lavish and frequently have a theme.
Source: Premier Cruise Lines.

Caribbean Night Dinner Selections

APPETIZERS

Tomato Juice   Mango Nectar   Fruit Punch

Seafood Cocktail Calypso   Fresh Pineapple with Rum

Bahamian Conch Croquette

SOUPS

Lobster Bisque   Jamaican Red Bean

Chilled Papaya Soup

SALADS

Tropical Salad
Crisp Greens, Watercress, Cucumbers and Radishes

Hearts of Lettuce with Carrot Curls

A choice of Blue Cheese, Goombay or Ginger Lime Dressing

ENTREES

Fillet of Bimini Grouper
Broiled and lightly flavored with a Spice Island Coriander Sauce

Caribbean Lobster Tail
Presented with Lemon Butter

Lamb Curry Port Royal
Diced tender Lamb in a spicy Curried Island Sauce with Pineapple as in the wicked days of old Port Royal

Roast Duckling a l'Orange
Crisp Duckling in a tasty light Orange Sauce

Beef of the Buccaneers
Chunks of Tenderloin marinated, skewered, broiled and served on Rice

Fried Plantains   White Turnips Coriander

Yellow Rice with Pigeon Peas

Amenities and Activities on Board

Most cruise ships offer similar amenities although these depend to some extent on the size of the ship and the target market. All cruise ships have the cabins, restaurants, lounges and sun decks described earlier. The number and their quality, however, varies. Only by examining ship profiles and deck plans in references and brochures can a counsellor be certain of the particular features of the ship being sold.

Cruise lines appreciate that passengers on a cruise are confined to the vessel. Onboard meals and activities therefore become critical to a client's pleasure. Considerable care and planning is spent on the preparation and service of meals. Even on long cruises, menus are generally not repeated. On a standard one-week voyage, each meal will have a different theme or focus. There may be a Caribbean Night, an Italian Night and so on (Figure 11.8). All cruise ships offer a Captain's Dinner, sometimes combined with the Farewell Dinner and sometimes as a separate occasion. These meals tend to be the most lavish and formal offered on a cruise.

Many cruises offer passengers a choice of two sittings for dinner. First sitting is usually around 6:00 p.m. while the second sitting is typically served about 8:00 p.m. Passengers will be asked to state their preference when they book their cruise or when they first board the ship. On the first day, the purser assigns passengers to a specific sitting and table (with seating for 2, 4, 8 or 10 as preferred). Passengers must then take dinner at the assigned table and chosen sitting for the remainder of the voyage. This procedure simplifies tipping procedures at the end of the cruise. Since the arrangements are made on a first come basis, clients should be advised to see the purser as soon as possible after boarding the ship. Older clients generally prefer to eat at the first sitting while younger ones usually choose the latter. The first sitting enables clients to participate in many of the daily activities and dine before the evening's events commence. Second sitting means that clients do not have to rush back from shore excursions or hurry their meals. Newer cruise ships are usually designed with sufficiently large dining rooms to allow all passengers to be served at the

same time. Breakfast and lunch on almost all cruise ships are based on an open seating concept and passengers may sit at whichever table they prefer.

Activities on board a cruise are planned around pastimes during the day

FIGURE 11.9
Cruises offer passengers a choice of day and evening activities. *Courtesy of CLIA.*

DAILY PROGRAMME*

*Based on composite Daily Programme.
All times may vary depending on specific port schedules.

THIS MORNING

Coffee and Danish Pastries are served from 7:00 am to 12:00 noon in the Satellite Cafe (5 Deck Aft). A light breakfast is served in the Satellite Cafe from 8:00 am to 10:00 am.

As an alternative, breakfast is served in the Meridian Restaurant at 7:00 am and 8:45 am.

9:30 **Quotations Quiz** with a prize for the most correct entry handed in by 3:00 pm at the Purser's office.
10:30 **Travel Talk.** Where to go, what to see and do and Custom hints, given by your Cruise Director. Showtime Lounge.
11:30 **Navigational Bridge Visit.** Reservation cards available in the Library.
11:30 **Interdenominational Church Service.** Theatre.
11:30 **Tote On The Ship's Run.** Can you guess how far the ship has travelled since leaving port until noon today? Funnel, Starboard Side.
11:30 **"Music in the Sun."** Indoor/Outdoor Center.

THIS AFTERNOON

Luncheon

A light buffet luncheon is available in the Satellite Cafe between noon and 3:00 pm.

As an alternative, luncheon is served in the Meridian Restaurant at Noon and 1:30 pm.

1:00 **An informal meeting** of Masons, Rotarians and all Service Club members. Indoor/Outdoor Center.
2:00 **Movie SPLASH** starring Daryl Hannah & Tom Hanks. Clipper Suite.
2:30 **The Casino** opens for your gaming pleasure. Indoor/Outdoor Center.
2:45 **Bridge.** Potpourri Room.
2:45 **Tennis Tournament.** Recreation Deck 8. Golf. Recreation Deck 8.
3:30 **Dance Class.** Showtime Lounge.
4:00 **Trapshooting.** 4 shots $2.00. Recreation Deck 7.
4:00 **Afternoon Tea** is available. Showtime Lounge.
5:15 **Teen Get-Together.** Lido Bar.
6:00 **BBC World Service News Broadcast.** State/Public Rooms & Open Decks.

THIS EVENING

The Captain's Cocktail Party.
The Captain and his Officers request the pleasure of your company for cocktails in the Indoor/Outdoor Center.
5:45 **Party** for guests on Main Sitting followed by dinner in the Meridian Restaurant.
7:45 **Party** for guests on Late Sitting followed by dinner in the Meridian Restaurant.
8:00 **Movie THE PURPLE ROSE OF CAIRO** starring Mia Farrow and Jeff Daniels. Clipper Suite.
9:30 **SHOWTIME,** presenting Caribbean Calypso & Fancy Dress Ball. Boat Deck Aft.
10:00 **Movie THE FALCON AND THE SNOWMAN** starring Timothy Hutton and Sean Penn. Clipper Suite.
10:00 **Dancing to Top Disco Sounds.** Indoor/Outdoor Center.
10:00 **Casino opens.** Indoor/Outdoor Center.
10:30 **Repeat of SHOWTIME** for passengers on Late Sitting. Showtime Lounge.
12:00 **Midnight Buffet.** Meridian Restaurant.

and entertainment in the evening (Figure 11.9). Both vary depending on the ship, the cruise and the market. Some cruises offer a wide range of daytime activities from gambling to skeet shooting and exercise classes. Others offer less variety. Most cruise ships offer passengers something to do on an almost continuous basis. However, clients are not obliged to participate; they may choose to relax by the pool or read a book if they prefer. All cruise ships feature live entertainment, dancing, movies and other pursuits. Although most events are included in the price of a cruise, passengers must pay for some activities, particularly those during the day. It is therefore important that counsellors examine the cruise brochure to help them explain the types of activities available and the costs involved. The activities as well as the itinerary should be matched to the client's needs and interests.

FIGURE 11.10
How cruises are listed in the OAG Worldwide Cruise and Shipline Guide.
Reprinted by special permission from the January-February 1990 issue of the OAG Worldwide Cruise and Shipline Guide. Copyright© 1990, Official Airline Guides, Inc. All rights reserved.

Cruise Ship Personnel

The crew of a cruise ship has two areas of responsibility; the ship and the passengers. Counsellors have little need to know the duties and responsibilities of those who actually sail the ship. They should, however, be familiar with the hotel staff and other crew members or cruise representatives who take care of their clients' needs on board.

The two officers that affect a passenger's enjoyment are the captain and the purser. The **captain** is in charge of the ship and is responsible for its operation, and for the performance of its officers and crew. The **purser** is the business manager on a voyage. The purser's office acts as a general enquiry bureau, arranges the sale of shore excursions and land transportation, holds passengers' valuables for safekeeping, and cashes travellers' cheques. Its duties are similar to those of a hotel front desk.

The **cruise director** may be an officer on board, but is more often a representative hired by the cruise line. Cruise directors supervise the staff and arrange the activities and entertainment on board. Each day, often in the late afternoon, the cruise director makes a presentation to passengers on the attractions and excursions available at the next port. The daily activities sheets delivered every morning to each cabin are also prepared by the cruise director.

Cruise ships employ stewards in a number of hotel functions to care for cabins and clients. A **steward** is any crew member who acts in a passenger service capacity. (Sailors are concerned with the actual operation of the ship.) Deck stewards arrange the rental of deck chairs and serve passengers on deck during the voyage. Cabin (or room) stewards are responsible for chambermaid duties, such as cleaning passenger cabins, making

IBERIA, CANARY IS., N. AFRICA

From BARBADOS GENOA LONDON SAN JUAN		BARCELONA KIEL MALAGA SANTA CRUZ TENERIFE	BREMERHAVEN LA GUAIRA NAPLES SOUTHAMPTON	CIVITAVECCHIA LE HAVRE PIRAEUS	FUNCHAL LISBON PORT EVERGLADES		
Sailing Dates	**No. of Days**	**Ship & Operator**	**Sail & Return**	**Itinerary**		**Cost Range**	**Table No.**
From **BARBADOS** 1990 Apr 3 — Apr 22	19	OCEAN PRINCESS OCEAN CRUISE LINES ALSO AVAILABLE AS 17-DAY CRUISE TO MALAGA, $2750 - $4495.	S 2200 R 0800	DEVIL'S IS., AMAZON RIVER, BREVES CANALS, BELEM, SAO VICENTE, DAKAR, SANTA CRUZ TENERIFE, GIBRALTAR, MALAGA, NICE (Terminates)		I/S 2995 - 3695 O/S 3950 - 4950	
BARCELONA 1990 May 20 — Jun 1	12	ROYAL PRINCESS PRINCESS CRUISES $250 SAVINGS FOR BOOKING AND DEPOSIT BY JANUARY 31.	S 2359 R 0800	LIVORNO, CIVITAVECCHIA, CANNES, GIBRALTAR, CASABLANCA, LISBON, LONDON (Terminates)		2640 - 8350	
BREMERHAVEN 1990 Jul 22 — Aug 1	10	VISTAMAR JAHN REISEN RATE SHOWN IN GERMAN CURRENCY.	S 2000 R 0800	SOUTHAMPTON, LISBON, TANGIER, PALMA, AJACCIO (Terminates)		1695 UP	

beds, and collecting laundry. Dining room stewards (or waiters) and bartenders serve meals and drinks. Some cruise ships also employ wine stewards who have particular knowledge in this area. On smaller ships, a steward may fulfill several of these functions. As in any quality restaurant, a maître d' arranges table reservations and supervises the entire dining room.

Cruise Industry References

Brochures, which are discussed below, are the main sales tools used by both cruise lines and travel counsellors to sell the product. Travel counsellors, however, should be familiar with several standard references which provide information on ships and their services. The *Official Steamship Guide International* is a monthly publication which lists the schedules and fares for cruises worldwide by destination, for cruises in various categories such as barge and canal cruises, for passenger freighters and for ferry services. It also contains ship profiles, shipline information and maps. *Ford's International Cruise Guide*, published quarterly, treats cruise information in a similar fashion but supplies more detailed descriptions of the ships. It does not show maps or provide shipline information. The *ABC Passenger Shipping Guide*, issued monthly, and the *OAG Worldwide Cruise and Shipline Guide* (Figure 11.10), updated every two months, cover similar topics as the previous two references but are more comprehensive. A relatively recent reference is the *Official Cruise Guide* which is published annually. This manual contains detailed descriptions of cruise ships and cruise lines, including ship specifications, cabin types and sizes, dining facilities, public areas, and other features. Sailing schedules are cross-referenced by departure date and port, and by destination. Minimum and maximum rates, and booking policies and procedures are also covered. Although these references include similar topics, each has a particular format and a different emphasis. Since subscriptions can be rather expensive, most travel agencies select one or two for office use.

The *CLIA Cruise Manual* is issued

FIGURE 11.11
The Thomas Cook European Timetable prints ferry as well as rail schedules.
Source: Thomas Cook European Timetable.

CROSS-CHANNEL

Table 1003   **SEALINK**   02

Sealink is the fleet name of the shipping services of British Ferries, and its partners French Railways (SNCF) and Zeeland S.S. Co. The Harwich–Hoek v. Holland service is operated jointly with Zeeland S.S. Co. Passengers without cars must report approx. 45 minutes before sailing time.

British Ferries		SNCF Ships		Zeeland S.S. Co. Ships
m.v. *Horsa*, 5,590 tons.	m.v. *St. Anselm*, 7,405 tons.	m.v. *Chartres*, 4,586 tons.	m.v. *Versailles*, 6,527 tons.	m.v. *Koningin Beatrix*, 31,189 tons.
m.v. *Hengist*, 5,590 tons.	m.v. *Vortigern*, 4,797 tons.	m.v. *Côte d'Azur*, 8,800 tons.		
m.v. *St. Christopher*, 7,399 tons.	m.v. *St. Nicholas*, 17,043 tons.	m.v. *Champs-Elysées*, 9,069 tons.		

HARWICH – HOEK VAN HOLLAND
Journey 6¾ hours (7½–8¾ hours for night sailings).

Sailings from Harwich Parkeston Quay‡:
1115 Daily except Dec. 25, 26.
2145 Daily except Dec. 25, 26.
Sailings from Hoek v. Holland‡:
1145 Daily except Dec. 25, 26.
2245 Daily except Dec. 25, 26.

DOVER – CALAIS
Journey 1½ hours‡.

Sailings from Dover Eastern Docks‡*:
0030 Daily Jan. 2–Apr. 12.
0001 July 16, 23, 30, 31.
0130 Daily Apr. 13–July 31.
0145 Daily Mar. 27–Apr. 12.
0215 Daily Jan. 12–Mar. 1.

DOVER – CALAIS continued
1015 Daily Apr. 13–July 31.
1115 Daily Mar. 27–Apr. 12.
1130 Daily Jan. 4–Mar. 26, Apr. 13–July 31.
1245 Daily Apr. 13–July 31.
1315 Daily Jan. 1–Apr. 12.
1400 Daily Apr. 13–July 31.
1500 Daily Jan. 4–Mar. 26.
1515 Daily Apr. 13–May 14, May 16–July 31.
1530 Daily Mar. 27–Apr. 12.
1630 Daily Apr. 13–July 31.
1645 Daily Jan. 1–Mar. 26.
1745 Daily Apr. 13–July 31.
1845 Daily Jan. 1–Apr. 12.
1900 Daily Apr. 13–July 13.
2015 Daily Mar. 27–July 31.
2030 Daily Jan. 1–Mar. 26.
2130 Daily Mar. 27–July 31.
2230 July 15, 22, 29, 30.

annually and is the best source of information on that organization's members and their ships. The manual provides detailed information on each member's sales policies and personnel, profiles and deck plans of their ships, company histories, and passenger services. The publication also gives numerous examples of menus and activities, plus port maps and a variety of other useful sales aids. *Garth's Profile of Ships*, a looseleaf binder that can be updated twice a year, not only presents profiles of almost 200 ships but also rates them for quality and efficiency. *Ford's Deck Plan Guide*, released annually contains large-size deck plans for over 130 ships. The company also publishes *Ford's Freighter Travel Guide* twice yearly. This book is the most complete reference for those interested in selling freighter travel. Although the *Thomas Cook European Timetable* (published monthly) is primarily a reference for rail services, it also provides schedules for connecting ferries (Figure 11.11).

Some counsellors use the weekly summary of shipboard sanitary inspections, issued by the United States Public Health Service, as a guide to a ship's quality. The department's Centre for Disease Control (CDC) has been conducting sanitary inspections of all passenger cruise ships arriving at U.S. ports since 1975. To pass, a ship must meet CDC standards in the following

categories; drinking water, refrigeration, food preparation, potential contamination of food, personal cleanliness of food handlers, and general cleanliness and repair. In total, 32 items are inspected, each of which can result in a loss of 20 points. Since a score of 85 or more of a possible 100 points is required to pass, failure in any one of the inspected items can result in a failure on the overall inspection. Counsellors should, however, be aware that although the summary is issued weekly the inspections are made only when a vessel visits the USA. It is therefore possible for a ship to fail an inspection, correct the fault, but still have the fault listed in the weekly report because a subsequent inspection has not been conducted. The weekly report should be considered as an indicator rather than as proof of a ship's standards. An occasional slip is understandable (even the QEII has failed the test) whereas constant failure to pass the inspection may be significant. The *ABC Star Service*, although primarily a hotel reference, also contains cruise ship evaluations (Figure 11.12).

Cruise Brochures

Brochures are a cruise line's main sales tool. Like those produced by tour operators, cruise brochures must not only provide clients with the information necessary to make a purchase decision but they must also contain sufficient reference material to be used by travel counsellors as sales manuals. The brochures of these two suppliers therefore share many similarities in content and format. As a rule, however, cruise brochures are of a higher quality and possess additional and unique features not generally found in ITC brochures.

Cruise brochures are lavishly illustrated with colour photographs of the ships, life on board, and various ports of call. Each company clearly pictures what it offers. Luxury cruises emphasize glamorous people in evening dress, sumptuous food displays, and exotic ports. Others show young people,

FIGURE 11.12 Cruise ships are assessed in the ABC Star Service. *Courtesy of Reed Travel Group.*

S.S. REGENT SUN, Regency Cruises, built in 1964, was refurbished in 1988 with new carpets, some remodeling, and some new furnishings. Ship's nine decks are served by five conveniently located elevators. Public areas include one outside bar, four lounges, casino, shopping arcade, hairdresser, card room, library-writing room, theater-meeting room. Entertainment, which features two orchestras, is staged in main lounge with multi-tiered seating. Second lounge is completely encircled by windows, providing excellent vistas of ocean and ports. Small disco has sea view and modern decor. Attractive dining room with good views serves generally good to excellent food and specializes in French cuisine. Active cruisers enjoy outdoor and indoor pools, gym with exercise machines, sauna, massage, aerobics classes, and a physical-fitness program. Computer instruction is also available. Well-maintained staterooms have full-length mirrors, wardrobes with little drawer space, mirrored vanities, twin beds, two music channels, phones, individual reading lights, air conditioning, and baths with showers (some with tubs).

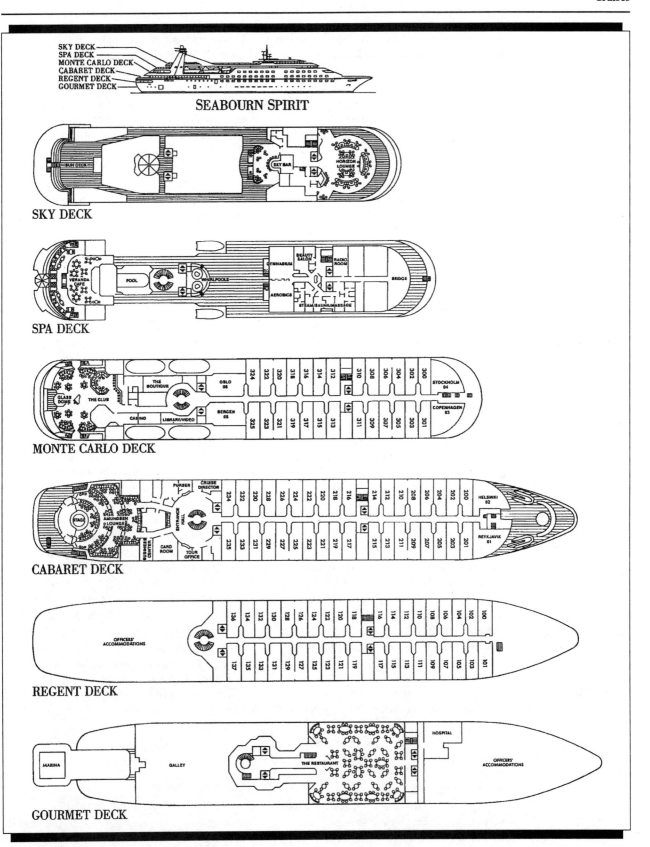

FIGURE 11.13
Deck plans help counsellors to locate cabins and facilities.
Reproduced from the CLIA Cruise Manual. Courtesy of CLIA.

casually dressed or enjoying the nightlife. These illustrations offer sales clues for counsellors in that they indicate the client types targeted by the particular vessel. For example, if brochure photographs show "sophisticated" couples and no children in evidence, it would not be wise to sell that cruise to families.

Brochures usually contain several sections, some of which correspond with the contents of a tour brochure. The cover states the cruise line's name, the ships in the fleet, the cruise or area being marketed, and the effective dates of the cruise program. The cruise line is generally described on the following pages. The ship's registry and the crew's nationality may be mentioned if they are a focus of the cruise or different from the country of registration. Several pages recount the features, facilities and activities on board ship. Descriptions of the ports of call and destination photographs are included to highlight the attractions, such as sightseeing, shopping, entertainment and nightlife, that can be experienced on shore excursions. Concrete sales information on the particular cruise program is presented after the introductory promotional segments. This relates to the itinerary, the cabin locations and layouts, and the rates for various cruise and accommodation options. Cruise itineraries and dates indicate the schedule, the route followed, the ports visited, the times spent cruising, and the hours in port. Diagrams and photographs of typical arrangements for various styles of suites and cabins are presented.

Most cruise brochures contain a deck plan for every ship in the program. A deck plan is a detailed map of each deck showing all facilities, public rooms and cabins (Figure 11.13). Two formats are used. Traditionally, deck plans are printed horizontally with the bow of the ship pointing to the right hand edge of the page, and with the top deck at the top of the page. Some deck plans align the diagrams vertically with the bow pointing to the top of the page and the topmost deck on the left. Cabins are generally colour-coded according to price.

Passenger cabins are numbered in ascending order from bow to stern; lower numbers are found towards the front of a ship while higher numbers are towards the stern. All even-numbered cabins are on one side of the vessel with odd-numbered cabins on the opposite side. Passengers in cabins near the front or on higher decks may sense the movement of a ship more than those accommodated on lower decks or near the rear. However, these cabins will generally be quieter and subject to less vibration.

Facts and figures on the ship are frequently printed on or near to the pages containing deck plans. As described earlier, this information can be used to assess a vessel's level of comfort and service. A schedule of cruise and accommodation rates is coordinated with the deck plan. Rates are determined by cabin type and by departure date. As with deck plans, rates are usually printed with the upper deck at the top and progress through the lower decks and less expensive cabins. The rates quoted are generally based on per person double occupancy. Exceptions to these prices, such as extra person charges and discounts for children, are printed at the bottom of the rate sheet. Port taxes and other additional charges will also be identified. Unlike airline tariff pages, rate sheets for cruise lines do not have a standardized format. As with tour brochures, counsellors must become familiar with the variations. Many cruise lines quote fares in U.S. dollars, although those represented by Canadian tour operators generally use Canadian currency. Counsellors must inspect a cruise brochure carefully to ensure that clients are informed of the appropriate currency.

Cruise Fares

Four factors influence the price of a cruise; its duration, the season, the quality of the particular ship, and the cabin selected (Figure 11.14). Longer cruises are more expensive than shorter cruises, although the daily cost may be the same.

WINTER
14- TO 20-DAY CRUISES

FT. LAUDERDALE TO
LOS ANGELES & HONOLULU

MS **ROTTERDAM VI** (ONLY 1,316 GUESTS)

This early January sailing is the prelude to the Inaugural World Cruise of our elegant new Rotterdam VI – and also her first cruise through the Panama Canal, both of which she will make with some very elegant touches: an entire deck of spacious suites served by a private lounge and concierge; a second dining room featuring Italian cuisine; deluxe staterooms with verandahs large enough to sun and party on.

Adventures along the way: our private island in the Bahamas, the Mayan ruins of Guatemala, the sunny Mexican Riviera, Hollywood, and Hawaii.

MS ROTTERDAM VI

STATEROOMS		CRUISE-ONLY FARES			
		TO LOS ANGELES 14 DAYS		TO HONOLULU 20 DAYS	
OUTSIDE DOUBLE		TARIFF	PS -25%	TARIFF	PS -25%
PS Penthouse w/verandah		$16,665	$12,499	$27,335	$20,502
S Suite w/verandah		11,915	8,936	19,165	14,374
A Deluxe w/verandah		9,125	6,844	13,995	10,496
B Deluxe w/verandah		8,815	6,611	13,505	10,129
C Large		7,275	5,456	10,955	8,216
D Large		7,145	5,358	10,735	8,051
E Large		6,965	5,224	10,465	7,849
F Large		6,795	5,096	10,155	7,616
FF Large		6,615	4,961	9,855	7,392
G Large		6,435	4,826	9,565	7,173
H Large		6,145	4,609	9,125	6,844
INSIDE DOUBLE					
I Large		6,155	4,616	8,845	6,634
J Large		5,985	4,489	8,455	6,341
K Large		5,805	4,354	8,115	6,086
L Large		5,645	4,234	7,955	5,966
M Large		5,465	4,098	7,605	5,704
N Large		5,195	3,897	7,165	5,374
* 3rd/4th Person		1,750	1,750	3,165	3,165
* Infant: Under Age 2		675	675	675	675
Port Charges & Taxes		372	372	405	405
Deposit Requirement		800	800	800	800
Cancellation Protection Plan			3% of Tariff		3% of Tariff

Fares in Canadian dollars and based on double occupancy.
* Based on sharing accommodations with two full-fare guests.
Single Partners Program: Categories F and K.
Single Occupancy: Categories PS through B at 190% of double occupancy; Categories C through N at 150% of double occupancy.
Stateroom Facilities: Refer to deck plans on pages 42 and 43 for specific facilities in each stateroom.

FROM FT. LAUDERDALE			JAN 5, 1998	
To LOS ANGELES			14 days from $3,897	
To HONOLULU			20 days from $5,374	
DAY	**DATE**	**PORT**	**ARRIVE**	**DEPART**
Mon	Jan 5	FT. LAUDERDALE, FLORIDA		5:00pm
Tue	Jan 6	Half Moon Cay, Bahamas	8:00am	5:00pm
Wed-Thu	Jan 7-8	At sea		
Fri	Jan 9	Cartagena, Colombia	7:00am	4:30pm
Sat	Jan 10	Enter Panama Canal at Cristóbal	7:00am	
		Transit Panama Canal		
		Leave the Canal at Balboa		4:00pm
Sun	Jan 11	Scenic cruising Golfo Dulce	9:00am	Noon
Mon	Jan 12	At sea		
Tue	Jan 13	Puerto Quetzal, Guatemala	6:00am	6:00pm
		(Antigua, Copán and Tikal tour options)		
Wed	Jan 14	Santa Cruz Huatulco, Mexico	Noon	7:00pm
Thu	Jan 15	Acapulco, Mexico	8:00am	11:00pm
Fri	Jan 16	Cruising the Mexican Riviera		
Sat	Jan 17	Cabo San Lucas	7:00am	4:00pm
Sun	Jan 18	Cruising the Baja coast		
Mon	Jan 19	LOS ANGELES, CALIFORNIA	8:00am	5:00pm
Tue-Fri	Jan 20-23	At sea		
Sat	Jan 24	Lahaina, Maui, Hawaii	8:00am	11:00pm
Sun	Jan 25	HONOLULU, OAHU, HAWAII	8:00am	

FIGURE 11.14
Duration and cabin category are among the factors that affect the price of a cruise.
Source: Holland America Line.

The cruise industry has seasons in the same way as destinations and fares vary accordingly. High season for the Caribbean is during the winter months whereas cruises in the Mediterranean and off Alaska are more expensive during the summer. Even though two cruises may follow the same itinerary for the same length of time and make the same number of port calls, their prices may be quite different because of the ships involved. Some are more luxuriously appointed or offer better service than others. Some have fewer cabins and more crew. The space ratio and the passenger/crew ratio influence the quality of the service on board and therefore the price charged. Counsellors can verify this by calculating these ratios for two similar cruises. The more expensive cruise ship generally has a higher space ratio and a lower passenger/crew ratio than its competitor.

Another consideration in the cost of a cruise is the itinerary and the number of port calls made. Both affect the length of a cruise. Further, port taxes are levied on a ship whenever it docks. These fees may substantially increase the price of a cruise, depending on the number of stops made and the charges applied. Cruise lines generally show port taxes as a separate item not included in the price of a cruise, however, counsellors must advise clients of these fees and add them to the amount collected for the cruise. Intangibles, such as a ship's reputation for food, entertainment and service, also contribute to the variation in cruise prices.

The above factors influence the fare charged for any cruise. The price of a given cruise, however, is based on the size and location of the cabin booked. A cabin's cost is determined by the amount of space it occupies, its bathroom facilities and its location. Suites and larger cabins are more costly. Larger cabins often have more extensive bathroom facilities, such as a bath rather than a shower, and may have twin or double beds rather than an upper and lower bunk. These features increase the fare charged for a cabin. Cabins on higher decks are considered more desirable because of the view they afford. Consequently they are more expensive. A general rule is that the higher the deck, the higher the fare. Cabins located amidships, where motion of the ship in heavy seas is felt less, have a higher price. Several other features affect the fare assessed. Outside cabins, which offer a view, are more expensive than inside cabins which have no portholes. Similarly, passengers pay more for cabins in a quiet location than for those beside stairways or service areas which may be noisy. Cabins at the extreme stern are sometimes considered undesirable because of possible vibrations caused by the propellers. Cruise lines place cabins in various categories according to the weighting of these factors. Each category is then assigned a price which varies only with the season and number of occupants.

A strong selling feature of cruises is that the fare paid is almost entirely all-inclusive (Figure 11.15). Cruise fares include the voyage from the port of embarkation to the ports of call on the itinerary and the debarkation port at the end of the cruise. Many cruise fares also include return air transportation between major cities and the cruise port. Accommodation in the category of cabin selected, cabin services, all meals and entertainment are also part of the fare paid by passengers. Not only does a cruise include all meals, but on most cruises clients may eat virtually around the clock if they wish. Since passengers are effectively captives when on board, food is extremely important to the success of a cruise. The result is that the restaurants on cruise ships constantly change their menus and consistently offer high quality food. If a ship does not dock at a port but instead anchors offshore, the cruise fare includes transfers for passengers by tender from ship to shore. A variety of activities, such as sports, casinos, entertainment, movie theatres, libraries, and social life in bars and discos, is also provided as part of the cruise. Clients also have access to the duty free shops, hairdressing salon, and other services available on a cruise ship.

Cruise fares do not generally include port taxes or personal expenditures such as tips, laundry and alcoholic beverages. On some ships passengers may be charged for some sports activities and for reserving deck chairs. Some cruise lines have a no tipping policy. Cruise brochures usually state the line's tipping policy, suggest the accepted amount and identify who should be tipped. Recommended tipping guidelines are sometimes provided in the information given to clients with their tickets. The average tip for cabin and dining room stewards varies between US$2.50 and US$4.00 per passenger per day each. Busboys are generally tipped half the amount of a steward. A couple on a 7-day cruise could therefore expect to budget about US$50-70 each for gratuities. Other personnel may be tipped at the client's discretion. All tips, with the exception of those to bartenders, should be paid at the end of the voyage. If a service charge is not included on bar bills, bartenders are usually tipped 15 percent as each cheque is paid. The wine steward may be tipped at the end of the cruise if wine is charged and not paid for at the time. Clients should be advised that they never tip an officer or cruise entertainment staff. Clients should also be aware that the U.S. dollar is the standard currency used on board most cruise ships sailing in the North American market; Canadian dollars are generally not accepted and they may be difficult to exchange since ships carry only a limited quantity of currency. Clients should therefore carry U.S. currency or travellers cheques.

Most cruises involve stops at ports of call, even if only for a few hours. Depending on the points of interest ashore, the entertainment facilities such as nightclubs and casinos, and shopping, the ship may stay overnight or longer. During such stops, passengers may go ashore to shop, see the local sights and generally absorb the atmosphere of the destination visited. Although passengers on a short cruise generally spend less than a day in each port, the cruise line will arrange a series of shore excursions. These are sightseeing tours or visits to local attractions operated by local tour operators as an optional extra. They are

---

ENJOY ALL THESE FABULOUS "FUN SHIP" FEATURES:

- 3, 4, 7, 10 or 11 day "Fun Ship" Cruise
- Fabulous Ports of Call
- "Welcome Aboard" Rum Swizzle Party
- Eight Great Meals and Snacks a Day Including Two Late Night Buffets (even breakfast in bed, if you like)
- Gala Captain's Dinner
- Captain's Cocktail Party
- Camp Carnival …Year-Round Supervised Children's Activities
- Complimentary 24-Hour Stateroom Service
- Pampering "Fun Ship" Service
- Wide Range of Entertainment, Including Different Nightclub Shows Each Evening At Sea
- Singles Cocktail Party
- Full Gambling Casino (not just Slots, but also Blackjack, Craps, Wheel of Fortune, Roulette and Caribbean Stud Poker)
- Nautica Spa Program
- Use of All Shipboard Facilities
- 3 Bands and Orchestras
- Choice of Three Pools, Including Children's Wading Pool
- Duty-Free Shopping On Board
- Briefings on Each Port of Call
- Gala Midnight Buffet (4, 7, 10 or 11 day only)
- Dozens of Activities
- First-Run Movies Featured Daily

---

not included in the cruise price. Clients who wish to participate can purchase tours from the purser or cruise director. Since transfers to shore are included in the price of a cruise, passengers may elect to explore a destination independently. Clients interested in independent touring should be advised of two points, especially when visiting smaller islands where a cruise ship's weekly visit may comprise the entire local tourist industry. Passengers should be prepared to negotiate the price of a tour, and there may be a scarcity of taxis and guides if

FIGURE 11.15
Cruise fares are almost entirely all-inclusive.
Source: Carnival Cruise Lines.

FIGURE 11.16
Cost comparison
chart.

Cost Comparison Chart

	Cruise	Tour Package
Company	_____	_____
Itinerary/Destination	_____	_____
Departure Date	_____	_____
Duration	_____	_____
Quality (deluxe, moderate, etc.)	_____	_____

Costs

	Cruise	Tour Package
Cabin/Room - double per person	$ _____	$ _____
Transportation (port/port)	0.00	_____
Ground Transfers	0.00	_____
Breakfast	0.00	_____
Lunch	0.00	_____
Dinner	0.00	_____
Midnight Snack	0.00	_____
Pool/Deck Activities	0.00	_____
Spa Facilities	0.00	_____
Parties	0.00	_____
Entertainment	0.00	_____
Disco	0.00	_____
Nightclub Shows	0.00	_____
Tips/Gratuities	_____	_____
Drinks	_____	_____
Port Taxes	_____	N/A
Air Fare including Tax	_____	_____
Destination Departure Tax	N/A	_____
Hotel Taxes and Service Charges	N/A	_____
Exchange	_____	_____

	Cruise	Tour Package
Total Cost	$ _____	$ _____
Less: Early Booking Discount	_____	_____
Grand Total	$ _____	$ _____
Per Diem Cost (Divide Grand Total by the number of days)	$ _____	$ _____

the cruise line has already booked all available transport. Passengers on longer cruises may have the option of taking tours lasting several days. Information on shore excursions is generally provided in the wallet containing a client's cruise ticket. This helps clients to budget their expenses. Some cruise lines offer passengers a package of shore excursions at a lower price than if bought individually. Shore excursions that can be booked in advance offer travel counsellors a chance to increase their commission.

The majority of cruise lines promote their product on a fly-cruise package basis which offers an air allowance or special add-on air fare. This merchandising concept (also called air/sea holidays) has proven quite successful. In fact, CLIA estimates that two-thirds of all its 1981 passengers arrived at their port of embarkation by air. Some lines regularly charter aircraft or block space on scheduled flights from various cities to the embarkation port.

Comparing the Cost of a Cruise and a Package Tour

Clients who have never taken a cruise frequently remark that cruises are more expensive than vacations at a resort. While this may appear true at first sight, counsellors can often negate this comment by preparing a cost comparison. As a professional, a counsellor should ensure that clients compare "apples with apples", especially when considering two different types of holiday such as a package tour and a cruise. This method may reveal that a cruise is no more costly than a comparable package tour and may indeed offer clients better value for money. The basis for such comparisons is the daily rate or *per diem* cost of the vacation. Counsellors who prepare these costings must ensure that the comparison is fair by choosing vacations of similar length and quality. The most important factor is to make certain that all known and predictable costs for both vacations

(whether or not they are included in the published price) are part of the calculation. After all costs for each vacation have been itemized and totalled, each is divided by the relevant number of days in the tour. The result is the daily cost of the cruise or package. Cruise prices commonly consist of all meals, accommodation, entertainment and most other costs, and in addition passengers can buy drinks at duty-free prices. Many tour prices, however, do not include meals and all require expenditures on taxis, entertainment and other "necessities" already in the cruise price. Only by calculating all potential costs and reducing this figure to a daily rate can a true comparison be made between alternative vacations. An example of a cost comparison chart is shown in this chapter (Figure 11.16). When making a cost comparison, the cruise and the package tour should be of similar quality (i.e., both deluxe vacations or both budget trips), to the same destination area (preferably with some stops in common), of comparable duration, and departing around the same date. Enter "0.00" or "included" for items that are part of the vacation price, and "N/A" (not applicable) for items that are irrelevant. This will help clients to clearly see the difference between a cruise and a package tour.

Selling Cruises

Cruises are marketed not as transportation but as a unique and pleasurable way of life. Travel counsellors emphasize the romantic mystique associated with cruising and the strong attraction of the sea. Since the shipboard experience forms the major part of a cruise vacation, cruise lines attempt to meet all of their passengers' needs. Cruise ships offer comfort, luxury, excellent food, amiable company and a variety of diversions for their clients to enjoy.

The rising popularity of cruising has prompted a spurt in the construction of cruise ships resulting in an overcapacity and a more competitive industry. Cruise lines not only compete with each other but also with tour operators offering package holidays. Marketing expertise is therefore essential if a cruise company is to be successful. In much the same way as in other sectors of the industry, cruise lines are becoming increasingly specialized. Several lines target exclusively at a specific income level and operate only one of budget, first class or luxury cruises. Some companies and ships appeal to a specific age group. Others are tied more closely to exotic destinations and the ports visited. Several cruise lines offer cruises based on a particular theme, such as nostalgia cruises featuring music and celebrities from a particular era. Others develop cruises around special interests such as culture, education, adventure or nature, such as voyages to the Galapagos Islands. A new field being explored by cruise lines is the use of ships for business meetings and incentive groups. All continue to search for new products and different market niches. The outcome is that clients may choose from a wide variety of cruises, varying in duration, ports of call and price. It appears that the only common feature shared by most cruises is travel by water. Counsellors who attempt to sell cruises on a single feature, such as price, are likely to mislead their clients.

Counsellors must decide whether to sell the cruise, the ship or the destination but they cannot make this choice until they determine their clients' motivations and needs. The itinerary and type of cruise must then be matched with these needs. Some clients cruise because they wish to enjoy the scenery. An appropriate cruise would therefore have a daytime cruising schedule and opportunities to admire the view. A voyage through the Alaska passage or a Rhine River cruise may meet their needs. Some wish to experience cruise life and others sail primarily to visit interesting ports of call. A Caribbean cruise which sails mostly at night and stops each day at a different island may appeal to these clients. Knowledge of ports of call and of life on board is therefore essential to properly

counsel clients. To some extent the choice depends on the client's preferences for an itinerary and how much time is spent at sea. Small ships are more suited to a variety of destinations and to small ports that the big ships cannot enter. Counsellors must be aware that not all cruise ships or cruise lines are the same. Again, the quality of the vessel and the type of passenger should be matched to the client's needs. It is important that clients know what to expect in terms of the ship, the clientele and the quality of the cruise.

Before attempting to sell a particular product, counsellors must qualify their clients by obtaining some background information. Clients who have not previously taken a cruise should be asked to describe their last holiday. Those who have cruised before should be probed to reveal what they enjoyed and disliked about the experience. Most returning cruise passengers report that the excellence of the meals is the most memorable aspect of a voyage. Cruise lines recognize the importance of fine cuisine in a confined environment and have therefore spent considerable time and money on providing high quality food services. In addition to three meals a day, cruises serve mid-morning coffee or bouillon on deck, afternoon tea, and a midnight buffet which often rivals dinner in the size and variety of its dishes. Counsellors can consult cruise lines or the *CLIA Cruise Manual* for examples of shipboard menus to learn of the choice of soups, sea foods, entrées and desserts available. Menus tend to become more sophisticated as the quality and price of a cruise rises. One of the pleasures of an ocean voyage is to taste dishes cooked in various styles. French, Italian, Swedish, Greek and Norwegian cuisine are some of the specialties one might expect to enjoy on a cruise. Several references identify a ship's registry and the nationalities of the crew and hotel staff. These suggest the style of food that passengers might expect on board. A copy of a typical daily activities sheet will help clients understand what is available for the all-inclusive price. In addition, clients need

FIGURE 11.17
Sample cruise
assessment form.

SHIP BASICS

Ship's Name: _____ Cruise Line: _____

Built: _____ Rebuilt/Refurbished: _____

Registry: _____ Crew Nationality: _____

Crew Size: _____ Passenger Capacity: _____ GRT: _____

Passenger/Crew Ratio: _____ Space Ratio: _____

CRUISE DETAILS

Cruise Length: _____ Departure Port: _____

Ports of Call: _____

Theme: _____

Clientele: _____

Price Range: _____

SHIP DETAILS

Facilities   Quality

of inside cabins: _____ _____

# of outside cabins: _____ _____

# of inside swimming pools: _____ _____

# of outside swimming pools: _____ _____

# of dining rooms: _____ _____ _____

# of theatres: _____ _____ _____

# of public rooms: _____ _____

# of shops: _____ _____ _____

Services   Quality

Entertainment: _____ _____

Activities: _____ _____

_____ _____

_____ _____

Meals: _____ _____

Atmosphere: _____ _____

Maintenance: _____ _____

Overall Assessment/Comments: _____

_____

_____

little extra spending money on a cruise.

Once the relevant client details have been discovered the next step is to select some cruise products which match this profile. To do so, counsellors must develop a method of evaluating cruises in terms of factors such as the ship size and reputation, cost, itinerary and shore excursions, shipboard and on-shore activities available, passenger/crew and space ratios, and type of clientele. An assessment form will be useful for this purpose (see Figure 11.17).

When selling a cruise, counsellors most often rely on the cruise company's brochure. The ship's deck plan and rate sheet are the essential sales tools used. Counsellors can use a deck plan to show their clients the complete layout of a ship, to identify cabin types and their location in relation to dining room, swimming pool, theatre, and other facilities, to give approximate cabin sizes (some brochures show dimensions), and to indicate their layout and amenities. A useful sales strategy is to mark or highlight high traffic areas (near steps and dining rooms, for example) in one colour and quiet areas in another. This not only visually reveals preferable cabin locations, but also supports price differences associated with them. By using the correct rate sheet in conjunction with the deck plan, a counsellor can state the price of each cabin type under consideration. Counsellors should recommend a cabin type or group rather than a specific cabin number or location. For example, consider a prospective client who seeks a two-bed outside cabin, amidships on "A" deck. The deck plan may reveal seven or eight cabins of that type, each of the same size, with the same furniture, and at the same fare. A counsellor cannot promise a specific cabin until a request for space has been confirmed by the cruise line. Further, to base a sale on the merits of one particular cabin may destroy the counsellor's sales attempt if that cabin has already been sold. In this regard, counsellors should treat the sale of a cabin in the same way that they would handle the sale of a hotel room; not by room number but by room type.

The general information printed at the end of a brochure provides important guidance for clients and counsellors (Figure 11.18). Counsellors sometimes disregard this section which can help them answer many client questions. It contains details essential to the sales process, such as terms for deposits and final payments, special rates for children and cancellation conditions, as well as useful client information on sailing times, baggage handling, table reservations, and passport and visa requirements.

The number of cities with the port and harbour facilities necessary to service cruise ships is limited but increasing. Most cruises from the east coast sail from New York City, Fort Lauderdale/Port Everglades, Port Canaveral or Miami. On the west coast, embarkation is frequently from Vancouver, Seattle, Los Angeles or San Francisco. San Juan has become important as a cruise port since the 1980s. Counsellors need to add facts on various ports to their store of product knowledge. The port maps reproduced in various references can help counsellors route their clients through the most convenient airport and help them find the correct departure dock. Since some cruise lines are based at particular ports counsellors should also be familiar with these details.

Overcoming Objections

Research indicates that less than five percent of the population has taken a cruise and that the majority of cruise passengers are repeat clients. This suggests that there is some buyer resistance to cruising but if this can be overcome, a client will usually be satisfied with the cruise experience. Some travellers are anxious about sailing and others have doubts about how well they would enjoy a cruise. Clients who are reluctant to buy a product frequently express their concerns in the form of an objection. Counsellors should never discount these statements, no matter how trivial they may appear. An appropriate response is to support the client's feelings

General Information

THIS IS NOT AN OFFER OR A CONTRACT EXCEPT THAT UPON PAYMENT OF A DEPOSIT ALL BOOKINGS ARE SUBJECT TO THE CANCELLATION PROVISION SET FORTH BELOW AND BY WHICH THE PASSENGER AGREES TO BE BOUND. THE ATTENTION OF THE PASSENGER IS SPECIFICALLY DIRECTED TO THE TERMS FOR CARRIAGE OF PASSENGERS AS SET FORTH IN THE CUNARD PASSAGE CONTRACT. COPIES OF THE TERMS OF THE PASSAGE CONTRACT MAY BE OBTAINED FROM A TRAVEL AGENT OR CUNARD. THESE CONTAIN IMPORTANT INFORMATION ON ITINERARY, LIABILITIES OF CUNARD, INDEPENDENT CONTRACTORS, HEALTH, IMMIGRATION, AND OTHER RELEVANT INFORMATION.

RESERVATIONS

Consult your CLIA cruise agent or call Cunard. Your entire trip can be booked with just one phone call. You must be a resident of the U.S. or Canada to book your cruise from this brochure.

PASSAGE CONTRACT TERMS/DEPOSIT

Bookings will be accepted solely on the terms of the Cunard Passage Contract. A deposit is required to secure a confirmed reservation as follows:
. Cruises of 20 days or less: 20% of full passage fare. The balance of the fare is required as follows:
. 60 days prior to sailing date for cruises of 20 days or less.
. 90 days prior to sailing date for cruises of 21 days or more.

PERSONAL FUNDS

American Express, Visa, MasterCard and Diners Club credit cards can be used to pay deposit, passage fare and some on-board expenses. Since personal checks cannot be cashed at the Purser's Office or accepted on board, most passengers prefer to carry travellers checks which may be cashed at the Purser's Office on board.

PHYSICALLY DISABLED PASSENGERS

Physical disabilities must be reported to the Company before Passage Contracts are issued. The Company reserves the right to refuse passage to anyone who, in the opinion of the Company's medical advisors, is in such a state of health or physical condition as to be unfit to travel. Advanced pregnancy is regarded as a physical disability and application for passage from pregnant passengers shall by accompanied by a medical certificate.

HANDICAPPED FACILITIES

There are a limited number of cabins available for passengers requiring entry to cabins with a wheelchair. However, for those passengers requiring assistance, it is recommended that they bring an attendant at their own expense. Reservations must be advised at the time of booking of any disabilities.

EMBARKATION

Embarkation generally begins 2 hours prior to departure. We regret that no visitors are allowed aboard the ship.

TRAVEL DOCUMENTS

All passengers traveling to Europe and the Panama Canal should be in possession of a passport valid for the period of the entire trip. This is to be presented at the pier, prior to embarkation, together with the passenger information form. Visa regulations vary depending on destination and citizenship and you should obtain details from the consulates of the countries that you wish to visit. U.S. and Canadian citizens on Caribbean and Hawaii cruises are not required to carry passports or tourist cards. Passengers are well advised, however, to carry documentary proof of citizenship such as a voter's registration card, copy of a birth certificate or passport.

ALIENS

Certain aliens may be required to be in possession of one or more of the following travel documents: U.S. Transit Visas, U.S. Sailing Permits, Alien Identification Cards, or unexpired Re-Entry or Non-Quota Visas. All such passengers are advised to check with the Bureau of Internal Revenue and the U.,S. Consulate Service to determine which documents they must obtain. All passengers other than U.S. and Canadian citizens must have valid passports.

VACCINATION CARDS

Neither vaccination certificates nor health cards are presently required. However, regulations vary from time to time depending on countries visited and world health conditions. Please consult your travel agent or public health office before departure.

SECURITY

In the interest of safety, all passengers and all baggage is screened and searched. Film should not be packed in your baggage.

VALUABLES

Fragile articles and valuables must be carried on and off the ship by the passengers themselves. Safe Deposit boxes are available free of charge at the Purser's Office.

CUNARDCARE TRAVELER'S PROTECTION INSURANCE

We strongly recommend that all passengers purchase the CunardCare comprehensive passenger travel insurance program which has been specially designed and economically priced exclusively for Cunard passengers. For complete details, see the ad on page 70, or contact your travel agent or Cunard.

BAGGAGE

All your baggage must be tagged with Cunard tags showing ship, sailing date and room number. We will send these to you before you sail. A reasonable amount of baggage will be accepted without charge for carriage in your cabin. Passengers embarking in New York may drop off their baggage early on the day of sailing between 8:00am-11:30am. Otherwise, they should arrive with their baggage at the New York pier at the time of embarkation. Ask your travel agent for airline baggage limitations.

BAGGAGE INSURANCE

The Company's liability for loss of or damage to fragile articles, valuables and/or baggage is limited by the Passage Contract. Therefore, it is recommended that all baggage be insured. CunardCare, Cunard's low-cost, comprehensive travel insurance program, includes baggage protection up to $1000 in the event of loss or theft. See page 71 for details.

CANCELLATION BY PASSENGERS

Cruises 20 days or less

Number of days before sailing written cancellation notice received	Cancellation Charge
Over 45	None
45-21	20% of full fare
20-1	50% of full fare
No show/No written notice	100% of full fare

Cruises 21 days or more

Number of days before sailing written cancellation notice received	Cancellation Charge
Over 90	None
90-60	25% of full fare
59-30	50% of full fare
29 or less	100% of full fare
No show/No written notice	100% of full fare

Specially reserved Concorde flights

Number of days before flight written cancellation notice received	Cancellation Charge
45-21	$450
20-1	$750
No show/No written notice	Full Fare

Cancellation notice must be put in writing and sent to Refund Department, Cunard P.O. Box 2947, Grand Central Station, New York, NY 10163.

Retroactive adjustments to Air-Sea package or round-trip fares, etc. are not permitted after the original date of departure. Passengers wishing to alter their return arrangements do so at their own expense.

ADVANCED OR DELAYED SAILINGS

In the event of strikes, lockouts, riots or stoppage of labor from whatever cause, or for any other reason whatsoever, the Company may at any time cancel, advance or postpone any scheduled sailing and may, but is not obliged to substitute another vessel and shall not be liable for any loss whatsoever to passengers by reason of such cancellation, advancement, postponement or substitution, except as otherwise provided in the Passage Contract.

SERVICES PROVIDED BY AIRLINES

Cunard reserves the right to choose the air carrier, routing and city airport from each gateway city. Within 45 days of departure, the air program is on a request basis. Airline tickets issued by Cunard are highly restrictive and often cannot be reissued, revalidated, or exchanged for another carrier or routing. Flight schedules cannot be changed by Cunard once your tickets have been issued. Any additional costs, including penalties for cancellations/rebooking will be made at the passengers' expense. All airline tickets issued in conjunction with Cunard air program are refundable only to Cunard. Any unused flight coupons must be returned to Cunard attention Air Refunds. Cunard will determine the amount of any refund due. If air ticket is lost, the passenger is responsible for the cost of replacement. Cunard has no responsibility for cost incurred due to altered travel plans caused by airline delays or for any act, omission, or event occurring while not on board its vessel. Cunard cannot confirm airline seat assignments, add frequent flyer numbers to airline records or request special meals. These services should be arranged by the passengers' travel agent directly with the airline.

BAGGAGE BY AIR

Passengers making part of their trip by air should note that airline baggage allowances are as follows: Two pieces allowed, maximum dimensions of each cannot exceed 62" (length and height and depth). Total dimension of both pieces not to exceed 106". NOTE: On Concorde flights baggage is not to exceed 1 bag per passenger or 3 bags per couple. See your Travel Agent for other requirements such as excess baggage, carry-on baggage, etc.

SERVICES PROVIDED BY INDEPENDENT CONTRACTORS

All shoreside tours and portions of other services described in this brochure are provided by independent contracts, including but not limited to airline carriers, shoreside tour operators and on board physicians. Cunard shall have no obligation or liability of any kind to passengers for acts or omissions in connection with or arising out of arrangements with independent contractors, including but not limited to airline carriers, shoreside tour operators and on board physicians since they are not agents for or employees of Cunard. For restrictions and other details on tours, see tour information, page 55.

FIGURE 11.18
Cruise brochures identify the terms and conditions that apply to the cruise. *Source: Cunard.*

and note that these are not unusual. The counsellor should then answer the objection. Some of the more predictable comments and suggested replies are discussed below.

- **Too expensive**. Brochure prices may appear high but when a counsellor prepares a cost comparison clients will often select a cruise because of its value for money.
- **Boredom and regimentation**. Clients may be concerned about feeling bored or being regimented on a cruise. Counsellors can emphasize the many activities organized on board for clients. Those who are not interested in these activities should be offered a cruise which spends a minimum of time at sea and makes a variety of port calls and shore excursions. Clients should also be made aware that they need not participate in organized activities that do not interest them. Only the lifeboat drill is mandatory. Even the restriction of fixed meal times can be avoided since many ships offer room service.
- **Confinement**. Clients may comment that cabins are too small and cruise ships too confining. A suitable reply is to emphasize the size of modern cruise ships (some as long as a football field), and the larger size of their cabins and public rooms. Counsellors should also point out the freedom of movement that passengers have, and remind their clients that they will likely spend little time in their cabins. Claustrophobic clients should be sold an outside cabin. Those who feel that a cruise is too limiting should be sold an itinerary with a different port call each day.
- **Seasickness**. Many travellers worry about becoming seasick on a voyage. Counsellors can help reduce these fears by pointing out that cruise ships have stabilizers to keep them steady under most conditions. Modern technology also permits ships to be aware of bad weather so that they can reroute to avoid storms and rough seas. Clients should be aware that drugs are available to counter motion sickness, and that cruise ships have a doctor on board. Counsellors should also attempt to sell cabin space on a lower deck and amidships where the vessel's motion will be less noticeable.
- **Too formal or need an expensive wardrobe**. At one time cruise lines were guilty of promoting the myth that clients needed a large and expensive wardrobe to take a cruise. Many cruise brochures showed photographs of professional models wearing lavish or formal clothes, a reminder of the class system that once prevailed on ships. However, the cruise industry today is based on a one-class system. Accommodation and facilities are recognized as first class and all passengers receive the same service no matter which cabin they occupy. Similarly, current brochures tend to reflect the image of the company's target market and the ship's usual clientele. Casual, lightweight sports clothes are the rule on most cruises during the day and for shore excursions. A suit or jacket and tie is appropriate for men in the evening, while women will be quite acceptable in a cotton or silk dress. Tuxedos and evening gowns are worn only by a small proportion of passengers, even on formal occasions such as the Captain's cocktail party or farewell dinner. Each ship and cruise line has a different style. Counsellors should also check with colleagues and former passengers. Clients who will be making shore excursions should be advised that clothing should be appropriate for the culture being visited. Many destinations frown on shorts and beachwear on city streets. Again, counsellors must apply their product knowledge of the destination and inform their clients accordingly. Cruises offer a relaxed atmosphere with many opportunities to mix and mingle. Repeat cruise customers cite the easygoing, friendly atmosphere aboard ship and the friendships that can be made through dining with the same people each evening and participating in activities.

Advantages of Cruises

Cruises offer a number of benefits to both clients and counsellors.

Advantages for Clients

Clients appreciate the all-inclusive and prepaid nature of cruises which helps them to budget more easily. Expenses are predictable as only drinks, tips, souvenirs and other personal items need be bought.

Cruises offer good value for money. Even though a client may have booked a budget cabin, service, meals and entertainment are first class. Clients therefore enjoy the benefits of a luxury vacation at a moderate price. They can eat as much as they wish, from gourmet meals to hamburgers, and they enjoy a high standard of personal service.

Cruises offer all the satisfaction of a resort vacation, such as sunbathing, casinos, nightly entertainment, sports and activities, combined with the charm of an ocean voyage and the excitement of visiting new places. The port calls made also make a variety of destinations, sightseeing and onshore activities possible. Passengers can experience different cultures, go shopping, view the scenery, or take part in activities when the ship docks. Cruises offer clients the opportunity for a safe adventure; clients can explore an exotic destination safe in the knowledge that they can return to the protection of their cabin and the comfort of a wonderful meal.

Since each cruise ship has its own character and different cruise lines try to tap different markets, cruises can attract all types of travellers from novices to old hands. They can be relaxing or active, of any duration from one day to several months, and tailored to general interests or market niches. Cruises offer passengers the flexibility to take part in everything or do nothing at all. Except for shore excursions, no prior plans are necessary so passengers can alter them at any time.

For many, the appeal is the experience of cruising and shipboard life. Every cruise ship has its own character and the ship becomes their destination. Many passengers become attached to a particular ship. These clients enjoy the relaxation of a cruise, the invigorating sea air, and the isolation from everyday cares. For others, the convenience of a cruise is the main benefit. Passengers pack and unpack only once, and are not subject to the strict timetable or confinement found on a coach tour.

Advantages for Counsellors

Travel counsellors gain several benefits from selling cruises. Since cruises are all-inclusive, counsellors earn commission on a larger total price than by selling simple tours or transportation and accommodation. Some shore excursions can also be booked in advance and these too are commissionable. Although cruises may initially be more difficult to sell, they enjoy a high satisfaction rating and the majority of cruise passengers are repeat clients. Once a counsellor starts to sell cruises, therefore, such clients should continue to return to the agency. There is less paperwork associated with cruise sales since the cruise line or tour operator issues the tickets, and provides the ticket wallet, tip sheets and other client details. Cruise fares are based on cabin category and sailing date, and include everything except port taxes. They are therefore easy for counsellors to calculate.

Disadvantages of Cruises

There are, however, those who criticize cruises and counsellors should be aware of some possible disadvantages of this product. Critics declare that cruises provide a shallow experience of countries and cultures. This may be a valid comment but many would say the same for any form of mass tourism. Some people comment that there is nowhere to go when a ship is at sea. This too is true, however, unless the person suffers from claustrophobia there is enough activity to keep most people occupied. Other negative comments, such as cruises are dependent on the weather and appeal only to older travellers have already been discussed.

Glossary of Nautical Terms

Accommodation Ladder.	A folding stairway used to gain access to a ship from ashore or from a tender alongside.
Aft.	The stern (rear) of a ship.
Aloft.	Above the highest deck; in, at or near the masthead.
Amidships.	The central part of a ship, midway between the bow and the stern.
Beam.	The breadth of a ship at its widest part.
Berth.	(1) A bed in a cabin. (2) A space at a pier for a ship to dock.
Bow.	The forward (front) extremity of a ship.
Bow Thruster.	A small engine at the front of a ship used to manoeuvre the vessel into position when docking.
Bridge.	Where the Captain and officers navigate and steer.
Bulkhead.	A partition or wall dividing the ship into cabins.
Bunk.	Bed.
Cabin.	A passenger's sleeping room (also called a stateroom).
Capstan.	A spindle used to wind in hawsers, cables or anchor chains.
Colours.	A flag or ensign showing the ship's nationality.
Companionway.	Interior stairway.
Crow's Nest.	Lookout platform on the top of the mast.
Disembark.	To land, or go ashore from a ship.
Dock.	Berth, pier or quay.
Doldrums.	The virtually breezeless oceans around the equator.
Draft.	The depth from the waterline to the lowest point of a ship's keel.
Embark.	To go aboard a ship; to begin a voyage.
Even Keel.	When the ship is in a vertical position.
Fathom.	Measurement of water depth equal to 6 feet.
Fender.	Protective material serving as a cushion between the side of a ship and the dock. Old tires are often used for this purpose.
Fore.	(Forward) In or towards the bow of a ship.
Free Port.	A port or place free of customs duty and most customs regulations.
Galley.	The ship's kitchen.
Gangway.	The opening in a ship's side and the ramp by which passengers embark and disembark.
Gross Registered Tonnage (GRT).	A commonly used designation of a ship's size, not a measure of weight but of a ship's volume in cubic feet. GRT is determined by dividing the total number of cubic feet enclosed by the ship's hull and superstructure by 100. One GRT = 100 cubic feet.
Hawser.	A large diameter rope or cable.
Helm.	The ship's entire steering mechanism.
Hold.	Lower cargo storage compartments.
Hull.	The frame of a ship, without the superstructure.
Inside Cabin.	A cabin with all interior bulkheads and no windows or portholes.
Keel.	Thick steel plate running from stem to stern along the bottom centre of the ship to which all vertical framing is attached.
Knot.	A unit of speed, meaning one nautical mile (6,080 feet) per hour. (A land mile is 5280 feet.)
Latitude.	Angular distance measured in degrees north and south of the equator. One degree of latitude is approximately 60 nautical miles.
Leeward.	Towards the sheltered (from the wind) side of the ship.
Line.	Any rope smaller than a hawser.
Log.	Daily record of the ship's speed and progress.

FIGURE 11.19
Glossary of nautical terms and abbreviations.

Glossary of Nautical Terms

Longitude.	Angular distance measured in degrees east or west of the prime meridian of Greenwich, England. Due to the earth's curvature, one degree of longitude varies from approximately 60 nautical miles at the equator to zero at the north and south poles.
Manifest.	A list or invoice of the ship's passengers, crew and cargo.
Moor.	To secure a ship to a fixed place by hawsers, cables or anchor.
Nautical Mile.	6,080 feet (15 percent longer than a land mile of 5,280 feet).
Outside Cabin.	A cabin with the hull of the ship forming one bulkhead.
Pitch.	The alternate rise and fall of the ship's bow.
Port.	The left side of a ship when facing toward the bow. Even-numbered cabins are usually on the port side.
Porthole.	A window in the ship's hull.
Prow.	The bow or stem (front) of a ship.
Quay.	European word for wharf or pier. (Pronounced "key".)
Registry.	The country under whose laws the ship and its owners are obliged to comply.
Roll.	The motion of a ship from side to side.
Rudder.	The metal fin at the stern used to steer the ship.
Running Lights.	Three lights (green on the starboard side, red on the port side and white at the top of the mast) required by international law to be lighted when a ship is in motion between sunset and sunrise.
Screw.	A ship's propeller.
Sitting.	Most ships have two sittings for dinner, usually about 6:00 p.m. and 8:0 p.m., which are reserved when a passenger books a cruise or boards the ship. Breakfast and lunch are usually open seating.
Stabilizers.	A set of underwater fins or vanes attached to the hull. Controlled by a gyroscope, stabilizers dampen or lessen a ship's tendency to roll from side to side in heavy seas.
Starboard.	The right side of a ship when facing towards the bow. Odd-numbered cabins are usually on the starboard side.
Stateroom.	A passenger's cabin or sleeping quarters.
Stem.	The extreme prow of a ship.
Stern.	The extreme rear of a ship.
Superstructure.	The structural part of a ship above the main deck.
Tender.	A smaller vessel, sometimes the ship's lifeboat, used to carry passengers between the ship and the shore when the ship is at anchor.
Trade Winds.	Those winds blowing from a westerly direction towards the equator.
Wake.	The trail of agitated water left behind a ship in motion.
Waterline.	The line painted on the side of a ship's hull which indicates the ideal portion of the ship to be submerged.
Weather Side.	The side of a ship exposed to the wind or weather.
Weigh.	To raise, as in to weigh anchor.
Windward.	Towards the direction from which the wind is blowing.

Some Common Nautical Abbreviations

MS	Motorship
MTS	Motor Turbine Ship
MV	Motor Vessel
SS	Steamship
STR	Steamer
TS	Twin Screw
TSS	Turbine Steamship

FIGURE 11.19

Reservations and Ticketing

Cruise lines ask that reservations for cruises be made at least four to six weeks in advance of the sailing date. Popular cruises, particularly longer voyages, sell out quickly. Clients should therefore be advised to book as early as possible. All cruise companies follow the same basic procedures for making reservations and issuing tickets. To make a cruise booking, a counsellor will call the cruise line's representative (which may be a tour operator), or its reservation or sales office. A counsellor must supply the reservations agent with the following information:

- Identify the agency and the counsellor.
- Request the ship by name, the departure date and the port of embarkation.
- State the category of cabin desired.
- Give the number in party and their names. (Provide the ages of any children in the group.)
- If space is available, provide the nationality and passport numbers of the clients.
- Specify the preferred meal sitting.
- Request any special dietary needs such as diabetic, Kosher or vegetarian meals.

If suitable space is available, the reservations agent will offer accommodation in the passenger's name for the chosen cruise, and will provide the counsellor with a locator number and an option date. The option date is the date by which the line requires the deposit specified in the terms and conditions of the company's brochure. An option date is usually seven days from the initial request. Failure to receive the deposit by the option date means that the line automatically places the confirmed reservation back in its inventory of cabins for that cruise. If a client declines the space, the counsellor should immediately notify the line so that the space can go back on the market.

An increasing number of cruises can now be booked through an airline CRS using a program such as Leisure Shopper in Galileo. This gives counsellors the ability to book clients, confirm cabin numbers, request dining room assignments, arrange pre- and post-tours, make special requests, and select special rates. By the end of 1996, the majority of all cruise capacity was available in these systems.

Similar to package tours, cruise lines request a deposit to protect the booking and as a sign of commitment and acceptance by the client. A deposit must be paid at the same time as the booking is made but usually no less than 45 days before departure. The deposit amount varies. Some companies charge from 10 to 25 percent of the cruise price while others ask for a flat fee of $200 to $400. Specific requirements are set out in the cruise line's brochures. When final payment is due, usually four to six weeks before the sailing date, an agency sends its client's money to the cruise company and the ticket is issued. Cruise tickets, sometimes called passenger contracts, are generally issued by the ship line. Before issuing a ticket, a cruise line will need detailed information on the client so that it can obtain immigration and customs clearance for passengers to disembark for shore excursions. The amount of information required depends on the cruise itinerary. More is required for visits to many foreign ports than to a few Caribbean ports. The cruise line arranges with each country visited for all passengers to be cleared in advance. After these arrangements have been completed, the cruise line sends the agency a ticket wallet containing tickets, airline tickets if included in fare, luggage tags, tips and information on the cruise, the ship and the ports visited, and contact addresses en route.

Counsellors deduct their commission prior to submitting the final payment to a cruise line. Commissions are deducted from the final payment only, not from deposits. Commission is paid only on the total cost of the cruise. Counsellors do not earn commission on port taxes or service charges.

When booking a Caribbean cruise, clients can be advised that Canadian and American passengers are usually excused from producing passports or tourist cards under "yacht privileges" granted to the ship by the host nation. However, passengers must always carry proof of citizenship such as a birth certificate, passport or citizenship certificate.

Guaranteed Accommodation

Occasionally a cruise line's reservation department may be unable to offer the requested accommodation as all such space has already been sold or is under option to others. As an alternative, the company may offer a counsellor's client guaranteed accommodation on the cruise in question. This guarantee is a firm commitment by the cruise line to provide accommodation. All cruise lines experience changed and cancelled reservations before a ship actually sails. They can therefore offer guarantees based on their anticipated turnover.

Guarantees are typically offered within the fare range or cabin category requested. However, there is an understanding that a specific room number will not be assigned to the passenger until later (perhaps just when the passenger boards the ship). Sometimes the stateroom ultimately assigned is superior in quality and price than that requested and paid by the client. Such passengers enjoy the benefits at no additional charge. Under a guaranteed arrangement, passengers are never assigned less expensive or inferior quality accommodation than they originally requested and paid for. Indeed, many experienced travel counsellors prefer to accept guarantees because history has shown that clients almost always obtain superior accommodation to that paid for.

If a cruise line's bookings are such that guaranteed accommodation cannot be offered, it may instead suggest that the client be put on a waiting list for the cruise. This assures the individual of a place in line if the accommodation should become available.

Review Questions

1. Briefly describe the development of the cruise industry.

2. Describe the different types of marine transportation which a travel counsellor may be asked to book.

3. What are the selling features of a cruise vacation?

4. Describe the responsibilities of the cruise ship personnel who deal with passengers.

5. Describe the various sections in a typical cruise brochure.

6. Discuss the factors which influence the cost of a cruise.

Research Assignment

Choose a cruise from a cruise line brochure and a package tour from a tour operator. Using a cost comparison chart, determine the per diem cost of each vacation. Make sure that the companies offer products of similar quality, to similar destinations and that the two vacations are of similar duration and depart around the same date. Recommend one of these holidays and give reasons for your suggestion.

References

ABC Passenger Shipping Guide, Reed Travel Group, 131 Clarendon Street, Boston, MA 02116, USA. Published monthly.

ABC Star Service from the above address.

CLIA Cruise Manual, Cruise Lines International Association, 500 Fifth Avenue, Suite 1407, New York, NY 10110, USA. Published annually.

Criuse Industry Annual, Nissen-Lie Communications, 441 Lexington Avenue, Suite 1209A, New York, NY 10017, USA. Published annually.

Ford's Deck Plan Guide, 19448 Londelius Street, Northridge, CA 91324, USA. Published annually.

Ford's Freighter Travel Guide from the above address. Annual subscription or single copy.

Ford's International Cruise Guide from the above address. Published quarterly in March, June, September and December and available by annual subscription or single copy.

OAG Worldwide Cruise and Shipline Guide, 2000 Clearwater Drive, Oak Brook, IL 60521, USA. Published every two months.

Official Cruise Guide, 500 Plaza Drive, Secaucus, NJ 07096, USA. Published annually.

Office of the Chief, U.S. Public Health Service, 1015 North American Way, Room 102, Miami, FL 33131, USA provides a weekly summary and detailed reports on the sanitary standards of specific ships.

Official Steamship Guide International, Subscription Department, Official Steamship Guide, 111 Cherry Street, New Canaan, CT 06840, USA. Published monthly.

Peterson, Garth. *Garth's Profile of Ships*, P.O. Box 34697, Omaha, NE 68134, USA or from the Forsyth Travel Library, Inc., 9154 West 57th Street, P.O. Box 2975, Shawnee Mission, KS 66201-1375, USA.

Thomas Cook European Timetable, P.O. Box 36, Peterborough PE3 6SB, England or from Thomas Cook Travel offices or the Forsyth Travel Library.

## Chapter 12

Travel Insurance

Chapter Summary

This chapter reviews the need for travellers to purchase insurance protection, discusses the business of insurance, and outlines the procedures associated with selling this product. Travel insurance terminology is defined and the types of travel insurance available are identified. The features of each type of travel insurance are then highlighted. Waiver forms and claims procedures are discussed. Examples of common situations are provided to assist counsellors to sell travel insurance products. The chapter concludes with a discussion of the industry's future.

Chapter Objectives

After completing this chapter you should be able to:

- Counsel clients regarding the need for travel insurance.

- Define and use travel insurance terminology.

- Identify and describe the types of travel insurance coverage available.

- List sales features and benefits of these insurances.

- Compare coverage offered by insurance companies and tour operators.

- Interpret travel insurance brochures and manuals.

- Calculate the cost of various insurance policies.

- Complete an insurance application for a client.

- Complete an insurance sales report form.

- Describe the need for and complete waiver forms.

- Describe and follow claim procedures.

The Need for Travel Insurance

Most travel agencies sell travel insurance as part of the range of travel products they offer to clients. Since provincial governments in Canada have greatly reduced out-of-province health coverage, travel insurance can no longer be considered a luxury or an extra service. Rather, it has become an absolute necessity for the travelling public. Selling travel insurance can not only benefit clients it can also generate significant additional revenue for agencies. Commissions for an agency can average between 20 and 40 percent of the premium paid. In some cases remuneration can exceed 40 percent through high sales volume and low loss ratios. In addition, by selling travel insurance an agency protects itself and its counsellors against potential lawsuits.

The topic of insurance naturally conjures up an image of misfortune. Few travellers wish to hear about possible hazards when planning a trip. Equally, travel counsellors are reluctant to introduce such matters as part of the discussion during the sales process. However, sometimes things do go wrong. It is therefore the travel counsellor's responsibility to broach the subject. The need for travel insurance must be stressed.

Everyone who travels needs travel insurance. Despite all precautions, travellers can't completely avoid risks that can occur during a trip or holiday. Accidents, sickness, death, fire, earthquakes, tornadoes, lightning, criminal assault, flight delays, flight accidents, severe weather conditions, theft and baggage delays do happen. These are just a few of the possibilities that travellers face. The consequences of these hazards range from unpleasant to calamitous. Their impact can be both physical and economic. A hospital stay for several months in a foreign country could represent the loss of most of a client's wealth. An injury may prevent a person from completing a planned trip or holiday. A rental automobile worth thousand of dollars can be wrecked in an instant. Baggage can be stolen in a few seconds.

In many of these cases, insurance helps individuals reduce the financial loss from such sudden and unexpected events. It operates by spreading this risk over a large number of people. Those who *could* suffer a loss but *do not*, help to repay the losses of the few who *do*.

Obviously, insurance does not prevent the physical occurrence from taking place. Owning an insurance policy will not keep an accident from happening or a hotel from burning down, nor a flight being delayed because of severe weather, nor a person from collapsing from a heart attack. However, it does help relieve the financial problems created by such events. To this extent, insurance plays an important part in maintaining an insured person's sense of security.

Although consumers cannot be forced to purchase travel insurance, counsellors must clearly explain the risks associated with the travel arrangements the client is purchasing. In the client's best interests a counsellor must recommend the purchase of an appropriate travel insurance plan which, at the moment of need, may prove to be the best investment the client will ever make. Figure 12.1 describes some typical situations where travel insurance is needed and suggests appropriate travel insurance products that can be recommended.

By clearly explaining the protection provided by travel insurance coverage, counsellors can help to ease their clients' concerns. For example, provincial health plans give adequate coverage when an illness or injury occurs at home. However, these benefits do not extend to all medical expenses incurred outside a person's province of residence. Some provinces have reduced out of province coverage to as low as $75 per day. Clients who suffer a mishap requiring medical attention on a business or vacation trip will not only have an unpleasant experience but they may also encounter serious financial consequences. They can avoid negative economic consequences by purchasing travel insurance to protect against any expenses beyond the limits imposed by provincial governments.

Situation:	What if a client's travelling companion (or host or family member) is hospitalized and the trip must be cut short or postponed?
Recommendation:	Clients need to remember that travel arrangements depend on more than just their own health. With Trip Cancellation and Interruption insurance a client will not suffer any loss even when a trip is cut short or postponed due to the illness of a travelling companion.
Situation:	What if clients' baggage did not arrive at their destination?
Recommendation:	The clients need Baggage and Personal Effects insurance so that they are not burdened with the cost of buying interim clothing and personal necessities.
Situation:	What if clients have cut short a trip because of a medical emergency and they have made non-refundable, prepaid travel arrangements?
Recommendation:	The clients need Trip Cancellation and Interruption insurance so that they are not financially penalized for an unforeseen difficulty.
Situation:	What if clients experience a medical emergency in a country where they do not speak the language?
Recommendation:	The clients need Emergency Hospital and Medical insurance, which among other features offers 24-hour contact to a worldwide assistance network and multilingual interpretation services.
Situation:	What if a client drives south for a holiday but is flown home as the result of a medical emergency?
Recommendation:	The client needs to know that Emergency Hospital and Medical insurance covers unusual situations like this. Not only would your client be flown home, but arrangements would be made to ship your client's vehicle back as well.
Situation:	What if clients have an accident with a rental car?
Recommendation:	Clients need Physical Damage Protection insurance to make sure that even a minor fender-bender doesn't ruin their vacation.
Situation:	What if the clients' return home was delayed because they were unable to travel after being discharged from hospital?
Recommendation:	The clients need Trip Cancellation and Interruption insurance so that they will be reimbursed for the unexpected costs of hotels, taxis, and telephone calls.
Situation:	What if a client misses a connecting flight because of bad weather or an illness?
Recommendation:	The client needs Trip Cancellation and Interruption insurance so that the costs of catching up with the remainder of the trip are covered.

FIGURE 12.1
Recommended travel insurance for particular situations.

FIGURE 12.2
**Definitions clearly
explain the terms
used in an
insurance brochure.**
*Source: Voyageur
Insurance Company.*

The following definitions apply when written in *italics* throughout this document.

Accidental bodily injury - bodily injury caused by an accident of external origin occurring during the period of insurance and being the direct and independent cause of the loss.

Antique automobile - an automobile which is more than 20 years old.

Bedside companion - a person of *your* choice who is required at *your* bedside while *you* are hospitalized during *your* trip.

Business meeting - a meeting scheduled before *your effective date* between companies with unrelated ownership, pertaining to *your* full-time occupation or profession and which is the sole purpose of *your trip*.

Health expenses vary considerably from one country to another and sometimes from one province to another. Travel insurance is designed to take account of this fact. For example, daily hospital rates in the United States are considerably higher than in Canada. Furthermore, a tourist may not always be referred to a general hospital but rather to a private hospital or clinic where daily rates are higher still. In either case, clients can reduce the risk only by purchasing travel insurance.

It is important that travel counsellors have a basic knowledge of insurance products, terminology and coverage. All are clearly defined in the brochures and manuals supplied by insurance companies selling travel insurance. Counsellors must carefully study these materials to become familiar with the features of travel insurance products. Several examples are presented for reference throughout this chapter. As well as knowledge of insurance products, travel counsellors must also be able to explain the consequences associated with purchasing a travel product. Most travel suppliers demand a deposit to confirm a reservation and almost all impose a penalty if the booking is not honoured or is not cancelled with sufficient notice. Clients can avoid many of these charges if they purchase suitable travel insurance. It is a travel counsellor's responsibility to advise clients of such penalties and to ensure that passengers fully understand the conditions connected with the purchase.

What is Insurance?

Most of us recognize the importance of planning even the simple activities of daily life. A part of this planning is to make provisions for events that might interfere with our plans and that might require the redirection of financial resources. The events, called **risks**, involve the possibility of economic loss. A person can protect against such financial losses through the concept of insurance. Insurance is a plan of risk management that, for a price, offers an individual (the **insured**) an opportunity to share the costs of possible economic loss through an organization called an insurer.

Risks, or **hazards** as they are sometimes called in the insurance industry, include personal, property, and liability risks. These risks can be handled through proper planning, or risk management. Insurance is an important part of managing the three main categories that involve risk.

- Personal risks include the uncertainties surrounding loss of life, health or wealth due to untimely death, illness, disability, unemployment or old age.
- Property risks deal with direct or indirect losses to personal or real property due to fire, wind, accident, theft and other hazards.
- Liability risks involve losses due to negligence resulting in bodily harm or property damage to others. Such damage could be caused by an injury on one's own property, by an automobile, by professional misconduct, or by other factors.

These three types of risk are considered insurable because they are **pure risks**. Pure risks are accidental and unintentional. There is no possibility of financial gain, only of financial loss. In contrast, speculative risks such as purchasing shares offer the chance of loss or gain and are not subject to insurance coverage.

What is Travel Insurance?

Travel insurance is a risk management plan underwritten and packaged by an insurer that is sold either directly to travellers or indirectly through a distributor of travel insurance products (often a travel agency). It is sold as protection against the three types of risk that may occur prior to or during a trip.

Travel Insurance Terminology

The insurance industry commonly uses a number of terms to describe the features of its products. Counsellors should be able to correctly use this vocabulary and explain it to clients.

Clients who purchase travel insurance are issued with a **policy** which describes in writing the particulars of the protection provided. The amount of protection is referred to as the **coverage**. It describes the total range of risks covered by the travel insurance policy as purchased by the client. For example, a client may be covered for out-of-province emergency hospital, medical and physician costs in excess of those paid by provincial health plans. The cost of insurance coverage is determined by a number of factors including the amount of protection desired. The price charged for a given insurance policy is its **premium**. Travellers purchase insurance protection for a specific length of time, usually equal to the duration of their trip. The length of time covered by a policy is known as its **term**.

Travel insurance is sold under certain **conditions**, in much the same way as other travel products. The conditions are the rules which govern the protection offered. They modify the application of the coverage in the travel insurance policy. For example, any claim for lost property covered under the policy will be adjusted and paid when the property remains not found after a reasonable time.

All insurance policies include a series of **definitions** which precisely describe many of the terms used (Figure 12.2). Thus if an insurance policy states that coverage is extended to members of the immediate family, then the insurance brochure will define everyone who falls into this category. Although most of the definitions have generically the same meaning, their interpretation and explanation may vary slightly from one insurer to another. The insurer and the agency management have a combined responsibility to ensure that counsellors are properly trained to fully understand the meaning and interpretation of the terms used by the agency's insurance supplier. As of August 1998, the insurance industry in Canada had yet to implement a standard interpretation of the terminology and definitions used for travel insurance products. However, some work has begun in this direction.

Travel insurance is also sold with a variety of **limitations** and **exclusions**. The limitations specify the maximum sum, usually a fixed dollar amount, which the insurer will pay on a claim made under a covered risk of the travel insurance policy. For example, out-of-pocket expenses shall not exceed $100.00 per day. A policy may also have an "aggregate limit" that restricts the total amount to be paid on any given claim. Exclusions on the other hand list any articles or circumstances which are not covered under the policy (Figure 12.3). For example, items such as tools and equipment used to earn a living on the trip are excluded from coverage under a lost luggage policy. Similarly,

FIGURE 12.3
Exclusions depend on the type of travel insurance purchased and vary from one company to another.
Source: John Ingle Insurance

Limitations and Exclusions

No benefits are payable for expenses incurred as a result of:

1. any pre-existing medical condition which relates directly or indirectly to cardiovascular (heart & blood vessels) conditions; cerebrovascular (stroke or TIA) conditions; respiratory conditions; gastro-intestinal disorders and/or cancer;
   and
   any pre-existing medical condition that was causing symptoms, or was treated or investigated whether or not it was deteriorating, or for which medication was changed in type or dosage during
   (a) the 90-day period immediately preceding your departure date, if you are age 64 or under; or (b) the one (1) year period immediately preceding your departure date, if you are between age 65 and 79;
   or
   any pre-existing medical condition if you are age 80 or older;

   unless you have prior written approval from INGLE Health that will amend this exclusion.

   IMPORTANT: If you do not qualify for medical benefits, you may apply for coverage under our medically underwritten policy by completing a Medical Questionnaire and submitting the information to INGLE Health for consideration.

2. any loss, sickness or injury occurring while the policy is not in effect;

3. hospital or medical treatment where the policy is specifically purchased to obtain such services, whether or not authorized by a physician;

4. any investigation or treatment recommended or scheduled prior to departure;

FIGURE 12.4
Extract from a rate guide that shows the premium can vary with age and length of coverage.
Source: Voyageur Insurance Company.

DAYS	AGE 0-24	AGE 25-59	DAYS	AGE 0-24	AGE 25-59
1	18	26	24	23	37
2	18	26	25	24	39
3	18	26	26	25	40
4	18	26	27	25	41
5	18	26	28	26	42
6	18	26	29	26	44
7	18	26	30	27	45
8	18	26	31	28	47
9	18	26	32	29	48

losses caused by circumstances such as war and pregnancy are not covered. In addition, the effects of any pre-existing conditions are generally not covered. Thus insurance companies are unlikely to compensate a person with a history of a heart disease who suffers a heart attack on a trip. Some companies charge an extra premium if the client is over 65 years of age since health problems are likely to increase with age.

Clients who experience an incident which is covered by their travel insurance must make a **claim** on their policy. The insurance company will then pay the clients or their dependents the appropriate amounts outlined in the policy. These are known as **benefits**. Benefits refers to help or compensation to which the insured is entitled under the risks covered by the travel insurance policy, for example, out-pocket-expenses incurred and redeemable under a covered risk. Certain policies apply a **deductible** to the payment of any benefits. This means that the insurance company will reduce the specified benefit sum by an exact, predetermined amount, for example, fifty dollars.

All policies also describe the **terms of the agreement** and **statutory conditions**. Terms of the agreement refers to the insuring agreement portion of the policy that binds both the insurer and the insured, once payment has been made and a policy issued. For example, all benefits will be paid in Canadian currency. Statutory conditions are the conditions established by statute and legally required by both parties to implement the insuring agreement. For example, the company shall be deemed not to have waived any condition of this contract, either in whole or in part, unless the waiver is clearly expressed in writing and signed by the company.

Today, most insurance companies offer **assistance**. This refers to help and assistance services via a 24-hour, seven days a week, worldwide telephone call centre at the disposal of the insured. The assistance is most commonly used in cases of emergency medical requirements and hospitalization. For example, the insurance company might arrange multilingual services for a client receiving medical treatment in a foreign country.

The Travel Insurance Business Transaction

As in the production of all goods and services, insurers offer their product (an insurance policy) to a buyer (the insured or policyholder) for a price (the premium). This price includes many factors such as an assessment of initial and continuing expenses (both actual and potential), the creation of a fund from which to pay claims, and a contribution to the insurer's investment income. The insurance company uses this investment income to support its overall operation and development, thus reducing the amount a policyholder pays. The process by which the premium is determined is called **rating** or **rate setting**. Premiums are printed in a rate guide which insurers supply to travel agencies (Figure 12.4).

The Travel Insurance Policy: A Legal Contract

At times people who sign an insurance contract have only a vague idea of what they are signing or purchasing. However, there is nothing "tricky" or mysterious about this. An insurance contract is simply a legal contract that binds both the insurance company and the policyholder to certain agreements. Although an insurance contract and an insurance policy can be thought of as equivalent, for this discussion let's make a distinction between them. We will consider that a:

- Policy is the written evidence of specific insurance protection.

- Contract is the legal description of the type and scope of insurance protection provided. A contract also identifies the rights and responsibilities of insurer and insured toward that protection.

Specific benefits or coverage are detailed in the insurance agreement. That is where purchasers will find a description of the protection they receive for the fee they have paid.

Components of a Legal Contract

A contract is simply a binding agreement between two or more parties. In common with all contracts, an insurance policy must have four basic components to be considered legally valid.

- A contract must be made by mutual consent. One party makes an offer; the other party accepts the offer. In legal terms this is called a "meeting of the minds".
- A contract must contain a "consideration". Consideration is what is exchanged (money or the premium in this case) for what is given (insurance coverage from loss). For the person insured, loss means the reduction in quality, quantity or value of property, finances or health. For the insurer, loss is defined as the amount of insurance or benefits for which the insurer is liable under the terms of the policy. When a policy is issued, the insurer assumes the risk in return for the payment of a premium by the insured.
- The parties making the contract must have the legal capacity to do so. Common law determines this capacity. For example, minors, intoxicated or insane people cannot enter into a contract.
- A contract must have a legal purpose.

Components of a Travel Insurance Policy

A legally valid contract exists when the above four conditions are met. As we have seen, an insurance policy is a legal contract that describes the specific insurance protection provided by the insurer. Just as an airline ticket is a contract between the carrier and the passenger, a travel insurance policy is a contract between the insurer and the policyholder. A travel insurance policy has several important components. All form part of the contract. These components can be divided into the following categories.

- Coverage and Benefits
- Definitions, Exclusions, Conditions and Limitations
- Worldwide Assistance Services
- Terms of the Agreement
- Statutory Conditions

Although these terms have already been discussed, it is important that counsellors become familiar with all aspects of the components that apply to the travel insurance products they sell. Clients depend on a counsellor's expertise and guidance to purchase the best (i.e., most appropriate) travel insurance coverage for their trip or holiday. If counsellors do not understand any part of these products, it is their responsibility to contact the insurance supplier for clarification. Both counsellor and insurance company must ensure that there is no misunderstanding in the sale of this product.

Travel Insurance Products and Services

Travel insurance was developed to provide protection when needed by travellers. It can be purchased to guard against almost any eventuality. Travel insurance products offer a number of different services. These services are listed below.

- Trip Cancellation and Interruption
- Baggage and Personal Effects
- Accidental Death and Dismemberment (AD&D)
- Emergency Hospital and Medical Expense
- Physical Damage Protection otherwise known as Collision Damage Waiver (CDW)
- Default Protection
- Assistance Services

FIGURE 12.5
Typical format for trip cancellation and interruption insurance premiums table.
Source: Voyager Insurance Company.

- Premiums are taxable at 8% when sold in Ontario and are non-refundable.
- This insurance can be sold to cover all travel arrangements, including air fare, hotel, car rental, etc. It may only be purchased at the time of initial deposit.
- Remember to cover the extra cost of a one-way economy air fare home and the unused prepaid travel arrangements, where applicable.

SUM INSURED BEFORE DEPARTURE	SUM INSURED AFTER DEPARTURE		
Up to	Up to $800	Up to $1500	Unlimited
100	16	19	22
200	19	22	28
300	22	26	33
400	25	31	38
500	28	36	44
600	30	42	49

Most insurers offer parts or all of the above services. With the exception of Default Insurance, each can be sold as a policy on a stand-alone basis. For example, for a fixed premium a client can purchase an Emergency Hospital and Medical policy only. Alternatively, the services can be combined to create a policy with more complete coverage. For example, a client might purchase an "all inclusive" policy consisting of Emergency Hospital and Medical, Trip Cancellation, AD&D, Assistance, Default and Baggage protection. Such products give clients coverage at a lower price than by purchasing the services individually. This text refers to these all-inclusive products as "Combination Insurance", however, insurers package their services in different ways and sell them under several different brand names and coverage.

An insurer's portfolio contains a variety of travel insurance products that are generally marketed under the headings listed below. Again, however, the product names vary from one insurer to another.

- Trip Cancellation and Interruption Insurance
- Baggage and Personal Effects Insurance
- AD&D Insurance
- Emergency Hospital and Medical Insurance
- CDW or Collision Damage Waiver Protection
- Combination Insurance
- Visitors to Canada Insurance
- Annual Plans

These products are subject to applicable exclusions, limitations, terms of the agreement and statutory conditions. All are clearly outlined in the policy of each insurer. Counsellors should acquaint themselves with all parts of the travel insurance product they provide their clients. This may seem complicated but insurance companies provide agencies with complete training programs designed to make counsellors familiar with their travel insurance portfolio.

Since travel insurance is complicated and varies from one insurer to another, it is wise to specialize in one product. This should be all encompassing to the agency and capable of meeting the needs of the great majority of its clientele. The most popular product sold by travel agents is the "all inclusive" version (here called Combination Insurance). The most popular individual policies are Trip Cancellation and Interruption, Emergency Hospital and Medical, and Baggage and Personal Effects.

The following discussion describes the features of these products and how to sell them.

Trip Cancellation and Interruption Insurance

This is an extremely important form of insurance protection which reimburses travellers for any financial loss caused by cancellation either prior to or after departure. This travel insurance therefore offers a solution which guards against unforeseen circumstances and allows travellers to book their trips without worry. A travel counsellor's prime responsibility is to ensure that clients are fully conversant with the nonrefundable penalties or additional costs applicable to the forms of travel contracted. Generally, when making a booking for an airline ticket, a tour package, a cruise or any similar type of travel product, cancellation penalties are applicable. If clients have to cancel, they could suffer financial loss. In this case trip cancellation and interruption insurance would cover the clients up to the dollar amount of coverage purchased for the risks outlined in the policy. Counsellors must inform their clients the moment they are at risk and advise them that travel insurance protection is available for certain risks.

Most charter flights, tour packages, cruises and land arrangements require a deposit of either 10 percent of the cost or a flat rate charge. The balance is generally due 42 days before departure. Special attention should be given to the cancellation conditions contained in all types of travel sold. For example, if a client should have to return earlier than planned, possible expenses include the cost of a full fare one-way air ticket home and the loss of any prepaid hotel reservation charges.

First class, business class and economy class air fares on regular scheduled service are valid for one year from the date of issue. These fares are offered at a premium price. However, passengers who cancel their flights can receive a total refund for any unused portion of the fare regardless of their reasons for not travelling. All other types of air fares are offered at a discount from these regular prices and are sold with a number of conditions and restrictions. A common condition is that a certain portion of the fare is nonrefundable if the passenger fails to travel as ticketed. (Some fares do, however, permit passengers to change flight arrangements for a fee.) Practically all tour packages also assess penalties prior to or after departure. The cancellation fees on such programs are often based on an increasing scale of penalties as the departure date approaches. Often, if a trip is cancelled within seven days of departure, the client will usually lose the total cost of the holiday. Most forms of transportation, cruises and land arrangements assess a similar form of cancellation penalty. As a result, there is a definite need for the protection afforded by trip cancellation and interruption insurance for all travel and no client should travel without it.

The insurance covers two possibilities; trip cancellation and trip interruption. Trip cancellation insurance covers the money a client has deposited or paid for a trip or holiday against the risks outlined in the policy. Trip cancellation refers to a covered event occurring prior to the commencement of the trip or holiday, which prevents clients from departing and thus exposes them to unforeseen financial losses. Trip interruption refers to an event occurring after the commencement of the trip or holiday that prevents a client from completing it, exposing the client to financial losses. Clients must be covered for both possibilities. The risks covered are outlined in the policy. Not all reasons for cancellation and/or interruption are covered. Coverage, benefits, terms, conditions, exclusions and limitations are clearly defined in the policy.

To sell this product, a counsellor must establish the dollar amount that the client could lose in case of a cancellation or interruption. Always choose the premium that ensures clients are adequately protected against both eventualities. To calculate this amount, first identify the applicable penalty prior to departure and the cost that the client is subject to in case of interruption (usually the price of a one-way airfare home). For example, the total cost of a tour could be $800.00 and be totally non-refundable if cancelled at the last minute. If the airfare to return from the destination is $1500.00, then the counsellor must ascertain that the insurance will cover this cost. Coverage varies among insurers. Once the potential financial loss has been established, the counsellor consults the insurer's rate guide (Figure 12.5) to determine the premium. The first column lists the sum to be insured before departure. Locate the figure that matches the maximum cancellation penalty. Beside this column are several others that show amounts insured after departure. Choose the column that will cover the client's return airfare. The box where the two figures intersect will show the correct premium to be charged. This product is usually rated on the cost of the trip prior to and after departure. If an agency has an automated travel insurance software package, then its CRS system will auto-price the policy. Clients who wish coverage for more than one type of policy pay the total of all the premiums calculated.

Trip cancellation and interruption insurance compensates passengers for financial loss on the nonrefundable portions of travel as a result of sickness, bodily injury, accident, jury duty or loss of life (Figure 12.6). People who simply change their minds and decide not to

What risks are insured?

Medical condition

1   *Your emergency medical condition.*

2   The admission to a *hospital* following an *emergency* of a member of *your immediate family* who is not at *your* destination, *your* business partner, *key employee* or *caregiver.*

3   The *emergency medical condition* of a member of *your immediate family* who is not at *your* destination, *your* business partner, *key employee* or *caregiver.*

4   The admission to a *hospital* of *your* host at destination, following an *emergency medical condition.*

5   The *emergency medical condition* of *your travelling companion.*

6   The *emergency medical condition* of *your travelling companion's immediate family* member, business partner, *key employee* or *caregiver.*

7   The *emergency medical condition* of *your immediate family* member who is at *your* destination.

Pregnancy & Adoption

8   Complications of *your* or *your* spouse's pregnancy arising in the first 31 weeks of pregnancy.

9   Complications of *your travelling companion's* or *your travelling companion's* spouse's pregnancy arising in the first 31 weeks of pregnancy.

10 *Your* or *your* spouse's pregnancy being diagnosed after *your* travel arrangements are booked, if *your* departure from *your departure point* is scheduled to take place in the 9 weeks before or after the expected date of delivery.

FIGURE 12.6
Accepted reasons for cancellation are identified in each company's brochure.
Source: Voyageur Insurance Company.

travel are not protected. The insurance protection also applies to circumstances occurring to near relatives (whether or not they are travelling with the insured) or a travelling companion. Similarly, many insurance companies will pay the upgrade fee or single supplement if a client's travelling companion cancels for acceptable reasons. Additional causes for claim are outlined in the insurance brochures. The premium rates vary depending on the type of travel. Coverage, benefits, conditions and exclusions are clearly defined in the brochures. These should be explained to clients at the time insurance is offered to avoid any misunderstanding if a claim is made. Many tour companies offer their own protection to cover cancellation penalties (Figure 12.7). Counsellors must determine which insurance policy offers the best protection for their clients and advise them accordingly.

Trip cancellation and interruption insurance must be purchased when the initial deposit is paid. The reason is clear.

If a client wishes to obtain protection for the deposit or any other amount paid prior to departure, it is obvious that the coverage must be purchased when the initial payment is made. Most other insurances may be purchased at any time prior to departure. Generally insurers allow up to two business days after initial deposit to issue the policy. Counsellors require authority from the insurer to issue policies beyond two days after initial deposit. Since this coverage takes effect the moment the policy is written, normally refunds are not allowed.

Baggage and Personal Effects Insurance

Baggage and Personal Effects refers to the baggage and personal effects owned and taken by a client on the trip or holiday. This coverage applies to baggage and personal effects against delay, theft, burglary, loss, fire or transportation hazards during a client's trip or holiday (Figure 12.8). Most people have a homeowner's policy or a tenant's package policy which provides some protection for personal effects while away from their residence. Many travellers feel that these policies provide sufficient protection under the "off premises" clause in such contracts. This is only partially true as the protection is not an "all risks" coverage. Further, all homeowner's policies contain some form of deductible or limitation for loss in the event of a claim. The purchase of baggage insurance reimburses for all loss, damage or theft not normally covered under a homeowner's type of policy.

Premiums for this coverage depend on the duration of the trip and dollar value purchased. This product can be sold on a stand-alone basis, combined with another non-conflicting stand-alone coverage, or it can be part of an all included travel insurance package plan. In the case of a stand-alone sale, the sale can occur at the very last moment prior to departure. As a rule, most baggage and personal effects plans have very low maximum dollar amounts of coverage per individual or family. As with all other coverage, it is subject to limits, exclusions and conditions as outlined in the policy. Coverage is valid anywhere in the world once the trip has commenced. In most cases, this coverage must be purchased prior to departure and for the whole duration of the trip or holiday. Most insurers do not allow the sale of this product where there is only a one-way trip.

This insurance is for personal effects or possessions which would normally be taken on a trip or vacation. It does not cover items used by the insured person to earn income during the term of the trip (e.g., a musician's instruments or equipment used by a professional photographer). Some forms of all risk baggage and personal effects insurance insure cash but only to a limit of $100.00 and only for robbery or hold-up. Further, there is a dollar limit placed on articles covered under the insurance. These limitations restrict the amount which can be claimed on any one item and also place a ceiling on the total claim per individual or family insured. These limits can be raised by purchasing additional coverage. Most people have a tendency to under-insure as they do not realize the value of the goods accompanying them nor are they aware of the limits imposed by insurance companies. Counsellors must bring both points to their clients' attention to ensure that they purchase adequate protection.

Clients who lose articles on a trip must follow certain reporting procedures which are outlined in brochures and policies. For example, a client who loses baggage at an airport must complete the airline's lost baggage form at that time. Similarly, if items are stolen a police report is usually required. Clients who fail to take such actions may find that their claim is denied by the insurance company.

Accidental Death and Dismemberment

This refers to death or the loss of one or more limbs as a result of an injury sustained by the insured during the period of coverage. This coverage is often referred to as 24-hour accident insurance, flight accident insurance or common carrier accident insurance. Coverage provides protection on trips anywhere in the world. It is effective for the complete period insured, 24-hours a day, against all types of accidents on all forms of transportation whether on land, sea or in the air. This type of product is offered automatically as a feature of some credit cards and is also available from airport insurance kiosks.

The policy must normally be purchased prior to departure and for the whole duration of the trip. Such coverage must not to be mistaken for health insurance. It applies only if there is death or dismemberment. Accident insurance does not provide any form of protection for expenses incurred through sickness or disease. Coverage can be bought on a stand-alone basis, combined with another non-conflicting stand-alone product or as part of an all-included package. Rates for this product are normally calculated according to the dollar amount of coverage chosen (Figure 12.9). As with other coverage, it is subject to limits, exclusions and conditions as outlined in the policy

Emergency Hospital and Medical Insurance

This insurance covers eligible emergency expenses incurred in excess of those covered by a client's provincial government health insurance plan and which occur outside the province of residence. It is important to note that this insurance is not a substitute for the coverage and protection provided in one's home province. The coverage applies only in the event of an emergency and is subject to the terms, conditions, limitations and exclusions outlined in the policy. One of the most common exclusions is that concerning pre-existing conditions discussed below.

FIGURE 12.7
Most tour companies offer their clients some form of cancellation protection.
Source: Horizon Holidays.

Cancellation charges:
Within 2 months of departure, 10% of cost. Within 1 month of departure, 25% of cost. After departure, 50% of remaining cost.

How to avoid cancellation charges:
By paying a non-refundable waiver fee with your deposit you are completely protected from cancellation charges on all travel arrangements provided by Horizon. Fee is per person:

$26 for travel under $1,500	$38 for travel under $5,000
$30 for travel under $2,500	$42 for travel over $5,000
$34 for travel under $3,500	

If you have to cancel, for any reason, your money is protected as follows:
Before departure: Full refund.
After departure: Refund of unused transportation, accommodation, meals, sightseeing, tipping and escort's services.
Emergency return: Included if air tickets originally issued by Horizon. Upgrade limited to one-way economy fare.

What risks are insured?

Direct physical loss of, or damage to, the baggage and personal effects *you* own and use during *your trip*.

What are the benefits?

1   Reimbursement of *your* losses up to the sum insured shown in the *insurance application/declarations*, subject to a maximum of $300 for any one item or set of items.

2   Reimbursement of up to $50 towards the replacement of one or more of the following documents: passport, driver's license, birth certificate or travel visa, in the event any one of these is lost or stolen.

3   Reimbursement as outlined under a) and b) below for necessary toiletries and clothing when *your* checked baggage is delayed by the carrier for 12 hours or more while on route and before returning to *your departure point* and *you* are covered under a Package Tour:
    a) $400 under Deluxe or Non-Medical Package Tour, and
    b) $200 under Standard or TravelCare® Package Tour.

What is not covered?

This insurance does not cover:

1   animals, perishables, bicycles except while checked as baggage with a common carrier, household effects and furnishings, artificial teeth and limbs, hearing aids, eye glasses, sunglasses, contact lenses, money, tickets, securities and documents, professional or occupational items, antiques and collector items, breakage of brittle or fragile articles, property illegally acquired, kept, stored or transported.

2   any claim arising from loss:
    a)   caused by wear and tear, deterioration, defect or mechanical breakdown;
    b)   caused by *your* imprudent act or omission;
    c)   of articles specifically insured on a valued basis by another insurer while this insurance is in effect;
    d)   directly in consequence of war (declared or not), act of foreign enemies or rebellion.

What conditions apply?

1   For Package Tour coverages, the principal sums are shown in the corresponding insurance chart contained in this booklet.

FIGURE 12.8
An example of the coverage, exclusions and conditions for baggage and personal effects insurance.
Source: Voyager Insurance Company.

Questionnaires

Many insurers have introduced a medical questionnaire (Figure 12.10). Depending on the insurer, this questionnaire acts as a rate qualifier, as a waiver for certain conditions or exclusions, or it can be used to establish deductible amounts. When completing a questionnaire a client must make **full and complete disclosure**. Providing false information in order to obtain a lower rate can invalidate the policy, leaving the client uninsured.

Top-up Insurance

Selling top-ups is part of today's travel insurance business. It is emergency medical coverage in addition to an existing out-of-country Emergency Hospital and Medical plan. There is sometimes a danger that a top-up plan could create a gap in a client's protection where coverage is not the same. Counsellors should not be tempted to combine two different plans just to make a sale. It is sound business practice and probably less expensive to sell a client one plan that covers everything. This will eliminate any grey area and be much simpler should a claim arise.

Add-ons or Extensions

Sometimes clients request an add-on or an extension to their policy. Generally, this will occur after the client has departed on the trip or holiday. Add-ons and/or extensions must be sold before the expiry date of the policy. Insurers usually approve these requests if there is no claim in progress and if the client's medical condition has not deteriorated. The insurer provides procedures for add-ons and/or extensions.

Deductibles

Some insurers have introduced deductibles to their medical policies that come into effect only if there is a claim. Deductible amounts vary and may be mandatory or optional. Clients must be advised at the time of purchase if the medical plan contains a deductible. Deductibles are described in dollar amounts or as percentages of the claim.

Pre-existing Conditions

Insurers normally address pre-existing conditions in the exclusions and/or conditions section of the policy. The term refers to an existing medical condition diagnosed by a physician from which the insured has either suffered or is suffering at the time of booking. During the period of coverage, this pre-existing condition is such that it could prevent a client from travelling and thus be the cause for cancellation and/or trip interruption. If this occurs the insured could be subject to financial losses because the pre-existing condition may not be covered (or only partially so) under the policy. A pre-existing condition may also require a client to seek or need medical treatment while on a trip. The same rule applies to the costs incurred for such medical treatment. In this case, the insured is responsible for part or all of the incurred expenses because of the pre-existing condition.

Depending on the status and severity of the pre-existing condition, insurers may cover it entirely, in part, or exclude it altogether. The degree of coverage depends on when the pre-existing condition occurred, or when it was treated during a fixed period of time prior to departure or the effective date of the policy. This exclusion however does not bar a client from the remainder of the coverage. The application of this clause differs among insurers. Counsellors must become familiar with the specifics of the pre-existing clause as defined by the insurance policy they are selling. As this has become an area where people can suffer catastrophic losses of some or all of their accumulated wealth, counsellors are obligated to clearly point out this section to their clients at the time of sale. Clients must read and fully understand this exclusion.

Some clients may not wish to discuss their medical situation with a counsellor. In such cases it is best to refrain from commenting on whether or not a pre-existing condition is covered. A counsellor's responsibility is to outline the risks, explain the policy and ensure that the client has proper protection or signs a waiver. If counsellors are in doubt regarding the topic of pre-existing conditions, they should refer clients to their family doctor and/or the insurer. If necessary, the doctor or insured can request clarification in writing from the insurer.

Variety of Emergency Hospital and Medical Plans

Because of the scope and risks associated with this coverage, many insurers offer a variety of plans from which consumers can choose. Short-stay medical plans are usually quite similar. Differences in plans more often occur when the plan caters to the long-stay or "snowbird" market. These plans are often divided into three categories identified as basic, standard and superior. Each category differs in price and usually establishes the difference between very low risks and very high risks. Insurers use a variety of qualifying features to distinguish

What risks are insured?
Your accidental bodily injuries, resulting in *your dismemberment, loss of sight* or death within 12 calendar months from the date of the accident.

What are the benefits?
The greatest of these benefits for all losses resulting from an accident:
1   100% of the principal sum for death, double *dismemberment* or *loss of sight* of both eyes, or
2   50 % of the principal sum for single *dismemberment* or *loss of sight* of one eye.

PRINCIPAL SUM	PREMIUM
$200,000	$8

FIGURE 12.9
An example of premiums and benefits for flight accident insurance.
Source: Voyageur Insurance Company.

the potential insured person's state of health. These include using questionnaires, requesting a letter from a doctor, and in certain cases obliging the client to visit a doctor prior to the sale of a policy.

Selling Emergency Hospital and Medical insurance coverage entails various elements that a counsellor must understand. This product is for Canadians holding a valid provincial health card, and is usually sold prior to departure. It is normally fully refundable if the trip does not occur. In some cases, insurers may refund unused portions of the policy. (This usually means an early return, and proof is required.) In both cases the insurer may levy an administrative fee. The exact amount of this administration fee is normally outlined in the policy or marketing piece provided by the insurer.

MEDICAL QUESTIONNAIRE
TO BE COMPLETED IN FULL AND SIGNED ONLY BY APPLICANT

B

In the **past 12 months**, have you had: YES   NO

3   a heart condition, for which you have taken or been prescribed medication (other than aspirin or cholesterol-reducing medication)?

4   a lung condition, for which you were hospitalized, took prednisone or other oral steroids or more than one puffer type, received home oxygen treatment, or needed a medication/treatment change (in type or dosage)*?

5   a stroke, mini-stroke or peripheral vascular disease?

6   both diabetes and high blood pressure?

* Please see reverse for definition of medication/treatment change (in type or dosage).

FIGURE 12.10
Portion of a medical questionnaire used to determine pre-existing conditions.
Source: Voyageur Insurance Company.

The premium for this product is usually based on age and the number of travel days. Some companies will not insure those over the age of 75 years (Figure 12.11). Duration can be up to 183 days. Extensions beyond 183 days usually require approval from the insurer.

Physical Damage Protection

This coverage, commonly called Collision Damage Waiver (CDW), refers to rental vehicles as rented by the policyholder. As a rule, persons other than the policyholder who are approved to drive the vehicle are, according to the rental contract, also covered by this policy. Generally, coverage compensates the policyholder against financial loss caused by physical damage or loss of the rented vehicle. This coverage also has dollar limit waivers and/or exclusions each of which are outlined in the policy.

Coverage applies to damage or loss to rented vehicles and can be purchased at any time prior to collecting the vehicle. The premium is based on the number of days that the vehicle is rented. Premiums are around $9.00 per day regardless of the number of persons that are contracted to drive. As premiums are calculated in Canadian dollars, they are usually much lower than those currently available at the destination. This protection can be sold on a stand-alone basis or combined with any other insurance coverage. As with all other coverage, it is subject to limits, exclusions and conditions as outlined in the policy.

Combination Insurance

At one time, clients who wanted insurance protection against the hazards discussed above had to purchase individual coverage for each area. The result was a rather large premium which led to buyer reluctance and inadequate insurance coverage. Insurance companies therefore began to offer a combination insurance package to overcome potential losses to both clients and insurance companies. Combination insurance provides a measure of protection against several possibilities for the payment of a single, lower premium. In this way a client can obtain more protection at a premium which is lower than for the various insurances purchased separately. A variety of plans are available so that clients may choose a blend of coverage that best suits their needs. Clients may also upgrade the coverage in any one or more of the categories by paying an additional premium. The premium charged is based on the duration of the coverage and the amount insured (Figure 12.12). Combination insurance has become extremely popular with travellers. It was originally designed for the "average" tourist but this type of combination insurance is now just as appropriate for FIT travellers. This type of insurance must be purchased prior to departure.

Tour operators noted the popularity of combination insurance and began to offer insurance protection that competed with the coverage available through combination insurance from the insurance companies (Figure 12.13). Travel insurance companies responded by improving the coverage and benefits in their package tour or comprehensive insurance. Package tour insurance generally offers coverage for emergency family transportation and so can be used for any type of travel including air only. Since the policy includes trip cancellation coverage, comprehensive insurance must be purchased at the time the initial deposit is paid. Package tour insurance provides the best value-for-dollar coverage a travel counsellor can offer.

FIGURE 12.11
Premiums for hospital and medical expense coverage depend on age and the trip duration.
Source: Reliable Life Insurance.

Benefits	Sum Insured
Medical & Other Expenses	$1,000,000
Repatriation Due To Death	$10,000
Cremation or Burial Costs	$3,000
Accommodation & Meals Expense	$3,000

NO. OF DAYS	AGES 0-54	AGES 55-69	AGES 70-75
4	14	20	30
8	20	36	52
15	36	52	94

Visitors to Canada Insurance

Usually, this coverage can be sold to anyone visiting Canada, Canadians normally not eligible for benefits under a government health insurance plan, persons on work or student visas, and immigrants to Canada.

Many travel agencies derive significant income by arranging prepaid travel for their clients' friends and relatives visiting Canada from overseas. Just as Canadians are not necessarily covered for medical expenses incurred outside Canada, foreign visitors to this country are not eligible for benefits from provincial health insurance plans. Clients should therefore be advised of the possible costs facing relatives or friends who meet with an accident or illness during their visit to Canada. Such visitors can obtain insurance coverage for hospital and medical costs at a reasonable fee. Insurers generally permit purchase of this plan at any time and it can be purchased for any duration up to 365 days. Unlike medical plans for Canadians holding a valid provincial health insurance card, this coverage is not excess coverage. Rather, it is usually primary; the insurer pays from the first dollar. However, it covers medical emergencies only. Rates for this product are normally based on the age of the insured and the duration to be covered (Figure 12.14). As with all other coverage, it is subject to limits, exclusions and conditions as outlined in the policy. It may be subject to a deductible before any benefits are paid.

Age of the Individual	Trip Length (Days)					Minimum Premium Per Policy
	1-15	1-30	1-90	1-183	183+	
Under 35	$1.75	$2.05	$2.35	$2.95	$3.65	$25.00
35-54	$1.95	$2.25	$2.50	$3.10	$3.85	$25.00
55-59	$2.50	$2.85	$3.55	$4.35	$5.40	$25.00
60-64	$3.80	$4.20	$5.25	$6.65	$8.10	$25.00
65-69	$4.80	$5.25	$6.90	$8.60	$10.75	$30.00
70-74	$7.60	$8.55	$9.55	$12.40	$14.85	$32.00
75-79	$8.85	$10.45	$11.85	$14.65	$22.10	$35.00
80 or Over	$11.90	$14.90	$15.10	$19.70	$23.90	$50.00

* Family rates are twice the single premium (based on the age of the eldest traveller).
* Premium rates are subject to change without notice.

Trip Length (Days)	Ontario Residents Add Sales Tax	Quebec Residents Add Sales Tax	DEDUCTIBLE OPTIONS PER PERSON
1-30	$0.24 per policy	$0.27 per policy	$ 500 Deductible Per Person - 5% off Total Premium
31-90	$0.72 per policy	$0.81 per policy	$ 1000 Deductible Per Person -
Over 90	$1.20 per policy	$1.35 per policy	10% off Total Premium (before Provincial Sales Tax)

- **Additional Trip Cancellation $5 per $100**, under age 70 (maximum $5,000)
- **Additional Trip Cancellation $8 per $100**, 70 or over (maximum $5,000)
- **Additional Baggage $0.30 per day per $100** of coverage (maximum $2,000)

Ontario Residents add 8% Sales Tax/Quebec Residents add 9% Sales Tax

FIGURE 12.12 Combination insurance packages often let clients select a blend of coverage to meet personal needs.
Source: John Ingle Insurance.

Annual Travel Insurance Plans

This product has gained in popularity since the early 1990s. Annual plans provide coverage for a fixed or unlimited number of trips (normally of short duration) during a period of 365 days. Some insurers offer top-up coverage to their own annual plans. This type of top-up does not create a problem for a client since it is the same basic product from the same company. These annual plans are particularly attractive to business people who travel often as part of their job. Some insurers automatically renew this plan and the agency receives a commission upon renewal. If an automatic renewal agreement does not form part of the initial policy, then the client needs to approve or request each renewal. The rate for this product is normally based on the type of plan selected and the age of the client (Figure 12.15). Some insurers will permit a client to choose either the date of purchase or the date of first usage as the start or effective date. In the case of first usage, the start date cannot be later than six months after the purchase date. As with all other coverage, it is subject to limits, exclusions and conditions as outlined in the policy.

Group Insurance Travel Plans

Agencies can obtain a special group policy to provide coverage for group tours that they organize. This form of insurance can be adapted to a specific benefit or for a combination of benefits. Group coverage simplifies administration by permitting agencies to issue a single group policy rather than having to write individual policies for each group member. As with annual policies, travel insurance companies can provide full details.

FIGURE 12.13
Most tour operators offer comprehensive insurance coverage.
Source: Sunquest Vacations.

All-Inclusive Coverage

- **Emergency Assistance Worldwide**
- **Trip Cancellation Insurance**
- **Emergency Travel Health Insurance**

Please ask your Travel Agent to explain all the terms, conditions, limitations and exclusions contained in your Certificate of Insurance.

Your insurance benefits include:

Trip Cancellation Insurance	
Hospital/Medical/Return Home/	
Air Ambulance	$2,000,000*
Trip Interruption and Delay	Unlimited
Meals and Accommodations	$800
Repatriation	$3,000
Flight Accident Insurance	$50,000
Common Carrier Accident	$20,000
Accidental Death & Dismemberment	$10,000
Dental Accident	$1,000
Family Transportation	$1,000
Return of Vehicle	$1,000
Baggage and Personal Effects	$800
Money Loss	$100

* For US residents and travellers not covered under a Canadian Government Health Insurance Plan, coverage is limited to in-hospital expenses up to $10,000

Other Products and Services

Insurers offer a number of other products and services.

Default of a Supplier

This coverage applies to a client's financial loss when a travel service supplier is unable to provide the services purchased by the client and/or return the monies that have been deposited or paid for such services because of insolvency or bankruptcy. Default coverage cannot normally be purchased on a stand-alone basis. It applies only when a client has purchased and paid for a travel insurance product that has Trip Cancellation and Interruption coverage. Insurers that offer this coverage usually include it as part of a plan or plans that include such coverage.

Summer Plans

These are a recent introduction to the marketplace and can be ideal for family summer drive holidays. The plan must be purchased prior to departure and usually permits multiple trips up to a fixed number of days during the period of coverage. Some insurers allow top-up to this plan as long as it is within the same portfolio of coverage. The rate is usually based on age only and is available for a fixed number of days. The plans are sometimes restricted to a number of days and a particular geographic area.

Assistance Services

Most insurers now include assistance services as part of their policies. These services are applicable mainly to the purchase of Emergency Hospital and Medical coverage. Assistance services can vary from one insurer to another. Generally these services include assistance with claims handling, multilingual services, direct payment to hospitals, contact of family, contact of family physician, repatriation, transfer arrangements for return transportation of children and/or family, help in finding an appropriate physician and/or medical facility, and pre-payment and arrangement of air ambulance. Most insurers provide this assistance service 24-hours a day, seven days a week through a call collect or 1-800 line.

It is of the utmost importance that clients be made aware of the contact number for assistance service. They should be instructed to call immediately in case of a medical emergency, prior to seeking medical treatment. Some insurers will reduce payment of a claim by as much as 30 percent if the client has not called the assistance number prior to seeking medical treatment or being hospitalized. It is essential that, at the moment of purchase, this condition be made clear to clients who choose plans containing emergency hospital and medical coverage.

As with all insurance coverage, the above plans are subject to exclusions, conditions, terms and limitations. Counsellors must become familiar with all the features of the insurance products they sell. If something is not clear, they should consult their supporting insurer.

Selling Travel Insurance

The provinces of British Columbia, Ontario and Quebec require the owner to hold a permit from the travel Registrar to operate a travel agency. In Ontario and Quebec this permit enables an agency to sell travel services, including travel insurance. In ~~Alberta and~~ British Columbia, an insurance license is required in addition to the travel agent's permit. The Provincial Superintendent of Insurance is responsible for issuing such insurance permits. In both Alberta and British Columbia an agent must be sponsored by an insurer in order to obtain an insurance permit. In British Columbia a counsellor must also pass a written exam. In this case, the agency's travel insurance supplier will work with counsellors to prepare for the exam.

Travel Insurance in the Sales Process

The subject of travel insurance must be included with every step of the travel sale process. Clients are at risk the moment they make a deposit or pre-pay a trip or holiday where financial penalties apply. Similarly, the moment clients leave their province of residence they are at risk. For these reasons, it is not advisable for counsellors to wait until the last minute to bring up the subject of travel insurance. Because of the risks involved, the topic must be brought to the attention of clients at the very moment a counsellor knows that they face a risk. It should be introduced naturally as part of the conversation during the sales process whenever cancellation or change penalties are mentioned, or when travel arrangements are being discussed. This can be done in a positive and reassuring manner by reminding clients throughout the sales process of the protection that is available with insurance. This approach permits clients to plan their trip or holiday with peace of mind. In addition, by making the subject of travel insurance part of a complete travel planning process, the task of completing the insurance sale becomes much easier for a counsellor, especially when it has been explained and stressed throughout the process.

Too often, counsellors end a sales presentation (or even the successful sale of a travel product) by asking clients if they want travel insurance. In the eyes of the clients, this only diminishes the importance and need for travel insurance. As a result, clients are often tempted to decline coverage.

Counsellors attempting to sell travel insurance will sometimes encounter objections from clients. Figure 12.16 describes some of the most common statements made by consumers when declining travel insurance products. The suggested responses are a guide only. It is a counsellor's duty to emphasize the importance of proper travel insurance coverage to protect a client against risks involved with travel.

The proper sale of a travel insurance policy will help prevent unpleasant situations for an insured client, the counsellor and the agency. In addition, it builds confidence in the client/counsellor relationship, resulting in loyal repeat business.

Policy Issuance

Most insurers have made it relatively simple to issue a travel insurance policy. Travel insurance can be sold through computer reservation systems, accounting software packages, manually and in some cases by calling a 1-800 line. Insurers require some basic information to validate a policy document. The information required is the policyholder's name and date of birth, the date of issue, the date of departure, the number of travel days, the return date, the destination, the plan purchased, the number of people insured and the applicable premium and tax. The counsellor and agency must also be identified on the document.

FIGURE 12.14
Visitors to Canada insurance coverage has various restrictions.
Source: John Ingle Insurance.

You are eligible for coverage if you are:
i)   a visitor to Canada, and
ii) not eligible or covered under a Canadian Government Health Insurance Plan, and
iii) under age 75.

Temporary visits to the United States are covered provided:
a)   the trip is 30 days or less, and
b)   the trip originates and terminates in Canada, and
c)   you are not a resident of North America.

DAILY PREMIUM RATES		
Maximum Sum Insured	under age 65	65-75
$ 5,000	$1.20	$1.85
$15,000	$1.80	$3.25
$25,000	$2.40	$3.60
$50,000	$2.80	$4.00
Optional AD & D	$ .30	N/A

- Minimum premium $20.00

FIGURE 12.15
Rates for annual
insurance
coverage.
*Source: The
Prudential.*

FIGURE 12.15
Rates for annual
insurance
coverage.
*Source: The
Prudential.*

ANNUAL PLAN

AGE	PRICE
Under 45	$ 54.00
45-49	$ 64.00
50-54	$ 74.00
55-59	$ 84.00
60-64	$ 124.00
65-69	$ 150.00
70-74	$ 200.00

• **Family Rates are double the single rates**

  Single: Coverage insures one person only.

  Couple/Family: Coverage insures any two persons and their children under twenty-one years of age.

• **Not available to persons 75 or over.**

• **Rates are for one year of coverage, however, no individual trip may exceed 30 days.**

• **Dependent Children must be travelling with their parents to be eligible for coverage.**

RATES ARE SUBJECT TO CHANGE

Automation

Computer reservation systems and automated accounting systems have simplified the transaction process and provide agents with features such as auto-pricing similar to airline ticketing. In some cases, accounting is done automatically and all details relating to travel insurance are printed on the client's invoice. In Canada, Galileo, Sabre, Global Matrix, PC Voyage and Voyageur provide accessible software programs that feature travel insurance products.

Manual Sales

Although most travel agencies in Canada are automated, policies can also be issued manually. For this an agent needs a rate guide and in some cases a validation form (Figure 12.17) to attach to the policy. The insurer will provide the agency with the required documentation.

Normally, the validation document has an audit copy for the insurer, a copy for the agency and a copy for the client. In some cases, a fourth copy is provided for claims purposes.

Where an agency has an automated system, travel insurance should be issued using the system. With this method the insurer knows that a client is insured and can act instantly should the client leave and require emergency medical assistance on the same day. When a policy is issued manually, an insurer may not know of a client's coverage until the paperwork has been received. To compensate for this, some suppliers request faxed copies of a manual sale when the client is travelling on the same day.

Internet

Some insurers have web pages but at this time they are not interactive. These web pages generally act as marketing/advertising pieces. They may provide a 1-800 number to call for information or to purchase insurance by telephone.

Closing the Sale

When a client purchases travel services that include travel insurance and makes a deposit or pays money to an agency, the counsellor must collect the premium and issue a policy immediately. Protection then applies at once. Counsellors should also make sure that the client receives the policy the same day. As the client accepts the insurance policy, the counsellor should advise the client to:

• Read all parts of the policy.
• Ask questions if anything is unclear.
• Take the policy on the trip.
• Copy and keep the contact number (call collect or 1-800) in a wallet or purse. Some insurers provide a wallet-size card that contains the numbers and instructions. Counsellors should advise their clients to carry this card at all times during the trip or holiday.

Tax Information

Revenue departments in Newfoundland and Labrador, Quebec and Ontario have implemented provincial sales tax on some travel insurance products (trip cancellation, baggage, packaged and CDW). In Quebec, the agency is responsible for collection and payment to the provincial government. In Ontario, and Newfoundland and Labrador the insurer is responsible for collection and payment to the appropriate provincial revenue department. Currently, rates vary from five to 15 percent of the premium. In agencies that are automated, the auto-pricing function calculates the tax owing and adds it to the premium amount. In non-automated agencies, counsellors must perform this calculation manually. Note that tax is not collected on CDW if the insured takes possession of the vehicle outside of the province where insurance was purchased.

Waiver Forms

It is a counsellor's duty to ensure that clients are aware of the travel insurance protection available. Counsellors assume this responsibility to give clients an opportunity to insure against unforeseen events and to protect themselves and their agency against charges of negligence. Many clients take advantage of the protection afforded by travel insurance, especially when the cost of insurance is weighed against the potential losses if a trip is cancelled or otherwise interrupted. Sometimes, however, clients refuse to purchase travel insurance. Counsellors must ask clients who decline travel insurance to sign a waiver form (Figure 12.18). This form indicates that the client was offered insurance, that the offer was rejected and that the client will not hold the agency responsible for any expenses incurred as a result of this refusal. The request to sign a waiver form forces the client to reconsider the consequences of refusing insurance coverage and frequently acts as a sales incentive.

Waiver forms were introduced after some counsellors were sued for negligence for not informing clients (who subsequently became ill or were injured on holiday) that protection was available. As in many travel industry law cases, the burden of proof is usually placed on the professional, that is, on the counsellor. A statement by a counsellor that a client was offered insurance is likely to be

FIGURE 12.16
How to overcome some common client objections.

Objection:	I am covered by my group or credit card plan.
Answer:	You may be covered but is the coverage you have complete? Does it cover all of the penalties associated with your trip or holiday? Do you have a copy of this policy and when was the last time you read it? The product we offer is of recent design and provides the latest available coverage. For your own benefit please check this with your insurer.
Objection:	I'm covered under my provincial health plan.
Answer:	Are you aware that your provincial plan covers a very limited portion of health care costs outside of Canada? On average, provincial health plans pay only between 10 and 25 percent of the average hospital costs outside your province.
Objection:	I'm sure I'm going. I never get sick.
Answer:	Unfortunately your good health isn't the only factor to be considered when thinking about travel insurance. Did you know that at least 50 percent of hospitalizations while on vacation are due to accident? Additionally, travel insurance covers the loss of baggage, damage to your vehicle and trip cancellation.
Objection:	I've no intention of cancelling my trip.
Answer:	Trip Cancellation and Interruption insurance also protects the people you care about and rely on. So, if your travelling companion gets sick and has to return home, you're not penalized. As well, if a business associate or a family member is hospitalized back home, you can return immediately.
Objection:	I've been shopping around and your insurance seems expensive.
Answer:	Like any purchase, it's very important to make sure you're comparing apples with apples. Comparing prices is only comparing numbers. Please check that your insurance provides as much coverage as the policy I recommended.
Objection:	I'm going to take my chances and not buy travel insurance.
Answer:	It's certainly your choice to take your chances but are you willing to risk losing all of your wealth to pay unexpected financial expenses? This is especially important to consider when you can purchase insurance that will protect you against a great many of these risks. However, if you decide not to purchase insurance please sign this waiver form. This form verifies that I did offer you travel insurance and that you declined to purchase it.

FIGURE 12.17
Sample validation form for manual sales.
Courtesy of Voyageur Insurance Company.

VALIDATION FORM to be issued in sequence NUMBER R 077804

Name of Insureds (Surname First)	Age	# of People Insured	Date of Issue	IATA NUMBER:
			DD / MM / YY	Travel Agency (Name and Address):
		Name of Issuer:		

Plan No.	Premium per Person	No. Per.	Total Premium	Payment of Premium Validates Coverage Circle the Plan Number(s) of Plan(s) Purchased	
1				All Inclusive Prior After Sum Insured $ Unlimited	Beneficiary (Estate unless Otherwise Specified)
2				Rest Assured™ Package ☐ single ☐ family	Departure Date: Day Month Year
3				Trip Cancellation/Interruption Prior After Sum Insured $ $	Return Date: Day Month Year
4				Excess Hospital/Medical ☐ single Unlimited ☐ family	Number of Days: (Include departure and return days)
5				Air Flight Common Carrier sum insured $250,000 24 Hour Accident sum insured $100,000	Destination:
6				Baggage and Personal Effects sum insured $1,500	IMPORTANT: To expedite claims forward this document (or copy) with completed Claims Form to
7				Visitors to Canada ☐ single maximum benefit $50,000 ☐ family	Mutual of Omaha. Payment: Cash: Credit Card:
8				Collision Damage maximum liability $50,000	Enroute ☐ VISA ☐ MC ☐ AMEX ☐
9				Air Flight Accident Sum Insured $	Expiry Date: MONTH YEAR Card Number:
Total Premium: $ (excluding tax)				**Tax:** $ (if any) **Total Paid:** $ (including tax)	Authorization Number: Client's Signature:

INSURED'S COPY

insufficient; proof is always required. Experience suggests that when no other evidence is available, a judge will usually take the word of the client over that of the counsellor. Signed waiver forms therefore offer a great deal of protection against such occurrences for both counsellors and agency owners. Agencies in some provinces include a waiver in the receipt issued to clients (Figure 12.19).

Despite all of a counsellor's efforts, some clients will still refuse insurance. It is their prerogative. If a client refuses to sign a waiver form, then the counsellor must clearly indicate on the client's invoice that the potential risks were explained, that proper insurance to cover these risks was offered and that the client subsequently refused. It is also prudent to indicate the date on which this offer was made to the client. The invoice must be given to the client as soon as possible after the refusal. Under no circumstances should the client depart on the trip before receiving this invoice. This process can only help the client and prevent potential lawsuits against the counsellor and the agency.

Claims Procedure

Most clients never have to make a claim. For those who do, this becomes the moment of truth for the counsellor, the agency and the travel insurance supplier. At this time the insurance policy ceases to be a mere piece of paper. It becomes a promise to pay.

The claims process can be quick and efficient if a client follows the instructions provided as part of the policy (Figure 12.20). Sometimes consultants will wish to assist a client by handling the claim. This is not recommended. While counsellors can assist clients, as they should, it is the client who has to make and submit the claim. Very often a client will ask a counsellor if a claim is payable or not. It is clearly **not** the job of a travel counsellor to be a claims adjudicator. Travel counsellors should not offer any comment on the outcome of a claim. That is clearly the job of the travel supplier's adjudicator. Insurers have trained adjudicators who specialize in settling claims quickly and efficiently.

Counsellors should instruct their clients

to read and follow the claim instructions very carefully, provide their clients with all the documentation that may be required by the insurer and ascertain that these are submitted as requested to the insurer. Insurers have specific procedures for dealing with travel insurance claims. Instructions for submission are usually by type of product such as Trip Cancellation or Emergency Hospital and Medical.

Usually when an insurer receives a claim a file is opened, dated, recorded and given a claim reference number. Under normal conditions, and when the insurer receives all the proper documentation as per written instructions, a claim is settled within seven to 14 days. The settlement of a claim means that either a cheque or a letter explaining the reason(s) for rejection is mailed to the policyholder.

Some insurers have refined the process of handling large Emergency Hospital and Medical claims. This happens when a client has called the contact number outlined in the assistance portion of the policy. Very often in these cases the insurer will handle all of the paperwork and deal with the other insurers or governments on behalf of the client. In such cases the client is almost never involved in the process.

Where a client has to submit documentation to a provincial government plan, a counsellor can provide the provincial health department contact information listed in this chapter.

Dealing with Travel Insurance Suppliers

Today travel insurance products and services are distributed in Canada by insurers, financial institutions, insurance brokers, insurance agents, associations, credit card companies, loyalty clubs, airlines, airport kiosks, travel wholesalers and retail travel agents. Although there are numerous distributors, many of the plans sold are underwritten by the same insurer. In the retail travel industry, Ingle Insurance, Reliable Life Insurance and Voyageur Insurance Company are the most common insurance companies.

An agency's supplier of travel insurance services is an associate and a partner for the benefit of their mutual

clients. An agency and its counsellors act on behalf of the insurer and as such need the full support of the supplier. The ultimate goal is to provide clients with products and services that meet their needs and consequently create a bond of loyalty that will grow over the years.

FIGURE 12.18
An example of a waiver form.
Source: Voyageur Insurance Company.

This **general waiver** form is supplied by:

Member of Royal Bank Financial Group™

I decline to purchase any of the following travel insurances that you, my travel agent, have offered and explained to me:

☐ Emergency Medical

☐ Cancellation & Interruption - Default of Supplier

☐ Flight Accident

☐ Baggage & Personal Effects

☐ Rental Car Physical Damage (CDW)

Consequently, I, the undersigned, will not hold you, my travel agent or the travel agency responsible for any expenses incurred from any sources as a result of:

a) my refusal to purchase travel insurance, or

b) my selection of the principal sums and/or sums insured of the insurance(s) I have purchased.

Client's Signature: _____

Date of Signature: _____

Travel Agent's Signature: _____
                                    (Witness)

Date of Travel: _____

Agency File #: _____

* Registered trade-mark of Royal Bank of Canada.
  Voyageur Insurance Company, licensee of the trade-mark.
™ Trade-mark of Royal Bank of Canada.
  Voyageur Insurance Company, licensee of the trade-mark.

FORM # 71

Travel Insurance has been explained _____

Accepted ☐   Declined ☐

Bought From   Type   Premium
_____ $ _____

Receipt of _____ By _____
                                    (Cash, Cheque, CC)

Balance of _____
                    (Price could be subject to change)

TOTAL PRICE _____
                    (Cdn. funds unless otherwise stated)

PASSENGERS HAVE BEEN ADVISED OF:

(a) the fact that the instructing Person has the authority to book the travel services covered by the receipt on behalf of the named passenger(s), and to keep the agent advised of any changes of plans, or contact addresses:
(if applicable)

(b) a non-refundable counselling fee of $ _____ will be charged by the travel agent, separate and apart from the supplier's cancellation provisions.

SEE REVERSE FOR CONDITIONS OF SALE

The following brochure(s) have been delivered to the instructing Person:

1._____ 2._____ 3._____

AGENT by his Authorized Rep. _____

THIS IS YOUR RECEIPT - CUSTOMER COPY

FIGURE 12.19 Agency receipts sometimes contain a waiver. *Courtesy of Saunders Travel Service.*

Selecting a Travel Insurance Supplier

Insurance is a highly specialized and complicated business. For this reason it is important to deal with quality insurance suppliers. Most agencies in Canada select one major supplier because of the legal responsibilities and high risks involved in selling travel insurance products. This also ensures that the agency will earn the highest possible commission rate. (Unlike other segments of the travel industry, it is not necessary for an agency to be appointed by all or most of the insurance suppliers in the marketplace.) In a few cases an agency may have a second supplier as a supplement. Some agencies select two or more suppliers to provide their clients with a variety of products, prices and services. In the final analysis, a distributing agency must select a supplier or suppliers that can meet the needs of its clientele. Counsellors do not participate in selecting an agency's travel insurance supplier; agency management makes that decision. However, sometimes a counsellor will have to choose between competing products carried by the agency. For example, clients may ask a counsellor to recommend between the coverage available from a travel insurance company and that offered by a tour operator. Whether it is the choice of an agency's supplier or a customer's coverage, counsellors and agency managers should thoroughly investigate suppliers and products before making the decision. The following questions can help them decide

- Can the supplier meet the client's needs?
- What is the financial stability of the supplier?
- What training and support does the supplier provide?
- What after-sale service is provided?
- How quickly does the supplier pay claims?
- What experience does the supplier have?
- What commission is paid?

Today, travel insurance has become a large part of travel agency revenue. At the same time, agencies and counsellors are subject to potential lawsuits when travel insurance sales are mishandled or not made. For these reasons it is of the greatest importance to select an appropriate insurance supplier. Choosing the correct travel insurance supplier plays a large part in an agency's success and future growth.

Appointment

The process for the appointment of a travel agency by an insurer varies from country to country. In Canada, insurers appoint distributor agencies on a commission basis to act on their behalf in the sale of travel insurance products. This is accomplished through an agreement called an appointment or accreditation. The document is normally negotiated between the supplier and the agency's management. The agreement deals with such issues as responsibilities, selling methods and commission. Generally, appointments contain provisions for termination that can be implemented by either party.

Representatives

Travel insurance suppliers generally appoint representatives in a given territory. Their function is to assist appointed distributors in marketing products. They also appoint, train, and help new agencies to set up the sale of travel insurance products. Proper training is probably the most important single factor affecting the distributor/ supplier relationship. A supplier is very dependent on its distributors for the sales and growth of its product in the marketplace. On the other hand, distributors depend on the supplier for competitive travel insurance products that will assist in acquiring travel insurance market share. As part of the relationship, the travel insurance supplier generally provides training programs for the distributors' employees. These training programs deal with all aspects of selling the product. Usually, training is conducted when launching new products or when new employees are hired. Training sessions can be held on site or at the supplier's business location. Some suppliers have produced audiovisual training tapes that permit counsellors to study at home. Some insurers have ACCESS-approved training programs

FIGURE 12.20
A description of claims procedures.
Source: Voyageur Insurance Company.

HOW DO YOU SUBMIT A CLAIM?

(Please tear out the Claim & Authorization form from the centre of this booklet.)

a) **Cancellation & Interruption Insurance,** *we* require:

- the fully completed Claim & Authorization form, and where applicable:
- *our medical questionnaire* (if the full value of the non-refundable portion of *your* prepaid travel arrangements exceeds $10,000).
- the attached Medical Certificate, fully completed by the legally qualified physician in active personal attendance and in the locality where the *medical condition* occurred stating the reason why travel was impossible.

- written evidence of the risk insured which was the cause of cancellation.
- complete original unused transportation tickets and vouchers.
- receipts for the prepaid land arrangements and/or subsistence allowance expenses.
- original passenger receipts for new tickets.
- reports from the police or local authorities documenting the cause of the missed connection.
- detailed invoices and/or receipts from the service provider(s).

b) **Emergency Medical Insurance,** *we* require:

- the fully completed Claim & Authorization form, and where applicable:
- *our medical questionnaire* (if *you* are covered under TravelCare® Gold, Silver or Bronze).
- original of all bills, invoices and receipts.
- proof of payment by *your* government health insurance plan and payment from any other insurer or benefit plan.

- the completed and signed Power of Attorney and Quebec Regie forms, if *you* reside in the province of Quebec.
- a complete diagnosis from the physician(s) and/or hospital(s) who provided the treatment, including, where applicable, written verification from the physician who treated *you* during *your* trip that the expenses were medically necessary.
In addition, for accidental dental expenses, *we* require proof of the accident.

c) **Accident Insurance,** *we* require:

- the fully completed Claim & Authorization form (please contact your local office for the appropriate form at 1-800-263-8944), and, where applicable:

- police reports, medical records, death certificate, autopsy or coroner's report.

d) **Baggage & Personal Effects Insurance,** *we* require:

- the fully completed Claim & Authorization form (please contact your local office for the appropriate form at 1-800-263-8944), and, where applicable:

- proofs of loss (copy of reports made to the authorities) or damage, ownership and receipts for the items claimed, in the event of a loss or of damage.
- proof of delay and receipts for purchases of necessary toiletries and clothing, in the event of a delay.

e) *Rental Car* **Physical Damage Insurance,** *we* require:

- the fully completed Claim & Authorization form (please contact your local office for the appropriate form at 1-800-263-8944),
- invoice and/or receipt showing payment of the car rental,
- a copy of the car rental agreement,
- brief description of the loss, and, where applicable:

- police report if the loss is over $500, or the *commercial rental agency* loss report.
- copy of the repair bill or estimate of repair cost.
- copy of *your* written record of pre-existing damages, as completed before *your* acceptance of the *rental car.*

**VOYAGEUR
INSURANCE
COMPANY.**
Member of Royal Bank Financial Group®

**403-44 Peel Centre Drive
Brampton, Ontario L6T 4M8
Telephone (905) 791-8700   Fax (905) 791-0254**

SALES REPORT
(for Ontario agents only)

Agency Name & Address

Voyageur
Agency Code

This report covers the period for (date)

From _____ To _____

* Please do not include provincial sales tax in gross sales calculation.

	Regular Policies (Other than TravelCare®)	**TravelCare® Policies** (Other thanTravelCare® Package Tour)	**TravelCare®** Package Tour Policies
Gross Sales* (total credit card & cash sales)	$ _____	$ _____	$ _____
Refunds (total credit card & cash refunds) less	– $ _____	– $ _____	$ N/A
Net Sales	= $ _____	= $ _____	= $ _____
Commission	X ____ % = _____	X 20 % _____	X 25 % _____
Net Premium (Net Sales less Commission)	$ _____	$ _____	$ _____
Add Provincial Sales Tax Total for Cash & Credit Card Sales	+ $ _____	+ $ N/A	+ $ _____
Total Payable	(1) $ _____	(2) $ _____	(3) $ _____

CREDIT CARDS

Number of transactions	$ _____
Total credit card sales **	$ _____
Less credit card refunds	$ _____
Total Credit Card Receipts	(4) $ _____

**** Total of credit card sales
should include PST where applicable**

COMMENTS

REMITTANCE CALCULATION

Total Payable
(1) + (2) + (3) $ _____

Less Total Credit Card
Receipts (4) $ _____

Amount due to/from
Voyageur Insurance Company   = $ _____

Enclosed are "Reporting Audit" copies of Policies

FROM # _____ TO # _____

FROM # _____ TO # _____

FROM # _____ TO # _____

Note: • For refunds or spoiled documents: a) retain "Issuing Office" copy,   b) include all other copies of the policies
         • You are responsible for the reporting of all policy stock issued to your agency

DATE: _____ SIGNED: _____

® Registered trade-mark of Royal Bank of Canada. Voyageur Insurance Company, licensee of the trade-mark.

FIGURE 12.21 Non-automated agencies must regularly report insurance sales. *Source: Voyager Insurance Company.*

where counsellors can acquire credits to help maintain their professional accreditation.

Supplier Documentation

The insurer provides all necessary documentation required by a distributor to sell its products. This documentation includes marketing material, rate guides, policies, validation forms, waiver forms, claims forms, reporting forms and periodic clarification notices. Counsellors must be familiar with all of these documents, as they are what bind the whole process together.

Generally, distributors that sell using a CRS receive their sales and activity reports from the supplier. Non-automated agencies, however, must generally send a periodic sales report (Figure 12.21) to the supplier. Since most insurers have added 24-hour assistance to their products, it is important that they receive these reports as frequently as possible in order to provide clients with the services they have purchased should the need arise. Some suppliers request faxed copies of sales where a manual sale has been completed and the client is travelling on the same day. As a rule, insurers require a full report on a weekly basis.

Communication between supplier and distributor is a key element of the relationship. This can take many forms such as feedback on new products, testing new ideas, working together to settle contentious claims, joint market promotions, and shared market analysis. Healthy communication between both partners is instrumental for growth and market penetration.

Today, Canadian travellers face far greater risk of financial loss than ever. This explains the exceptional growth of travel insurance sales over the last ten years. Travel insurance has become a very important part of the modern traveller's requirements and planning process.

The business of travel insurance worldwide is changing. In Canada, various provincial governments are considering recommendations for change in the laws affecting how travel insurance is sold. Many global insurers recognize the opportunities such shifts will bring and are moving to benefit from them. As we proceed into the next century and a global marketplace, the future will bring new products, new distribution methods, new insurers and, most of all, new challenges in the business of travel insurance sales and services.

Without doubt, travellers will face a maze of products, travel suppliers, and distribution methods. This alone will make the purchase of a travel insurance policy a complicated affair. Consumers will have a need to consult an expert in the field. Travel counsellors have the opportunity to be that expert. This will mean keeping abreast of changing client needs and the travel insurance products available, which will necessitate a closer relationship with the travel insurance supplier. Tomorrow's successful counsellor will understand and grasp the opportunity presented by travel insurance sales. Those who choose to become acknowledged as experts will enhance their potential for additional income and moreover secure their future as a recognized professional travel counsellor.

Review Questions

1. Discuss the reasons why travellers should be counselled to purchase travel insurance.

2. Define the terms premium, exclusions and benefits.

3. Name and describe three types of travel insurance.

4. Compare the premium, coverage, benefits and exclusions offered by a tour operator with that available through a competing travel insurance company.

References

All travel insurance companies provide underwriting guides (manuals), brochures and specimen contracts to enable counsellors to become fully conversant with the features and procedures of travel insurance coverage.

For additional information on provincial health insurance plans, the telephone numbers and addresses are listed below. These contacts can be used by counsellors or referred to clients for information on coverage and/or claims questions.

Alberta: Alberta Health Medical Services Plan, P.O. Box 1360, Edmonton AB, T5J 2N3, Telephone (403) 422-1954, 1 800-310-0000, Fax (403) 422-3552.

British Columbia: P.O. Box 2000, Victoria BC, V8W 2Y4, Telephone (250) 386-7171, 1 800-663-7100, Fax (250) 952-2964.

Manitoba: Manitoba Health, P.O. Box 925, Winnipeg MB, R3C 2T6, Telephone (204) 786-7221, 1 800-392-1207, Fax (204) 783-2171

New Brunswick: Medicare, P.O. Box 2500, Fredericton NB, E3B 7J3, Telephone (506) 453-2161, Fax (506) 453-2726.

Newfoundland: Department of Health, P.O. Box 8700,   Confederation Building, West Block, St. John's NF, A1B 4J6, Telephone (709) 729-4928, Fax (709) 729-4009.

Nova Scotia: Department of Health, P.O. Box 488, Halifax NS, B3J 2R8, Telephone (902) 424-5999, 1 800-563-8880, Fax (902) 424-0615.

Northwest Territories: Department of Health, 2nd Floor, ICC Building, Inuvik NT, X0E 020, Telephone (403) 979-7400, 1 800-661-0830, Fax (403) 979-3197.

Ontario: Ministry of Health, P.O. Box 9000, Kingston ON, K7L 5A9, Telephone (613) 546-3811 (Call local office collect), Fax (613) 545-4399.

Prince Edward Island: Health and Community Services Agency, P.O. Bop 6600, 35, Douses Road, Montague PE, C0A 1R0, Telephone (902) 368-5858, Fax (902) 838-2050.

Quebec: RAMQ, Quebec QC, G1K 7T3, Telephone (418) 646-4636(Quebec), (514) 861-3411(Montreal), 1 800-561-9749.

Saskatchewan: Department of Health, 3475 Albert Street, Regina SK, S4S 6X6, Telephone (306) 787-3261, 1 800-667-7523, Fax (306) 787-3761.

Yukon: Health Services, P.O. Box 2703, Whitehorse YT, Y1A 2C6, Telephone (403) 667-5725, 1 800 661-9498, Fax (403) 393-6486.

## Chapter 13

Sales

Chapter Summary

The role of a travel counsellor is to sell travel products that match their clients' needs. This chapter reviews procedures and techniques for accomplishing this function. Initially, the marketing and promotion activities of retail travel agencies are examined. The study of sales, as a component of marketing, naturally follows this introduction. This comprises a general review of sales, a detailed account of the six stages of the sales process, and how they can be applied in person or by telephone. The chapter closes with some suggestions for sales success.

Chapter Objectives
After completing this chapter you should be able to:

- Distinguish between sales and marketing.

- Discuss travel agency marketing and promotion activities. Describe the importance of counsellor selling skills for retail travel agencies.

- Define three types of prospects.

- Follow the steps in the sales process.

- Discuss sales strategies.

- Apply product knowledge and use sales tools in a sales interview.

- Compare strategies for closing a sale.

- Practise telephone selling skills.

Marketing

Chapter 3 reviewed types of travellers, the reasons why people travel, and client needs and motivations. Questioning and listening skills, and how these could be used to determine client needs, motivations and expectations, were also examined. This chapter considers how a counsellor's knowledge of client needs and travel products can be applied to a sales process by using similar questioning and listening skills. Sales is generally accepted as a subdivision of marketing. A brief overview of marketing is therefore presented prior to a closer study of sales and selling skills.

Marketing encompasses all the operations that put the sellers and potential buyers of a product in contact with each other and that attempt to convince these prospective buyers to purchase the particular product. Marketing a product is a complex process that involves research, development, pricing, distribution, promotion and sales. In the travel industry, most of these marketing operations are performed by the destinations, governments and other suppliers that actually provide the products and services. Travel agencies are simply the distributors of these products

and services. However, agencies have an enormous influence on the sale of travel products since they provide the location where sellers and potential buyers meet.

Travel agencies are highly competitive as they tend to sell similar travel products at comparable prices. They must therefore market their services to attract clients. Typically, a travel agency's marketing activities involve setting basic policies which position the agency. Agency policies determine which travel products and suppliers are sold, what types of clientele are targeted, accounting procedures, and promotional activities. These decisions are taken by the owner and/or manager. Some agencies develop a marketing plan to help them clarify and implement their policy decisions. Once the basic policy has been established, travel agency marketing consists primarily of promotion and sales.

Travel Agency Promotion

Just as marketing brings buyers and sellers together, promotion is any business activity that either directly or indirectly contributes to the acceptance of a product, service, person or idea. All travel agencies must engage in some form of promotion if they are to remain viable. Advertising and publicity are the two types of promotional activities in which travel agencies become most involved. The extent to which a travel agency engages in promotional activities is governed by six interrelated factors:

- Objectives
- Audience
- Budget
- Staff Capability
- Type of Agency
- Promotional Medium

Objectives

An agency's primary promotional objective is to generate new business. However, promotional activities are also used to stimulate business during slow periods and to maintain existing business when competition increases. The general goal of generating business provides a framework for determining specific objectives. For example, an agency's goal may be to tap a new market within the community segment it serves, to stem a loss of clientele to a competitor, or to introduce a new agency service. An agency beginning a new venture in creating and operating tours will have the successful promotion of these products as one of its objectives. In general, an agency's promotional objectives are generated by the challenges, projects and new developments facing it.

Audience

Defining these challenges, projects and new developments will, in most instances, identify the audience. For example, an agency about to open a new branch office in a shopping plaza must identify the target group for its promotional campaign. Individuals who regularly patronize the plaza, those living nearby, and people working in the immediate area (the groups are not necessarily the same) would typically be considered as potential clients. Before an agency can decide on an effective promotional strategy, it must know the composition of this potential clientele and the mass media to which it is exposed.

Budget

Promotional activity is generally limited only by money and talent (and if one has money, talent can be hired). Although a limited promotional budget can be a handicap, it should not necessarily prevent an agency from considering a promotional campaign. It will, however, affect the strategy. For example, metropolitan newspapers generally have high advertising rates because they have mass circulation and serve a large area. However, the region served by such papers is generally too large to be practical for most travel agencies. Thus they would not benefit from an extensive advertising campaign in such a daily, and the high cost would not be the best use for the agency's promotional budget. However, there are alternatives. For example, direct mail advertising to a specifically targeted group costs less and is more effective. How the budget is used rather than its amount is the key factor.

Staff Capability

Budget limitations reduce the number of promotional options available to an agency. Depending on the staff's creative abilities, however, an agency can sometimes compensate for its budgetary deficiencies. If staff members have creative writing skills, for example, an agency can inexpensively produce a regular newsletter. This is in fact a valuable promotional vehicle.

Type of Agency

Different agencies have different promotional objectives depending on their size, type of business, and clientele. For example, large agencies may wish to stress their size and stability while smaller agencies may hope to create an image of personal service. Similarly, a corporate agency might try to attract more clients by emphasizing its experience and efficiency while an agency specializing in leisure travel might highlight its counsellors' knowledge of the world.

Promotional Medium

The medium selected for a promotional campaign must correspond with an agency's objectives. For example, an agency whose goal is to increase the number of corporate clients might advertise in prestigious business journals while one that is promoting tours might select local television as a suitable medium.

Advertising

Advertising (sometimes called persuasive communication) is any paid form of non-personal presentation and promotion of ideas, goods or services by an identified sponsor. (The sponsor is the individual or company that purchases the announcement and thus dictates the content of the message presented.) The basis of advertising is an acronym, AIDA. AIDA represents the four reactions (attention, interest, desire and action) which all advertisements try to achieve. A successful advertisement must first capture an audience's attention; next, it must stimulate the audience's interest; having generated an interest, it should create a desire for the product; finally, an advertisement should cause an audience to act, preferably by purchasing the product. Advertising employs three categories of media to accomplish its goals:

- Mass Media
- Direct Mail
- Other Forms

Mass Media

In terms of advertising, the mass media consist of print media (newspapers and magazines) and audiovisual media (radio and television). These are feasible channels of promotion, on either a national or regional basis, only for large multibranch agencies such as chains and franchises. Medium size agencies can benefit by advertising in local versions of these media, such as a community newspaper or a local radio station. Their audience is within easy geographic access to the agency and, if the product is appealing, this type of travel advertising will probably be beneficial. Even these restricted methods may, however, exceed the means and requirements of a small agency catering only to a portion of a community. Such an agency might consider the use of an urban weekly serving its particular geographic region.

One way for an agency with a limited budget to advertise in the mass media is to take advantage of advertising "hooks". Many suppliers such as carriers, larger hotels and resorts, and tour operators sponsor national advertising. Local agencies are often encouraged to become associated with these products and companies by tying into the advertisement. For example, an airline might announce the introduction of a new, low airfare. Travel agencies can, for a nominal fee, "hook" on to the nationally sponsored advertisement by purchasing space to print their name, address and telephone number below it. This identifies the small company (the agency) with a larger one (the airline) and so gives it an image of strength.

Cooperative advertising is another method employed by travel agencies. Cooperative advertising is simply a sharing of costs between, for example, a tour operator and a travel agency. Print media are typically used for this. The type of newspaper or magazine selected is usually proportional to the size of the travel agency. Larger agencies can afford to share costs in larger and more expensive publications. The copy for a cooperative advertisement is usually provided by the supplier and generally consists of an advertising matrix. This is a predesigned advertisement to which the name, address and telephone number of the travel agency can be easily added. Such advertising makes the talents of professional writers and artists available to an agency. It is usually provided by the supplier at no cost.

Direct Mail

Direct mail is an effective form of advertising that all agencies can employ, no matter what their size or budget. In this strategy, an agency selects a target group to receive product or promotional information directly, either by mail or through door-to-door delivery. For example, consider a travel agency that wishes to locally promote a tour targeted at those aged 18-35. The agency may decide to deliver the tour information to all residents living in a nearby adults only apartment building. Although not totally accurate, the technique may work if most of the residents fit the target category. Another option is to target the market more closely by purchasing mailing lists from clubs or associations whose members fit the description. Mailing lists can also be bought or developed from local directories. A mass mailing to a large geographic area tends to be expensive and the returns rarely merit the outlay. However, it is a productive way to reach small groups of addressees.

A sales letter to past and prospective clients is the most widely used form of direct mail. It is particularly valuable in maintaining contact with past clients. Such clients should be considered a source of repeat business and the basis for generating new business. Given the present level of automation in most travel agencies, it is a fairly straightforward matter to develop mailing lists from an analysis of the agency's own client list. Information can then be mailed to former clients who fit the target description or who have previously bought a similar product.

A periodic newsletter, which serves as both a promotional tool and an information vehicle, is another common direct mail piece. Many carriers and other suppliers produce materials specifically for direct mail promotion. These can be easily adapted or included in agency newsletters.

Circulars and flyers are generally distributed door-to-door within a specific area with little regard for the targeting associated with mailed pieces. They are most often used to make announcements, such as the opening of an agency, a special offer, or a travel film evening.

Other Advertising

Other types of advertising range from simple and inexpensive promotions, such as the use of novelties (key chains, calendars, pens, luggage tags), to exotic and expensive devices like cinema advertising or skywriting. Most agencies do not have the budget or need for many of these techniques. However, suppliers often use outdoor advertisements (posters, signs, billboards, balloons and busboards) to transmit their message. Earlier chapters discussed the most common form of travel advertising, catalogues and brochures. Many suppliers also use items such as directories, references, programs, menus or placemats, to carry their message to the public or to promote their product to travel agencies. Community involvement can also be a successful and relatively inexpensive method of advertising a company. For example, an agency may decide to sponsor a local sports team, or donate prizes (particularly travel-related) for a community draw.

Publicity

Advertising tries to stimulate demand for a product, service or business, or advance its image or reputation, by paid means. Publicity, sometimes called public relations or PR, attempts to similarly present the product, service or idea to the audience, but without payment by a sponsor and with no overt intention to generate sales. Publicity tries to make a company or product more familiar to potential clients. PR spreads its message by distributing commercially significant news about a company, product or service. The goal is to have this information published or reported favourably through newspapers, magazines, radio, television, or any other medium.

PR is often thought of as a "free" means of promotion. In practice, however, it is free only in the sense that a direct payment is not normally made to the company or organization that delivers the message. A successful publicity program demands considerable time, money and effort for planning and execution. Since they involve no direct payment, publicity releases must be designed to satisfy two groups: the medium's audience (e.g., newspaper readers, radio listeners and TV viewers); and the medium's controller (e.g., the newspaper editor or program producer). Not only must the publicity material meet the standards of the medium, as set by its controller, but it must also convince the controller that it will be of interest to the medium's audience. If it meets these criteria the controller will publish the material as news or present it as entertainment.

One advantage of publicity is that it is not sponsored promotion and is therefore perceived by an audience to be more credible and acceptable. However, publicity has a disadvantage in that its creator lacks control after the publicity material has been distributed. Once it has been issued, the originator has no way of knowing whether it will be published, or if it will be published in an acceptable manner.

Public relations is sometimes confused with the promotional techniques already discussed. Some of the confusion arises from the use of the phrase to mean three different things. First, PR often means image or reputation as in, "That company has good public relations". It is also used to describe a philosophy. For example, the statement, "She has a good PR sense" indicates that someone has a natural understanding of those things which impact on reputation. Finally, it embraces formal and informal techniques used to bolster the image of an organization or person. The present discussion considers public relations in the third sense, the furtherance or maintenance of a travel agency's or counsellor's public image. This public image is influenced by a wide range of factors ranging from an agency's physical appearance to the actions and knowledge of its counsellors. Honesty and sincerity are the keys to successful public relations. Anything else eventually rings false. (There is an adage often quoted by professional PR practitioners,

"No matter how much whipped cream you spread on a dung heap, the stench still comes through!") Travel agencies can generate publicity and achieve a positive PR image in at least six ways:

- New Developments
- Newsworthy Events
- Community Involvement
- Achievements
- Self-Generated
- Travel Films and Talks

New Developments

Innovations are frequently newsworthy. Notice of the first agency in an area to install a new electronic travel brochure system would be an interesting news story calling attention to the agency involved. Editors might be intrigued by the introduction of unusual tours or a new type of vehicle rental service. Trade publications would probably print an announcement concerning an agency's office relocation, the appointment of new personnel, or the participation of agency staff as part-time faculty at a college travel program. These releases would also be considered newsworthy to a smaller paper serving the agency's local community.

Newsworthy Events

Sales promotion activities have already been discussed. Many of these actions can also generate publicity. For example, an agency may enter a float in a winter carnival parade which may warrant a publicity picture. Advance arrangements can be made for pictures to be taken and delivered with a news release to the local newspaper. (Pictures for newspaper publication should be black and white.) Similarly, if a travel counsellor is to address a local service club, an advance announcement should be sent to the community paper. (A large metropolitan daily is unlikely to give coverage to such an event.) If the subject of the speech is a report on some unusual travel experience, a community paper may consider that it deserves a follow-up story. If the subject is sufficiently unusual, or particularly topical, it may even receive coverage in the metro daily.

Community Involvement

Some people, by virtue of their personality, interests or energy, participate in numerous activities in addition to their work, social and family commitments. They can be found in every town and in all occupations, including travel counsellor. Such individuals invariably gravitate towards volunteer work; they chair committees, serve on executive boards, work with charitable organizations, or run for elective office. Although publicity is rarely the motive for such involvement, these activities have promotional potential. Some ventures, such as running for public office, automatically receive coverage in the media. Other projects require prepared announcements. For example, a travel counsellor's election to the board of the Canadian Institute of Travel Counsellors is unlikely to become public knowledge without the aid of publicity efforts, although it would most likely be reported in the travel trade papers.

As well as involvement in personal interests, agencies and counsellors may also consciously support their local community. For example, counsellors might participate in local educational programs by offering to share their knowledge of geography and world events at a high school. Alternatively, they may subscribe to charitable organizations, community and welfare projects, or sponsor a local athletic team. Indications of community support are sometimes as simple as providing travel posters for a charity dance using an international theme.

Achievements

Agency and counsellor achievements can raise a company's profile in the industry and in the community. For example, a release on a travel counsellor who receives an industry award for special achievement will be well received by both trade and consumer publications. An agency's record sales volume with a particular supplier, however, would generally be of interest only to the trade media.

Self-Generated

Newspaper travel sections are popular with the public and are an important means of arousing interest in travel. These same pages represent a potential publicity medium for creative travel counsellors. Travel sections not only print publicity releases from carriers, tour operators and travel agencies, they provide a variety of travel-oriented articles for potential tourists and armchair travellers. Many of these columns are written by the journal's regular staff. However, freelance travel articles are also sought and published. For travel counsellors with writing talent, these pages provide a ready-made publicity opportunity and an enthusiastic market for first-hand accounts of travel experiences.

Radio and television, including cable TV, can be an effective avenue for publicity. The growth of cable TV has led to an increased demand for Canadian content in broadcast programming. Several local radio stations and cable TV systems have responded favourably to the idea of a weekly travel show hosted by an area travel counsellor. The counsellor is naturally identified as a travel expert with a particular (named) agency.

Travel Films and Talks

One of the most successful promotional techniques for a travel agency is to organize an evening event where counsellors show travel films and talk on the subject. Almost every organization, association, social or religious group, regularly looks for program material for its members. Such groups offer numerous opportunities for an alert agency to promote the services of its counsellors as speakers. Almost all tourist boards, many tour operators and other suppliers, and other organizations invest heavily in the production of travel films. There are literally thousands to choose from and new shows appear daily. These programs find extensive exposure on television, in theatres and in public meetings. They also provide an excellent promotional medium for travel agencies. As most are available at no charge, or for a nominal fee to handle shipping, they are an inexpensive way for agencies and counsellors to make themselves known to groups. Many travel counsellors pursue formal training in public speaking (Dale Carnegie and Toastmasters, for example, offer excellent programs). Such expertise and its availability can be publicized by sending formal letters to organizations in the area the agency serves. These letters should be mailed in the late winter or early spring when programs normally are planned for the following season.

None of these publicity suggestions have a measurable promotional value. Indirectly, however, they can produce benefits beyond any generated by an investment in advertising or sales promotion. Almost all provide an opportunity for counsellors to make personal contacts and other people are the most influential means of stimulating an interest in travel.

Sales

The AIDA theory suggests travel advertising and sales promotion can successfully gain attention, create interest, arouse desire, and prompt action. With few exceptions, however, the action taken is more likely to be contact with a travel agency than the immediate purchase of the product. When this occurs, as either a telephone or personal inquiry, the expert sales person (the counsellor) takes over.

The main reason clients deal with a travel agency is to receive service; they seek the benefit of the information and guidance a counsellor can provide. Travel counsellors deal with their clients directly, either face to face or by telephone. Thus, they are involved in personal selling. Personal selling comprises three principal categories: field sales (or external selling) which entails calling on clients; internal sales; and telephone sales. For the most part,

counsellors in a travel agency deal primarily with internal sales and telephone sales, although they sometimes perform external sales functions. Counsellors involved in generating corporate or group travel business, and representatives of various travel suppliers, spend more time on external sales activities.

This text focuses on a counsellor's ability to determine client needs and to find suitable travel products to meet these needs. However, travel counsellor duties are not limited to researching products, making reservations and issuing tickets. They are actively engaged in travel counselling. While the core of travel counselling may be the matching of client needs and travel products, its purpose is to sell travel products. Counsellors must remember that though they may deal in dreams, they are involved in the business of travel. And the purpose of any business enterprise is to make a profit. More than any other factor, a travel agency's survival depends on the selling skills of its counsellors.

The selling function is more than handing out brochures or answering questions on how much it costs to fly to Acapulco. When counsellors provide clients with tour brochures, they must be prepared to explain their contents and the implications associated with each product. However, no travel agency, tour company or airline, can exist by simply supplying free information and advice to the public. Counsellors must do more than tell, they must sell. This, in essence, is counselling. If a client is not entirely satisfied with a tour because it restricts the choice of accommodation, then the counsellor must seek an alternative tour which permits upgrading. Similarly, if a client wishes to extend the length of a tour beyond the basic period, the counsellor must attempt to find a tour that meets this wish. Counselling implies not only determining the client's motivations, needs and interests, answering questions, researching travel products for a suitable match, and making recommendations which most closely meets these needs, it also presupposes that the counsellor must persuade the client to accept the recommendations by purchasing the product from that agency. This principle applies whether the client is travelling for pleasure or on business.

Sales Prospects

Potential purchasers of a product are described as prospects. People who contact a travel agency in person, in writing or by telephone, fall into one of three categories:

• Specific Prospects
• Qualified Prospects
• Uncommitted Prospects

Specific Prospects

Specific prospects are committed to a definite course of travel action. They know exactly what they want, where they are going, how to get there, and what they will do on arrival. This group includes business travellers, experienced FIT travellers, and often the person travelling for specific family reasons. This type of client requires a travel counsellor to do little more than make a booking, although some research may still be necessary. The counsellor's prime responsibility is to obtain the information needed to process the client's requests. The client generally expects a minimum of conversation, a maximum of efficiency, and a speedy transaction. Specific prospects, however, still present a counsellor with opportunities to counsel and sell related services such as a rental car or travel insurance. If a counsellor recognizes some service that may make the client's travel more pleasant or more successful, an attempt should be made to sell it. A client may have overlooked these services and the counsellor's competence will be appreciated.

Qualified Prospects

Most people who enter a travel agency are described by sales experts as qualified prospects. This means they are potential customers interested in purchasing the products being offered, as opposed to people who browse through bookstores or visit a local car dealer's showroom without any serious thought of buying. Qualified prospects are generally committed to travel. They want to travel, are prepared to travel, and have a travel budget. However, they may be unclear about the type of holiday they want. They may not have decided on a destination, or know what they want to do when they arrive. Frequently, they have no knowledge of fares, routes, hotel rates, what clothes to take, or even the weather to expect. They look to a travel counsellor for help, advice and guidance on these and related matters. It is with qualified prospects that counsellors become most involved in the sales process discussed below.

For many reasons, some of these uncertain but likely customers may not actually voice their confusion and need for help. Some people are reluctant to state their wishes to a stranger (the counsellor); others are rather suspicious of what they will be told; still others are afraid of feeling embarrassed if they cannot afford the trip they have in mind. It is therefore crucial that counsellors have an awareness of motives, needs, expectations and behaviourial patterns. Without this knowledge, they cannot hope to understand their clients or meet their needs.

Uncommitted Prospects

Uncommitted prospects are those people who make enquiries at a travel agency but are not committed to any course of action.

This type of person may be a waste of time, similar to the individuals who like to kick tires and sit in new cars but have no intention of buying. They are sometimes known as "shoppers". They may wish to travel, but do not know when or cannot really afford to. Their desire may be merely a passing fancy which will not, or cannot, be realized. They may have contacted the agency on a whim, or be the type who collects travel brochures and information simply to feed a dream that will never come true.

However, they may in fact be prepared to invest in a vacation and ready to commit to a plan immediately.

Uncommitted prospects present the greatest challenge for travel counsellors. If counsellors do not take them seriously and treat them indifferently, they may be turning away a highly profitable sale. Conversely, if counsellors treat them as qualified prospects they may invest a significant amount of time in a hopeless cause. Knowledge of human behaviour permits a counsellor to more easily probe a prospect's intentions to determine whether the person is a potential client. Uncommitted prospects should never be pressured into making a commitment or declaring their intentions. This will simply drive them away and reduce the likelihood that they will return as a committed or qualified prospect. A travel counsellor who cannot elicit any information can simply suggest some alternatives, provide supporting literature and leave the next move up to the individual.

Sales Strategies

The demands on travel counsellors may appear excessive. They must have comprehensive product knowledge of a vast industry, and they must be able to quickly assess people, almost on the first impression. The sales process, however, can help to reduce these requirements to a few simple principles and strategies.

The principal sales strategy used by travel counsellors, and the basis of this textbook, is one built on satisfying the client's needs. This is a sophisticated approach which can be modified according to a counsellor's personal style and the client's individual requirements. It is characterized by a low pressure, conversational manner where the counsellor's recommendations are based on needs revealed and mutually agreed on during discussions with the client. The technique used to sell a tangible item generally includes a demonstration or presentation of the product. The method followed to sell vacation travel, however,

has more in common with an interview or conversation than with a one-directional presentation. Vacation counsellors rarely make formal presentations, however, the qualifying stage can be lengthier than for other products or services. On the other hand, outside sales people such as counsellors who solicit group, corporate and incentive clients are frequently called on to make a formal presentation of their agency's services and experience. The presentation is typically based on a standard format which may be modified somewhat by prior research on the particular client. It demands other, more forceful sales strategies which tend to ignore individual differences and treat all prospects alike. Prospects have few opportunities to provide input other than as a prescribed response. Although counsellors in an agency at times include elements from these strategies, they are generally ineffective for selling travel because they do not fully address the needs of the client.

The Sales Process

The sales process can be as simple as booking a flight in response to a telephone request, or as complex and demanding as helping a client to plan and select a vacation. Business clients and other travellers who typically know what they wish to purchase, generally require only that a counsellor be able to efficiently process the request. Pleasure travellers, however, tend to be more vague in their demands. They may be unfamiliar with the products available and may not even have decided on a type of vacation or destination. This complicates the sales process and compels a counsellor be more creative in responding to them. There are at least six steps in the sales process:

- Prospecting
- Qualifying
- Making Recommendations
- Overcoming Objections
- Closing the Sale
- Following Up

The number of steps in the process, the degree to which each is followed, and the specific sales strategy used, depends on the product, the client and the situation. The following discussion refers principally to the more complex sales process necessary to sell vacation travel through a travel agency. Counsellors that sell other types of travel may use or emphasize different strategies. Such deviations from the standard travel sales process are therefore noted.

Before examining the sales process in detail, readers are advised to review the questioning and listening skills discussed in Chapter 3. These same skills are necessary for a sales interview. When ascertaining a client's needs, a counsellor is qualifying that client for a type of travel product. This dialogue leads to a recommendation to purchase a particular product based on the counsellor's knowledge of the subjects presented in Chapters 4 through 12. Counsellors generally start a sales conversation by asking open-ended questions which supply the background information required. As the sales interview continues, a counsellor will introduce closed questions that promote a specific response. This narrows the search for a suitable product and leads to the counsellor's ultimate goal which is to close the sale by asking to make a reservation.

Prospecting

Prospecting is the term used for the process of identifying and seeking new clients. The prospecting activities of agencies specializing in pleasure travel will most likely be restricted to the development of personal contacts, direct mail schemes, and sales promotion activities. Agencies involved in corporate, group or incentive travel are more actively involved in prospecting for clients. Successful prospecting demands thorough planning and research. Before approaching a potential client, an agency will try to determine the client's need for the agency's services, its potential budget, and who makes the decision regarding the purchase of travel services. Agency personnel may try to learn this information by making cold calls in person or by telephone, or they may follow up sales leads. Once a potential client has been identified by prospecting, an agency will try to arrange an appointment to make a formal presentation on its services.

Qualifying

Before any product can be sold, the potential purchaser must be qualified by the seller. This applies to all products and all buyers. Qualifying the buyer essentially means obtaining the information necessary to make the sale. Part of prospecting for corporate accounts is to prequalify the company prior to making a sales presentation. In terms of selling travel in an agency, the basic information required can be found by asking the client five simple questions:

- Where is the client going? (Destination.)
- When is the client travelling? (Dates.)
- How long is the trip? (Duration.)
- Who is travelling? (Number of people.)
- What level of service is required? (Price and value.)

To business travellers, these are closed questions which can be answered in a definite manner. They already have the answers and the counsellor's task is simply to process the request. Other prospects, however, may not have the answers. They may not even be committed to travel. The first phase of the qualifying process is therefore to determine whether the prospect is a qualified or uncommitted prospect. Having established that a prospect is indeed seriously considering a vacation, a counsellor can then proceed through the five basic qualifying topics. One additional question must be added to qualify pleasure travellers:

- Why? (Reasons for travelling.)

The answer to this question is complex and varies for each individual. The counsellor's assignment is to determine the type of vacation experience desired. A counsellor also needs to know how flexible the prospect is in terms of the basic qualifying information, particularly dates and price. These demand the use of open-ended questions which draw out the client.

Although the basic qualifying questions are straightforward, they cannot be presented as a checklist or in rote form. In addition, they provide insufficient information to adequately qualify a pleasure traveller for the next step in the process, making a recommendation. Counsellors must be tactful and sensitive when probing a prospect. It is also important not to jump to conclusions or judge a client by appearance. To gather the information they need, counsellors must learn how to control a conversation with their clients. Naturally, the conversation should be based on the framework provided by the sales process. However, no two sales conversations can be exactly alike. No two counsellors think or act alike; no two prospects respond in the same way to a question. A formula for controlling the conversation cannot be applied in the same way to every client interview. There must therefore be some flexibility in how a counsellor follows the steps. A conversation may be sidetracked by questions asked and observations made by the prospect. Listening to the prospect is an equally important part of the selling process. By listening, a counsellor learns about the client's tastes, prejudices and desires. The use of open-ended questions permits a counsellor to keep the conversation on the desired path. It facilitates the counsellor's goal which is to sell the client a recommended product. Closed questions provoke a response, such as yes or no, which effectively end the conversation. The counsellor must then try to restart the conversation or take a new approach. The counsellor has then lost control of the conversation, even if only temporarily.

Counsellors use probing questions to qualify a client for specific travel products and services. For example, clients might be asked why they want to travel, what aroused their interest, where they have

travelled before, as well as what they did and enjoyed on that vacation. Such questions help travel counsellors to build a picture of the client's real needs. A simple inquiry can reveal valuable information which may send the conversation in several directions but will ultimately qualify some aspect of the purchase. For example, a conversation on a client's previous vacations naturally leads to further insights into the client's tastes and interests. If this reveals that the client enjoyed rafting on the Amazon River and backpacking through the Himalayas, it is unlikely that this person will enjoy two weeks on the beaches of Barbados, unless this change of style is specifically indicated. Similarly, a prospect who has not travelled before will naturally guide a counsellor towards questions on the client's lifestyle, interests, hobbies and what the client might like to do on a vacation. Such questions and their responses help counsellors to make recommendations on suitable destinations for either the experienced or the novice traveller.

A client's previous experience can also be used as a measure of the quality of service sought. For example, a counsellor may pose some questions on accommodation such as which hotel the client previously stayed at, and what the client liked or disliked about it. Even if the travel counsellor is not familiar with the particular property, its quality can be assessed from secondary questions and standard references. These questions help the counsellor recommend a hotel suited to that client's tastes and budget. For example, if a client comments that a particular hotel lacked on-premise dining facilities and had no room service or health club, it is fairly safe to assume that a better quality of accommodation offering all amenities is desired. Again, if the client is a first-time traveller the counsellor will likely have to ask direct questions concerning what the client considers important. For example, if a client is considering a beach resort destination, is it important that the hotel be on the beach or is across the street from the beach acceptable?

One part of the qualifying phase which can disturb counsellors is when and how to introduce the question of budget. If a counsellor simply asks how much a client is willing to spend, it can save time and prevent the embarrassment of suggesting something too cheap or too expensive. However, if the subject is broached too early in the conversation, the prospect may feel awkward and be reluctant to answer. A counsellor must first win the prospect's confidence. The question also assumes that the client knows how much travel arrangements cost. This is frequently not the case. In general, counsellors should be guided by their interaction with the client. Careful questioning will reveal the extent of the client's knowledge. By describing the features and benefits of the travel products, as discussed below, a counsellor will help clients to understand their value. This will facilitate a discussion of the client's budget.

Another area to be probed is the extent of information and misinformation possessed by the client. For example, a client's interest may have been stimulated by an extensive off-season advertising campaign promoting a January vacation in London, England. The campaign may have focused on the thrill of old London, the glittering theatre productions, and the exciting nightlife. The client, however, has been given only part of the information. The client may have given no thought to the inclement weather that can befall the British capital at that time of year. It is a counsellor's role to make the client aware of such facts so that a travel decision can be based on all the information. Part of a counsellor's function is to ensure that clients are not unpleasantly surprised by what they find; that their expectations are clear and realistic.

Counsellors base their suggestions and recommendations on the details revealed by prospects during the sales conversation. The greater the amount of relevant information that can be gathered, the more accurate and suitable will be the recommendations. The key is to ask the right questions and to listen carefully to the answers.

Making Recommendations

By establishing a client's travel motives, the qualifying stage provides the basis for making a recommendation. Once a counsellor has an idea of what the client is looking for, tours, cruises or other travel plans that might satisfy these needs can be proposed. During this stage of the sales process, a counsellor's ability to apply product knowledge and use sales tools becomes particularly important. Preparation is essential as a lack of product knowledge will quickly turn a prospective sale into a lost sale. The demands of product knowledge and client counselling may suggest that a travel counsellor must spend considerable time searching for a specific product that meets the client's particular needs. However, good sales people know their product. To sell tangible goods, experience with the product is essential. For travel products, however, the most important part of product knowledge is knowing where to find the information required, how to interpret it, and how to evaluate it. Competent counsellors are familiar with the information available in airline computer systems and in standard references. They know exactly where material is stored for easy retrieval. Further, they are conversant with the brochures and other inventory in their agency. Of course, product knowledge goes beyond simply understanding the material contained in brochures. It includes a general knowledge of geography, history and current affairs. Tariff and ticketing skills, destination knowledge, and familiarity with other segments of the travel industry, are necessary to complement this general background. Counsellors must also maintain and update their knowledge by reviewing circulars, announcements, mailings and trade papers on a daily basis. In total, product knowledge makes a counsellor highly familiar with a package of travel arrangements. Every element of this knowledge will be required during the sales process.

Using Sales Tools

Brochures help to show a client what to

expect. A client can become disappointed or even wary when a counsellor has done a good job of selling a product but cannot provide pictures to substantiate verbal descriptions. However, it is mistaken to expect a tour brochure or any other travel literature to sell a holiday or convince a prospect. A travel brochure is a sophisticated sales tool which requires intelligent use. Its contents must be explained and interpreted by an expert, a travel counsellor. A handful of literature shoved into a prospect's hands is usually ineffective, discourteous and a waste of resources. A brochure should not be given to a prospect unless the counsellor is also prepared to highlight and explain its contents.

The qualifying process will uncover the prospect's wishes and interests. The counsellor combines this information with a knowledge of the travel products in the office to guide in brochure selection. It is important to be selective when choosing brochures to review with a prospect. No more than three brochures should be picked from those that are closest to filling the client's needs.

When making recommendations from a brochure, a counsellor can use a felt pen to mark, circle or underline features believed important to the prospect. Draw arrows or highlight features which appeal to expressed interests and tastes. This procedure immediately personalizes that brochure for the prospect. (Counsellors should gain practice in reading and highlighting brochures upside down. This is often required as the client is generally seated across a desk and is reading the literature in the normal fashion.)

Counsellors must be impartial when selecting brochures and recommending a product. They must deal with the dilemma of being both counsellors to their clients and representatives of an agency and supplier. Their recommendations, however, must always be based on what is best for the client. This may not necessarily be the same as what is best for the agency or a particular supplier. For example, a prospect may remark that it would be less expensive to wait for a last minute sell-off than to book early. Although this is sometimes the case, it is not always so. Further, the sell-off product is not necessarily the best for the tour operator, the travel agency or the consumer. The tour operator sells at a lower price (and perhaps makes no profit on the sale), the agency earns less commission, and the consumer has a limited choice of product. Not only do the tour operator and agency earn more from clients who book early, but the clients benefit by having more choice and more time to decide; they can comparison shop and choose a vacation that meets all their needs. The counsellor's recommendation must be based on whichever product more closely matches the client's requirements.

However, a client will not accept a recommendation simply because it is suggested by a counsellor. In addition to meeting the client's needs, the product must provide maximum satisfaction within the client's budget. The recommendation stage is when product knowledge and effective selling techniques are most critical. Counsellors commonly use three methods to convince clients to accept their proposals:

- Proof
- Endorsement
- Value

Proof

Proof is the most compelling argument. A counsellor must offer conclusive proof that the proposal will satisfy the client's reasons for travelling. Further, this proof must be factual, must be subject to testing, and should strongly suggest that the client will lose nothing by accepting the recommendation. Counsellors must have qualified and listened effectively to their clients if they are to offer proof. Only by responding to the client's concerns can proof be provided. One way to sell in this manner is through features and benefits.

Features and Benefits

A feature is a characteristic of a product or service that is always valid. A benefit describes what the feature does for a client. Counsellors must explain features and sell benefits. This requires two steps. First, the feature must be explained in terms understood by the client. For example, if one flight is nonstop and another is direct, does the client understand the difference between them? An explanation of a feature should reveal its advantage. Once the advantage is clear (convenience and time savings, in this case), the benefits (more time at the destination, arriving well-rested) become plain. Counsellors also sell by relating a product's features to the client's expressed interests and tastes, and then explaining how these features benefit (or meet the needs of) the client. For example, consider a client who wishes to relax at a beach resort. A recommended hotel may feature all rooms with a balcony overlooking the beach; the benefit is that clients can enjoy an ocean view, the sea breeze and the sunset. Benefits must not only offer a prospect value, they must also have an emotional appeal. Some features and benefits are more difficult to explain than others, particularly as a feature may have different benefits for different clients. For example, a cruise may feature several ports of call. For one client the benefit may be the chance to explore new cultures. Another, however, might see this as providing an opportunity to experience the variety of shipboard life and shore excursions. Since travel products tend to promote a number of features, and since a client cannot benefit from them until or unless they are used, counsellors must clearly explain all features and benefits.

Endorsement

Counsellors can support their recommendations with endorsements. The endorsement of someone other than the counsellor is often more persuasive than a counsellor's personal recommendation. For example, clients might be shown unsolicited letters of approval from others who enjoyed the experience. Specific examples of other clients who had similar concerns but who benefited by accepting the proposal could also be cited. The counsellor's task is to

demonstrate how the prospect can obtain the same results. This requires knowledge of one's clients.

Counsellors sometimes find that referring to their own experience reassures a client who is unfamiliar with the product. A personal recommendation can be influential. If a counsellor has visited the proposed hotel, the client can be told and informed of the reasons why it was enjoyed. Personal recommendations can be useful but they must be used with care. A client may not like what the counsellor likes, and may not pay the same rate or be treated in the same way (especially if the counsellor's experience was a fam trip). However, a personal recommendation can reassure clients who are unsure and reluctant to make a commitment.

Value

Most clients seek value for money as much as, if not more than, the lowest price. A recommendation will be more easily accepted if a counsellor can demonstrate its economic value. This technique is often used to propose a cruise instead of a land-based holiday. As discussed in Chapter 11, a cost comparison of the two types of vacation will often confirm the value offered by an apparently more expensive cruise.

Most people do not like being pressured into accepting travel proposals. They must be convinced by gentle, rational persuasion. Including specific statements and motives expressed by the client during the qualifying stage acknowledges the client's needs and strengthens a counsellor's claims. Illustrating points by referring to brochures and other visual materials also reinforces a recommendation and helps the client to follow the reasoning. When travel counsellors make recommendations they should be enthusiastic but not oversell or exaggerate the benefits of the product. For example, "All the rooms in the hotel are huge and beautifully appointed" is overselling whereas "All the rooms are quite large, and most are adequately appointed" simply reflects the truth. Although counsellors should try to paint word pictures for their clients, it is important to avoid using clichés such as "tranquil", "blue waters", "romantic", or "moonlit nights". Similarly, clients should not be told how to react. For example, a statement such as "This resort seems to fit your desire for privacy" is preferable to "You'll love it!" These are not only matters of poor speech; clichés also tend to make people sceptical and may lead to legal problems if the client's experience is not as described by the counsellor.

Overcoming Objections

It is important for counsellors to confirm that they and their clients reach a mutual understanding. Throughout a sales interview counsellors must regularly review the conversation to verify their understanding of the client's statements. However, there may still be times when a client resists or objects to the counsellor's point, even though there previously appeared to be agreement. Naturally, there will also be occasions when a client simply disagrees with a counsellor. Since neither are unusual in such conversations, counsellors must be ready to deal with them. A counsellor faced with this situation has only two options; either to concede the client's point, or to defend the position and overcome the client's resistance or objection. In both cases, however, a counsellor must acknowledge the legitimacy of the client's feelings. The next step is to separate the point from the main discussion, analyze it and then respond. The objection or resistance should not be permitted to adversely affect decisions and arrangements already settled. If a counsellor agrees with the point, an alternative should be offered; if the counsellor disagrees, it should be overcome.

Client resistance can be summarized under four main headings: psychological; social; ignorance; and commitment.

Psychological resistance is most often encountered when a client feels pressured into making a decision. Counsellors can overcome this type of resistance by reiterating the argument and reconfirming the client's agreement of each point. The counsellor should progressively restate the product's benefits and how they meet the client's needs. As a last resort, a counsellor can tactfully point out that the client's resistance is simply postponing a decision which must be made and that a delay may cause later disappointment (for example, if the product sells out).

When clients respond to a suggestion by stating that they must consult with their spouse or travelling companion it is known as **social resistance**. Counsellors must generally accept this wish, however, they should indicate the importance of reaching a decision quickly to avoid future disappointment.

Sometimes a client resists a counsellor's recommendation because of **ignorance** or prejudice. This is a sensitive area and one that can be difficult to draw out of a client. The client may not be aware of certain facts relating to the product or destination, or may be opposed because of prejudice. Unless a counsellor can identify such lack of knowledge or feelings from the conversation, it will be almost impossible to counter them or offer an alternative.

Sometimes client resistance is communicated by a general unwillingness to make a **commitment**. At some point in the sales interview a client may begin to exhibit vague signs of discomfort such as fidgeting or distraction, or may state a need to "think it over". It is important that a counsellor maintain the dialogue so that these feelings can be expressed and the reasons determined. It may be that the client feels guilty and is questioning the need to spend money on a vacation rather than paying off debts or purchasing something more essential. In this situation, a counsellor can try to reassure the client that a vacation is a deserving (and perhaps necessary) use of the client's resources. To overcome a lack of commitment, a counsellor must discover the reason and respond to the concern.

Objections tend to be more specific and thus more easily identified than resistance. Clients will often state their objection quite clearly whereas counsellors may have to probe for the real reasons behind a client's resistance. Most objections arise because the counsellor has not fully qualified the client during the sales interview. Thus they can often be overcome by reviewing these elements. Client objections can usually be reduced to three areas: the product; the dates; and the price. (Note that these are three of the five basic areas necessary to qualify a client.)

If clients object to a product by stating, for example, that the hotel is unsuitable or that they do not like a particular airline, the simple solution is to offer an alternative. The fact that the product is unsuitable implies that it does not meet the client's needs. The counsellor must therefore ask more questions to determine the client's true needs. Similarly, if the objection is to the dates or duration, an alternative can be offered by ascertaining those that would be suitable. If a client objects to the price (usually that it is too high), the counsellor should review the discussion on features and benefits and try to find out their relative importance to the client. In essence, this means separating the features and benefits into those the client "must have" and those which the client would "like to have". This objection can sometimes be overcome by comparing the features and benefits of the recommended product with those of a lower priced option. This generally leads the client to either take the counsellor's recommendation or settle for less and stay within budget.

Upgrading

Making recommendations and overcoming objections are natural parts of the sales process. A counsellor's goal in this process is to reach the closing stage as quickly as possible. However, such conversations frequently present opportunities for a counsellor to try to upgrade the sale. Upgrading, sometimes called suggestive selling or selling up, occurs when a counsellor recommends a more expensive product or an additional service that the client had not previously considered. Counsellors should attempt to upgrade a sale whenever they see an opportunity to offer a client better value

or more convenience. The implication is that these benefits are worth the additional expenditure and they should be presented in this light. They are not simply a ploy to increase the counsellor's commission. This type of suggestive selling is generally done just before or just as a sale is being finalized, although it can also form part of the qualifying and recommending stages.

When used effectively, upgrading increases agency commissions and frequently ensures that a client has a better vacation. However, selling up requires skill. Too much pressure may offend a client. To upgrade a sale a counsellor must relate the additional component to the product being sold. The comparison should use features and benefits deemed important by the client during the preliminary conversation. Typical examples of upgrades are the purchase of additional stopovers en route, a higher category of cabin or room, a sightseeing tour, transfers, and theatre or event tickets. Travel insurance should be offered to every client whether or not it is requested. (This offer is mandatory in some jurisdictions.) In addition, clients who make simple travel arrangements, for example, the purchase of airline tickets only, should be asked if they require accommodation or a rental car at the destination. All three are products which can quickly lead to an upgraded sale and increased customer satisfaction.

Inexperienced counsellors often make two common errors; they forget to offer an upgrade, or they offer the client the cheapest product possible. These omissions can be avoided if a counsellor listens carefully to clients. A standard rule is that clients who inquire about an upgrade generally want it. For example, if a counsellor is booking a flight for a business traveller and the client asks the price of business or first class service, the interest is obvious and it is the counsellor's responsibility to pursue it. Similarly, not all clients want the lowest price. In fact, most seek the best value and this is frequently not the least expensive product. Counsellors must be sensitive to their clients' needs and feelings. A client might be insulted by the offer of a budget hotel room, the lowest category of cabin on a cruise, or an economy class air fare. It is an error for a counsellor to assume that a client cannot afford a particular travel arrangement. Counsellors should not impose their values or interests on clients. They must also try to become aware of and break any stereotypical images they may possess. For example: not all business people travel first class and on an expense account; not all senior citizens have a budget based on a limited pension; and not all families are looking for moderately priced accommodation.

Closing the Sale

For a counsellor, closing the sale means making the reservation and getting the client to make a commitment by leaving a deposit. Few clients, even specific prospects such as business travellers, initiate this stage of the process. It is a counsellor's responsibility to approach the client. Before beginning the closing process, counsellors should verify that their clients have no more questions. During closing, counsellors must explain the steps necessary to complete the travel arrangements and specifically state the action required of the client. These points include reservations and deposit requirements, cancellation charges, and final payment procedures. All are described in the relevant tariff regulations, brochure conditions or other product references. In the current climate of increased consumer awareness, clients will be satisfied with nothing less than what they have been promised. This relates to the risks of overselling discussed above. Counsellors must be careful not to promise anything they know to be incorrect, or anything that is not contained in the product brochure or reference. In addition, counsellors must clarify and separate where their responsibilities end and where those of the supplier begin. They must not accept responsibility for things they cannot control.

The two main considerations in closing a sale are when to initiate the procedure and how to do so.

When to Close

Since clients rarely offer to close a sale, counsellors must be alert to signs that indicate their willingness or readiness to move to this stage. Clients provide clues to this moment through their words and body language. Verbal clues are often in the form of a question about booking procedures. For example, a client may ask when the final payment is due or how much time is available before a decision must be made. Sometimes clients indicate their readiness with a positive statement such as "That's just what I was looking for". On other occasions clients describe their requirements and the counsellor must simply meet them. A client's body language also conveys a message. When a client shows signs of agreement with a recommendation such as a nod of the head, or of interest in a suggestion such as leaning forward, it is usually time to begin closing the sale. Conversely, gestures such as a shake of the head or crossed arms tell a counsellor that there is still some resistance to be overcome.

There is no set time or point in a sales interview for a counsellor to introduce closing. It may emerge very early in a conversation or it may require a counsellor to go through every step in the sales process.

How to Close

The traditional strategy counsellors use to close a sale is to ask their clients if they may check availability. This is known as a trial close. This request forces the client to either agree with or object to the suggestion. Consent permits a counsellor to proceed with closing whereas an objection provides an opportunity to continue the conversation. This strategy can also help speed a client's decision, particularly if space is limited. If the product is not available, a client will often take a second choice rather than risk ending up without a holiday. Most offers of space involve an option date, a date by which the client must commit to the purchase by leaving a deposit. This makes clients aware that something suitable is available, that they must make the next move, and that they will suffer no financial loss if they decide to decline the offer.

A second closing method is known as an assumptive close. This techniques assumes that the client is ready and willing to buy the product; only the details need be finalized. It is characterized by the counsellor asking the client a secondary question such as "How will you pay, by cash, cheque or credit card?" or "Which date would you prefer?" Some counsellors use a variation on this approach which assumes that their clients can always afford the best; they sell from the top down. They might use as phrase such as, "I know it's important that you arrive fresh for your business meeting; shall I book first class?"

Some counsellors prefer to summarize the chief benefits before asking for the business. This review allows a counsellor to highlight the main sales points and relate them to specific views previously expressed by the client. It also provides an opportunity for the client to confirm whether the plans are suitable and for the counsellor to change or upgrade them.

A counsellor can occasionally use a special offer as an inducement to close the sale. For example, suppliers sometimes offer a price reduction if a product is purchased and fully paid by a given date. This incentive is particularly appealing to budget-conscious travellers.

At other times, the sales conversation comes down to one final concern or objection which threatens the whole process. Alert counsellors approach such situations by confirming with the client whether this is the last remaining obstacle. If a client admits that this is so, there is an added incentive for both counsellor and client to find a solution. If the issue can be resolved, the client has no other reason to prevent the counsellor from closing the sale.

Sometimes a counsellor cannot close a sale because the client has been offered too many options. However, this only occurs if the counsellor has failed to properly qualify the client during the process. The solution is to reduce the number of alternatives and thus simplify the client's decision. In general, clients should never be given a choice of more than three alternatives.

The simplest method of closing a sale is also the most direct. A counsellor may simply ask the client for the sale or booking. This can be an effective strategy but counsellors must be careful not to harm the progress made in the sales conversation. Asking a prospective client for a deposit can quickly close a sale or may cause the client to balk. However, asking for a sale too early in the process can result in an objection or a lost sale. Conversely, some counsellors fear rejection and therefore do not ask for the sale. Closing requires sensitivity to clients' reactions.

No matter how skilful or how experienced a counsellor is, there will be occasions when a closing attempt fails. However, the counsellor should never be the first to end the conversation. It is a counsellor's responsibility to persuade a client to purchase travel; it is the client's responsibility to accept or reject these overtures. Even if a sales interview is unsuccessful, a counsellor should remain pleasant and thank clients for their time and interest. If a client wishes to "think it over" rather than make an immediate commitment, the counsellor must be sure to obtain the client's name, address and telephone number. Most prospects do not object to giving this basic information, especially if the counsellor explains that it is required to make a reservation. The counsellor should then follow up the prospect within 48 hours or at a prearranged time. A telephone call can quickly ascertain whether the client needs additional information or alternative recommendations. Such a follow up indicates professionalism and displays a counsellor's personal interest in the client. If the client decides not to travel at the present time, the information gathered should be added to the agency's mailing list. This permits periodic follow up through newsletter or other mailings likely to be of interest. When the client is ready to travel, it is likely that the agency and counsellor that showed a continuing interest in the individual will be selected to make the travel arrangements.

Following Up

Following up when a client returns from vacation is an effective way of selling future trips. This personal contact can be just as important to a client as the first impression created by a counsellor. Some agencies send letters or evaluation questionnaires while others prefer the personal touch of a telephone call. Following up has several benefits. It lets a counsellor thank the client for the business and provides an opportunity to obtain feedback. These comments naturally help maintain a counsellor's product knowledge and develop further insight into the client. They also give the counsellor a chance to deal with complaints. Simply by keeping in touch, a follow up call maintains good customer relations by showing an interest in the client. This alone can promote repeat business. Counsellors can also maintain this relationship by calling to thank a client for new business referred to the agency, or to report on new tours, cruises or other holidays which might be of interest. Following up helps to build repeat business.

Telephone Sales

Many travel managers argue that the ability to sell by telephone is the most important sales skill required by counsellors. Agents report that the majority of business travel arrangements and about half of all vacation plans are made by telephone. Many counsellors sell almost exclusively by telephone; they rarely see their clients and use only the phone and an airline CRS. Selling on the telephone, or telemarketing, follows basically the same procedure as selling directly to a client in an agency. Clients must still be qualified, recommendations made, and objections overcome before a sale can be closed by telephone. The telephone has proven to be a particularly effective tool for the prospecting and qualifying phases of a sale.

Although the same sales procedure is followed, the communications process is different. A telephone conversation does not provide counsellors with clues such as gestures or other body language to interpret their clients' reactions. Words, voice tone and manner become more important in a telephone conversation and, to some extent, pacing or pauses replace gestures as nonverbal expressions of communication. Counsellors also have more difficulty controlling a telephone conversation since a caller can receive information and then simply hang up. It is more difficult to make an exit in person.

Many people make their initial contact with an agency through a telephone conversation with one of the counsellors. It is therefore important to create a positive impression which suggests efficiency, sincerity, courtesy, warmth and cooperation. Since telephone callers cannot see the counsellor, they form impressions of the counsellor and by extension of the agency solely from the words used and the manner in which they are spoken. When talking on a telephone, the counsellor is the company. The following guidelines will help create the desired impression and make selling by telephone easier and more effective. The suggestions apply not only to telephone conversations but generally to all speech.

If the voice is warm and friendly, courteous and helpful, customers will enjoy dealing with the counsellor and with the agency. Remember the person cannot see you or your smile. Every time you make or receive a call, your company is judged by your voice, by what you say, and by how you say it. A satisfactory voice is natural and pleasant to the listener. It should sound clear and alert. People rapidly lose interest if they cannot understand what is being said. It is therefore essential to speak distinctly. Similarly, an alert voice indicates that the speaker is interested in what the caller has to say. Enthusiasm is contagious and is a further indication of the counsellor's interest in the caller and the topic. However, enthusiasm should not be confused with increased speed. If a counsellor speaks too quickly, the listener cannot keep up and may not hear an important sales point. Similarly, a prospect who is given too much information in a short time will be unable to absorb it. Enthusiasm also implies expressiveness. Good speech has pleasant sound variations whereas a dull, monotonous voice stifles personality. Remember that a caller does not usually have access to a brochure or other reference material. Counsellors must therefore try to paint word pictures to help the caller visualize the feature or trip being contemplated.

Whenever possible, address the caller by name. This is the most effective way to give an impression of personal service and interest. Counsellors should maintain a professional manner but be careful not to be overly familiar. It is important to pay attention to the caller, particularly as the communication process is limited in a telephone conversation. One would not expect a counsellor to rustle papers or focus on someone else during a personal conversation. The same rules of courtesy apply in any telephone conversation. Thus, counsellors should resist the use of slang terms and technical jargon, which may confuse a caller, and expressions of impatience or annoyance. It takes only a few seconds to maintain customer satisfaction on the telephone by taking the time to be helpful. It may take months to restore an agency's goodwill if a counsellor is abrupt, discourteous or disinterested. Finally, a counsellor should always thank the caller before hanging up.

Since a prospect's words and voice tone convey a message in the same way as do a counsellor's, it is equally important for a counsellor to be a good listener. Counsellors cannot change a client's negative reaction if they do not know it exists. A short pause after each sales point permits the prospect to catch up and allows the counsellor to gauge the reaction. If the caller does not ask a question or make a comment, the counsellor should ask a question or encourage an opinion. Listening not only shows respect, it also helps determine whether the client actually heard what was said and its effect. Listening also

indicates what else a counsellor might say to develop the sales process.

When using a telephone the mouthpiece should be about one half inch from the speaker's lips. Greet the caller pleasantly, and identify yourself and the agency. Be sincere and enthusiastic, but be yourself. Talk as though you were face to face with the person calling. Telephone enquiries should be treated in the same way as a walk-in client. A counsellor should ask the five basic qualifying questions. A simple way to obtain this information by telephone is to offer to send the caller relevant literature. Further qualifying questions will reveal the type of prospect who is calling. At the appropriate moment in the conversation, or in a follow up call soon after, the counsellor should invite the caller to visit the agency at a specific time to continue the sales process. If the caller is making a reservation, the counsellor will require additional information to complete the booking. The caller should be asked for an address and for home and business telephone numbers. The counsellor will also need to know how the client will pay for the trip, and whether the documents will be picked up at the agency or delivered to the client.

A common complaint on telephone technique is the use of the hold button. Most people dislike being put on hold (just ask a counsellor who is trying to reach an airline or tour operator), however, this is sometimes unavoidable. If a caller must be put on hold, the counsellor should first ascertain whether the client wishes to wait, wants to leave a message, or would prefer to receive a return call. Surveys indicate that people become restless after waiting about 17 seconds. Counsellors (or someone in the agency) should therefore check with callers frequently to reassure them that they have not been "forgotten" and to determine whether they still wish to hold. If a counsellor is requested or offers to return a call, it should be made as soon as possible. This indicates that the client is important to the counsellor. Do not avoid returning a telephone call because the requested information has not yet been obtained. It is better to give a progress report in a return call than to avoid the client. Delays are irritating to most clients. If a client must wait, either in person or by being put on hold, the counsellor should make a sincere and natural apology before beginning the conversation.

Sales Success

The sales process involves similar steps whether a prospect makes a telephone inquiry or walks in to an agency. Further, all travel agencies sell basically the same products at similar prices. The only differences are the counsellors and the service or satisfaction they give their clients. Travel counsellors are therefore central to an agency's sales success.

This textbook has focused on the technical skills necessary for sales success; product knowledge and communications. Sales strategies and techniques have been reviewed. The technical basis of travel counselling means that sales people can be trained (or train themselves) to be successful. However, sales experts cite some personal qualities and characteristics that can help one master these skills. Good counsellors are friendly, self-confident and enthusiastic. They treat clients as important individuals, not as an intrusion or an irritation. Successful sales people never take an old client for granted. They talk about their clients' needs, wishes and objectives for travel, not their own, and they do so in a clear and effective manner. Successful counsellors choose their words carefully to avoid misunderstandings and offer concrete examples to clarify their meaning. They do not use technical jargon or relative terms such as "walking distance" or "nearby" which simply confuse clients. Keeping clients informed is also a part of good communication. Successful counsellors promptly respond to requests, reservations and trips, with answers, confirmations and follow up evaluations. They understand the importance of creating a positive first impression and recognize that they must sell themselves before they can sell a product. This is particularly so for travel products which emphasize image. A professional appearance, personal hygiene and good posture are essential to convey an appropriate image. Neither do good counsellors forget the importance of the final impression; they always thank clients for their business. Between the first and last impression, they are tactful and conscientious. When they have no clients, professional sales people are self-disciplined and continue to maintain their skills through self-education.

Selling travel as a travel counsellor is a rewarding profession. Career success is based primarily on listening to clients' needs and on treating each person as an individual, rather than on exactly imitating the sales techniques described above. Develop your personal sales style by adapting these techniques to suit your personality and that of your clients. Sales success will follow.

Review Questions

1. What promotional strategies would be effective for a small, independent travel agency located in a community with a large number of middle-income, single apartment dwellers? Why?

2. Compare the different types of prospects.

3. Discuss the information needed to qualify a prospect. How does this differ for pleasure travellers and business clients?

4. Describe the typical stages in the sales process.

5. Describe closing strategies and occasions when each might be successfully applied.

6. How do the techniques used by a counsellor to sell on the telephone differ from those used in face-to-face selling?

References

The American Society of Travel Agents has produced a series of sales training videotapes and has two booklets, *Professional Travel Selling Skills* and *Market Research: Gateway to Profits* to help counsellors develop their sales and marketing skills. They are available from ASTA, P.O. Box 23992, Washington, DC 20026-3992, USA.

The Canadian Institute of Travel Counsellors offers two sales training modules through distance education. The courses, titled *Making the Sale* and *Maintaining a Diverse Clientele*, incorporate ASTA's training videos. Further information on these and other distance education courses are available from CITC, Suite 209, 55 Eglinton Avenue East, Toronto, Ontario M4P 1G8.

Cruise Line International Association likewise has sales training videotapes, titled *Principles of Professional Selling* and *Group Sales Made Easy*, which offer sound advice for selling cruises. The association also regularly hosts a series of sales training seminars throughout North America. Information can be obtained from CLIA, 500 Fifth Avenue, Suite 1407, New York, NY 10110, USA.

## Chapter 14

Administration

Chapter Summary

This text began by outlining the role of a travel counsellor in a retail travel agency. A professional travel counsellor was described as someone who could identify a client's travel needs and match them with an appropriate product. This ability demands both client knowledge and product knowledge. The sale of a suitable travel product to the client was proposed as evidence that this knowledge was being applied. However, a travel counsellor's job does not end when a reservation is made and a deposit is collected. Even after the client has paid the balance owing on the travel arrangements, the counsellor still has several responsibilities to fulfill. In this chapter, these responsibilities have been categorized as administration; however, they encompass more than the processing of paper and records. A travel counsellor's post-sale functions include not only the administrative aspects of processing sales, that is, the accounting and reporting procedures to be followed, but it also includes following up with clients, handling complaints and ensuring that the agency functions efficiently by using a proper filing system. A travel counsellor must also maintain a professional manner in all dealings with clients, colleagues, and suppliers. The topic of professionalism and how it can be maintained is therefore discussed. Every ending naturally seems to lead to a new beginning and to the future. For readers whose goal lies beyond the function of a retail travel agency employee, this manual ends with a brief discussion of some of the procedures involved in opening a travel agency.

Chapter Objectives
After completing this chapter you should be able to:

- Describe and use agency accounting procedures.

- Use BSP terminology.

- Explain the function of the Billing & Settlement Plan and how it relates to airlines and travel agencies.

- Organize documents for a BSP sales report.

- Prepare a sales report and an agency authorization slip.

- Recognize the different filing systems used in retail offices.

- File and maintain supplies of office materials, brochures and documents.

- Describe the need for time management skills.

- Receive a client enquiry, set up and maintain a client file.

- Identify the various office machines used in retail offices and describe their function.

- Maintain good customer relations.

- Handle customer complaints effectively.

- Describe the importance of professionalism and how it can be acquired and maintained.

- Identify some steps which can be taken to avoid litigation.

- Describe the functions of a trade association.

- List the major travel and tourism trade associations and identify their goals.

- Prepare a fam trip report.

- Describe the procedures to open a travel agency.

- Describe the process for obtaining an appointment from IATA and ATAC.

Profitability

The prime objective of any business is to make a profit. Travel agencies are no different in this regard. An agency cannot continue to operate without earning a profit, or worse suffering a loss. Either condition eventually leads to unemployment for the agency's counsellors. As a result, counsellors must be aware of the profitability of every sale.

A profitable sale is one in which the commission exceeds the cost of making that sale. Counsellors can ensure that their sales are profitable in any of several ways. Some are based on individual initiative while others are prescribed by management policies. Some of the ways to increase profitability are:

- Sell products that offer a higher commission rate. Some agencies have implemented this solution as company policy by selling only preferred suppliers. This reduces the choice that the agency offers the public but ensures that the agency earns an override commission rate.
- Upgrade sales by selling additional and/or higher rated services.
- Increase productivity. For example, many counsellors find that they can process sales much more quickly using an airline CRS. Not only do automated systems speed the research process, they also significantly reduce the time taken to issue airline tickets. These systems increase efficiency and reduce paperwork thus freeing more of a counsellor's time for selling. Although a given sale may not be more profitable, the larger number of sales that can be made in a day raises the agency's profitability.
- Set consultation fees. Some agencies assess consultation fees (which are sometimes waived if a sale is made). This not only discourages "shoppers" but also partially compensates counsellors for the time they spend with clients.
- Collect cancellation and service charges.
- Refuse to offer extended credit terms.

It is possible to eliminate unprofitable sales by other methods, most of which are matters of agency policy and thus determined by agency management. Although the methods may be beyond the control of an individual counsellor, it is the counsellor's responsibility to be aware of management policies.

There are occasions, however, when it is sound business sense to complete an unprofitable sale. For example, consider a counsellor's options if a client, whose company is one of an agency's largest corporate accounts, requests special services such as delivery of tickets on a low commission sale. The cost of performing these services may exceed the commission on the sale. However, should a counsellor refuse the client's request there is a strong possibility that the agency will lose the account. More likely, as this is a rare request by a major client, the agency would deliver the tickets and maintain its record of customer service and good customer relations. The sale would ultimately be profitable as the client is satisfied and the corporate account would remain with the agency. Another common example of an unprofitable sale is the processing of clients' frequent flyer plan benefits. These take time to arrange and yield little commission income to an agency. Again, however, most agencies will complete these arrangements to ensure their clients remain satisfied. In general, a counsellor should consciously process an unprofitable sale only as a service to a client.

Accounting Procedures

All travel agencies conduct financial transactions. These transactions must be processed and recorded in a specific manner, for both legal and financial reasons. The process of recording this information is called accounting. Accounting helps an agency to track its income and expenses. The difference between the two determines whether an agency makes a profit or a loss. The basic principle of accounting is that all transactions must balance. For example, if an agency collects a payment from a client, it must generally make a payment to a supplier. Accounting systems vary from one travel agency to another. Some use an automated process while others use manual procedures. Some systems are in-house, that is, all functions are handled by agency staff on the premises; others are external, that is, the accounting procedures are performed away from the agency by a separate individual or company that specializes in accounting. Some agencies expect counsellors to process much of their own accounting transactions; others employ a full-time bookkeeper solely for this purpose. No matter which system is encountered, a counsellor should understand standard bookkeeping terms and procedures.

The simplest way to explain standard bookkeeping terms is to analyze the transactions required to process a sale. The following example examines how a counsellor would process a simple FIT trip for a couple to Portugal. After consulting with the clients, the counsellor makes the following arrangements:

- Air transportation: Ottawa/Lisbon return $968 per person.
- Transfers: Lisbon airport/Ritz Hotel one way $19 per person.
- Hotel Accommodation: Ritz Hotel $89 per person per night double.
- Tour: Grand Tour of Portugal $1189 per person.
- Comprehensive Insurance: $105 per person.

The tour company confirms all reservations and the counsellor then calculates the costs. The couple is asked to pay the required deposit of $200 per person for the tour and $100 per person for the air transportation. Note that the comprehensive insurance must also be paid at the same time as the deposit. Once the agency accepts the deposit it acknowledges a commitment to the clients. In essence, a deposit formalizes the agreement made between the agency and the client. The counsellor then issues a receipt for the amount paid and gives a copy to the client. A **receipt** is a legal document acknowledging payment of money and protects both the client and the agency. It should provide a clear description of the goods or services purchased and the amount paid, as well as the date and details of the agency and client (names, addresses and telephone numbers). Receipts usually contain an identification or record number. The number of copies in a receipt varies depending on the system used by the agency. There are usually at least three copies; one for the client, one for the agency's client records, and one for the agency's accounting purposes. The counsellor or agency bookkeeper then forwards the appropriate deposit or payment (usually in the form of a cheque) to the relevant principals. Each principal in turn issues a receipt to the agency to prove payment. Just as the client's deposit represents a binding agreement between agency and client, the acceptance of this deposit by a tour company (or other principal) represents a commitment to perform the contracted services. A copy of these documents is usually placed in the client file which has been created for the trip.

After the deposit has been paid, the clients will generally have a period of time before they must pay the outstanding balance of the travel arrangements. Tour companies usually require full payment about six weeks prior to departure. Payment procedures, however, will be clearly described in the terms and conditions of the relevant reference used to sell the travel product. To ensure that the clients meet their obligations, the counsellor sends them an invoice in advance of the due date. An **invoice** is an accounting document that is the opposite of a receipt; it indicates that a payment is owed. It contains similar basic information as a deposit (agency and client details, date and an identification number). The invoice describes the booking, notes the total cost of services less any deposits paid (if applicable), and identifies the balance due from the client. To keep the client's account in proper order it is imperative that the invoice be checked for accuracy. An invoice that overcharges a client is embarrassing to the counsellor and can be annoying to the client. An under-collection is equally embarrassing for the counsellor and, if irreversible, unprofitable for the agency. Again, one copy is sent to the client, one retained in the agency's client file, and one copy sent to the accounting department. An invoice clearly shows the client what services have been reserved and the cost of these services. It also lets the agency know what has been done and the income to expect. The contents of an invoice generated for the FIT client would be similar to that shown in Figure 14.1.

The details of the deposit received need not be itemized as these will have been described on the original receipt. There is a credit (or plus balance) of $810.00 in the client's account with the principal. Typically, the deposit collected equals the deposits required by the travel principals according to the terms of the brochure or tariff. Thus the agency's client account has neither a credit nor debit (negative balance). If the deposit collected by an agency exceeds the deposits remitted to travel principals, the client has excess funds in the agency's client account which will be applied to the balance of the arrangements. If an agency collects insufficient funds to cover necessary deposit payments, the agency's client account will have a debit balance. This is unprofitable to the agency as a counsellor or bookkeeper must now use agency funds to cover the client's deposit. This is risky because it creates a negative cash flow position for the agency. In addition, the client may cancel the

arrangements and the deposit paid with agency funds may be irretrievable. Let us assume that in this case the deposit collected is equal to the necessary disbursements and proceed.

The client must pay the balance of the travel arrangements on or before the due date on the invoice (see Figure 14.1). When this amount is collected by the agency, the counsellor will mark the invoice "paid" and return it to the client. Alternatively, some agencies issue a receipt for this payment and include the invoice number as a reference. The formats of invoices and receipts, as well as the procedures used to process them, vary from one agency to another (see Figure 14.2).

The counsellor or bookkeeper is then ready to calculate and retain the appropriate commission, make the final payment to the principals, and close the accounting segment of the client's file. The disbursement to the tour company is calculated as follows:

FIGURE 14.1
Sample invoice.

ABC Agency, 4567 Rideau Canal Boulevard, Ottawa, Ontario K2Z 2Z9
Telephone: (613) 555-1234

Mr. M. Parliament   Invoice #: X90123
123 Laurier Boulevard   Date: May 15, 1990
Ottawa, Ontario
K1X 1X0

Re: Air Transportation to Lisbon via Air Lisboa APEX Fare

Depart Aug. 1 Return Aug. 13	2 @	$968.00	$1936.00
Transportation Tax	2 @		$40.00
80.00			
Transfers Lisbon Airport to Ritz Hotel			
(Estoril Transfer Service)			
Return Trip Basis	2 @	$38.00	76.00
Accommodation for two nights, double basis			
including tax, s.c. and breakfast Aug. 2			
and Aug. 12 per person/per night	2 x 2 @	$89.00	356.00
Grand Tour of Portugal by Eurosol			
Aug. 3-12 Lisbon/Lisbon	2 @	$1189.00	2378.00
Comprehensive Insurance	2 @	$105.00	210.00

TOTAL FOR ALL SERVICES   **$5036.00**
Less Deposit Paid Including Insurance
2 @ $200.00 plus 2 @ $100 plus $210 insurance   810.00
BALANCE DUE ON OR BEFORE (DATE)   **$4226.00**

Saunders Travel Service Co. Ltd.
1859 Eglinton Ave. W.
Toronto, Ont. M6E 2J3
(416) 781-5596

RECEIPT #	№ 4350
RECEIPT DATE	
REFERENCE #	

PASSENGER INFORMATION:

SOLD TO:

COMPANY / PASSENGER NAME	ADDRESS	AGE (if under 18)	PASSPORT INFORMATION (Citizenship)
1.			
2.			
3.			
4.			

_____ Passport Required _____ Visa Required _____ Health Requirements

TRAVEL SERVICES PURCHASED:

DESTINATION	DATE	ACCOMMODATIONS
TOUR COMPANY		CARRIER (If Known)

BRIEF DESCRIPTION OF TRAVEL SERVICES: _____

Travel Insurance has been explained _____

Accepted ☐   Declined ☐

Bought From _____ Type _____ Premium

$ _____

Receipt of _____ By _____
(Cash, Cheque, CC)

Balance of _____
(Price could be subject to change)

TOTAL PRICE _____
(Cdn. funds unless otherwise stated)

PASSENGERS HAVE BEEN ADVISED OF:

(a) the fact that the instructing Person has the authority to book the travel services covered by the receipt on behalf of the named passenger(s), and to keep the agent advised of any changes of plans, or contact addresses:
(if applicable)

(b) a non-refundable counselling fee of $ _____ will be charged by the travel agent, separate and apart from the supplier's cancellation provisions.

SEE REVERSE FOR CONDITIONS OF SALE

The following brochure(s) have been delivered to the instructing Person:

1. _____ 2. _____ 3. _____

AGENT by his Authorized Rep. _____

THIS IS YOUR RECEIPT - CUSTOMER COPY

FIGURE 14.2
Some agencies use multipurpose forms which combine invoice, receipt and insurance waiver details.
Courtesy of Saunders Travel Service.

ABC Agency to Eurosol

Tour Cost 2 @ $1189.00	$2378.00
Less commission 10%	237.80
	$2140.20
Less deposit paid previously	
(Deposit receipt #A123)	400.00
Balance enclosed	$1740.20

The final payments for the other components of the travel arrangements will be similar, with the exception of the air transportation portion which is discussed below under BSP.

Calculating Commission

Commissions keep an agency operating and it is essential that counsellors accurately determine both the rate and amount of commission. Ensure that commissions are calculated on the total sales figure (before deposits have been subtracted) less taxes and service charges (on which commission is never earned). Whenever possible, commission should be deducted from the final payment and retained by the agency. This means instant earnings for an agency rather than waiting for the principal to return commissions due. It is a counsellor's responsibility to be familiar with commission rates and to communicate these to the agency accounting staff.

Calculating Refunds

Cancellations often occur and these can happen for many reasons. If any of the travel arrangements involve cancellation penalties, the travel principal may impose fees on the client and deduct them from the refund made. Refunds are not made directly to the client, however, but instead are forwarded to the agency to reimburse the client. If no cancellation fees are involved, the amount refunded to the client will be the full amount paid; either the deposit, or the total cost of the arrangements if full payment was made. The agency receives no commission as it is recalled. Consider the procedure if the couple in the above example cancel their trip to Portugal after final payment has been made. Assume that the deposit of $200.00 per person was retained by the tour operator as a cancellation fee.

Eurosol to ABC Agency

Tour Cost $1189.00: Commission 10%

Amount paid by	
agency for tour	$2140.20
Less cancellation penalty:	
2 @ $200.00	400.00
Cheque enclosed	$1740.20

ABC Agency to Mr. Parliament

Amount paid by	
client for tour	$2378.00
Less cancellation penalties	400.00
Cheque enclosed	$1978.00

The difference in the cheques ($237.80) is equal to the commission amount originally retained by the travel agency. Since all figures balance, all original accounting transactions must be accurate and the refund is simply a reversal of the original entries. If complete and accurate, the original information permits prompt handling of refund cheques from suppliers and subsequent cheques to clients.

A client's chief concern may be the return of funds paid to the agency. Quick and efficient processing of client refunds is therefore an important part of a travel counsellor's job. Cancellation is often caused by factors beyond the client's control. By receiving a refund without aggravation the client will be encouraged to return to book another trip. This response to the situation may recover part of the lost profit by ensuring repeat business.

If a supplier's cancellation penalties prevent a client from receiving a full refund, an insurance claim can be made to recover the balance of the funds provided that the client purchased insurance coverage and has a valid reason for cancellation.

Forms of Payment

There are several ways of paying for business transactions. The most common forms of payment for travel agency clients, however, are by cash, cheque or credit card. When clients pay by cash or cheque, it is the agency's responsibility to distribute the payments to the appropriate supplier. This procedure was described earlier. When clients pay by credit card, the agency's responsibility is to issue a credit card form. The client receives a copy of the charge form as a receipt. In some jurisdictions, however, it is mandatory to issue a travel agency receipt as described above. In practice, a counsellor must obtain authorization from the credit card company before a client can incur the debt. Suppliers are not paid directly by travel agencies for credit sales of their products. Rather, the supplier is paid by the bank that issued the credit card to the client.

Currency Conversions

Confidential tariffs and many other references used by travel counsellors display product prices in a foreign currency, either the local currency or U.S. dollars. Since clients usually pay for their travel services in Canadian funds, counsellors must be able to convert rates quoted in another currency to their equivalents in Canadian dollars. Accurate exchange rates can be found in the Friday edition of *The Globe and Mail* and in airline computer reservation systems. Foreign exchange tables often show two different exchange rates. Counsellors must be able to understand the difference between them and how they are used to convert currencies. One form shows the value of one unit of foreign currency in Canadian dollars. For example:

U.S. dollar: USD 1.00 = CAD 1.3734
British pound: GBP 1.00 = CAD 2.1847
Japanese yen: JPY 1.00 = CAD 0.016210

Note that these rates are used only to illustrate the calculation. Current rates must always be obtained from reliable sources such as those described above. To convert a foreign currency to Canadian dollars, simply multiply the price quoted in the foreign currency by the exchange rate given in the table.

Example 1. A city tour of San Juan is quoted at USD 17.00 per person. How much does the tour cost in Canadian dollars?
USD 17.00 x 1.3734 = CAD 23.35.

Example 2. The double room rate at the Drumrossie Hotel in Inverness, Scotland is quoted at GBP 62.50. What is the cost in Canadian dollars?
GBP 62.50 x 2.1847 = CAD 136.55.

FIGURE 14.3
Some common accounting terms.

Accounting Terms

Travel counsellors should be familiar with the following accounting terms:

Account	A record of financial transactions.
Credit	A balance in an account that shows an income, either earned or owed. It is a positive balance.
Debit	A balance in an account that shows a debt or expense, either paid out or owing.
Disbursement	Payment.
Invoice	An itemized list of services or goods specifying the price and terms of sale.
Receipt	A written acknowledgement of the receipt of money or goods.

Example 3. A single room at the Moriguchi Prince Hotel in Osaka is priced at JPY 8500. How much is this in Canadian dollars?

JPY 8500 x 0.016210 = CAD 137.79.

Exchange rates are also quoted in the opposite manner. That is, the rates do not express the currency in Canadian dollars as described above but instead quote the value of one Canadian dollar in foreign currency terms. (Again, rates are used for illustrative purposes only.) For example:

CAD 1.00 = USD 0.7281
CAD 1.00 = GBP 0.4577
CAD 1.00 = JPY 61.69

This type of listing is the converse of the previous one. In such cases, one divides the rate quoted in another currency by the exchange rate to obtain its equivalent in Canadian dollars. Using the same rates quoted in the above examples, the calculation is as follows.

Example 1. San Juan city tour quoted at USD 17.00. The rate of 17.00 divided by 0.7281 = CAD 23.35.

Example 2. Double room at the Drumrossie hotel priced at GBP 62.50. The price of 62.50 divided by 0.4577 = CAD 136.55.

Example 3. Single room at the Moriguchi Prince Hotel quoted at JPY 8500. The quote of 8500 divided by 61.69 = CAD 137.79.

Since one form of exchange rate is the inverse of the other, the type of rate can be easily converted. For example, if the rate is given in a foreign currency (USD 1.00 = CAD 1.3734) it can be converted to the other form by division. Thus, 1.00 divided by 1.3734 = 0.7281 and CAD 1.00 = USD 0.7281.

Bank Rates

Counsellors and clients also encounter two different exchange rates in their dealings with banks. The **bank selling rate** (BSR) is the exchange rate that a bank charges an individual who wishes to buy currency. For example, if a counsellor must purchase a foreign currency draft to pay a supplier or a traveller wishes to buy foreign currency traveller's cheques, the bank will calculate the currency exchange at the BSR. The BSR is higher than the official exchange rate to cover the bank's risk and administrative costs.

The **bank buying rate** (BBR), on the other hand, is the exchange rate a bank pays to a customer to purchase currency from an individual. For example, if a client takes Canadian dollar traveller's cheques to Britain and exchanges them in London, the British bank will use the BBR for Canadian dollars to calculate the conversion to British pounds. Similarly, if a client returns from a vacation with excess U.S. dollars and wishes to change them back to Canadian dollars, the rate of exchange will be the BBR for U.S. dollars. The BBR is lower than the official rate of exchange to again cover the bank's risk and administrative costs.

Thus customers lose money whenever they buy or sell currency from a bank. To limit the number of transactions, counsellors should advise clients to match their traveller's cheques with the currency of their destination. If Canadian dollars can be readily exchanged at a destination, clients can choose to buy cheques in either Canadian dollars or the local currency. Either choice will involve only one currency conversion. However, counsellors should encourage clients not to change too much money into local currency as funds that are not spent must eventually be converted to Canadian dollars. This will result in another bank transaction and a further loss of money.

Billing and Settlement Plan

Accounting procedures for recording airline transactions differ from those discussed above. A special system called the Billing and Settlement Plan (BSP) was implemented by IATA to process and report sales of air transportation on its member airlines. These accounting procedures are discussed in detail in the *BSP Canada Manual for Passenger Sales Agents* published by IATA. Any travel agency that wishes to sell international air transport for commission must be appointed by IATA and sign a Passenger Sales Agent Agreement with the association. Such appointed agents must follow a series of rules laid down by IATA. The most important rules (or resolutions) are printed in the *IATA Travel Agent's Handbook and Guide to Automation*. The BSP Manual is actually an attachment to Resolution 850 and covers the procedures that apply to Canada. These instructions include the correct entries for traffic documents (so that the processing centre can accurately calculate the net amount due) and administrative forms completion.

Before BSP was introduced to Canada in 1978, each airline supplied its own ticket stock to travel agencies. When a ticket was sold, the correct carrier's stock had to be used. Furthermore, agencies were required to submit a sales report to every airline with which it transacted business. The ticket formats and the procedures for reporting sales differed from one carrier to another. The result was a cumbersome and confusing system. BSP standardized and simplified the procedure. The new system introduced a single format for all documents, and replaced multiple reporting procedures with a single sales report to a central processing centre and a single payment to a central clearing bank. BSP has been extremely beneficial for travel agencies. It has allowed all agencies to benefit from computerized processing not only in terms of saving labour time, but it has also improved the ability of agency managers to analyze their sales and markets. Currently, about 4000 travel agency locations are on the BSP system in Canada. Three-quarters of these agencies use automated ticketing devices. Each year over 13 million transactions are processed through BSP.

The BSP process begins when an agency orders and then receives a supply of tickets and administrative forms. Travel agencies are responsible for the safekeeping and accounting of all traffic documents. When the inventory arrives, a counsellor must therefore immediately check that all supplies are received as outlined on the invoice. A register or other record of ticket numbers is maintained so that the agency can track them. Tickets should be issued in numerical sequence to facilitate record keeping. A ticket is issued each time air transport is purchased. As described earlier, the audit and agent coupons are detached and retained by the counsellor before the ticket booklet is given to the client.

Preparing a BSP Report

Although each agency generally designates one individual to prepare its BSP reports, all counsellors should be able to perform the operation. It is important to prepare the report in a location where there is sufficient space for the documents and where the individual can work undisturbed. There are several steps in the process. The following overview of BSP reporting procedures is not intended to replace the BSP Manual which is the official reference.

All airline sales must be reported to BSP each week on particular dates set by BSP at the beginning of the year. The reporting period begins on Monday morning and ends the following Sunday. An agency must submit its sales report to BSP for the period to arrive no later than 5:00 p.m. the following Wednesday. If an agency does not comply with BSP reporting deadlines it may be declared in default and all ticket stocks and other BSP materials removed without notice. Shortly after the end of a reporting period, usually on the following Monday, each agency prepares its sales report. This report summarizes all cash and credit sales, refunds, exchanges, and other relevant transactions.

Compile Documents

The first step in the process is to gather the audit coupons from airline tickets sold during the reporting period and separate them into two groups: manual four-coupon and OPTATs. Place each group in numerical order according to the ticket number and verify that none are missing. Airline tickets should be issued in sequence and all must be reported. Generally, these groups of audit coupons will therefore contain some which have been voided. The person preparing the report should next inspect the audit coupons to ensure that the commission and destination boxes have been completed. The former ensures that the agency will receive prompt payment for the commissions earned and both contribute information to sales summaries which are provided by BSP to each agency. If everything is in order, the documents are then separated and reassembled in two batches according to the form of payment. (Voided tickets are kept in a separate pile.) Although the tickets need not be retained in numerical order, such an arrangement helps to locate specific documents if there are questions on a sales report at a later date. One group contains all tickets paid by credit card while the other is for those paid by cash. Cash is a form of payment other than a credit card. It includes traveller's cheques, cheques and certified cheques. All other relevant documents should be gathered and assembled in a similar manner. These documents include audit coupons from all traffic documents (such as MCOs), credit card charge forms, and agency debit and credit memos.

Calculate Sales Totals

The BSP Manual not only specifies the contents of a sales report, but also indicates the order in which these items must be submitted. Credit sales are placed before cash sales in the completed report and therefore counsellors are advised to follow this order when preparing the parts of a report.

Total credit sales are determined by adding the amount in the total box (fare plus applicable taxes) of all audit coupons in the credit sales group. BSP requires that a paper tape record of this addition

be included with the report. Such a record provides a useful means of checking for errors. In addition to the audit coupons from tickets, there may be coupons from ticket exchange notices for additional collections paid by credit. All such amounts are added on the tape. Similarly, any credit card refunds are deducted on the tape. The final amount is the total for credit sales. As a check that this figure is correct, the counsellor must prepare a second tape. On the second tape the amount in the total box on each credit card charge form is added and credit card refunds should be deducted. The total on this second tape must be the same as on the first tape to ensure that the credit sales are in balance. If the totals are in agreement, the words "Credit Sales" are written at the top of each tape. The agency's name, address, IATA code number and authorization number, and the date when the reporting period ends are also entered on the tape. The tapes and supporting documents are then banded together.

A similar process is followed to determine the cash sales total. Ticket sales are again calculated first by adding the amount in the total box of all audit coupons paid by cash. Refunds, debit and credit notes, agency underpayments, and the like are listed below the ticket sales. The amounts for additional collections paid by cash, debit memos and recall commission statements are added on the tape. Cash refunds, credit memos and authorization shortage notices are deducted on the tape. The amount of any sales summary adjustment notice will be added or subtracted depending on the circumstances. Note that the cash sales tape not only includes the amounts from tickets paid by cash, but also any other payments which an agency must make to BSP, such as for shortages in previous sales report calculations. The process is then repeated on a second paper tape to verify that the total sales figure is correct. If the two totals agree, the calculation is likely to be accurate. One tape is marked "Cash Sales" and completed in the same manner as the credit sales tapes. Similarly, the tape and supporting documents are banded together. The second tape is attached to the agency's batch of agent's coupons and kept as an office record.

Calculate Authorized Amount

The next step in the process is to calculate the amount that will be withdrawn from the agency's account to cover all sales for the reporting period. This is a two-part process. First, the total on the credit sales tape is added to the total on the cash sales tape. The total sales figure is then multiplied by 0.06 and the resulting product deducted from the cash sales total. The remaining figure is the authorized amount (see Figure 14.4).

BSP recognizes that agencies receive payments for cash sales which can be deposited in their accounts. Credit card charges on the other hand are billed directly to the client by the credit card company. However, an agency is entitled to earn commission on both types of sales. BSP testing indicated that a figure of six percent was a reasonable estimate of commission income from credit card sales since agencies must issue credit card refund notices. Since an agency actually collects the funds for cash transactions only, the six percent is deducted from the total cash sales amount to allow for commissions earned on credit card sales. Note that the authorized amount identifies the maximum figure which can be withdrawn from an agency's bank account. It does not affect the actual commission which is calculated by the processing centre. Adjustments are

therefore made and these amounts, too, are included in subsequent sales reports.

Assemble Report

A completed sales transmittal consists of various items which must be assembled in a specific order (see Figure 14.5). At the top of the sales transmittal materials are two copies of the sales report settlement authorization form. This form is validated in a ticket imprinter which reproduces the agency's information and report preparation date. The remainder of the form is completed by entering the last date of the reporting period, agency name, IATA number, authorization number, telephone number, and the authorized amount. The form must be signed by an authorized person. The types of sales being reported are also noted on the form (see Figure 14.6). The paper tape showing how the authorized amount was calculated is attached to the authorization form. These pieces are followed by the credit sales adding machine tapes banded to the credit sales audit coupons and supporting credit documents. Next is the cash sales adding machine tape which is banded with the cash sales audit coupons and supporting documents. Audit coupons of void tickets comprise the final group of documents. All materials are placed in an envelope and mailed or delivered to the BSP processing centre in Winnipeg to arrive by the due date. Agencies retain a copy of the sales report settlement authorization form for their records. Similarly, the agent coupons from all traffic documents issued are stored. Agencies also keep the agent coupons and all flight coupons from void tickets but destroy the covers.

BSP reporting as described is for an office with a manual accounting system. When a sales report is completed using an automated accounting system, BSP receives the actual amount of the tickets with the correct commission amount deducted. Instead of tapes, computer printouts are used.

FIGURE 14.4
An example of how the authorized amount is calculated.

Cash Sales	$18,045.95		$18,045.95
+ Credit Sales	9,577.50		
Less	$27,623.45	x 0.06	1,657.41
Authorized Amount			**$16,388.54**

444

BSP Processing

Once the processing centre is in possession of the agency settlement authorization, it acts as an accounting service for the carriers and travel agencies. It separates the documents submitted by each agency and distributes them to the accounting department of the particular airline whose CIP was used. The processing centre also advises the clearing bank of the authorized amount to be withdrawn from each agency's account to pay for the reported sales. This sum is then disbursed proportionately to the appropriate airlines. Since the sales authorization slip submitted with the sales report empowers the clearing bank to withdraw the specified amount from an agency's bank account, there must be sufficient funds in the account to meet this payment. If the account is not capable of paying the authorized amount, the agency is in default and all BSP materials and ticket stock may be removed without notice.

When an airline receives the documentation from the BSP processing

FIGURE 14.5
The order in which a BSP report must be assembled.
Source: IATA.

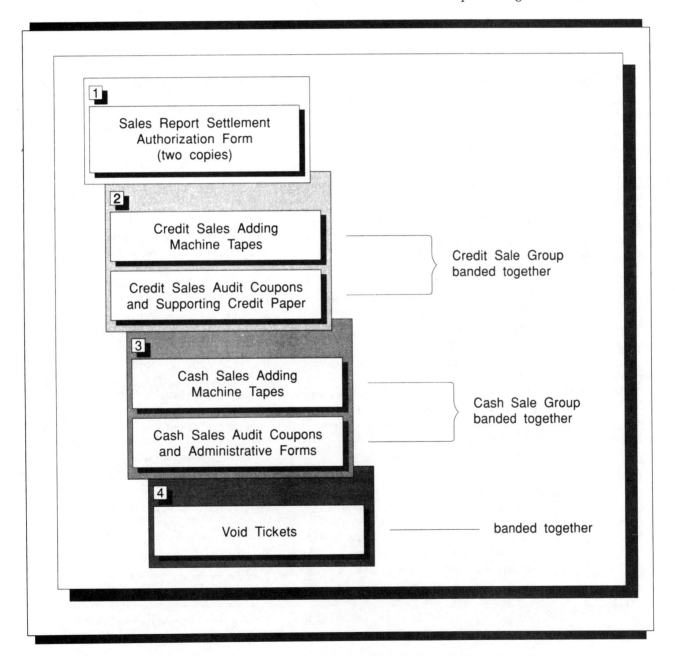

445

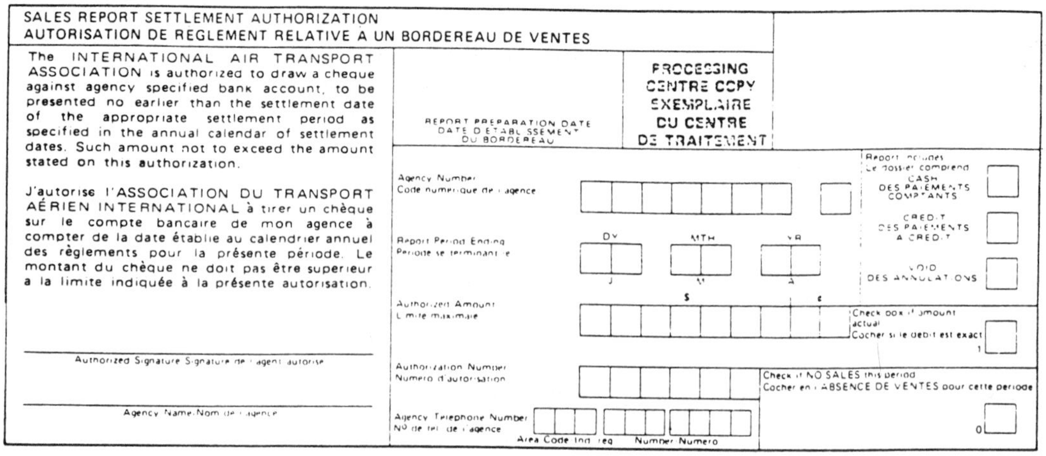

SALES REPORT SETTLEMENT AUTHORIZATION
AUTORISATION DE REGLEMENT RELATIVE A UN BORDEREAU DE VENTES

The INTERNATIONAL AIR TRANSPORT ASSOCIATION is authorized to draw a cheque against agency specified bank account, to be presented no earlier than the settlement date of the appropriate settlement period as specified in the annual calendar of settlement dates. Such amount not to exceed the amount stated on this authorization.

J'autorise l'ASSOCIATION DU TRANSPORT AÉRIEN INTERNATIONAL à tirer un chèque sur le compte bancaire de mon agence à compter de la date établie au calendrier annuel des règlements pour la présente période. Le montant du chèque ne doit pas être superieur a la limite indiquée à la présente autorisation.

Authorized Signature Signature de l'agent autorisé

Agency Name Nom de l'agence

REPORT PREPARATION DATE
DATE D'ETABLISSEMENT
DU BORDEREAU

PROCESSING
CENTRE COPY
EXEMPLAIRE
DU CENTRE
DE TRAITEMENT

Agency Number
Code numerique de l'agence

Report Period Ending
Periode se terminant le

DY J | MTH M | YR A

Authorized Amount
Limite maximale

$ ¢

Authorization Number
Numero d'autorisation

Agency Telephone Number
Nº de tel. de l'agence

Area Code Ind. reg. Number Numero

Report includes
Le dossier comprend

CASH
DES PAIEMENTS COMPTANTS

CREDIT
DES PAIEMENTS A CREDIT

VOID
DES ANNULATIONS

Check box if amount actual
Cocher si le debit est exact 1

Check if NO SALES this period
Cocher en l'ABSENCE DE VENTES pour cette periode 0

FIGURE 14.6
A sales report settlement authorization form must be completed for each BSP report.
Source: IATA.

centre, its accounting personnel review the coupons submitted to verify that the correct fares were charged. Agencies that have charged incorrect amounts receive an adjustment notice from the carrier for a refund or an additional payment. A carrier receives all coupons which have been validated on its CIP because the airline whose CIP is used is responsible for all administrative and commission costs involved in processing a ticket. However, other carriers frequently transport passengers holding a ticket which is not validated on its own CIP. To receive payment for this service, a carrier must send its flight coupons to the accounting department of the sponsoring airline.

Within two weeks of submitting a sales transmittal, each agency receives a Travel Agent Sales Summary Report (Figure 14.7). This is a computer printout of its sales that lists each transaction including void tickets, and provides summaries of the total sales, fares, commission, cash and credit sales, sales by airline, and various other analyses. Agencies also receive a monthly summary of sales (fares and commission) by destination, a summary by airlines, and month and year to date totals. These reports are an extremely important part of an agency's accounting records. They can be used for comparisons against previous year's sales, for marketing trends, to anticipate busy times of the year, to assist with staff planning for busy periods, and to identify overall sales figures.

Handling Refunds

It was noted that cash refunds are processed through BSP by completing a cash refund notice and listing the amount as a credit on the cash sales summary tape. An agency can make an immediate refund to the client for a cash sale and then simply deduct this amount directly from the sales report. Credit card refund transactions, however, are handled in a different manner. The client simply has the refund amount applied as a credit on the next credit card statement while the agency must complete a credit card refund form. When BSP receives this form, it is sent to the responsible airline. Since the sale was cancelled, the agency must return the commission on the original ticket. The refund amount is then listed as a debit on the cash sales paper tape for the next reporting period.

Filing Systems

Travel agencies and their staff are constantly at risk of being overwhelmed by the daily flood of information they receive. In addition to regular mail, agencies receive trade papers, brochures, flyers, destination announcements, supplier information, tariff bulletins, client confirmations, accounting forms and a host of other material. Each type of information is treated differently but all must be sorted and either distributed or filed for future use. As with an accounting system, each agency selects its own filing procedures. Although no single filing system can possibly meet the needs of every travel agency, any suitable arrangement must possess the following qualities:

- Easily accessed by all personnel.
- Readily apparent order that permits information to be quickly located and retrieved.
- Efficient use of available space.
- Separate file sections for brochures storage, accounting records, client files, and other categories.
- Regularly maintained so that information is current.

Some agencies assign one particular individual the responsibility of organizing and maintaining the office filing system. However, all counsellors must be familiar with the procedures used. Most offices arrange materials in two main categories; supplies and storage files. As a rule, filing should be completed as soon as possible after the information arrives in the office. It is not only easier to file a small amount of material daily, but this approach also helps ensure that files remain current. To guarantee that the system is up-to-date, excess and outdated material must be discarded immediately. For example, supplier brochures should be replaced each time a new season's brochure is issued. Some agencies, however, maintain historical files of older material for reference purposes. A filing system's effectiveness is improved by regular

FIGURE 14.7
An example of the type of sales information which agencies receive from BSP.
Source: IATA.

TRAVEL AGENT SALES SUMMARY

INTERNATIONAL AIR TRANSPORT ASSOCIATION — ASSOCIATION DU TRANSPORT AERIEN INTERNATIONAL

9740 418288 0912   69 84840 2 XYZ TRAVEL LIMITED   514 555 6960   07 SEP 80 18 SEP 80   1.70   1

11	12	13	14	15	16	17	18	19	20	21	22	23	24
016	3016273865 3			50.00	92	50.00	VC	.00					50.00
015	3059479627 1			800.00	92	800.00	VC	85.00-					715.00
016	3016273865	1		EXCH									
014	3352341234 6	3		461.00	91	450.00	8.00	36.00-		4.00	3.00	US	425.00
227	3352341404 6			236.87	91	222.87	7.00	15.60-		9.00	6.00	XD	221.27
081	3468124355 2		Q1	1,682.43	8	1,674.43	10.00	167.44-	8.37	3.00			1,523.66
081	3658124356 3	34		CONJ									
018	3458124357 4		C	602.85C	2	594.85	8.00	47.59-		3.00			47.59-
	3468124358 5			VOID									
001	3468124359 6			.00		.00		.00					.00
001	3442126993	1234		EXCH									
014	3468124360 0			750.00	62	736.00	10.00	73.60-		8.00	6.00	XT	676.40
	3468124361 1			VOID									
018	3468124362 2		N	120.00-C	41	120.00	8.00	9.60-					9.60
018	3451137611	34		EXCH									
007	3468124363 3			22.00-	9	22.00-	7.00	1.54					20.46-
007	3246118293	12		EXCH									
026	3452937860	1234		860.00-	81	849.00-	10.00	84.90		8.00-	3.00-	US	775.10-
00	0 51234567 4			ADJ	12								18.50
01	0 72139312 1			ADJ	31								127.65-
01	0 40087360 4			ADJ									7.66
00	0 30045007 4			ADJ									2.92
	0 35007170 0			ADJ									269.00
AGENT TOTALS				3,581.15		3,537.15		329.19-	8.37	12.00	12.00		2,962.09

AGENT SETTLEMENT RECONCILIATION

64 TOTAL FARES	3,537.15
65 TOTAL TAXES	44.00
66 TOTAL SALES	3,581.15
67 LESS CREDIT SALES	482.85-
68 LESS COMMISSIONS	329.19-
ADJUSTMENTS	184.61
49 PENALTY CHARGES (LATE REPORTING)	8.37
50 NET REMITTANCE DUE	2,962.09
51 AUTHORIZED NO 123456 AMOUNT	3,315.20
51B 1st DRAFT	2,962.09
2nd DRAFT	.00
52 REFUND AMOUNT	.00
53 SHORTAGE NOTICE AMOUNT	.00

AGENT TAPE RECONCILIATION

54 TOTAL CASH SALES	3,036.30
55 ADJUSTMENTS	184.61
56 TOTAL CASH AMOUNT	3,282.91
57 AGENT CASH TAPE AMOUNT	3,282.91
58 CASH DIFFERENCE	.00
59 TOTAL CREDIT SALES	482.85
60 AGENT CREDIT TAPE AMOUNT	702.85
61 CREDIT DIFFERENCE	220.00

updating. In addition, obsolete information is useless and can lead to problems.

Different types of information are generally filed in different ways. However, most divisions tend to be filed alphabetically. For example, destination information is typically arranged by area or continent and then sorted alphabetically by country within each category. Brochures of tour operators servicing these destinations are also placed in the appropriate file but usually in a separate section. Agencies sometimes create tour operator files. Each file contains one copy of all of the company's brochures and other relevant information. Some agencies build additional tour files such as those based on types of tour, types of transport used, types of activity, special interests, and themes. The variety of ways in which tour and destination information can be filed means that most agencies have duplicate copies of the materials. This system has the advantage that references can be quickly located no matter how a client poses a question. For example, a client may inquire about a particular company's tours, ask about ski tours, or may wish to know about a winter vacation in Switzerland. No matter how the inquiry is phrased, a counsellor will most likely be led to the same brochure. The disadvantage of multiple filing categories is that it is more difficult to ensure that brochures in all categories match and are current. Whenever a counsellor updates a brochure in one section, all other file divisions must also be checked. If a filing system is too complicated, discrepancies are more likely to occur.

Tariffs are generally filed in a central area where counsellors can easily reach them. Rate sheets from individual carriers are commonly filed alphabetically by airline. Amendments to tariffs and rate sheets must be filed immediately to ensure that counsellors quote fares accurately.

By law, accounting records must be kept for a specific period of time. These records consist of the agent's copy of traffic documents and vouchers, invoices,

receipts and cheques. BSP forms are handled as described earlier. Other records are usually filed in numerical order. If an agency retains an external accountant, most records are stored at the accountant's office. Only the most current information will be kept on the agency's premises.

Client Files

The most important set of files for counsellors are the client files. A client file is a comprehensive record of all the transactions made on behalf of the client. At the minimum it contains a single booking form recording the details of the client's arrangements. A client file, however, can consist of several additional items such as notes made from conversations with the client, suppliers and reservations agents, fare calculations, references checked, and copies of vouchers and other documents issued. Client files must be absolutely clear so that other counsellors can understand all transactions should it be necessary for them to deal with the client.

Client booking forms vary in both content and format depending on the agency (see Figure 14.8). A good booking form has clear headings and sufficient space to record the necessary details. It generally contains sections for entering booking information, reservation status, the name of the reservations agent, and confirmation numbers. There will also be an area to note payments and collections. It must be accurately and legibly completed so that any other counsellor can read and interpret the information.

There are at least two categories of client files; active and inactive files.

Inactive files require no further work. The clients have already returned from their trip and all accounting and other procedures have been completed. These records are usually kept on file for about three years and then discarded. They are used to develop mailing lists for promotions and newsletters, and for agency sales and marketing analyses. Inactive files are usually stored

BOOKING SHEET

DATE	AGENT	INVOICE NUMBER	RECORD LOCATOR	CLIENT NUMBER

PASSENGERS	AGE	HOME PHONE	BUSINESS PHONE
		ADDRESS	
		PASSPORT	
		VACCINATION	
		VISA	
		INSURANCE	

CITY FROM	TO	CARRIER	FLIGHT	CLASS	DATE	TIME DEPART	ARRIVE	DATE	STATUS	SIGN	AMOUNT

HOTEL / CAR RENTAL	CITY / LOCATION	IN	OUT	NIGHTS	RATE	STATUS	SIGN	AMOUNT

SPECIAL REMARKS:

AMOUNT	$
AIR TAX	$
HOTEL TAX AND SERVICE CHARGE	$
INSURANCE	$
OTHER	$
TOTAL AMOUNT.	$
DEPOSIT PAID	$
BALANCE DUE	$

FARE BASIS _____

TICKET # _____

TICKET # _____

TICKET # _____

INSURANCE OFFERED CLIENT

☐ DECLINED

☐ ACCEPTED

_____ INITIALS

METHOD OF PAYMENT:
☐ CASH   ☐ CHEQUE   ☐ CREDIT CARD

NO. _____

TYPE _____ EXP. DATE _____

Product 3019 Available from NEBS Ltd . Midland ON L4R 4V9

FIGURE 14.8
A sample booking form. The format of such forms varies from one agency to another.

alphabetically in a central file.

Active files are those of clients who have not yet travelled or that require additional work or information. Client files may be further divided into business clients (companies) and vacation clients (individuals). These may be sorted in several ways depending on the agency policy or manager's preference. The most common methods are:

- Alphabetical by client or company name in a central file.
- By departure date in a central file.

Alternatively, counsellors may file alphabetically or by departure date but keep their own client files at their desk.

Processing Client Files

A client file is opened for each of an agency's individual or company clients. A new booking form is completed for each trip showing the relevant client and supplier information. Basic information such as the date the inquiry is received, requested travel dates, and customer name and contact details are entered on every file. As reservations are made, the specifics are written on the booking form. If applicable, due dates for deposit and final payment are noted at this time. Counsellors also insert additional information such as the documentation necessary, the method of payment and the insurance purchased or declined. On vacation files, counsellors note the date that tickets will be picked up. Commercial files, however, note whether (and how) tickets will be delivered and the file reference number. Once a client has completed a trip, the file is maintained in the active category until all accounting processes have been completed. It is then transferred to the inactive category.

In addition to client files that record travel details, there may be another set of client files that help counsellors build profiles of their clients. These files, often kept on index cards, are developed from an agency's inactive files and are used for marketing and sales purposes. As well as the standard information such as name, address and contact number, they may

contain information on a client's tastes and preferences, frequent flyer plan member number, credit card number and expiry date, and similar details. Such files not only speed the booking process, thereby increasing a counsellor's efficiency and professionalism, but they also help increase customer satisfaction by providing information which assists counsellors to better service their clients' needs.

Some agencies file correspondence separately from client files. An alphabetical system is generally used.

Automated agencies use the Passenger Name Record (PNR) built on an airline CRS as the basic client file. However, a manual file system is still necessary to hold other documents and information created in the process of selling travel. Similarly, counsellors in automated agencies can build client profiles on an airline CRS thus eliminating the need for index cards or corresponding client files. Airline CRSs also have a queue system to help remind counsellors when payments are due or tickets must be issued. This removes the need to record such items in a desk calendar.

Office Machines

In the course of an average day, counsellors may be required to operate a number of standard office machines in addition to the typewriter and computer keyboard needed to transact regular business. Although most agencies possess similar equipment, the particular model and manufacturer differs and so, therefore, do the operating instructions. When a counsellor starts work with a company, someone in the office usually shows the individual the particular techniques required.

As far as a counsellor is concerned, the most important piece of office equipment is the agency's telephone. These differ from home models in that they have the ability to hold and transfer calls, as well as other features. A counsellor must feel comfortable with the practical aspects of telephone use before competent telephone techniques can be exercised. The importance of these skills cannot be overestimated as clients often make their first contact with an agency by telephone.

Fax (or facsimile) machines have spread rapidly throughout the business community in a remarkably short period. These machines are part telephone, part photocopier and part computer. A fax machine works by scanning a printed message and converting this to a digital code which is transmitted over a telephone line to another fax machine. The receiving machine decodes and reprints the digital message. Faxes save time and money, and are simple and convenient to use. They are faster than many other means of communication and they reduce the chances of misunderstanding because information is printed. This electronic mail device has become an increasingly commonplace means of communicating with suppliers and clients.

In today's business environment it is imperative that travel counsellors become experienced in accessing the Internet. Many businesses and leisure clients prefer communicating via email. This fast and inexpensive tool allows communication anywhere in the world between agents, clients and suppliers. Professional travel agents can use the Internet to make reservations, research travel destinations, access travel information for their clients, print out pictures and/or descriptions of hotel rooms and ship cabins, and provide up-to-date travel reports.

Counsellors may also be called on to operate photocopiers, postage machines, calculators, cheque imprinters, videotape players, film projectors, and perhaps also an automatic coffee maker. Most people are familiar with how much of this equipment works. When a new machine is encountered, someone experienced in its use can be requested to give instructions.

Customer Relations

The travel industry is based on people contact. Travel counsellors must relate to and with other people every day. How well they do so, contributes in large measure to their personal satisfaction, their career success, and consequently to the success of their agency. Maintaining good customer relations really means communicating with clients. If counsellors cannot communicate effectively with their clients, then clients are likely to feel that the agency and its personnel are unconcerned with their welfare and satisfaction. The result is that those clients will eventually take their future travel business elsewhere. Such action has serious repercussions for an agency. Agencies only have two sources of business; new clients and repeat customers. Since a large part of developing new clients is selling them on the agency and its counsellors, it is easier to repeat a sale to an existing client than to find and convince a new one. Once a customer has been sold on an agency, that client is unlikely to look elsewhere as long as satisfaction is maintained. Thus, good customer relations and client satisfaction preserve an agency's client base. However, agencies grow by acquiring new clients. Some new business comes from the referrals and recommendations made by satisfied clients. If existing clients are not satisfied, there will be no such referrals. In addition, new clients who approach an agency based on a friend's recommendation are already partially sold on the agency and its services. This makes the counsellor's sales assignment easier. It is important that travel counsellors remember that career success demands more than knowledge and technical skills. Success also demands that counsellors practise good customer relations. These are determined by a variety of personal factors including appearance, ability to communicate, organization and time management, and attitude toward others.

The importance of creating a strong first impression and of developing sound communications skills was emphasized earlier. Sending clients on a trip with a positive impression of the counsellor is just as important as the impact of the first meeting. Counsellors can help to foster this view when clients visit the agency to pick up their tickets. This provides counsellors with an opportunity to check documentation, answer any last-minute questions, and generally ensure that clients are suitably prepared. Some counsellors like to review the complete itinerary chronologically and indicate when and where each ticket or voucher must be presented. This routine reduces the chances of misunderstandings and may help a counsellor to spot and resolve last minute problems.

Counsellors must develop strong organizational ability and sound time management techniques to cope with the constant demands and deadlines, and to keep the vast amount of information current and accessible. Without these skills, they are likely to be overwhelmed by their workload. Clients are likely to lose confidence in a counsellor they perceive as disorganized and unprepared. One way to develop time management skills is to make a record in a desk journal of all tasks to be performed on given days. Many counsellors prefer to use their computer terminal for this purpose. Daily obligations include assignments set by management, as well as action prompts such as dates when client payments are due or when tickets must be issued. These reminders of jobs to do eventually become quite routine. First thing each morning, a counsellor should review and add to the daily job list. The major challenge in developing time management skills is in setting priorities and following them. A counsellor's next step is therefore to rank the tasks according to their urgency. Some duties must be performed on certain days. For example, final payments are due on specific dates and BSP reports must be completed on given days. Such crucial assignments should be completed as soon as possible; they must, however, be concluded by the end of the day. Travel counsellors often have difficulty accomplishing their identified duties because of intrusions such as telephone calls and walk-in clients. Such interruptions contribute to the stress experienced by travel counsellors.

More important than the qualities of a positive appearance and strong organizational ability, however, is one's attitude to others and to one's work. Attitudes are formed early in life and can be extremely resistant to change. However, no other factor is likely to play such an influential role in one's career success and personal satisfaction. Improved customer relations leads to greater customer satisfaction and more repeat business. Two simple guidelines will help counsellors to strengthen their customer relations skills.

- Treat others as one would wish to be treated.
- Look for the positive rather than the negative in people and their behaviour.

These attitudes can be easily forgotten in the pressure of business and under the stress of personal problems. However, imagine a society lacking the common courtesies and social graces that lubricate the wheels of human relationships. A smile, a firm handshake, or a sincere word of welcome are simple acts that require little effort. However, they are priceless actions that distinguish a considerate, sensitive person from one who is self-centred and indifferent. Successful travel counsellors have the ability to overcome the daily pressures of their work and focus attention completely on the needs of their clients.

Handling Complaints

No matter how conscientious and careful a counsellor may be, things still sometimes go wrong and clients return to the agency to lodge a complaint. A counsellor's response to such complaints is determined largely by their nature and what the client seeks in the way of compensation. Some complaints are trivial while others are serious and legitimate. Some problems are caused by a counsellor's actions while others are totally beyond a counsellor's control. All complaints, however, must be treated in the same professional manner. How counsellors handle complaints is a reliable measure of their customer relations skills.

The first thing a counsellor must do is listen sympathetically to the client's story. No matter how minor the complaint, clients must be treated with respect. It is important not to interrupt and to let clients express the problem in their own words. Although a counsellor need not remain mute, it is counterproductive to argue, blame someone else or deny responsibility. Similarly, counsellors should not assume they are at fault or act defensively. Once clients have released their emotions, counsellors can ascertain the facts of the case and deal with them. It is helpful to take notes as the client relates the problem and as the discussion progresses. Counsellors should probe until they are satisfied they have all the information. Sometimes a complaint is registered as one problem but as the counsellor continues with the questioning, other facts are exposed and the real reason for the complaint becomes apparent.

Complaints tend to fall into a few categories. The complaint may be trivial, such as a comment that the people were rude or the weather was terrible. In this case, counsellors must be sympathetic and attempt to placate the client. However, no apology is necessary nor should responsibility be assumed. The counsellor's challenge is to be pleasant and then if possible turn the conversation in a positive direction (perhaps to the pleasures of the trip) before ending the discussion. Essentially, the counsellor must try to make the client leave the agency feeling positive about the counsellor's role or response to the affair.

Other complaints are almost as trivial, such as flight attendants were discourteous or the hotel room was drafty. Expressions of sympathy are again in order. However, if such complaints are repeated by several clients at different times, the counsellor has acquired a valuable piece of product knowledge

concerning the particular suppliers. Failure to act on this information by informing the supplier and refusing to book further clients until service was improved would be negligent.

Some complaints, however, are legitimate. Perhaps a hotel did not honour a confirmed reservation or a sightseeing bus broke down and no replacement was provided. Counsellors must recognize the seriousness of such problems, ascertain responsibility and attempt to resolve the situation to the client's satisfaction. If an error was made, it is essential that counsellors remain sympathetic, even if it was the client's fault (such as forgetting to reconfirm a flight or misreading a date). If the problem was caused by the counsellor or agency, then the error should be admitted and an apology made. Some form of compensation will most likely be required. Appropriate settlement can be difficult to determine since a client cannot truly be reimbursed for a spoiled vacation. If a choice is possible, for example, a refund or a discount on a future trip, counsellors should ask the client's preference.

Complaints frequently develop as a result of the negligence of third parties. They may be caused by suppliers or other situations that a counsellor cannot control. In such cases, counsellors have two choices. They can refuse to become involved and refer the client to the party responsible for the problem. While there may be some justification in this course of action, it is a poor example of customer relations. Alternatively, they can offer to help, perhaps by negotiating on behalf of the client. Counsellors should always ask clients to document such third party problems in writing. This has two purposes; it not only provides the counsellor with a detailed record of the circumstances, but it also verifies that the client is serious in registering a complaint. Those who do not feel strongly will simply not provide the required statement. Counsellors who approach a supplier on behalf of a client must try to find a solution that satisfies both the client and supplier. It is also important to act professionally with the supplier so that a positive agency-supplier relationship can be maintained.

Whatever the problem, every attempt should be made to ensure that it is not repeated. The simplest way to reduce complaints is to control the situations that cause them. Although this is not always possible, there are some steps which counsellors can take to lessen the chances that problems will occur. Some complaints result because a counsellor overlooks something. Such errors of omission can be reduced if counsellors make a habit of double-checking all reservations, calculations and documents. They can also be diminished by reviewing every detail with clients. For example, it is an error to assume that a client is aware of a requirement such as the necessity of a passport or the need to reconfirm a flight. Other complaints arise because of something a counsellor does. Such errors of commission are usually reported as client dissatisfaction with the supplier of the product. For example, a major source of complaints concerns the supplier information that counsellors provide to their clients.

Clients regularly recount that the information in brochures is insufficient, inappropriate, or changes. Cost and pricing issues such as hidden costs, complicated and confusing price structures, arbitrary pricing practices and price changes, are also cited. When counsellors hand a brochure to a client they must accept some responsibility for its contents. Counsellors can prevent some of these complaints from arising by carefully selecting the suppliers they sell. Other complaints occur when there is a mismatch between a client's expectations and the delivery of the product. This type of grievance can be reduced if counsellors are honest in their assessment of the products and realistic in the advice and suggestions they offer. This ensures that clients clearly understand the quality of the services purchased.

Client complaints can be valuable sources of information for counsellors. Each complaint reveals an aspect of the client and thus enhances a counsellor's knowledge in that domain. Similarly,

those who honestly report problems are valuable sources of information about suppliers and destinations.

It is important to document all complaints and to keep notes of all conversations with the client and suppliers. These should be retained in the client's file. However rare, client grievances sometimes end in court. If this situation does occur, the evidence will mainly be the client's recollections, the counsellor's memory and the documents in the client file. For this reason, it is important that counsellors explain the terms and conditions of the contract they make by purchasing a travel product. These are described in the relevant brochure, tariff or other reference source. Part of this procedure is to point out which companies actually perform the services and thus are responsible for the activities. Many clients think that the travel agency is the supplier. This misconception should always be corrected. When a counsellor names the tour operator, airline or other supplier that will provide the service, it is called **disclosing the principal**. Such a declaration is a feature of all business legislation, particularly of the travel acts which apply in some provinces. Similarly, counsellors must ensure that clients sign a waiver if they refuse an offer of insurance. Many agencies place all such information on a receipt which is given to the client (see Figure 14.2). This form identifies the relationship between client and supplier, states the agency's responsibilities, and often has a waiver or disclaimer noting that insurance was offered and declined. Such efforts will be documented in the client file and can be used as evidence to support a counsellor's case. Failure to document actions or obtain a client's signature will mean that the case is determined on the basis of each party's memory of the circumstances and on their credibility in the eyes of the judge. Judges have typically chosen to accept the client's rather than the counsellor's version in such cases. Travel counsellors have certain responsibilities as professionals. If they fail to meet their obligation to provide accurate advice and maintain proper records, a judge has little choice but to support the lay person's claim.

Professionalism

One definition of a profession is a vocation that involves advanced learning. On the basis of this description, there are many occupations that can arguably be described as professions. By extension, professionalism is defined as the qualities or typical features associated with a profession or its practitioners. These characteristics are more difficult to identify. However, certain qualities are recognized as depicting professional behaviour. The degree to which travel counsellors possess these qualities and how they express them reflects on their reputations and that of their agencies.

Honesty

The principle of *caveat emptor* (let the buyer beware) still holds sway in many sales industries. Travel counsellors who embrace this philosophy, however, deserve neither the label "professional" nor the title "counsellor". Professional travel counselling is based on what the client needs, not on what the counsellor wants to sell. A client makes an unstated admission merely by approaching a travel counsellor; "I don't know as much as you. I need your help and advice." Similarly, by agreeing to service that client's travel needs a counsellor assumes an obligation to find the most suitable product for the client. This relationship demands complete honesty. Travel counsellors do not deliver the products they sell. They simply make recommendations based on their perception of the best possible product for their clients' travel needs. A counsellor's ability to assess client needs therefore becomes a critical element in the process. This process contains an implied acknowledgment that the most suitable product may not be a perfect match. The recommended product may have some limitations. If a counsellor recognizes

such disadvantages, the client should be informed and encouraged to discuss alternatives. It is a counsellor's responsibility to guide clients through the promotional material provided by suppliers since the client relies on the counsellor's experience, contacts and knowledge.

Accuracy

Counsellors must be accurate as well as honest in their dealings with clients. Before quoting prices to clients, all calculations should be verified to prevent costly and embarrassing errors. Advice should be factual and information comprehensive. If a departure tax is assessed at the destination airport, clients should be informed to ensure that this does not come as a surprise. Clients must also be reminded of the obvious as well as the "small print" items. For example, counsellors should make sure that clients are aware of check-in times and locations as well as the need to reconfirm flights. Comments should be clearly stated and free of technical jargon and other terms that clients may misunderstand. The better that a counsellor can prepare clients, the more closely will their expectations match the services delivered. This reduces the chances of client disappointment and thus the possibility of complaints and problems.

Ethics

It is important for counsellors to maintain professional integrity in their dealings with both clients and suppliers. This means more than being honest and accurate; it means acting in an ethical manner. Ethics are the professional and personal standards that govern business interactions. Particular behaviour is unethical if it breaks the law, if it violates guidelines set by an employer or professional association, or if it conflicts with an individual's principles. Although the subject of ethics is extremely broad and open to interpretation, there are some common principles with which everyone agrees. The following examples provide an indication of the scope of the topic. It is considered unethical to:

Ethics: a code of morals or standards of a person or profession

un-ethical → things that go against guidelines set out by employer or professional association or against your own principles

CITC

- illegal

- Deliberately misrepresent a product to a client.
- Sell a product to someone who does not qualify, e.g., cannot afford the purchase or cannot obtain the necessary documentation.
- Recommend a product that benefits the counsellor rather than the client, e.g., to gain points towards a prize or a higher commission instead of to meet the client's needs.
- Disclose confidential information to clients, suppliers or others.
- Remove client files or client lists when leaving one agency's employ for another.
- Make duplicate reservations to prevent others from selling the space.

Some organizations, such as ACTA and CITC which are discussed below, have developed codes of conduct for their members (see Figure 14.9). Such guidelines help direct counsellors to the correct decision when faced with an ethical dilemma. Agencies are legally responsible for the actions of their employees and therefore they should provide direction through office policies and guidelines.

Trade Associations

Another part of being a professional is to make contact with others in the same field. Most people develop formal and informal networks to help them advance in their chosen career. Membership in professional and trade associations not only provides these links but often denotes a commitment to the chosen occupation. Such organizations are found in almost every industry and tourism is no exception.

A feature of many associations is that their members are typically competitors in the business world. However, an association's purpose transcends these differences and emphasizes the concerns shared by the members. Associations are usually formed to achieve a common purpose or to transact business which will be mutually beneficial to the industry and its members. Any collection of individuals or companies that experience common concerns, needs or regulations can benefit by forming an association. Some groups require a unified voice and numerical strength to make representations to government. Others associate for informational or promotional purposes. Trade organizations are the modern equivalent of the early craft guilds which were formed to protect the interests of their members. Labour unions, professional associations such as the Canadian Bar Association, and business groups like the Canadian Manufacturers Association are typical examples of the existing range of organizations. Trade associations deal with issues in specific industries and have three main purposes:

- Protection
- Promotion
- Information

Protection

Associations are formed to protect their members' interests. All associations therefore develop criteria for membership. These may be extremely liberal; for example, applicants must be interested in the association or particular industry to become a member. Or entry can be based on experience, qualifications, financial stipulations and other standards. This mechanism protects members by restricting entry to unqualified applicants. Some professions have attained legal recognition for their members such that individuals or companies cannot operate unless they are members of the association. For example, IATA's membership is restricted to scheduled airlines and travel agencies cannot earn commission from the sale of international air transport unless they meet the association's criteria. On an individual level, membership in a law society is a prerequisite for practising the profession. At this time, however, professional qualifications are not required to work in the travel industry.

Associations attempt to protect their members by soliciting governments to

FIGURE 14.9
The CITC Code of
Conduct.

CANADIAN INSTITUTES OF TRAVEL COUNSELLORS
INSTITUTS CANADIENS DES CONSEILLERS DE VOYAGES

CODE OF CONDUCT

I   Preamble

All members of the Canadian Institutes of Travel Counsellors shall adhere to the following Code of Conduct. By joining the Institute, each agrees to abide by the Code, and acknowledges that a failure to comply may lead to disciplinary action or termination of membership.

This Code recognizes that professional travel counsellors have responsibilities to a number of different people and groups, in the day-to-day course of practising their profession. It sets forth the general principles by which those responsibilities ought to be executed by a Certified Travel Counsellor.

II   Responsibility to the Public

The CITC Certified Travel Counsellor shall:
(a) Convey to the public the image of a competent professional;
(b) Maintain a high degree of knowledge, continually reconfirming existing abilities and acquiring new expertise, on his or her own, by taking advantage of upgrading resources available to him or her;
(c) Be honest, accurate, and display a high standard of integrity and objectivity when expressing opinions;
(d) Avoid exaggeration, misrepresentation, innuendo and all other unprofessional sales and advertising techniques; and
(e) Exercise due care and discretion in the choice of suppliers and their products within the parameters set by the employer.

III   Responsibility to the Client

The CITC Certified Travel Counsellor shall:
(a) Treat every client transaction as confidential unless authorized by the client to release information;
(b) Counsel each client accurately and impartially in accordance with that client's best interests;
(c) Advise clients of all relevant documentation and information, such as fees, taxes, cancellation charges, insurance policies, passports, visas, health certificates, and terms and conditions of travel; and
(d) Endeavour to advise the client of relevant facts relating to the destination or the services purchased.

IV   Responsibility to fellow CTCs

The CITC Certified Counsellor shall:
(a) Seek no unfair advantage over his or her fellow member;
(b) Share with his or her fellow member the lessons of experience and study;
(c) Treat his or her fellow member with the respect warranted by his or her professional status; and
(d) Refrain from doing or saying anything that could disparage the dignity of the profession.

V   Responsibility to Employer

The CITC Certified Travel Counsellor shall:
(a) Properly represent the employer in all matters;
(b) Abide by any formal or informal practices, policies, Manual of Office Procedures, dress code, or other such statement of principle by the employer;
(c) Shall obtain the employer's consent prior to using his or her position to gain advantage for self, family or friends; and
(d) Attend to his or her responsibilities in such a manner as to allow a fellow employee easily to assume responsibility of a file in the event that it becomes necessary.

VI   Responsibility to Suppliers

The CITC Certified Travel Counsellor shall:
(a) Comply with the instructions and procedures issued by suppliers with respect to the sale of their products, and meet his or her obligations to the suppliers;
(b) Abide by any conference regulations to which the supplier is bound; and
(c) Refrain from suggesting or making duplicate reservations or bookings, and shall release promptly all unsold or cancelled space.

New one given on 29 MAR 04.

acknowledge the organization's membership criteria and points of view. In addition, many organizations try to influence government to introduce, modify or repeal legislation affecting the particular industry. The creation of provincial travel legislation and subsequent amendments to these regulations are due in part to the lobbying conducted by various trade associations.

Membership in an association also helps protect individuals by providing strength in numbers. This permits members to speak freely and to support controversial positions which may arise.

Promotion

Associations promote their members' interests by advertising in the consumer and trade media. Since an association speaks for all its members, advertising is an inexpensive way for an individual member's views to be expressed. Sometimes advertising is simply used to publicize all members. Costs are borne by the organization from the revenue it generates. The membership's interests are also promoted when an association lobbies or negotiates on their behalf. For example, an association may push for legal recognition and political rights, demand better salaries and working conditions, press for higher commission scales, or seek more recognition for its members' services. Representation by an organization simplifies negotiations and strengthens the individual's negotiating position.

Information

An important function of an association is to inform members, the industry, government and/or the public. Associations meet regularly and publish newsletters to keep their members informed and to solicit feedback. Many associations also assume an educational role to ensure that their members' information is accurate and their skills current. Examinations, training programs and publications are some of the educational benefits offered to members. Industry visibility is maintained through trade shows, conferences, press releases and trade publications. Associations also communicate their views to governments through position papers and other lobbying activities. Regular media advertising keeps the public informed of the benefits provided by the association and its members.

Association Operations

Most associations are set up as non-profit organizations. This means that any surplus earned by the association is retained and used to benefit the membership. Revenue for association operations comes from membership fees, conferences, educational programs, publications and other items which the association considers appropriate to offer members. Some organizations generate income from social events, some sell accessories that members find useful in daily business operations, and others offer benefits such as insurance plans. Associations generally assess an annual membership fee which must be paid to maintain one's membership status. There may also be initiation fees. The cost of individual membership typically depends on the membership category and, for corporate associations, the size of the company (measured by sales or number of employees) and the number of branches.

Depending on the association's membership criteria and goals, the majority of associations have three main categories of membership:

active or full membership; allied, affiliate or associate membership; and other types of membership for special circumstances. Full members have a direct interest in the affairs of the association, such as travel counsellors in CITC, airlines in IATA, or travel companies in ACTA. As a rule, only active members can vote in association proceedings and be elected to office. Associate members support the association's goals and may benefit from its work but frequently are not eligible for full membership. They may be in the process of meeting the association's membership standards or they may simply not qualify for full membership. For example, the operations manager of a tour company may join CITC or a travel school may join ACTA. Some become affiliate members to develop a network of industry contacts. Other categories of membership are offered to suit a variety of circumstances. For example, an organization may create categories such as student member, honourary member or retired member.

Membership in most trade associations is at an individual's discretion; it is voluntary rather than mandatory. Furthermore, the non-profit nature of associations and their generally small revenue base means that they frequently rely on a few full-time paid staff and many volunteers to run the organization's affairs. Association policy is usually developed by an executive or board of directors elected by the membership. Typically, these too are voluntary positions although larger associations sometimes pay for the services, either directly to the individual or to the person's company, if considerable release time is required.

Many trade associations have been discussed at different points in this text. It is therefore unnecessary to repeat the information on the WTO, IATA, ICAO, ATAC, CLIA and the like. However, there are several others, each of which serves a separate community within the travel industry. Travel counsellors should have a working knowledge of their roles.

ACTA: Association of Canadian Travel Agencies

ACTA is a rather different trade association in that it represents different interest groups in the travel industry under one umbrella. It has achieved this by developing different groups of full membership for retail travel agents, wholesale tour operators, and travel service suppliers. Each group has an equal voice in the affairs of the association. ACTA is a corporate trade association; the company becomes a member rather than the individual.

More accurately, an agency, operator or supplier joins the local provincial association which in turn belongs to ACTA National. ACTA was created in 1977 and is based in Ottawa.

ACTA deals with government and international associations such as IATA and UFTAA. It is very active in the aviation industry and sits on a joint council created by IATA to deal with agency-airline relationships in Canada. ACTA encourages industry education and together with CITC established ACCESS, a body set up to standardize education and to offer professional credentials through examination and continuing professional education. ACTA sponsors an annual conference which is one of the Canadian travel industry's main events. The ACTA conference includes a large trade show and a number of seminars. ACTA also conducts promotional campaigns on behalf of its members and offers a number of other benefits. The association has a code of ethics which members agree to follow when becoming a member. The code governs the relations between members, and between members and the public.

CATO: Canadian Association of Tour Operators

CATO was formed in 1986 and is based in Toronto. The association consists of about twenty of the largest ITC tour operators in Canada whose specific concerns and interests caused them to band together. These companies account for about 80 percent of all tour packages sold in Ontario. Most, but not all, of the members also belong to ACTA. Since its inception CATO has worked closely with ACTA to develop a set of recommended practices for travel agents, tour operators, suppliers and consumers. Many of these suggestions were subsequently adopted by the Ontario Government when it modified the Travel Industry Act in 1988. The failure of a large tour company and charter airline in 1990 prompted the association to extend its efforts both nationally and provincially for changes to the relevant travel legislation.

CITC: Canadian Institutes of Travel Counsellors/Instituts Canadiens des Conseillers en Voyages

CITC represents the individuals who make a career in the travel industry whereas ACTA represents the businesses involved. CITC is a national organization composed of provincial or regional associations. It is similar to ACTA in that individuals become members of a particular local association whose representatives set policy for the national organization. CITC's national office is located in Toronto. Separate institutes serve British Columbia, Alberta, Saskatchewan, Manitoba, Ontario, Quebec and the Atlantic region. Historically, CITC was originally established in Ontario during the 1960s. The other associations were incorporated over the following years.

CITC focuses on the education and professionalism of travel counsellors. Prior to 1990, CITC administered a national examination and offered the CTC (Certified Travel Counsellor) and FCTC (Fellow of the Institute) designations based on education and experience. The development of ACCESS in cooperation with ACTA has strengthened the CTC/CTM designation and shifted CITC's activities towards training programs, instructional materials and conferences. The organization's main interest, however, continues to be the professional development of its members.

UFTAA: Universal Federation of Travel Agency Associations

Just as the United Nations offers a forum for the countries of the world, UFTAA provides the same opportunity for each country's travel trade associations. Thus ACTA and similar national associations belong to UFTAA. The organization's head office is located in Belgium. IATA negotiates travel agency commissions with UFTAA rather than separately with each national association.

ASTA: American Society of Travel Agents *Equiv y ACTA in CAN.*

ASTA was established in 1931 and, with over 20,000 members, is the travel industry's largest association. Whereas ACTA attempts to represent all facets of the Canadian travel industry, ASTA speaks only for retail travel agents. It promotes its members' interests to government, suppliers and the public, and tries to protect the travelling public through educational courses, home study programs and newsletters for its members. Full membership is available only to those travel agencies which meet ASTA's membership standards. These criteria essentially relate to the length of an agency's business experience and the duration it has held appointments from supplier associations. There is also an allied category of membership open to suppliers, hotels, tour operators and related companies.

ARTA: Association of Retail Travel Agents

ARTA is smaller than ASTA and has a different philosophy. It is solely an educational association of retail agents and offers no allied membership category. Full membership in ARTA is dependent on an agency's appointments but it has no requirement based on industry experience.

ICTA: Institute of Certified Travel Agents *Equiv CITC in CAN*

ICTA is an American organization whose goals are similar to those of CITC in Canada. The association has an educational program directed at senior counsellors and management personnel which leads to the designation CTC. Candidates must successfully pass examinations in four areas, present a research paper or seminar evaluation report, and possess at least five years' travel industry experience to gain the credential. ICTA also produces instructional materials and training programs for junior travel counsellors.

Area Trade Associations

Most of the organizations discussed above have memberships that are based on similar types of business or occupation. However, there are other trade associations that have been formed specifically to promote tourism to or within a specific area. Conventions and visitors associations are the most obvious example of this type of organization. However, larger regions also cooperate for the same promotional purposes. The best known in Canada of these associations are TIAC, ANTOR, ETC, PATA and CTA.

TIAC: Tourism Industry Association of Canada

TIAC exists to meet the needs of all suppliers to the travel industry in Canada. Any company that has an interest in Canadian domestic tourism may join. Its membership ranges from hotel chains to seasonal lodges and from international air carriers to small scale transportation outfits. Restaurants, banks, oil companies, souvenir manufacturers and a multitude of other companies associated with the travel industry have also joined TIAC. The organization is based in Ottawa and receives government financial support.

ANTOR: (Association of National Tourist Office Representatives)

ANTOR's membership is open to representatives of national and provincial government tourist offices. This group regularly gathers at informal meetings to exchange views on matters of mutual interest within the travel industry. ANTOR has over 60 members in Canada.

ETC: European Travel Commission

This organization was established in 1948 and is based in Dublin. The ETC is a more formal organization than ANTOR and comprises the 24 European national tourist associations. Its goals are to increase tourism to Europe through marketing activities, and to provide opportunities for members to exchange ideas and experiences. The ETC produces conferences, workshops and trade shows, and advertises in trade papers. It has operated in Canada since 1979.

PATA: Pacific Asia Travel Association

PATA was formed in Hawaii in 1951 to develop and promote travel to and within the Pacific Area. Any country bordering on the Pacific Ocean is eligible to participate in the association's activities. PATA's membership criteria are the most liberal of any of the trade associations discussed. Any individual, company or organization conducting business to or within the area, or interested in the association's objectives, may become a member. PATA is organized in a number of worldwide local chapters and has in excess of 15,000 members in over 60 countries. Each chapter's objectives and activities vary according to the interests of its members. However, all subscribe to the common goal of strengthening travel industry expertise through education and professional development. PATA regularly distributes a trade journal and is involved in marketing research, promotion, an annual conference, and regional trade shows called Patamart.

CTO: Caribbean Tourism Organization

CTO's goals are similar to those of other area trade associations. All Caribbean countries are eligible for membership. The CTO promotes the Caribbean region through marketing, information programs and educational activities.

Continuing Education

Continuing education is a part of being a professional and many professional associations demand that their members keep up-to-date to maintain their status. Few industries change as much or as frequently as the travel industry. This constantly changing situation places considerable pressure on travel counsellors and makes it essential that they continue their education. Some methods for doing so, such as attending courses, seminars and industry presentations, were reviewed in an earlier chapter. However, theoretical training alone is insufficient in the travel industry; it must be tempered with experience. ACCESS (ACTA/CITC Canadian Educational Standards System) was introduced in 1990 to meet this need. ACCESS certification at the counsellor level is acquired through a combination of an examination of theoretical knowledge, industry experience, and continuing education credits. A management level credential can be earned through further study. This system not only provides a blend of theory and practice, it also encourages counsellors to maintain their skills and knowledge.

Familiarization Trips

Fam trips are one of the best and most enjoyable ways for counsellors to continue their education. The topic of fam trips was introduced in Chapter 4 as a means of acquiring product knowledge. This section examines the subject more closely. A fam trip is a training device (in fact, sponsors now frequently describe them as educational tours) that can be turned into a sales tool. It is not a reward in the sense of a holiday although some managers use them as rewards for productivity. Most fam trips follow a standard format which comprises:

- Visits to several hotels to inspect their rooms and facilities.
- Visits to sightseeing attractions so that counsellors can acquire first-hand information for their clients.
- Meeting local industry representatives and residents in their own environment to discuss culture, facilities, shopping and the like.

Most suppliers are enthusiastic about fam trips as they raise counsellor awareness and increase bookings. Successful fams accomplish two

purposes; they acquaint counsellors with the product and they show the most effective way to sell it. Unless counsellors apply the knowledge gained during a tour by building sales, the experience will be worthless. Fam trips help to build a counsellor's confidence; they permit a counsellor to say "I've been there" and this can have a strong influence on clients.

Fam Trip Guidelines

Before deciding to participate in an educational tour, counsellors should study the itinerary to ensure that the experience will be beneficial and productive. The tour schedule should allow time to relax and absorb information. Tours that include too many attractions and inspections in a limited time simply overload and exhaust the participants. Fam trips should be judged on their educational value not on the pleasure they promise. There should also be sufficient opportunity to be a tourist and experience the destination as a client does. Counsellors on a fam trip will gain maximum benefit for themselves, their employers and their colleagues if they research the destination prior to departure. This provides a framework for the tour and may help avoid unexpected and unwanted surprises. Participants should also set objectives and prepare specific questions on the destinations, facilities and attractions to be visited. Before leaving check whether agency co-workers require particular information on specific hotels, tours, and the like. Many agencies set sales targets which are based on office rather than individual sales. If this is the case, it will pay fam trip participants to teach their colleagues how to sell a destination.

There are several tips which can enhance the educational value of a fam trip. The most practical suggestion is to wear comfortable walking shoes when making inspections. It is difficult to absorb information and be interested in the surroundings if one's feet are sore and tired. Counsellors should attempt to relate each of the destinations and facilities visited to particular target markets. Compare features with price to assess the product's value. How a counsellor personally feels about a destination, attraction or facility is irrelevant on a fam trip (although the reasons for these feelings often provide insights into how various client groups might perceive them). Since fam trips are offered only to destinations interested in attracting tourists, it is a counsellor's task to identify which destinations would appeal to different types of clients. Recognizing the features that make them appealing is the basis for selling the destination.

Ask questions and make notes rather than try to rely on one's memory. Incorrect information is worse than no information at all. Some counsellors record their tours on audio or video tape. A still camera can also be useful, particularly a polaroid which allows an individual to immediately note the location and assessment. Experienced counsellors often take along the relevant tour brochures, deck plans and other sales material in which additional notes can be made. These can be particularly useful for inspections of cruise ships. If high activity areas (e.g., near steps and dining rooms) are highlighted in one colour and quiet areas (e.g., reading rooms) in another colour, it is easy to see which cabins are more desirable. This guide can then be used to locate and inspect desirable areas. Since a cruise ship is a destination in itself, it is important to allow enough time to experience the atmosphere on board and the attitude of the staff. Similarly, the amount of open deck space and the number of available deck chairs should be checked to ensure that passengers will not feel overcrowded. Tour brochures can be used to make hotel comparisons and to note how the hotels differ from their pictures and descriptions. Most hotel managers provide counsellors with brochures and rate sheets. Ask to see all the categories of rooms including those at the minimum, moderate and maximum rates. The various checklists provided in other chapters of this text can also be used as a basis to assess destinations, hotels, resorts, attractions, facilities, cruise ships and tours. Other observations

and headings can then be added as appropriate.

Remember that sponsors offer fam trips to encourage sales. This also means that participants receive special treatment not accorded to the typical visitor. It is therefore important to take the time to experience the destination in the way that "real" tourists might. For example, local sightseeing tours can be extremely beneficial. Local tours, especially city sightseeing tours, help counsellors to develop a reliable overview of a destination, provide a sense of direction and distances in a large city, and help assess the quality and competence of the services. Time spent in any travel activity is time spent increasing one's knowledge. This makes counsellors more valuable to their agency and more professional to their clients. It can also lead to increased commissions. It is also useful to travel by local ground transportation since most familiarization tours are designed for groups and conducted by charter coach. References often provide details of timetables and fares for local transit, but only by riding in a taxi or city bus can one decide whether to recommend the mode of transport to clients. Notes on the cost and travel times, for example from a major hotel to a shopping or theatre district, and whether the fare is metered or must be haggled over, enhance knowledge and help build a complete picture of a destination. If possible, take a train to a nearby town or attraction and assess the service. Perhaps rent a car for a half day and do some individual touring. Such activities can be fun as well as functional. They provide the level of detail that FIT clients often seek and give all clients the benefits of the counsellor's experience.

Since most hosts put on their "best face" for visiting fam groups, many counsellors make time to see additional hotels in their "natural" condition. Such unscheduled hotel inspections give counsellors an opportunity to see the "true" nature of a property and its operation, such as the times when rooms are made up, or how well the front desk and restaurant service clients. Properties chosen for unannounced visits are those which particularly interest counsellors or are sold frequently by their agency. Similarly, if a fam is sponsored by a luxury tour operator, for example, counsellors should also check budget and moderate properties in the area to supplement their knowledge of the destination. Most hotels are quite willing to show travel counsellors their property.

At each stop on the itinerary it is appropriate to thank the various hosts. A small note of thanks at the end of the tour is also appreciated.

Fam Trip Behaviour

Fam trips are sponsored by tourist boards, airlines, tour operators and other suppliers, and offered to travel counsellors at a reduced cost. Furthermore, many agency managers pay the tour costs for their staff. These facts mean that in addition to guidelines which can enhance their experience, counsellors have certain responsibilities to fulfill. They must behave professionally and abide by the rules set by sponsors and employers. Failure to behave in accordance with the recommendations discussed below can result in counsellors being asked to leave a tour and return home. In such cases, the individuals are responsible for the cost of their transportation home (at full fare).

Educational tours are generally by invitation and almost always restricted to members of the travel industry. They are neither a privilege nor a right. They are certainly not holidays; their purpose is strictly educational. Counsellors are responsible for ensuring that their documents, vaccinations and other requirements are in order. Dress codes should be observed at all times. Most airlines have fairly strict dress requirements for travellers on passes. Whether counsellors are inspecting hotels or attending a hosted function, neat and appropriate attire is required at all times. Counsellors on a fam trip represent not only themselves but also their company and the principals associated with the tour. Participation in the complete tour is compulsory, including all presentations

and functions. During presentations do not engage in side conversations. This is not only rude but it also means that the individual will miss the purpose of that visit. Since time is usually limited, the itinerary is frequently quite hectic. Punctuality is therefore more than common courtesy, it is essential. Tardiness inconveniences and irritates other group members and can disrupt the schedule, especially if all participants do not stay at the same hotel. It is equally unacceptable to sleep on buses; counsellors who stay up late should not count on sleeping the next day.

There are also some rules of personal behaviour that should be followed. It is considered unprofessional to conduct personal business during tour activities. Most itineraries include some free time for such projects. Similarly, it is inappropriate to complain during the tour. Complaints should be made as constructive criticism to the proper personnel after the trip has been completed (or, if essential, privately at the time). Grievances voiced to other group members are irrelevant and unprofessional. It can be awkward to the host if a counsellor asks for special favours (such as bringing friends). During refreshment and social breaks, each person must be prepared to pay their own way. A mooch is never popular. Excessive drinking, foul language and boorish behaviour are equally embarrassing and have no place on educational tours. Romances can make other members of the group uncomfortable, especially if flaunted. Participants are supposed to be responsible adults and are expected to behave accordingly.

Fam Trip Reports

Most agency managers request that their staff prepare a comprehensive report of the tour within seven days of returning. The report not only provides evidence of how much the counsellor has learned by participating in the tour, but also helps build a resource file which can be accessed by other counsellors in the office. It is also both courteous and

HOTELS

HOTEL NAME				
STAR RATING				
YEAR BUILT/ RENOVATED/ PRESENT CONDITION				
ROOMS: MIN-MAX SIZE/RATE APTS: MIN-MAX SIZE/RATE				
SPECIAL FEATURES				
HOTEL STAFF ATTITUDE				
GUESTS: INCOME/AGE BRACKETS				
NEIGHBOURHOOD: TYPE/NOISE, ETC.				
MILES/KM TO: • AIRPORT • NEAREST TOWN (SPECIFY) • NIGHTLIFE AND RESTAURANTS				
LOCAL TRANSPORT				
TOUR OPERATORS USING HOTEL				
GENERAL IMPRESSION/ COMMENTS Please circle one of: • S – stayed in hotel • W – walked through	S W	S W	S W	S W

FIGURE 14.10
Agency managers may ask counsellors to complete hotel assessment forms on fam trips.
Source: Carlson Wagonlit.

Destination Profile

DESTINATIONS/ITINERARY	DATES VISITED	STAR RATING

GENERAL DESCRIPTION/OVERALL IMPRESSIONS

TOURS/SIGHTSEEING/ENTERTAINMENT/SHOPPING

AVERAGE COST/DAY DINING EXPENSES (LOCAL CURRENCY)

OTHER COMMENTS

TRANSPORTATION/CARRIER COMMENTS

GROUND OPERATOR COMMENTS

BRANCH/CITY/PROV., _____

TRAVEL CONSULTANT _____

SIGNED _____ DATE _____

FIGURE 14.11
Some agencies use standardized forms for a counsellor's fam trip reports. *Source: Carlson Wagonlit.*

informative to forward a copy of fam trip reports to the host. Reports must be objective for colleagues and tour hosts to benefit from them. Some agencies encourage counsellors to make a presentation to their colleagues during regular staff meetings. An objective fam trip report contains a summary of the official itinerary, notes deviations and additions to this, and evaluates the tour in terms of the quality of the product and its suitability for various client groups. The report should be supported with evaluation forms and checklists, such as those presented in earlier chapters, with relevant brochures and with other references. Since one use for fam trip reports is as an office resource, they must have a clear format which is easy to read. Brevity is important. Fam trip reports are not intended to be college essays; they are an additional sales tool. Brief phrases under bold headings will make a report easier for all counsellors to read and use. Some agencies provide hotel critique cards for counsellors to complete on a fam trip (see Figure 14.10). These are then filed in the agency so that all staff can use them as references. Some agencies use standardized reporting forms so that information can be quickly located (see Figure 14.11). No matter which format or style is used, fam reports are usually retained in alphabetical order in a central destination file.

Travel counsellors are fortunate to be engaged in a profession where the job can be learned in such an enjoyable and inexpensive manner. Those who take maximum advantage of these opportunities acquire knowledge that translates into better client service. This not only increases their income but also enhances their professional image.

Counsellors can continue their education on a formal basis through courses and seminars, and in other structured situations such as fam trips. However, the nature of the travel industry and its intimate relationship with the everyday world means that counsellors must necessarily learn from a variety of other sources. It is essential that counsellors have a sound knowledge of current affairs by regularly reading newspapers and magazines or by viewing television news. Tourism has an impact on so many facets of life that almost every event has some bearing on tourism in the surrounding area. Counsellors must remain current on the political climate throughout the world, as well as the business climate, currency markets and changes in lifestyle. Travel has become a popular topic in both consumer publications and on television. Such consumer-oriented media frequently provide information that is also useful to professional travel counsellors. The media both shapes and reflects current trends and attitudes, and thus provide insight to future client tastes and markets. Reports of events can spark an interest in or adversely affect travel to the location. Entertainment is equally influential in setting the travel agenda.

How to Start a Travel Agency

For some people, the challenges of travel counselling are not enough. They seek the additional challenge of owning and operating a travel agency. Some people decide on this course of action early in their professional lives while others set different personal and professional goals. Almost all counsellors, however, give at least some thought to the subject during their career.

The process can be simple or complex depending on the amount of legislation in the particular province and the type of travel products that the prospective owner wishes to sell. If the agency is located in one of the provinces without specific travel legislation and if the intention is simply to sell packaged tours, a travel agency can be opened as simply as any other type of retail sales business. If the agency is located in B.C., Quebec or Ontario, however, provincial travel regulations demand that the agency be licensed. If the intention is to sell scheduled airline tickets as well as charter flights from tour operators, the agency will also require approval by IATA and the other airline conferences.

The first step in opening a travel agency is compliance with local provincial legislation. This applies in the provinces of Quebec, Ontario and British Columbia as discussed in Chapter 1. Each province has consumer-oriented legislation designed to protect the purchasers of travel services. Legislation was considered necessary because of the unusual nature of the travel industry; it is one of the few businesses where customers are asked to pay the full purchase price well in advance of the delivery of the goods or services bought, thereby depriving them of one of their most effective levers in obtaining satisfaction, that is, a refusal to pay.

Similar legislation and requirements for registration exist in the three legislated provinces. Some of the common general rules with which an owner must comply are:

- The agency owner must be 19 years or older.
- The agency location must be open to the public during normal operating hours and be a permanent place of business.
- The agency must operate under a registered name.
- The registration certificate must be prominently displayed at the office for which it was issued.
- The certificate must be returned if the license is revoked or the agency goes out of business.

To obtain a license one must complete an application for registration. The application is frequently a common form used by the ministry concerned to register other types of businesses such as real estate brokers or motor vehicle sellers. An agency cannot open for business until the application is processed and a registration certificate issued. The processing procedure usually takes two to three weeks if the application is in order.

Each administration is supervised by a Registrar who administers and enforces the act and its regulations in the relevant province. Specific details of the act, copies of the appropriate act and regulations, application forms, and answers to particular questions can be obtained by contacting the Registrar at the address provided at the end of this chapter. In provinces without specific travel legislation, travel agencies must comply with the regulations that apply to opening any type of business.

Obtaining Appointments

Most agencies rely on the sale of airline tickets as their principal source of income. It is, of course, possible to operate a travel agency without offering these products but commission income is likely to be relatively small. Alternatively, an agency can sell airline tickets by purchasing them for cash directly from the carriers and then reselling them to clients. However, this would be strictly a customer service; the agency would earn no commission from such sales. Before a travel agency can earn commission on the sale of scheduled airline tickets, it must first apply for approval to IATA for international journeys and to ATAC for domestic sales. If approved by these airline conferences, the agency will be recognized as an appointed passenger sales agent. This not only lets the agency earn commission, but also makes it unnecessary for the agency to pay cash in advance for the tickets. An IATA appointment lets agencies join the BSP system which debits their bank account on a weekly basis. Agencies can also seek appointments from CLIA and VIA Rail to sell cruise and rail products respectively. Appointment procedures try to protect customer's payments by encouraging professionalism in the sales and distribution system.

The *IATA Travel Agent's Handbook and Guide to Automation* is the basic reference for rules and regulations which appointed agencies must follow. It is also useful as a day-to-day guide for managers. The publication contains certain IATA Resolutions (or rules) which describe an agent's duties plus others that relate to an agent's work. The rules cover everything from who is eligible for reduced rate transportation and how to apply for this, to the role of the travel agency commissioner and reservations procedures. The procedure to obtain an IATA appointment is summarized (Figure 14.12) and a code of reservations ethics is included. The handbook, which is updated periodically, is automatically sent to approved agency locations.

The initial step is to decide which air carrier conference appointments are desired. IATA's and ATAC's geographic jurisdictions and functions are described in Chapter 6. Both relate only to scheduled air travel, not to charters. What IATA does internationally, ATAC does domestically. At one time ATAC had a separate set of criteria and a separate appointment process. In 1986, it aligned its criteria with those of IATA and it has since contracted out to IATA the task of administering the process. Application forms are available from IATA or member carriers. The same form is used to apply for approval from either or both IATA and ATAC. The application form

FIGURE 14.12
The IATA approval and appointment process.
Source: IATA.

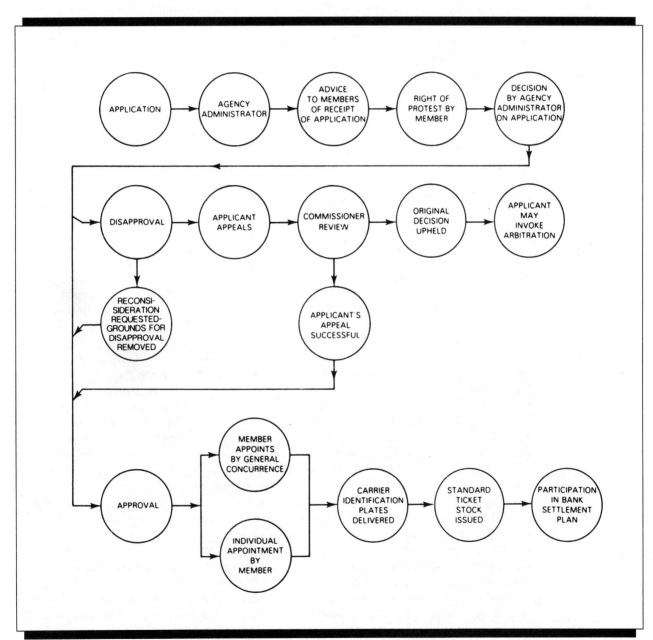

gives IATA a profile of the applicant. IATA approval is subject to scrutiny in several areas. Part I of the application covers general information such as a description of the applicant and type of business (e.g., corporation, sole proprietorship). Part II investigates the agency's business and customer relationships to ensure that there are no conflicts of interest or history of malpractice. In Part III, IATA seeks details of the agency's premises. The agency's personnel, specifically their professional experience, are outlined in Part IV. Security procedures are noted in Part V of the application and any other information is described in Part VI. The application must be signed by an authorized representative and witnessed by a Notary Public. Applications must include exterior and interior photographs of the premises showing the location of the office safe, a copy of the agency's provincial license where applicable, financial statements, and the appropriate fee. Completed applications are submitted to the association's Agency Administrator and receipt will be acknowledged within one week.

To receive an appointment, IATA currently requires that the travel agency have two or more full-time employees. One of these individuals must posses at least two years' experience in retailing, promoting and supervising, gained within the previous five years. The other person must have a minimum of one year's experience within the preceding three years. This requirement is strictly enforced by IATA. All conferences have similar personnel standards. Regarding an agency's financial stability and equity, IATA awards points for meeting various parts of the financial criteria. A number of specific financial ratios are calculated using a different formula for each. Agencies must attain a minimum number of points for these ratios in order to receive an appointment. IATA's security criteria try to ensure that an agency's precautions are such that it would be relieved of liability for damage, loss, theft, robbery, burglary or fraudulent misuse of traffic documents from premises.

After receiving an application, the Administrator advises all IATA members of the application. Carriers then have 30 days to inform IATA if they feel that the application should be denied. Such a view must be supported with reasons. An on-site inspection is scheduled during this period to view the agency's security arrangements. If an agency's application is acceptable the appointment is granted, usually within 90 days. If not acceptable, the agent can rectify the problem or appeal to the Travel Agent Commissioner for Canada. Should the Commissioner also reject the application, the applicant can ask the Agency Administration Board to reconsider the decision. In the event that the initial finding is reconfirmed, any appeal by the applicant is referred to an independent arbitration board.

Once granted an appointment, the agency receives its IATA numeric identity code and a list of carriers on whose behalf it can issue tickets. The agency must sign a Passenger Sales Agency Agreement with IATA that outlines the rights and obligations of the agency with respect to the carriers. IATA's Director General signs on behalf of all IATA carriers. IATA's sales agency agreement permits agencies to sell airline tickets, however, an agency must also approach each airline to acquire its CIP to issue tickets. An agency's right to collect commission on the sale of scheduled airline tickets, granted by the appointment procedure, is often made retroactive to the date on which the application was filed.

The appointment procedure is intended to satisfy IATA that an agency has sufficient capital and expertise to operate, satisfactory security measures regarding ticket stock and imprinters, and proof that it will promote and sell air travel on the services of all IATA members. Applicants must not only meet IATA's criteria but must also maintain these standards on an ongoing basis in order to retain their appointments. Agents must notify IATA of changes to the name, ownership or location of the agency. Each change involves refiling an application together with the appropriate documentation.

Review Questions

1. Discuss ways that a travel agency can increase its profitability.

2. Describe the BSP reporting process.

3. Explain the purpose of client files and describe their contents.

4. What types of complaints do counsellors receive and how should they be handled?

5. What are the goals of travel industry trade associations?

6. Discuss the criteria for registering a travel agency and obtaining an IATA conference appointment.

Research Assignment

Select one non-tourism story from each of the following areas of a current daily newspaper: international news; business; arts and entertainment. Briefly summarize the report and then discuss how it might affect Canadian travel to the country or region where the story originated.

References

Association of Canadian Travel Agents (ACTA), 1729 Bank Street, Suite 201, Ottawa, Ontario K1V 7Z5.

American Society of Travel Agents (ASTA), 1101 King Street, Alexandria, VA 22314, USA.

BSP Canada Manual for Passenger Sales Agents, International Air Transport Association, 2000 Peel Street, Montreal, Quebec H3A 2R4.

Canadian Institute of Travel Counsellors of Ontario (CITC-Ont), Suite 209, 55 Eglinton Avenue East, Toronto, Ontario M4P 1G8, Tel: (416) 484-4450, Fax: (416) 484-4140.

Cruise Lines International Association (CLIA), 500 Fifth Avenue, Suite 1407, New York, NY 10017, USA.

Institute of Certified Travel Agents (ICTA), 148 Linden Street, P.O. Box 82-56, Wellesley, MA 02181, USA.

IATA Travel Agents Handbook and Guide to Automation, International Air Transport Association (IATA), 2000 Peel Street, Montreal, Quebec H3A 2R4.

International Civil Aviation Organization (ICAO), International Aviation Square, 1000 Sherbrooke Street West, Montreal, Quebec H3A 2R2.

Registrar, Loi des Agents de Voyage, Ministere du Tourisme, de la Chasse et de la Peche, 150 est Boul. St.-Cyrille, Quebec City, Quebec G1R 4Y1.

Registrar, TICO (Travel Industry Council of Ontario) 1200 Bay Street, Suite 1100, Toronto, Ontario M5R 2A5, Tel: (416) 975-0818, Fax: (416) 975-9141.

Registrar of Travel Services, Travel Agents Registration Act, Government of British Columbia, 411 Dunsmuir Street, Vancouver, B.C.

Tourism Industry Association of Canada (TIAC), 130 Albert Street, Suite 1016, Ottawa, Ontario K1P 5G4.

Universal Federation of Travel Agents Associations (UFTAA), Rue Defacqz, Boite 1, 1050 Brussels, Belgium.

World Association of Travel Agents (WATA), 37 quai Wilson, 1211 Geneva 1, Switzerland.

World Tourism Organization (WTO), Capitan Haya 42, 20820 Madrid, Spain.

Bibliography

Selected Bibliography

Ames, Margaret. *The Travel Agency of D.C.: A Job Simulation*. 2nd ed. Cincinnati, OH: South-Western Publishing Co., 1991.

Ang, Roxanne S.L. *Airline Tariff and Ticketing: Domestic*. Toronto: Canadian Institute of Travel Counsellors of Ontario, 1992.

Ang, Roxanne S.L. *Airline Tariff and Ticketing: International*. 3rd ed. Toronto: Canadian Institute of Travel Counsellors of Ontario, 1992.

Axtell, Roger. *Do's and Taboos Around the World*. Toronto: John Wiley and Sons, Inc., 1985.

Baud-Bovy, Manuel, and Fred Lawson. *Tourism and Recreation Development*. Boston, MA: CBI Publishing Co., 1977.

Blum, Ethel. *The Total Traveler by Ship*. New York, NY: Hippocrene Books, Inc., 1988.

Bryant, Carl L., Isaac Reynolds, and Teresa A. Poole. *Travel Selling Skills*. Cincinnati, OH: South-Western Publishing Co., 1992.

Burkart, A.J., and S. William Medlik. *Tourism, Past, Present, and Future*. London: Heinemann, 1981.

Burke, James F., and Barry P. Resnick. *Marketing and Selling the Travel Product*. Cincinnati, OH: South-Western Publishing Co., 1991.

Burton, Rosemary. *Travel Geography*. London: Pitman, 1991.

Cleverdon, Robert. *The Economic and Social Impact of International Tourism on Developing Countries*. London: The Economist Intelligence Unit, 1979.

Coltman, Michael M. *Introduction to Travel and Tourism: An International Approach*. New York, NY: Van Nostrand Reinhold, 1989.

Coltman, Michael M. *Tourism Marketing*. New York, NY: Van Nostrand Reinhold, 1989.

Coyle, John J., Edward J. Bardi and Joseph L. Cavinato. *Transportation*. 2nd ed. St. Paul, MI: West Publishing Co., 1986.

Curran, Patrick J.T. *Principles and Procedures of Tour Management*. Boston, MA: CBI Publishing Co., 1978.

Davidoff, Philip G., and Doris S. Davidoff. *Financial Management for Travel Agencies*. Albany, NY: Delmar Publishers Inc., 1988.

Davidoff, Philip G., and Doris S. Davidoff. *Sales and Marketing for Travel and Tourism*. Englewood Cliffs, NJ: Prentice-Hall, Inc., 1983.

Davidoff, Philip G., and Doris S. Davidoff. *Worldwide Tours: A Travel Agent's Guide to Selling Tours*. Englewood Cliffs, NJ: Prentice-Hall, Inc., 1990.

Davidoff, Philip G., Doris S. Davidoff, and J. Douglas Eyre. *Tourism Geography*. 2nd ed. Englewood Cliffs, NJ: Prentice-Hall, Inc., 1995.

Davidson, Rob. *Tourism*. London: Pitman, 1989.

de Kadt, Emanuel. *Tourism: Passport to Development?* Washington, DC: Oxford University Press, 1979.

de Souto, Martha Sarbey. *Group Travel Operations Manual.* 2nd ed. Albany, NY: Delmar Publishers Inc., 1992.

Dervaes, Claudine. *The Travel Dictionary.* Tampa, FL: Solitaire Publishing, 1989.

Doswell, Roger. *Case Studies in Tourism.* London: Barrie and Jenkins Ltd., 1978.

Doswell, Roger. *Further Case Studies in Tourism.* London: Barrie and Jenkins Ltd., 1979.

Dumazedier, Joffre. *Sociology of Leisure.* New York, NY: Elsevier, 1974.

DuPont, Herbert L., and Margaret W. DuPont. *Travel with Health.* Englewood Cliffs, NJ: Prentice-Hall, Inc., 1981.

Edington, John M., and M. Ann Edington. *Ecology, Recreation and Tourism.* Cambridge: Cambridge University Press, 1986.

Ehret, Dr. Charles and Lynne Scanlom. *Overcoming Jet Lag.* New York, NY: Berkley Publishing, 1983.

Feifer, Maxine. *Tourism in History: From Imperial Rome to the Present.* New York, NY: Stein and Day, 1986.

Foster, Dennis L. *Destinations: North American and International Geography.* 2nd ed. New York, NY: Glencoe/McGraw-Hill, 1994.

Foster, Dennis L. *First Class: An Introduction to Travel and Tourism.* 2nd ed. New York, NY: Glencoe/McGraw-Hill, 1994.

Foster, Dennis L. *Sales and Marketing for the Travel Professional.* New York, NY: Glencoe/ McGraw-Hill, 1991.

Foster, Dennis L. *The Business of Travel: Agency Operations and Administration.* New York, NY: Glencoe/McGraw-Hill, 1991.

Freedman, Jacqueline and Susan Gersten. *Traveling Like Everybody Else: A Practical Guide for Disabled Travelers.* New York, NY: Adama Books, 1987.

Fremont, Pamela. *How to Open and Run a Money-Making Travel Agency.* Toronto: John Wiley and Sons, Inc., 1983.

Frommer, Arthur. *The New World of Travel.* Englewood Cliffs, NJ: Prentice-Hall, Inc., 1988.

Fruehling, Rosemary T. and Constance K. Weaver. *Electronic Office Procedures.* Toronto: McGraw-Hill, 1987.

Fuson, Robert. *Fundamental Place-Name Geography.* 5th ed. Dubuque, IA: Wm. C. Brown Co., 1981.

Gee, Chuck Y. *Resort Development and Management.* East Lansing, MI: American Hotel and Motel Association Educational Institute, 1981.

Gee, Chuck Y., James C. Makens, and Dexter J.L. Choy. *The Travel Industry*. 2nd ed. New York, NY: Van Nostrand Reinhold, 1989.

Gee, Chuck Y., Dexter J.L. Choy, James C, Makens, and Kevin B. Boberg. *Professional Travel Agency Management*. Englewood Cliffs, NJ: Prentice-Hall, Inc., 1990.

Gee, Gordon E. *Calculations for the Leisure, Travel and Tourism Industries*. Toronto: Hodder and Stoughton, 1991.

George, Ben. *Where in the World, When in the World? An Introduction to Travel Geography and International Time*. Englewood Cliffs, NJ: Prentice-Hall, Inc., 1989.

Godwin, Nadine. *Complete Guide to Travel Agency Automation*. 2nd ed. Albany, NY: Delmar Publishers Inc., 1987.

Gold, Hal. *The Cruise Book: From Brochure to Bon Voyage*. Albany, NY: Delmar Publishers, Inc., 1990.

Green, William and Gordon Swanbonough. *An Illustrated Guide to the World's Airliners*. New York, NY: Arco Publishing Inc., 1982.

Gregory, Aryear. *The Travel Agent: Dealer in Dreams*. 4th ed. Englewood Cliffs, NJ: Regents/Prentice-Hall, Inc., 1993.

Gunn, Clare A. *Tourism Planning*. 2nd ed. New York, NY: Taylor and Francis, 1988.

Harris, G., and K. Katz. *Promoting International Tourism*. Los Angeles, CA: The Americas Group, 1986.

Hart, E.J. *The Selling of Canada: The CPR and the Beginnings of Canadian Tourism*. Banff, Alberta: Altitude Publishing Ltd., 1983.

Hatt, John. *The Tropical Traveller: An Essential Guide to Travel in Hot Climates*. New York, NY: Hippocrene Books, Inc., 1984.

Hawkins, Donald E., Elwood L. Shafer and James M. Rovelstad, editors. *Tourism Planning and Development Issues*. Washington, DC: George Washington University, 1980.

Hayes, Greg and Joan Wright. *Going Places: The Guide to Travel Guides*. Boston, MA: The Harvard Common Press, 1988.

Hecker R.N., Helen. *Travel for the Disabled: A Handbook of Travel Resources and 500 Worldwide Access Guides*. Portland, OR: Twin Peaks Press, 1985.

Hong, Evelyne. *See the Third World While It Lasts: The Social and Environmental Impact of Tourism with Special Reference to Malaysia*. Penang, Malaysia: Consumers' Association of Penang, 1985.

Holloway, J. Christopher. *The Business of Tourism*. 3rd ed. London: Pitman, 1989.

Holloway, J.C., and R.V. Plant. *Marketing for Tourism*. London: Pitman, 1988.

Howell, David W. *Discovering Destinations*. 3rd ed. Englewood Cliffs, NJ: Prentice-Hall, Inc., 1992.

Howell, D., R.A. Ellison, M. Bateman Ellison, and D. Wright. *Passport: An Introduction to the Travel and Tourism Industry.* 2nd Canadian ed. Toronto: ITP Nelson, 1998.

Howell, David W. *Principles and Methods of Scheduling Reservations.* 2nd ed. Englewood Cliffs, NJ: Prentice-Hall, Inc., 1987.

Hudman, Lloyd E. *Tourism: A Shrinking World.* Toronto: John Wiley and Sons, Inc., 1980.

Hudman, Lloyd E., and Donald E. Hawkins. *Tourism in Contemporary Society: An Introductory Text.* Englewood Cliffs, NJ: Prentice-Hall, Inc., 1990.

Hudman, Lloyd E., and Richard H. Jackson. *Geography of Travel and Tourism.* Albany, NY: Delmar Publishers Inc., 1990.

Jackson, Ian. *An Introduction to Tourism.* Melbourne: Hospitality Press, 1989.

Jefferson, Alan and Leonard Lickorish. *Marketing Tourism: A Practical Guide.* London: Longman, 1988.

Kaiser, Charles, Jr., and Larry E. Helber. *Tourism Planning and Development.* Boston, MA: CBI Publishing Co., 1978.

Kelly, Edward M., Editor. *Perspectives: Leisure Travel and Tourism.* Wellesley, MA: Institute of Certified Travel Agents, 1986.

Krippendorf, Jost. *The Holiday Makers.* London: Heinemann, 1987.

Landry, Janice L., and Anna H. Fesmire. *Explorations: Travel Geography and Destination Study.* Englewood Cliffs, NJ: Prentice-Hall, Inc., 1994.

Landry, Janice L., and Anna H. Fesmire. *The World is Out There Watching: An Introduction to Travel and Tourism.* Englewood Cliffs, NJ: Prentice-Hall, Inc., 1994.

Lattin, G.W. *The Lodging and Food Service Industry.* Lansing, MI: Educational Institute of the American Hotel and Motel Association, 1989.

Lavery, Patrick, and Carlton Van Doren. *Travel and Tourism: A North American-European Perspective.* Huntington, Cambs.: ELM Publications, 1990.

Lehmann, Armin D. *Travel and Tourism: An Introduction to Travel Agency Operations.* 4th ed. Indianapolis, IN: Bobbs-Merrill Co. Inc., 1980.

Lehmann, Armin D., and Diane Embree. *Travel Agency Policies and Procedures Manual.* Albany, NY: Delmar Publishers Inc., 1988.

Lundberg, Donald E. *The Tourist Business.* 6th ed. New York, NY: CBI, Van Nostrand Reinhold, 1990.

Lundberg, Donald E. *The Travel Agent.* Englewood Cliffs, NJ: Prentice-Hall, Inc., 1983.

Lundberg, Donald E., and Carolyn B. Lundberg. *International Travel and Tourism.* Toronto: John Wiley and Sons, 1985.

Lyne, Clare. Editor. *Leisure Travel and Tourism.* Wellesley, MA: Institute of Certified Travel Agents, 1989.

MacCannell, Dean. *The Tourist: A New Theory of the Leisure Class*. New York, NY: Schocken Books, 1976.

Mancini, Marc. *Conducting Tours: A Practical Guide*. Cincinnati, OH: South-Western Publishing Co., 1990.

Mancini, Marc. Selling Destinations: *Geography for the Travel Professional*. Cincinnati, OH: South-Western Publishing Co., 1992.

Marks, Ronald B. and Petra T. Soden. *Personal Selling: An Interactive Approach*. 3rd ed. Toronto: Allyn and Bacon, Inc., 1989.

Maslow, A.H. *Motivation and Personality*. New York, NY: Harper and Row, 1954.

Mathieson, Alister, and Geoffrey Wall. *Tourism: Economic, Physical and Social Impacts*. New York, NY: Longman, 1982.

Mayo, Edward J., and Lance P. Jarvis. *The Psychology of Leisure Travel*. Boston, MA: CBI Publishing Co., 1981.

Medlik, S. Editor. *Managing Tourism*. Oxford: Butterworth-Heinemann Ltd., 1991.

Metelka, Charles J. *The Dictionary of Tourism*. 2nd ed. Albany, NY: Delmar Publishers Inc., 1986.

McIntosh, Robert W., and Charles R. Goeldner. *Tourism: Principles, Practices, Philosophies*. 6th ed. Toronto: John Wiley and Sons, Inc., 1990.

Middleton, Victor T.C. *Marketing in Travel and Tourism*. London: Heinemann, 1988.

Mill, Robert Christie. *Tourism: The International Business*. Englewood Cliffs, NJ: Prentice-Hall, Inc., 1990.

Mill, Robert Christie, and Alastair M. Morrison. *The Tourism System: An Introductory Text*. 2nd ed. Englewood Cliffs, NJ: Prentice-Hall, Inc., 1992.

Mitchell, G.E. *Designing and Escorting Group Tours*. Elmsford, NY: National Publishers, 1988.

Morrison, Alastair M. *Hospitality and Travel Marketing*. Albany, NY: Delmar Publishers Inc., 1989.

Murphy, Peter E. *Tourism: A Community Approach*. New York, NY: Methuen, 1985.

Neulinger, John. *The Psychology of Leisure*. Springfield, IL: Thomas, 1974.

Noble, Cinnie. *The Disabled Traveller: A Guide for Travel Counsellors*. Toronto: Canadian Institutes of Travel Counsellors, 1991.

Nyy, Linda. *Travel CounSELLing*. Englewood Cliffs, NJ: Prentice-Hall, Inc., 1989.

Pearce, Douglas. *Tourism Today: A Geographical Analysis*. Toronto: John Wiley and Sons, 1987.

Pearce, Douglas. *Tourist Development*. New York, NY: Longman, 1981.

Pearch, E.A., and Gordon Smith. *The Times Books World Weather Guide*. New York, NY: Random House, Inc., 1984.

Plog, Stanley C. "Why Destination Areas Rise and Fall in Popularity." *Cornell Hotel and Administration Quarterly*. Vol. 14, No. 4, February 1974.

Pond, Katherine L. *The Professional Guide: Dynamics of Tour Guiding*. Toronto: Nelson, 1993.

Porterfield, James D. *Selling on the Telephone*. Toronto: John Wiley and Sons, Inc. 1985.

Powers, Tom. *Introduction to the Hospitality Industry*. Toronto: John Wiley and Sons, 1988.

Poynter, James M. *Corporate Travel Management*. Englewood Cliffs, NJ: Prentice-Hall, Inc., 1990.

Poynter, James M. *Tour Design, Marketing, and Management*. Englewood Cliffs, NJ: Prentice-Hall, Inc., 1995.

Poynter, James M. *Travel Agency Accounting Procedures*. Albany, NY: Delmar Publishers, Inc., 1990.

Poynter, James. *Foreign Independent Tours: Planning, Pricing and Processing*. Albany, NY: Delmar Publishers Inc., 1989.

Quest, Miles. Editor. *Horwath Book of Tourism*. London: The Macmillan Press Ltd., 1990.

Reason, James. *Man in Motion: The Psychology of Travel*. New York, NY: Walker, 1974.

Reilly, Robert T. *Handbook of Professional Tour Management*. Albany, NY: Delmar Publishers Inc., 1982.

Reilly, Robert T. *Travel and Tourism Marketing Techniques*. 2nd ed. Albany, NY: Delmar Publishers Inc., 1988.

Ritchie, J.R. Brent, and Charles R. Goeldner. *Travel, Tourism and Hospitality Research: A Handbook for Managers and Researchers*. Toronto: John Wiley and Sons, Inc., 1987.

Robinson, H. *A Geography of Tourism*. London: Macdonald and Evans, 1976.

Rosenow, John E., and Gerreld L. Pulsipher. *Tourism: The Good, The Bad, and The Ugly*. Westport, CT: AVI, 1979.

Sakmar, Dr. Thomas et al. *Passport's Health Guide for International Travelers*. Lincolnwood, IL: Passport Books, 1986.

Smith, Stephen L.J. *Tourism Analysis: A Handbook*. London: Longman, 1989.

Smith, Valene L. *Hosts and Guests: The Anthropology of Tourism*. Philadelphia, PA: University of Pennsylvania Press, 1977.

Starr, Nona S. *Marketing for the Travel Industry*. Wellesley, MA: Institute of Certified Travel Agents, 1984, 1990.

Starr, Nona S. *Viewpoint: An Introduction to Travel, Tourism and Hospitality*. Toronto: Houghton Mifflin, 1993.

Starr, Nona and Karen Silva. *Travel Career Development*. 4th ed. Boston, MA: Houghton Mifflin Company, 1990.

Stevens, L. *Guide to Starting and Operating a Travel Agency*. 2nd ed. Albany, NY: Delmar Publishers Inc., 1983.

Swinglehurst, Edmund. *Cook's Tour: The Story of Popular Travel*. New York, NY: Sterling Publishing Co., 1982.

Thompson, Douglas. *How to Open Your Own Travel Agency*. San Francisco, CA: Dendrobium Books, 1987.

Thompson, Douglas. *Profitable Direct Mail for Travel Agents*. San Francisco, CA: Dendrobium Books, 1989.

Thompson, Douglas and Mary Millar-Marshall. *Travel Agency Bookkeeping Made Simple*. San Francisco, CA: Dendrobium Books, 1987.

Thompson-Smith, Jeanie M. *Travel Agency Guide to Business Travel*. Albany, NY: Delmar Publishers Inc., 1988.

Timmons, Veronica. *Tourism and Travel: Focus Canada*. 3rd ed. Vancouver, B.C.: Timmons and Associates, 1989.

Trowbridge, Keith W. *Resort Timesharing*. New York, NY: Simon and Schuster, 1981.

Turner, Louis, and John Ash. *The Golden Hordes: International Tourism and the Pleasure Periphery*. London: Constable, 1975.

Van Harssel, Jan. *Tourism: An Exploration*. 3rd ed. Englewood Cliffs, NJ: Prentice-Hall, Inc., 1994.

Wahab, S.E. *Tourism Management*. London: Tourism International Press, 1975.

Wahab, S.E., J. Crampon and L. Rothfield. *Tourism Marketing*. London: Tourism International Press, 1976.

Webster, Susan, and Ralph Phillips. *Group Travel Operating Procedures*. New York, NY: Van Nostrand Reinhold, 1983.

Weiss, Louise. *Access to the World: A Travel Guide for the Handicapped*. New York, NY: Henry Holt & Co., 1986.

Weissmann, Arnie. Editor. *The Weissmann Travel Report: Travel Geography and Destinations*. Austin, TX: 49th & H. Inc., 1989.

Witt, Stephen F., and Luiz Moutinho. *Tourism Marketing and Management Handbook*. London: Prentice Hall International (UK) Ltd., 1989.

World Tourism Organization. *Role and Structure of National Tourism Administrations*. Madrid: WTO, 1978.

World Tourism Organization. *Tourism Multipliers Explained*. Madrid: WTO, 1981.

Young, George. *Tourism, Blessing or Blight?* Baltimore, MD: Penguin Books, 1973.

Zedlitz, Robert H. *Getting a Job in the Travel Industry*. Cincinnati, OH: South-Western Publishing Co., 1990.

Zvoncheck, Juls. *Cruises: Selecting, Selling, and Booking*. Elmsford, NY: National Publishers, 1988.

Index

A

ABC - see Advance Booking Charter
ABC Star Service 71
Academic Journals 90
Accommodation 22, 110, 261
    Amtrak 214
    European rail 219
    guaranteed 282, 381
    history and background 262
    VIA rail 208
Accounting
    procedures 435
    terms 436
Accuracy 455
ACTA 459
Activities 113
Administration 45, 433
Advance Booking Charters 184
Advertising 32, 412
Air Fares
    add-on 181
    international 179
    types 168
    used for tours 182
Air Regulations, International 153
Air Tariff 69, 174
Air Transport Association of America 30, 302
Air Transport Association of Canada 30, 469
Air Travel
    development 144
    selling 159
Airline Equipment 159
Airline Fares and Tariffs 168
Airline Marketing and Promotion 157
Airline References, Standard 69
Airline Regulation 145
Airline Ticketing 190
Airline Tickets 191
Airline Tour Order 193
Airlines 20
    charter 151
    classification 150
    commuter 151
    domestic 153
    foreign 153
    mutual cooperation between 156
    owned by tour operators 322
Allocentrics 58
Amtrak
    accommodation and services 214
    equipment 212
    fares 215
    reservations and ticketing 215
ANTOR 461
Apparent Flying Time 121
ARTA 460
Assessment Form
    hotel 278
    cruise ship 373

ASTA 460
ATA - see Air Transport Association of
    America
ATAC - see Air Transport Association of
    Canada
ATPCO Passenger Tariff Set 69, 170
Attitudes 56
Attractions and Sightseeing 111

B

Backhaul, One-Way 182
Baggage Handling 165
Bank Rates 441
Barges 353
Barriers to Travel 52
Bermuda Agreement 11
Bibliography 473
Bilateral Agreements 155
Billing and Settlement Plan 441
    manual 69
    processing 445
    report preparation 442
Bonding 16
Brochures
    cruise 364
    tour 331
BSP - see Billing and Settlement Plan
Bus Operators 21
Bus Transportation 242
    Europe 245
    North America 244
Buses, Types 243
Business Practices Act 15
Business Travellers, Needs 54

C

Canada Customs for Returning Residents 135
Canadian Government and Tourism 9
Canadian Government and Tourism
    Legislation 12
Car Leasing 257
Car Rental 21, 247
    charges 252
    sales features 49
Car Renters, Qualifying 251
Carriers
    off-line 153
    regional 151
    scheduled 151
    trunk 151
Cash Refund Notice 195
Catalogues 73
Catering 163
CATO 459
CBIT - see Contract Bulk Inclusive Tour

Chain Agencies 35
Charter Airlines 151
Charter and Tour Tickets 195
Charters, Advance Booking 184
Check-In Procedures
    air 164
    hotel 287
Chicago Convention 11
Cholera 130
Choosing an Agency 32
Circle Trip 168
Circle Trip Minimum 182
CITC 460
    code of conduct 457
Claims Procedure 402
Classes of Service
    air 162
    cruise ships 356
    European rail 218
Classification of Airlines 150
Classifying Groups 48
Clearing Houses 82
CLIA - see Cruise Lines International
    Association
Clients 86
    advice for car rental 256
    files 448
    knowledge 44
    motivations, needs and expectations 59
    relations 451
Clock System, The 24-Hour 118
Combination Passes 232
Combining Fares 182
Commercial Hotels 264
Commercial Travel 37
Commission 30
    calculation 439
Common Law 13
Commuter Airlines 151
Compensation Fund 16
Competition Act 13
Complaints 452
Computer Systems 75
Confidential Tariffs 305
Connecting Flight 168
Consolidated Tour Manual 305
Consolidators 188
Consumer Protection Act 14
Continuing Education 461
Contract Bulk Inclusive Tour Fare 184
Contracts 324
Convenience 33
Convention and Visitors Bureau 9
Convention Travel 40
Conversion
    currency 440
    time 120
Cook European Timetable 70, 71, 222
Cook Overseas Timetable 71, 237
Cost-Benefit Analysis 100
Costing
    cruise 371
    FIT 310
    independent tours 309
    ITC packages 325

Costs & Benefits of Tourism Development 100
Couchettes 219
Credit Card Charge Form 195
Credit Card Refund Notice 195
Cruise Brochures 364
Cruise Industry 348
    references 363
Cruise Lines International Association
    cruise manual 70, 363
Cruise Ships 356
    amenities and activities 360
    assessment form 373
    classes of service 356
    passenger-crew ratio 360
    personnel 362
    space ratio 359
Cruises 347
    abbreviations 379
    advantages 377
    brochures 364
    cost comparison 370
    disadvantages 377
    fares 366
    growth 349
    history 349
    overcoming objections 374
    selling 371
    terms 378
    types 351
CTO 461
CTM - see Consolidated Tour Manual
Cultural Attractions 111
Cultural Impacts 99
Currency
    conversion 440
    regulations 139
Customer Relations 451
Customs Procedures 135
CVB - see Convention and Visitors Bureau

D

Deadhead 321
Demographic Research 48
Deregulation in the USA and Canada 146
Destination
    analysis 106
    development phases 100
    knowledge 104
    primary 102
    secondary or stopover 102
    tourist 92
Development
    tourism 93
    types 102
Dining and Entertainment 112
Direct Effects 96
Direct Mail 412
Direct Service 168
Disclosing the Principal 454
Discretionary Travel 50
Documentation
    tour operator 341
    travel 124

Domestic Airlines 153
Domestic Fares and Tariffs 170
Domestic Passenger Tariffs 172
Domestic Routing Guide 172
Domestic Rules Tariff 173
Domestic Tariff, Using the 170

E

Economic Impacts 95
Effective Listening 60
Elapsed Flying Time 121
Elasticity 67
Entertainment, Dining and 112
Entry Requirements for Visitors to Canada 130
Environmental Impacts 97
Escorted Tours 315
ETC 461
Ethics 455
Ethnic Travel 39
Eurail
    Europass 231
    flexipass 232
    passes 233
    saverpass 231
    youthpass 232
Eurailgroup 233
Eurailpass 231
Eurailtariff 70, 225, 233
European Rail
    equipment 218
    fares 225
    schedules 222
Excursionists, Definition of 3
Expenses, Fixed and Variable 31

F

Factors Determining Individual Travel
    Behaviour 54
Familiarization Trips 83, 462
    behaviour 464
    co-workers 83
    guidelines 462
    reports 464
    selection process 85
Fare Construction Principles 180
Fare Restrictions 169
Fares
    add-on 181
    Amtrak 215
    combining 182
    cruise 366
    European rail 225
    international books 175
    lowest combination 182
    specified 181
    VIA rail 209
Fares and Tariffs
    airline 168
    domestic 170
    international 174
Ferries 353
Ferry Flight 321
Filing Systems 446

Flag Carrier 156
Flight Reservations 189
Flyer 72
Flying Time, Apparent and Elapsed 121
Ford's Deck Plan Guide 70
Ford's Freighter Guide 70
Ford's International Cruise Guide 70
Foreign Airlines 153
Franchises, Travel Agency 36
Freedoms of the Air 155
Freighters 352

G

Gateways 155
General Interest Tours 298
GIT - see Group Inclusive Tour
Glossary
    hotel terminology 270
    nautical terms 378
Government and Legislation 11
Grand Tour 5
Ground Transportation 241, 246
Group Inclusive Tour Fare 183
Group Tours 312
Group Travel 39
Groups
    classifying 48
    reference 57
Growth of Tourism 6
Guidebooks, Travel 117

H

Hague Protocol 11
Health Requirements 130
Hepatitis 134
Higher Intermediate Point 182
HIP - see Higher Intermediate Point
Honesty 455
Hospitality Industry, Importance of 263
Hotel and Travel Index 71
Hotel Representatives 268
Hotels
    assessment form 278
    booking procedures 283
    business relations 289
    checking in and checking out 287
    checklist for quality 277
    commercial 264
    commission arrangements 288
    grading 271
    group bookings 284
    ownership 264
    personnel 271
    meal plans 283
    rates and charges 279
    resort 265
    specialization 267
    terminology 270
    types 264
    WTO classification system 272
Hub and Spoke Routes 148

I

IAMAT - see International Association for
    Medical Assistance to Travellers
IATA - see International Air Transport
    Association
ICAO - see International Civil Aviation
    Organization
ICTA 460
IIT - see Individual Inclusive Tour
Impacts of Tourism 94
Incentive Tours 298
Incentives, Sales 40
Inclusive Tour Charter
    costing 327, 336
    creation of program 320
    regulations 330
Inclusive Tours 313
Independent Air Tours 301
Independent Tours 300
Independent Travel Agencies 34
Individual Inclusive Tour Fare 184
Individual Travellers 51
Insurance, Travel 383
    annual 397
    claims procedure 402
    dealing with suppliers 403
    group 397
    need 384
    selecting a supplier 404
    selling 398
    terminology 387
    types 386
    waiver forms 401
    what is 386
Intangible (Product) 64
International Air Fares 179
International Air Regulations 153
International Air Transport Association 11, 12,
    30, 153, 301, 441
    appointments 468
    traffic conferences 174
    ticketing handbook 69
International Association for Medical
    Assistance to Travellers 134
International Certificates of Vaccination 132
International Civil Aviation Organization 12,
    153
International Driving Permit 140
International Fares and Tariffs 174
International Fares Books 175
International Route Structures 155
International Rules, Routings and Mileages
    Books 177
International Tariff, Using 175
International Tourism Legislation 11
ITC - see Inclusive Tour Charter

K

Knowledge 57
    destination 104
    product 45, 68

L

Leakages 96
Legislation, Tourism 11
Licenses, Vehicles 139
Licensing Levels 151
Linear Routes 148
Listening, Effective 60
Live Flight 321
Load Factor 325
Lowest Combination of Fares 182

M

Malaria 133
Manila Declaration 8
Man-made Attractions 111
Marine Transportation 21
    standard references 70
    types 352
Marketing 410
    airline promotion 157
Maslow's Hierarchy of Needs 53
Maximum Permitted Mileages Books 179
MCO - see Miscellaneous Charges Order
Meal Services (European Rail) 221
Mileage System 181
Miscellaneous Charges Order 193
Montreal Agreement 11
Motivations, Needs and Expectations 59
Motives 55
Motorcoach Tours 313
Motorhomes and Specialty Vehicles 257
MPM - see Maximum Permitted Mileages
Multiplier Effect 96
Municipal By-Laws 17

N

National Governments and Tourism 8
National Transportation Act 13
National Transportation Agency 13, 146, 330
Natural Attractions 111
Nautical Abbreviations 379
Nautical Terms 378
Needs
    business travellers 54
    Maslow's hierarchy 53
    pleasure travellers 52
Neutral Units of Construction 180
Nondiscretionary Travel 50
NTA - see National Transportation Agency
NTO - see Tourist Boards
NUC - see Neutral Units of Construction

O

OAG - see Official Airline Guides
Objections, Overcoming 374, 424
Off-Line Carriers 153
Office Machines 450
Official Airline Guides 69, 166

Official Canada Bus Guide 71
Official Hotel and Resort Guide 71
Official National Motor Coach Guide 71
Official Railway Guide 70
Official Steamship Guide International 70
OHRG - see Official Hotel and Resort Guide
One-Way Backhaul 182
Open Jaw 168

P

Packages 325, 342
Passenger Tariffs, Domestic 172
Passenger-Crew Ratio 360
Passports 124
PATA 461
Payments
    forms of 440
    tours 339
Personnel
    cruise ship 362
    hotel 271
Phases in Destination Development 100
Pleasure Travel 38, 52
Political Impacts 94
Presentations 79
Primary Destinations 102
Principal, Disclosure of 454
Product
    analysis 338
    checklist for tours 340
    knowledge 45, 68, 87
    launches 82
    travel 63
Professionalism 455
Profitability 434
Promotion
    airline 157
    travel agency 410
Prospects, Sales 417
Psychocentrics 58
Psychographic Information 49
Publications 23, 77
Publicity 413

Q

Questioning Skills 59

R

Rail Accommodation and Services 208, 214
Rail Equipment 206, 212, 218
Rail Fares 208, 215, 225
Rail Passes 230
Rail Schedules, European 222
Rail Travel 199
    advantages 202
    Britain 234
    Canada 205
    Europe 215
    development 200

disadvantages 204
United States 211
worldwide 237
Railroad Organizations 216
Railroads 21
Rate Sheets 73
Reasons for Travel 50
Recreation and Entertainment 23
Reference Groups 57
References
    accommodation 292
    administration 471
    air travel 198
    client 62
    cruises 382
    destinations and documentation 142
    ground transportation 260
    rail travel 239
    sales 431
    tourism industry 25
    tours 345
    travel counsellor's role 46
    travel insurance 408
    travel product 89
Refunds
    BSP 446
    calculation 439
    European rail 234
Regional Carriers 151
Registration 15
Religious Pilgrimages 39
Repeat Clientele 33
Representative Companies 23
Representatives
    hotel 268
    tour operator 325
Reputation, Travel Agency 32
Research Assignments
    administration 471
    cruises 381
    destinations and documentation 141
    tourism industry 24
    tours 345
Reservations
    Amtrak 215
    car rental 254
    cruises 380
    European rail 232
    flight 189
    tour 338
    VIA rail 211
Resort Hotels 265
Resorts
    grading 271
    summer 265
    winter cold 265
    winter warm 266
    year-round 266
Review Questions
    accommodation 292
    administration 471
    air travel 198
    client 62
    cruises 381
    destinations and documentation 141

Review Questions
    ground transportation 260
    rail travel 238
    sales 431
    tourism industry 24
    tours 344
    travel counsellor's role 46
    travel insurance 407
    travel product 88
Role of a Travel Counsellor 43
Route Structures 148, 155
Routes
    hub and spoke 148
    linear 148
Routing Guide, Domestic 172
Routing System 180
Rules, Routings and Mileages Books,
    International 177
Rules Tariffs, Domestic 173
Russell's Guides 71

S

Sales 405, 412
    ability 45
    closing 426
    conferences 40
    follow up 428
    incentives 40
    process 418
    product knowledge 87
    prospects 417
    strategies 418
    success 430
    telephone 428
Scheduled Carriers 151
Secondary Effects 96
Secondary or Stopover Destinations 102
Selling
    air travel 159
    cruises 371
    travel insurance 398
Seminars 83
Service Industry, Travel Agency 31
Sightseeing 246, 307
    and attractions 111
    and events 112
Sleepers 220
Smallpox 131
Social Impacts 98
Sources of Product Knowledge 68
Space Ratio 359
Special Interest Travel 39
Special Needs Tours 298
Specialization
    hotels 267
    train services 238
Specified Fares 181
Standard References 68, 70, 71, 89
Statutory Laws 13
Supplier Information 72
Surcharges 328

T

Tariff
    air 69, 174
    confidential 305
    domestic 170
Telephone Sales 428
Terminology
    accounting 436
    hotel 270
    insurance 385
    nautical 378
The 24-Hour Clock System 118
Thomas Cook European Timetable 70, 71, 222
Thomas Cook Overseas Timetable 71, 237
Through Service 168
TIAC 461
Ticket Exchange Notice 195
Ticketing
    airline 190
    Amtrak 215
    cruises 380
    European rail 232
    IATA handbook 69
    VIA rail 210
Tickets
    airline 191
    tour operator 341
TIM - see Travel Information Manual
Timeshare 289
Timetables 75
Tour Brochures 331
Tour Escort 317
Tour Operators 22, 299
    airlines owned by 322
    contracts 324
    documentation 341
    inbound 319
    negotiations 320
    outbound 319
    representatives 325
    role 318
    tickets 341
    vouchers 341
Tour Order, Airline 193
Tour References, Standard 71
Tour Reservations 338
Tour Wholesalers 22, 299
    benefits of dealing with 308
    role 308
Tourism
    Canadian government 9
    definition 2
    growth 6
    history 4
    impacts 94
    national governments 8
Tourism Canada 10
Tourism Development 93
    costs and benefits 100
Tourism in Canada 4
Tourism Legislation
    Canadian government 12
    federal framework 13
    provincial framework 14

Tourist 3
Tourist Boards 8, 23
Tourist Cards 128
Tourist Destinations 92
Tours 293, 294
    airline promotion 331
    classification 297
    costing 309, 325, 336
    definition 294
    escorted 315
    general advantages 298
    group 312
    inclusive 313
    independent 300
    independent air tours 301
    motorcoach 313
    packages 325
    payments 339
    product analysis 338
    product checklist 340
    recommending 334
    reservations 338
    types 295
Trade Associations 24, 456
    area 461
    operations 458
    purpose 456
Trade Papers 77, 90
Trade Shows 81
Traffic Conferences, IATA 174
Transfers 246, 307
Transportation Suppliers 20
Travel Agency 24
    appointments 468
    business 37
    cooperatives or consortiums 37
    description 28
    expenses 31
    franchises 36
    how to start 467
    income 29
    independent 34
    organization 34
    reputation 32
    size 33
    types 33
Travel Counsellor
    definition 41
    job description 42
    reasons for study 43
    role 44
Travel Distribution Systems 17
Travel Documentation 124
Travel Fairs 81
Travel Guidebooks 117
Travel Industry Segments 20
Travel Information Manual 71
Travel Insurance 23, 383
Travel Legislation
    bonding 16
    compensation fund 16
    registration 15
    specific 15
Travel Planner Hotel and Motel RedBook 71
Travel Product 63

Travel Trade Publications 77, 90
Traveller Tips 140
Travellers, Individual 51
Trunk Carriers 151
Trust Accounting 16
Type of Journey 168
Type of Service 168

U

UFTAA 456
Universal Credit Card Charge Form 195

V

Vaccination, International Certificates 132
Vehicles and Licenses 139
VIA Rail
    accommodation and services 208
    equipment 206
    fares 208
    reservations and ticketing 211
Visas 127
Visit Friends and Relatives (VFR) 50
Visitors to Canada, Entry Requirements 130
Vouchers 341

W

Waiver Forms 401
Warsaw Convention 11
Wholesale Travel 22
World Tourism Organization 2, 8, 10, 12
    hotel classification system 272
WTO - see World Tourism Organization

Y

Yellow Fever 130